Sunset
South Pacific
TRAVEL GUIDE

DARROW M. WATT

Yacht anchors in protected waters off a French Polynesian island.

By the Editors of
Sunset Books and Sunset Magazine

LANE PUBLISHING CO.
Menlo Park, California

Golden sands and clear waters await visitors at Kaiteriteri on New Zealand's South Island.

CHRIS GILBERT

Your passport to the South Pacific

The vast island continent of Australia and the scenic lakes and mountains of New Zealand are increasingly popular destinations in the South Pacific. Here, too, are the coral atolls and jagged peaks of partially submerged mountains that make up the thousands of tropical islands scattered across the Pacific.

Sunset Books has long offered a number of guides to these areas. Now, to better serve travelers to several destinations, we've combined them into one volume. Let it be your companion while you fish off New Zealand's coast, marvel at Australia's marsupials, or explore a secluded South Pacific island.

Front cover: *Twilight on the Tahitian waterfront. Photograph by Richard Rowan.* **Back cover:** *Photographs by Bruce Moss (top) and Chris Gilbert (bottom).*

Sunset Books
  Editor, David E. Clark
  Managing Editor, Elizabeth L. Hogan

Second printing July 1987

CONTENTS

Australia

A comprehensive guide to the land down under,
from its cosmopolitan cities to its
rugged, untamed outback. Descriptions of the
Great Barrier Reef, the bush country,
and Australia's unique plant and animal life.
Festivals and sports events to enhance your visit.

New Zealand

A tour of this young country of lofty mountains,
lush farmlands, and clear waters, where Maori and
British cultures blend. Special attractions,
including skiing in the Southern Alps, trekking
on the Milford Track, and sampling a Maori
hangi in Rotorua.

Islands of the South Pacific

A look at the enchanting islands of Polynesia,
Melanesia, and Micronesia,
strewn over thousands of miles in the South Pacific.
A range of recreational opportunities—
cruising among Fiji's islands, scuba-diving in
Truk Lagoon, and deep-sea fishing in the Samoas.

Sunset

Australia
TRAVEL GUIDE

By the Editors of Sunset Books
and Sunset Magazine

Lane Publishing Co. • Menlo Park, California

Edited by **Joan Erickson**

Design: **Cynthia Hanson**

Illustrations & Maps: **Joe Seney**

Cover: Sydney's sculptural Opera House, overlooking the harbor, has become an internationally known landmark of Australia. Photographed by Darrow M. Watt.

Sunset Books
Editor: David E. Clark
Managing Editor: Elizabeth L. Hogan

Second printing July 1987

 Library of Congress Catalog Card Number: 86-82155. ISBN 0-376-06066-2. Lithographed in the United States.

Acknowledgments

For assistance in the gathering of information and manuscript checking, we would like to thank the following: Australian Tourist Commission, New South Wales Tourist Commission, Canberra Tourist Bureau, Victorian Tourism Commission, Tasmanian Department of Tourism, South Australian Department of Tourism, Western Australian Tourism Commission, Northern Territory Tourist Commission, and Queensland Tourist & Travel Corporation.

Photographers

Australian Information Service: 71 top left. **Australian Tourist Commission:** 6, 11 top left, 14 bottom, 19 top right and bottom, 38 bottom, 51 all, 54, 59 bottom, 62, 66 top, 79 all, 87 top, 90 top, 95, 98 bottom, 106 top right, 111, 119, 122. **Dave Bartruff:** 35 right. **Margaret Betchart:** 43 bottom right. **Brian Brake, Photo Researchers, Inc.:** 11 bottom, 90 bottom. **Canberra Tourist Bureau:** 46. **Ken Castle:** 82, 87 bottom, 106 top left. **Joan Erickson:** 30 top, 38 top, 43 left, 59 top, 66 bottom, 71 top right, 74, 103. **James Gebbie:** 98 top. **George Holton, Photo Researchers, Inc.:** 19 top left. **Esther Litton:** 106 bottom. **Bruce Moss:** 43 top right, 114 bottom. **New South Wales Department of Tourism:** 71 bottom. **Qantas Airways Ltd.:** 3, 11 top right, 127. **Richard Rowan:** 27 bottom, 35 left. **Joan Storey:** 14 top left, 27 top. **Marie Ueda, S.F. Photo Network:** 30 bottom. **Darrow M. Watt:** 22, 114 top. **Nikolay Zurek:** 14 top right.

Maps have been provided in each chapter for the purpose of highlighting significant regions, routes, and attractions in the area. For detailed road maps of Australia, check with automobile clubs, insurance or travel agencies, or government tourist offices.

Lifeguards in surf boat crash through waves.

CONTENTS

Australia

Kilometers
0 50 100 200

0 50 100 200
Miles

—— Principal Roads (sealed)
—— Secondary Roads (sealed)
- - - - Unsealed Roads

How far is it?

Australia is a large country. Places that seem close to each other on a map might, in reality, be a good distance apart. The chart below indicates distances by road between certain towns.

Sydney/Melbourne	893 km/555 miles
Melbourne/Adelaide	755 km/469 miles
Sydney/Perth	4,135 km/2,569 miles
Perth/Albany	407 km/253 miles
Perth/Port Hedland	1,818 km/1,130 miles
Sydney/Brisbane	1,027 km/638 miles
Brisbane/Cairns	1,826 km/1,135 miles
Cairns/Mackay	786 km/488 miles
Mackay/Brisbane	1,044 km/649 miles
Alice Springs/Darwin	1,532 km/952 miles
Alice Springs/Ayers Rock	468 km/291 miles
Canberra/Sydney	309 km/192 miles
Canberra/Melbourne	661 km/413 miles

Arafura Sea

win Arnhem Land
Jim Jim Crossing
Katherine

Gulf of

Groote
Eylandt

Carpentaria

Coral Sea

Cooktown
Port Douglas
Green Island
Cairns
Dunk Island

GREAT

Cape York Peninsula

Atherton
Tableland

Townsville

BARRIER

Hayman Island
Proserpine
Lindeman Island
Brampton Island

Tennant Creek

Mount Isa

78

Northern

Queensland

Mackay

REEF

Territory

Ross River

Longreach

66

Rockhampton

Great Keppel Island
Heron Island
Gladstone

ice Springs

1

CDONNELL
NGES

Birdsville

71

Fraser Island

Ayers Rock

sert

South

Coober Pedy

Australia

Andamooka

1

Broken Hill

New South Wales

FLINDERS RANGES

32

Brisbane
Gold Coast

Tenterfield

Glen Innes
Armidale

Port Augusta

stralian

Bight

Port Lincoln

Spencer Gulf

Gulf St. Vincent

Adelaide

Mildura

Kangaroo
Island

1

8

79

Swan Hill

16

Bendigo

75

Mt. Gambier

Lorne

Port Phillip Bay

King Island

39

15

Dubbo

39

32

Bathurst

20

39

A.C.T.

31

Albury

Victoria

Melbourne

Bairnsdale

Bass Strait

Flinders Island

Port Macquarie

GREAT DIVIDING RANGE

Katoomba

Newcastle

Sydney

Canberra

Cooma

Eden

1

Lakes Entrance

Tasman Sea

Burnie

Launceston

Queenstown

Tasmania

Hobart

Richmond
Port Arthur

5

INTRODUCING AUSTRALIA

An ancient continent filled with inviting contrasts

Australia is a faraway country of sunburnt red earth. It's a city called Sydney and an ultramodern Opera House. It's kangaroos and koalas, bleating sheep and well-tanned cattle drovers. Australia is all of this and much, much more—nearly 8 million square km/3 million square miles, in fact—and filled with a remarkable range of travel experiences.

Comparable in size to the United States (excluding Alaska), Australia is an island continent in the South Pacific. It's the only continent with just one nation on it, and, geologically, it's believed to be the oldest continent on the earth. In the northwest corner of Western Australia, researchers recently found a fossil-laden rock 3.5 billion years old: the oldest known evidence of life on the globe.

Separated from other land masses early in its youth, Australia developed separately. Unique plant and animal life, native only to Australia, resulted from this separate development. One of the most unusual feats of Mother Nature is the country's marsupials: kangaroos, koalas, wombats, and Tasmanian devils. Raucous kookaburras, beautiful lyrebirds, and graceful black swans also claim Australia as their native home. Along with unusual fauna are fascinating flora like the eucalypt (gum tree). Varieties of these trees are found all over the world today, but they had their beginnings in Australia. For more information on Australia flora, see page 70.

A land of contrasts

The country offers a myriad of topography and color— rich red plains, blue green mountains, deep green pasturelands, and turquoise lagoons. Much of Australia's center, though, is a flat plateau of red earth occupying about three-fourths of the continent. Little rain falls in this outback area to nourish the vegetation. Though maps

Masters of the situation, these hard-working sheep dogs help rider herd flock of Merinos around twisted gum tree. Pastoral scene is repeated throughout world's top wool-producing country.

show many rivers flowing into central Australia, most streams go dry before they reach the huge salt flats that are called lakes, but which fill with water only in the wettest years.

Yet even in this apparently monotonous landscape there is striking beauty in the rocky peaks and red-walled chasms of the MacDonnell Ranges or the hulklike mass of Ayers Rock. To the south of these attractions the treeless Nullarbor Plain breaks off into dramatic, sheer cliffs of the Great Australian Bight.

Variety in landscape

The continent's principal mountain chain, the Great Dividing Range, is also varied in character. Paralleling the country's eastern coast for almost 4,023 km/2,500 miles, the Great Dividing Range includes the alpine peaks of the Snowy Mountains near Canberra, the gum-tree-covered Blue Mountains of New South Wales, and the jungle-clad mountains of Queensland. The country's most important river, the Murray, begins in the Great Dividing Range, then flows about 2,575 km/1,600 miles along the New South Wales-Victoria border and through South Australia to the Indian Ocean.

The well-watered foothills of the Great Dividing Range contain fertile farmlands and rich, tree-dotted pastures of grazing sheep and cattle. Here you'll find fast-running streams, leafy glades, and tumbling waterfalls.

In contrast, Australia's coastline (nearly 37,047 km/ 23,021 miles) contains miles of golden sand beaches, secluded coves, expansive bays, and dramatic headlands. It rates high on the country's list of scenic attractions. The eastern and southeastern coast is home for many Australians. In fact, all but one of the country's capital cities— Canberra— have the ocean at their doorsteps.

Then there are the tropical rain forests of the northern section of Australia which lie in the tropics above the Tropic of Capricorn. Here you'll find forests reminiscent of those in Asia and Africa where orchids grow wild and leafy tree ferns thrive. Brilliantly colored birds flit through these vine-tangled forests and even a crocodile or two might lurk in a swampy clearing.

One of Australia's great natural wonders—The Great

Barrier Reef—lies in this tropical region. Stretching in lazy arcs along the Queensland coast, the reef is really a series of reefs and underwater shoals. It includes one of the largest coral collections in the world—more than 350 varieties. In these clear, warm ocean waters, the reef supports a fascinating array of flora and fauna; it's a living laboratory for those who study marine life.

Varying climates

Seasons in Australia are the reverse of those in the Northern Hemisphere. Summer lasts from December through February, autumn from March through May, winter from June through August, and spring from September through November.

As the landscape of Australia varies, so does the climate. Summers in semi-tropical Sydney can be more humid than in Melbourne, and Melbourne's winters can be cooler than Sydney's. In both cities, sunshine intermingled with moderate rainfall can be expected the year around.

As you travel farther inland, the climate becomes warmer and much drier. In the arid interior, winter temperatures average 23°C/73°F, while summer temperatures can soar to 43°C/118°F or even higher. Rainfalls are few and far between.

The tropical northern coastal areas of Australia are hot and humid the year around, with temperatures averaging between 27°C/80°F and 33°C/91°F. Darwin, on the north coast, really has only two seasons—"the wet" and "the dry." The wet or monsoon season runs from November to April, and the dry season from April to October.

Australia's people

Of Australia's 15½ million people, 7 out of every 10 live in the country's major cities. As city people, they enjoy things that urban life can provide—modern shopping complexes, good restaurants, and an array of cultural events. Although they may work in the heart of the city, they live in sprawling nearby suburbs, in homes complete with gardens and outdoor barbecues much like those of the American West.

Beyond the cities and their suburban sprawl is the vast, little-populated outback of Australia. This is a land of rambling sheep and cattle stations—some of them bigger than some European countries. The men and women who live on these stations are tough and self-sufficient. The nearest neighbor might be a several-hour drive away from the veranda-trimmed homestead, light aircraft the best way to get into town. Station children learn their lessons by radio—the School of the Air (see page 107).

The good life. Australia is a country rich in natural resources. It's the world's leading producer of lead and zinc; it also exports copper in large quantities. Discoveries of vast iron ore deposits in Western Australia add to this mineral wealth. In addition the country is the world's biggest wool producer.

All this wealth contributes to the good life that many Australians enjoy. To most Australians, work is only part of their lives. With long hours of sunshine and pleasant weather much of the year, Australians want time to enjoy the outdoors and to enjoy their country.

Although many Australians don't live in the bush or the outback, the beautiful country beyond the city's doorstep is never far from mind. On weekends and during vacations, Australians love to escape to the country to fish, bushwalk, camp, or picnic. The "bush" is considered the wild country just beyond the city. The "outback" is farther away and far more desolate and rugged. Both hold an attraction for city-dwelling Australians.

Australians love outdoor sport whether it be bushwalking, swimming, sailing, golf, or tennis. When they are not playing, they are enthusiastically watching such outdoor sports as soccer, rugby, or Australian Rules football.

Along with this love of sports goes a love of gambling. Betting the horses is extremely popular. Nearly every Australian has purchased a lottery ticket at some time.

Roots in England. Many Australians come from British stock. Australia is part of the British Commonwealth, and the influence of England is evident in the fact that Australians drive on the left side of the road, and enjoy morning and afternoon tea.

The distinctive British pattern of speech is also evident, though altered somewhat by vigorous Australian idioms and pronunciation changes. As in England, apartments are "flats," candies are "lollies," and crackers are "biscuits." Then there are Aussie terms like "back of beyond" which means far away in the outback and "dinkum" which means honest or genuine.

Cosmopolitan influences. Many newcomers—immigrants from Europe since World War II—have added zest and an international flavor to Australia. Nearly one-third of Australia's people are first or second-generation immigrants. A large portion of these new arrivals are from the British Isles; other immigrants include Europeans (Dutch, Italians, Greeks, Yugoslavs, Spaniards, Scandinavians, Hungarians, Czechoslovaks, Turks, Poles, and Icelanders), North and South Americans, Asians, and Arabs.

Something for everyone

With Australia's diversity in landscape and lifestyle, the country can accommodate its many visitors with varied interests—from the person who enjoys the cosmopolitan life of the big city to the person who wants to ride a camel through the outback and sleep under the stars.

Big city offerings

Australia's larger cities—Sydney, Melbourne, Adelaide, Perth, Canberra, and Brisbane—offer high-rise hotels, gourmet restaurants, and cultural opportunities. Visitors can attend a performance of the opera at Sydney's famous Opera House or a concert at Melbourne's Victorian Arts Centre. The Adelaide Festival, held in March on even-numbered years, offers visitors a bonus of 22 days of cultural performances and art exhibits. Sydney's Australian Museum provides a glimpse of Aboriginal artifacts, and Fremantle's Maritime Museum near Perth takes you back to the 16th century, with relics of Dutch explorers. Canberra's National Gallery houses Australian, European, Oriental, and American art.

(Continued on page 10)

Australia—A brief history

Australia's first inhabitants came from Asia about 40,000 years ago. Some traveled across a land bridge (now submerged); others came by raft or canoe. Descendants of these first Aborigines still live in Australia today.

Thousands of years later, 2nd century European geographers were suggesting that a large land mass existed at the southern end of the world. Otherwise, they said, the earth couldn't possibly remain upright. They called this southern land mass "Terra Australis Incognita," which appropriately means "Unknown South Land."

The discovery. As early as the 1500s, Portuguese exploring the East Indies may have sighted Australia. A Portuguese navigator, Pedro de Quiros, thought he had found the "southern continent" when he discovered the New Hebrides in 1606. That same year Willem Jansz of the Dutch East India Company discovered and charted 322 km/200 miles of the north Australian coast. This is the first recorded discovery of Australia.

During the 17th century, Portuguese, Dutch, and British navigators carried out preliminary explorations and charting of the country's northern and western coastline. Abel Tasman discovered the island of Tasmania in 1642 and named it Van Dieman's Land. These early explorers gave dour accounts of the country, characterizing it as "the barrenest spot upon the globe." It was dismissed as being an improbable area for development, with nothing of commercial value, so interest in the continent lapsed for three-quarters of a century.

Credit for the "rediscovery" of Australia goes to the intrepid English explorer, Captain James Cook. On April 29, 1770, Cook cast anchor in Botany Bay near the site of Sydney's present-day airport. He charted the whole eastern coast and took possession of it for the British calling it New Wales. Having seen Australia's lush east coast, he was able to send glowing reports back about possibilities for colonization.

Settling Australia. With the American Revolution, England lost a place to transport the overflow of convicts from its innumerable prisons. England's jails and prison ships were overcrowded, and the country was in search of new territory to settle. Australia seemed a good alternative, so Britain sent a shipment of convicts under the command of Captain Arthur Phillip to establish a settlement in Australia. In a simple ceremony on January 26, 1788, Phillip unfurled the Union Jack at what is now Sydney, drank to the King's health, and set to work building the colony of New South Wales.

During the next 80 years, another 100,000 convicts were transported to Australia. With them were free settlers willing to endure the hardships of a strange land to make a new life. At first the going was rough. Crops failed, stock escaped, supply ships were delayed. But slowly, painfully, the colonists succeeded in the most difficult pioneering effort in history.

One of the most important developments during the country's early history came from the experiments of Captain John MacArthur. In 1801, he began breeding sheep for a fine wool. The results of his experiments—the Australian Merino—produce some of the finest wool in the world.

Exploring a strange land. Australia's first settlements were along the coast and transportation between them was primarily by boat—the inland regions seemed too inhospitable for overland travel. Gradually, however, Australians began to see what was beyond their "back door." In 1813 William C. Wentworth's expedition crossed the Blue Mountains west of Sydney. Between 1827 and 1829 Charles Sturt charted much of the Darling River and its tributaries, and in 1841 Edward Eyre walked the entire southern coast of Australia across the Nullarbor Plain to the west coast.

Along with the success of these first explorations, there were some tragic failures. Ludwig Leichardt and his party disappeared in 1848 while attempting to travel overland from Queensland to Perth. The Burke and Wills expedition ended in death for both men during their 1860 attempt to cross Australia from south to north.

Beginnings of a nation. The discovery of gold by Edward Hargreaves in 1851 brought a tide of immigration that doubled the population in 10 years. New South Wales peacefully achieved responsible self-government in 1855, and by 1890 the rest of the colonies had followed suit. Federation came quickly—January 1, 1901, saw the birth of the Commonwealth of Australia.

With the exception of a brief uprising during the gold rush period, the nation's history has been one of unbroken domestic tranquility. The city of Darwin was bombed by the Japanese in 1942, but no enemy troops have ever set foot on Australian soil. Australian troops fought with distinction in two world wars and in conflicts in Korea and Vietnam.

The government. Since 1901 Australia has been governed as a federal commonwealth, with both federal and state parliaments modeled on a thoughtful mixture of British, American, Canadian, and Swiss democracies. A prime minister heads the national government, and a premier leads each of its six states: New South Wales, Victoria, Queensland, South Australia, Western Australia, and Tasmania. Governors in each of the states, along with a governor general, represent the British Crown in Australia.

In addition to states, Australia has several territories. On mainland Australia are the Northern Territory and the Australian Capital Territory (A.C.T.), site of Canberra, the nation's capital city. Six more territories—ranging in size from tiny Christmas Island to Australia's holdings in the Antarctic—lie outside the continent.

One feature of Australian politics is that enfranchised adults are required to vote, under penalty of fine.

...Continued from page 8

Outdoor enthusiasts will love the many parks and waterways of Australia's cities. You can row a canoe on the Yarra River in Melbourne or the Swan River in Perth, or sail a boat on Sydney's beautiful harbor. Golf, tennis, cycling, and jogging are among activities available.

A glimpse of history

Sights throughout Australia speak of Australia's early days. The Rocks, one of Sydney's restored areas, is where a nation began after Captain Phillip's convict ships anchored in Sydney Cove in 1788. To the south in Tasmania, other convicts toiled under harsh conditions at Port Arthur's penal colony.

Australia also has a number of folk museums that show life the way it was in Australia's early years. Swan Hill's Pioneer Settlement in northern Victoria is a re-creation of a 19th century Australian inland river town. Sovereign Hill Goldmining Township, also in Victoria, evokes memories of Australia's gold rush era. This historical park re-creates the town of Ballarat during its first 10 years of development following the discovery of gold in the area in 1851. For a real gold rush ghost town, journey out to Coolgardie in Western Australia. During its heyday, this town was considered queen of the gold fields.

A taste of the grape

Wine-country touring in Australia can be every bit as interesting, educational, and fun as it is in France or California. Australia's wines are diverse. So are the wineries; they range from small to large and family-owned to cooperative, some in historic chateaux, others in modern, functional structures.

You'll find most of the wine-producing vineyards concentrated in three states—South Australia, New South Wales, and Victoria. Other smaller wine-producing areas are located in Western Australia, Queensland, and Tasmania. No matter which of these regions you visit, you'll find that wine people are friendly and enjoy sharing with you the story of how they make their wines; and frequently they'll allow you to sample their product.

Heading the list of wine-producing regions is the Barossa Valley just north of Adelaide in South Australia. Other South Australia wine regions you can tour include the Clare Valley, Southern Vales, Coonawarra, and Murray River. In New South Wales you can go touring and tasting in the Hunter River Valley or the Riverina District. In Victoria take a trip to Rutherglen or the Great Western District.

The lure of the wild

Lovers of the great out-of-doors will not lack opportunity to commune with nature in Australia. The country has 500 national parks, from the rugged, rocky beauty of the Flinders Ranges to the white sands of the Great Barrier Reef islands, set aside to preserve and protect a variety of terrain, vegetation, and wildlife.

In Australia's many fauna parks you can feed a kangaroo or lorikeet, or hold a koala. Especially noteworthy are the Cleland Conservation Park near Adelaide, the Currumbin Bird Sanctuary on the Queensland Gold Coast, and the Lone Pine Koala Sanctuary near Brisbane.

Still other outdoor experiences include adventure tours in the outback or a tropical rain forest. These Australian adventure tours are numerous and varied (see page 15 for more information on them).

Rockhounds with an inclination to strike it rich can take their picks to remote opal mining areas like Coober Pedy, Andamooka, or Lightning Ridge. Lovers of farming and ranching can spend time at one of Australia's many cattle or sheep stations.

Traveling Down Under

You can reach Australia from North America, Europe, Southeast Asia, the Orient, many South Pacific Islands, New Zealand, and South Africa. More frequent air service has made access quick and easy; more than two dozen international air carriers serve the country.

Air travel has made a voyage by ship a rare experience, though many cruise lines still call at several Australian ports.

Tours to Australia are numerous. You can choose from escorted tours, independent tours, special interest tours, and adventure tours. The choice depends on what you want to spend and what you want to see and do. Because of the number of options available for your trip to Australia, it's wise to seek the advice of a knowledgeable travel agent to help plan your trip.

Getting there by air

Both direct and connecting flights link Sydney with major North American cities. Airlines providing service from the United States include Qantas, Continental, Air New Zealand, United, and UTA French Airlines. Qantas, Canadian Pacific, Continental, and Air New Zealand provide service from Canada.

Sydney, Melbourne, Cairns, and Brisbane are important arrival cities for international flights from North America, but Darwin, Perth, Townsville, Adelaide, and Hobart all have international airports too.

A variety of discount air fares are now available to travelers heading for Australia. Traveling independently, visitors can take advantage of several Advance Purchase Excursion (APEX) fares. The seasons you travel will dictate the round-trip cost. There are different low, shoulder, and peak season rates for each direction of travel. Air fares fluctuate a great deal; the amount of time spent in Australia and the miles traveled will affect the cost of your ticket. Consult a travel agent for specific rates.

Getting there by boat

In this jet age, not many passenger ships sailing from the United States stop at Australian ports. A number of cruise lines—Royal Viking, P & O, Salen Linblad Cruising, Society Expeditions, Cunard, Sitmar, Royal Cruise Line, and Princess Cruises—include Australia in their world or circle-Pacific cruise itineraries. These cruises often stop at some South Pacific islands and at least one New Zealand port. Sydney, Melbourne, Adelaide, Perth, Darwin, and Hobart are the usual Australian ports-of-call.

Aboriginal drovers herd cattle (above) on a station in Northern Territory outback. Some Australian stations are larger than some countries.

Grim determination shows on faces of lifeguards marching with military precision (right) at summer surf carnival. After parade, guards take to boats in a show of speed and skill.

Sleek horses and groomed sheep parade toward reviewing stand at a Royal Show (below). Annual event is renowned for livestock and agricultural exhibits.

Sports— A way of life

To Australians, sports are more than a mere pastime or form of recreation— they're a way of life. A zest for living only partially explains their sports-mindedness. Their fanatical loyalty and competitive spirit develop from rigorous physical training at school, a continuing drive to beat the other fellow, and the double advantage of a favorable climate and a high standard of living.

Sports to watch

You can learn a great deal about the Australian's love for sports if your travels include a sports event. Popular spectator sports in Australia include horse racing, football (Australian Rules, rugby League, rugby Union, and soccer), and cricket.

Horse racing. Most pervasive of the spectator sports is horse racing. Many Australians have a natural love for gambling and this sport of kings allows them to place their bets. Throughout the year, you'll find races being run somewhere—from small country meetings to colorful major events attracting thousands of spectators. Races are usually run on Saturday, but you'll also find them held midweek. (In Canberra, races are run on Sunday as well.)

The biggest horse race—in number of spectators and impact on Australians—is the Melbourne Cup (see page 63). Other major racing events during the year include the AJC (Australia Jockey Club) Derby held at Randwick Racecourse in Sydney in October, and Melbourne's Caulfield Cup also in October. These big meets are always sellouts requiring advance arrangements; your travel agent can usually make them for you.

You place your bets for the races at windows operated by the Totalizator Agency Board (TAB), the state-controlled betting organization which uses the pari-mutuel machine, an Australian invention. (The Aussies also were the first to introduce the photo-finish camera.) You'll also find TAB "shops"—betting agencies—in most cities throughout the country, enabling you to bet on the big races whether or not you can attend.

On a smaller scale are the bush or picnic meetings, and they provide an even better way to get to known Australians. Bush horse racing has no season; races are held throughout the year. Some of these bush meets are on race tracks with stands, while others are simply a course marked out with stakes. Often the picnic is almost as important as the race, with sumptuous spreads for frontier appetites.

Still another form of horse racing is harness racing— called "trotting." With the advent of night race meetings and legalized betting, this sport has increased in popular-

ity. The harness-racing season runs from October through July.

Football mania. Each year many Australians are gripped with a seasonal passion second to none when it comes to numbers of avid, highly partisan followers. Australian Rules football is said to have greater support per person than any other field sport in the world today, though it's played only in Australia where it was invented.

The game's most avid followers are perhaps in Victoria where Melbourne is the center for club matches that can draw 100,000 spectators. The area's twelve professional league teams do battle in 6 league games each Saturday from April to September. The finals, held in September, attract even greater crowds. "Aussie Rules" is also played and enthusiastically supported in each of Australia's other states.

Still another football game—League (professional) rugby—has its own group of strong supporters in New South Wales and Queensland. Union (amateur) rugby finds fans in rural areas. Soccer (association football) is played throughout Australia.

Cricket. This English game has an avid following in Australia during the summer season (October to March). It was first played in Sydney in 1803, but not until 1877 did the Australians feel qualified to hold their first test match with England. Their first victory on English soil came in 1882, and since then they've bested the English at their own game a number of times.

International Test Matches—Australia versus England or another cricket-playing country—are held in capital cities every second year from December to February. All states except Tasmania play each other twice a season (at home and away) for the Sheffield Shield, symbol of cricket supremacy in Australia.

Lawn bowls. Every Saturday, and often on workdays as well, you can watch white-clad members of lawn bowling teams rolling their black balls down immaculately kept greens toward a white "kitty" or "jack"—the target. The point of the game is to get as close to the target as you can with your black ball.

Bowling greens seem to be everywhere—in capital cities and in small country towns. As a visitor, you're welcome to watch; and if you're interested, it's relatively easy to get an invitation to participate. However, you must wear traditional whites for tournament play. The sport's major event, the Australian Gold Coast Winter Bowls Carnival, is held in July along the Gold Coast and attracts more than 1,000 entries.

Sports to play

With more than 80 sports enthusiastically played down under, there's something for everyone, so you shouldn't miss the opportunity to enjoy your favorite sport while in Australia.

Tennis. Australians are avid tennis players. This fact is evident in the number of top players the country has produced. In all major city areas, you'll find a wealth of public and private courts with equipment for hire. There are both hard courts and beautifully maintained lawn courts. If you belong to a club at home, you can almost always get honorary privileges at clubs in Australia.

Golf. Australia's golf courses challenge every type of golfer, from the tournament-hardened professional to the casual amateur. As Australia's big cities enlarged, the greenbelt of golf courses remained where they were placed 40 to 60 years ago. As a result, many of the top golf courses are less than a 30-minute drive from a city center.

You can choose your style, playing a round on a public course or on a private course with a club member. Capital cities have a number of excellent public courses where green fees are modest and clubs can be hired. Leading country clubs welcome visitors introduced by a member and some have reciprocal arrangements with overseas clubs. If you are a member of a club at home, ask your club's secretary-manager for a letter of introduction to the Australian club and have him include your handicap.

Deep-sea fishing. The incredible variety of fish in the seas surrounding Australia attracts fishermen from around the world. The best season is between November and May, though sharks are caught the year around. Fishermen claim the prime area is along Australia's eastern and southeastern coast—particularly off Queensland, New South Wales, South Australia, and Tasmania.

The best ocean fishing is in the waters off northern and southern Queensland; the waters of southern New South Wales—around Sydney and the Bermagui-Eden area; and off Tasmania's rugged southeastern coast. In South Australia, most favored waters are Streaky Bay; the mouth of Spencer Gulf near Port Lincoln; and the prolific waters of Backstairs Passage, between Kangaroo Island and the mainland. Tuna fishing is so good around the island of Tasmania and off the South Australia coast that annual tuna tournaments are held at both places—off Eaglehawk Neck in Tasmania in March or April and at Port Lincoln, South Australia, in January.

Numerous game fishing charter boats and water safaris are available. Charter and tariff information is available from the Australian Tourist Commission.

Stream and lake fishing. The Australian Alps, lying between New South Wales and Victoria, offer many mountain streams and lakes teeming with good-size brown and rainbow trout. Among the best of these spots is massive Lake Eucumbene, formed by the big Snowy Mountain hydroelectric scheme southwest of Canberra. Thousands of fingerling trout are released each year into this huge reservoir by the New South Wales Fisheries Department.

Still another good fishing spot is Tasmania. Some of Tasmania's good fishing streams and lakes are rarely visited by fishermen, and the quality and size of trout are very high. Best Tasmanian haunts are the northwest coastal rivers, the highlands, the Huon Valley area in the south, and the upper reaches of the Derwent River.

An inland fishing license is compulsory. Regulations governing closed season and bag limits vary from state to state. In most states the fishing season is from September through

April. In Tasmania, the season is from November to April on lakes, and from September through April for inland streams and estuaries. At Lake Eucumbene there's fishing year around.

Skiing. Australia's snowfields are skiable from June through September. Well-known ski resorts include Thredbo Village, Perisher Valley, and Smiggin Holes—all in the Snowy Mountains of New South Wales. In Victoria, areas such as Falls Creek and Mounts Buller, Hotham, and Buffalo offer good skiing.

Skiers will find lodging, shops, restaurants, and ski schools at the resorts. Slopes are reached by chairlifts, T-bars, Poma lifts, and rope tows.

The surf world

Australia has beaches to suit everyone—from wading children to daring surfers to people who just want to relax and bake in the sunshine. During Australia's warm summer months—November to March—people flock to the beaches to do just that. This is also the time of the surf carnival (see page 28).

Surfing. Australians love to surf. Body surfing became popular in the early 1900s, but it wasn't until 1915 that Hawaii's Duke Kahanamoku introduced board riding at Freshwater Beach, Sydney.

Surfers may be reluctant to tell you their favorite beaches (preferring to keep the traffic to a minimum), but the eastern coast, from Melbourne to north of Brisbane, has good surfing beaches as does the western coast near Perth.

Skin and scuba diving. Stretching 2,012 km/1,250 miles north and south along the Queensland coast, Australia's Great Barrier Reef provides a paradise for skin divers and underwater photographers. Bright sunlight shafts down into the coral-studded depths, providing an almost ethereal atmosphere for divers. Fascinating coral grottoes and colorful tropical fish provide an enthralling setting.

Heron Island and Green Island, the major coral island resorts along the reef, are the two main areas for skin divers and photographers. Divers prefer them for the marine life, ease of accessibility, and availability of equipment and service. A number of diveboats journey out to the Great Barrier Reef, providing day trips from the mainland and island resorts, as well as extended trips where you live on board overnight or longer.

Yachting. You'll find this sport nearly as popular as surfing. On weekends, the country's harbors, bays, and rivers come alive with sailboats. Club and interclub races are exciting to watch.

Good sailing areas include Sydney Harbour, the Derwent River at Hobart, Adelaide's Gulf St. Vincent, Perth's Swan River, Melbourne's Port Phillip Bay, and Brisbane's Moreton Bay and Brisbane River. One of the best places to sail is the Whitsunday Passage off the Queensland coast.

If you are a member of a yacht club at home, you may be given facilities privileges at an Australian sailing club. Those with sailing know-how can charter a boat with or without a crew.

Waves crash on headland facing Bermagui, a quiet village known for its excellent fishing. Popular for holidays, town is near the lively resort of Narooma.

Sydney Tower's golden capsule offers observation floors and restaurants, lofty perches for viewing city's mix of historic and modern architecture.

Day's changing light adds muted brilliance to the Olgas (below), massive weathered rocks rising above flat central plains.

A word about tours

There's a multitude of packaged tours on the market today, so before planning your trip to Australia, investigate the types of tours available. With some tour packages, you travel in a group escorted by a tour guide and have a set itinerary. Still other tours offer you the independence of designing your own trip and setting your own pace at package discount prices. For those of you with special interests, there are trips designed with you in mind.

Escorted tours. Varying in length from about 18 to 36 days, these tours can feature Australia only, or Australia and New Zealand, or even Australia, New Zealand, Tahiti, and Fiji. Some even include Papua New Guinea in the country combination. Tours featuring a number of destinations usually include only a few of Australia's highlights—Sydney, the Snowy Mountains, Melbourne, and Canberra. Tours focusing just on Australia include a number of capital cities as well as the Alice Springs area and the Great Barrier Reef.

These escorted tours usually include transportation, accommodations, some meals, and sightseeing.

Traveling independently. There are fly/drive tours, fly/coach tours, fly/camper-van tours, fly/rail tours, and fly/tour packages available. With these packages you get a round-trip ticket to Australia, a pass for the type of transportation you want to use, and a pass for selected hotels (except on the camper-van tour). You set the pace you want to travel and select your destinations.

Special interest tours. Whether you're an avid golfer, an enthusiastic rockhound, or a cattle rancher who wants to learn more about cattle raising Down Under, Australia's expansive country has something to offer. Special golf tours feature play on Australia's top courses. Ranchers can learn more about Australia's agricultural development on tours to sheep and cattle properties; skin divers can explore the beauty of the Great Barrier Reef on diving tours designed especially for them. Tours for rockhounds include fossicking in the opal fields of Coober Pedy and Lightning Ridge. Tasting tours for wine connoisseurs go to two of Australia's wine regions—the Hunter and Barossa valleys. There are tours for horse breeders, bird watchers, anglers, and horticulturists.

These tours often include round-trip air fare, accommodations, and transportation within the country, as well as a tour guide.

Adventure tours. For the person who likes to rough it a little, there are adventure tours in Australia to the outback and country areas. You travel away from tourist roads and accommodations consist of a sleeping bag and tent. There are four-wheel-drive safari trips into North Queensland's rain forests, white-water raft trips on the upper Murray River in Victoria, camel treks into South Australia's North Flinders Ranges, alpine hikes into the Snowy Mountains, and bicycle trips around Tasmania.

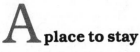

A place to stay

Accommodations in Australia are as varied as the landscape itself and range from modern high-rise hotels with first-class facilities to comfortable motels, serviced apartments, resort cabins, youth hostels, trailer parks (the Australians call them caravan parks), and campgrounds.

In general, travelers can expect a more limited choice of lodgings outside the major urban and resort centers. Outback facilities cannot always offer air-conditioning and private bathrooms; but they often compensate with good home cooking and a family atmosphere. Your hosts can offer valuable information about local attractions and road conditions.

It's advisable to make advance bookings for accommodations since Australians enjoy traveling themselves and accommodations are sometimes tight, especially during holiday periods. Though varying from state to state, these holiday periods are generally the summer holidays—a week or two before Christmas through the end of January; May holidays—one or two weeks in mid-May; August holidays—two or three weeks beginning mid-August to late August, mid-September (Queensland and Western Australia), or early October (Northern Territory); Easter—a few days before and after Easter. If you are planning your trip during any of these periods, confirmed reservations are essential, particularly in vacation areas. This applies not only to accommodations but also to transportation from place to place.

Accommodation bookings can be made with your travel agent before you leave for Australia or, upon your arrival, with the state tourist board office or a local travel agent.

Note that standard check-out time in Australia is generally 10 A.M. (some hotels 11 A.M.).

Hotels, motels & serviced apartments

The wide choice of accommodations in and near Australia's major cities and resort areas is tailored to every taste and budget. There are high-rise hotels featuring restaurants, shops, and cocktail lounges. The Wrest Point Hotel-Casino in Hobart, Tasmania, includes a gambling casino; you'll find similar hotel-casinos in Launceston, Tasmania; in Townsville and on Queensland's Gold Coast; in Alice Springs and Darwin in the Northern Territory; and in Perth, Western Australia.

In addition to plush hotels, there are simple but comfortable private hotels, guest houses, and cottages.

Built mainly in recent years, Australian motels, motor lodges, and motor inns enjoy a high reputation. You'll find them in and near major cities, in smaller towns, and in resort areas. They range from four or five-unit "family" motels to luxurious high-rise establishments. Most motel rooms—like many hotels—provide refrigerators and facilities for preparing coffee and tea; restaurants are often attached to the motel. A unique room service feature in many motels is a special delivery hatch for your tray. Your food is delivered through the outer door of this hatch which is then closed, you can then open the inside door to retrieve your meal in complete privacy.

The serviced apartment is another accommodation option in capital cities and major resort areas. Consisting of one to three rooms, as well as a bathroom and a kitchen, these apartments are generally fully equipped with cooking and eating utensils and linens. Prepared meals are not usually available on the premises.

Youth hostels

Affiliated with the International Youth Hostel Federation, the nearly 130 hostels in Australia vary in size and in the facilities they offer. You'll find youth hostels in every state; for more information, write to the Youth Hostels Association, 118 Alfred Street, Milsons Point, New South Wales 2061. You'll also find additional accommodations at YMCA and YWCA facilities.

For more information contact...

The Australian Tourist Commission (ATC) can be a helpful source of trip-planning information.

In the United States, ATC offices are located at 2121 Avenue Of The Stars, Suite 1200, Los Angeles, CA 90067 and at 489 Fifth Avenue, 31st Floor, New York, NY 10017.

The free *Great Aussie Holiday Book* is available in the United States by phoning 1-800-445-4400.

The Australian Tourist Commission's head office is located at 324 St. Kilda Road, Melbourne, Victoria 3004, Australia.

Each of Australia's states and territories operates a tourist bureau or travel center in the United States (see below). For addresses of state tourist offices in Australia, check "The essentials" feature in each chapter.

New South Wales Tourist Commission
2049 Century Park East, Suite 2250
Los Angeles, CA 90067

Victorian Tourism Commission
2121 Avenue Of The Stars, Suite 1270
Los Angeles, CA 90067

Northern Territory Tourist Commission
2121 Avenue Of The Stars, Suite 1230
Los Angeles, CA 90067

Queensland Tourist & Travel Corporation
611 North Larchmont
Los Angeles, CA 90004

South Australian Department of Tourism
2121 Avenue Of The Stars, Suite 1200
Los Angeles, CA 90067

Western Australian Tourism Commission
2121 Avenue Of The Stars, Suite 1210
Los Angeles, CA 90067

Tasmanian Department of Tourism
2121 Avenue Of The Stars, Suite 1200
Los Angeles, CA 90067

Australian Home Accommodation
209 Toorak Road, Suite 4
South Yarra, Victoria 3141, Australia

Farm Holidays
9 Fletcher Street
Woollahra, N.S.W. 2025, Australia

Host Farms Association
'Fairview'
Gnarwarre, Victoria 3221, Australia

Camping out in Australia

A number of trailer parks—caravan parks—are located near big cities and towns as well as out in the country. You can enjoy the economy of these parks without having to haul along your own trailer: many of the parks have on-site vans (house trailers) for hire at very reasonable rates. These are usually equipped with stove, refrigerator, eating and cooking utensils, linens, etc.

If you want to travel in a camper-van, a number of rental car agencies have camper-vans for hire that are fully equipped (sometimes at a small extra charge).

Some caravan parks have specially designated areas for tent camping. You'll also find regular campgrounds throughout Australia and in some of the country's many national parks.

Farm holidays

If you want to enjoy the country life, you can choose from a number of farms (stations) that offer accommodations. It's an excellent way to meet Australians and enjoy some warm hospitality.

Accommodations on these stations can vary from very plush to very spartan. In some places, you might stay in your own separate cottage; in others you might be in the station owner's home, eating with the family and sharing their bathroom facilities.

While on the farm, you're on your own to do whatever you wish, including the farm chores. You can also fish in a nearby creek, swim in the family swimming pool (or waterhole), or go for a horseback ride.

A list of stations offering farm holidays is available from each state's tourist board and from the addresses at left.

Meet an Australian

There are several "bed and breakfast" plans that feature a stay with a local family. Your accommodations might be a waterfront home near Sydney, a beach-side house on the Gold Coast, or a sheep property in Victoria.

For more information, contact Bed and Breakfast International (Australia), 396 Kent Street, Sydney, N.S.W. 2000, Australia.

Traveling around a vast country

Australia is a vast land of nearly 8 million square km/3 million square miles, much of it sparsely populated because people tend to live in or near capital cities. The distances between these centers are great, but seem even greater because of their empty openness.

The quickest way from city to city is by air. Roads between cities generally have only two lanes.

The following tells you the length of time it takes to travel between certain cities. From Sydney to Alice Springs, it takes about 3 hours by air and 56 hours by bus. The trip from Sydney to Brisbane takes a little over an hour by air and almost 18 hours by bus. The distance between Sydney and Melbourne can be covered in little over an hour by air, but takes 14½ hours by bus.

Flying around Australia

Early in Australia's history, the country realized the importance of air service in linking isolated towns. The first route flown was between Geraldton and Derby in Western Australia in 1921. In 1922, Queensland and Northern Territories Aerial Services Limited (now known as Qantas, the country's international carrier) began flights between Cloncurry and Charleville, Queensland.

Today, frequent air service links all of Australia's cities and many smaller towns. Both Ansett Airlines and Australian Airlines (formerly Trans-Australia) have routes throughout Australia. East-West Airlines has an extensive network in New South Wales with additional service to other states. Kendell Airlines connects cities and towns in New South Wales, South Australia, and Victoria.

Air New South Wales flies to points within New South Wales, and to Ayers Rock. Ansett N.T. covers the Northern Territory and flies to Cairns. Ansett W.A. connects the vast reaches of Western Australia to Darwin and Alice Springs. Air Queensland provides service within this state. In addition to these larger airline companies, numerous small airlines provide regional services.

Discounts. Although Australia's airline services can be convenient, they also can be expensive. Several discount packages are available to help reduce the costs of Australian air transportation. We mention a few of the available discounts below. Since fares vary from season to season—and even from week to week—always consult a travel agent for the latest information on ticket fares and restrictions.

Airlines offering discount packages include Ansett Airlines, Australian Airlines, East-West Airlines, Air New South Wales, and Kendell Airlines. Many of the discounted fares are offered only to persons holding international airline tickets. In some cases, these tickets must be either an excursion or promotional airfare to qualify for the domestic air carrier discount. These discount tickets may have to be purchased prior to arrival.

Both airpasses and discount airfares are available. Some airpasses allow unlimited mileage on the carrier's routes with a maximum number of days to complete the journey. Still other airpasses set limitations on the number of miles traveled within a specified time frame. Stopover restrictions may also apply. Airfare discounts usually range from 20 to 35 percent and a minimum number of sectors may be required.

Reservations. As with hotel accommodations, it is advisable to make advance reservations for flights, especially during holiday periods. You can make your reservations through your travel agent or, in Australia, with the airline office concerned.

Riding the rails

Australia's network of rail lines provides numerous rail travel opportunities. The principal lines follow the east and south coasts, linking the principal cities of Cairns, Brisbane, Sydney, Melbourne, and Adelaide. Lines from Adelaide connect with the line between Sydney and Perth—the famous *Indian-Pacific* run (see page 96)—and with a line to Alice Springs.

In addition to this major network of interstate rail service, there is intrastate service as well as suburban rail service in metropolitan areas.

Discounts. If you plan to travel a good deal on Australia's trains, you might want to purchase an Austrailpass entitling you to unlimited, first or budget-class rail travel on interstate, intrastate, and metropolitan trains. Sleeping berths and meals are extra. You can purchase a pass for 14 days (with a 7-day extension available), or 1, 2, and 3 months, depending on your needs. The pass must be purchased before you go to Australia. The agent is Tour Pacific/Australian Travel Service, 1101 E. Broadway, Glendale, CA 91205.

In addition to the Austrailpass, there are all-lines tickets which offer unlimited rail travel within a particular

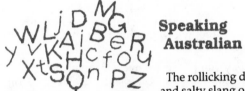

Speaking Australian

The rollicking dialect and salty slang of the Australians reflect a nimble-witted humor unique to Australia. Although English is the country's official language, an Australian's interpretation of this language might prove mind-boggling to a visitor.

First, the pronunciation of words can be different. The letter *A* takes a long sound, either as long *i* (eye) or somewhere between *a* and *i*. Thus, "Good day, mate" is pronounced "Goo'dye, mite." More obvious in pronunciation is the disappearance of the letter *r* in the middle or last syllable of a word. Thus Melbourne is pronounced Mel'bun.

A number of Australia's colorful words and expressions might put you *up a gum tree* (in a quandary). *Bo-peep* (take a look at) some of the words and expressions listed in the next paragraph and *give it a burl* (try it) yourself.

One of the most commonly heard expressions is *fair dinkum* which means absolutely true or genuine. Other vigorous Aussie terms you might hear include *beaut* (an exclamation of approval), *galah* (a fool), *wowser* (a straight-laced person, a spoil sport), *crook* (sick), *cobber* (a friend, also *mate*, *sport*), *squatter* (large landowner), *jumbuck* (sheep), *billabong* (water hole), *tucker* (food), or *drink with the flies* (drink alone). Of all Aussie slang terms, *bloody* is the most commonplace. You hear it everywhere except in polite English households—where youngsters, particularly, bloody well better not use it.

Aussie expressions can be an enjoyable challenge. Just remember that the key to communications is friendliness. Smile, and somewhere along the way you're bound to hear the friendly greeting: "Goo'dye mite; 'owyer goin'? Can I shout yer a beer (buy you a beer)?"

state for a designated period of time. Check with the state Public Transport Commission office or the state tourist office for more information. These can be purchased after your arrival in Australia. Some states also feature package tours using public transportation.

Making reservations. Australia's rail services are also popular with Australian travelers, so it is important to book in advance, if possible. This is especially true of the *Indian-Pacific* run between Sydney and Perth.

For reservations, contact your travel agent or the Railway Booking office in the capital city where your first rail trip begins.

Taking to the road by bus

Whether you want to sightsee your way through Australia, or just travel between a few major cities and see a little scenery along the way, Australia has three bus companies to fill your needs. Traveling the highways and byways of Australia are Ansett Pioneer, Greyhound, and Deluxe coachlines. Coaches usually have air conditioning, toilet facilities, fully adjustable seats, picture windows, and a driver versed in sights along the way.

Part of the fun of traveling by bus is planning your own itinerary and stopping where you want. It's also a great way to meet Australians.

Discounts. If you plan extensive bus travel in Australia, investigate the various special plans. Periods of validity vary by company and plan, but most range between 10 and 90 days. Most must be purchased before arriving in Australia.

Ansett Pioneer Express offers the "Aussiepass" and "Super Aussiepass", covering fast inter-city service on its coaches throughout Australia (including Tasmania, on Redline coaches); some sightseeing is also included. The "Super Aussiepass" includes limited accommodations at Flag Inns.

Deluxe Coachlines' "Koalapass" offers unlimited travel on its express network for periods from 10 to 90 days.

Greyhound's "Aussie Explorer" offers a series of wide-ranging circular tours on express coaches, valid for up to 12 months; you begin the journey anywhere along the route but must travel in one direction without backtracking. The Greyhound Bus Pass offers unlimited travel over its express coach network. Both plans include discounts on selected accommodations, sightseeing tours, and rental cars.

Tours. A variety of package tours which include daylight transportation, informed commentaries, and accommodations depart from capital cities regularly. Run by a number of different bus companies, these tours can range from 2 or 3 days to 8 weeks.

Still another bus tour features camping out. Rather than hotels, you stay in a tent you pitch yourself and help with the cookout. These tours can range from a long weekend to a 44-day tour around the country.

Reservations. Talk to your travel agent about discount passes and reservations. As with train and air travel, buses are a popular form of local transportation, particularly during holiday periods. In Australia, you can make bus reservations through the office of the bus line on which you want to travel.

Taking to the road by car

Cars are especially convenient for day trips out of major cities and resort areas. They give you the freedom to explore what you want at the pace you want. However, be prepared to drive on the left side of the road and on two-lane thoroughfares in many areas. Major highways linking capital cities are paved, but you'll find that roads between smaller towns can be gravel, and in remote outback areas the road might be nothing more than a two-wheel track.

If you are thinking of exploring all of Australia by car, bear in mind that beyond cities, distances are great and towns sometimes few and far between. For longer journeys, it might be best to take an air-conditioned train or bus or a domestic plane flight.

Renting a car. You'll find rental car agencies throughout Australia. Companies include Avis, Budget, Hertz, Letz, Natcar, and Thrifty.

To rent a car you'll need a valid driver's license from home. Minimum rental-age varies from 21 years old to 25 depending on the rental agency. Foreign car insurance is not valid in Australia. Compulsory third party insurance will be automatically added to your car rental charges.

All sizes of automobiles are available for hire. In the warmer climates of Alice Springs, Cairns, or the Gold Coast, you might want to rent a mini-moke. This open-air, jeeplike vehicle is an economical, breezy way to travel short trips. Some rental car agencies also rent self-contained camper-vans accommodating up to 5 people.

Driving tips. First—fasten your seat belt. It's against the law not to wear your seat belt; and failure to do so can result in a fine.

Next, remember that you drive on the left side of the road. If you're a pedestrian, you look to your right instead of left before you step off the curb to cross the street. Speed limits are generally 60 km/36 miles per hour in cities and towns and 100 km/60 miles per hour in Australia's open country.

Traveling in the remote outback on dirt tracks is not really advisable for the inexperienced. Tracks can sometimes become confusing or disappear. Flash floods are not uncommon. If you must head into rough country on a dirt track, check out road conditions with local residents before you go, and leave your destination and time of arrival with someone before you leave. Take along an extra supply of water and gas, and if your car does break down, stay near it, don't wander off.

A word of warning about Australia's wildlife. In the country areas—on both paved and unpaved roads—kangaroos as well as domestic livestock have been known to stray onto the road at dusk and become blinded by headlights. Hitting a 2-meter/6-foot kangaroo can be very damaging to you and your car. Australians who travel country roads often have steel guards on the front of their cars as protection against wandering wildlife.

Going for a cruise

Don't overlook the possibility of seeing some of Australia by boat. The *M.V. Abel Tasman*, an 850-passenger/car ferry, sails between Melbourne and Devonport, Tasmania. The

Angler nets catch in New South Wales stream. Trout fishing, good in many spots throughout Australia, is particularly rewarding in the state of Tasmania.

Immaculately clad members of local lawn bowling team roll balls down well-kept turf during tournament.

Brightly colored sails catch the wind. Weekends find eager yachters hoisting spinnakers in Sydney Harbour.

overnight sailing, which takes about 14½ hours, can be rough at times.

Still another water option is a calm, leisurely 5 or 5½-day cruise aboard a paddle wheel boat on the Murray River. Amenities include comfortable cabins, pleasant sun decks, and good food. There are also shorter day trips on the Murray.

If you want to skipper your own boat, you can rent a houseboat in several places, including the Hawkesbury River near Sydney and the Murray River. These houseboats come fully equipped with stove, refrigerator, toilet, water supplies, cooking and eating utensils, linens, etc.

Dozens of fully equipped, big-game fishing boats, available for charter, dock at Cairns, Port Lincoln, and Kangaroo Island (South Australia), and at Tasmanian harbors. In most of the major coastal cities, you can charter yachts or boats for light fishing or cruising.

Know before you go

The following pertinent information will help you plan your trip—from documents you'll need to enter the country to items you should pack in your suitcase.

Entry formalities

In order to enter Australia, you'll need a valid passport and a visa. Visitor visa application forms are available from Australian consular offices in Los Angeles, San Francisco, New York, Chicago, Washington, D.C., Honolulu, Houston, Ottawa, Toronto, and Vancouver.

Inoculations. Only visitors arriving from an area infected with smallpox, yellow fever, or cholera are required to have a valid International Certificate of Vaccination showing inoculation against these diseases.

Customs. The only duty-free items you're allowed to bring into Australia are your personal effects including 200 cigarettes or 250 grams (approximately a half-pound) of tobacco or cigars as well as a liter (approximately a quart) of liquor.

Sporting equipment and camping gear are admitted without duty, but the importation of firearms and ammunition is restricted, subject to approval by state police authorities. Reasonable limits are placed on the importation of radios, tape recorders, tape players, dictating machines, and record players.

Strict controls are maintained on the importation of animals and plants and on the transport of plants between the various Australian states.

Currency. Australia has a decimal currency system. As in the United States, $1 equals 100 cents. Australian notes come in denominations of $2, $5, $10, $20, $50, and $100; coins are minted in denominations of 1 cent, 2 cents, 5 cents, 20 cents, 50 cents, and $1. You may bring in any amount of personal funds into the country, but you can't take out more than the amount you brought in.

International credit cards that are accepted include American Express, Diners Club, Carte Blanche, Visa, Mastercard, and their affiliates. Usage may be restricted in small shops and in smaller towns and country areas.

Departure tax. A A$20 departure tax is assessed departing travelers, payable in Australian currency. Transit passengers are exempt from payment of the tax.

What to pack

Except for business and certain evening functions, casual, informal clothing is the rule. Australians reserve their formal attire for opening nights and diplomatic functions. Men might want to bring along a coat and tie for dinner at more elegant restaurants in the larger cities.

Remember that the seasons are reversed in the Southern Hemisphere. If you visit Australia between November and March (summer), be sure to include lightweight clothes for warm weather, a sweater for air-conditioned rooms, and your swimsuit, sunglasses, and suntan lotion. It's warm all year in the northern tropical areas of Australia, but winters in the southeastern states can be cool and rainy, so bring along warm clothing, a lined raincoat, and an umbrella.

Some useful items. If you are traveling into Australia's Centre (Alice Springs area), bring along durable, casual clothes, good walking shoes, and a sunhat. Winter evenings in this area can be chilly. People going to the Great Barrier Reef will want to bring along a pair of tennis shoes for reef walking. Still another useful item is insect repellent to ward off flies and mosquitoes.

Electrical appliances. Electric current in Australia is 220-240 volts A.C., and 50 cycles. Leading hotels usually have 110 volt outlets for razors and small appliances, but for larger appliances such as hairdryers, you'll need to bring along a converter and a special flat three-pin adapter plug to fit into outlets.

A few other details

Here are still more helpful items of information to familiarize you with Australia.

What time is it? When it's noon in Perth, it's 1:30 P.M. in Darwin and Adelaide and 2 P.M. from Cairns down to Hobart. Australia has three time zones: Eastern Standard Time is 10 hours ahead of Greenwich mean time; Central Australian Standard Time is 9½ hours ahead; and Western Standard Time is 8 hours ahead.

During the summer months, most of Australia (except Queensland, Western Australia, and Northern Territory) set their clocks ahead for daylight savings time.

There's an 18-hour time difference between Sydney and San Francisco, which means that when it is 10 A.M. Monday in Sydney, it is 4 P.M. Sunday in San Francisco. This time difference will vary with daylight savings time.

To tip or not to tip. In Australia, tipping is a reward for good service. It is the customer's prerogative; restaurants do not add a service charge to the bill. A tip of 10 to 15 percent is customary at first-class restaurants if you feel you've had good service. You can tip baggage porters about A20 to A30 cents per suitcase.

Measuring up. Some years ago Australia converted to the metric system of weights and measures, so a small, wallet-size conversion table might be helpful in your travels.

Australia's many special events

Whether you prefer concerts or rodeos, flower shows or football, you'll find plenty of activities to suit your taste on Australia's calendar of events. The major regularly scheduled events are covered below.

January—March

New Year's Day (January 1). This public holiday is celebrated with surf carnivals and horse race meetings (including Perth Cup in Western Australia).

Festival of Sydney. A month-long series of art and cultural events held in January.

Australia Day. A national holiday observed the last Monday in January, it commemorates the founding of the first settlement at Sydney in 1788. Events include the Royal Sydney Anniversary Regatta in Sydney Harbour plus ceremonies and parades throughout the country.

Royal Hobart Regatta. In early February, this several-day aquatic carnival in Tasmania features sailing, swimming, and rowing events plus fireworks and parades.

Festival of Perth. Held mid-February to mid-March, this cultural festival in Western Australia includes a foreign film festival, concerts, opera, and ballet.

Moomba Festival. An annual event held in Melbourne in late February or early March, the festival features art exhibitions, concerts, street theater, and a parade.

Adelaide Festival. This festival is held in March on even-numbered years. It is a 3-week concentration of art exhibits plus performances in music, drama, and dance by visiting international artists and Australian artists.

Canberra Festival. This 10-day March festival celebrating Canberra's birthday includes cultural and sports events.

April—June

Royal Easter Show. The most popular of the country's agricultural shows, it is held in Sydney in early to mid-April.

Anzac Day. On April 25 this solemn holiday commemorates the 1915 landing of the Australian and New Zealand Army Corps (ANZAC) at Gallipoli in Turkey during World War I. War heroes of this and later conflicts are remembered with massive parades, memorial services, speeches, and sporting events.

Barossa Valley Vintage Festival. Held during late April in odd-numbered years, this festival heralds the harvest of this area's wine grapes.

Bangtail Muster. Horse racing, a rodeo, and cattle roundup are features of this event held in early May in Alice Springs.

Camel Cup. In May this well-known camel race is held in Alice Springs.

Beer Can Regatta. Beer cans are the building materials for speedboats, sailboats, and rafts that race on Darwin Harbour on this public holiday in June.

July—September

Doomben Ten Thousand. In the first half of July, this winter carnival horse race is held in Brisbane.

Royal Shows. Held in August, the Brisbane Royal Show is noted for its unusual display of Queensland's tropical plants and flowers. Other Royal Shows featuring agricultural displays are held in September in Melbourne, Adelaide, and Perth.

Rugby football finals. Rugby League and rugby Union grand final competitions are held at Sydney Cricket Ground in September.

Australian Rules football finals. Some 100,000 spectators turn out at Melbourne Cricket Ground to watch the four September games of these fast-moving finals.

October—December

Henley-on-Todd Regatta. This yacht race is held on a dry riverbed in Alice Springs in early October.

Royal Hobart Show. An agricultural show, it is held in mid-October in Tasmania.

Jacaranda Festival. Events at this October festival in Grafton, New South Wales, include parades, floral displays, and sporting events.

Spring Racing Carnival. A week-long series of horse races in Melbourne culminates in the Melbourne Cup in early November.

Melbourne Cup. Australia's richest handicap race, it is held on the first Tuesday of November at Flemington Race Course in Melbourne.

Cricket matches. They are held November through March in cities and towns across the country; international matches are held in state capitals from late December to early February.

Surf carnivals. Teams of volunteer lifeguards give spectacular displays of lifesaving techniques (see page 28). On weekends and holidays, December through March, on beaches in New South Wales, Queensland, Victoria, and South and Western Australia.

Carols by candlelight. Outdoor caroling in Melbourne's Myer Music Bowl, Sydney's Hyde Park, and in other cities and towns throughout Australia in mid-December.

Boxing Day. A national holiday, it falls on December 26 and marks the start of the Sydney-Hobart Yacht Race, Australia's yachting classic for ocean cruisers.

S Y D N E Y

In New South Wales, urban bustle or rural quiet

The heart of New South Wales is Sydney, the state's capital and the largest city in Australia. With a population of three million, Sydney is a bustling center for industry, business, and manufacturing as well as a major world port. Spreading over about 1,736 square km/670 square miles, the city seems to stretch from an undulating coastline in the east to the horizon in the west, north, and south.

Where the city's thriving metropolitan area ends, the bush of New South Wales begins. Since most of the state's residents live in the Sydney metropolitan area, the rest of the state's 803,109 square km/310,000 square miles are wide-open spaces—a playground for those who want to enjoy the outdoors.

New South Wales's superb coastline—including golden beaches, dramatic headlands, and quiet bays and river estuaries—are a haven for swimmers, surfers, and fishers. Bushwalkers can enjoy the Blue Mountains just west of Sydney or travel north to the New England area where trees turn vibrant red and gold in the fall. Throughout the state are numerous national parks where visitors can enjoy Australia's outdoor offerings.

Sydney—A zestful city

The key to Sydney's splendor is its harbor. It gives the city a pronounced maritime character and an immense vitality. From a number of vantage points throughout the city you can enjoy the harbor's beauty—its quiet coves, its dramatic headlands, and its wooded peninsulas. Beyond the water of the harbor are the coastal beaches—alluring expanses of golden sand that stretch north and south along the Pacific Ocean.

All this water plus a warm, subtropical climate makes Sydney an outdoor city. The residents are outdoor people who enjoy such pastimes as surfing, swimming, boating, fishing, water-skiing, and sun-bathing.

The sail-shaped roofline of Sydney's Opera House provides a dramatic backdrop for outdoor dining. The complex includes concert and opera halls and a playhouse.

Summer daytime temperatures average 26°C/78°F. When the temperatures do soar to 38°C/100°F, residents can escape to the beaches or to the Blue Mountains. Winters are mild, with daytime temperatures averaging 13°C/55°F.

The feeling of Sydney is vital, breezy, brash, and busy. It's a place with a zest for life.

Getting your bearings

Geographically Sydney is divided into Sydney proper on one side of the harbor and North Sydney on the other. The city's famous Harbour Bridge spans the bay to link these two metropolitan areas.

Many of the sights are clustered in the central city area—Sydney proper; those in North Sydney can be easily reached by ferry from Circular Quay, or by train. In fact the heart of Sydney seems to be Circular Quay (pronounced *key*).

Within minutes you can walk from the quay to the Opera House and Harbour Bridge and to one of Sydney's best viewing spots—the 48-story Australia Square Tower on George Street—where you can survey the entire city in a painless orientation course.

Australia Square Tower—a round building in Australia Square—has its observation terrace on the 48th floor. From here, you have an impressive, 360-degree view of the city, including the bustling harbor, the historic Rocks area, and the constantly changing downtown skyline. The terrace is open daily from 10 A.M. to 10 P.M.

Sydney Tower, atop the Centrepoint commercial complex on Pitt Street, provides another vantage point. The 298-meter/984-foot tower's central shaft is topped with a golden capsule. Inside this capsule is an observation deck, open daily, and a pair of revolving restaurants.

Seeing the city

Like many of the world's major cities, Sydney is a contrast of old and new. There are soaring glass and steel skyscrapers and the dramatic white sails of the Opera House, offset by interesting old historical buildings.

Captain Arthur Phillip and 1,000 convicts set foot on the shores of Sydney Cove in 1788. Today, you can see some of this settlement's buildings in The Rocks—a his-

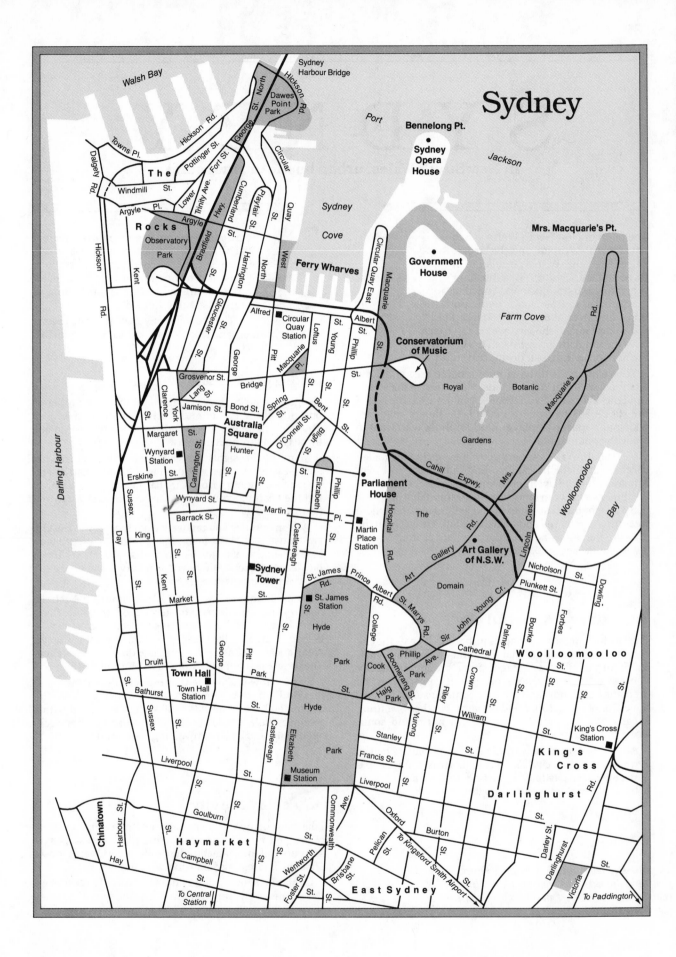

Sydney

toric area of Sydney that is being restored. In other sections of Sydney you'll see some of convict-architect Francis Greenway's buildings, as well as some of Sydney's early gracious mansions.

Besides historic offerings, Sydney has a number of modern shopping centers for visitors to browse through, and museums and galleries to enjoy. Sydney's entertainment scene runs the gamut from the bright neon lights of King's Cross to drama and opera productions at the Opera House.

Sydney Opera House

An improbable collection of curving walls that soar 70 meters/230 feet above Bennelong Point, this may be the most talked-about building in the world. Certainly it has become an international symbol of Australia, surpassing with ease the kangaroo and the koala. From its inception in 1956 to its completion in 1973, the building was the source of endless local arguments and discussions.

It all started when the New South Wales government

The essentials

Australia's largest and most internationally minded city is well endowed with ample comforts for the traveler.

Getting there. Australia's internal and external transportation networks have their hubs at Sydney.

Air. International service to and from Sydney is by Qantas and foreign flag carriers from New Zealand, the United Kingdom, continental Europe, the Orient, Southeast Asia, and North America.

Domestic flights by Ansett, Australian, East-West, and Air New South Wales link Sydney and other state capitals. Other New South Wales towns are served by Air New South Wales and East-West Airlines.

Kingsford Smith International Airport is about 30 minutes south of downtown by taxi or bus.

Sea. Pacific cruise ships call at Sydney, most of them docking downtown at Sydney Cove.

Rail. Direct routes link Sydney with Brisbane, Perth, Canberra, and Melbourne. Train connections west can also be made from Melbourne to Adelaide, Alice Springs, and Perth.

Accommodations. Like most Australian cities, Sydney has a welcome concentration of hotels and restaurants in the main shopping and business districts.

Major hotels include Boulevard, Chateau Sydney, Hilton International Sydney, Holiday Inn Menzies, Hyatt Kingsgate, Inter-Continental Sydney, Old Sydney Inn, Ramada Gazebo, Regent of Sydney, Rushcutter Traveldge, Sebel Town House, Sheraton Wentworth, Southern Cross-Sydney, and Wynyard Traveldge.

Food and drink. An unofficial census gives Sydney 3,000 restaurants, a number that includes at least one for every major ethnic cuisine in the world. Sydney's own chief claims for gastronomy center around local seafoods, especially Sydney rock oysters, a white-fleshed fish called John Dory, snapper, and salt-water crayfish. Sydney's reigning dish for everyman is the meat pie, as common here as the hamburger is in Chicago.

The most prestigious wines of New South Wales come from nearby Hunter River Valley, the reds mostly Shiraz, the whites mostly Semillon. Producers include old standbys Lindemans and McWilliams, and such smaller cellars as Tyrrells and Lake's Folly.

Tooheys and KB Reschs are popular Sydney beers.

Getting around. Central Sydney is so compact that feet can do most of the traveling, but an excellent public transport system is there to be used.

A loop subway stops at Town Hall, Wynyard, Circular Quay, Martin Place, St. James, and Museum stations; another line links Martin Place (downtown) with King's Cross and Bondi Junction.

The Sydney Explorer Bus travels an 18 km/11 mile loop around the city daily from 9:30 A.M. to 5 P.M., stopping at 20 tourist attractions en route. Full-day tickets can be purchased on the bus or from the Travel Centre of New South Wales.

Ferries provide quick cross-harbor service and routes to ocean beaches (see page 29).

Public transportation maps are available from the Urban Transit Authority, 11 York Street, or the Travel Centre of New South Wales, 16 Spring Street.

Taxis and rental cars are abundant.

Tours. Half and full-day bus tours cover city sights, southern beaches, northern suburbs, Blue Mountains (see page 39), Hawkesbury River (page 40), and Hunter Valley (page 41). Most tours leave from Circular Quay West. Hotel pickup can also be arranged.

Half and full-day train tours take in the Blue Mountains, Old Sydney Town, Hawkesbury River, and Hunter Valley.

For a bird's-eye-view of the city, try a helicopter or bi-plane flight over the harbor and northern beaches. Scenic seaplane flights are also available.

For more information. The Travel Centre of New South Wales, 16 Spring Street, Sydney 2000, is open weekdays from 8:30 A.M. to 5 P.M.

decided to build an opera house on Bennelong Point—a beautiful headland bounded by Sydney Harbour on three sides and the Royal Botanic Gardens on the fourth. The government asked architects from around the world to submit designs for a building on the site. From the 223 entries submitted, that of Danish architect Joern Utzon was selected.

Utzon's sketches showed a building unlike any other in the world, its soaring roof structure resembling a cluster of billowing sails, a fitting design for a building nearly surrounded by a harbor alive with boats. But Utzon's submission was only a schematic presentation of sketches. He had not been required to submit any final plans with such particulars as engineering details and cost estimates.

Though Utzon's design was free as the wind on paper, the concrete problems of constructing it were another matter. From inception to completion, the building took 17 years. Part way through the project Utzon resigned. Costs, originally estimated at $12 million, rose through the years to more than $100 million. (Sydney proved it is a sporting town; a lottery paid the bills in just 2 years.)

The final results of all the years of problems and frustrations is one of the most exciting buildings in the world. It's a vast complex housing some 90 rooms under its soaring roofs: a concert hall seating 2,700, an opera hall accommodating more than 1,500, a playhouse seating 600, and smaller halls for recitals and receptions. There are also two restaurants on the premises.

To get a feeling for the building, take the long stroll around it to study its form and shape. You'll note upon closer inspection that the roof tiles that create the white soaring sails of the Opera House aren't really white at all. Instead they are an intermingling of off-white glossy tiles with buff-colored matte tiles, a combination that reflects the mood of the daytime hours—from early morning until dusk.

After your leisurely stroll around the outside, take one of the guided tours offered, Monday through Friday from 9 A.M. to 4 P.M. to see how some of the unconventional qualities of Utzon's exterior have been matched by uncommon touches in the great concert halls by Australian architect Peter Hall. In the symphony hall, finished with thousands of narrow, vertical strips of wood, a narrow tier of seats runs behind the orchestra, allowing conductor watchers an unparalleled opportunity to see (if not hear) the shadings of orchestral playing. The opera theater, contrarily, has its front and side walls and the backs of all its seats painted mat black, so as to focus every bit of attention on the stage.

Good as the tours are, the Sydney Opera House is at its best when crowded for a performance. The outer halls were deliberately underplayed to put audiences into the forefront just as the inner halls were shaped and finished to benefit the performers.

You can book a package tour, dinner, and performance as much as 12 months in advance through travel agents or Qantas, or you may book directly by writing to Tourism Marketing Section, Sydney Opera House, GPO Box 4274, Sydney 2001. For schedules of performances in the current year, write the Australian Tourist Commission. (For additional information on types of performances given in the Opera House, see "The lively arts," page 33.)

On Sundays—weather permitting—there is free outdoor entertainment around the Opera House between noon and 8 P.M. You'll see everything from street theater to jazz bands.

There is no parking at the Opera House. If you're driving into town to attend a performance, park your car at the Domain Parking Station. A special bus will take you to the front steps.

Sydney on The Rocks

If you want to discover what Sydney's architecture was like in the early days, before the advent of soaring glass-and-steel skyscrapers, take a trip to The Rocks. To Sydneysiders, this area includes the entire western promontory of Sydney Cove. It was here that working parties of convicts from Captain Phillip's First Fleet began to chisel out the beginnings of a town.

The history of this area of Sydney has not always shown man at his best, but it has been colorful. The area's rocky terrain stifled development. Good roads and decent drainage were impossible. Instead a series of alleyways and dead end streets appeared. Soon these were lined with taverns, hovels, flophouses, gaming houses, and brothels. In 1855 The Rocks had 37 taverns with intriguing names like "Hit and Miss" and "Live and Let Live." The area became the haunt of sailors, harpies, whores, and bands of thugs. The 1900s brought bubonic plague to the area, and in the rat hunts that followed, whole areas of The Rocks were razed. Still further destruction took place in the 1920s, when more buildings were destroyed to make way for the Sydney Harbour Bridge approaches. In the 1970s the Sydney Cove Redevelopment Authority was formed to salvage what was left of The Rocks and revitalize and renovate it.

As you stroll the streets of The Rocks, you'll see this redevelopment. Many buildings have already been partly or fully restored. Courtyards have been paved, and gas lamps added. Many buildings now house antique stores, arts and crafts shops, galleries, and restaurants.

The best way to explore The Rocks is on foot. Start your explorations at The Rocks Visitors' Centre at 104 George Street. It's open from 8:30 A.M. to 4:30 P.M. weekdays, and 10 to 5 on weekends and public holidays. Here you can see a film on The Rocks and get a useful map and other information on the area. There are guided tours of The Rocks daily from the Argyle Centre on Argyle Street. Phone ahead (27-6678) for tour reservations.

The following are some points of interest you'll want to see during your Rocks exploration. (You'll also want to take a look at nearby Pier One, Sydney's oldest shipping terminal. It's now an entertainment complex with a variety of shops and restaurants.)

Along George Street. Sprinkled along George Street are a number of bars, sandwich shops, and specialty shops including a shop for left-handed people and a shop selling seashells. The Orient Hotel, at the corner of Argyle and George streets, was built in 1850 and has been faithfully restored.

The Geological and Mining Museum, 36 George Street, contains one of the best displays of geological specimens in the Southern Hemisphere. Here you'll see mineral ores, fossils, and gemstones. The building was built in 1902 as an electric light station. Hours are 9:30 A.M.

Lingering over lunch, shoppers enjoy an oasis created by leafy trees and curtains of water. King's Cross area, center of nighttime activity, abounds with noise and neon.

Future lifeguards enjoy surf and sand at one of 34 grand beaches within easy reach of downtown Sydney.

Surf carnival time

It's a warm summer day at the beach and the scene about to unfold is uniquely Australian. Several groups of bronzed lifeguards in distinctive swim suits and headgear march along the beach with military precision. At the head of each column, a member carries the club pennant. The groups come to a stop and stand at parade rest. Then the action begins. The lifeguards launch surf boats into the pounding surf, stage demonstration rescues of swimmers in distress, and race boats.

The event is a surf carnival whose participants are volunteer members of surf lifesaving clubs. You'll find one or more such carnivals on the beaches of Sydney almost any weekend from December through March, and less frequently during the summer on other beaches in New South Wales, Queensland, Victoria, South Australia, and Western Australia.

The first lifesaving club was originated at Bondi Beach in Sydney in 1907 (with the motto "Vigilance and Service") to help save swimmers who tired in the rough surf or were caught in the riptide. Today there are 160 affiliated clubs with more than 25,000 members and an amazing record of rescues—more than 7,000 yearly.

Surf rescues are carried out by several methods including by belt and reel and by boat.

Belt and reel rescue squads are seven-man teams. One member, wearing a belt and trailing a light line attached to a large reel on shore, swims out to a swimmer in trouble. While he holds the swimmer, the reel men bring them both back to the beach. In a surf carnival, competing teams are judged on precision and speed.

Surf boat squads are five-man teams (four rowers and a helmsman). Boats are used when the surf is too rough for a lifeguard or when the swimmer is too far offshore. The five life-jacketed members launch their boats into the crashing surf and row through the breakers to reach the swimmer in distress. The most thrilling event for spectators at a surf carnival occurs when these surf boat teams row out through the breakers, round a buoy, and race back to the beach.

---

to 4 P.M. weekdays, 1 to 4 P.M. on Saturdays, and 11 A.M. to 4 P.M. on Sundays.

Lower Fort Street. Next, head out to Dawes Point Park at the tip of the promontory. From here you get a good view of The Rocks, including the peaked roofs of the remodeled Campbell's Storehouses, home of the Australian Wine Centre. You can also see the Opera House.

High above Dawes Point Park's grassy expanse tower the approaches to the Sydney Harbour Bridge. Walk under the bridge and over to Lower Fort Street. Several gracious old Georgian buildings line this street—an area where prosperous merchants lived. Numbers 59 and 61 are particularly elegant, and so is Bligh House (number 43). Built in 1833, this was the home of Robert Campbell Jr., son of the colony's first merchant. Today, this historic building is occupied by the Australian College of General Practitioners.

Of an entirely different order is the Hero of Waterloo Hotel, a pub with an interesting history. During the 1800s, ships' crews were hard to find. It is said that a trapdoor in the floor of this bar helped to fill a few captains' orders. Unwary imbibers were dropped to a tunnel below and hauled off to sea. Note that some of the windows of the hotel are only painted on—when the hotel was built, there was a tax on window glass.

Argyle Place. Continuing another block up Lower Fort Street, you'll come to Argyle Place, a delightful corner of old Sydney just below Observatory Park. Terrace houses and cottages trimmed in a variety of iron lace border a true village green that is shaded by giant trees and lighted by gas lamps. The restored houses on this street were built between 1830 and 1880.

Sydney's second oldest church stands facing one corner of the green. The cornerstone of the Church of the Holy Trinity—better known as Garrison Church—was laid in 1840. After its completion, it became the official garrison church for the English Queen's Regiments stationed at Dawes Point. Note the beautiful stained-glass east window that depicts the Holy Trinity.

Observatory Park. This rolling stretch of parkland shaded by large Moreton Bay fig trees overlooks Argyle Place and the harbor. From this sandstone bluff, you get a good view of Sydney Harbour Bridge. The Observatory, built in 1858, is open 10 A.M. to noon weekdays (except Wednesday when it closes at 5 P.M.), and weekends from 1 to 5 P.M. You can get to the park by climbing the flight of stairs located opposite the Argyle Place green.

Argyle Cut. Descending the stairs, head down Argyle Street through the damp Argyle Cut. Construction began on this tunnel in 1843. Pick-wielding convicts struggled to hew the tunnel out of solid rock. It was later widened to accommodate cars.

Argyle Arts Centre. Just beyond the tunnel is the brick Argyle Arts Centre. It's located in the old bond stores built between 1828 and 1881. At one time goods were delivered into the cobblestone central courtyard by horse and carriage. Today, the Argyle Arts Centre, open daily from 10 A.M. to 5:30 P.M., features a number of shops where browsers can watch craftspeople at work on silverware, copperware, leather goods, pottery, stained glass, and art enamels.

Cadman's Cottage. On George Street, not far from where Argyle Street intersects it, is Cadman's Cottage—a simple, cream colored building dating from about 1816 and believed to be the oldest building still standing in the city of Sydney. Originally called the Coxswains' Barracks, it was home for the government boatswains, including John Cadman, the Overseer of Government Craft, who gave it his name.

Heart of the harbor

Sydney Harbour is huge, one of the world's largest. But the heart of it nestles in the few hundred meters of shore-line between the Opera House and The Rocks. Sydney had its origins in this cove in 1788, when Captain Phillips landed on the spot. The first pier was called Semicircular Quay. Today, the main one is Circular Quay. It's only a name—the quay is not even semicircular.

Circular Quay may be the heart of the city as well as the harbor. At least this is where many of its arteries of transportation come together. Ferries and hydrofoils depart from six jetties for destinations as close as straight across the harbor or as distant as its mouth, 11 km/7 miles east. Passenger ships dock just alongside. In front of the ferry building, elevated commuter train tracks lead into Sydney. Higher still, Harbour Bridge looms against the skyline, the quick connection to North Sydney.

The Circular Quay's recent redevelopment included

***

Cruising Sydney Harbour

Sydney has one of the most beautiful harbors in the world. In size alone it outdoes the harbors of some other major world cities, its watery expanse lapping against more than 290 km/180 miles of shoreline. There are secluded beaches, quiet coves, inviting bays, soaring headlands. In some places, homes march to the shore's edge and marinas extend their arms into the water. In other places, wild native bushland reaches to the bay's edge, and man is but a visitor.

To enjoy this exceptional harbor, as well as get a different perspective of Sydney's skyline, take a ride on a tour boat or one of the ferry boats leaving from Circular Quay.

The city's ferries sail at frequent intervals daily until 11 P.M. Some of their routes are as scenic for sightseeing as they are efficient for commuting, and they let you rub elbows with a variety of Sydneysiders. During commute hours, business people travel to and from their jobs on ferries. In the afternoons, legions of schoolboys wearing short flannel pants and caps with sewn-on insignias use the ferries to head for playing fields or home. On weekends, families and outing groups board the ferries for relaxing excursions.

Short ferry trips. Two ferry lines leave from Number 6 Jetty. The shortest ride goes to Kirribilli and gives you a panorama of the city skyline, the Opera House, and the Harbour Bridge—all on a round trip taking only 20 minutes.

Another ferry stops at Lavender Bay, across the harbor from Circular Quay, and then goes to McMahon's Point.

From Number 5 Jetty, ferries leave for Taronga Zoo and Hunter's Hill. At the zoo you can see such Australian natives as the koala, kangaroo, and emu, along with performing seals and dolphins and a host of other creatures (see page 34).

The ferry to Hunter's Hill takes you under the Sydney Harbour Bridge (an impressive view) and makes stops at Darling Street Wharf, Balmain, Long Nose Point Wharf, Parramatta Wharf, and Valentia Street at Hunter's Hill.

From Number 4 Jetty, one ferry goes to Kirribilli and on to Neutral Bay. Another crosses the harbor to Mossman, with stops at Musgrave Street, Cremorne Point, and Old Cremorne. On this trip you have spectacular views of the Opera House, the bridge, and the eastern suburbs of Double Bay and Watson's Bay.

The longest regular ferryboat run is the trip from Number 3 Jetty to Manly, covering 11 km/7 miles in 35 minutes. You can also get to Manly by hydrofoil from Number 2 Jetty in about 17 minutes. To better see the harbor, it's good to travel one way by ferry. At Manly, there are a number of beaches to explore.

Harbor cruises. The Urban Transit Authority has a 1½-hour Sydney Harbour scenic cruise that leaves from Circular Quay at 1:30 P.M. on Wednesday, 2:30 P.M. on Saturday and Sunday. You sail along the southern shores of Port Jackson and cruise up Middle Harbour before returning to Circular Quay by way of the north shores of the main harbor. Another scenic cruise operating at 2 P.M. on Sunday covers the Upper Harbour and the Lane Cove and Parramatta rivers.

Captain Cook and Southern Cross cruises offer an assortment of harbor cruises that include the Parramatta and Lane Cove rivers. Interesting commentary accompanies each cruise. Most of the cruises last 2 hours, though several are longer. Captain Cook has morning and afternoon coffee cruises, plus luncheon and dinner cruises, and on the M.V. *Southern Cross* there are morning coffee, luncheon, and dinner cruises.

The *Sydney Harbour Explorer* catamaran cruise schedules stops along the way so passengers can disembark for a swim or lunch.

All cruises leave from Circular Quay.

For more information on cruise details, contact the Travel Centre of New South Wales (see page 25).

Fine view of Sydney and its harbor diverts attention from performing seal at Taronga Zoo. Ferries from Circular Quay bring visitors daily to spend some time among the park's inhabitants.

Humpback Sydney Harbour Bridge, dubbed "the coat hanger" by locals, links the glittering lights of the downtown area with suburban North Sydney.

the upgrading of ferry docks and the commuter train station. A new covered walkway will connect the area with the neighboring Sydney Opera House.

Harbour Bridge. Just west of Sydney Cove and Circular Quay, this bridge looms on the skyline. Called "the coat hanger" by Australians, this mass of metal is the world's second largest single-span bridge after the Kill van Kull Bridge between New Jersey and Staten Island, New York. The views from the bridge are worth a walk across it. You can take a train back from Milson's Point station.

Fort Denison. Within view of the Opera House stands a stone fortress on a tiny rock island in the middle of Sydney Harbour.

The island, nothing more than a bleak lump of rock, was first used as a place of confinement for incorrigible convicts. A fort was built on the island in 1857, during the Crimean War, to protect Sydney from invasion.

Today, the island fort serves as a maritime tide observation station. Tours of the island, conducted by the Maritime Services Board Tuesday through Saturday, must be booked in advance by calling 240-2111 ext. 2036. Sights to see at the fort include old cannons and stairways too narrow for an invader to swing a cutlass.

Greenway was here

The Opera House was not Sydney's first controversial building, Utzon not its only flamboyant imported architect. Early in the 19th century, Francis Greenway set an example that remains impressive. Some of the best of his work is along Macquarie Street, within easy walking distance of the Opera House.

Greenway arrived in Australia as a convict, his original death sentence for fraud having been commuted by the English courts to 14 years' transportation to New South Wales. The exiled architect befriended New South Wales's Governor Macquarie, who soon discovered his talents. Greenway became Acting Government Architect, and quickly demonstrated the temperament that put him in Australia.

The governor's desire for grandeur and Greenway's desire to produce it left a rich legacy of buildings.

Conservatorium of Music. When it was built in 1817, this elaborate white building was to be the stable for the governor's horses. An even more elaborate building was planned as the governor's house. The colonists were horrified at the useless ornateness of the stable that Francis Greenway designed.

In 1914 the stable was converted and became a center for musical instruction for New South Wales. Regular concerts are held at the conservatorium.

Hyde Park Barracks. This building, at the end of Macquarie Street on Queen's Square, was designed in 1819 by Greenway as a convict barracks. Governor Macquarie was so pleased with the building that he granted Greenway a full pardon. Today, the barracks is a museum of the state's history. A model of the original barracks is included among the displays.

St. James' Church. Built on Queen's Square in 1819, it is one of the few churches designed by Greenway. It is a fine example of Georgian architecture and is noted for its cop-

per-sheathed spire and its pleasing proportions. This symbol of another architectural era contrasts sharply with surrounding glass and steel skyscrapers that tower high above it.

Grandeur other than Greenway's

Besides the work of Francis Greenway, Sydney has preserved a number of other buildings of architectural merit and historical interest.

The Old Mint. On Macquarie Street not far from Hyde Park Barracks, this is one of the surviving wings of the Old Rum Hospital—so named because the three colonists who built it (between 1811 and 1816) did so in exchange for a virtual monopoly on the colony's rum trade. The structure's simple design and side verandas are typical of buildings constructed in the British colonies during this era.

From 1855 to 1926, the building was part of the Royal Mint. Today, it houses a museum.

Parliament House. The central portion of this building, on Macquarie Street a short distance from the Old Mint, is also part of the Old Rum Hospital. (The section of the Old Rum Hospital between Parliament House and the Old Mint was torn down and replaced by Sydney Hospital.)

First occupied by the State Legislature in 1829, Parliament House has an interesting interior. You can arrange to visit Parliament House by phoning the Deputy Sergeant-at-Arms.

General Post Office. A monumental example of Renaissance-inspired architecture by James Barnet, this massive building extends along Martin Place between Pitt and George streets.

In 1942 the building's clock was dismantled and stored away. It was feared that Japanese raiders during World War II could use the tower as a landmark. Finally, in 1964—with some difficulty in fitting all the pieces—the tower was reconstructed.

Town Hall. You'll find the seat of Sydney's city government three blocks west of Hyde Park. Located on the corner of George and Park streets, the building was begun in 1866. It includes a large concert and assembly hall and one of the world's finest pipe organs. Until the advent of the Opera House, this building was the city's main concert hall. Town Hall is open weekdays from 9 A.M. until 5 P.M.

Stately homes

During the 1800s many elegant mansions were built in Sydney. Surrounded by gardens, they were showcases, centers of Sydney's social life. A few of these graceful ghosts from the past have been preserved to be enjoyed today.

Elizabeth Bay House. Built in 1838 for the colonial secretary of New South Wales, Elizabeth Bay House is one of the city's most graceful mansions. John Verge designed the Regency house, open Tuesday through Friday, 10 A.M. to 4:30 P.M.; Saturday 10 A.M. to 5 P.M.; and Sunday noon to 5 P.M. The house is located at 7 Onslow Avenue, Elizabeth Bay.

Vaucluse House. This colonial-style house was once the home of William Charles Wentworth, chief architect of the New South Wales Constitution. You approach the house through beautifully landscaped grounds featuring palm trees, ferns, gum trees, and Moreton Bay figs. The interior of the house is decorated with 1800s period pieces. There's even a wine cellar complete with wine press, as well as a coach house with a display of antique carriages.

Servants' quarters near the stable have been converted into a history museum. In four rooms are displayed portraits of governors; memorabilia of the Blue Mountains Expedition that Wentworth participated in; Wentworth family possessions; and items of Sir Henry Browne Hayes, the first owner of the Vaucluse property. (The small house he built on the property was incorporated into Wentworth's larger house.) Vaucluse House is open daily, except Mondays, from 10 A.M. to 4:30 P.M.

Museums & galleries

In just three stops, visitors to Sydney can look into the continent's natural history, its art—both Aboriginal and Western—and some of the odder moments of the history of flight.

Australian Museum. Located near the corner of College and William streets across from Hyde Park, this museum features Australian natural history and includes an extensive Aborigine section. Don't miss the Hall of Fossils' impressive stegosaurus skeleton or the Marine Hall with its large aquarium, wave tank, and mangrove and coral reef dioramas.

The museum is open Tuesday through Sunday from 10 A.M. to 5 P.M., and Monday from noon to 5 P.M.

The Power House Museum. The Ultimo Power Station, on Mary Ann Street in Ultimo, provided Sydney's electricity from 1900 to 1964. Today, it is a museum with exhibits on science and the applied arts. The enormous exhibition halls and galleries provide a unique setting for such diverse displays as a vintage car from the 1920s, a monoplane, an assortment of box kites, a complete railway station and New South Wales' first locomotive, one of Australia's first manufactured cars, a collection of Japanese swords, and numerous gadgets from Australian inventors. There are also several participatory science exhibits—good activities for travelers with children.

Guided tours through the Power House Museum are available, but feel free to explore on your own. After viewing the exhibits, you'll want to investigate the museum's other facilities: a library, a cafeteria, and a gift shop crammed with unusual souvenirs. The building itself has an interesting history; you can take in a film that describes its progression from power station to museum.

The museum is open daily from 10 A.M. to 5 P.M.

Art Gallery of New South Wales. Appropriately, this building is located on Art Gallery Road in the center of The Domain. Its permanent collection includes many paintings by Australians as well as Europeans. You can visit the gallery Monday through Saturday from 10 A.M. to 5 P.M., and on Sunday from noon to 5.

Shopping around

Sydney is a mecca of shopping centers. Nearly every new high-rise building in the downtown area seems to have an underground shopping arcade filled with colorful shops offering a fascinating variety of merchandise. Things to shop for in the Sydney area include opals, Aboriginal woodcarvings, and sheepskin products.

Downtown shopping. Sydney's main shopping district is bounded by Martin Place, George, Park, and Elizabeth streets. Within this area you'll find large department stores like David Jones, Grace Brothers, and Waltons, as well as sprawling shopping arcades such as Piccadilly, Imperial, Strand, Royal, and MLC Centre. One of the area's largest is the four-level Centrepoint Shopping Arcade that runs between Pitt and Castlereagh streets and connects Grace Brothers and David Jones department stores.

Martin Place, extending from George Street to Macquarie Street, provides a resting place for foot-weary shoppers. The paved pedestrian plaza has seats intermingled with trees, flowers, and a fountain. At lunch time on weekdays, workers and shoppers alike gather to hear free entertainment in the plaza's amphitheater.

The Cenotaph on Martin Place memorializes Australians who died in war. Every Thursday at 12:30 P.M. there is a changing of the guard ceremony here.

Market days. Paddy's Market, located at the Darling Harbour end of Liverpool Street, offers a variety of goods, including fresh produce, confections, flowers, pets, art, jewelry, clothing, and leather goods. The market is open Saturday and Sunday from 9 A.M. to 4:30 P.M.

In Flemington, the Flemington Markets' 1,172 stands offer fruit, vegetables, and goods of every description. It's open Fridays, Saturday mornings, and Sundays.

Neighborhoods of note

Beyond the city's central district, you'll find other destinations worth a visit. Though they're not far from downtown, unless you're a dedicated walker it's best to seek out these spots by bus or taxi. City sights bus tours also include them in their itineraries.

Paddington. Once you've arrived in this charming suburb 5 km/3 miles southeast of downtown, a good way to explore it is on foot. Called "Paddo" by locals, this charming community offers visitors narrow streets lined with beautifully restored Victorian terrace houses as well as restaurants, antique shops, and art galleries.

The area—a former working-class suburb—has in recent years become a fashionable place to live that is close to the city. The area's narrow terrace homes sharing common walls have been elegantly restored to their former 1800s grandeur, complete with iron lace balconies.

Chinatown. You can enjoy the sights, sounds, and smells of China in this bustling neighborhood around Harbour and Hay streets. The area is packed with locals Friday through Sunday—so schedule your visit on a Monday, Tuesday, Wednesday, or Thursday.

You'll see some nice terrace houses on Jersey Road (off Oxford Street), Queen Road, Five Ways, Union, Stafford, Healey, Goodhope, Gurner, and Cambridge streets.

On Oxford Street you'll see the immense Victoria Barracks—a good example of colonial military architecture. Built in the 1840s by convict labor (as were many of the buildings of this period), the barracks is still used by the military. There's a changing of the guard ceremony at 10:30 A.M. Tuesdays (February to November). Following the ceremony is a tour of the barracks and military museum. The museum is also open the first Sunday of the month.

Darlinghurst. The major points of interest in this suburb are the Old Gaol and Darlinghurst Court House.

In the 19th century the Old Gaol was notorious for harshness. Public hangings here attracted large crowds. The building on Forbes Street is now part of East Sydney Technical College. Begun in 1835, the Old Gaol consists of a massive wall surrounding a collection of austere buildings that radiate from a round house that once was a chapel. Patterned after the Eastern Penitentiary in Philadelphia, the sandstone gaol was constructed over a long period by the inmates.

Next door to the Old Gaol you'll find the Darlinghurst Court on Taylor Square. The central portion of this impressive colonnaded building—reminiscent of Greek Revival architecture—was designed by Mortimer Lewis in 1837.

The lively arts

Sydney supports more music and theater with more enthusiasm than a good many cities whose populations exceed its mere three million.

The focal point for both music and theater is, not surprisingly, the Opera House. The Australian Ballet Company, the Sydney Dance Company, and the Sydney Theatre Company all perform here. But the Opera House is only the focal point, as the city boasts other major auditoriums and theaters.

Less formal performances at nightclubs are just as abundant. The center of nightlife is in the neon-lighted King's Cross area, but the purely Australian experience of the league club is worth seeking out too.

Music. Sydney has an appetite for music of every stripe. Fittingly for a city with such an opera house, it has one of the largest per capita opera audiences in the world. Major singers from abroad appear with the regular company and in recital. (One of the visiting performers has been Dame Joan Sutherland.)

The Opera House also is home to the Sydney Symphony Orchestra. Its season is supplemented by visiting orchestras, chamber groups, and recitalists. (Examples include the Warsaw Philharmonic, The Tokyo Quintet, and flautist James Galway.)

Jazz has been healthy in Sydney since the 1940s, and still is. Fans will remember the Australian Jazz Quartet from the 1950s, and genuine veterans may recall Graeme Bell's New Orleans-style band. These days, Sydney boasts many fine jazz bars including Don Burrows Jazz Club at the Regent of Sydney. The annual October Manly Jazz Festival is one of the biggest jazz festivals in the world.

The January Festival of Sydney features operas, pop concerts, and symphony performances.

In addition, there's free entertainment year-round in Sydney. Nearly every Sunday, there are free chamber music concerts at the Opera House, with additional outdoor entertainment on the promenade. There are brass band concerts in Wynyard Park and lunchtime classical music performances at the Conservatorium of Music and St. Stephen's Church on Macquarie Street.

Theater. The city has a dozen permanent theaters in operation including the Ensemble, Elizabeth, and Nimrod theaters.

League clubs. These are the social headquarters (and, to a considerable degree, the financial support) of local football teams. Local residents must be members to enter, but many clubs welcome overseas visitors as guests after telephoned inquiries. The attractions include live entertainment (often big names), poker machines (slot machines to Americans), restaurants, and—not least—a chance to rub elbows with Australians on their own grounds.

Some of these clubs also have swimming pools, saunas or steam rooms, and gymnasiums.

Sydney outdoors

Sydney is blessed with an average of 342 sunny days each year. All this pleasant weather makes for an outdoor city; Sydneysiders flock to nearby golden beaches, a beautiful harbor, golf courses, and tennis courts at every chance. During weekday noon hours downtown workers flee their offices for the pleasure of a stroll in a nearby park. When outdoorsy people aren't getting exercise themselves, they watch spectator sports.

A stroll through the park

The eastern section of Sydney's city center is dominated by three beautiful parks—the Royal Botanic Gardens, The Domain, and Hyde Park. Starting at Farm Cove, this parkland area stretches south to Liverpool Street. In Sydney's eastern suburbs you'll find still another large park—Centennial Park.

The Royal Botanic Gardens. These gardens, sweeping down to the curve of Farm Cove, are renowned for their beauty and design. More than 400 varieties of plants, shrubs, and trees from around the world grow throughout the park's 27 hectares/67 acres. Lawn areas are interspersed with oblong flower beds and dotted with fountains and sculptures. Azalea Walk is in full bloom around mid-September; the rose garden stays fragrant with blossom from early spring into autumn, the Pyramid Glass House features lush tropical varieties. The park is open from 8 A.M. to sunset. (Government House, near Bennelong Point, is in the park, but not open to visit. It is the home of New South Wales's governor.)

The Domain. This open stretch of grassland south of the Royal Botanic Gardens is an ideal place to play a little football or cricket, fly a kite, or give a public speech. On Sundays some of Sydney's orators climb onto their soapboxes (ladders these days) to do just that. They speak on everything from religion to politics, and small crowds gather to listen.

Hyde Park. Stretching from Queen's Square to Liverpool Street, Hyde Park is the most central of the large city parks. Near the city's main shopping district, it provides an excellent resting spot for weary shoppers and a noon-time retreat for office workers. The two-block park is graced with tree-lined walks, a multitude of benches, expansive lawns, and beautiful flower gardens.

Hyde Park has several attractions. Archibald Fountain at the park's north end spews forth dramatic streams of water amid striking bronze statuary. The fountain commemorates the French and Australian alliance during World War I. At the other end of the park is another war memorial—The Anzac Memorial.

Centennial Park. This park of ponds, grasslands, and bush in Sydney's eastern suburbs was established during the country's 1888 centennial year. It was also the site of the January 1, 1901 ceremony establishing the Australian Commonwealth.

Today, the park is enjoyed by equestrians and cyclists. Horses are available for hire (phone 39-5314) and bicycles for rent (phone 357-5663 or 398-5027).

The large park also has sports grounds for rugby, soccer, cricket, field hockey, and baseball.

A trip to the zoo

On a north shore promontory overlooking the harbor and downtown Sydney, the Taronga Zoo offers visitors not only an amazing variety of wildlife but also an exceptional view. In fact, *taronga* in Aborigine means "view over the water."

The most pleasant way to visit the zoo is to take a 15-minute ferry ride from Circular Quay (Number 5 Jetty) to the wharf at the base of the zoo area, from where you ride a zoo bus to the top entrance. It's all down hill from there. The zoo's enclosures and gardens stretch downslope to the harbor. You leave the zoo through the bottom entrance, only a few steps from the wharf. At Circular Quay you can buy a package ticket that includes the ferry, bus, and admission.

The zoo has more than 3,000 mammals, birds, reptiles, and fish. Among them are a number of Australia's creatures. In the Platypus House you can watch these elusive monotremes swimming around a water tank from 11 A.M. to noon and from 2 to 3 P.M. In the Nocturnal House, day becomes night so you can see the beautiful cuscus and graceful gliding possums. Strolling through the Rainforest Aviary—a special walk-through wire cage filled with tropical trees and vines—you'll see a number of colorful Australian birds flitting about. Of course there are kangaroos and koalas in the park. There's also an aquarium and a petting zoo for children.

At the zoo's seal show, you might find it hard to concentrate on the performers. From this area of the zoo you have an outstanding view of the harbor and city.

Throughout the zoo, the emphasis is on an open, natural environment for the animals. Instead of cages, there are moated enclosures wherever possible.

The zoo is open daily from 9 A.M. to 5 P.M.

Miles of golden beaches

Sydneysiders claim they have more golden beaches than any of the Pacific islands, and it's true. Within Sydney's city limits are 34 magnificent beaches, most within easy reach of downtown. On summer weekends and holidays, Sydneysiders flock to these beaches to soak up the sun, swim, and catch the big waves on their surfboards. The popular swimming and surfing season is October through March, though a few hardy people use the water the year around.

Most of Sydney's beaches are easily reached by public transportation. Fast hydrofoils as well as more leisurely ferries transport people to Manly. Other beaches can be reached by bus.

Northern ocean beaches. One of the best-known northern beach areas is Manly, at the mouth of Sydney Harbour. With four ocean beaches, this resort area offers a variety of swimming and surfing possibilities. The huge tank at Manly Marineland features all kinds of local sea creatures, including giant turtles, rays, and sharks. Seals perform daily at noon and 2 P.M., with an extra show at 4 P.M. on weekends.

Beyond Manly, the beach world stretches another 40 km/25 miles north to the entrance to the Hawkesbury River. Beaches include North Steyne, Queenscliff, Harbord, Curl Curl, Dee Why, Collaroy, Long Reef, Narrabeen, Warriewood, Mona Vale, Bungan, Newport, Bilgola, Avalon, Whale, and Palm Beach. Favorites among surfing beaches include Dee Why and Collaroy.

Southern ocean beaches. Along the coast south of Sydney Harbour, you'll find about 32 km/20 miles of good beaches. The closest is famous Bondi Beach. Other beaches include Tamarama, Bronte, Clovelly, Coogee, Maroubra, and Cronulla. The best surfing beaches are Bondi, Maroubra, and Cronulla.

Inside the harbor. Within Sydney Harbour, a string of beaches stretches along the southern shore from Rushcutters Bay east to Watson's Bay: Seven Shillings at Double Bay, Rose Bay, Nielson Park and Camp Cove. Along the harbor's northern shores, the well-known beaches are Balmoral, Edwards, Chinaman's, and Clontarf.

A word about sharks. Sharks are found in Sydney's waters. Because of the shark threat, most of the harbor beaches are safeguarded by shark nets. On surf beaches—where nets can't be used—aerial and ground patrols keep a lookout for sharks. It's best to swim only between marker flags at patrolled beaches. If you hear a siren or bell while you are in the water, get ashore immediately; a shark has been spotted.

The harbor, naturally, is not sharkproof outside the netted areas, so don't dive off a boat into the harbor. Unprotected river estuaries also can be dangerous.

One other menace in Sydney's waters is the Portuguese man-o-war, appearing in armada strength every summer in the ocean and estuary waters. Their poisonous sting is itchy and painful.

Other sports to enjoy

In Sydney you can sample a variety of sports—from a number of water sports to those where both feet are on the ground.

Water sports. Besides surfing and swimming, Sydneysiders enjoy other water-oriented activities. Heading the list is boating. Weekend sailors ply the waters of the harbor

The Rocks, site of Sydney's beginnings, was once the haunt of sailors and thugs. Today's visitors stroll past art galleries, antique shops, and quaint restaurants.

Neat geometrical design is consistently repeated in Paddington's rooftops. Sydney's southeastern suburb boasts restaurants, taverns, antique shops, restored Victorian residences, and an art colony.

and nearby rivers. If you want to join them, you can charter boats at many waterfront resorts in Sydney Harbour, at nearby rivers including the Hawkesbury, and at Broken Bay north of Sydney.

There are also snorkeling and scuba diving off the coast of New South Wales. Scuba equipment can be rented at Pro-Diving Services in Maroubra. For more information on scuba diving, contact the New South Wales Government Travel Centre.

Fishing. One of the best places for deep-sea fishing is out of Coff's Harbour, 579 km/360 miles north of Sydney. You'll also find good fishing out of Port Stephens and Bermagui. Deep-sea catches can include marlin, Spanish mackerel, barracuda, and albacore. For boat charter information, contact the Game Fishing Association located in Sydney.

Fresh-water fishers can cast their lines into the rivers and streams of nearby mountain areas, including the Blue Mountains as well as the Hawkesbury River. You'll need an inland angling license, which you can obtain from the Department of Fisheries in Sydney.

Golf. For the golfer, public courses are available and some championship private clubs open their courses to visitors, especially on weekdays. These clubs include the New South Wales Golf Club and The Lakes Golf Club. For more information on Sydney area golf courses, contact the Secretary of the New South Wales Golf Association in Sydney.

Tennis. Sydney has both public courts and private tennis clubs. Club players seeking more information may contact either the New South Wales Lawn Tennis Association or the New South Wales Hardcourt Tennis Association. Public play courts are listed in the telephone book Yellow Pages.

Eating & drinking Australian-style

During your travels around Australia, there's no reason to go hungry or thirsty. Today, Australia offers a pleasant variety of both good food and good beverages.

Culinary specialties. The influx of immigrants from all over the world has had its effect on the cuisine of Australia. Restaurants reflect this international influence, with offerings from Hungarian goulash to coq au vin to beef Wellington on the same menu.

Aside from a number of good international selections, one of Australia's best offerings is seafood. Sydney rock oysters, for instance, are an excellent appetizer. Incidentally, when you're looking for appetizers on a menu in Australia, look at "entrées"—the main course is something separate.

Other good Australian seafoods you'll want to try include Queensland barramundi, John Dory fish, coral trout, Moreton Bay bugs (miniature crustaceans), Queensland mud crab, large king prawns, and large crayfish whose tails are exported to the United States as "Australian lobster tails."

For those who prefer steak, Australian menu offerings include steak and eggs, carpetbag steak (beef stuffed with oysters), and chateaubriand. Also try Australia's roast spring lamb in mint sauce, or perhaps lamb chops.

No matter what you order for a main course in Australia, you'll discover that you get more than enough to eat. In addition to the meat or fish, you'll usually get three vegetables—one of them a potato.

Among Australian staples is the meat pie, particularly popular as a fast-food item. These pies consist of meat and gravy in a crust, and Australians love to pour tomato sauce all over them.

If you go on a bush picnic or an organized cookout with a tour group, you might get to sample damper bread and billy tea. Damper is made from unleavened wheat flour, mixed with water and then kneaded. The dough is placed in a heavy cast-iron pot that is then put in a hole in the ground and covered with hot coals to bake. You wash down the delicious results with billy tea, simply prepared in a tin can over a campfire.

Something to drink. Australia's national drink is beer, and Australians consume it with gusto. There are more than two dozen breweries in Australia producing more than 70 different brands of beer—strong and hearty and with a higher alcohol content than U.S. beers. Some Australian states are currently trying to lower the alcohol content of beers served in their state.

Beer is served in glasses of different sizes that are called by different names—names that vary from state to state. For example, in New South Wales and Western Australia a "middy" is a 10-ounce glass of beer; in other states the term "middy" might not be even used. A "pony" and a "schooner" are among other beer glasses you might hear about.

For a long time Australians didn't drink much wine. Many people order beer with their meals, but wine has become a popular accompaniment to meals as well. The country produces a number of first-rate wines that rival those of California and France. Among Australian wine selections you'll find Moselle, Semillon, Rhine Riesling, Claret, Cabernet Sauvignon, Shiraz (Hermitage), and Pinot Noir, as well as sherries, ports, and champagnes.

Bushwalking. There are a number of walking trails not far from Sydney where hikers can enjoy the out-of-doors. You'll find good trails to the north at Ku-ring-gai Chase National Park, to the west in the Blue Mountains, and to the south in Royal National Park. For more information on bushwalking, contact the New South Wales Federation of Bushwalking Clubs in Sydney.

Horseback riding. From sunrise to sunset, horseback riders exercise in Centennial Park. Horses (and instruction, if desired) are available at a number of riding stables listed in the Yellow Pages.

Sports to watch

In this sports-minded city, you also have a wide variety of spectator sports to choose from.

Racing. Sydneysiders love a good horse race. The city has six race tracks, with Randwick—5 km/3 miles from down-town—the closest and principal track. Randwick's big races are held in the spring and fall, but races are scheduled throughout the year at Canterbury, Rosehill, and Warwick Farm, a little farther from city center.

Trotting races are held Friday nights under the lights at Harold Park, a short distance from the city. Greyhounds race on Saturday nights at Harold Park or Wentworth Park.

Football. Though four codes of football (Australian national code, rugby League, rugby Union, and soccer) are played in Sydney, perhaps the most popular is professional rugby League football. Played throughout New South Wales and Queensland, this game includes international matches between Australian teams and teams from England, France, and New Zealand. Games are played during the winter months (March through September) at the Sydney Sports Ground at Moore Park (south of Paddington) and at other ovals in Sydney.

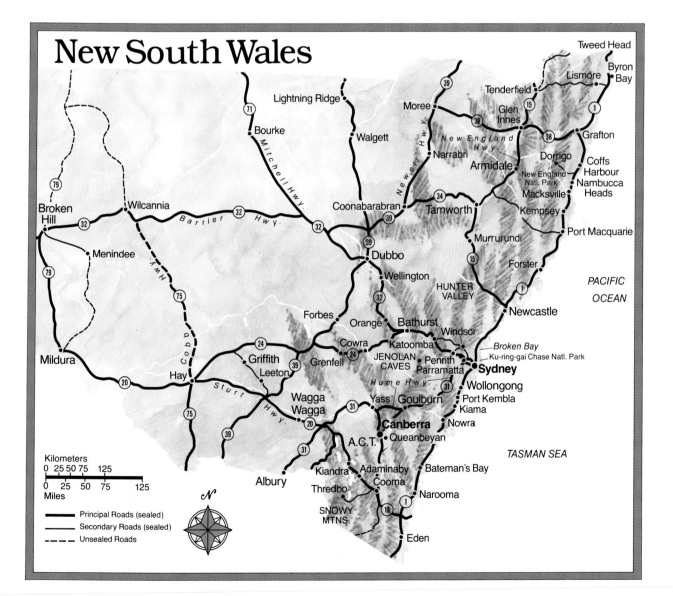

Turreted tops of Three Sisters in the Blue Mountains provide vistas of surrounding countryside. This is a vacation land of plummeting waterfalls, fern-filled gorges, and hidden caves.

Costumed soldiers lounge at ease in Old Sydney Town, a re-creation of Sydney Cove in the late 1700s and early 1800s.

Cricket. Sydney's summer sport is cricket. On Saturday mornings at 11 during the cricket season (October through March), you can watch cricket being played at the Sydney Cricket Ground in Moore Park. Check the newspapers for cricket international test matches between Australian teams and teams from England, New Zealand, India, Pakistan, and the West Indies.

Sailboat racing. Both on weekends and during the week, you'll find the harbor dotted with sailboats, their brightly colored sails catching the breeze. Some are out for a pleasure sail; others are there to race. The yachting season runs from September through May with races and regattas held nearly every weekend. Races that are particularly popular are those between "18-footers." Sailed by a crew of four, these little boats dart back and forth across the harbor at amazing speeds. The 18-footers club is at Double Bay.

Sailors turn out in full force each year for the start of the big Sydney-Hobart Yacht Race, December 26.

There's no need to stand on the sidelines to watch the harbor races—every Saturday during the racing season, you can follow the boats in a spectators' ferry. Catch the ferry at Circular Quay at 2 P.M.

West to the Blue Mountains

Through a dreamlike blue haze, the Blue Mountains rise from the plains just 65 km/40 miles west of Sydney. Part of the Great Dividing Range that runs along Australia's eastern seaboard, these mountains provide a popular, nearby vacation retreat for Sydney residents. There are opportunities for golf, swimming, tennis, horseback riding, rock climbing, and bushwalking, and for people who just want to enjoy the scenery. Vistas include deep fern-filled gorges, wide ravines, steep cliffs, and plummeting waterfalls.

From a variety of good vantage points, you can discover that the mountains do indeed appear blue, an effect caused by the eucalyptus forests that cover the area. Droplets of oil from the gum tree leaves refract the light of the sun, creating a blue haze.

You can get to the Blue Mountains on a 1-day tour out of Sydney. There is also daily train service from Sydney Central Railway Station to Katoomba and Leura, or you can drive yourself. Accommodations in the Blue Mountains include hotels, motels, holiday flats, cottages, cabins, caravan parks, and campgrounds.

The Katoomba resort area

Katoomba, 104 km/65 miles from Sydney, is the main resort center for the Blue Mountains. From here you can visit Echo Point Lookout, where you'll have a good view of forested Jamieson Valley and the massive weathered sandstone formation known as the Three Sisters. From Echo Point, take the Giants' Stairway into the valley. Lookouts and rest stops along the 916-step descent help make the trip a little easier.

Blue Mountain rides. Across from Echo Point, enjoy more of the Blue Mountains on two different rides.

The Scenic Skyway gondola travels on a cable high above the Jamieson Valley floor. From this lofty vantage point, you can see cascading waterfalls, vertical cliff faces, and miles of bushland.

Nearby, you can take another ride whose surprising descent might leave you momentarily white-knuckled. The Scenic Railway—perhaps the steepest railway in the world—drops you 213 meters/700 feet through a tunnel into the valley in a matter of seconds. At the bottom you can leave the rail car and hike to Katoomba Falls or Leura Falls. Like the skyway, the Katoomba Scenic Railway runs on a regular basis from 9 A.M. to 5 P.M. daily.

Still another ride awaits you near Lithgow, about 40 km/ 25 miles from Katoomba. On weekends the Zig Zag Railway steam train winds through tunnels and along stone viaducts. When it was built in the 1860s, the Z-shaped track, which descends the eastern slopes of the Blue Mountains, was considered an engineering feat.

Tribute to a great artist. In Springwood, 30 km/19 miles from Katoomba, you can tour the home and grounds of Norman Lindsay's estate. Lindsay was one of Australia's best-known artists and writers, and the home—now converted to a museum and gallery—houses some of Lindsay's oil paintings, etchings, manuscripts, and sculptures, as well as a collection of model ships. There are beautiful views of the Blue Mountains from the grounds of the estate. The home is open Friday through Sunday from 11 A.M. to 5 P.M.

Jenolan Caves

Among the Blue Mountains scenic highlights are the Jenolan Caves 77 km/48 miles southwest of Katoomba. Famous for their stalagmites, stalactites, pillars, canopies, and shawls, these limestone caves are among the most spectacular and extensive formations of their type in Australia. Used by Aborigines for centuries, these caves were first discovered by European settlers in 1838 when a stockman tracked a bushranger (highwayman) to his hideout in them.

There are two types of cave formations—great natural archways and underground "dark" caves. You can explore the open archways on your own, but you'll need a guide for the dark caves. Nine of the dark caves have been developed—lighting, pathways, and stairs have been added for easy exploration. Cave inspection tours are held at regular intervals between 10 A.M. and 4 P.M. daily.

Part of the attraction of the Jenolan Caves is their location in a 2,428-hectare/6,000-acre wildlife sanctuary. Aside from exploring the beauty of the caves, you can wander through bushland and perhaps see wallabies scramble about. Along the well-graded trails outside the caverns, many birds can be spotted—among them bright-plumed rosella parrots, satin bowerbirds, Blue Mountain parakeets, kookaburras, and cockatoos. In summer the reserve gains added color as masses of wildflowers come into bloom.

Sydney tour operators include Jenolan Caves on some tours to the Blue Mountains. Daily train service is also available from Central Station in Sydney with a connecting bus tour from Katoomba to Jenolan on certain days. You can stay overnight at Jenolan Caves House.

Three historic towns

If you drive to the Blue Mountains, you can add a bonus to your trip by including a trio of historic old towns: Parramatta, about 24 km/15 miles west of downtown Sydney, and the sister towns of Windsor and Richmond, 21 km/13 miles and 29 km/18 miles northwest of Parramatta. Among Australia's earliest settlements, they contain buildings dating back to the late 18th and early 19th centuries. Most of the historic buildings are open to visitors.

Parramatta. Settled in 1788 less than a year after Sydney's founding, this inland town was Australia's second permanent settlement. At the time of its establishment, many felt the town was located in the wilderness. Today, it is part of the sprawling metropolitan area of Sydney.

Parramatta has a number of historical sites worth looking at. The Old Government House (1799) in Parramatta Park was the country residence of Australia's first governors. This graceful white building with its green shutters and imposing pillars is open Tuesday through Thursday, and Sunday.

The Elizabeth Farm House was constructed in 1793 by John Macarthur, a pioneer of the wool industry. It's a long building with a sloping roof and pillared veranda.

The colonial Georgian Experiment Farm Cottage (1798) marks the site of Sydney's first wheat farm. There's a museum of farm implements in the cottage cellar. Take note of the cottage's courtyard paved in convict-made bricks, and the garden of violas and herbs.

Windsor. Many of Windsor's buildings of the 1800s were designed by convict-architect Francis Greenway. The Georgian-style St. Matthew's Anglican Church, built in 1820, is one of them. Faithfully restored in 1965, the brick church is considered by some to be the finest example of Georgian architecture in the country. Its cemetery has headstones dating from 1810.

Another Greenway creation is the Court House. Built in 1822 by convict labor, this sandstone structure has also been carefully restored. It's a fine example of early-day craftsmanship.

Other interesting Windsor buildings include the Toll House (1814 or 1816), used for the collection of tolls on the Fitzroy Bridge until 1887 and now restored and fitted with period furnishings. You'll find more 19th century furnishings plus farm equipment in the Hawkesbury Museum. John Tebbutt—discoverer of Tebbutt Comet—lived in Windsor and you can visit his home and small garden observatory.

Richmond. Still another town that abounds in old buildings is Richmond. Hobartville (1828) is a Greenway-designed residence. Special features include "bush-rangerproof" doors and barred cellars.

Other buildings include Toxana House (1860), now a historical museum; St. Peter's Anglican Church (1837–1841), with a graveyard where many of the area's pioneers are buried; and Woolpack Inn (1830s), which provided lodging for early-day travelers.

Gold rush region

To the west, just beyond the Blue Mountains, is the region known as New South Wales' "Golden West." More than 100 years ago, pioneers and bushrangers flocked to this area in search of gold. Discovery of payable gold in New South Wales occurred not far from Bathurst. Today, the area's riches come mainly from wool, wheat, fruit, and vegetables. But old gold mining settlements like Sofala, Hill End, and Wattle Flat can still be explored, and it's always possible that some gold can be found in the area.

A good center for exploring the gold rush region is Bathurst on the Macquarie River 208 km/129 miles west of Sydney. This sedate settlement of red brick and blue granite is Australia's third oldest city (1815). From Sydney, you can get to Bathurst by train, plane, bus, or on a coach tour.

To the north

A short distance from downtown Sydney are the winding waterways of the Hawkesbury River and the bushlands of Ku-ring-gai Chase National Park. Nearby, Old Sydney Town re-creates the Sydney Cove of the 1800s. The Hunter Valley, an easy day's drive from Sydney, is known for its fine wines.

Farther north are the verdant plateaus of New England and the sweeping North Coast. Several days could easily be spent exploring this area of New South Wales on a circle trip from Sydney or en route to Brisbane.

The Hawkesbury River

The Hawkesbury River flows wide and winding through New South Wales bush and farmland before it empties into Broken Bay 32 km/20 miles north of Sydney. When Sydney was young, the river's course cut through rich alluvial lands where wheat prospered. The river soon became the region's principal waterway to these farmlands. Produce was transported downriver, then across Broken Bay, and south along the coast to Sydney. For many years—beginning in the late 19th century—paddle wheel steamers plied this river on regular runs.

Though the wheat has gone, agriculture is still important to the area, with fruit orchards, market gardens, and farms all along the river; and though paddle wheelers have disappeared, boats—mainly recreational—still ply the river.

Sydney residents and visitors both can enjoy the recreational pleasures of the Hawkesbury River. The area is ideal for cruising—either in your own rented boat or on a tour boat. Dense vegetation edges the river along much of its lower reaches. Palms, ferns, and gum trees grow along the banks. Waterfowl follow its course, and the raucous laughter of the kookaburra (bird) can be heard from the woods along the way. In the Broken Bay estuary, towering headlands overlook the river waters.

One-day tours. Sydney firms offer tours of the North Sydney area that include a short boat ride in the Pittwater and Broken Bay estuaries. Other cruises go up the Hawkesbury River.

Leisurely cruising. If you have several days to cruise on the Hawkesbury, you can rent a boat and explore it on your own. You'll find a selection of small cruisers available at a number of places in the Hawkesbury River area.

No boating license is needed. You'll find plenty of overnight anchorages and small refueling/restocking stops along the way. During the peak vacation period (from Christmas holidays through April or May), you must reserve a boat well ahead.

Also available are 2- and 4-night Hawkesbury River cruises aboard a 140-passenger luxury vessel.

Once on the river, you can set your own pace, stopping at historic old river towns en route. At Ebenezer you can visit the Presbyterian Church. Completed in 1809, it's the oldest church in use by an Australian congregation. A short distance upriver from Ebenezer, Windsor is one of Australia's oldest settlements (see page 40). Some 20 historic buildings, now restored, have been assembled at Wilberforce in the Australiana Folk Village. Also on display are a working ferry and a model of the first train to run from Sydney to the Hawkesbury Valley.

Ku-ring-gai Chase National Park

This vast bushland reserve on the southern banks of the Hawkesbury River, only 24 km/15 miles north of Sydney, offers rugged sandstone plateaus that are rich in native plants and wildlife. Area fauna include swamp wallabies and a small colony of koalas. Between July and November, the area's wildflowers display their colors, and tiny honeyeater birds come to drink the nectar.

In the national park, you can swim, fish, bushwalk, and boat. Boats may be hired at Bobbin Head, Brooklyn, and Terrey Hills.

Several Sydney tour operators include Ku-ring-gai Chase National Park in tours of the northern suburbs, or you can drive there on your own.

Old Sydney Town

About 72 km/45 miles north of Sydney is Old Sydney Town, a re-creation of Sydney Cove as it appeared in the time of Governor Bligh at the beginning of the 19th century.

Built on a hilly, lightly wooded site, the 101-hectare/ 250-acre park slopes down to a large body of water representing Sydney Cove. Around this cove are unpaved roads and paths dotted with tents, tiny convict gang huts, church, courthouse, jail, and houses of the free settlers and freed convicts. In the cove, the brig *Perseverance* is tied up at Hospital Wharf. Building continues in the park, giving visitors a chance to see the evolution of the township from its beginnings to about 1810.

All the personnel of Old Sydney Town wear the costumes of the period, portraying convicts, soldiers, magistrates, and free settlers. Each day they act out the events of the period. There are speedy court hearings, public floggings, flintlock pistol duels, and street dancing. Craftspeople—blacksmiths, coopers, wheelwrights, seamstresses, candlemakers, and tinsmiths—can be seen at work.

Old Sydney Town is open Wednesday through Sunday from 10:30 A.M. to 5 P.M. Sometimes in the evenings there are special "sound and light" shows that feature a tour of the town and a recounting of the history of the colony's first days.

It's about an hour's drive to Old Sydney Town, or you can take the train from Sydney's Central Station to Gosford—a 1½-hour scenic trip through wooded hills. From the Gosford Railway Station, you can take a bus to the park. The State Rail Authority has a special rail/bus tour from Sydney; there are bus tours from Sydney as well.

Lake Macquarie

About 149 km/90 miles north of Sydney is this pleasant seaboard lake with more than 160 km/100 miles of shoreline. Because of the lake's size, the Royal Australian Air Force was able to use it as a major seaplane base during World War II. Today, it's a popular vacation spot for swimming, water-skiing, fishing, and boating. There also are a golf course, tennis courts, and lawn bowling greens. A guided boat tour from Belmont's main jetty gives you a close look at the lake.

Accommodations in the area include motels, campgrounds, and a caravan park.

Hunter River Valley

It takes only a few hours by car to drive the 208 km/130 miles north from Sydney to the Hunter River Valley, noted for its wineries and vineyards.

The largest wineries in the area are located near Cessnock and Pokolbin, about 32 km/20 miles west of Newcastle. Australia's oldest wine-producing area, the Hunter River Valley combines coal mining with its vineyards. As a result, Cessnock resembles a busy mining center more than a picturesque wine town, but the cellars and winery buildings around Pokolbin have the traditional look of a wine region.

Fine red and white wines are produced here including red shiraz and cabernet and white semillon and chardonnay. Wineries known in other parts of Australia, such as McWilliams and Lindemans, welcome visitors as\do most of the smaller local wineries.

There are both motels and hotels at Cessnock and Pokolbin. Some Sydney bus tours include the Hunter River Valley.

The North Coast & New England

The scenery of northeastern New South Wales varies from coastline blessed with golden beaches and banana plantations to tablelands of dairy farms, deep valley gorges, and rain forests.

The North Coast. This narrow strip of land—known as "The Holiday Coast"—extends from Forster (north of Newcastle) 550 km/342 miles to Tweed Heads on the Queensland border. A chain of quiet resorts and tiny fishing villages marks this coast, whose bays, inlets, and beaches offer water sports enthusiasts chances to fish, water-ski, scuba dive, boat, swim, and surf.

At Port Macquarie, 430 km/267 miles north of Sydney, seascapes and beaches are the principal attractions. Pacific Drive offers cliffs, headlands, and pocket beaches for viewing. Sea Acres, a 31-hectare/77-acre sanctuary for flora and fauna located between Pacific Drive and Shelly Beach, 5 km/3 miles south of Port Macquarie, has been preserved as one of the few surviving corners of true primeval rain forest on the New South Wales coast.

(Continued on page 44)

Australia's wonderful wildlife

The first Europeans to explore Australia were amazed at the animal life they saw. Who'd ever heard of a duck-billed mammal with fur that laid eggs, or a bird that could make sounds like a buzz saw, or a hopping creature that carried its young in a pouch? These amazing animals didn't exist in Europe, and it was hard for people back home to believe the explorers' stories. But exist they did and still do, their development the result of Australia's millions of years of isolation from the rest of the world's land masses. In essence, Australia is a living museum of rare and unusual species.

You won't find kangaroos hopping around the streets of Sydney, but you will find them and Australia's other unique creatures in protected areas that provide a natural habitat for the animals. Australia has made an outstanding effort to protect its natural environment and wildlife by establishing more than 200 sanctuaries and national parks. By visiting some of these reserves, you can observe many of the country's 400 kinds of native animals as well as over 1,200 species of birds—half of them unique to Australia.

Check with the government tourist bureau in the capital of each state you visit for a list of the sanctuaries in that area. The following paragraphs tell a little about some of the animals and birds you might have a chance to see.

Marsupials. Animals whose newborn live in their mothers' pouches and nurse for the first 4 or 5 months after birth are marsupials. Australia has more than 170 marsupials, including the kangaroo, koala, wombat, and Tasmanian devil.

Perhaps the most popular of the marsupials is the koala. (Note that it's not a bear.) With woolly fur, big eyes, and a button nose, this animal is considered cuddly and cute. But a word of warning—its claws are sharp. Koalas make their home in gum trees and their diet consists of only a few dozen different types of eucalyptus leaves.

The other well-known Australian marsupial is the kangaroo. This animal has a place of honor—along with the emu—on the Australian coat of arms. There are more than 50 types of kangaroos ranging from great red kangaroos that stand 2 meters/6 feet tall to rat-size quokkas. Both wallaroos and wallabies are also in the kangaroo family. Members of the kangaroo family can be found on grassy plains, in rocky hills, and even in swamps.

The kangaroo has huge hind legs, small forelegs, and a stout, elongated tail it uses as a prop when grazing or standing. When stirred into flight, kangaroos can bound away at great speeds. The red and gray ones have been known to jump more than 6 meters/20 feet and do speeds of up to 48 km/30 miles per hour.

A baby kangaroo is called a "joey." At birth the baby is about an inch long, blind, and furless. By natural instinct the newborn makes its way through the mother's fur into her pouch; the pouch seals itself, and joey stays there until it can hop out to nibble grass and plants. The pouch continues to be used as an emergency shelter—a frightened joey dashes headlong into it, often leaving the long hind legs dangling outside.

Mammals that lay eggs. Monotremes are the lowest order of mammals—unique egg-laying animals whose eggs hatch into mammals. Once hatched, the young are suckled. The combination of laying eggs and nursing the young dumbfounded English and French scientists who studied the first monotremes brought back from Australia in the early 1800s. Australia possesses the only two extant monotremes: the platypus and the echidna.

The adult platypus is less than ½ meter/2 feet in length. This duckbilled, fur-coated, webfooted animal has a large, flat furry tail which is used as a rudder when swimming. The platypus's talents include burrowing, swimming, and diving.

The echidna—really a spiny anteater—resembles a porcupine in size and appearance. Like the platypus, the spiny anteater is an egg-laying mammal of prehistoric vintage; it is the only remaining kin of the platypus.

Though the echidna comes in several varieties, the best known are a short-legged variety living on the Australian mainland, and two long-beaked, densely furred species living in Papua New Guinea. All echidnae are burrowers—masters at disappearing into the sand.

For bird watchers. Australia's birds vary in size from the tiny weebil to the stately emu. There are black swans with scarlet beaks and feet, and a host of brightly plumed parrot family members like lorikeets, cockatoos, ringnecks, rosellas, and budgerigars.

Appearing with the kangaroo on Australia's coat of arms, the emu is considered the most outstanding of the country's unusual birds. The powerfully built, brown-feathered, 2-meter/6-foot bird resembles the ostrich. Though emus can run at high speeds, they can't fly; they graze in flocks on the plains and in wooded country.

The lyrebird lives in the mountain forests of the east coast between Melbourne and Brisbane. He can project his own rich melodious voice up to a quarter of a mile or convincingly mimic birdcalls ranging from a kookaburra's raucous laugh to a thornbill's treble. The bird can even mimic a buzz saw. One of the most outstanding features of the male lyrebird is his spectacular courtship dance.

Also known for its sound is the country's most popular bird—the kookaburra. Because of the bird's rollicking laugh, it has been nicknamed the "laughing jackass." The kookaburra's laugh can be heard everywhere—even in the cities and suburbs.

Ranger introduces a wombat at
Urimbirra Fauna Park near Victor Harbor.
This paunchy marsupial is a nocturnal animal
that's happy in mud.

Cuddle a koala (above) at Lone Pine Koala
Sanctuary near Brisbane. Many parks offer
opportunities to hug Australia's favorite
marsupial.

Alert red "roo", Australia's largest
marsupial, can leap up to 20 feet and travel 30
miles an hour.

...Continued from page 41

Banana plantations surround Coff's Harbour, a holiday center for fishing, skin diving, and spear fishing. Northwest of Coff's Harbour is Bruxner Park Flora Reserve, a tropical jungle of vines, ferns, and orchids (blooming in September). Bird watching is good here. Kangaroos, emus, and other Australian animals and birds may be seen at Kumbaingeri Wildlife Sanctuary, 16 km/10 miles north of Coff's Harbour.

Both planes and trains serve several of the area's major towns from Sydney. You'll find accommodations including motels, hotels, caravan parks, and campgrounds all along the coast.

New England. The northern reaches of the Great Dividing Range form an immense tableland—an expansive plateau known as New England. These highlands mix rich farmlands with cattle and sheep holdings. One of the best times to visit New England is in autumn when the landscape is vibrant with fall color, thanks to the first settlers in this area, who planted an array of European deciduous trees including oaks, elms, poplars, and silver birches.

Center for the area's activities is Armidale, 566 km/352 miles north of Sydney. Here you'll find the University of New England, Armidale Teacher's College, a technical college, and several secondary schools. Besides the many schools, Armidale has several cathedrals with noteworthy spires.

A number of motels and caravan parks provide comfortable accommodations in Armidale. The fastest way to reach Armidale from Sydney is by air. It takes about 9 hours by train, 8 hours by car.

Fossicking. Admirers of topaz, diamonds, and sapphires might want to take a side trip to Glen Innes and Tenterfield at the northern end of the New England plateau. Several sapphire reserves have been set aside in the Glen Innes and Invernell areas. Before you begin, you will need to get a fossicker's license from the Department of Mines in Sydney.

New England National Park. About 80 km/50 miles east of Armidale, New England National Park is similar topographically to the Blue Mountains. But it is far less populated and relatively undeveloped.

Some of the best scenery is found along the eastern escarpment, where the tablelands suddenly drop off to the lush subtropical forest below. A trail winds along the edge of the escarpment. Only experienced bushwalkers are advised to descend to the valley floor.

Dorrigo State Park just east of New England National Park gives easy access to the valley rain forest. Here you can take a nature walk through subtropical foliage of huge tree ferns, palms, and orchids. Throughout the area are waterfalls, streams, and cascades.

South of Sydney

South of Sydney, the Princes Highway (1) winds along the coast of New South Wales through the industrial cities of Wollongong and Port Kembla. Then the landscape changes to an area of uncrowded surfing and swimming beaches and miles of rich farm and dairy lands. This is the Illawarra Coast. Here you'll find resort towns and tiny fishing villages, open pastureland, river valleys, and cedar forests. The Princes Highway eventually rounds the southeast corner of the continent, crosses the border into Victoria, and heads westward to Melbourne.

You can see some of the Illawarra on day tours out of Sydney, or you can drive down the coast on your own. There's also air and rail service to Nowra, Wollongong, Bateman's Bay, and Kiama. Along the coast, you'll find motels, hotels, caravan parks, and campgrounds. If you like you can drive from Sydney to Melbourne—a 893-km/555-mile trip. Though the road is paved and well maintained, it does become narrow and winding after Kiama.

Besides the Illawarra Coast, southern New South Wales has another interesting region to explore—the Riverina wine district, an inland, irrigated region that produces some fine wines.

Royal National Park

Only 32 km/20 miles south of Sydney, this national park is a popular retreat for Sydney residents on weekends and holidays. The 14,892 hectares/36,800 acres of bushland include plenty of opportunities for scenic drives and pleasant bushwalks. The park's coast has good surfing beaches. From August through November, wildflowers come into bloom.

Park facilities are not highly developed, but you will find sites for picnicking. There are camping areas at Bonnie Vale and Audley.

The Illawarra coast

South of the Royal National Park, the Princes Highway bends toward the coast. At Sublime Point, 366 meters/1,200 feet above the sea, you get a sweeping view southward along the Illawarra coast as far as Kiama. You'll find another good view point just south of Sublime Point at the top of Bulli Pass.

In the waters off this stretch of coast, half of Australia's fish catch is taken. Salmon fishermen congregate here, and you'll see their net dinghies and power boats anchored offshore and in the little ports along the way.

South of Wollongong, Princes Highway veers inland. For a better coastal view, take the coastside road. You hug the ocean through Port Kembla and see Lake Illawarra—a body of water popular with water-skiers, fishers, and swimmers. The little fishing port of Shellharbour, just south of the lake, is a quiet, pleasant seaside resort with a motel, caravan park, and campgrounds.

Kiama. Lighthouse buffs will be interested in the lighthouse in Kiama, built in 1886 and still in operation. At the foot of the lighthouse, a blowhole funnels a huge jet of spray skyward.

Kiama is situated on the Minnamurra River. About 18 km/11 miles upstream, you can see the river cascading into a deep, rock-strewn gorge. Walking paths provide pleasant opportunities for exploring the subtropical rain forest.

South of Kiama, Princes Highway follows a tortuous route along cliffs and beaches through the little town of Geroa at the mouth of Crooked River; along Seven Mile Beach, famous as the take-off point for Kingsford-Smith's flight across the Tasman Sea in the *Southern Cross*; past the fishing resort of Greenwell Point, Currarong, and Jervis Bay.

Kangaroo Valley. Inland from the Princes Highway, about 22 km/14 miles northwest of Nowra, is an area of pastoral charm. Rain forests, grazing land, and bush offer visitors a variety of scenery to explore. Trails for hiking and horseback riding are well developed. An interesting stone castellated bridge—the Hampden Bridge—crosses the Kangaroo River in the valley. The river, with its chain of pools, is popular with anglers.

Popular recreational pursuits include fishing, canoeing, and swimming. Camping facilities, cottages, and cabins are available in Kangaroo Valley Village.

Nowra. This town on the Shoalhaven River has become popular with vacationers from both Sydney and Canberra. The river follows a rugged course through forest-covered ranges, and the sights include waterfalls, caverns, and interesting rock formations. A sizeable town, Nowra has a good assortment of hotels, motels, cabins, caravan parks, and campgrounds.

Bateman's Bay. This bay, 277 km/172 miles south of Sydney, marks the southern extremity of the Illawarra district. The bay was first sighted by Captain Cook in 1770 and named after Captain Bateman of the sailing ship *Northumberland.*

The small village has an old-world atmosphere and offers beautiful seascapes. Famous for its oysters and crayfish (which can be bought right off the boats), the town is popular with Canberra residents. Favorite area activities include surfing, swimming, fishing, and boating. Motels, a guest house, caravan parks, and campgrounds provide a variety of accommodations.

A wine region

Also south of Sydney, but far inland from the Illawarra Coast, you'll find the productive vineyards of the Riverina District. Nearly 60 percent of New South Wales's wines come from this district located about 644 km/400 miles southwest of Sydney and 322 km/200 miles northeast of Melbourne. The vineyards here thrive on a warm climate and an irrigation system watering some 80,936 hectares/200,000 acres through a canal system fed by the Murrumbidgee River.

The principal town is Griffith, situated on the main irrigation canal. You can reach the area by air, rail, or express bus from Sydney. You'll find hotels, motels, caravan parks, and campgrounds.

McWilliams has three wineries here; Wynn's and Penfold's are the other big names in the area. These contrast with a number of smaller wineries. The area produces both table and fortified wines.

Other trips from Sydney

There are two other side trips you can take from Sydney if you have the time. By air, you can take excursions to the Snowy Mountains southwest of Sydney and to Lightning Ridge northwest of Sydney.

Even though the Snowy Mountains (see page 53) are closer to Canberra, many visitors reach the area from Sydney. Daily flights go into Cooma from Sydney, as do rail, bus, and tour services.

If you want to see what some of the real outback looks like, take a tour to Lightning Ridge. There are both 1 and 3-day tours into this dry, dusty frontier land.

Lightning Ridge is the source of the ''black'' opal—one of the most valuable opals in Australia. The first of these opals was discovered in 1907, and by 1914, area opal production had reached its peak. Today, fossickers still come to the area to search abandoned mines and sift through heaps in search of opal fortunes. With a fossicker's license, you too can hunt for that elusive fortune.

Lightning Ridge is 772 km/480 miles northwest of Sydney—about 2½ hours by plane.

Visiting a sheep station

Beyond Sydney and its metropolitan area lies the bushland of New South Wales—the ''outback.'' Here sheep roam, and beauty prevails in wide open spaces, rolling pasturelands, and gum trees.

Several tour operators offer day trips to this area. One such tour operator flies you to Dubbo, a rural community of 21,000 on the Macquarie River 402 km/250 miles northwest of Sydney. Beyond the town are the vast open reaches of Australia and the rich farming area of the Macquarie Valley.

During your day's tour of the area, you might see a sheep and lamb auction and visit a sheep station to see sheep shearing, wool grading and packing, and sheep dogs at work. You'll have a barbecued lunch under the shade of the gum trees and learn how to throw a boomerang. A trip to Dubbo's open range zoo is also on the tour itinerary. Here you'll make friends with—and hand-feed—some of Australia's animals.

Still another tour goes to Cowra, a 55-minute flight from Sydney. This day trip also includes a visit to a sheep station and other features like those at Dubbo. Coach tours also leave Sydney to visit sheep properties near the towns of Mittagong, Bowral, and Moss Vale, all southwest of Sydney. In fact, wherever you travel in Australia you'll find sheep stations to visit.

CANBERRA

Australia's national capital is one grand design

Australia's national capital was planned for only $3,500. That's right—$3,500.

In the early 1900s, the country's leaders recognized a need for a capital, but neither Sydney nor Melbourne was willing for the other to win this honor. So the Australian Capital Territory (A.C.T.) was created at a compromise location between the two cities, and an international competition was established to plan a capital city. Chicago landscape architect Walter Burley Griffin won the competition and the $3,500 prize money in 1911, when the broad valley that now holds Canberra was little more than a home for grazing sheep.

A planned capital city

Parliament convened for the first time in Canberra in 1927, but it was a sparse place still. In fact, world wars, bureaucratic disagreements, and lack of funds kept development at a crawl until the 1950s. Today, Canberra's population stands at more than a quarter million—but there's still enough space between buildings to make the city seem more like a gigantic college campus than a teeming metropolis.

Like Brasilia and other planned cities, Canberra is of interest to vacationing visitors principally for its monumental architecture, museums, and fine parks.

Canberra is distinct from Australia's other major cities. Planned as the national capital, it was designed and built mainly to hold parliament and the other arms of national government. It's also home to numerous foreign embassies and legations. Unlike Australia's other major cities, Canberra does not border on the ocean—so summers are warm here, winters chilly.

Seeing the grand design

The key to putting Canberra's development into perspective is the Regatta Point Planning Exhibition. This build-

Canberra, the well-planned capital city, borders on Lake Burley Griffin. Water jet commemorates 200th anniversary of Captain Cook's voyage; in background is the National Library.

ing is located in Commonwealth Park, on Lake Burley Griffin's north shore near Commonwealth Avenue Bridge. It houses a collection of models, photos, and diagrams that give you a clear understanding of how this planned city works. The exhibit is open daily from 9 A.M. to 5 P.M.

Of particular interest are color reproductions of Walter Burley Griffin's 1911 plan for his dream city. An excellent audio-visual presentation shows the main events of Canberra's growth. After the presentation step onto the terrace, from where you can see the spacious core of Canberra. Then, to get the big picture, head for the top of Black Mountain or Mount Ainslie.

Canberra's Telecom Tower sits atop Black Mountain. From its viewing platforms and revolving restaurant at 870 meters/2,842 feet, you get a 360-degree sweeping panorama that encompasses Canberra, its three satellite cities, plus distant rivers and valleys with the Brindabella Range as a backdrop. The tower is open daily from 9 A.M. to 10 P.M.

Opposite the Civic Centre sits Mount Ainslie. The view from its summit (842 meters/2,762 feet) offers the best appreciation of Walter Burley Griffin's grand design.

As you look at Canberra along the central axis of the Parliamentary Triangle, immediately below you is the big green dome of the Australian War Memorial. Leading from there to the lake, you see the broad double strip of Anzac Parade. Follow this line across the lake, and you'll see the white facade of the present Parliament House. Immediately behind it is the nearly-completed new Parliament House on Capital Hill, apex of the triangle.

South of the lake

Standing on the lake shore, between the two bridges that form the sides of the Parliamentary Triangle, are the National Gallery, the High Court, the National Library, and the National Science and Technology Centre (scheduled to open in 1988). Behind these are the original Parliament House and the new Parliament House.

Parliament House. Facing Lake Burley Griffin just below Capital Hill, "The House"—as it is known in the capital—is an attractive white building set amid trim lawns, trees, and colorful gardens. But in spite of its established appearance, Parliament House is, and always has been, temporary.

Canberra

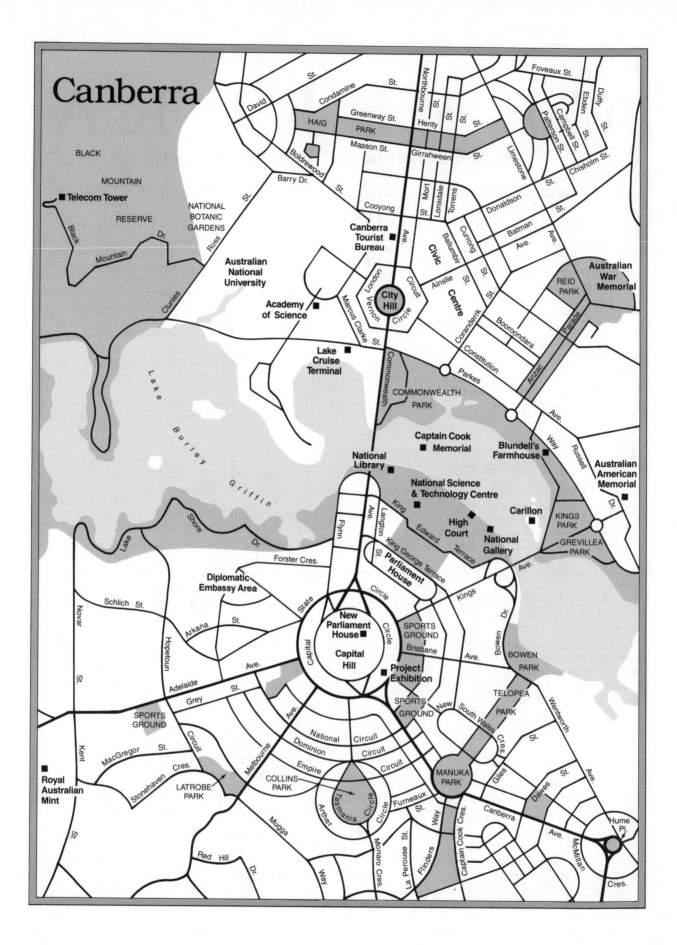

BLACK
MOUNTAIN
RESERVE

NATIONAL
BOTANIC
GARDENS

■ Telecom Tower

Black

Mountain

Dr.

Clunies

Ross

Barry Dr.

David

St.

HAIG
PARK

Condamine

St.

Greenway St.

Masson St.

Cooyong

Boldrewood

St.

St.

Girrahween

Northbourne

Henty

St.

St.

St.

Mort

Lonsdale

St.

Ava.

Ballumbir

Currong

St.

Torrens

St.

Foveaux St.

Ebden

Patterson St.

Campbell St.

St.

Duffy

St.

Chisholm St.

Limestone

Donaldson

St.

Batman

Ave.

Canberra
Tourist
Bureau ■

Civic
Centre

London

Vernon

Marcus Clarke

Circuit

Ainslie

City
Hill

Circle

St.

St.

Coranderrk

Constitution

Booroondara

REID
PARK

Australian
War
Memorial

Anzac

Parade

Australian
National
University

Academy
of Science ■

Lake
Cruise
Terminal ■

Commonwealth

St.

COMMONWEALTH
PARK

Parkes

Ave.

Australian
American
Memorial ■

Russell

Way

Dr.

Lake

Burley

Griffin

Captain Cook
Memorial ■

Blundell's
Farmhouse ■

National
Library ■

National Science
& Technology Centre ■

King

Edward

High
Court ■

Carillon ■

KINGS
PARK

National
Gallery ■

GREVILLEA
PARK

Shore

Dr.

Lake

Flynn

Ave.

Langton

St.

King George Terrace

Terrace

Ave.

Forster Cres.

Parliament
House

St.

Circle

Kings

Schlich St.

Diplomatic
Embassy Area

Arkana

State

St.

Circle

New
Parliament
House ■

SPORTS
GROUND

Brisbane

Bowen

Dr.

BOWEN
PARK

Novar

St.

Hopetoun

Capital

Ave.

Capital
Hill

Circle

Ave.

TELOPEA
PARK

Wentworth

Adelaide

St.

Grey

Project
Exhibition ■

SPORTS
GROUND

New

South Wales

Cres.

St.

SPORTS
GROUND

Kent

St.

MacGregor

Circuit

St.

Melbourne

Ave.

National

Dominion

Circuit

Circuit

MANUKA
PARK

Giles

St.

Dawes

Ave.

■ Royal
Australian
Mint

Stonehaven

Cres.

LATROBE
PARK

Empire

COLLINS
PARK

Tasmania

Circle

Circuit

Furneaux

St.

Captain Cook Cres.

Canberra

Ave.

McMillan

Hume
Pl.

Mugga

Arther

Circle

La Perouse Cres.

Way

Flinders

St.

Red Hill

Way

Dr.

Monaro Cres.

Cres.

When the building was constructed in 1927, city planners intended to use it for only about 50 years. After that a larger building would replace it. However, it has taken time for those plans to be realized. The new Parliament House now sits atop Capital Hill and will open in 1988, Australia's bicentennial. A nearby project exhibition, open daily from 9 A.M. to 6 P.M., provides information about this new building.

In the meantime, you can stroll through the colonnaded foyer of the current Parliament House. King's Hall has a fascinating collection of paintings and portraits, including a painting depicting the opening of the first Parliament in Canberra. Among the documents preserved there is one of three surviving originals of the Inspeximus Issue of the Magna Carta, dated 1297. This aged parchment document is carefully preserved in a transparent capsule filled with argon and fitted with a filter to reduce fading.

As you enter King's Hall, the Senate chamber is to the right and the House of Representatives to the left. Each chamber has a visitors' gallery where you can watch proceedings when Parliament is in session, normally from March through May and August through November, on Tuesdays, Wednesdays, and Thursdays. In daytime, the Australian flag flies over the chamber that is in session. At night, lights are used: red for the Senate, green for the House.

It is not necessary to get tickets in advance for the Senate visitors' gallery. However, it is recommended for the House. You can pick them up at Parliament House a day or two in advance, or write: Principal Attendant, House of Representatives, Parliament House, Canberra 2600.

Parliament House is open daily from 9 A.M. to 5 P.M. Conducted tours of the building are available when Parliament is in recess.

The National Library. This 5-story building is north of Parliament House and overlooks Lake Burley Griffin. It houses several million books, plus maps, photos, plans, prints, and films. Of particular note are a number of original papers, including Captain Cook's journal for the years 1768 to 1771: a description of his voyage of discovery to Australia on board the *Endeavor*.

The library's exhibition areas—the lower ground floor, the foyer, and the mezzanine—feature changing exhibits of outstanding materials from the library. Don't miss the cannon in the foyer. It's one of the six cannons thrown overboard when Captain Cook's *Endeavor* struck a reef off the coast of Queensland in 1770. An American expedition recovered this bit of history nearly 200 years later.

Leonard French's stained-glass windows add beautiful splashes of color to the foyer. Symbolizing the planets, the windows capture the morning sun in reds, oranges, and golds on the north side, and transform afternoon sun rays into blues, greens, and violets on the south side. (French also created the stained-glass ceiling in the Great Hall at Melbourne's National Gallery.)

The exhibition areas are open Monday through Thursday from 9 A.M. to 10 P.M., and Friday through Sunday from 9 to 4:45.

National Gallery and High Court. These strikingly modern buildings stand side by side on the lake shore just east of the National Library. The two buildings were designed and developed as one project; they're connected by a footbridge.

Inside the gallery, an extensive collection of Australian (including Aboriginal), Southeast Asian, European, and American art fills 11 exhibit areas. A sculpture garden is outdoors. The gallery is open daily from 10 A.M. to 5 P.M.

The High Court building has glass walls that soar to 26 meters/87 feet on the building's north and south sides, exposing angled cornices to sunlight and creating a feeling of light-drenched spaciousness. The courtroom walls (15 meters/50 feet tall) are paneled in red tulip oak brought from a Queensland rain forest. You can visit the High Court between 9:45 A.M. and 4:30 P.M. daily.

Royal Australian Mint. Australia's coins as well as the coins of several other Pacific and Asian countries are produced at the Royal Australian Mint on Denison Street, just off Adelaide Avenue west of Capital Hill.

(Continued on page 50)

The essentials

The information below will help you plan your trip to Canberra.

Getting there. Canberra is served by air, rail, and bus.

Air. Domestic flights by Ansett, Australian, and Air New South Wales from Sydney and Melbourne, with service also from Sydney on East-West Airlines. The airport is 20 minutes from downtown by bus or taxi.

Rail. Direct service from Sydney daily. From Melbourne, rail to Yass, then bus (1 hour ride) to Canberra.

Bus. Direct service from Sydney (4½ hours), Melbourne (9 hours). Bus tours are also available from both cities.

Accommodations. Major hotels include Canberra City Travelodge, Canberra International Motor Inn, Canberra Parkroyal-Canberra, Canberra Rex, Hyatt Hotel-Canberra, and Noah's Lakeside International.

Food and drink. Local specialties include trout, lamb, and beefsteaks; there's also a wide range of ethnic cuisine available. Several small local wineries produce good-quality red and white table wines.

Getting around. Public buses serve downtown and the suburbs. A day ticket on the Canberra Explorer tourist bus allows unlimited travel with stops at key Canberra attractions. Buses run every 45 minutes to 1 hour. Taxis and rental cars are plentiful.

Tours. Full or half-day bus tours are available. Drive-yourself tours are made easy with five tour routes marked with arrowed signposts.

For more information. The Canberra Tourist Bureau, Jolimont Centre, is open from 8:30 A.M. to 7 P.M. daily. The Visitor Information Centre (Northbourne Avenue near Morphett Street) is open daily (except Christmas) from 8:30 A.M. to 5 P.M.

...Continued from page 49

You can take a self-guided tour of the facility and, through windows in the visitors' gallery, see the step-by-step production of the coins. The mint is open Monday through Friday from 9 A.M. to 4 P.M.

Embassies and legations. Seventy countries have diplomatic missions in Canberra. Most embassies are south and west of Capital Hill, scattered through three of the city's suburbs—Red Hill, Forrest, and Yarralumla. Many of the embassy buildings reflect the architecture of their country. For example, the Thai embassy has a golden roof with upswept corners, and the red brick, colonnaded, American embassy is reminiscent of colonial Virginia. Both the Indonesian and Papua New Guinean buildings have exhibit areas open to the public.

Government House. Another impressive building, historic Government House, sits at the end of a tree-lined drive at the southwestern end of the lake. This several-story white building, with beautifully landscaped grounds extending to the lake's edge, was built by early Canberra Valley settlers as Yarralumla Homestead. Later enlarged, it is today the official residence of the governor-general. Neither the grounds nor the residence are open to the public. However, you can get a good view of both from a lookout point off Lady Denman Drive on the western boundary of the grounds.

North of the lake

While Capital Hill and the area south of Lake Burley Griffin are devoted mainly to the working arms of national government, the north side of the lake is where the cultural and social life of the city is centered. Ringing the downtown are monuments, museums, schools, and a diverse array of attractions.

The Civic Centre. Around City Hill is the civic and business heart of Canberra. In Civic Square stands the dramatic Ethos statue symbolizing the spirit of the community. At the head of the square sits the Canberra Theatre complex. Concerts, ballet, opera, and major stage shows are presented in the 1,200-seat Canberra Theatre. Other productions are presented in the more intimate 300-seat playhouse.

Shopping around. Sheepskins, leather goods, opals, and Aboriginal arts and crafts are just a few of the unusual items you can find in Canberra shops. Many of the shops are conveniently located near Civic Square in shopping complexes that include large department stores as well as tiny boutiques and gift shops.

Children (and adults who are young-at-heart) will love Petrie Plaza's colorful merry-go-round. From 1914 to 1974, this delightful ride stood on the Esplanade at Melbourne's St. Kilda beach. Canberra purchased the merry-go-round for more than 10 times the price of its master plan—$40,000.

Canberra's city shops are open Monday through Thursday from 9 A.M. to 5:30 P.M., Friday from 8:30 A.M. to 9 P.M., and Saturday from 8:30 A.M. to noon.

Questacon. Located on Elouera Street near the Civic Centre, this participatory science exhibition features more than 100 working "hands-on" displays. Questacon will double in size when it moves to the new National Science and Technology Centre in 1988. Questacon is open Monday through Friday from 10:30 A.M. to 4:30 P.M.

National Museum of Australia. While the museum itself will not be completed until the 1990s, a Visitor Centre is open. It overlooks the construction site—an 88 hectare/ 220 acre peninsula at the western end of Lake Burley Griffin. Here, you can view exhibits from the museum's wide-ranging collection as well as models and plans of the museum project. It's open from 10 A.M. to 5 P.M. daily (Mondays from 1 P.M.).

National Film and Sound Archive. The exhibits in this National Trust-classified building focus on Australian movie, radio, and television productions. Located in McCoy Circuit at the edge of the University campus, it's open from 10 A.M. to 4 P.M. daily.

Academy of Science. Some call it The Martian Embassy. This igloo-shaped building, across the street from the National Film and Sound Archive, consists of a copper-sheathed concrete shell, 46 meters/150 feet in diameter, resting on arches set in an encircling pool. It was designed by Sir Roy Grounds, a Melbourne architect. Though not open to the public, it is worth a look for its exterior design.

Australian War Memorial. One of Australia's most popular tourist attractions is the Australian War Memorial at the end of Anzac Parade—a broad boulevard east of City Hill. This handsome building with its huge copper dome serves as a dramatic memorial to Australians who gave their lives in the service of their country, from the Sudan war in 1885 through Vietnam.

Tribute is paid to these war dead in the building's central courtyard. Here, on either side of the Pool of Reflection, are arcaded galleries whose walls contain bronze panels inscribed with a Roll of Honour. At the end of this courtyard is the Hall of Memory with its copper dome, mosaic walls, and beautiful stained-glass windows.

Two floors of exhibition area within the memorial tell the tales of war through paintings, sculptures, photos, and historic relics. Large dioramas vividly depict historic battle scenes. The building houses a massive array of war implements including a Lancaster bomber, a Spitfire fighter plane, tanks, shells, and torpedos. Sections of the museum will be closed for periods during the next 10 years during a major rebuilding and expansion program.

The Australian War Memorial is open daily from 9 A.M. to 4:45 P.M. The building's closing is announced by the sounding of the Last Post.

From the steps of the memorial, you can look down the broad expanses of Anzac Parade and across the lake to Parliament House. Anzac Parade, completed in 1965, honors the cooperation of the armed forces of two nations—Australia and New Zealand.

Australian-American Memorial. Standing at the head of Kings Avenue, this 79-meter/258-foot aluminum spire commemorates the contribution made by the people of the United States to Australia's defense in World War II.

The Royal Military College. In Duntroon, a suburb just east of the Australian-American Memorial, you'll find Australia's West Point. Here the country's regular army officers receive their training.

On ceremonial occasions the college is the scene of

Skiers congregate on the Snowy Mountains. This is Australia's major skiing area, easily reached from Canberra.

Blundell's Farmhouse, one of Canberra's first buildings, was erected in 1858. Across the water in the background stands the original Parliament House.

much pomp and circumstance. Colorful pageantry includes Beating the Retreat in March and October.

The college grounds are open for inspection. At 2:30 P.M. Monday through Friday (except from November through March), you can take a guided tour.

Blundell's Farmhouse. In this city where so many buildings are new, historic Blundell's Farmhouse provides a contrast. It was built in 1858 by pioneer Robert Campbell for his ploughman. The house, still on its original site, sits on Wendouree Drive in Kings Park overlooking Lake Burley Griffin.

Three of the cottage's rooms have been furnished with pieces dating from the mid-1800s. It is open daily from 2 to 4 P.M. and also from 10 A.M. to noon on Wednesday. It's closed Mondays and Wednesdays during winter.

Australian Institute of Sport. This sprawling complex, one of the world's most advanced sport training and competition centers, is located in the satellite city of Belconnen, 10 minutes from Canberra. Here, there are facilities for ten Olympic sports—basketball, gymnastics, volleyball, rowing, soccer, swimming, tennis, track and field, water polo, and weightlifting. Tours begin at the Swimming Hall Saturdays at 2 P.M.

Canberra outdoors

Many of Canberra's outdoor activities are centered around Lake Burley Griffin in the heart of the city. The lake is not only Canberra's major scenic attraction, but also the city's recreational center. Along its 35-km/22-mile shoreline, you can follow lakeside drives and walking paths, picnic in well-developed recreation areas, or stroll across grassy open spaces. The lake itself offers swimming, boating, and fishing. Besides the vast parklands surrounding Lake Burley Griffin, Canberra's open spaces also include large bushland reserves within a short distance of the city.

Seeing the lake. One of the best ways to experience Lake Burley Griffin is to take a cruise on the 11-km/7-mile-long lake. One-hour cruises depart at noon from the Ferry Terminal at West Basin near Marcus Clarke Street, and two-hour cruises depart at 1 P.M. There are also luncheon and dinner cruises.

One memorable feature of the lake is the Captain Cook Memorial Water Jet. Located near Regatta Point just east of the Commonwealth Avenue Bridge, the jet can send up a dramatic water column of more than 137 meters/450 feet. It was installed in 1970 as a memorial to mark the 200th anniversary of Captain Cook's discovery of eastern Australia. The water jet operates daily from 10 A.M. to noon and 2 to 4 P.M., plus summer evenings.

Still another dramatic lake attraction is the carillon on Aspen Island just west of the Kings Avenue Bridge. The 53-bell-carillon and its tower surrounded by graceful white pillars was a gift from the United Kingdom on Canberra's 50th jubilee. The tower's Westminster chimes ring daily every quarter hour from 8 A.M. to 9 P.M., and there are carillon recitals on Wednesdays and Sundays. The tower is open for inspection on weekends.

Parks and gardens. Several interesting parks line the shores of Lake Burley Griffin. Commonwealth Park, along the northeastern shore of the lake, has been landscaped to include marsh gardens and a children's play area. Thousands of flowering plants add color to the park the year around. Weston Park's adventure playground, on the lake's southwestern shore, features a play area that includes tree houses, a miniature lake with islands and bridges, a maze, and a miniature railway.

The National Botanic Gardens primarily provide a place to enjoy and study plants. Stretching across the lower slopes of Black Mountain, the gardens contain plants from all over Australia grown under conditions similar to their native environment. You can stroll through shady fern glens made humid by artificial misting or enjoy the colorful profusion of acacias in bloom in an area devoted to the growing of this Australian native. On the garden's Aboriginal Trail, you'll learn what plants were used by Aborigines for food, clothing, and weapons. The gardens are open daily from 9 A.M. to 5 P.M. with guided tours Sunday at 10 A.M. and 2 P.M.

Canberra has 105 km/65 miles of paved cycleways and bikes can be rented near the Ferry Terminal at West Basin. Small boats are also available for rent at West Basin.

Two public 18-hole courses lure golfers (Canberra also has several private clubs). For information on tennis, contact the A.C.T. Lawn Tennis Association, P.O. Box 44, Dickson 2602.

Side trips from Canberra

Sheep stations and satellites compete for the attention of visitors looking beyond Canberra for manmade changes of pace from the central city. Then there is always the opportunity to get into the Australian bush at the expense of only a few miles of travel.

Sheep stations

A trip to a sheep station is easier from Canberra than from any other major city in Australia, for the surrounding countryside is still grazing land, just as it was in the early 1900s when the valley was selected as the site of the national capital. Local tour operators offer day visits to sheep stations. These tours include outdoor barbecue lunches, demonstrations of sheep dogs at work, and sheep shearing, and—as an added bit of local color—boomerang throwing.

Stars and space

Students of the stars and deep space will be interested in two nearby attractions.

Mount Stromlo Observatory. Housed in the large silver domes on Mount Stromlo, off Cotter Road 16 km/10 miles west of Canberra, are the telescopes of Australian National University's Department of Astronomy. The visitor center at the 188-cm/74-inch telescope is open daily from 9:30 A.M. to 4 P.M.

Space tracking stations. Two space tracking stations are located about an hour's drive southwest of Canberra. Under the control of the United States' National Aeronautic and Space Administration (NASA), they're part of a worldwide chain of tracking stations.

Of the two, only Tidbinbilla (40 km/25 miles from Canberra) is open to the public. Here, you'll find a visitors' information center with model spacecraft, audio-visual presentations, and photos that tell the story of man's exploration of space. The information center is open daily from 9 to 5.

Nearby bushlands

Several bushland reserves near Canberra offer visitors an opportunity to enjoy some native flora and fauna.

Rehwinkel's Animal Park. Here, just 24 km/15 miles north of Canberra via the Federal Highway, you can meet kangaroos, koalas, and other native fauna in natural surroundings. It's open daily from 10 A.M. to 5 P.M.

Tidbinbilla Nature Reserve. A variety of Australian wildlife dwells in the natural surroundings of this reserve 40 km/25 miles southwest of Canberra, near the Tidbinbilla tracking station. Unspoiled hilly bushland offers a chance for scenic walks on winding trails as well as a number of secluded picnic spots.

In a special enclosure, you can see kangaroos, koalas, and emus close up. The reserve is open daily from 9 A.M. to 6 P.M., and the special enclosure is open daily between 11 and 4.

Cotter Reserve. Canberra's original reservoir (Cotter Dam), 23 km/14 miles west of the city, preserves some bushland, but also has been developed with picnic and campsites. There also is good river swimming nearby in the Cotter and Murrumbidgee rivers.

The Snowy Mountains— An all-year playground

Some of Australia's most rugged and dramatic scenery is found about 161 km/100 miles southwest of Canberra in the Snowy Mountains—the highest range on the continent. In this corner of New South Wales are deep fern gullies and lush hillside forests, snow-capped mountains and flower-dotted alpine meadows, and clear, bubbling streams and deep blue lakes.

Much of the area has been set aside as Kosciusko National Park, making it an ideal spot for both summer and winter vacationers. Besides an abundance of recreational possibilities, the area offers detailed looks at one of the world's most extensive engineering projects—the Snowy Mountains Hydro-Electric Scheme.

Kosciusko National Park. This 6,134 square km/2,368 square mile park is Australia's largest national reserve. Its towering mountain peaks, cascading streams, and majestic forests are enjoyed as a summer and winter playground.

Between June and September, skiers swish down the slopes of towering Mount Kosciusko—at 2,230 meters/7,316 feet the highest peak in Australia. Park resorts shuttle skiers to their favorite runs on chairlifts, T-bars, and Poma lifts. Cross-country skiing is also popular. Summer activities include hiking, fishing, trail riding, tennis, golf, and touring the nearby Snowy Mountains Hydro-Electric Scheme. The park's summer alpine wildflowers—including buttercups, everlasting, and heath—come into brilliant bloom around November.

The Yarrangobilly Caves, in the northern portion of the park about 97 km/60 miles from Cooma, will interest spelunkers. Four large limestone caves have been developed for visitors and contain a variety of stalactites, stalagmites, canopies, and flowstone.

Kosciusko resorts can be found in the southern part of the park at Thredbo Village, Perisher Valley, Smiggin Holes, Mount Kosciusko, Guthega, Digger's Creek, and Wilson's Valley. Resort accommodations include hotels, motels, lodges, and guest houses.

Snowy Mountains Hydro-Electric Scheme. The Snowy Mountains Authority has set up inspection tours for visitors to this vast engineering project that was begun in 1949 and completed in 1973. Sixteen dams have been built and ten power stations installed, some of them buried in the hills. More than 145 km/90 miles of tunnels have been hewn through the mountains, and 97 km/60 miles of aqueducts have been constructed. As a result, water from the abundant Snowy River has been diverted from the unproductive eastern slopes of the mountains into the Murray-Murrumbidgee river system on the west side, thus generating electricity and providing irrigation water for a large amount of productive farmland.

The project has created an additional bonus for sports enthusiasts—a group of lakes, of which the largest, Lake Eucumbene, contains nine times the volume of water in Sydney Harbour. Anglers will be glad to know that Eucumbene, Lake Jindabyne, and Tantangara Reservoir are stocked with trout all year. Other area sport activities include water-skiing, windsurfing, and boating. Accommodations can be found at Jindabyne, Adaminaby, Anglers Reach, Buckenderra, and Braemar.

Seeing the Snowy Mountains. Cooma is the gateway to this mountain country and the area's transportation center. By air, the town is a half-hour from Canberra, about an hour from Sydney or Melbourne. It is easily reached by rail, bus, or car. Situated 106 km/66 miles from Mount Kosciusko, Cooma is an excellent starting point for tours of the national park and the remarkable Snowy Mountains Hydro-Electric Scheme. The town's accommodations include motels, caravan parks, and campgrounds.

In addition to area tours originating in Cooma, several Melbourne and Sydney tour operators feature tours which include the Snowy Mountains; and there are tours from Canberra into the region. The Snowy Mountains Authority has also set up inspection tours of certain installations for visitors.

MELBOURNE

Victoria neatly packages a stately city, fine beaches, snowy peaks

In a country where distances are measured in the thousands as often as the hundreds, where Texas would be a middle-sized sort of state, Victoria is small. In fact, it is almost 10,000 square miles smaller than Oregon.

Size is no handicap, though, for this is one of those happily compact regions where a great city—Melbourne—is flanked on one side by warm ocean waters and on the other by beautiful mountains. The history of the place encompasses a greater gold rush than California's. On Victoria's innermost border is a river big enough to carry steamboats. The state has deserts, named, forthrightly, Big Desert and Little Desert. (It also has a region we cannot resist mentioning, Sunset Country.) Between river and deserts, it has wine valleys.

And for all of this, Victoria is purely Australian, full of tree ferns, eucalyptus forests, koalas, lyrebirds, and all the other exotics that come to mind.

Melbourne—A dignified capital

Instead of the frenetic tempo usually associated with a metropolis, Melbourne has a quiet dignity. There's a sense of culture, graciousness, beauty, and unhurried growth and prosperity. In spite of the city's position as Australia's financial hub, there still exists a sedate charm. Broad avenues are lined with beautiful deciduous trees, and intermingled with today's glass and steel are elegant Victorian-era buildings.

Don't let Melbourne's conservative appearance fool you. The city does hum.

Fine theater productions and concerts are staged the year around. In addition, Melbourne is a mecca for the fashion-minded because it is Australia's major fashion center. The boutiques and department stores reflect this.

Melbourne is also perhaps the most sports-minded city in Australia. Tens of thousands flock to Australian Rules football games, as well as horse races and cricket matches.

The activity-oriented spirit of Melbourne is perhaps best revealed during the annual Moomba Festival. Each March, as summer yields to autumn, the city kicks up its heels in the 10-day Moomba, a zesty celebration of the arts, sports, and sheer fun in living.

The Royal Botanic Gardens, one of the city's many parklands, is considered one of the best in Australia. Within a half-hour's drive south of downtown are a host of good beaches for water sports enthusiasts, and to the east the lush Dandenong Ranges offer hikers and picnickers a number of pleasant spots.

What Melbourne is, above all else, is big. The city and its suburbs spread far inland from Port Phillip Bay and the mouth of the Yarra River, as far as the lush Dandenong Ranges. A population of 2.9 million lives in 59 separately named communities within the 1,852 square km/715 square miles of Melbourne.

The heart of the city

Melbourne is a city for strolling.

In spite of extensive redevelopment, its compact center retains an old-world, 19th century character. Amid today's skyscrapers, many of its early Victorian-style buildings still stand, reminders of the city's history and tributes to gold rush boom times.

Even downtown, wide, tree-lined boulevards capture the essence of the city—spaciousness and greenery—before they plunge into a luxurious greenbelt of parklands rare by any standard for their generous proportions. Some of these parks are so close to offices that they are favorite lunchtime retreats for workers, offering instant respite from urban pressures.

The heart of the inner city, called the Golden Mile, contains the government and commercial hub of Melbourne, its chief shopping street, and the main hotels and theaters. The perimeters are the Yarra River on the south, Spencer Street on the west, LaTrobe Street on the north, and Spring Street on the east.

For a bird's-eye view of downtown Melbourne, go to the observation deck of the AMP Building at the corner of Bourke and Williams streets. Viewings, restricted to once daily Monday through Friday at 1:40 P.M., can be arranged through the security guard. The top of the Shrine of Remembrance (see page 57) on St. Kilda Road provides good views of the downtown skyline and parklands.

Broad, tree-lined boulevards like Collins Street typify Melbourne's famed Golden Mile. Electric trams make city-exploring enjoyable and inexpensive.

Landmarks. The greatest of Melbourne's public buildings are in or adjacent to the Golden Mile, all within walking distance of each other.

Victoria's legislature meets at State Parliament House, on Spring Street opposite the end of Bourke Street. Between 1901 and 1927 the Federal Parliament also met here. This neoclassic building with its Doric columns was begun in 1856; it's still considered unfinished today. A simple rectangle, it lacks the north and south wings and imposing dome included in the architect's original drawings. Weekdays there are guided tours of the building.

From the steps of State Parliament House, you have a clear view of the Princess Theatre on Spring Street. This elaborately decorated structure was built in 1887 for Queen Victoria's Jubilee, and still is being used for legitimate theater.

South on Spring Street, the Old Treasury Building borders on Treasury Gardens. Built between 1859 and 1862, it is considered an excellent example of Italian Renaissance. At one time its underground vaults held £100,000,000 in gold from the fields at Ballarat and farther north. (Today the building houses many state government offices.)

At the corner of Flinders and Swanston streets stands the Flinders Street Railway Station. Built in the 19th century, the French Renaissance building with its two clock towers and copper dome is one of the busiest railway stations in the world. Suburban commuters rush through it daily. Clocks telling departure times of suburban trains line the facade above the main entrance.

One of Melbourne's finest examples of 19th century Gothic Revival architecture is just a few blocks northeast

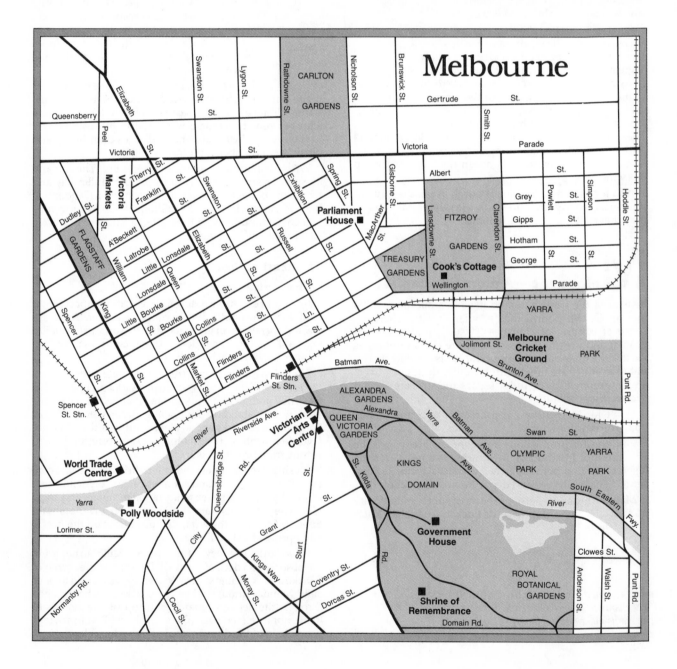

of the State Parliament House. The triple spires of St. Patrick's Roman Catholic Cathedral rise from a spot at the corner of Gisborne and Albert streets. Construction on the cathedral began in 1863. The west portal and spires were added in 1939.

You'll find another impressive cathedral across from the Flinders Street Railway Station. Designed by William Butterfield, the church is another good example of post-Gothic Revival architecture. It was the second Anglican cathedral—it replaced St. James Old Cathedral in 1891.

St. James Old Cathedral, once located on Little Collins Street, was moved to its present location at the corner of King and Batman streets in 1914. Completed in 1842, it served as Melbourne's Anglican cathedral for a half-century. This historic church retains its original box pews and furnishings, including a baptismal font donated by Queen Victoria.

Though LaTrobe's Cottage—the first Government House—may be beyond casual strolling range, it still belongs in a tour of landmark buildings as a reminder of the beginnings. It is located in King's Domain park.

LaTrobe's Cottage was shipped prefabricated from England in the late 1830s and erected on a site near what is now Melbourne Cricket Ground. The small, weatherboard building served as home for Lt. Gov. Charles LaTrobe during his term of office, 1839 to 1854. The cottage was moved to its present site and restored by the National Trust. Open daily from 10 A.M. to 4:30 P.M., the house still has many of its original furnishings.

Also in King's Domain is the Shrine of Remembrance, an impressive memorial to Victoria's war dead. It was designed so that a ray of sunlight falls on the Rock of Remembrance at the 11th hour of the 11th day of the 11th month, the exact moment of the armistice ending World War I.

For serious shoppers. Melbourne is Australia's major fashion center. Tree-shaded Collins and Bourke streets are noted for department stores and boutiques.

Two of the city's major department stores—David Jones and G.J. Coles—are located on Bourke Street. The huge Myer department store on the Bourke Street Mall (between Elizabeth and Swanston streets) is the largest department store in the Southern Hemisphere. The mall, a one-block section of Bourke Street, is closed to all vehicular traffic except trams.

At the top end of Collins Street, between Spring and Swanston streets, some of Melbourne's most exclusive (and expensive) fashionable boutiques specialize in imported designer clothes. Georges—an exclusive department store on Collins Street—has fine women's and men's wear and household goods. The nearby Figgins Diorama features 40 boutiques in a restored Victorian building.

A dozen arcades—filled with tiny shops offering a surprising array of merchandise—branch off from the city's main shopping streets. The oldest, Royal Arcade, dates from 1870. Other arcades include Block Arcade with entrances on Collins, Little Collins, and Elizabeth streets; and the Australian Arcade under the Hotel Australia.

Most of Melbourne's stores are open from 9 A.M. to 5 P.M. Monday through Thursday, 9 to 9 on Friday, and 9 to noon on Saturday.

(Continued on page 58)

The essentials

The capsule version below is what you need to know about getting to and around Melbourne, and enjoying your stay there.

Getting there. Melbourne is served by air, sea, rail, and bus.

Air. International service by Qantas and foreign carriers. Domestic flights by Ansett, Australian, Air New South Wales, East-West, and Kendell airlines. Tullamarine Airport is 23 km/14 miles from downtown by bus or taxi.

Sea. International cruise ships put in at Port Melbourne. A suburban train takes you from piers to city center.

Rail. Interstate trains provide regular service to and from other state capitals. Spencer Street Station adjoins downtown area.

Bus. Ansett Pioneer, Greyhound, Deluxe, and VIP journey between Melbourne and other state capitals.

Accommodations. Major hotels in the downtown area include the Melbourne Hilton International, Rockman's Regency Hotel, Noah's Hotel Melbourne, Regent of Melbourne, Menzies Rialto, Hyatt on Collins, Windsor Hotel, and Southern Cross. A short tram ride up St. Kilda Road are the Travelodge and Parkroyal. *Note:* You may find it hard to obtain reservations during Australian Rules finals (late September), Melbourne Cup Week (early November), and Moomba Festival (March).

Food and drink. Local specialties are led by the whiting, a white-fleshed saltwater fish, followed by other seafoods such as prawns, lobsters, and oysters. A wide range of ethnic cuisine is available. For an unusual dining experience with gourmet food plus a city tour, try the Colonial Tramcar Restaurant. Yarra River dining includes a floating restaurant, the Melbourne Lighter, or one can rent Bar-B-Boats complete with gas barbecues.

Local beers include Carlton, Crown Lager, Crest Lager, Fosters, and Victoria Bitter. Wines of note come from Best's, Brown Bros., Bullers, and Seppelt.

Getting around. Local transportation includes an extensive tram system, an underground train loop, and bus service. There's also an extensive suburban train system operating from Flinders Street Railway Station. Bargain (2-hour, daily, weekly) local and multi-neighborhood travel tickets are available. The City Explorer Bus does a circular tour of Melbourne, stopping at city attractions.

Tours. Several full or half-day tours of city available. Regional tours to Dandenongs (page 64), Phillip Island (page 73), Wilson's Promontory (page 67), Lorne and Great Ocean Road (page 68), and Ballarat and Sovereign Hill (page 60). Also available: spring wildflower tours into the Grampians (page 69), winter ski tours (page 69), and 1 and 2-day weekend excursions into Victoria on a restored, vintage steam train, *The Melbourne Limited.*

For more information. Victour, 230 Collins Street, Melbourne 3000.

...Continued from page 57

For an uncommon shopping experience, stroll through Queen Victoria Market, a few blocks north of the Golden Mile via Elizabeth Street. Tuesdays, Thursdays, Fridays, and Saturdays, the century-old market has everything—fruits, vegetables, fish, meat, clothing, and much more. On Sundays it becomes a craft market. Additional craft items are featured at the Meat Market Craft Centre in North Melbourne.

Beyond the city center, inner suburbs like South Yarra, Prahan, Camberwell, and Toorak have shops specializing in antiques. South Yarra's and Toorak's boutiques sell trendy fashions.

Victorian Arts Centre

This complex of three buildings, located on St. Kilda Road across from Queen Victoria Gardens, is the focal point for many of Melbourne's cultural events (see page 62). Included in the complex are the Melbourne Concert Hall, Theatres Building, and the National Gallery.

The circular-shaped, 2,600-seat Concert Hall lies closest to the Yarra River with a riverside promenade along one border. The hall's interior reflects the colors and textures of Australia: wool for carpeting and seat covers, leather for lining the foyers, and native woods for the stage, wings, and floors. Works by famous Australian artists decorate the entrance walls, and a gigantic light sculpture of brass and steel reflects light from spotlights scattered through all five floors of the complex. The Concert Hall building is also home to the Performing Arts Museum and its changing exhibits.

The Theatres Building, set between the Concert Hall and the National Gallery, is topped by a 115-metre/377-foot spire. Inside are three theaters—the 2,000-seat State Theatre, the 880-seat Playhouse, and the versatile 420-seat Studio.

Guided 1-hour tours of the Concert Hall and Theatres Building are offered daily between 10 A.M. and 5 P.M.

You approach the National Gallery by crossing a bridged moat. The front window is highly unusual: two sheets of glass with a water curtain flowing between them. More surprises await you inside the gallery. The soaring stained-glass ceiling is a breathtaking sight; designed by Leonard French, it took 6 years and 10,000 pieces of glass to complete.

Museums in Melbourne

The story of Melbourne and Victoria's past is told through exhibits in several Melbourne museums.

The Old Melbourne Gaol and Penal Museum, at the corner of Russell and LaTrobe streets, provides an excellent opportunity to discover what imprisonment was like in 19th century Melbourne.

It was here that the infamous bushranger, Ned Kelly, was hung in November 1880. (Kelly and a band of fellow highwaymen terrorized the countryside during gold rush days, ambushing gold escorts and robbing banks.) The hangman's scaffold and Kelly's bullet-dented armor are on display, gruesome reminders of rough and tumble times during Victoria's early days. The Old Gaol, now open to visitors daily from 10 A.M. to 5 P.M., has been carefully renovated.

The National Museum on Russell Street offers special insights into things uniquely Australian—Aboriginal weapons, domestic articles, and ceremonial objects, as well as mammals, birds, reptiles, and minerals. To most Australians the museum's prime exhibit is Phar Lap, the Australian chestnut gelding who—before meeting a taxidermist—won 37 races in the 1930s. The museum is open from 10 A.M. to 5 P.M. Monday through Saturday, and 2 to 5 P.M. on Sunday.

Museum of Chinese Australian History. Located in Chinatown, on Cohen Place, the exhibits trace the history of the Chinese in Australia from the gold rush of the 1850s onward. The museum is open weekdays (except Tuesdays) from 10 A.M. to 4:30 P.M., and weekends from noon to 4:30 P.M.

Melbourne Maritime Museum. The showpiece of this museum is the restored barque *Polly Woodside*, a square-rigged ship built in the 1880s. The museum is located at the corner of Normanby Road and Phayer Street in South Melbourne. Open weekdays from 10 A.M. to 4 P.M., and weekends from noon to 5 P.M.

A short trip away

Not all of Melbourne's great landmarks and points of interest nestle into the downtown. The suburbs contain a fine zoo, the University of Melbourne campus, and some extraordinary houses.

An elegant age. Como House, off Williams Road in South Yarra, reflects the elegant prosperity of the Victorian era in Melbourne. Overlooking the Yarra River, this stately mansion is one of Melbourne's oldest residences and one of the few remaining, unspoiled historic mansions. It was home for the Armytage family for nearly a century before it was sold to the National Trust in 1959. Much of the original furniture remains.

The gardens, laid out following suggestions of the famous botanist Baron von Mueller, were once the scene of annual cherry picking parties. If the trees didn't produce a sufficient crop, the boughs were hung with ripe cherries purchased for the event.

Two other historic homes worth a visit are Rippon Lea in Elsternwick and Werribee Park Estate in Werribee. Rippon Lea, a polychrome brick mansion built in the 1860s, is surrounded by beautifully landscaped gardens.

The expansive grounds of Werribee Park Estate include a golf course, picnic grounds, children's playground, zoological park, equestrian center, and large formal garden. The estate's 60-room Italianate mansion, built in the 1870s, features lavish furnishings.

Como House and Rippon Lea are open daily from 10 A.M. to 5 P.M. Werribee Park Estate is open Friday through Tuesday from 10 A.M. to 5 P.M.

Zoological Gardens. You'll find grounds beautifully landscaped with Australian flora as backdrops to koalas, kangaroos, wombats, echidnae, emus, and fairy penguins at the Zoological Gardens located in the corner of Royal Park near the University of Melbourne.

The emphasis at this zoo is to preserve a natural environment for the animals. At the Lion Park you can watch lions stalking the savanna below from the safety of an enclosed bridge. The orangutans and chimpanzees at the

(Continued on page 62)

Sky-piercing spire tops the Theatres Building at the Victorian Arts Centre, venue for Melbourne cultural events.

Gog and Magog preside over the Royal Shopping Arcade in Melbourne's Golden Mile. Ornate ironwork adorns the arcade's arched dome; glossy boutiques and gift stores fill the mall.

Australia's golden bonanza

The story of Australia's gold rush begins on the banks of California's Sacramento River in 1849. An Englishman, out to gain his fortune in the California gold fields, recognized the similarity of the Mother Lode terrain to a valley in the mountains behind Bathurst, New South Wales. Though 18 years had passed since Edward Hargreaves had seen that valley, he returned to Australia, struck out across the Blue Mountains, and immediately found gold beside Summer Hill Creek.

News of the discovery soon emptied Australia's cities. Melbourne, drained of its citizens, offered a £200 reward to the first person to find a gold field within 100 miles of town. In July 1851, gold was discovered at Clunes, and in August, at Ballarat—the richest alluvial gold field the world has ever known. Discoveries at Bendigo and Mount Alexander followed soon after.

The gold was easily won. So rich were the alluvial deposits that the output of Bendigo and Ballarat alone nearly equaled that of all the California fields. By the middle of 1852, adventurers from all over the world were pouring into Melbourne and fanning out across Victorian bush—"forty-niners" from California, New Englanders, Texans, Irish, English, Europeans, and Chinese—100,000 in one year alone. Port Phillip Bay became a forest of masts—at one time about 500 ships were anchored in Sandridge. Many of these were empty, deserted by their crews who set off to seek their fortunes in the fields. (Shanghaiing became a popular form of obtaining a new ship's crew.)

Almost overnight, towns sprang up in the bush, at first just canvas and clapboard cities, but soon replaced by ornate neoclassic stone structures that reflected the area's new-found wealth.

Australia's bushrangers (highwaymen) also joined the rush to the gold fields. But their method of obtaining riches was far different from that of the hard-working digger. Bands of bushrangers swept the countryside, ambushing gold escorts and robbing banks. Many of the country people admired these dapper individuals and their deeds soon were immortalized in Australian folk ballads.

Today you can easily reach this colorful, historic area of Victoria from Melbourne by daily coach or rail service. There are also full-day coach tours to Ballarat and Sovereign Hill as well as Bendigo.

Ballarat. Located in hilly country 113 km/70 miles west of Melbourne, Ballarat was a small farming community until Thomas Hiscock found gold near Buninyong cemetery in 1851. The area's alluvial gold fields turned out to be the richest in the world.

In 1854, Ballarat witnessed Australia's only civil war—the Eureka Stockade rebellion. At this time, the Crown technically owned all the land and claimed the gold mines as property of the government. However, the Crown didn't lay claim to the gold found on the land. Instead, they required diggers to have a license which cost 30 shillings per month. Many diggers—unlucky in their search for gold—couldn't afford this amount and didn't pay it. Soon the police were stopping everyone, demanding to be shown licenses. Harrassment and corruption became common. A group of 150 diggers, angered by oppressive government policies and the arrogance of the police, declared themselves independent. Though they were overwhelmingly defeated, the rebellion of the diggers resulted in sweeping reforms.

Ballarat retains much of its Victorian atmosphere, with 1860s stone buildings and churches bordering tree-lined avenues. Among interesting places to visit are the Eureka Stockade Memorial, site of the original stockade; Adam Lindsay Gordon's Cottage; the Botanic Gardens, containing the famous Begonia House (center of the annual March begonia festival); and "Ercildoone," a pioneer homestead built by the Learmonth brothers around 1859.

Of particular note is the Gold Museum located a short distance southeast of Ballarat across from Sovereign Hill Goldmining Township. Through a variety of well-done displays and graphics, the museum tells the story of gold and the part it has played in the history of mankind.

There are displays showing precoinage of valuable gold items from ancient civilizations. Gold coins from around the world, including coins from Australia, Great Britain, Europe, the Middle East, the Americas, India, and Africa, are presented—accompanied by graphics describing historical facts, and relating interesting anecdotes about the country's gold coins. Modern uses of gold in today's industries are also illustrated.

In a special section of the museum you can study a bas-relief map that shows the location of places where gold was discovered in the Ballarat area, plus the types of nuggets found at each site.

More than 20 hotels and motels, as well as guest houses, caravan parks, and campgrounds provide comfortable accommodations for visitors.

Sovereign Hill Goldmining Township. This historical park, a short distance southeast of Ballarat, evokes memories of the gold rush period. Set near land once mined by the diggers, the park re-creates the town of Ballarat during its first 10 years of development following the discovery of gold in the area in 1851.

Many aspects of mining life are exemplified, from the first gold diggings through the development of an established town. In Red Hill Gully Diggings you'll see windlasses, shafts, whims, and the tents in which early diggers lived. At the Gold Commissioner's tent, you can buy a "miner's right" to pan for gold in the nearby creek.

A fascinating array of buildings—re-created from drawings and photographs of the time—line the township's main street. Strolling its wooden sidewalks, you can stop in the confectionary shop for a "lolly," get your name printed on a "wanted" bulletin at the *Ballarat Times* office, or attend a production at the Victoria Theatre.

At the far end of town is a reconstructed quartz mine. Descending to its depths, you'll learn of mining techniques used between 1860 and 1918.

Eating establishments at Sovereign Hill include the New York Bakery and the United States Hotel. Sovereign Hill's Government Camp has family, bunk-bed accommodations and is also an associated youth hostel.

Bendigo. About 153 km/95 miles northwest of Melbourne, Bendigo ranked second to Ballarat in gold production. Its record year was 1856, when 661,749 ounces were taken from the fields. Today, Bendigo is a prosperous agricultural center, with the third largest sheep market in the country.

As in Ballarat, the wealth of the gold fields found its way into the construction of many ornate, neoclassic public and commercial buildings. Some of Australia's finest examples of Victorian architecture line the city's streets. A number of them have been classified by the National Trust as notable buildings. Included among noteworthy structures are the Town Hall, the Post Office, the Law Courts, several banks, a couple of churches, the old police barracks, the Shamrock Hotel, and the Temperance Hall. The Fortuna Villa is an outstanding example of a Victorian mansion.

One of the town's main attractions is the Central Deborah Gold Mine, which has been restored to working condition with a boiler, compressor, poppet legs, winding equipment, and blacksmith's shop. The Central Deborah Gold Mine was the last deep reef mine to close on the Bendigo gold fields. When it closed, the mine's main shaft extended through 17 levels and was 396 meters/1,299 feet long. There are guided tours of the mine daily between 10 A.M. and 5 P.M.

A good way to take a brief tour of the town is on the "Talking Tram" from the Central Deborah Gold Mine. The trip takes you on an 8-km/5-mile ride through town, to the Tramways Museum, and out to the Chinese Joss House at Emu Point before it returns to its starting point. The running dialogue covers many of Bendigo's historical sights.

Other town highlights include the Bendigo Art Gallery where you can enjoy a fine collection of Australian and French impressionist paintings. The new Bendigo Steam and Oil Engines Museum (open the last Sunday of each month) has a number of working models.

On the outskirts of town is an interesting pottery factory—one of Australia's oldest, established in 1857. Here you can buy famous Epsom stoneware that has been salt-glazed in vintage kilns heated by wood and coal.

If you decide to stay in the area, you can choose from 25 hotels and motels, several caravan parks, and campgrounds.

Castlemaine. This small gold mining town is located south of Bendigo.

During gold rush days, Castlemaine played an important role as the gold fields market center for the gardens and or-

chards in the area. The Castlemaine Market, built in 1862, stands as a reminder of this era. Renovated in 1974, the building now houses a museum of old photos of gold rush days. These photos feature the gold fields and show what living conditions were like for the diggers. They are the work of Antoine Foucherie, a French photographer who visited Castlemaine in 1857–58. Also included in the market/museum are early maps and plans of the area and other gold mining memorabilia.

At Pennyweight Flat, on the outskirts of town, tombstones tell of the harshness of life on the gold fields. Many diggers and members of their families went to early graves, the victims of numerous diseases that ravaged the crowded gold camps.

You'll find hotels, motels, and caravan parks in the area.

Maldon. Still another historic town lies south of Bendigo not far from Castlemaine. Located on the slopes of Mount Tarrangower, Maldon is a well-preserved town of the gold mining era. It is the only town entirely protected by the National Trust of Victoria. Maldon's main street is lined with an interesting assortment of shops with wide front verandas. Included among noteworthy buildings are the Holy Trinity Church, the Court House and Police Lock-up, and the Maldon Hospital. The Folk Museum, housed in the old Council Offices, contains a wealth of interesting gold rush items.

Just outside of town, you can see evidence of gold mining days—grass-covered mounds, the tailings of early diggings. You can also tour Carmen's Tunnel, a 468-meter/1,535-foot tube carved out of solid bluestone, and view the Beehive Mine Company chimney.

The area around Maldon is known for unusual rock formations with such descriptive names as The Sphinx, The Judge, and Witch's Head. In spring, the hills are ablaze with wildflowers.

Area accommodations include hotels, motels, and caravan parks.

Beechworth. This old mining town—about 241 km/150 miles northeast of Melbourne (via the Hume Highway to Wangaratta)—had a role in the saga of Australia's notorious bushranger, Ned Kelly. This is "Kelly Country." Ned and his gang roamed the hills around the town and Kelly was imprisoned in Beechworth's jail in 1881.

Established in 1852, Beechworth has an excellent collection of well-preserved historic buildings including the historic jail and several stone churches. The powder magazine, built in 1859, tells of the time when large amounts of blasting powder were necessary for nearby gold mining operations. The town's museum contains an interesting collection of pioneer relics.

Just outside of town are abandoned gold mines. If you like, you can do a little gold panning in nearby streams. There's also a trout farm where you can sink a line to catch your dinner.

Area accommodations include hotels, motels, and caravan parks.

Wild ducks and black swans *gather for a handout at Royal Botanic Gardens, one of Melbourne's popular parks.*

...Continued from page 58

Ape Complex swing and play in freedom in open-air, moated enclosures.

The zoo, open daily from 9 A.M. to 5 P.M., has both a souvenir shop and snack bar.

University of Melbourne. Founded in 1854, this was Australia's second university—but the first to admit women. It's located in Parkville, about 3 km/2 miles from the city. The avenue of palms leading to the main entrance was planted with seedlings brought back from the Middle East by Australian soldiers after World War I. As you stroll around the campus, you'll discover the Percy Grainger Museum, displaying the personal effects of the noted composer-pianist, and some striking murals by Douglas Annand.

The lively arts

Melbourne's entertainment scene is highly varied, ranging from concerts and opera to night clubs and discotheques.

Primary venue for many cultural events is the Victorian Arts Centre (see page 58). The Melbourne Theatre Company stages a variety of plays in the Playhouse, and the Playbox Theatre performs in the adjacent Studio. The State Theatre, also in the Theatres Building, is home to the Australian Ballet, Australian Opera, and Victorian State Opera. Performances are staged throughout the year.

Between April and October, the Melbourne Symphony Orchestra performs in the Melbourne Concert Hall.

One of the peak months for theater and almost every other kind of performance is March, during the great festival called Moomba (pronounced Moo-mba). Along with theater and music, there's an open-air art show, sailing regattas, horse shows and horse races, parades, carnival rides and a fireworks finale.

In September, the Spoletto Melbourne Festival of Three Worlds features music and theater performances by Australian, American, and Italian artists.

If you're visiting Melbourne between November and April, take advantage of free outdoor concerts—symphony, pop groups, ballet—at the Sidney Myer Music Bowl. The bowl, in the King's Domain on St. Kilda Road, has a tentlike roof of aluminum and steel housing the sound shell and stage. During the winter, the music bowl's stage area becomes an ice-skating rink.

Other free entertainment is also held throughout the city in gardens and squares between November and April. There are free Sunday concerts the year around in the National Gallery's Great Hall on St. Kilda Road and in the Melbourne Town Hall on Swanston Street.

A swinging night life hasn't been part of the Melbourne scene since the boom days of the Australian gold rush, when Lola Montez entertained the diggers. Today, though, you'll find night clubs as well as theater restaurants and a growing number of discotheques. Rock and jazz music livens the scene at some pubs and wine bars in the city and its suburbs.

For more information on Melbourne's lively arts, pick up a copy of *This Week in Melbourne* from the Victour office.

Sports to watch

If you want to watch Melbournians cast aside their Victorian reserve, any major sports event will do, but football and horse racing are the surest bets.

The phenomenon known as Australian Rules football is at its best in Melbourne. The 12 professional teams in the Victorian Football League represent district clubs throughout the Melbourne area, and some of the rivalries are fierce. Six matches are held each Saturday during the April to September season. The finals pit the two top teams at the Melbourne Cricket Ground before Super Bowl-sized crowds of 100,000. (See page 12 for more on the game of Australian Rules football.)

Just as fervently followed is horse racing, held the year around both midweek and Saturdays at Flemington, Caulfield, Moonee Valley, and Sandown race tracks.

Flemington is the home of the Melbourne Cup, an internationally famous racing event held on the first Tuesday in November. On this special day the entire nation comes to a halt to hear the race on radio, or see it on television. Meanwhile, all Melbourne is at the track, when huge amounts of champagne and betting money flow. On this occasion, gentlemen wear gray top hats and dark morning suits, and ladies splash color through the stands with wacky, wonderful hats. The Melbourne Cup is part of the Spring Racing Carnival which includes a line-up of important horse races.

Harness racing meets are held the year around at the Moonee Valley Racecourse.

Greyhounds race at Olympic Park on Batman Avenue in East Melbourne, and at Sandown Park in Springvale.

Soccer adds to the excitement of the summer sports season. The highest level is found at Ampol Cup contests on January and February nights.

December through February is the season for international test cricket matches, played at the Melbourne Cricket Ground.

Fun in the sun

For those who'd rather play than watch, Melbourne provides plenty of opportunities.

The city beaches. During the summer months, Port Phillip Bay comes alive with summer sports activities. Sunbathers and swimmers will enjoy beaches around the bay. St. Kilda, Elwood, Brighton, and Sandringham are some of the best, and they are all within a half-hour of downtown by car or train. You'll find good boating and sailing at Sandringham, Black Rock, Mordialloc, and Frankston, as well as near town at Albert Park Lake. Water-skiing is also popular on the bay.

For more information on sailing, contact the Royal Melbourne Yacht Squadron on the Lower Esplanade in St. Kilda. Water-skiers can get additional information from the Victoria Water-Ski Association in Elwood. Boats and water-skis are available for rent around the bay at beach resorts.

Closer to town is the Yarra River, a good place for paddling a hired canoe or dinghy. There are also boats for hire at Albert Park Lake. The less ambitious might want to take a riverboat cruise on the Yarra, departing from Princes Walk near Princes Bridge.

There's good deep-sea fishing at Westernport Bay and Lakes Entrance. The major catch is the bluefin tuna. Freshwater anglers should contact the Victour office on Collins Street for more information on inland lake fishing.

Tennis. Players will find both grass and hard courts in Melbourne. The Secretary of the Lawn Tennis Association (50 Commercial Road, South Yarra) has information on private clubs offering guest privileges. Public tennis courts for hire are listed in the phone book's Yellow Pages. Melbourne hosts the Australian Open Tennis Championship each year in January.

Golf. There are about 3 dozen public courses in the Melbourne area. Private clubs will usually grant guest privileges if you can arrange for an introduction by a member or if arrangements are made through your home club. Royal Melbourne Golf Club heads the list of private clubs. It's considered one of the best courses in Australia and is well-known for its sand traps. Melbourne hosts the Australian Open Golf Championship each year in November.

Jogging and cycling. A 4-km/2-mile jogging trail runs along Alexandra Avenue near the Royal Botanic Gardens and King's Domain. Bikes are available for rent near Princes Bridge and opposite the Royal Botanic Gardens on the south side of the Yarra.

Parks and gardens

Melbourne enjoys a wealth of beautiful parklands beginning literally at the heart of the city and fanning out through the farthest suburbs.

King's Domain, capstone of the system, is just across the Yarra River from Flinders Street Railway Station via the Princes Bridge.

The park rises gently from the banks of the Yarra alongside St. Kilda Road. It merges with the Royal Botanic, Alexandra, and Queen Victoria gardens to form a huge parkland of more than 214 hectares/530 acres of beautiful gardens, expansive lawns, and recreation grounds.

The Royal Botanic Gardens, south of King's Domain, is one of Melbourne's oldest and most beautiful parks. The site was selected in 1845.

(Continued on page 64)

...*Continued from page 63*

Stroll through its glades of majestic, venerable trees—some planted by such famous personalities as Prince Albert, Dame Nellie Melba, Alfred Lord Tennyson, and the Duke of Edinburgh. A plaque on a gum tree proclaims the spot where Melbournians celebrated their "separation" from New South Wales in 1851.

The beautiful landscaped gardens include manicured lawns, colorful flower beds, and three lakes where wild ducks and black swans congregate. The park's plantings include Norfolk pines, Japanese cedars, magnolia and oak trees, ferns, camellias, rhododendrons, azaleas, and cacti and succulents. In the southwest corner, the Tropical Plants Glasshouse contains exotic plants.

Alexandra Gardens, a section of the park directly next to the Yarra, is a popular lunchtime retreat for downtown office workers. Next to it, Queen Victoria Gardens has a 10,000-plant floral clock as its focal point.

Still more gardens await exploration. At the east end of Collins Street are Fitzroy Gardens and the adjacent Treasury Gardens. Magnificent elms shade these plots laid out in the late 1850s. Broad open lawns provide places for pleasant picnic lunches. There are also several pond areas trimmed in lush flowering bushes and flanked by an occasional bench for quiet contemplation.

Here, amid lawns and flowers, you can see whimsical Fairy Tree—carved by the late Australian sculptress, Ola Cohn—and a miniature Tudor village that delights children of all ages. Nearby, a conservatory displaying seasonal flowers is open daily from 10 A.M. to 4:45 P.M.

In the Fitzroy Gardens, surrounded by lawns and covered with ivy brought from England, is one of Melbourne's historic monuments—Captain Cook's Cottage. It was brought to Melbourne from England in 1934 to commemorate Melbourne's first centennial the following year. The cottage was probably built by Cook's father around 1755. Though it can't be verified that James Cook ever lived in the house, it's assumed he must have returned often to visit his father. Be sure to explore the tiny 18th century cottage garden with herbs such as rosemary and thyme, old-fashioned rose bushes, red and black currant bushes, and a hawthorn hedge.

Carlton Gardens, a 24-hectare/60-acre park of lawns and flowers, also contains Exhibition Building. Topped by an exotic dome and minarets, it was constructed for the International Exhibition of 1880, and still is used for trade shows. Another Melbourne park of great charm is Flagstaff Gardens on King Street opposite St. James Old Cathedral.

Nearby mountain retreats

The mountains just east and north of Melbourne provide a pleasant respite from the city's bustle. There are fern-filled forests, a wildlife sanctuary, resort towns, and an antique steam train ride.

Dandenong delights

In less than an hour, you can leave downtown Melbourne behind and travel to the deep fern gullies and forested hills of the Dandenong Ranges. These gray green hills provide a pleasant topographical backdrop to the city's northern and eastern suburbs as well as a nearby, quiet retreat for city dwellers.

Many Melbournians have built homes in the seclusion of the wooded hills, their own touches of trees and shrubs adding color to the natural landscape. Nearly every season has something special to offer—camellias in spring, tulips and rhododendrons in summer, and red and gold leaves in autumn.

Throughout the Dandenongs are a number of pleasant walks, drives, and picnic spots. Good roads wind through the area, making it a fine day's outing from Melbourne. Suburban electric trains as well as coach tours also journey into the Dandenongs. The following are a few places you'll want to see during your Dandenong excursion.

Ferntree Gully National Park. Heading into the Dandenongs on the Burwood Highway (Route 26), you stop first at Ferntree Gully National Park, located 34 km/21 miles east of Melbourne. This park has magnificent tree ferns and tall gum trees, and you'll stroll through cool, fragrant valleys where ferns grow over the pathway creating a delicate green tunnel. Wildlife in the area includes swamp wallabies, platypuses, echidnae, lyrebirds, and whipbirds.

Puffing Billy. Children and adults alike will enjoy a ride on this famous old narrow-gauge steam train that chugs through wooded hills, fern gullies, and flower farms between Belgrave and Emerald. Some trips continue on to Lakeside. You can hop aboard at Belgrave just a short distance from Ferntree Gully National Park. The trip generally operates weekends, public holidays, and special school holidays. Menzies Creek—one of the stops on the line—has an interesting Steam Museum featuring locomotives and early narrow-gauge rolling stock.

Sherbrooke Forest. Just 8 km/5 miles north from Belgrave on Monbulk Road, you'll come to one of the gems of the Dandenongs—Sherbrooke Forest. A favorite with bush ramblers, it's also one of the best places in Australia to observe lyrebirds. You'll hear their mimic calls and perhaps see them on forest trails. The male on occasion displays his beautiful tail in a courtship ritual. Road signs remind you to watch: "Drive Carefully—Lyrebirds Cross Here."

William Ricketts Sanctuary. Still farther north you'll discover a world of eerie beauty at the William Ricketts Sanctuary. As you walk along trails between giant ferns, the sculpted clay forms of Aborigines—carved by Ricketts—seem almost alive in the filtered green light of the rain forest. The sculptor has spent most of his life depicting the faces and legends of Australian Aborigines.

Mount Dandenong. Nearby Mount Dandenong is the highest point in the ranges—633 meters/2,077 feet. From the lookout, you can see Port Phillip Bay and Melbourne across patches of farmland and forested slopes. At the summit a restaurant takes full advantage of the view.

Beyond the Dandenongs

The foothills of the Great Dividing Range—just north of the Dandenongs and a few hours from Melbourne—have both charming towns and one of Australia's most attractive wildlife sanctuaries.

Sir Colin MacKenzie Wildlife Sanctuary. This fascinating natural refuge is near Healesville, 63 km/39 miles northeast of Melbourne. Here koalas, kangaroos, wombats, and a variety of birds live in conditions closely resembling their native habitat.

Also known as the Healesville Sanctuary, this wildlife park began as a research station and is home to the first platypus bred in captivity. The sanctuary houses some of these elusive duck-billed creatures in a glass tank where you'll see them swimming about.

Half-day coach tours travel from Melbourne to the sanctuary, which is open daily from 9 A.M. to 5 P.M.

Mountain resorts. Mountain air, unspoiled bushland, lakes, streams, and plentiful wildlife lure vacationers to resort towns like Healesville, Marysville, and Warburton. Activities in these mountain towns include trail riding, fishing, golf, and tennis. Bushwalkers enjoy short tracks leading through forests to waterfalls. Nearby Mount Donna Buang is Melbourne's closest snowfield for winter skiing.

Kinglake National Park. Waterfalls and magnificent mountain ash trees are highlights of this park on the southern slopes of the Great Dividing Range. It's located 20 km/12 miles northwest of Healesville and 64 km/40 miles north of Melbourne. From the summit of Bald Hill within the park, visitors have wonderful views across the forest and fern gullies toward Melbourne and Port Phillip Bay. Kangaroos, wallabies, lyrebirds, and many other species of birds unique to Australia make their home in the park.

Natural bridges carved by wave action
are part of a scenic stretch of coastline
preserved in Port Campbell National Park
along Great Ocean Road.

It's wool harvesting time at a Victoria
sheep station. Guests can watch or shear;
secret is to keep sheep relaxed.

By the beautiful sea

Somewhere close to Melbourne is the kind of salt-water shoreline you want. Within a few hours of the city are two great, sheltered bays, miles of straight-edged sand facing open ocean, and a whole series of gloriously rugged headlands, and you can have any one of the lot populated either thickly or hardly at all.

Port Phillip Bay stretches away from Melbourne, a broad, open expanse of water 61 km/38 miles long, and just as wide. Westernport Bay, its neighbor to the east, is the opposite—a narrow circle of water between the mainland and, in its center, French Island.

The greatest and most rugged of the headlands, Wilson's Promontory, has been preserved as a national park. The sea has pounded against the shore here for centuries, whittling the rocks into curious shapes. Just upcoast is the sparsely populated Gippsland Lakes region; its one beach stretches for 144 km/90 miles. Popular pastimes are boating, fishing, strolling, and hiking.

The surfing and sunning beaches run westward from the mouth of Port Phillip Bay, facing Tasmania across Bass Strait. Still farther to the west are the warm-water beaches collectively known as the Australian Riviera.

Mornington Peninsula

The beaches of Mornington Peninsula—a boot-shaped promontory separating Port Phillip Bay from Westernport Bay—are a playground for residents of Melbourne and its suburbs.

Easily reached by electric train and shoreline highway, these beaches offer a diverse assortment of water sports opportunities. The calmer waters of bayside resorts bordering protected Port Phillip Bay provide good opportunities for swimming, water-skiing, sailing, and surf sailing (wind surfing).

On the opposite side of the peninsula, ocean "back" beaches facing Bass Strait—Portsea Surf Beach, Sorrento Ocean Beach, Rye Ocean Beach, and Gunnamatta Surf Beach—offer fantastic surfing possibilities.

Resort areas like Flinders and Shoreham on Westernport Bay feature surfing as well as fishing and scuba diving. Water sports equipment including boats for hire for sailing and fishing are available at many of the resorts.

Collins Bay, at Sorrento, is a good spot for picnicking and shell collecting, and rock hounds can hunt for gemstones in outcroppings along the beach near Shoreham on Westernport Bay. You'll find golf and tennis are readily available.

Points of interest. At Arthur's Seat, near Dromana, a chairlift transports sightseers to the summit for panoramic views of both bays, Phillip Island, and the orchards and small farms of the peninsula itself.

The fashionable resort of Sorrento, near the peninsula's tip, is the site of a part in Victoria's history. In October 1803, Lt. Col. David Collins landed here and attempted to establish a colony—the first in Victoria. However, the colony's success was short-lived, and it was abandoned in 1804. The area became popular in the late 1800s when a resort was built, and paddle steamers were employed to transport vacationing Melbourne residents to Sorrento. Today, you can zoom across Port Phillip Bay on a wave-piercing catamaran, the *Spirit of Victoria,* which stops at bayside towns, including Sorrento. It leaves from Melbourne's Station Pier, Friday through Sunday.

Accommodations. The Mornington Peninsula has a variety of accommodations from hotels to caravan parks.

Wilson's Promontory National Park

Jutting into Bass Strait—223 km/139 miles southeast of Melbourne—this mountainous and windswept peninsula is one of Victoria's most popular national parks.

"The Prom," as it is affectionately known, possesses a grand beauty. Heavily wooded mountains descend to the edge of white sand beaches and massive granite headlands. Deep gullies shelter pockets of luxuriant rain forest, and open heaths come alive with colorful wildflowers in spring and summer. Wildlife, including wombats and wallabies, roam the forests and heathlands. You may be fortunate enough to spy one or two.

Holiday lodges and caravan and camping areas at Tidal River Camp provide accommodations for leisurely enjoyment of this wildly beautiful place. Out of Melbourne, there are 1-day excursions into the area by coach.

Gippsland Lakes region

Good highways lead from Melbourne to Gippsland, a popular resort district in southeastern Victoria. It's known for rich farmlands, coal and oil fields, forests, rivers, an extensive stretch of beach, and large navigable lakes.

Ninety Mile Beach. East of Wilson's Promontory is an unbroken stretch of beach extending northeast in an almost straight line for nearly 145 km/90 miles. Named for its length, Ninety Mile Beach is relatively undeveloped, making it ideal for surfing, surf fishing, and undisturbed beach walking. Fishers try for salmon, trout, snappers, greybacks, tiger flatheads, and flounder. Good spots to explore this area from include Bairnsdale, Lakes Entrance, Paynesville, and Metung.

The lakes. Inland from Ninety Mile Beach, the Gippsland Lakes run parallel to the shoreline for more than 80 km/50 miles. In some places these waterways are separated from the ocean by only a narrow ribbon of land.

Because the lakes are connected, they are ideal for long leisurely days of cruising. You can take organized launch trips from Paynesville or Metung or rent your own boat to sail. Nearly every type of craft is available for hire, including well-equipped four and six-berth cruisers. You can book craft through the Victour office on Collins Street in Melbourne.

Swimming and fishing are excellent. In the tidal waters you'll find bream, perch, mullet, and skipjack; lakes and streams abound with blackfish, perch, and bream. From many of the lakes you can hike over extensive dunes to Ninety Mile Beach.

Lakes National Park on Spermwhale Head is ideal for picnics. Flowering wattles, tea trees, and ground orchids add patches of brilliant color to the park in winter and spring.

Getting to the lakes. The Gippsland Lakes region is easily accessible from Melbourne by car, or you can take a train as far as Bairnsdale and then a bus. There are also coach and rail tours from Melbourne. Some coach tours traveling between Melbourne and Sydney include the lakes area in their itineraries.

Accommodations. Lakes area resort towns have a variety of modest accommodations in small hotels, motels, guest houses, holiday flats, and caravan and camping parks.

Southwest Riviera

Route 1—the Princes Highway—and fast rail service connect Melbourne with Geelong, 72 km/45 miles southwest of Melbourne. From Geelong—Victoria's largest provincial city—you can reach sheltered beaches on the nearby Bellarine Peninsula or head southwest along the Great Ocean Road to the popular ocean beaches of the Southwest Riviera.

Though basically a regional commercial center—wool-selling headquarters and busy port—Geelong itself is an attractive city with extensive parklands. Geelong has a large number of hotels, motels, and caravan and camping grounds.

Bellarine Peninsula. There are several pleasant holiday resorts along the shores of this peninsula not far from Geelong. The area offers sheltered swimming beaches, boating facilities, and good fishing grounds, as well as opportunities to play tennis and golf. Surfing is best on the southern beaches below Point Lonsdale.

You'll find comfortable accommodations in hotels, guest houses, and motels in the Portarlington area (inside Port Phillip Bay), Queenscliff-Point Lonsdale (on the headland at the entrance to the bay), and in Ocean Grove and Barwon Heads (both on the ocean side of the peninsula). Campers will find well-equipped parks in most local peninsula towns.

The Great Ocean Road. One of Victoria's most scenic routes is along the Great Ocean Road, which follows the coast southwest of Melbourne for nearly 322 km/200 miles. The highway begins just south of Geelong at Torquay and winds south and west to Warrnambool. It skirts sheer cliffs, parallels golden sand beaches, and traverses the forested slopes of the Otway Ranges.

Along the way, at seaside towns like Torquay, Anglesea, Airey's Inlet, Lorne, and Wye River, visitors will find swimming, surfing, boating, fishing, tennis, and golf. At Anglesea's golf course, you'll have to share the green with grazing kangaroos.

The Otway Ranges meet the ocean at Lorne. You can bushwalk through groves of giant eucalyptus and fern-filled valleys, surfcast, or laze away the days on a wide, golden strand of beach.

Beyond Apollo Bay, the road turns inland, crossing the Otway Ranges, and then returns to the ocean west of Port Campbell. Here, brown, yellow, and orange cliffs have eroded into a series of natural bridges and rock stacks. Particularly interesting are the rock formations named the Twelve Apostles: a dozen rock stacks of varying sizes. Port Campbell National Park comprises a 30-km/19-mile stretch of this spectacularly beautiful coastline. Offshore islands in the area support many birds. Mutton Bird Is-

land, just offshore near the mouth of the Sherbrooke River, is the nesting ground for a large number of mutton birds. At sunset, you'll see the adults returning to their young with food.

At the resort town of Warrnambool in the center of rich dairy farming country, you can rejoin Princes Highway and return to Melbourne along the inland route. Or you can continue along the coast to the old whaling town of Port Fairy and then on to Portland, another whaling town with numerous historic sites.

Resort towns all along the Great Ocean Road offer visitors a choice of accommodations—hotels, motels, and caravan and camping parks.

Victoria's rugged west

West and northwest of Melbourne the countryside varies from rolling farm and grazing lands to rugged hills and forested mountains. You can sample vast sheep stations, wild Australian bushland, and gold rush boom towns. (To learn more about Ballarat and other gold rush towns see page 60.)

Visiting a sheep station

It is said that much of Australia's wealth has been shorn from the backs of sheep. Traveling west from Melbourne, you'll pass through Victoria's rich grazing land—rolling, pastoral fields edged with stands of pines and gum trees. A number of working sheep properties welcome visitors. Here, discover what it's like to live on a station today, as well as learn what it was like to be a pioneer settler homesteading this area in the mid-1800s.

Naringal. At this historic working station near Cape Clear (161 km/100 miles west of Melbourne), you can watch the Australian pastoralist at work and, if you like, participate in the duties of the station yourself. As a guest you'll be able to watch sheep mustering and shearing and learn how wool is graded. Naringal, established before 1845, is still owned by descendants of the founding family. You can also visit the family's original slab timber hut and see the private cemetery. Both are reminders of the hardships endured by Victoria's pioneer settlers.

At Naringal, you can enjoy gracious living in the family's beautiful homestead or stay in a self-contained cottage or in dormitory-style accommodations. It's an easy drive from Melbourne via Ballarat.

Glenisla Homestead. Founded more than 140 years ago, this property (305 km/190 miles west of Melbourne) also ranks among Victoria's oldest.

The historic homestead complex was built in 1873 by a great-grandfather of the current owners. Constructed of local sandstone, the site is listed with the Australian National Trust. Guest accommodations are in the main house and adjacent courtyard buildings.

In addition to sheep station activities, there are guided tours from Glenisla to the Grampian Mountains to see the diversity of plant and animal life (see page 69). Glenisla can be reached by car, bus, and plane.

Other stations. Farm stays are available at other stations throughout Victoria. Accommodations and activities vary. In some cases, guests may have to bring food and linens. For information on farm stays, contact the Victour office.

Victoria's Farm Shed. This indoor farm animal display center, on the Princes Highway an hour's drive east of Melbourne, provides a quick look at Australia's livestock and farm activities. There are twice-daily shows featuring livestock identification, sheep shearing, cow milking, and sheep dogs working. It's open daily from 9 A.M. to 5 P.M.

The Grampians

The stark, sandstone ridges of the western edge of the Great Dividing Range rise from the surrounding plains some 266 km/165 miles west of Melbourne. Over the centuries, wind and water have eroded the Grampians' red bulk into weird and unusual shapes with descriptive names like The Lady's Hat, Mushroom Rock, and The Fallen Giant.

For thousands of years, Aborigines occupied the Grampians. Many sacred ceremonies and initiation rites were performed here. The stories of these early residents are told in the interesting rock paintings of Grampian mountain caves.

Bushwalkers traversing the area on short or long hikes can enjoy cascading waterfalls, awesome lookout points, and plentiful wildlife such as kangaroos, emus, echidnae, koalas, and platypuses. The towering cliffs and craggy rock faces offer some stiff challenges to rock climbers. Anglers can work well-stocked lakes.

During the spring and early summer months (August to December) the Grampians are colorfully carpeted with wildflowers—wild fuchsias, ground orchids, wattle, and flowering peas. There are nearly 1,000 native plant species.

During wildflower season, all-day tours from Melbourne give visitors a good opportunity to enjoy the region's wildflowers, scenery, and wildlife. If you want to linger awhile longer, you'll find comfortable accommodations in Hall's Gap in the heart of the Grampians and in Ararat, Horsham, and Stawell.

Ski country

Melbourne residents enjoy the ski areas of the Snowy Mountains (see page 53), but Victoria also has its own ski country in the Southern Alps, stretching south and west from the Snowy Mountains. Here the terrain is gentle, with long, hazard-free runs—ideal for ski touring. The best skiing comes during the latter part of the season (late August and September) when the snow has been compacted. Skiers will find that powder snow is virtually unknown in the area.

Occasional years of light snowfall make some of Victoria's resorts chancy—but you can generally count on good snow conditions from mid-June to mid-September at Mount Buller, Mount Buffalo, Mount Hotham, and Falls Creek.

Winter isn't the only season to enjoy Victoria's mountain playgrounds. Most of the area's resorts operate the year around. In spring, the mountains are a patchwork of alpine flowers. Summer activities include camping, trout fishing, horseback riding, bushwalking, and mountain climbing.

From Melbourne you can reach the area by car or by flying to Albury and going the rest of the way by coach.

Mount Buller

Victoria's busiest ski resort is Mount Buller (1,800-meter/5,907-foot elevation), only 241 km/150 miles by road from Melbourne. Ski runs descend three sides of the mountain peak. Providing transportation to the top are ten Poma lifts, seven T-bars, and three chairlifts.

Accommodations include a chalet, a motel, a pension, and a lodge.

Mount Hotham

The most reliable snowfall in the entire region occurs at Mount Hotham (1,862-meter/6,109-foot elevation). But this is also the most difficult of the four resorts to reach because of road and weather conditions. Distance from Melbourne is 373 km/232 miles. Mount Hotham is close enough to the Mount Buffalo ski area (both are off the same road) that you can stay at one resort and enjoy skiing at both.

Used primarily by intermediate and experienced skiers, the area has four Poma lifts, a chairlift, and two T-bars. Hotham Heights, on the slopes of the mountain, has two lodges, one chalet, and a few apartments.

Mount Buffalo

With an elevation of 1,723 meters/5,654 feet, Mount Buffalo presents snow conditions less predictable than those at the other three major resorts. For skiers there are three Poma lifts and a chairlift.

The area is not only a winter vacation spot, though. Mount Buffalo National Park, 322 km/200 miles from Melbourne, is a year-round resort with good opportunities for swimming, boating, fishing, horseback riding, and bushwalking. The massive rock face of Mount Buffalo is popular with mountain climbers.

The area has two hotels and several smaller commercial chalets.

Falls Creek

The ski village at Falls Creek nestles in a natural bowl deep in the heart of the Bogong High Plains, 380 km/236 miles from Melbourne. The bowl not only forms a natural trap for sunshine (promoting spring skiing) but also provides excellent beginners' slopes. The resort's international-standard runs are the site of an annual international race, the Ross Milne Memorial Slalom, held in July or August.

The area offers skiers a chairlift, six Poma lifts, and four T-bars in a carefully integrated system that can lift 5,500 skiers per hour. Accommodations are available in about a dozen lodges.

Mother Nature shows off in full flower

Artists glorify it in their paintings, writers dramatize it in their prose, and Australian suburbanites escape to it on their vacations. "It" is the Australian bush, less than a day's drive from most of Australia's major metropolitan areas.

The term "bush" applies to rain forests, tropical jungle, rolling hills covered with scrub, forests of gums or conifers, and even grasslands. Much of this bush boasts a profusion of colorful blossoms and pervading fragrance. Sailors say they can smell the sharp, medicinal scent of gum trees (eucalyptus) far out to sea.

Gum trees. Perhaps the most prolific of Australia's native plants is the eucalyptus—commonly called gum tree. It's as Australian as the kangaroo. More than 700 different species have been identified, and many have colorful pungent blossoms—scarlet, coral, white.

The prolific gum tree comes in a variety of shapes and sizes, and grows in nearly all parts of Australia. The eerie white ghost gum sinks its roots into the dry earth of outback regions around Alice Springs, while the twisted snow gum survives the frigid winters of the alpine highlands. In the mountains of eastern Victoria, in parts of Tasmania, and in southwestern areas of Western Australia, stand dense forests of giant gums, some 91 meters/300 feet tall. Smaller varieties of gum trees are found in the drier woodlands. These trees, having an open structure and small leaves, attain a height of only about 6 meters/20 feet. Still other vinelike, crawling varieties of gum trees exist along the fringes of the country's desert areas.

Like Australia's other flora and fauna, the gum trees have been separated by ocean from the rest of the world since prehistoric times. But this doesn't mean they're unknown. In fact gums are among the most transplanted trees in the world. They were first planted in California for windbreaks more than 100 years ago, and now more than 150 varieties grow in California and Arizona. Other countries that have imported and planted gum trees include Italy, Russia, India, and China. In total, they're found in 73 countries.

A profusion of wildflowers. Many of Australia's native plants are found nowhere else in the world. Sturt desert peas stretch like a red carpet across vast tracts of inland desert; dainty white snow daisies brighten the slopes of the Australian Alps; and more than 600 varieties of orchids lend their beauty to the steamy rain forests of the north.

Western Australia alone grows more than 7,000 species of wildflowers and flowering shrubs and trees, many found nowhere else. For eons, the southwestern corner of Australia was virtually a floral island, isolated from the rest of the continent and other land masses by the Indian Ocean on the west and south and by the desert areas to the east and north. Because of this isolation, unique and unusual plants developed.

Among the most colorful of Western Australia's plants are the unusually shaped kangaroo paw in vivid green and red, the Geraldton wax flower with either white or deep rose flowers, the *Banksia coccinea* with its scarlet conelike flowers, and pine grevillea, its big spikes of deep orange flowers crowning plants growing 6 meters/ 20 feet high. There are also gray smokebush and blue leschenaultia.

For a strange shape there is the blackboy with its spear-shaped blossom. Related to the lily, it grows about 1½ meters/5 feet tall, and the "spear" can add another 2 meters/6 feet to its height. The bush blossoms along its spear, bearing hundreds of tiny flowers.

Two native plants are carnivorous—the pitcher plant and the rainbow plant, both designed to attract insects. The pitcher plant's lure is a pitcherlike flower full of sweet nectar, and the rainbow plant attracts with rainbow-colored, threadlike leaves.

Other interesting plants. The acacia, found in some variety over most of the continent, has gained national fame. It appears on Australia's coat-of-arms. In early days, colonists used acacia branches to make "wattle and daub" huts, resulting in the name "wattle" becoming attached to the acacia. More than 600 species are found in Australian gardens, parks, and street plantings, and as part of the bush.

Perhaps not as prolific but equally interesting is the baobab tree. Found mainly in northwest Australia, this tree possesses an unusual shape—a bulging base that can have a circumference of 18 meters/60 feet. The water collected in this base helps the tree survive during long periods of drought. Some baobab trees are probably 2,000 years old. Hollowed-out baobab bases have even been used as temporary, overnight jails for prisoners being transported to town. One such prison tree can be found near Derby in Western Australia. Although the tree has been hollowed out, it goes on living.

Still other Australian plants include bottle brush, cycads, and coral trees. In the country's tropical north, you'll find flame, pawpaw, and Davidson's Plum trees. Although the growing of macadamia nuts is a big industry in Hawaii, the macadamia nut tree's native home is Queensland, Australia.

Ghost gum gleams in sunshine, its far-flung branches rising high above bushwalkers' heads. Rich green leaves make a strong contrast to stark white bark.

Fluffy Golden Wattle, an acacia that blooms profusely throughout the country, is Australia's national flower.

Regal Waratah was chosen for New South Wales's floral emblem. This flower is one of more than 6,000 species of wildflowers, flowering shrubs, and trees in Australia.

Murray River country

Australia's most important waterway—the Murray River—flows westward from the mountains of northeast Victoria through the state's quiet pastoral land of orange groves and farmsteads. Its meandering path delineates Victoria's border with New South Wales.

The river was once a great trade route providing access to hard-to-reach inland towns. Hundreds of paddle steamers plied the Murray's length, bringing in supplies and taking wool bales out to market. Today, the Murray River's waters provide irrigation and hydroelectric power for New South Wales, South Australia, and Victoria.

You can drive along the river on the Murray Valley Highway, which parallels the water from Albury northwest to Mildura, near the South Australia border. Or you may prefer a leisurely cruise on the river out of Echuca, Swan Hill, or Mildura. These main river towns can be reached by rail from Melbourne. There's also air service to Mildura and Swan Hill, and Melbourne tour operators have coach tours of the valley that include these towns.

All three areas have accommodations—hotels, motels, and caravan and camping parks. The best times to visit the Murray River region are spring, autumn, and winter; summers can be very hot.

Echuca, a river port town

Once a roistering river port, Echuca sits at the junction of the Murray, Campaspe, and Goulburn rivers—206 km/128 miles north of Melbourne. In the 1800s more than 200 boats docked here annually to unload and load goods. Echuca was considered Victoria's second largest port and the largest inland port in Australia.

The restored Port of Echuca, major setting for the television mini-series "All the Rivers Run," recreates these early days. Moored at the red-gum wharf are two historic paddle steamers, the *Adelaide* and the *Pevensey*. A diorama in the wharf's cargo shed depicts wharf activities over 100 years ago. Nearby restored buildings include the Bridge Hotel, built in 1858, and the Star Hotel, built in 1867.

From Echuca, you can take 1-hour river cruises on the P.S. *Canberra* and the P.S. *Pride of the Murray*. Two-night cruises are available on the P.S. *Emmylou*.

Neighboring marshes provide good fishing and duck hunting possibilities. Barmah State Forest, a well-known bird watching territory, lies only 32 km/20 miles northeast of Echuca.

Swan Hill's Pioneer Settlement

One of Australia's most interesting outdoor folk museum villages sits on the banks of the Murray River at Swan Hill 338 km/210 miles northwest of Melbourne.

Visitors enter the Pioneer Settlement by strolling through the paddle steamer *Gem*, once queen of the Murray. On the other side of the ship's gangplank is a re-creation of a 19th century Australian inland river town complete with general store, print shop, stereoscopic theater, saddler's shop, stagecoach office, fire station, and pioneer log cabin. Tradesmen, dressed in period costume, demonstrate skills such as blacksmithing and wood turning. At Jimmy Long's Bakery, hunger pains can be quieted with freshly baked bread.

There are steam engines that work and horse-drawn vehicles to take you for a ride through town. Throughout the settlement are everyday household and agricultural items used by the pioneers, including farm implements and windmills.

A highlight of a visit to the Pioneer Settlement is a cruise on the Murray River on the paddle steamer *Pyap*. Several trips leave the settlement's wharf daily. The boat sails leisurely around the river's sweeping bends, beneath overhanging red gums, and past old historic homesteads.

Other Pioneer Settlement attractions include an art gallery and restaurant, both located on the paddle steamer *Gem*. The restaurant features such local delicacies as wichety grub soup and yabbies (freshwater crayfish) caught nearby. You might want to follow a dinner on the *Gem* with a special evening sound-and-light tour through the settlement. A daytime tour takes you by bus to Murray Downs Station, an historic sheep property; you return on board the paddle steamer *Pyap*. Reservations are recommended for both these tours. The Pioneer Settlement is open daily from 8:30 A.M. to 5 P.M.

Other Swan Hill attractions

While in the Swan Hill area, you'll want to explore a number of other attractions, including a museum, a homestead, and a bird sanctuary.

Military museum. This museum, in downtown Swan Hill, houses memorabilia from every war in which Australians have fought, from the Crimean War to Vietnam. Museum items include arms, uniforms, documents, and letters.

Tyntynder Homestead. Just 17 km/11 miles north of Swan Hill is the pioneer Tyntynder Homestead. Built in 1846, it evokes the gracious living of an era when paddle steamers plied the Murray and the homestead was the area's social center. Items of interest include an old wine cellar, costume museum, station store, and furnishing and implements of the time.

Kerang. About 60 km/37 miles southeast of Swan Hill (between Swan Hill and Echuca) is a spot of special interest to bird watchers. The town of Kerang, located on the Loddon River at the junction of the Murray and Loddon highways, is surrounded by marshlands. Here enormous flocks of ibis make their home. In fact, Reedy Lake is thought to be the world's largest ibis rookery. Over 130 species of birds have been identified in the area where blinds have been set up for bird watching.

Mildura, an inland resort

This prosperous small city is the center of an irrigated fruit growing area 557 km/346 miles northwest of Melbourne. Its warm, mild winter climate makes it an inland holiday resort during Victoria's colder months.

The city is home port for the 1912 paddle steamer *Melbourne*. This historic boat plies the waters of the Murray on 2-hour morning and afternoon cruises, departing Mildura's wharf daily except Saturday. A 2-hour lunch cruise is offered daily on the paddle steamer *Avoca*, with 4-hour dinner cruises on Saturday nights and 4-hour disco cruises on Friday nights. A 5-day Murray River cruise on the paddle steamer *Coonawarra* departs Mondays and includes accommodations and meals. You can book passage for this trip through the Victour office in Melbourne.

Besides an exciting collection of river vessels, Mildura also lays claim to the longest bar in the world: 87 meters/ 285 feet of drinking space. It's a claim you can verify for yourself at the Working Men's Club. Other attractions include Rio Vista, a stately home that serves as a museum of local history as well as an art gallery featuring more than 200 paintings. In adjacent Rio Vista Park, you'll see a display of pioneering machinery including an engine used to pump water from the Murray River into Mildura's irrigation channels.

Houseboats are available for rent in the Mildura area, and there is good fishing in nearby backwaters of the Murray River. A colony of koalas inhabits nearby Lock Island.

Hattah Lakes National Park, 80 km/50 miles south of Mildura, is the home of many varieties of water birds, including large nesting colonies of ibis. In the spring, you'll find a profusion of wildflowers too.

Victoria's wine country

The state of Victoria was once Australia's major wine producer. Then, at the close of the 19th century, the plant louse *phylloxera* (which earlier had played havoc with French and California vineyards) found its way to Victo-ria. The devastating *phylloxera* infestation was finally contained and several of Victoria's wine regions are again producing wines.

Rutherglen

This region of vineyards, about 278 km/173 miles northeast of Melbourne near the Murray River, has staged one of the state's strongest recoveries. It is considered one of the oldest winegrowing regions in Australia, the first plantings having taken place in 1851. Almost wiped out in 1899 by the vine disease, it was among the first areas to plant resistant strains.

Today the Shiraz grape does particularly well, and each winery treats it a bit differently. This region also produces some delicate white wines, sherry, and dessert wines that have a good reputation.

A number of wineries in the area are worth a visit. Among them are Campbell's, Bullers, Rosewood, All Saints, Morris, Stanton and Killeen, Jones, St. Leonards, Mt. Prior, Fairfield, Pfeiffer, and Jolimont.

Great Western district

Another important Victorian wine area is near the town of Ararat, 203 km/126 miles northwest of Melbourne along the foothills of the Grampians. The first vines were planted here by French immigrants in 1863; today, most of the vineyards are owned by the big Seppelt winery. Known primarily for its champagne, the area also produces some fine dry red wines.

Seppelt's, 16 km/10 miles west of Ararat, has an underground champagne cellar. Other area wineries include Best's, Boroka, Donoview, Mt. Langi, and Montara.

Penguins on parade

One of the most enjoyable tours out of Melbourne is the excursion to Phillip Island, 145 km/90 miles south of the city at the entrance to Westernport Bay. Every night, the year around, tiny fairy penguins stumble ashore at Summerland Beach and parade in squadrons up the beach to their burrows.

The show begins at dusk and lasts about a half-hour to an hour. Spotlights play across the sand, picking up one dark form, then another, and another, as up from the surf they strut, undaunted by the nearness of humans. For them the day's hunt for food is over and they can return to their rookeries to feed their young and rest.

Eudyptula minor is the world's smallest penguin—less than a foot tall. Though several penguin species visit the Australian coast, the fairy penguin is the only one to breed there, nesting amid grass tussocks, in crevices, and in burrows—as many as 200 penguins to the acre.

Besides penguins, Phillip Island offers visitors a variety of other wildlife. You can see one of Victoria's largest fur seal colonies off the westernmost tip of the island, and the island has a thriving koala colony. Other island attractions include a Dairy Centre, chicory kilns, Wool Centre, and a motor and antique museum.

Both day and overnight-coach trips are available from Melbourne to Phillip Island to view the penguins. The island is a 1½-hour drive from the city and is connected to the mainland by a bridge. There's also ferry service from Stony Point. People with limited time might want to take the Penguin Express tour, flying to the island from Melbourne in a light aircraft.

Phillip Island, a popular recreation area for Melbournians, has hotel and motel accommodations and camping and caravan facilities.

TASMANIA

The emerald isle where Australians escape to play

Dangling like a pendant south of Australia's mainland, tiny Tasmania often gets overlooked on world maps. Yet it is one of the country's most fascinating tourist destinations for overseas visitors—and a favorite holiday retreat for Australians.

The island's 427,000 residents prefer to be called Tasmanians rather than Australians. A sixth of the island's inhabitants are direct descendants of convicts. The island was settled in 1803 as a British penal colony, then called Van Diemen's Land. Most of its development was done by convict labor under military supervision; approximately 70,000 prisoners were sent here between 1803 and 1850. Convict traffic stopped in 1853, and in 1856 the island's name was changed to Tasmania in honor of its discoverer, Dutch explorer Abel Tasman.

For many visitors, though, the lure of Tassie (as it is affectionately called) lies not in historical mementos but in the island's scenic variety: from blustery western coastline, over rugged mountain ranges, through tranquil valleys, to east coast fishing ports and beach resorts.

Thanks to the second highest rainfall of any Australian state, much of Tasmania is covered by dense vegetation. Winter dusts mountaintops with snow; clouds of apple blossoms blanket lush, green hills and valleys in spring; and the autumn countryside glows with reds and golds of imported oaks, willows, poplars, and elms. Clear streams cascade through gorges and merge into rivers spawning enough trout to attract anglers from around the world.

Tasmania is graspable, a compact isle only 314 km/195 miles wide and 296 km/184 miles long (a bit smaller than Ireland). Most of its diverse attractions are easy to reach. Two good bases for exploring the countryside are Tasmania's capital, Hobart, in the south, and Launceston in the north.

Hobart—A capital city

Historic Hobart, capital of Tasmania, has a lot in common with Sydney: it was founded only a few years later (1804);

Children frolic among ruins of Port Arthur, infamous penal colony on tip of Tasman Peninsula. Guided tours of the buildings include nearby Isle of the Dead cemetery.

it owes its beginnings to a penitentiary; and its setting is similar, if not more impressive.

Surrounding one of the world's finest deep-water harbors, the city covers the broad lower valley of the Derwent River. Providing a spectacular backdrop is Mount Wellington—snow-clad in winter, forested and green the rest of the year. On a clear day, the 22-km/14-mile ride up to the Pinnacle (the 1,270-meter/4,166-foot summit) provides an unobstructed view of the harbor, the city's eclectic mixture of colonial architecture and modern high-rises, and a good portion of south and central Tasmania, as well.

Getting your bearings

Hobart proper lies on the west bank of the Derwent, linked to suburbs on the eastern shore by the soaring Tasman Bridge. Much of the town's historical heritage centers on the waterfront. Along the harbor, ships' bows loom over the side streets, and fishing vessels, draped with nets and green glass buoys, prove irresistible to photographers.

Sandstone warehouses and stores date back to the whaling days of the 1830s. Close by are the winding streets, Georgian cottages, and tiny gardens of the city's first settled area—Battery Point.

North of the city stretches the vast parkland called the Queen's Domain and the adjoining Royal Botanical Gardens. To the south lies Sandy Bay, about 3 km/2 miles from the city center, where the 21-story Wrest Point Hotel-Casino and adjacent Hobart Convention and Entertainment Centre dominate the scene.

First stop for visitors to this bustling city of over 180,000 should be the Tasbureau (downtown at 80 Elizabeth Street). Open weekdays from 8:45 A.M. to 5:30 P.M. and weekends and holidays from 9 to 11:30 A.M., the Tasbureau offers maps and brochures of major tourist attractions and accommodation information, operates city sightseeing tours, and arranges a variety of tours to other Tasmanian destinations.

Mementos of the past

Hobart's Georgian and Victorian eras have been preserved in many fine old buildings. Several museums also provide a peek into the past.

Battery Point. A number of early buildings remain at Battery Point, an apt name for a promontory once dominated by a gun battery overlooking the harbor. Hobart's original settlement is a fascinating district of narrow streets, winding lanes, and grassy squares. Its homes, public houses, and stores date back to the 1850s and days of sea captains, sailors, and shipwrights. On Saturday mornings there are Battery Point walking tours that leave from Franklin Square.

Constitution Dock and Salamanca Place. Sleek pleasure boats have taken the place of old whaling ships at Hobart's seaside doorstep. Constitution Dock marks the end of the famous Sydney/Hobart Yacht Race in December, and is the site of the annual Royal Hobart Regatta, largest aquatic event in the Southern Hemisphere, in February. Nearby Salamanca Place warehouses are now homes for restaurants and shops. On Saturday mornings the place becomes the open-air Salamanca Market, a colorful collection of stalls, singers, and bands, where locals and tourists browse for trash and treasure.

Collections of history. Van Diemen's Land Folk Museum, 103 Hampden Road, is housed in one of Hobart's earliest colonial homes. Built in 1836, the carefully preserved furnished residence shows how the gentry lived in those times. The museum is open weekdays from 10 A.M. to 5 P.M., weekends from 2 to 5 P.M.

Other museums downtown include the Tasmanian Maritime Museum, exhibiting historic material on seafaring in Tasmania, located at the rear of St. George's Church on Cromwell Street (open daily from 2 to 4:30 P.M.); the Tasmanian Museum and Art Gallery, containing tragic but fascinating relics of the state's extinct Aborigines as well as early colonial paintings and sketches, at 5 Argyle Street (open daily from 10 A.M. to 5 P.M.); and the Post Office Museum, housing historic information on the post and telegraph in Tasmania, at 21 Castray Esplanade (open weekdays from 9 A.M. to 5 P.M., and Saturday from 9 to 11 A.M.).

The Model Tudor Village, 827 Sandy Bay Road, will delight both adults and children. A faithful reproduction of an English 16th century hamlet, this scale model is historically authentic down to the clothing of the 2-inch-high residents. The village is open daily from 9 A.M. to 5 P.M.

You can have Devonshire tea at Shot Tower, located at Taroona 11 km/7 miles from Hobart. The landmark tower was erected in 1870; the adjacent factory (now containing a museum and gallery) was built in 1855.

Shopping around town

Articles made from the island's natural resources make interesting mementos. The usual gimmicky souvenir finds its way onto store shelves, but you can find good substitutes by visiting art and craft shops, galleries, antique stores, and craft workshops. Look for local gemstones, wooden products made from Huon pine, pottery, metalwork, framed art, shellcraft, and antiques. Leatherwork is increasingly popular; best buys are handbags, wallets, and key cases.

You'll find several modern shopping centers downtown, including the Cat and Fiddle Arcade (Elizabeth to Murray streets) where an animated mural enacts the old nursery rhyme every hour on the hour. Look for antique shops around Battery Point.

Most shops are open Monday through Thursday from 9 A.M. to 6 P.M., and 9 A.M. to 9 P.M. on Friday. Some stores are open on Saturday from 9 A.M. to noon.

After dark

Hobart has a variety of good places to dine, ranging from the revolving restaurant atop the Wrest Point Hotel-Casino to more romantic little spots at Battery Point. However, in some cases restaurants may have early closing hours, and be closed on Sundays.

There are theaters, cabaret shows, and ubiquitous discos around town, but most of the nightlife centers around the casino. Here, you can watch a Las Vegas-type revue or join the throng at the tables. Most of the games people play are known world-wide, but there is one unique Australian game, Two-Up. Though it is played throughout the continent, it is played legally only in the casino. Two-Up is fast and fascinating. You bet on whether two coins will fall heads or tails after they have been thrown up in the air simultaneously by a "spinner" in a pit below the gambling circle. If the coins do not land on the same side, it's a "do-over"; after five "do-overs" in a row, everybody loses except the house.

Things to do outdoors

Tasmania is an outdoor playground for sports enthusiasts and spectators. Around Hobart visitors can enjoy golf, tennis, squash, swimming, and boating. Horse racing is held at Elwick Racecourse throughout the year; the Hobart Cup takes place in February. Major trotting events include the Tasmanian Pacing Championships held in December.

Courses, courts, and links. For a list of public tennis courts for hire in Hobart and around the island, contact the Tennis Centre, 2 Davies Avenue. Squash courts are listed in the telephone directory. Rosny Park, in Bellerive suburb, is a public golf course offering prebooked starting times and equipment rental. Here, you can pick up a list of island golf courses open to the public.

Aquatic sports. Bayside beaches close to Hobart include Nutgrove, Long Beach, Bellerive, Sandy Bay, and Kingston. The Derwent Sailing Squadron and the Royal Yacht Club invite members of an affiliated club to get on the water. Guests of the Wrest Point Hotel-Casino can rent boats; other boat rental agencies are found in Sandy Bay and Hobart.

During the summer months, various half-day and day sightseeing cruises operate to Bruny Island and New Norfolk and along the D'Entrecasteaux Channel. Check with the tourist bureau for more information.

Get into the bush. Mt. Wellington, crisscrossed by walking tracks, is a good introduction to bushwalking. Among the most popular is a 3 km/2 mile walk from the Springs to the Pinnacle, past the Organ Pipes. For walking tour maps and guides, stop by the National Parks and Wildlife Service, 16 Magnet Court, Sandy Bay. For more information on bushwalking throughout Tasmania, check with the Tasmanian Wilderness Society, Liverpool Street, Hobart 7018.

Fishing. Game fishing is big sport off the coast of Tasmania. Bluefin tuna run the year around at Eaglehawk

Neck (on the Tasman Peninsula south of Hobart); check with the Tasbureau on boat charters. Several surf-fishing beaches around Hobart, good for catching flathead, mullet, and perch, include jetties at Sandy Bay, Lindisfarne, and Bellerive. The fishing season opens in early January, but each area sets its own season closing date. For a copy of the brochure, "Fishing Code for Anglers in Tasmania," check with the Tasbureau office in Hobart.

One excursion from Hobart includes the Plenty Salmon Ponds. In spite of its name, this is where the first brown and rainbow trout were introduced into the southern hemisphere—in 1864. You can look at the fish here, but you can't go fishing. In addition to a piscatorial museum, the salmon ponds have a tea room and spacious lawns for strolling.

Excursions from Hobart

Radiating from Hobart are regions displaying Tasmania's diversity. To the southwest lies the Huon Valley, source of most of the state's apples. Westward is a wilderness area so rugged that it remains unpopulated and virtually unexplored. Northwest of Hobart are the mountains and national parks. The sheep-raising Midlands stretch due north from Hobart toward Launceston. Farther afield, there's good skiing in the inland mountains of the lightly inhabited northeastern corner, and resort towns and white sand beaches are scattered along the east coast. The Tasman Peninsula off the southeastern coast was the site of the Port Arthur penal colony.

You can explore many of these areas on day trips from Hobart, and most trips can be booked through the Tasbureau office.

Port Arthur's old penal colony

The last of the penal settlements, Port Arthur on the tip of the Tasman Peninsula 100 km/62 miles southeast of Hobart, is Tasmania's number one tourist attraction. Guides show visitors through the ruins of this monument to misery, abandoned in 1877.

Most of the 12,500 prisoners who spent time in this penal settlement were second offenders, under conviction for crimes committed after their deportation to the colony. Many spent their time at Port Arthur learning some trade and were later released to become useful citizens of the infant colony. For the incorrigible prisoners, however, there was harsh discipline.

Prisoners literally built their own prison. Ruins of the since-burned settlement include the prison church, an exile cottage, commandant's residence, and model prison where the "silent system" of punishment replaced the lash. The former lunatic asylum now houses an audio-visual theater and musuem.

Escape from this prison was not easy. On Eaglehawk Neck, the peninsula's narrow land bridge, vicious dogs were chained; only a few inches separated hound from hound. Guards patrolled the line continuously.

Within a few miles of Eaglehawk Neck, the sea has carved several interesting sights. Stretching from the rugged cliffs into the sea is the Tesselated Pavement, a vast plaza of rectangular paving blocks laid out by nature in one of her more orderly moods.

Nearby is an impressive blowhole, as well as Tasman's Arch, a bridge of land whittled away over the centuries by the crashing waves, now far, far below. At Devil's Kitchen you look straight down into a cauldron of churning, roaring surf, hemmed in on three sides by sheer cliffs.

The essentials

Getting there. Tasmania is served by air and sea from the mainland.

Air. Australian Airlines, Ansett Airlines, and East-West Airlines provide air service to Tasmania from Melbourne and Sydney. Air New South Wales also flies to Tasmania from Sydney.

In addition to Hobart International Airport, there are domestic airports at Launceston, Devonport, and Wynyard. Hobart's airport, 22 km/14 miles outside town, is served by bus and taxi.

Sea. The M.V. *Abel Tasman* passenger/vehicle ferry crosses Bass Strait three times weekly from Melbourne to Devonport. The crossing takes about 14½ hours.

Accommodations. Most major hotels are in Hobart and Launceston Major hotels in Hobart include Four Seasons Downtowner, Four Seasons Westside, Lenna of Hobart, Sheraton-Hobart, South Port Town House, and Wrest Point Federal Hotel-Casino. Hotels in Launceston include Four Seasons Great Northern, Colonial-Launceston, Penny Royal Launceston, South Port Town House, and Launceston Federal Country Club Hotel-Casino.

Other types of accommodations include colonial cottages, host farms, guest houses, and villas and flats.

Food and drink. Tasmania has the country's freshest, tastiest fish, home-grown fruit, and some restored colonial buildings where memorable meals and fine Devonshire tea are served. The usual range of ethnic cuisine is available only in Hobart. Watering holes around the state include everything from licensed historic pubs to the posh Federal-Hotel casinos at Launceston and Hobart. Try the local cider, beer, and wine.

Getting around. Transportation on the island is good, with most main towns connected by daily coach service from Hobart. There is daily air service from Hobart to Launceston, and other cities around the island. Because the island is so compact, rental cars are a good bargain if you wish to explore out-of-the-way spots. Local drive-yourself firms usually offer one-way rentals. Tasmania is also good for camper-vans; a number of caravan parks are located throughout the island.

Tours. Half-day city tours of Hobart, Burnie, Devonport, and Launceston are available from the Tasbureau. Scenic air tours are a great way to see the island.

For more information. Tasbureau, 80 Elizabeth Street, Hobart 7000.

Orchards & seascapes

On a 145-km/90-mile loop trip southwest from Hobart—heading for the Huon Valley on Route B64 (the Huon Highway) and returning on Route A6 along the D'Entrecasteaux Channel—orchard views combine with seascapes. A winding side road branches off the Huon Highway, leading you up to the top of Mount Wellington.

The island's first apple tree was planted in 1788 by the botanist accompanying Captain Bligh on the *H.M.S. Bounty*, when the ship anchored at Adventure Bay off Bruny Island south of Hobart. Much of the island's history is recorded in the Bligh Museum at Adventure Bay. Car ferries operate between Kettering and Barnes Bay, North Bruny.

Route A6 continues south beyond the Huon district, past dairy farms, sawmill towns, and tiny seaside hamlets. A popular stop along the way is the vineyard and winery in Cygnet. From the end of the road at Southport, you can drive west about 16 km/10 miles into the hills to Hastings Caves. A number of guided tours daily lead spelunkers into the lighted caverns. Just a few kilometers away is a thermal pool with an average year-round temperature of 27°C/81°F. Also nearby are the Lune River, a haven for gem collectors, and the Ida Bay Railway, a narrow-gauge, open-sided excursion train that operates daily during the summer tourist season.

Also southwest of Hobart lies Hartz Mountains National Park, a superb hiking area of forests and lakes, with peaks rising above 1,255 meters/4,117 feet and providing sweeping views over southern Tasmania. Sir Edmund Hilary noted this park contained "some of the wildest and most spectacular scenery I have ever seen." Perhaps it will be here that you encounter your first Tasmanian devil, a ponderous marsupial who earns his name by his half-scream, half-snarl cry. More elusive would be the Tasmanian tiger (really a wolf); no authenticated sighting has taken place in years. Watch out for the Tasmanian snakes when you do any back-country bushwalking. There are only three, all poisonous: the copperhead, the whip, and the tiger.

Mount Field National Park

Another easy 1-day trip from Hobart by coach or car is through the Derwent Valley to Mount Field National Park, with its 16,260 hectares/40,180 acres of mountains, rain forests, lakes, and streams.

Passing through hop fields you reach New Norfolk, a town that has received "historic" classification by the National Trust. At the Oast House you can take tea after visiting a hop museum and art gallery. Other historical buildings include St. Matthew's Church, oldest in Tasmania; the Bush Inn, built in 1815; and the Old Colony Inn, chock-full of history and antiques.

About 40 km/25 miles beyond is Russell Falls; here you'll enjoy watching a beautiful series of cascades dropping 36 meters/118 feet into a lush gorge, green with rain forest plants and tree ferns. Between July and October, the slopes of nearby Mount Mawson become a popular ski resort; in summer the mountains are alive with hikers.

Beyond the park, the Gordon River Road continues westward about 80 km/50 miles into the wilderness, along a route that many people consider Australia's most spectacular mountain highway. Every turn of the road reveals another range of mountains.

At the end is Lake Pedder, a natural lake now filled beyond its shoreline as part of Tasmania's hydroelectric system. The lake and its companion, Lake Gordon, comprise the largest inland fresh-water storage in Australia. Popular among anglers for its giant trout, Lake Pedder has a number of boat ramps. A launch offers scenic lake cruises. Camping is available, as are motels and guest houses.

The Midlands

Ross and Oatlands—in the Midlands—and the town of Richmond, across the Derwent 27 km/17 miles northeast of Hobart, are probably the best preserved of Tasmania's villages.

Founded in 1814, Ross is noted for its three-arched bridge built by convict labor; a village store operated by the same family for more than a century; and the Scotch Thistle Inn, restored as a restaurant. Each year on the first Saturday in November, the town holds a 1-day rodeo that attracts riders from all over Australia.

Oatlands, 84 km/52 miles north of Hobart, was established in 1826 as a military camp and stopping place for coaches traveling between Hobart and Launceston, to protect travelers against the notorious bushrangers (highway robbers).

Richmond's special features include the six-arched stone bridge, Australia's oldest span, built across the Coal River in 1823; the oldest Roman Catholic Church in Australia, completed in 1837; and the Richmond Gaol (jail), built in 1825. You can wine and dine in one old home and buy antiques in another.

Elsewhere on the island

Beyond the Hobart area, scenic highway routes lead to Tasmania's other towns and attractions.

Launceston, the state's second largest city, is the hub of northern Tasmania. From here you can make a number of excursions to coastal resorts and the lake district in the center of the island. Fine beaches and rich farmlands line the northwestern coast, while the wild region of the west holds some of Tasmania's most spectacular scenery.

The Launceston district

Set in pleasant, hilly countryside 64 km/40 miles inland at the head of the Tamar River estuary, Launceston is a provincial city of 88,000. Three scenic highways and good bus connections link it with Hobart in the south. The city has a number of hotels and motels, including the Colonial Motor Inn, housed in a structure built in 1847.

The town's parks and private gardens are among the best in Australia. European trees, particularly oaks and elms introduced by early settlers, and flowering shrubs flourish in Launceston's mild, moist climate, reminding many travelers of rural England.

(Continued on page 80)

Early colonial architecture is found in Launceston. Tasmania's second largest city is also known for its fine gardens and parks.

Boats tie up at Constitution Dock in Hobart. Bush-covered Mount Wellington provides backdrop for Tasmania's largest city.

...Continued from page 78

The Tasbureau, at the corner of Paterson and St. John streets, is your best source of information about Launceston. The Explorer Bus is a good way to see the town. You can also book tours ranging from a half-day jaunt around town to day trips to a seaside resort.

Cataract Gorge. In 10 minutes you can walk from the city center to famed Cataract Gorge, an awesome rocky corridor chewed out by the South Esk River on its way to join the Tamar. The rapids are especially exciting after a heavy rain in the highlands. On the north face of the gorge, a path, illuminated at night, leads along the cliff to First Basin. Here, in a picturesque setting, are a restaurant and swimming pool. You can cross the river on a breathtaking chairlift ride or by a wriggling suspension bridge.

Parks and gardens. Stretching north of Tamar Street is City Park, the most centrally located of the town's parklands. This oasis harbors a miniature zoo and a conservatory displaying begonias, cyclamen, and other hothouse blooms.

At the Punchbowl Reserve and Rhododendron Gardens, south of the city along Punch Bowl Road, a large variety of native birds, beasts, and reptiles live among natural surroundings.

Historic beginnings. Penny Royal World, on Paterson Street, is a fascinating collection of restored buildings that include a working cornmill (vintage 1825), miller's quarters, wheelwright's shop, threshing room, windmill, blacksmith's shop, gunpowder mill, arsenal, cannon foundry, museum, tavern, and restaurant. A paddle steamer takes visitors for a cruise on the Tamar River. Penny Royal World is open daily 9 A.M. to 5 P.M.

Franklin House, 6 km/4 miles from Launceston, was built by convict labor in 1838. It later became a school house and is now restored with furniture and fittings of the era. The home is open daily from 9 A.M. to 5 P.M.

Entally House, 13 km/8 miles south of Launceston at Hadspen, is an excellent example of early colonial architecture. Built in 1820, the restored mansion was once the home of a Tasmanian premier. Exceptional antiques inside and other interesting estate buildings make this dwelling a Tasmanian showplace.

Ben Lomond. One of Tasmania's two major ski areas, Ben Lomond lies in a rocky mountain plateau in the northeastern part of the state, about an hour's drive from Launceston. During ski season (July, August, September) a daily bus runs between Launceston and Ben Lomond; there are no overnight accommodations.

The Great Lake. Southwest from Launceston 120 km/75 miles is one of Australia's leading trout fishing resorts. Lying 1,034 meters/3,392 feet above sea level, the lake is also part of Tasmania's hydroelectric system. Visitors' galleries are located at power stations around the lake.

East coast resorts

Tasmania's east coast, paralleled by the Tasman Highway, is famed for its mild climate, beautiful beaches, fishing, and swimming facilities.

Of numerous popular coastal holiday resorts, the principal ones are St. Helens, Scamander, Bicheno, Coles Bay, Swansea, and Orford. A variety of accommodations are available throughout this area and range from motels and older guest houses with cabins, to self-contained villa units. There are also caravan campgrounds.

St. Helens, 265 km/165 miles northeast of Hobart and 165 km/103 miles east of Launceston, has a large sheltered bay popular for fishing and boating. Good surf beaches line the open coast, and forest streams winding from the north and west offer excellent trout fishing.

Bicheno and Triabunna on the coast are old whaling towns where people still make their living from the sea. You can arrange for fishing trips with local fishers.

At Coles Bay you can explore secluded coves, swim from snow-white beaches, scale rocky cliffs, or stroll leisurely along quiet, bush-edged trails. The small guest house stands at the base of The Hazards, 305-meter/1,000-foot-high hills of red granite. Adjoining the town is Freycinet National Park—a combination seaside resort and bushwalking and mountain climbing haven.

Tasmania's best-known park

The best-known wildlife sanctuary and scenic reserve in Tasmania is Cradle Mountain-Lake St. Clair National Park in the western half of the state, covering an area of 126,148 hectares/311,725 acres. From Devonport on the north coast, the park is a 1½-hour drive. Lake St. Clair, at the southern end of the park, is 175 km/109 miles north of Hobart on the Lyell Highway.

A favorite among hikers is the 83-km/52-mile, 5-day trek through the park from Waldheim Chalet at Cradle Mountain to Cynthia Bay at the south end of Lake St. Clair, with overnight stops at huts along the way. Cradle Mountain Lodge near Waldheim provides accommodations in the lodge or in self-contained cabins.

The wild west

The most unusual and fascinating part of Tasmania is the island's wild western region. This part of the state ranges from tracts of unexplored wilderness, to bare, stark hills in the Queenstown area, and Aboriginal rock carvings at Marrawah in the far north.

Tasmania's western region has been put under the protection of the World Heritage Council. The Western Tasmania Wilderness National Parks World Heritage Area consists of three national parks—Cradle Mountain-Lake St. Clair National Park, the Franklin-Lower Gordon Wild Rivers National Park, and the South West National Park.

The area can be explored on guided hikes, 4-wheel drive expeditions, cruise boat and rafting trips, and scenic air tour excursions. In the mountains, beware of a phenomenon called the "horizontals." Saplings grow to a certain height, then blow over to lie parallel to, but above the ground. This creates an area that looks like solid ground, but isn't.

A good way to get a glimpse of the area is to take the Lyell Highway into Queenstown, 256 km/159 miles northwest of Hobart. En route, you'll pass through Cradle Mountain-Lake St. Clair and Franklin-Lower Gordon Wild Rivers national parks. From the nearby coastal town of Strahan, take a boat trip up the Gordon River.

Queenstown. This is the largest township on the west coast (about 4,500 people), prospering from nearby copper mining. Before the turn of the century, the surrounding hills were green with trees and dense undergrowth. But then the smelters started to process copper ore, the timber was cut for fuel, and resulting sulphur fumes denuded the slopes. Heavy rains washed away topsoil, and the rocks became stained in shades of chrome yellow, purple, gray, and pink. Ore processing changed in 1922, and plant life is slowly returning.

A wilderness boat trip. The only developed port on the west coast is Strahan, west of Queenstown on the northern shore of Macquarie Harbour. Fishing boats and ships handling lumber sail in and out of the port.

Strahan is the starting point for boat trips across the harbor toward Settlement Island, Tasmania's first infamous penal colony, and into the wilderness surrounding the Gordon River.

The northwest corner. From Queenstown, the Murchison Highway crosses rugged mountains to reach Burnie, a timber and agricultural center on the northern coast. From Burnie, Route A2 heads west across the Cape Country and ends at Marrawah, where ancient Aboriginal rock carvings can be seen inside caves overhanging the shoreline.

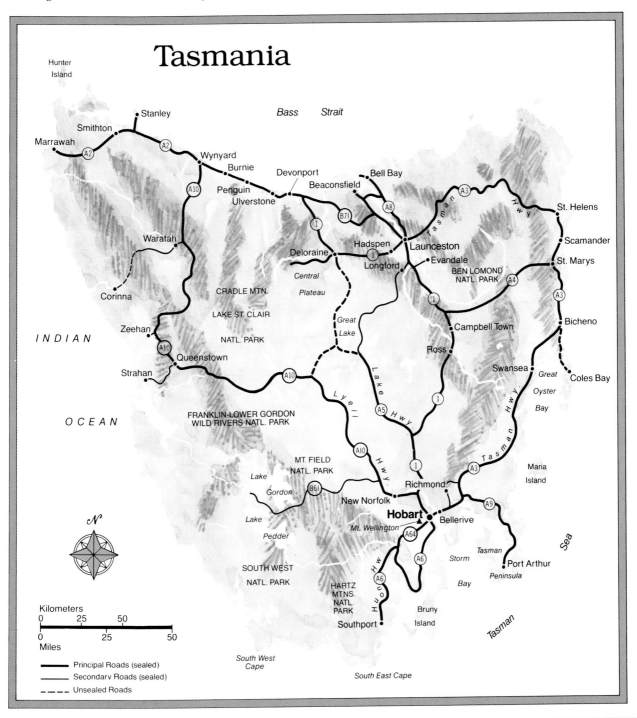

ADELAIDE

South Australia's beach resorts & wine valleys begin at town's edge

South Australia is at once a source of greater contrasts and smaller ones than its two great neighbors, New South Wales and Victoria. And, as a result, it is a much different place to visit.

Most Australian states have fertile coastal edges posed against bleak interior deserts, but in South Australia the line seems closer and sharper. It does not take long to get from the lush gardens of Adelaide to the bony, sun-bleached ribs of the Flinders Ranges, but the more dramatic point is that most of the journey is across rich, green agricultural land.

That greater contrast is also the key to the smaller contrast, which is that Adelaide does not dominate the rest of South Australia in the ways that Sydney and Melbourne dominate their states. Rather, farm districts ease through the suburbs and right into the edge of the city. Or, maybe, the city eases out into the farms. Either way, Adelaide is closely linked to the countryside around it. Visitors find themselves as much tempted to poke around in the countryside as downtown.

South Australians also manage to blur the boundary between land and sea. Sailors, swimmers, and surfers in and around Adelaide make the beaches of St. Vincent Gulf and other resort shores look as if fully a quarter of the population is amphibious. There remains plenty of room in the water for visitors.

The local populace is pleased that its state was not developed by convict labor. Philosopher Edward Gibbon Wakefield developed a plan to generate capital by paying laborers enough to encourage them to buy land. The successful idea must have come from the heart. Wakefield devised it while serving time in Newgate Prison in London, England.

Adelaide—A city of parks

Despite its sizable population (over 1 million), Adelaide manages to retain many of the charms of a much smaller

Part of the vast greenbelt encircling Adelaide, the Torrens River adds to the city's recreational possibilities. Pedal boats can be rented near the Festival Centre.

city—partly because some of its streets are lined with colorful buildings that would not look out of place in Western movies, and partly because it has a superior park system even by Australia's high standards.

With implausibly fair weather, with a ring parks around town, open spaces in the Mount Lofty Ranges on one side and the spacious St. Vincent Gulf on the other, Adelaide is attuned to the outdoors. Adelaide revels in outdoor sports, including motor racing—the city is host to the annual Australian Formula One Grand Prix. However, both outdoor and indoor venues are used for the biennial Adelaide Festival, a 3-week art, music, and dance event.

Getting your bearings

Adelaide is an easy city to get to know. The key is compactness, the result of the well-designed 1836 plans of Colonel William Light, South Australia's first surveyor-general.

The business heart of Adelaide throbs within a square mile centering on Victoria Square. Many of Adelaide's corporate offices, banks, stores, hotels, and public buildings flank the wide, tree-lined streets and broad squares that seem to be the hallmark of every Australian city.

Circling this inner city are the great parklands that dominate the shape of Adelaide. Through the northern section of these parks flows the Torrens River, dammed in front of the Festival Theatre to form a lake.

Beyond the river is North Adelaide—a suburb of large, old homes and bluestone cottages. In this pleasant suburban area you will find Light's Vision. The statue of Colonel Light stands on top of Montefiore Hill. From the hill you can get a commanding view of the city.

Central Adelaide walking tour brochures are available from the South Australian Government Travel Centre at 18 King William Street. You can also pick up general information and maps on Adelaide and South Australia here.

Strolling through the park

Because Adelaide is so definitively shaped by its 688 hectares/1,700 acres of parks, they are the best places to begin an acquaintanceship with the city.

Showplace of Adelaide's parklands is the Botanic Gardens and Park in the northeast parklands. Here, you'll find 16 hectares/40 acres of native Australian vegetation.

(Continued on page 84)

...Continued from page 83

A world-renowned collection of water lilies grows in the park's lakes.

Next to the Botanic Park is Adelaide's compact zoo. It's open daily from 9:30 A.M. to 5 P.M. During summer months, a launch sails along the Torrens River between the zoo and the Festival Theatre.

The parklands not only provide a pleasant place to stroll, but also feature facilities for a number of recrea-tional pursuits—golf courses, tennis courts, cycling paths, and jogging tracks.

Touring the central city

Within the square created by Adelaide's parklands, is the city's central shopping and business district—a conglomeration of 19th century architecture and modern high rises.

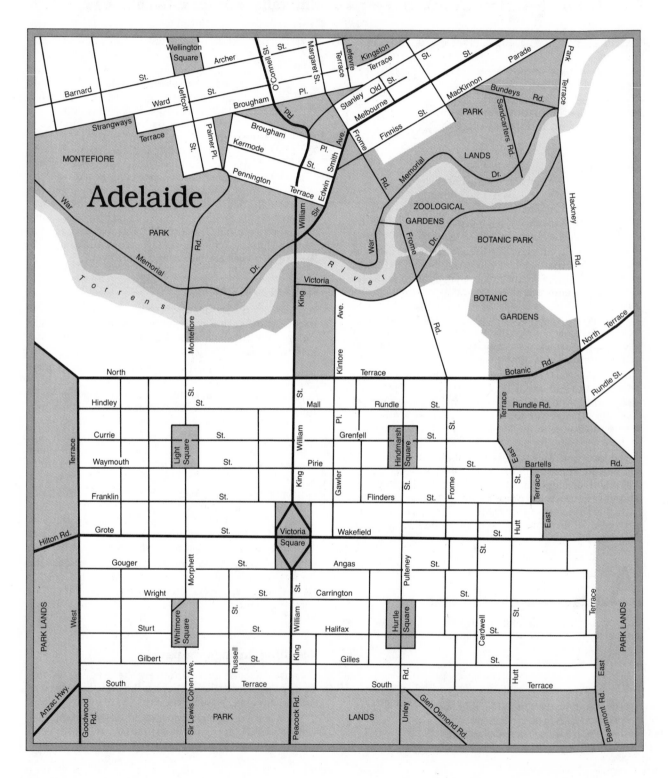

The city's parkland atmosphere extends into this commercial hub with numerous tree-shaded squares. Victoria Square—marking the exact center of the city—is filled with trees and features a statue of Queen Victoria.

One of the city's main thoroughfares—King William Street—heads north and south from Victoria Square. With its median strip of lawns and flowers, it is considered the widest capital city street in Australia. Lining King William Street are most of the city's banks, insurance offices, town hall, and post office. These latter two buildings—opposite each other—have imposing clock towers.

Another main tree-lined boulevard—North Terrace—runs in an east/westerly direction at the north end of city center. Important buildings along this thoroughfare include Parliament House, Holy Trinity Church (Adelaide's oldest), Government House, South Australian Museum, Art Gallery, State Library, and University of Adelaide.

Following are some of the major attractions for visitors.

Art Gallery. Located on North Terrace near its intersection with Pulteney Street, this gallery houses a fine collection of Australian paintings, ceramics, and sculptures as well as works of British, European, and American artists. The gallery is open daily from 10 A.M. to 5 P.M.

South Australian Museum. Near the Art Gallery, this museum houses large collections of regional natural history and Aboriginal and Melanesian artifacts. Take note of the giant Diprotodon skeleton on the ground floor of the museum. It's believed to be an ancestor of today's wombat. The museum is open daily.

Historic home. On North Terrace opposite the Royal Adelaide Hospital stands Ayers House. This beautiful 19th century bluestone residence was once the home of Sir Henry Ayers, one of South Australia's earliest premiers. Today it houses the headquarter offices of the South Australian National Trust, a historical museum, a posh restaurant, and a bistro. The house is open weekdays (except Monday) from 10 A.M. to 5 P.M. and on weekends from 2 to 4 P.M.

North Adelaide. On the north side of the Torrens River (a long walk from town center) is this interesting suburb with its bluestone cottages, old hotels, and new restaurants. North Adelaide was the city's first fashionable residential area. You can still see fine 19th century colonial mansions as well as simple cottages. Good streets to explore include Stanley, Melbourne, and Archer streets, and Le Fevre Terrace.

Shopping around

Adelaide's main shopping area is concentrated in the pedestrian-only Rundle Street Mall between King William Street and Pulteney Street. On it are many of the city's large retail department stores (Myer's, David Jones, John Martins of South Australia) as well as cafes, boutiques, and movie houses. Several small shopping arcades branch off tree-shaded Rundle Street with its flower boxes, sculptures, and fruit carts.

Shops in Adelaide are open weekdays from 9 A.M. to 5:30 P.M. and Saturdays from 9 A.M. to 11:30 A.M. On Fridays many of the downtown stores are open until 9 P.M.

The essentials

Here are a few basics to help you in planning and taking a trip to Adelaide.

Getting there. Adelaide is served by air, rail, and bus.

Air. Interstate domestic flights by Ansett and Australian airlines with intrastate service by Kendell Airlines. Adelaide International Airport is 6 km/4 miles from downtown by bus or taxi.

Rail. Interstate trains provide regular service to and from other state capitals. The terminal is 2 km/1 mile from downtown.

Bus. Ansett Pioneer, Greyhound, and Deluxe have regular service between Adelaide and other capitals.

Accommodations. Most major hotels are in the downtown area; try the Adelaide Parkroyal, Gateway Inn, Hilton International-Adelaide, Hyatt Regency Adelaide, Hotel Adelaide, Adelaide Travelodge, South Park Motor Inn, Old Adelaide Inn, and Barron Town House.

Food and drink. Seafood from nearby waters heads the list of local specialties—crayfish, prawns, whiting, yabbies, and rock lobsters. One local dish, a "floater," is also a favorite. It consists of a meat pie floating upside down in pea soup with a dab of tomato sauce on top. Pie carts, operating nights and Sundays, are adjacent to the General Post Office.

South Australia has five good wine districts—the Barossa, Southern Vales, Clare, Murray River, and Coonawarra—whose wines are featured on Adelaide restaurant menus. Major local beers include West End, Southwark, and Coopers.

Getting around. Extensive city-operated bus system in city as well as out to suburbs. Free "Bee-line" bus follows downtown shopping circuit—Victoria Square to Railway Station along King William Street. City's only tram travels between Victoria Square and beach suburb of Glenelg. Extensive surburban train system operates from Adelaide. City circle bus links tram, rail, and bus services. Also several rental car agencies in town rent both cars and motor scooters.

Public transport maps available at South Australian Government Travel Centre.

Tours. Half-day tours include city sights. Regional tours (some half-day, some full-day) include Mount Lofty Ranges (see page 86), Victor Harbor (page 89), Kangaroo Island (page 91), the Murray River (page 93), Barossa Valley (page 92), and Southern Vales (page 92). Also available are longer tours to Flinders Ranges (see page 93) and cruises on Murray River (page 93).

For more information. South Australian Government Travel Centre, 18 King William Street, Adelaide 5000. Can also arrange tours and accommodations. Open Monday through Friday from 8:45 A.M. to 5 P.M., Saturday from 8:45 to 11:30 A.M., and Sunday from 10 A.M. to 2:15 P.M.

Buying an opal. South Australia's opal mines (see page 88) make Adelaide one of Australia's best cities for opal shopping. Small workshops in the city cut and polish opals on the premises to make custom jewelry you can purchase. Most of the major jewelry stores and department stores also stock a good range of opal jewelry.

Antique hunting. On North Adelaide's Melbourne Street, several old buildings have been restored to house antique shops. (There are also a number of exclusive boutiques in the area.) Other antique dealers can be found along Unley Road and King William Road near Hyde Park.

Arts and entertainment

The focus of Adelaide's entertainment scene is the Festival Centre. Many of Adelaide's cultural events are held in this modern complex on the banks of the Torrens just north of North Terrace off King William Road.

The Festival Centre, built for the Adelaide Festival, includes a 2,000-seat auditorium (Festival Theatre), a 612-seat drama theater (The Playhouse), a 360-seat experimental theater (The Space), a 2,000-seat open-air amphitheater, and a broad plaza with concrete sculptures. Hourly guided tours are held weekdays from 10 A.M. to 3 P.M. and Saturdays from 10:30 A.M. to 3 P.M.

Both the Adelaide Symphony Orchestra and State Theatre Company perform at the Festival Centre. The center also hosts international performers on tour. (The Stuttgart Ballet and Vienna Boys' Choir are among recent visitors.) During the summer months the open-air amphitheater is the venue for free concerts.

The State Opera of South Australia performs at the Opera Theatre on Grote Street.

Adelaide Festival. Biennially—during the first 3 weeks of March in even-numbered years—the Adelaide Festival brings together fine performers of every kind from Australia and abroad. Rudolph Nureyev, Dave Brubeck, the Royal Shakespeare Company, London Philharmonic, and the Kabuki Theatre of Japan are among the roster of past performers.

The list of activities during the festival includes opera and ballet performances, jazz and symphony concerts, folk dancing, comedy, and drama. Art and sculpture fill the galleries and spill over into outdoor exhibits. Floral displays provide color in the gardens. Processions and pageantry complete the festival's calendar.

The core of all the events is the Festival Centre but activities occur everywhere—streets, parks, smaller theaters, sports arenas, and playgrounds.

Adelaide Casino. This city's only casino is housed in the beautifully refurbished former railway station on North Terrace. In addition to gaming tables, the casino has a restaurant and five bars.

Sports to watch

The city's main sports ground is the Adelaide Oval, in parklands on the north side of the Torrens River. During the summer months cricket is played here and during the winter months fans enthusiastically gather to support Australian Rules football.

Horse races are run weekly at Victoria Park Racecourse, in parklands southeast of the city or at Morphetville near Glenelg. Other tracks include Cheltenham, 8 km/5 miles to the northwest. There's harness racing from October through July at Globe Derby Park in Bolivar.

Recreational possibilities

The city's parklands offer a rich range of activities.

Boating. The Torrens River—flowing gracefully through the city's northern parklands—is ideal for quiet boating. You can hire rowboats and pedal boats on the river bank near the Festival Centre.

Golf. It's just a short walk from city center to the Municipal Golf Links in the northern parklands; there are two 18-hole courses.

For more information on Adelaide's golf courses check with the South Australian Golf Association on War Memorial Drive in North Adelaide.

Tennis. Adelaide is one of the last great bastions of lawn tennis in the world. The city also has a number of hard courts. (The most notable public complex is Memorial Drive Tennis Courts next to the Adelaide Oval in the northern parklands.) For-hire courts are listed in telephone book Yellow Pages. For information on club play contact either the South Australian Lawn Tennis Association, P.O. Box 220, Goodwood 5034, or the South Australian Hard Court Tennis League, Inc., P.O. Box 202, Goodwood 5034.

Beautiful beaches

Adelaide's beaches stretch along the coast from Outer Harbor in the north to Seacliff in the south. Along their 32-km/20-mile expanse, you'll find good swimming in the calm waters of St. Vincent Gulf. Most of these beaches are less than a 30-minute drive from the city. A special streetcar even takes beachgoers from Victoria Square in downtown Adelaide to St. Vincent Gulf. Buses and trains also serve the area.

Principal resorts along this coast include Largs Bay, Semaphore, Grange, Henley Beach, Glenelg, Brighton, West Beach, and Seacliff.

Peaceful, quiet hill country

The sometimes steep, sometimes rolling hills that hem Adelaide tightly against the sea are serene pleasures within themselves. Along winding roads, green meadows with grazing sheep give way to orchards, which in turn give way to tiny villages tucked into forested folds.

Called the Mount Lofty Ranges, these hills hold some predictable charms in the form of parks and wilderness reserves, and some unpredictable ones in the forms of art colonies, a German village that holds one of the largest beer fests outside of Bavaria, and a museum of motorcars and other machines.

Spring and fall are the finest seasons for visiting the district. In spring the orchards come alive with fragrant blossoms; in fall, poplars, birches, and maples light the hillsides with fiery reds and golds.

Driving distances are easy. There also are full and half-day tours into the region from Adelaide.

With regal waves and smiles, queen and court parade through city streets at the Barossa Valley Vintage Festival. This great Australia winemaking region lies north of Adelaide.

Froufrous and furbelows adorn century-old Botanic Hotel on North Terrace in Adelaide.

Cleland Conservation Park. This inviting concept in wildlife sanctuaries allows people to walk among animals that roam free in natural habitats. The park is divided into five areas, each featuring animals that live together in the wild. Visitors can meet more or less eye to eye with red and gray kangaroos, tammar wallabies, swamp wallabies, red-necked wallabies, and such waterfowl as pelicans, cormorants, and black swans. A walk-through aviary gives close-up looks at rosellas, parrots, and lorikeets in flight. (Wombats, koalas, and dingoes must live in enclosures for the protection of one or both parties.) The park, 13 km/8 miles southeast of Adelaide, is open daily from 9:30 A.M. to 5 P.M.

Hahndorf is home to the great beer festival, held each January on Australia Day. All year around it is home to the descendants of settlers who fled to South Australia in 1839 to escape religious persecution in their homeland.

The half-timbered German cottages and houses lining the main street have been converted to an array of shops, crafts galleries, and restaurants. Of particular note are the Hahndorf Academy, which houses a German folk museum and the adjoining Heysen Art Gallery, which holds paintings by Sir Hans Heysen.

Hahndorf is 40 km/18 miles southeast of Adelaide.

Birdwood Mill. Northeast of the city, an old flour mill built in 1851 now houses Australia's Museum of Technology's collection of Australiana.

Inside the mill, you'll find old diving equipment, washing machines, stoves, gramophones, and drinking glasses. An adjacent new building houses the National Motor Museum's 135 old jeeps, racing cars, fire engines, and automobiles.

Birdwood is about a 50-minute drive from Adelaide.

A diverse shore

The coast of South Australia around Adelaide looks as if it had been cut with a scroll saw. Deep bays and peninsulas alternate in bewildering numbers—all to the benefit of sailors, surfers, fishers, and scenery watchers.

Opal fossicking at Coober Pedy

As your small plane begins its descent to the runway at Coober Pedy, you might feel you're landing on the moon. The dry, red outback soil below you is pock-marked with small craterlike surface diggings—remnants of opal mining.

More than 100 million years ago, the sea covered this area of Australia, laying down sediment and entrapping the silica solutions that developed into opals. The gems are found in sandstone, below layers of rock and jasper.

Miners at Coober Pedy, and Andamooka to the southeast, dig out more than $4 million worth of opals annually. About 75 percent of the world's opals come from these areas. Some miners use modern equipment such as blowers to bring up earth from the mines. Others scar the ground with giant earth-moving equipment, making deep cuts in search of opals. Still others rely on the old mining techniques, using just picks, shovels, windlasses, and buckets.

Above the ground, it's impossible to distinguish on sight persons who have struck it rich and those living off credit. Everyone avoids displaying wealth, for fear of claim jumping.

In Aborigine, Coober Pedy means "man in hole." It's an appropriate name, for nearly half of the 3,000 residents of Coober Pedy live underground—even the church is underground. The reason for this molelike existence is the area's soaring summer temperatures, which can reach 49°C/120°F. Average underground house temperatures stay around 19°C/65°F the year around.

These underground homes are usually quite spacious and comfortable. The prosperous miner might even have wall-to-wall carpets, a stereo, and a cocktail bar. The largest such dugout, Aladdin's Cave, has 11 rooms and a huge workshop-store.

If you're feeling lucky, you may want to dig for opals too. In addition to a Precious Stones Prospecting Permit from the Mines Department in Adelaide, you'll need a pick and shovel and a strong back. If you try this during the heat of summer, take heed from local miners who work their claims while temperatures are cooler—between 3 and 10 A.M.

Tours of Coober Pedy usually include an underground home, the church, nearby mining fields, and the Umoona Mine. You can tour this old mine and purchase opals from the underground shop. Opals, mounted or unmounted, are available in Coober Pedy at prices considerably lower than in larger cities.

Coober Pedy is 966 km/600 miles north of Adelaide. You can get there from Adelaide by bus or Opal Air, which operates eight-seater Cessnas on a regular schedule. Packaged tours on Opal Air can include Coober Pedy, Ayers Rock, and on to Alice Springs on Connair. Coach tours and 1-day air tours are also available from Adelaide. There are bus and air tours to Andamooka too. Accommodations in Coober Pedy and Andamooka are limited to a few motels and a guest house.

In addition to Coober Pedy and Andamooka, you can visit gem mining areas at Lightning Ridge in far northern New South Wales (home of the famous black opals) and in the Anakie District of Queensland, an important sapphire-producing area where good stones can still be found near old diggings.

For visitors from afar, there are two main choices south of Adelaide, and two more northwest. The southerly choices are the Fleurieu Peninsula and Kangaroo Island. The northerly options are Yorke and Eyre peninsulas. All four offer resorts and wilderness with equal ease.

Fleurieu Peninsula

The Fleurieu Peninsula coast touches the waters of both St. Vincent Gulf and the Southern Ocean. A varying seascape includes secluded bays with calm waters, broad beaches with rolling surf, and rocky headlands where waves crash endlessly. Inland are wine vineyards, almond orchards, forests, and undulating pasturelands.

You can visit the Fleurieu Peninsula on a 1-day tour from Adelaide. If you wish to stay longer, you'll find accommodations at Victor Harbor, Port Elliot, and Goolwa.

Victor Harbor. The largest and most popular seaside resort on the peninsula is Victor Harbor, 84 km/52 miles south of Adelaide. On Encounter Bay, the town's harbor

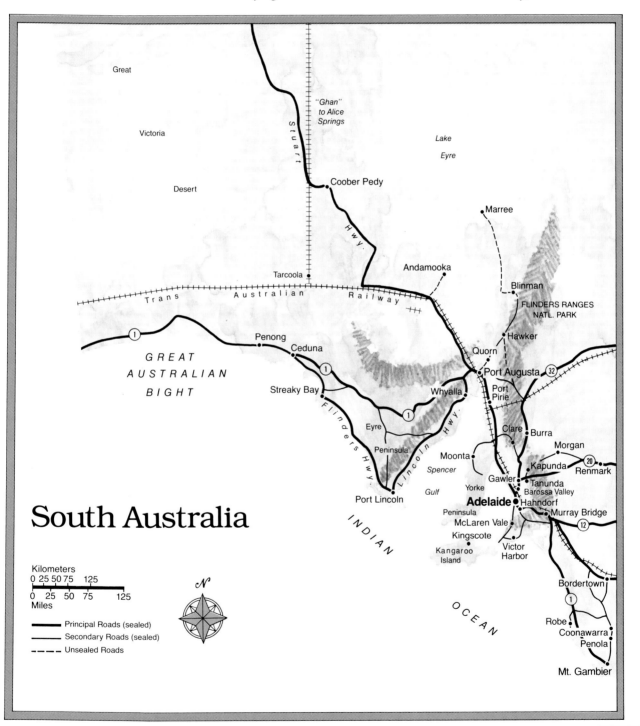

South Australia

Slowing to cross *a waterhole, four-wheel-drive vehicle ventures deep into the Flinders Ranges, a land of peaks and ravines tapering into desert.*

Amusing to tourists, *sign is no laughing matter to people who know the danger of hitting a kangaroo. Outback drivers protect cars with ''kangaroo guards.''*

is protected from the ocean by Granite Island. This rocky knob, joined to the mainland by a causeway, is buffeted by giant rollers crashing against its windward side, throwing spray high into the air. On the island's harbor side—facing the town—you can swim and study marine life in sheltered pools along the causeway.

Urimbirra Fauna Park. In the natural setting of this park—5 km/3 miles from Victor Harbor—you can see many of Australia's animals, some enclosed and some not. Wandering among giant gum trees, you'll see kangaroos, wallabies, emus, koalas, dingoes, wombats, and Tasmanian devils. The park also has an excellent Nocturnal House where you'll see Australia's night creatures.

Coorong National Park. Winding around Encounter Bay and heading south, you'll come to Coorong National Park. It consists of a narrow sandspit of sand dunes plus a shallow salt-water lagoon behind the beach area. This lagoon is the breeding rookery for pelicans, crested terns, and silver gulls.

You can best view the lagoon breeding area from Princes Highway (1).

Unspoiled Kangaroo Island

Australia's third largest island lies 113 km/70 miles southwest of Adelaide at the entrance to St. Vincent Gulf. Much of the island's original character remains—abundant wildlife, splendid beaches, secluded coves, rugged headlands, and wind-sculptured boulders. Here you can also enjoy Australia's animal kingdom. Walk among the seals at Seal Bay or explore Flinders Chase National Park and see the koalas and platypuses.

It's a 40-minute trip by air to Kangaroo Island from Adelaide. A car ferry from Port Adelaide makes the journey in 6 hours. And there's a one-day aerial tour from Adelaide.

Main centers. Largest of the island resorts is Kingscote on the north coast. It offers many safe beaches, a sea front swimming pool, jetty, and the main shopping area.

American River, southeast of Kingscote, is a holiday resort in a woodland setting. The waterway is not really a river, but an arm of the sea separating Dudley Peninsula from the rest of the island.

Penneshaw, on the Dudley Peninsula, looks 13 km/8 miles across the strait (called Backstairs Passage) to the mainland. An attractive town with a white sandy beach, jetty, and sheltered anchorage, it has a rocky promontory populated with fairy penguins.

A ferry service operates between Cape Jervis and Penneshaw; coach service links Cape Jervis and Adelaide.

Flinders Chase National Park. At the western edge of the island—about a 1½-hour drive from Kingscote—you can explore this refuge for Australian fauna and flora. Roads wind through the 54,950-hectare/135,787-acre park, and there are trails for bushwalking. Here you'll find kangaroos, wallabies, emus, Cape Barren geese, and goanna lizards. The animals are so tame that visitors have to guard their picnic hampers against hungry marauding kangaroos. Emus will even peck on your car window begging for handouts. Visitors can dine in an enclosure while the kangaroos and emus look on beseechingly from the other side of the fence.

Beautiful Yorke Peninsula

Like a long leg, the Yorke Peninsula stretches into the sea between St. Vincent Gulf and Spencer Gulf. With beautiful beaches along both these waterways, the peninsula is an ideal spot for a coastal holiday with activities like surfing, fishing, swimming, and boating. Inland, good roads wind through golden wheat and barley fields and lush pasturelands.

The peninsula's towns, including Wallaroo, Kadina, Moonta, Maitland, Ardrossan, and Port Vincent, are just a few hours' drive from Adelaide. Accommodations in the area include hotels, motels, and caravan parks.

One of the best times to visit Yorke Peninsula is in springtime when the wildflowers decorate the landscape. The peninsula is ablaze with yellow daisies, brilliant red flame bushes, and golden wattles.

Copper mining towns. In the late 1800s, copper was discovered on the Yorke Peninsula, and the resulting boom lasted for about 63 years. Boom towns included Kadina, Moonta, and Wallaroo.

Men from Cornwall, England, immigrated to work the mines, and you can still see their Cornish miners' cottages as well as abandoned mines and slag heaps. In Moonta, you can visit the Mining Museum located in the former Mining School.

The area's Cornish heritage is evident during the celebration of Kernewek Lowender. This Cornish festival—held on the long weekend in May in odd-numbered years—features wheelbarrow races, street dances, a Cornish feast, a village green fair, crowning of a festival king and queen, and the eating of Cornish pasties. Activities are centered in Wallaroo, Kadina, and Moonta.

Innes National Park. At the "toe" of the Yorke Peninsula, you can explore this 6,000-hectare/14,827-acre wilderness of mallee scrub and spectacular coastal scenery. There are wonderful beaches, coves, and bays.

Eyre Peninsula, a water playground

Lying between Spencer Gulf and the Great Australian Bight, Eyre Peninsula forms a giant triangle, with the towns of Port Augusta in the northeast, Ceduna in the northwest, and Port Lincoln at the southern tip.

The Eyre Peninsula's landscape includes grainfields, bushlands, and sheep pastures. In the northeastern part of the peninsula are iron ore mines at Iron Knob and Iron Monarch, and steel factories along the eastern coast.

Coastal offerings. As with the Yorke Peninsula, the area's greatest attractions are its shores. The coast surrounding Port Lincoln—the peninsula's major resort town—is long and deeply indented, with great seas for yachting, quiet inlets for swimming, and endless beaches with rolling waves for surfing. People who fish usually find the sea generous whether tackled from beach, jetty, rock, or boat.

A festival. The calm waters of Boston Bay where Port Lincoln is situated provide safe anchorage for Australia's biggest tuna fleet. Each year on the last weekend in January, this fleet is heralded with the Tunarama Festival. Honoring the opening of the tuna fishing season, the 4-day festival includes the blessing of the fleet, a sailpast of boats, parades, and feasting.

Getting there and accommodations. The hub of the peninsula's resort activities is Port Lincoln. Daily air service links this town with Adelaide. There's also bus service via Port Augusta. Motels, hotels, and guest houses are located in Port Lincoln, and there's a nearby caravan park.

Mount Gambier's crater lakes

Mount Gambier, a large commercial center near the Victoria border 483 km/300 miles southeast of Adelaide, takes its name from an extinct volcano rising above the town. Inside the mountain's shattered top are three beautiful crater lakes.

Perhaps the best known of the lakes is Blue Lake. Annually at the end of November, Blue Lake mysteriously changes color from slate gray to bright blue. Between January and March, the lake slowly reverts to its former gray.

You can get to Mount Gambier by daily air or coach service. There is also rail service from Adelaide. There are hotels, motels, and campgrounds.

Wine country

In this, Australia's largest winegrowing state, vineyards begin at the edges of Adelaide and sprawl everywhere sea breezes reach, and a few places where they don't.

The most famous single district in the country, the Barossa, is a broad, shallow upland valley little more than an hour's drive north of the city. Its near neighbor and one of its closest competitors is the Clare Valley. Flanking Adelaide on the south is the district called Southern Vales, where vines and suburban houses compete for space on a narrow shelf above the sea.

South Australia's other two wine districts demand longer travels. Far to the south is Coonawarra, a tiny but treasured source of red wines. It is most easily visited as part of a trek to Mount Gambier. Inland, south and east of Adelaide, the largest district of them all flanks the Murray River. It is as much visitable for rides on paddle wheel passenger boats and for fishing as for winery touring.

Barossa Valley

Heading the list of well-known wine-producing regions not only in South Australia but in the entire country is the Barossa Valley. This premier winemaking region is located only 64 km/40 miles northeast of Adelaide. The valley with its gentle rolling hills, vineyards, orchards, and market gardens stretches 29 km/18 miles from Lyndoch in the south past Nuriootpa in the north.

A bit of history. The valley was originally settled in the 1840s mainly by Prussians and Silesians. Lutherans, they came to Australia to escape religious persecution in their homeland. These settlers planted the first vines in 1847 near Tanunda and Rowland flats.

The valley's towns have retained an old-world look, with solid stone houses, old German cottages, and carefully cultivated gardens set along neat tree-lined streets. The Lutheran religion still predominates, and at the center of each town is a Lutheran church with its belfry.

Area wineries. The valley has about 40 wineries. Included in this lengthy list are Orlando, Chateau Yaldara, Penfolds/Kaiser Stuhl, Seppelt, and Yalumba.

Many of the Barossa Valley wineries are still family owned. Some boast castlelike buildings and clock towers reminiscent of the winegrowing districts of the fatherland. You'll find impressive stone buildings at Yaldara, Tanunda, Seppelt's, Yalumba, and Penfolds.

Behind the handsome facades, the wineries of the Barossa Valley offer hospitality. Many have guided tours showing the various steps of wine production from grape crushing (in season) through fermenting to bottling. You can also taste and purchase the wines they produce. The Barossa is noted for its fine table wines, but also produces sherry and brandy. Check locally for the hours the wineries are open.

During odd-numbered years, the Barossa Valley celebrates the vintage with a large-scale, 7-day festival in late March or early April. Activities include processions, feasting, wine sampling, grape stomping contests, folk dancing in German costumes, and crowning of a Vintage Queen. Headquarters for all these activities is Tanunda.

You can drive to the Barossa on your own or take a full-day coach tour from Adelaide. You'll find accommodations (hotels, motels, and caravan parks) at Lyndoch, Tanunda, Nuriootpa, and Angaston.

Clare Valley

About 136 km/83 miles north of Adelaide is a smaller district with considerable charm. Within Clare Valley are the towns of Clare and Watervale.

Clare—named after County Clare, Ireland—is a peaceful agricultural center with unusual bluestone cottages and other buildings dating back to the area's settlement in the early 1800s. The surrounding countryside offers vineyards divided by woodlands and scenic gorges. One unique way to explore the area is in a Cobb & Co. horse-drawn coach. A special weekend tour, starting at Waterloo, includes gourmet dinners, picnic lunches, and a 4-hour coach journey to historic Martindale Hall near Mintaro. This Georgian-style mansion was featured in the Australian film *Picnic at Hanging Rock.*

There are in the district about 12 wineries, including Chateau Clare, Mitchell Cellars, Sevenhill Cellars, Robertson's Clare Vineyards, and Wendouree Cellars. Wines produced in the area include whites, reds, and sherries.

You'll find accommodations (hotels, motels, and caravan parks) in Auburn, Watervale, Penwortham, Sevenhill, and Clare.

Southern Vales district

Still another wine district—the Southern Vales—is to be found about 32 km/20 miles due south of Adelaide on the Fleurieu Peninsula (see page 89). The charm of this area is the large number of small, family-owned wineries you can explore. Nearby are the southern coast's beaches.

Winery touring. About 40 wineries have regular visiting hours Monday through Sunday. Area wineries include Reynella, Old Clarendon, Maxwells, Hardy's, Kay Bros., and Sea View. The Southern Vales district is known for its red wines in particular.

Bushing Festival. McLaren Vale is the scene of this 7-day festival in October. Activities include wine tasting, winery tours, dancing, and an Elizabethan feast in costume.

Ol' Man Murray

Rising in the Australian Alps between Melbourne and Canberra, Australia's longest river—the Murray—flows for much of its 2,589-km/1,609-mile route between Victoria and New South Wales, forming those states' boundaries. However, near the end of its run, it meanders through 644 km/400 miles of South Australia. Just before it terminates its course at Encounter Bay, it widens into Lake Alexandrina.

Constantly changing its course over the centuries, the river has left a wide swath of rich bottom land now used for vineyards, orchards, and dairy farms. The riverfront towns serve not only as farming centers for these agricultural regions, but also as river resorts. The river provides excellent opportunities for fishing (no license required in South Australia), water-skiing, and boating.

From Adelaide, there's a coach tour to Goolwa at the mouth of the Murray River. There's also regular coach service from Adelaide to Goolwa, Murray Bridge, Loxton, Renmark, Barmera, Berri, and Mannum.

You'll find accommodations (hotels, motels, caravan parks, and campgrounds) all along the river. Fully self-contained houseboats are also available for rent.

Wineries. The development of irrigation along the Murray River opened this great river valley to productive vineyards between 1915 and 1930. Extensive vineyards around the towns of Barmera, Berri, Loxton, and Renmark provide the grapes for a number of winery cooperatives, as well as for small, independent wineries. All are open for inspection; check locally for visiting hours.

Dessert and appetizer wines were the early specialties of this area, but table wines of sound quality and reasonable price are rapidly increasing in volume.

River cruises. At one time the Murray River was an important trade route for Australia's inland cities. Wool, grain, and timber were transported down the river and supplies shipped up the river. With the advent of rail transport, this river traffic died. Today's river traffic consists mainly of pleasure craft and small passenger boats.

A variety of passenger vessels cruise the Murray. Among the favorite trips: The *Murray River Queen*, an 86-passenger, diesel-powered paddle wheeler, takes 5½ days on a trip from Goolwa to Swan Reach. The 120-passenger, paddle wheeler *Murray Princess* cruises from Renmark to Loxton and back. The paddle wheeler *Proud Mary* offers both 5-day and weekend cruises on the river.

Coonawarra

The most southerly of South Australia's wine districts, Coonawarra, lies 435 km/270 miles southeast of Adelaide close to the Victoria border. The rich volcanic soil of this region produces some of Australia's most sought-after red wines.

The area remains unspoiled farm country. Among area wineries are Mildara, Wynn's, Lindeman's Rouge Homme, Penfold's, Hungerford Hill, Redbank, and Brand's. Most have weekday visiting hours.

The rugged outback

Few places on the face of the earth are less hospitable to man than the Australian outback, that vast area occupying all but the coastal rim of the continent.

Nearly two-thirds of South Australia is outback, yet only 1 percent of the state's populace lives in it. A handful of station owners and opal miners endure a place where temperatures can touch 49°C/120°F and where rains come so seldom that the huge watershed called Lake Eyre goes for years at a time without so much as a puddle to justify its name. But when the rains come, they come. The lake gets deep enough for swimming every so often, and once it even had enough water to allow a shipwreck.

Dry or wet, the outback is no place to go alone as a stranger. Distances are cruelly long, roads few, and water questionable. But if the outback appeals to you at all, go, for this is dramatic country. Settlements in the Flinders Range and at the old silver mines of Broken Hill provide quick samplers. There are also tours from the Flinders area that get you deep into the outback.

The colorful Flinders Ranges

The Flinders Ranges provide a majestic slice of the outback. Rising abruptly from the plains near Crystal Brook (193 km/120 miles north of Adelaide), these spectacular mountain ranges offer 800 km/500 miles of multicolored cliffs, granite peaks, and razor-backed ridges. Steep gorges, many cut by creeks and cooled by deep water holes, have majestic gum trees.

The beauty of the Flinders lies not only in their ruggedness, but also in colors that change with the light of day. At sunrise, they are flaming rust and red; as the day progresses they mellow to blues, purples, and rich browns. Still more color comes to these mountains in September and October when wild hops, daisies, and Sturt peas all brighten the terrain after a spring rain.

You'll find that the Flinders Ranges' coolest months are April through October. Six-day coach tours from Adelaide provide the easiest way to visit the Flinders Ranges. Secondary roads can be primitive and treacherous after heavy rains; floods are not uncommon. Hotels, motels, caravan parks, and campgrounds are available in the main resorts of Wilpena Pound and Arkaroola, and in other smaller towns throughout the ranges.

Broken Hill—City of silver

To the world's mining community, Broken Hill represents one of the greatest mineral discoveries of the past 100 years. Chanced upon in 1883 by a range-rider, it has since become known as the world's largest silver-zinc-lead lode—152 meters/500 feet wide and as much as 610 meters/2,000 feet deep.

Though Broken Hill is located in New South Wales (1,190 km/739 miles west of Sydney), it is only 48 km/30 miles over the border from South Australia and most easily reached from Adelaide (402 km/250 miles southwest). Kendell Airlines operates between Adelaide and Broken Hill. There's also rail and bus service.

PERTH

In Western Australia, a pleasant city & rich hinterlands

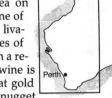

Perth is the principal urban area on Australia's west coast, and it's one of the country's prettiest and most livable cities. In and near Perth, miles of uncrowded beaches bask beneath a reliable sun. Not far inland, good wine is made, and the remains of a great gold rush still cough up an occasional nugget.

The vast state of Western Australia is three times the size of Texas. With more than a million square miles of land and a population not much over one million, it makes the American West look crowded. Eight out of 10 people live in or near Perth, making for a startling difference between cosmopolitan city and hinterland.

For many years Western Australia found itself left off the itineraries of many foreign visitors to Australia because it is so remote from the major east coast cities. However, now that Perth is Australia's gateway to Asia and a growing headquarters for mining, visitors have become numerous. Perth received still more recognition as a travel destination when it hosted sailing enthusiasts from around the world during the America's Cup races in 1986–87.

Perth—A booming capital

In 1829, Perth's founders chose their city's location for its beauty. They plotted their first few streets in low, rolling hills on the right bank of the Swan River where it broadens almost into a bay just before running into the Indian Ocean. Little did they realize their small start would grow to a thriving metropolitan area with 1 million people.

The first wave of growth and prosperity didn't come until the turn of the century, when gold was discovered east of Perth, in Coolgardie and Kalgoorlie. The second wave has yet to crest; with the recent discovery of iron and other minerals in the north, the city booms anew.

In spite of its growth, Perth retains the beauty that first attracted its founders. Residents still enjoy the Swan River for its swimmable waters, and its banks as public parklands. Throughout Perth, in fact, parks with flower gardens and ornamental lakes soften the harshness of urban concrete and glass.

In town or out, it is easy to be outdoors. The city enjoys a year-round average of 8 hours of sunshine a day, yet temperatures remain mild. Even in the hottest month, February, the thermometer averages a comfortable 24°C/75°F. When temperatures start to soar, a cooling, after-noon sea breeze—affectionately called the "Fremantle Doctor"—regularly blows in from Fremantle on the Indian Ocean. It's no wonder, then, that even the city's musicians and actors move outdoors for part of their seasons, and that the whole populace swims, surfs, sails, or otherwise plays in the sun.

With the city's downtown charms amplified by mile after mile of sweeping sandy beaches along the Indian Ocean, and the Darling Range offering limitless bushwalking possibilities a short distance to the east, it's no wonder Perth is so oriented to the outdoors.

The urban core

Perched on the far edge of Australia, Perth looks toward Asia as well as back to Australia's European or English heritage. The result is a diverse cosmopolitanism reflected in every aspect of life from music to food to sport.

Landmarks. Downtown Perth is a city of old and new. Because of today's prosperity in Western Australia, countless high-rises have sprung up in the downtown area. Preserved in the shadows of these glass and steel towers are some of Perth's first major buildings, richly textured classics painstakingly built by convict labor imported a few years after the city was founded. Many of these reminders of Western Australia's pioneers can be found downtown in the Barrack Street area.

At the corner of Hay and Barrack streets, Perth's Town Hall resembles an English Jacobean market hall complete with clock tower. It was built by convicts between 1867 and 1870. Around the corner on St. George's Terrace is the colonial-style Treasury Building dating from 1874.

Perth's oldest public building, the Old Court House, sits sheltered among trees in the Supreme Court Gardens. Built in 1836, the Georgian-style building today houses the Law Society of Western Australia behind its stately columns.

At the head of tree-lined St. George's Terrace, Barracks Archway stands in front of the modern brick home of the state parliament. Built in Tudor style, the brick arch is all

Christmas decorations add color to Perth's Hay Street Mall. Pedestrian promenade between William and Barrack streets allows car-free shopping and provides umbrella-shaded spots for resting.

that remains of barracks that housed soldier settlers in the 1860s. When Parliament is not in session, visitors can tour Parliament House at 11:15 A.M. and 3:15 P.M. Monday through Friday.

Across the Narrows Bridge in South Perth, the Old Mill, where Perth's first flour was ground, today houses a folk museum of early colonial artifacts. Visitors are welcome on Saturdays from 1 to 4 P.M., and on Sundays, Mondays, Wednesdays, and Thursdays from 1 to 5 P.M.

Museum and art gallery. The Western Australia Museum (entrance on Francis Street) features exhibits from the state's gold rush days, the skeleton of a blue whale, the Mundrabilla meteorite, and an Aboriginal gallery. Perth's first jail, built in 1856, has been extensively restored and is now part of the museum complex. The Old Perth Gaol, one of the city's best examples of colonial architecture, houses historical displays on western Australia's early days.

Hours are 10:30 A.M. to 5 P.M. Monday through Thursday, and 1 to 5 P.M. Friday through Sunday.

Near the museum, you can browse through the Western Australia Art Gallery (47 James Street). The collections include both traditional and contemporary paintings, prints, drawings, and sculptures. The gallery is open daily from 10 A.M. to 5 P.M.

Shoppers' paradise. Opals and other gemstones, Aboriginal arts and crafts, and Western Australian iron ore jewelry are the most distinctively local products. Shops and stores are equally distinctive.

Three blocks of Hay Street, between William and Barrack streets, have been set aside as a pedestrian promenade where shoppers can stroll or stop to relax on seats beneath giant parasols. Where cars once parked, trees in movable pots add a softening touch of greenery.

Branching away from this central mall are traffic-free shopping arcades called Piccadilly, National Mutual,

City, Trinity, Plaza, and Wanamba. London Court is of special note. This narrow walkway may make you feel you have stepped back in time to 16th century London. In it, some 50 small shops are housed in Tudor-style buildings. Noteworthy clocks mark the court's entrances.

Normal shopping hours are from 8:30 A.M. to 5:30 P.M. Monday through Friday, 8:30 A.M. to 1 P.M. on Saturday. Most stores stay open until 9 P.M. on Thursday.

After the sun goes down. During the Festival of Perth—February and March—the city is alive with plays, films, and music in both indoor and outdoor settings. But festival time isn't the only busy time for the performing arts.

The Perth Concert Hall on St. George's Terrace and the Perth Music Shell in Supreme Court Gardens hold concerts by the Western Australia Symphony and other well-known orchestras.

Both the Civic Theatre Restaurant and the Comedy Dinner Theatre offer dinner and live entertainment. The Western Australian Theatre Company performs in the Playhouse Theatre.

On Wellington Street, the 8,000-seat Perth Entertainment Centre hosts performances by pop performers (and is also the site of tennis tournaments and boxing matches). Some of the city's larger hotel cocktail lounges book live entertainment. The Burswood Island Resort casino is one of the world's largest.

A useful source of entertainment possibilities is *This Week in Perth,* available in hotels or from the Western Australian Government Travel Centre.

Things to do outdoors

The people of Perth spend as much time outdoors as they can. The mild climate lends itself to a multitude of recreational endeavors, many of them water-related. Australian Rules football, horse races, yacht races, and lawn bowls are favored spectator sports.

(Continued on page 99)

All aboard the Indian-Pacific

In today's fast-paced world where speedy transportation is the key, it's nice to know that Australia offers visitors a more leisurely form of travel on a great train—the *Indian-Pacific.*

As it makes its runs between Perth and Sydney, this train allows its passengers to really see some of the Australian countryside. During its 3,959-km/2,460-mile journey, the *Indian-Pacific* stops at places like Kalgoorlie, a town with an interesting gold rush past, and streaks across the Nullarbor Plain, a treeless expanse with the longest straight stretch of railroad track in the world.

There are times when you think that Australia's entire

landscape is nothing but clumps of blue green bushes, a scattering of gum trees, and endless red earth. Then the scene from the train window changes and becomes a more pastoral green, with rolling hills and grazing sheep. Throughout the journey, there is always the possibility of spotting Australian wildlife—perhaps even an emu or kangaroo.

Passengers making this 65-hour journey from coast to coast ride in air-conditioned comfort. Both first-class and economy fares include all meals as well as sleepers. Among other luxuries are an observation lounge, bar, and music room complete with a piano.

If you want to climb aboard for a ride on the *Indian-Pacific,* be sure and make your reservations well in advance for this popular trip. The *Indian-Pacific* runs three round trips a week between Perth and Sydney.

The *Trans-Australia Express* makes the run between Perth and Port Pirie two times a week with connections to Adelaide.

Western Australia

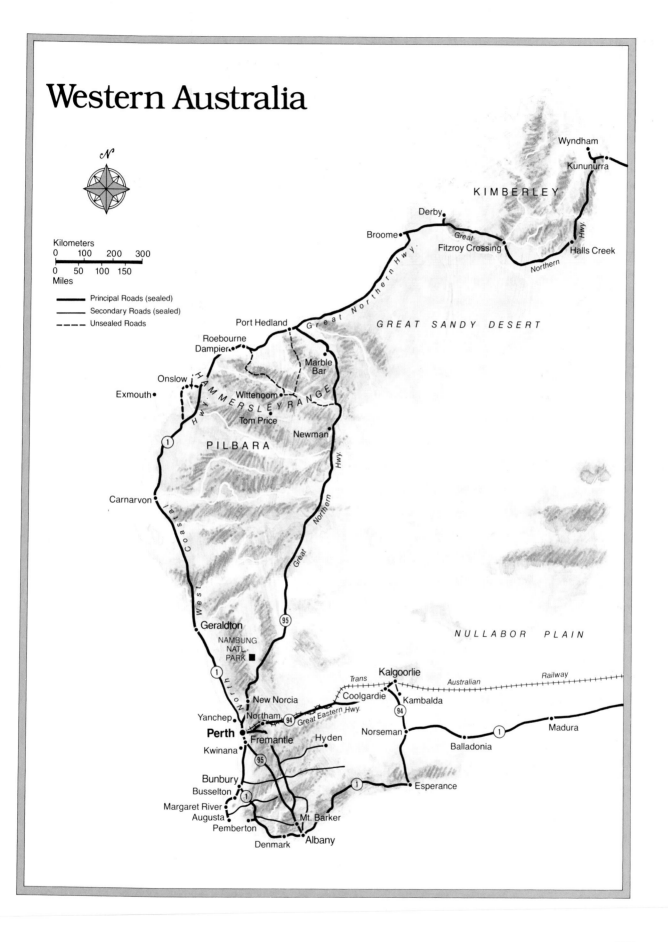

N

Kilometers
0   100   200   300

0   50   100   150
Miles

Principal Roads (sealed)
Secondary Roads (sealed)
Unsealed Roads

KIMBERLEY

Wyndham
Kununurra

Derby
Broome
Great Fitzroy Crossing
Northern Halls Creek
Hwy.

GREAT SANDY DESERT

Great Northern Hwy.

Port Hedland
Roebourne
Dampier
Onslow
Exmouth
Marble Bar
Wittenoom
Tom Price
HAMMERSLEY RANGE
Newman
Hwy.
PILBARA
Northern
Carnarvon
Great
West Coastal Hwy.

(1)

NULLABOR PLAIN

95

Geraldton
NAMBUNG NATL PARK

Kalgoorlie
Trans Coolgardie Kambalda   *Australian*   Railway
1
New Norcia   94   *Great Eastern Hwy.*   94
Yanchep   Northam
Perth   Norseman   1   Madura
Fremantle   Hyden
Kwinana   Balladonia
95
Bunbury
Busselton   1   Esperance
Margaret River
Augusta   Mt. Barker
Pemberton
Denmark   Albany

High-necked black swans, native to
Australia, eagerly accept food from
cautious visitors at Lake Monger outside
Perth.

Zooming in for a closer look, vacationers
watch boat heading into Lake Argyle.
Australia's largest man-made lake is a
recreation area for bush walking, fishing,
and water sports.

Strolling through the park. Perth offers a variety of verdant parklands. The pride of the city is King's Park—a short bus trip or drive southwest of downtown. The 405-hectare/1,000-acre reserve features both natural and cultivated bushland.

Footpaths and roads wind through the park. You can purchase guidebooks and a map at the entrance kiosk. Mount Eliza, at the northeast end of the park, provides views of Perth and the distant Darling Range.

From August through October, you can delight in a myriad of wildflowers—labeled with wonderfully descriptive names such as bacon and eggs, kangaroo paw, one-sided bottle-bush, and white spider orchid.

At the eastern end of Hay Street, you can retreat into Queen's Gardens with its lakes, footbridges, lily ponds, sloping lawns, and weeping willow trees. Children will adore the Peter Pan statue—a replica of the one in London's Kensington Gardens.

The Zoological Gardens in South Perth house rare native animals in a garden setting. Don't miss the walk-through aviary, the wallaby enclosure in a bushland setting, and the nocturnal animal house. The zoo is open daily from 10 A.M. to 5 P.M. You can reach the zoo via the Barrack Street ferry or a bus crossing the Narrows Bridge.

Sports to watch. In Perth, as in Melbourne, Adelaide, and Tasmania, Australian Rules football has an avid following: nearly a million spectators a year pack club ovals.

Cricket matches (including International Test Matches) are held at the Western Australia Cricket Association Oval at the end of Hay Street in East Perth.

Saturday horse race meetings—another popular Perth pastime—are held winters at Belmont Park and summers at Ascot. Gloucester Park Raceway in East Perth features Friday evening harness racing October through July. Richmond Raceway in Fremantle also hosts monthly harness races. To see greyhounds racing, go to the Cannington Dog Track on Albany Highway on a Saturday night.

Fun in the sun. Perth is an ideal city in which to enjoy outdoor sports. Water activities head the list.

West of the city stretch miles of Indian Ocean beaches. Skilled surfers will want to check out Cottesloe, City, and Scarborough beaches. For gentler waters try Leighton or North Beach.

The Swan River supports all forms of aquatic sports—yachting, speedboat racing, swimming, canoeing, rowing, and water-skiing. Crawley Beach near the University of Western Australia and Como Beach south of Perth are both ideal for sun-bathing.

Those who fish can work fresh or salt water. Deep-sea catches include blue marlin, mackerel, and tuna. Charter boats berth at Barrack Street Jetty and Fremantle. Freshwater fishers will find good summer trout fishing in rivers and dams south of Perth.

You'll need a license for fresh-water fishing or for catching crayfish and prawns. For more information about licenses and fishing in Western Australia stop by the head office of the Fisheries and Fauna Department at 108 Adelaide Terrace in Perth.

For golf, Wembley—one of a dozen public courses in Perth—is a challenging 18-hole test. For a quick workout, the 9-hole Embleton course serves well.

Public tennis courts are scattered throughout the city. Contact the Perth City Council Parks & Gardens section for information on booking a court.

Downriver to Fremantle

Fremantle, just 19 km/12 miles downriver from Perth, is the city's port and Australia's main western gateway to the Indian Ocean. Yachts competing in the America's Cup challenge races in 1986–87 docked at Fremantle's expanded marina facilities.

Established as a colony in 1829 by Captain Charles H. Fremantle, the town retains the feeling of those early colonial days—narrow streets, a city square with a fountain, and architecture emphasizing Dutch gables and Gothic cloisters. Many of the early stone buildings were built by convict labor.

Museums. The colony's first insane asylum, built in the 1860s, now houses the Fremantle Museum and Arts Centre. The old building, located on Finnerty Street, is considered one of the finest examples of convict colonial architecture in Western Australia.

The museum's exhibits trace Fremantle's colorful history, and the Arts Centre includes displays of ceramics, textiles, and paintings. The museum is open 10:30 A.M. to 5 P.M. Monday through Thursday, and 1 to 5 P.M. Friday through Sunday. The Arts Centre is open 10 A.M. to 5 P.M. daily, and 7 to 9 P.M. Wednesday evenings.

Still another example of Fremantle's early architecture is the Round House Gaol at the end of High Street. Built in the 1830s, this 12-sided building with eight cells served as the colony's first jail. Today, it is a historical museum, open Wednesday through Sunday.

The Martime Museum, in a restored building on Cliff Street, houses memorabilia from wrecked ships, antique weapons, and old photographs. It is open afternoons, Wednesday, and Friday through Sunday.

Fremantle Markets. More than 100 stalls filled with an exotic array of seafood, fruits and vegetables, herbs and spices, and handicrafts lure passers-by into Fremantle Markets at Henderson Street and South Terrace. Operating since 1897, they resemble old European markets. They are open Friday from 9 A.M. to 9 P.M., Saturday from 9 A.M. to 1 P.M., and Sunday from 11 A.M. to 5 P.M.

How to get there. Suburban trains and buses connect Perth and Fremantle. Half-day tours feature a river cruise to Fremantle from Perth.

Escape to Rottnest Island

This popular summer resort lies just offshore from Fremantle opposite the mouth of the Swan River. The tiny, low-lying island offers beautiful beaches and clear waters teeming with colorful marine life.

In 1917 Rottnest was declared a permanent public reserve and wildlife sanctuary. The island is home for the rare marsupial known as a *quokka*. The first Dutch seamen to see this midget-size kangaroo mistook it for a rat, thus the island's name—"Rats' Nest."

From 1850 to 1903, the island served as a penal settlement. Convicts built many of the limestone buildings you'll see in your island exploration.

The essentials

Perth serves as Australia's gateway to the Orient, and so is a busier transportation hub than its isolation might suggest.

Getting there. Perth is served by air, sea, rail, and bus.

Air. International service by Qantas and foreign flag carriers. Domestic flights to and from other states by Ansett, Australian, and East-West airlines. Flights within the state by Skywest and Ansett W.A. airlines. Perth's airport is 11 km/7 miles from downtown; bus and taxi services are available.

Sea. International cruise and passenger/cargo ships call at Fremantle, 19 km/12 miles west of Perth. Taxis, trains, and buses link piers with city center.

Rail. The famous *Indian-Pacific* train connects Sydney with Perth. The *Trans- Australia Express* connects Perth with Port Pirie. (See page 96.)

Bus. Ansett Pioneer, Greyhound, and Deluxe travel between Perth and Adelaide on the Eyre Highway. Hardy visitors may consider driving this same highway, but the desolate Nullarbor Plain makes the trip a grueling one.

Tours. Eastern-based tour operators offer package trips to Perth and rest of Western Australia as supplements to regularly scheduled trips.

Accommodations. Major Perth hotels include the Ansett International, Burswood Island Resort, Merlin, Parmelia Hilton International, Perth Ambassador, Perth Parkroyal, Orchard, Sheraton Perth, and Transit Inn. Fremantle area hotels include the Esplanade Plaza, Observatory City Resort, and Fremantle Tradewinds.

Food and drink. Local seafood is abundant and savory. Try Westralian Dhufish (succulent white meat), rock lobster (locally named crayfish), crab, and tiger prawns. Fare includes ethnic, national, and Asian cuisines.

Local wines from Swan River Valley vineyards include Houghtons and Sandalford. Major local beer is Swan Lager. (Unlicensed restaurants allow customers to bring own bottles for modest corkage fee.)

Getting around. Metropolitan Transport Trust operates bus, train, and ferry services within city and to suburbs as distant as Fremantle. For map and information, visit that office's information bureau, 125 St. George's Terrace. The free clipper-bus service circles the city Monday through Saturday; trips to Perth's scenic spots are made Sunday mornings and afternoons. Ferries to South Perth use Barrack Street Jetty. Taxis are plentiful.

Tours. Full and half-day city tours are available. Also available are tours to Fremantle (see page 99), Rottnest Island (page 99), Swan Valley vineyards (this page), Yanchep Park (this page), Darling Range (this page), and to a number of beach towns south of Perth (page 101).

For more information. Holiday W.A. Travel Centre, 772 Hay Street, Perth 6000.

Accommodations and activities. Even the island's accommodations reflect the history of Rottnest. The Lodge was the original prison complex and the Quokka Arms Hotel was once a summer residence for Western Australia's governors. Other island accommodations include cottages and a camping area where you can rent tents or bring your own camping gear. It's advisable to reserve accommodations well in advance.

Since the island has no private cars, bicycles are the most popular form of transportation. The less energetic can take a half-day bus tour.

How to get there. Ferries and hydrofoils travel daily to Rottnest, many by way of Fremantle. The ferry takes about 2 hours; by hydrofoil it's only 65 minutes. There is also air service to the island from Perth.

Other nearby jaunts

By bus tour or car, it's easy to visit a number of other interesting destinations during your stay in Perth. Here are a few trips you might want to consider.

The Darling Range. A trip to the Darling Range, 26 km/16 miles east of Perth, takes you into the 1,619-hectare/4,000-acre John Forrest National Park. Its scenic drives wind through the park, and hilltop view points provide sweeping vistas out across the plains to the sea. Facilities include a swimming pool, picnic areas, walking tracks, and sport grounds.

This wooded country, laced with streams and waterfalls, and ablaze with wildflowers in spring, was once an Aboriginal camping ground. Nearby is the Mundaring Weir (dam), starting point for a 563-km/350-mile pipeline to the eastern gold fields. The old No. 1 pumping station for the weir has been turned into a museum.

Yanchep Park. This 2,428-hectare/6,000-acre bushland reserve preserves not only wildlife and flora but also beautiful limestone caves. Located only 51 km/32 miles north of Perth, the coastal park has several small hotels, a golf course, tennis courts, a man-made lake, an aquatic entertainment center, and a swimming pool.

Daily tours explore the caves. In Crystal Cave—the main grotto—a quiet underground stream reflects images of stalactites and stalagmites. Other park attractions include a large koala colony and spring wildflower walks.

Swan Valley vineyards. A half-hour trip up the Swan River from central Perth brings you to the heart of Western Australia's wine country. There you can visit over 20 wineries including Houghtons, Sandalford, and Valencia. Bus and boat tours are available from Perth.

Beyond Perth

Perth and its environs, however attractive, are only a small part of Western Australia. The rest includes a southwest coast rich in beach resorts, explorable caves, forests, and wildflowers. To the northwest, colorful fishing villages dot the coast. Inland, rich mineral deposits have resulted in other attractions, and Lake Argyle provides recreational facilities. Due east are gold fields and ghost towns.

Into the southwest

Perth's residents flock to the southwest on vacation. Though they can sun-bathe, swim, surf, fish, sail, and play golf and tennis at home, in the southwest they can enjoy the same pleasures far from city pressures.

The major coastal resort towns all have hotels, motels, caravan parks and campgrounds near their beaches. Bunbury and Busselton are just down the coast from Perth; Augusta sits at the tip of the continent where the Indian Ocean gives way to the Great Australian Bight. Albany is on the bight. All of these towns are served by buses and trains; tour operators even make loop trips of the area.

Spelunkers' paradise. At the southwestern tip of the state stands a limestone cliff riddled with caves for almost 97 km/60 miles.

Along with stalactites and stalagmites, viewers can see rarer shawls—thin sheets of limestone projecting at right angles from the cave walls. Beautiful underground rivers flow through some of these caves, while quiet lakes mirror the fragile beauty of others. Four of these caves—Yallingup, Mammoth, Lake, and Augusta Jewel—have been developed with walkways and lights for tourists.

Hardwood giants. In a rain-soaked region near Pemberton, magnificent forests of karris loom out of the landscape. The karri is a huge species of eucalyptus. One giant, the Gloucester Tree, cradles one of the world's highest natural fire lookouts—61 meters/200 feet above the forest floor.

Wildflower country. Few places can boast such a profusion of wildflowers. Indeed, many of the species are unique to Western Australia.

From August to October, large areas of the southwest are carpeted with brightly colored spring wildflowers. While blue is the predominant color, you'll also see brilliant yellows, pale pinks, and glowing reds. One of the most notable places to find flowers is around Albany.

East to the gold fields

In the 1890s the shout of "Gold" rang out from the tiny communities of Coolgardie and Kalgoorlie, and the rush was on. Eager for riches, prospectors came in droves from the eastern Australian colonies and other parts of the world. From Fremantle, they rode on horseback or in camel-drawn coaches. Many even walked the entire 550 km/342 miles behind their wheelbarrows.

Towns appeared overnight at the peak, when as many as 200,000 prospectors roamed the rolling plains. Once the easy pickings on the surface were gone, these communities died as quickly as they were born. Coolgardie has become a ghost town, leaving Kalgoorlie the only active community.

At the turn of the century, Kalgoorlie's "Golden Mile" was known as one of the world's richest square miles of rock, yielding more than 34 million ounces of gold. Today the take is greatly reduced. But even if the easy pickings are gone, it's still worth looking around. In 1979, a local father and son prospecting team found a nugget weighing about 120 ounces worth $50,000 the day they dug it up. Visitors are allowed to poke about for the price of a miner's right.

For the quieter gold speculators, the former British Arms Hotel, which once housed the miners, now serves the public as the Golden Mile Museum, housing mining memorabilia. A short distance south of town, the Hainault Tourist Mine lets visitors descend 62 meters/203 feet into the earth by elevator on several daily tours.

Coolgardie, located west of Kalgoorlie, is probably Australia's most famous ghost town. Today, all that remains of the roaring boom town of 15,000—once known as the queen of the gold fields—are a few hotels, the Railway Station Museum, the Goldfields Museum, and a few crumbling stone buildings. Coolgardie is currently being restored as a gold rush memorial.

If possible, visit the gold fields during the winter months of June, July, and August. Summers—December through March—can be unbearably hot. Accommodations include campgrounds, small motels, and hotels.

A train rightly called *The Prospector* makes the 8-hour journey from Perth to Kalgoorlie. Passengers on the *Indian-Pacific* or *Trans-Australia Express* trains may stop off at Kalgoorlie. There's also air service from Perth. Local tour operators offer a variety of tours as well.

The remote north

The northern part of Western Australia is a frontier giant just beginning to feel its strength. Machines are beginning to tap rich deposits of iron ore and other minerals that could determine the financial future not only of the state, but also that of all of Australia.

For visitors, the principal charms range along the coast in a series of sweeping beaches and fishing villages. Inland, on the Kimberley Plateau, a manmade lake with nine times more water than Sydney Harbour is the main attraction. The mining district around Pilbara is at once surprisingly civilized and astonishingly beautiful with gorges and other natural scenery.

Nambung National Park. Located 257 km/160 miles north of Perth, Nambung is famous for its Pinnacles Desert. The "pinnacles" studding this coastal desert were once forest trees—but the forest is petrified now, the trees turned into odd-looking limestone pillars by the forces of time, wind, and weather. The pillars range from 1 to 5m/3½ to 17 feet in height; bright white sand surrounds them. Tours from Perth explore this area.

The Kimberley Plateau. The broad, high plains of the plateau have been carved by an unexpected wealth of water into pyramids and other dramatic shapes. But the most unexpected feature of the whole region is Lake Argyle. The harnessing of the Ord River and other northern streams formed the lake, which dwarfs Sydney Harbour. Lake Argyle Tourist Village has ample accommodations.

The Pilbara. The reason behind the quickening development of Western Australia is the mineral wealth buried in the Hamersley Range.

The Hamersley Iron Company's model town called Tom Price has such comforts as public swimming pools and tennis courts to cheer visitors, but the red-rock gorges of the Fortesque River System are the major attraction in this region. A rough but passable mine road between Tom Price and Wittenoom touches the finest gorges: Dales, Wittenoom, Yampire, and Hamersley.

NORTHERN TERRITORY

From the tropics of Darwin to the outback of Alice Springs

Australia's Northern Territory is one of the world's last frontiers. Massive and empty, it stretches roughly 1,600 km/1,000 miles from north to south and 933 km/580 miles east to west. Covering nearly a sixth of Australia's land area, the Northern Territory provides a multitude of scenic contrasts. In the north, commonly referred to as the Top End, there are tropical bushlands and swamps. Farther south is the Centre, in the heart of Australia. Here you'll find the rugged beauty of the MacDonnell Ranges, the massive bulk of Ayers Rock, and a landscape of scrub and gum trees.

Only two towns of any size will be found in the territory—Darwin, the capital on the northern coast, and Alice Springs, in the geographic center of the continent.

Darwin, a tropical capital

Darwin is not only the governmental center for the Northern Territory, it is also the gateway to a land rich in tropical vegetation and wildlife. Within easy reach of the capital, you can visit areas where wild water buffaloes roam and crocodiles bask in the sun.

Nearly half the Top End's residents (65,000) call Darwin home. Darwin is an international gateway to Southeast Asia. It is also a strategic commercial center.

Built on a peninsula on the eastern shore of Port Darwin, the city has not always had a happy history. The town, located in the middle of the Indian Ocean cyclone belt, has been hit directly by devastating cyclones (hurricanes) three times—in 1897, 1937, and most recently in 1974. During World War II, Darwin was the target of numerous Japanese air raids. But like the phoenix, each time the city meets destruction it rises anew.

Today, Darwin is a modern city of well-planned commercial and residential areas, attractive public gardens, recreation parks, and tree-lined streets.

When planning a trip to Darwin, take into account that the Top End has just two seasons—"the Wet" and "the Dry." The season known simply as "the Dry" (April to October) has warm, cloudless days and balmy nights. It's a pleasant time to visit Darwin and its environs. Heavy rains and high humidity, however, prevail during "the Wet" or monsoon season from November through April. Roads become flooded and impassable and excursions impossible.

Sightseeing in Darwin

Darwin offers sightseers modern city buildings; a few historical buildings including the Government House; the N.T. Museum of Arts and Natural Sciences with its historical displays; the Artillery Museum at East Point, complete with World War II blockhouses, command posts, and observation towers; and the Indo Pacific Marine, a collection of tanks filled with sea life.

Parks and gardens. Darwin's 14-hectare/34-acre Botanical Garden features tropical flora—frangipani, hibiscus, coconut palms, poinciana, and bougainvillea. In contrast, Yarrawonga Park, 21 km/13 miles southeast of town, is a small, private zoological garden that allows you a close look at wild water buffaloes, brolgas, emus, dingoes, and snakes.

A little shopping. Darwin's stores offer a wide range of Aboriginal products. The Arnhem Land Aboriginal Art Gallery, corner of Knuckey and Cavenagh streets, carries fabric designs, woodcarvings, and paintings.

Fun in the sun

Warm tropical weather makes Darwin ideal for swimming, skin-diving, water-skiing, sun-bathing, sailing, fishing, and beachcombing. Among the best of the silver-sand beaches are Mindil, Casuarina, and Dripstone. Swimming is impossible, however, between October and May because of the sea wasps (jellyfish) floating near the surface; their poisonous tentacles can produce fatal stings.

Ascending Ayers Rock is only for the physically fit, though chain rail gives climbers a boost. The less active can await companions' return on thoughtfully placed benches at base.

THE CLIMBING OF THE ROCK
IS DIFFICULT AND DANGEROUS.
THE PARK AUTHORITY ACCEPTS
NO RESPONSIBILITY FOR INJURY
OR LOSS OF LIFE TO ANY PERSON.
RESCUE GEAR IS AVAILABLE AT
THE RANGERS OFFICE.

· BY ORDER OF THE BOARD · AL ROSE CHAIRMAN ·

Fishing. Deep-sea fishing is ideal off the coast of Darwin. Catches include queenfish, Spanish mackerel, and coral trout. Fresh-water offerings include barramundi.

Tennis and golf. For information on tennis, contact the Northern Territory Tennis Association on Gilruth Avenue. The Darwin Golf Club on McMillans Road allows public play.

Sports around the clock

The hot climate fails to dampen the Australians' zest for recreation, with some 40 active and spectator sports available. Three codes of football are played. Both men and women compete in hockey. Basketball is played at night; during the day, baseball, cricket, and softball keep people busy.

One event unique to the area is the Beer Can Raft Regatta. The regatta is held in early June each year at Mindil Beach. Some 60 to 80 boats, built only of beer cans or soft drink cans, hold a 1-day regatta. Some are sailing craft, some paddle boats, some speed boats with 100-horse-power motors—all competing in different classes. Some of the boats use six to eight thousand empty cans in their construction, but with Darwin such a hot and thirsty land, there's no real shortage of building material.

Excursions from Darwin

Darwin serves as an excellent base from which to explore the surrounding countryside. Your excursions can include geological and wildlife phenomena and Aboriginal rock paintings.

The outback region of the Northern Territory is a living museum, populated by animals and birds that are—in many cases—the last remaining specimens of some of the world's most unusual wildlife. You can watch emus running through the mulga and saltbush, kangaroos standing up to survey the land, and dingoes circling safari camps like trained dogs. Along the swamp coastline and near water holes, you'll find the air thick with birds. Pelicans catch fish in the shallows of the swamps and long-legged spoonbills dabble in the marshes. Lagoons and northern rivers abound with giant barramundi (a superb table fish), saratago, catfish, mullet, and saw fish.

Darwin tour operators arrange excursions including the best of these attractions, with travel by coach, launch, car, jeep, or light aircraft. For a full listing of trip possibilities, contact the Northern Territory Government Tourist Bureau in Los Angeles (see page 16 for address).

Close-in excursions

Several close-in attractions may be reached on your own, or on a local tour.

Magnetic anthills. These wedge-shaped architectural wonders can be found at Howard and Berry springs, 24 km/15 miles and 64 km/40 miles south of the city. You'll see thousands of these hard mud mounds, some reaching 6 meters/20 feet in height and 2 meters/6 feet in width. White termites (not ants) construct these hill nests on a north/south axis—thus the name ''magnetic anthills.''

Fogg Dam Bird Sanctuary. Thousands of birds gather in and around the water lily-covered reservoir of this sanctuary, 58 km/36 miles southeast of Darwin. Nearby, wild buffalo tread the open plains. Sunrise is a good time to visit the sanctuary—just before the light of day, an eerie quiet pervades the area. As the sun brightens the landscape, this quiet gives way to a deafening sound of animals awakening to a new day.

Nearby are the remains of an experimental rice farm at Humpty Doo.

Aboriginal rock paintings

Among the wild red rocks and forests of the Northern Territory, Aborigines dream of times now past. Their cultural roots in Australia go back more than 30,000 years—that's how long ago scientists think the first Aborigines began to arrive from the north.

The Aborigines recorded their dreamtime (beginnings of time) with paintings on cave walls and on the sides of smooth cliffs beneath outcroppings. These were the same places where elders instructed young men in tribal ways, and where a *corroboree* (dance festival) enacted their story in music and dance.

The rock paintings were made with colors created by mixing pulverized rock with water—yielding white, red, brown, pink, and yellow ocher. There seems to be two styles of art: X-raylike paintings depicting both internal and external organs, and realistic paintings. The paintings chronicled great hunts and included intricate designs involving kangaroos and other marsupials. Some portrayed misfortunes, which the artists blamed on a colorful array of evil spirits or on the half-human, half-animal ancestral beings they believed were the inhabitants at the beginning of time.

Tribesmen claim that many of the older, single-line drawings were not done by men at all but by a spirit people called Mimi. They were credited with the ability to melt into cliffs by blowing on the rocks and to leave their shadows on the wall.

For centuries, retouching and new rock painting kept alive the myths of the secret places. With the shifting of tribes and passing of elders, though, many of the secrets of the Aborigines remain locked within the paintings.

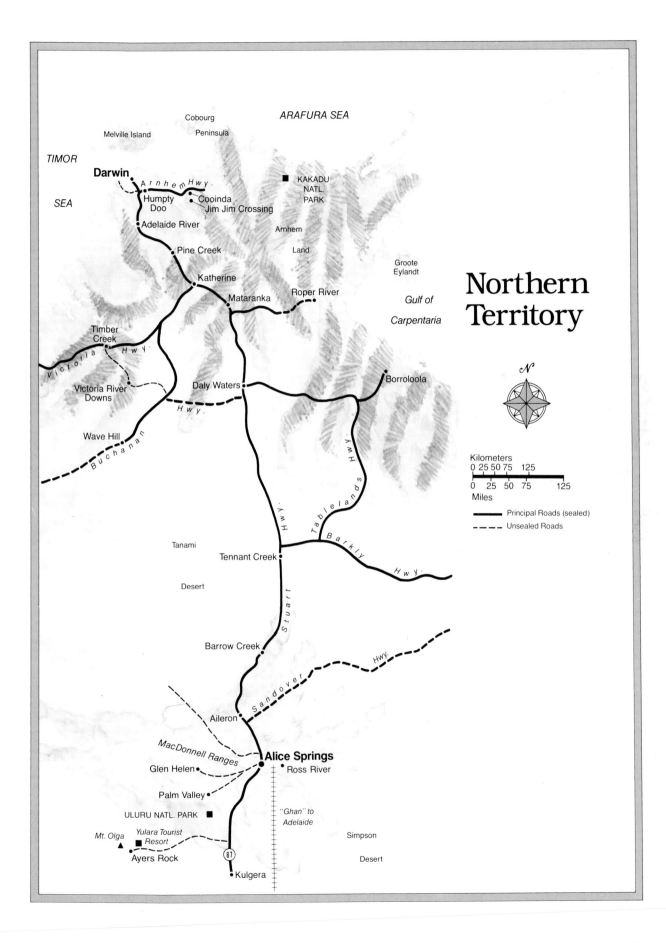

TIMOR

SEA

ARAFURA SEA

Cobourg
Peninsula

Melville Island

Darwin

Arnhem Hwy.

Humpty
Doo

Cooinda
Jim Jim Crossing

KAKADU
NATL.
PARK

Adelaide River

Arnhem

Pine Creek

Land

Katherine

Groote
Eylandt

Mataranka

Roper River

Gulf of

Carpentaria

Timber
Creek

Victoria _Hwy._

Daly Waters

Borroloola

Victoria River
Downs

Hwy.

Wave Hill

Buchanan

Tanami

Tablelands Hwy.

Barkly

Hwy.

Tennant Creek

Desert

Stuart Hwy.

Barrow Creek

Sandover _Hwy._

Aileron

MacDonnell Ranges

Alice Springs

Glen Helen

Ross River

Palm Valley

ULURU NATL. PARK

"Ghan" to
Adelaide

Mt. Olga

_Yulara Tourist
Resort_

Simpson

Ayers Rock

(87)

Desert

Kulgera

Northern
Territory

_N_

Kilometers

0 25 50 75   125

0   25   50   75   125

Miles

———— Principal Roads (sealed)

- - - - Unsealed Roads

Bottomless boat races are a feature along dry bed of the Todd River (below) at Alice Springs. This annual Henley-on-Todd Regatta was once cancelled because of water.

At Katherine Gorge, flatbottom excursion boats take passengers gliding through waterways edged by high cliffs. Aboriginal paintings cover canyon walls.

Ancient Aboriginal rock paintings awe visitors in Kakadu National Park. Fascinating art is believed to be more than 30,000 years old.

Kakadu National Park. The dry season (May through October) is the best time to visit this World Heritage List national park. Located 150 km/93 miles east of Darwin, this area is noted for its abundance of wildlife including birds, kangaroos, wallabies, and water buffaloes. The park's landscape includes marshlands, a eucalyptus forest, escarpments, and waterfalls.

The Aboriginal paintings found at Nourlangie Rock Artsite and Ubirr (Obiri Rock) Artsite are prime attractions. There's also a boat cruise on the Yellow Waters Lagoon, home of saltwater crocodiles.

You can reach Kakadu National Park via the Arnhem Highway. Accommodations include campgrounds and two motels. In addition to local coach and flightseeing tours from Darwin, many Northern Territory tours, featuring Ayers Rock, Alice Springs, Katherine, and Darwin, also include Kakadu National Park in their itineraries.

Katherine & Katherine Gorge

The town of Katherine, 354 km/220 miles south of Darwin, is the gateway to Katherine Gorge National Park. Here you'll find hotel, motel, and caravan park accommodations. There's also tourist park accommodations 13 km/8 miles from the gorge at the Springvale Homestead. Built in 1878, this homestead on the Katherine River is thought to be the area's oldest building.

You can reach Katherine by air or express bus from Alice or Darwin.

Katherine Gorge is located 35 km/22 miles northeast of Katherine. It features waterways edged by 61-meter/200-foot cliffs. During the dry season, 2-hour flatbottom boat tours take you along the Katherine River through the gorge. Canyon walls have Aboriginal paintings; trees grow at strange angles; and bird nests are tucked away small caves. Other canyon wildlife includes kangaroos, wallabies, crocodiles, dingoes, and echidna. The park also has a number of marked walking trails.

A town called Alice

"Down the track" from Darwin lies Alice Springs, the Northern Territory's other major town. Located in the center of the continent, isolated Alice Springs is surrounded by Australia's outback—a vast wilderness of spinifex grass, mulga trees, and rambling cattle stations. Alice's nearest neighbor of any size to the south is Adelaide, 1,320 km/820 air miles away. Darwin is 1,532 km/952 road miles to the north.

An oasis in Australia's "Red Heart," Alice is an attractive town of 25,000 nestled in a bowl of ancient, weather-carved red rock mountains. Its main streets are lined with modern buildings of concrete and glass.

For the visitor, Alice Springs is a "two-stage" town. The first stage concerns points of interest in the town itself, and the second, attractions in the surrounding area.

The tourist season for Alice Springs extends from April to October, a period of warm days (about 27°C/80°F), little humidity, and cool evenings—much like the winter season in Arizona. Days are clear and bright with about 9 hours of sunlight. During the rest of the year, temperatures soar to 38°C/100°F and above.

Exploring the town

Alice is a compact town, easily explored on your own or on a half-day tour. You might want to begin your exploration on Anzac Hill where you'll get a panoramic view of the city. The following are some other sights you'll want to explore.

The Old Telegraph Station. Alice Springs really began 3 km/2 miles from its current location. An overland telegraph repeater station was established here in 1872. The nearby water hole was named Alice Springs after the wife of the superintendent of telegraphs, Charles Todd. The tiny town which sprang up near this telegraph station was called Stuart. When the post office moved to Stuart, the town's name was changed to Alice Springs.

Today, the buildings of the old telegraph station—in operation from 1872 to 1932—have been restored and are part of a national park. The park—a favorite with picnickers—is open from 9 A.M. to 7 P.M. daily.

Royal Flying Doctor Service. The Flying Doctor base is located on Stuart Terrace between Todd and Simpson streets. From here, doctors give medical advice by radio to ranchers a long distance away. When needed, these doctors can fly in light aircraft to the scene of an emergency. The base is open for tours weekdays and Saturday mornings.

School of the Air. Two-way radios at the outback cattle stations are used for education as well as for emergency medical information. From the School of the Air headquarters on Head Street, school lessons are broadcasted to station children in remote areas. On weekday afternoons between 1:30 and 3:30, you can hear tapes of children at outback homesteads as they take part in lessons conducted by two-way radio.

Panorama Guth. The beauty of Central Australia is captured in an extraordinary circular (360°), 61-meter/200-foot painting exhibited in this gallery. Dutch artist Henk Guth created it to be viewed from a specially constructed platform. The floor in front of the painting is covered with rolling sand hills and shrubbery, adding dimension to the artwork.

Pitchi Richi. This unusual name belongs to a most unusual bird sanctuary 3 km/2 miles south of town. Here you'll find some of the dreamlike sculptures of William Ricketts. Placed in an outdoor setting of trees and rocks, his sculptures of Aborigines possess a haunting beauty. (The William Ricketts Sanctuary near Mt. Dandenong in Victoria also features sculptures by this famous Australian artist.)

Open 9 A.M. to 5 P.M. daily, Pitchi Richi also serves as an open-air museum for pioneer equipment.

Emily Gap Camel Farm. It hasn't been that long since Alice was supplied by camel caravans. These "ships of the desert" were the prime means of transportation for explorers, prospectors, and other pioneers in the area during the 19th century. When motorized vehicles finally came to the Centre, the camels were released to run wild. It's estimated that more than 20,000 camels roam wild today in the outback.

The Emily Gap Camel Farm just outside Alice has recaptured and domesticated some of these camels. You can ride a camel here. It's open daily from 8 A.M. to 5 P.M.

Araluen Arts Centre. Just minutes from downtown Alice is the town's art center; its definitely "outback" architecture blends well with the surrounding landscape. In addition to an art gallery, the center contains a 500-seat theater, a convention center, and a bistro.

Close to the arts center, you'll find the Central Australian Aviation Museum.

Shops in Alice are normally open from 9 A.M. to 5:30 P.M. Monday through Friday, and Saturday morning from 9 A.M. to noon. Some shops extend hours to 9 P.M. on Friday nights.

The essentials

The information below will help you plan your trip.

Getting there. The Northern Territory is served by air, rail, and bus.

Air. Regularly scheduled flights by Ansett and Australian airlines travel to and from most state capitals into Darwin and Alice Springs. Air New South Wales and East-West Airlines fly to Ayers Rock from Sydney. Ansett N.T. flies within the Northern Territory and to Ayers Rock from Alice Springs. International service into Darwin by Qantas and foreign-flag carriers. Each town's airport is about a 20-minute trip from downtown.

Rail. The interstate train providing regular service to Alice Springs from Adelaide with connections from other state capitals is *The Ghan.*

Bus. Ansett Pioneer, Greyhound, and Deluxe have service between Alice Springs and Adelaide with connecting service to more distant capitals. All three companies travel between Alice and Darwin, and Alice and Ayers Rock.

Accommodations. Major hotels in Darwin: Sheraton Darwin, Beaufort Darwin, Diamond Beach Hotel-Casino, Four Seasons Darwin, Darwin Travelodge, and Rodeway Phoenix. In Alice Springs: Lasseters Casino Hotel, Sheraton Alice Springs, Four Seasons Alice Springs, Gap Motor Hotel, Territory Motor Inn, and Oasis Motel. In the Yulara Tourist Resort at Ayers Rock: Sheraton Ayers Rock, and Four Seasons Ayers Rock.

Food and drink. Darwin's local specialty is barramundi, a fresh-water fish with a delicate flavor. Other local specialties in the Northern Territory include buffalo steaks and dates grown near Alice. Chateau Hornsby, located 15 km/9 miles southeast of Alice Springs, is Central Australia's only winery.

Getting around. Alice Springs has no public transport, but there are plenty of taxis. Darwin has bus service as well as taxis. Both towns are easily explored on foot.

Tours. Tours of Alice Springs include city sights, MacDonnell Ranges' attractions, and Ayers Rock. Special camel treks are also available, including a trip to Chateau Hornsby for lunch or dinner. Tours of Darwin can include Kakadu National Park and Katherine Gorge.

For more information. The Northern Territory Government Tourist Bureau offices are located at 31 Smith Street, Darwin 5790 and 51 Todd Street, Alice Springs 5750.

Sports to enjoy

You can enjoy a game of golf at the 18-hole Alice Springs Golf Club, or hire a public tennis court at Traeger Park (courts can be reserved at the Council offices on Hartley Street). If you enjoy spectator sports, you'll be glad to know that Alice Springs residents are avid followers of Australian Rules football and competitions are held on Sundays, April through September, at the Traeger Park sporting complex.

Horse racing is another favorite. Every Saturday the horses race at the Central Australian Racing Club south of town. Picnic race meetings, held annually, are a real social occasion for those who live in the sparsely populated outback. Picnic race meetings are held in May at Aileron and Renner Springs, in June at Barrow Creek and Brunette Downs, and in early August at Harts Range. Often the picnic is as important as the horse race.

Other Alice Springs spectator sports include baseball, cricket, and rugby.

Festival time

Rousing, rollicking annual events in Alice Springs include the Bangtail Muster and Camel Cup in May, and the Henley-on-Todd Regatta in early October.

Bangtail Muster. The name Bangtail Muster dates back to the early cattle station practice of cutting the tips off the tails of cattle. After mustering, these tips were collected and counted to determine the number of cattle being shipped. Events at a Bangtail Muster include a light-hearted procession and a series of sporting events.

Camel Cup. This event features a full day of camel races. The results of some of the races can be hilarious since camels can be quite unpredictable. Parties and fireworks follow the races.

Henley-on-Todd Regatta. This "regatta" is held in the dry river bed of the Todd River which "flows" through Alice Springs. It consists of a full program of "aquatic" events—races of skiffs, yachts, and bottomless canoes—but minus the water. Instead of wind or oar power, these makeshift craft are propelled over the course by the legs of their occupants. A highlight of the regatta is the Australia Cup—a battle between yachts representing Australia, the United States, and other international competitors.

Excursions from Alice

The MacDonnell Ranges—running in dramatic parallel ridges east and west of Alice—harbor tree-shaded canyons, steep-walled chasms, deep reflecting pools, and stands of stark, white-barked ghost gums. Beyond the drama of these mountains, visitors can travel further south to awesome Ayers Rock and the Olgas.

Roads to all of the closer MacDonnell Ranges' attractions are paved. Other attractions are reached by dirt road and, in some cases, four-wheel-drive track. The best way to see many of the attractions is on a tour. Alice Springs tour operators offer both short and long tours to points of interest in the MacDonnells. You can tour Ayers Rock by air, air and coach, or coach.

East of Alice

Although much of the MacDonnell Ranges are west of Alice Springs, the East MacDonnells have both scenic and historic value.

Emily and Jessie gaps. Just 8 km/5 miles east of Alice is the natural break of Emily Gap. Steep, jagged cliffs rise from a narrow sandy plain flooded by Emily Creek during heavy rains.

Another 11 km/7 miles east is Jessie Gap—another dramatic cut in the Heavitree Ranges of the MacDonnells. In your exploration of the MacDonnell Ranges, you'll discover that gaps like Emily and Jessie are common. Each cleft in these rocky mountains has its own character and beauty.

Trephina Gorge. Beautiful red cliff walls soar above the broad, sandy expanse of Trephina Creek in this reserve 80 km/50 miles east of Alice. Huge red gum trees line the usually dry creek bed. Nearby are the John Hayes Rockholes where steep rock walls shelter a series of inviting pools.

Ross River Homestead. If the prospect of a visit to a central Australian "dude" ranch appeals to you, try a stay at the Ross River Homestead located about 80 km/50 miles east of Alice Springs. A stay here offers time to see the East MacDonnells, and experience ranch life including horseback riding and a bush barbecue complete with damper bread and billy tea.

Your accommodations are rustic, comfortable cabins and you dine in the old Love's Creek Homestead—a whitewashed mud and stone-wall home built in 1898.

To the west of Alice

A series of dramatic gorges lie west of Alice. As with sights in the East MacDonnells, access to points of interest is not always by paved road.

Simpsons Gap National Park. Just 19 km/12 miles west of Alice is this gap with walls that soar to 150 meters/492 feet in height. Rock wallabies live here.

Standley Chasm. The walls of this spectacular chasm are no more than 5 meters/18 feet apart at their widest point. Midday, when the sun reaches into this narrow chasm, these walls glow a brilliant red and gold. Standley Chasm is 53 km/33 miles west of Alice Springs.

Glen Helen Gorge. The Finke River cuts through this gorge with its scenic rock formations 132 km/82 miles west of Alice. In addition to magnificent scenery, there are lodge accommodations.

Ormiston Gorge. Some say this feat of nature, 132 km/82 miles west of Alice, is more impressive than the Grand Canyon. Towering red and purple rock walls are reflected in permanent pools. In places the floor of this gorge is a chaotic jumble of huge boulders, worn into rounded shapes by Ormiston Creek—a raging torrent when it floods.

Finke Gorge (Palm Valley) National Park. About 145 km/90 miles west of Alice, the Finke River has carved out a huge rock canyon of rich red walls. Groves of lush prehistoric palm trees—some believed to be 5,000 years old—thrive in this canyon. A natural rock amphitheater in the valley is the site of many ancient Aboriginal rituals.

Ayers Rock, a massive monolith

The huge bulk of Ayers Rock rises abruptly from a flat plain 451 km/280 miles southwest of Alice Springs. It looms above the plain like a sleeping monster, some 348 meters/1,143 feet high with a perimeter of 8½ km/5½ miles. It is one of the world's largest monoliths—a spectacular natural wonder.

Touring the Rock. You can experience the majesty of the Rock on a walking, coach, aerial, or car tour.

Aborigines called it "Uluru" and considered it a holy place surrounded by legends. You can see Aboriginal rock paintings in some of the caves at its base. Actually, this monolithic wonder is pitted with caves, depressions, crevices, and holes carved by wind and weather. When it rains, water quickly fills the depressions near the top and then cascades down the Rock's sides in glistening waterfalls. To appreciate its spectacular colors, view the Rock at either sunrise or sunset. At these times, if the sun isn't covered by clouds, the Rock will glow a brilliant red.

Climbing the Rock. For the fit, climbing Ayers Rock is an important part of the "visit to the Rock" ritual. On the Rock's western face, a path has been marked to the top. There's also a sign at the start of the climb warning people that it can be dangerous; this is especially true when the Rock is wet or there are strong winds. Rubber-soled shoes are a must.

The first section of the climb is made easier by a post-and-chain safety rail along the steepest section of the Rock. A faded white line then marks the way along the last two-thirds of the trek which includes the negotiation of some steep holes and valleys. Only some of these depressions have helpful post-and-chain safety rails. At the summit, you can sign a guest book, rest, and enjoy the views below—endless flat plains and red sand dunes covered with spinifex, mulga, eucalyptus, and desert oak, relieved by the domes of the Olgas in the middle distance. The way down isn't much easier than the climb up, and it's not uncommon to see people clinging to the chain rail while they slowly make the last section of the steep descent on the seat of their pants.

The Olgas

About 32 km/20 miles west of Ayers Rock rise the spectacular domes of the Olgas. This group of more than 30 smooth-faced, dome-shaped monoliths of varying sizes separated by deep ravines covers a 36-square-km/14-square-mile area. Mount Olga, the largest, rises 549 meters/1,800 feet above the plains.

There are coach tours from Ayers Rock to the Olgas.

Both Ayers Rock and the Olgas are part of Uluru National Park. In years past, many park visitors traveled round-trip from Alice Springs, an arduous journey. Accommodations at Ayers Rock were few and rustic. Today, the Yulara Tourist Resort complex, 20 km/12 miles northwest of Ayers Rock, has modern accommodations, restaurants, and shops. The resort was built outside the park's boundary to protect the environment.

GREAT
BARRIER
REEF

A watery wonderland of coral reefs & tropical islands

Most maps of the world show a dotted line off the northeast coast of Australia, running from the continent's waistline all the way north to Papua New Guinea. Labeled the "Great Barrier Reef," it encompasses a series of coral reefs, shoals, cays, and islands–the biggest collection of coral in the world, 2,012 km/1,250 miles long and ranging in width from 16 km/10 miles to 241 km/150 miles.

Most of the vast area enclosed by the Great Barrier Reef is water. A long series of detached reefs—true coral islands (some submerged, many awash with booming surf, a very few topped with sand and perhaps some shrubbery and trees)—define the eastern edge or Outer Reef.

Between the mainland and the Outer Reef is a north-south passage dotted with rock-and-soil islands, once part of the mainland's coast ranges. Most of these larger, high-rise islands (tops of partly submerged mountains) also have coral reefs in the water around them. Of the island tourist destinations listed in this chapter, only Green and Heron islands and the Low Isles are true coral cays; Lizard Island, though situated on the Outer Reef, is a continental island.

At its northern end (along the Cape York Peninsula) the Outer Reef is barely 10 km/6 miles offshore; to the south, opposite Gladstone, the reef lies 100 km/62 miles or more from the coast.

Barrier Reef ecology. The unassuming architects of this "eighth wonder of the world" are coral polyps, colonies of tiny anemonelike creatures thriving in the tropical waters off the Queensland coast. Succeeding generations secrete protective limestone shells upon the skeletons of their forebearers, but at such a slow rate that the creation of the Great Barrier Reef took millions of years.

As in other habitats, a fierce, competitive, yet finely balanced food chain exists among the many creatures of the reef. Sharks and turtles feed on lesser marine life; the survivors feed on still smaller creatures, and so on.

Unfortunately, something went very haywire in nature's balance of feeder and food on the reef. A sudden incursion of crown-of-thorns starfish, the coral's worst enemy, wiped out entire coral communities. Government skin divers fought and destroyed about 50,000 of the spiny invaders before too big a dent was made in the reef. According to some environmentalists, the imbalance was caused by the over-hunting of the giant triton clam (a natural enemy of the starfish and prized for its shell) and by pollutants carried to reef waters by Queensland rivers.

When to visit. Time and tide are important if you're going to make the most of any reef visit. Weatherwise, late August through November is best for cruising, "reefing" (wandering along the exposed coral barrier), and viewing; some say May is good. At all times, winds are unpredictable. Caution is advised from late November through March when coastal beaches can be plagued with venomous sea wasps (jelly fish); and January through March is monsoon season, with winds at their worst.

The reef puts on its best monthly show during the full or new moon, when the tide is at its lowest. Tide tables are published in advance for the year. For reef walking, check tide depths; low tide on the reef usually means a foot or so of water—more than 1½ feet makes difficult walking. Snorkelers and scuba divers can see even more of the underwater wonders of the reef; in some places, the reef is a vertical wall of living coral. Glass-bottom boats and semi-submersible viewing vessels make it easy to see coral while staying dry.

Reef offerings

Island resorts between the mainland and Outer Reef—as well as numerous scheduled cruises, sightseeing trips,

Setting sail from Shute Harbour on the northern Queensland coast, boat heads through Whitsunday Passage toward island resorts along the Great Barrier Reef.

and package tours—make it easy to enjoy the wondrous Great Barrier Reef.

Planning your stay is important. Visitors can decide on a cruise among the islands, a flight around the reef, or a resort stay at one or more islands.

Reef walking is a revelation to those who have never done it—a chance to actually see coral formations and marine life first hand. Giant sea clams spit water at you, plants shrink inward if touched, and sea anemones wave wickedly. Best color and formation are at the reef's outer edge—a solid coral runway interspersed with pools of stranded multi-colored fish.

When exploring, wear rubber-soled shoes—coral cuts are painful, infect easily, and heal slowly. Walk carefully

The essentials

Here is basic travel information to help you reach and explore the gateway cities to the Great Barrier Reef.

Getting there. The gateway cities are served by air, rail, and coach.

Air. Ansett, Australian, and East-West airlines provide daily flights from the south, primarily via Brisbane, to Cairns, Townsville, and other tropical centers. Air Queensland and Air Whitsunday provide service within the state. Both Cairns and Townsville have international airports. Qantas flies to Cairns from the U.S. west coast (via Honolulu).

Rail. Australia's extensive rail system reaches as far north as Cairns. The Sunlander and Queenslander operate between Brisbane and Cairns on a regular basis; the Sunlander making the trip in 37 hours and the Queenslander in 34 hours. The Capricornian journeys between Brisbane and Rockhampton in 14 hours.

Bus. Ansett Pioneer, Greyhound, and Deluxe coachlines travel daily between Brisbane and Cairns, making intermediate stops along the Queensland coast.

Accommodations. Major Cairns hotels include the Pacific International, Tuna Towers, Ramada Reef, Kewarra Beach, Four Seasons Cairns, and Quality Inn-Harbourside; in Townsville try the Sheraton Breakwater Hotel-Casino, Townsville International, and Townsville Travelodge. (For island resorts, see pages 115–117.) Book all accommodations in advance.

Food and drink. The area's specialties are fresh seafood and fresh tropical fruit. The price of island accommodations generally includes full board.

Getting around. Island resorts are reached by plane, helicopter, or launch from nearby coastal cities. Boats and local airlines make regular trips to the Outer Reef from coastal cities and island resorts.

Tours. Coastal Queensland and Great Barrier Reef island tours depart from Brisbane and major cities.

For more information. Check with the Queensland Government Travel Centre, 12 Shields Street, Cairns, 4870, or the Far North Queensland Promotion Bureau Ltd., 44 McLeod Street, Cairns 4870.

and test the coral for solidity before putting your weight on it. Do not disturb formations, and replace anything turned over. If you plan to touch anything, it's a good idea to wear gloves. And don't break off a piece of coral—it's protected by law.

Cruising the reef

Great Barrier cruises—4 to 5 days in length—sail through the Whitsunday Passage calling at resort island beaches and exploring reef areas.

The M.V. *Elizabeth E* sails from Mackay Harbour Mondays and returns Thursdays, and the M.V. *Roylen Endeavor* sails Mondays and returns Fridays. Both visit Whitsunday islands and reef areas. The M.V. *Coral Princess* departs Townsville Mondays, returning on Fridays. This trip includes visits to Hinchinbrook and Dunk islands, a 2-night stay on Magnetic Island, and reef viewing in the *Yellow Submarine*. Special packages are available that include the standard cruise plus additional nights at a resort.

One-day cruises to the Outer Reef depart regularly from island resorts as well as Queensland coastal towns.

Reef flightseeing

Many visitors discover that the most dramatic way to experience the beauty of the reef—other than gliding through its waters as a skin diver—is to skim the surface in a low-flying plane or helicopter.

Between the Queensland coastal cities and the Outer Reef, passengers get a memorable view of transparent, iridescent waters revealing the mass of coral beneath. Thousands of islands, heaps of coral sand, and lagoon-crowned reefs sparkling like gems can be seen along the deep channel-threaded waterway.

Seaplanes fly out to the reef at low tide. Reef walkers are transferred to a boat and ferried to a point on the coral platform where they can step ashore.

Underwater observatories

Visitors who want to see the reef's underwater life without getting their feet wet will enjoy the Underwater Coral Observatory adjacent to Hook Island in Whitsunday Passage.

Sunk in the midst of inner coral reefs, the steel chamber of the all-weather, air-conditioned, carpeted observatory has a viewing floor 10 meters/32 feet below deck level. Through its huge glass windows, visitors enjoy an extraordinary underwater view of coral polyps, exotically colored tropical fish, and other sea life, all undisturbed in their natural habitat.

Another coral observatory is on Green Island, off Cairns (see page 115). It is not as large as the Underwater Coral Observatory, but it boasts views of even more spectacular formations and reef life.

Island life

On the resort islands, life revolves around the sea, the tides, the reef, and cruising. Varied activities mingle to create a fascinating vacation. You can go reefing (if the weather and tides are right) or sports fishing; sailing, windsurfing, or snorkeling; take a lazy swim or go skin diving; go for a long walk on the beach or climb hills lush with pine forests, rain forests, or bush; do a little bird watching; or just sit under a coconut palm and watch the surf.

Evening entertainment ranges from luaus to nightclub shows and dancing. Some islands feature guided reef-walking tours and bird watching. Some resorts offer tennis, golf, and even horseback riding.

Away from the hotel, you will find your island much the way nature left it. A National Parks Act protects flora and fauna; trails are well-kept and markers unobtrusive; native bush and birds are undisturbed.

Island dress is casual. The atmosphere is casual, easy, and relaxed. Visitors roam the islands in swimsuits, loose shirts or shifts, and thongs (or bare feet).

For reefing, wear rubber-soled sandals, tennis shoes, or even boots. As we've mentioned previously, coral cuts are painful, infect easily, and heal slowly. Slacks and long-sleeved shirts provide additional protection against scrapes and cuts should you slip and fall.

Island vacationers may also want a shade hat, sun glasses, large beach towel, a sweater for cool evenings or late launch outings, flashlight, camera, lightweight raincoat, and suntan lotion. Many islands have a shop where you may pick up miscellaneous items, in addition to coral specimens, shells, and shell jewelry.

Resorts, plain and fancy. Accommodations run the gamut from rustic to modern, but there are no high rises. A few islands are limited to salt-water showers.

Relaxed comfort rather than luxury is the keynote, with a few notable exceptions. Daily rates per person vary; most but not all resorts include all meals in their rates. Usually each island has only one resort, reinforcing the atmosphere of restful isolation.

Island resorts serve a full range of food, with emphasis on fish of all kinds and tropical fruit. If you like, you can gather some of the huge local oysters yourself, eating them raw or tossing them into a fire to steam.

During winter (April through September), the reef islands and adjacent coast are prime vacation spots for Australians, so reservations should be made well in advance. Some resorts close down from January to March; others lower their rates during off-season.

Your travel agent can be helpful in arranging your accommodations and transportation. Full schedules and booking information can be obtained from the Queensland Tourist and Travel Corporation in Los Angeles (see page 16).

For the sports-minded

Island resorts and gateway cities offer a wide range of activities for the ocean lover. Game fishing is spectacular; diving gets you down into the life of the reef; and boating on your own lends mobility.

Game fishing. Whether you've been fishing for years or have yet to experience the thrill of your first strike, the Great Barrier Reef ranks among the world's best places to enjoy the sport. An ever-increasing number of game fishers, attracted by record catches of black marlin and sailfish, are drawn to this area.

The major deep-sea fishing center for Great Barrier Reef

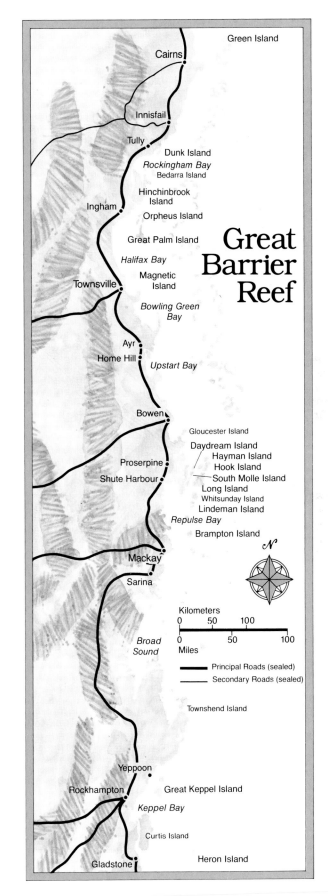

Great Barrier Reef

Green Island
Cairns
Innisfail
Tully
Dunk Island
Rockingham Bay
Bedarra Island
Hinchinbrook Island
Ingham
Orpheus Island
Great Palm Island
Halifax Bay
Magnetic Island
Townsville
Bowling Green Bay
Ayr
Home Hill
Upstart Bay
Bowen
Gloucester Island
Daydream Island
Hayman Island
Proserpine
Hook Island
Shute Harbour
South Molle Island
Long Island
Whitsunday Island
Lindeman Island
Repulse Bay
Brampton Island
Mackay
Sarina
Kilometers
0   50   100
0   50   100
Miles
Broad Sound
━━━ Principal Roads (sealed)
─── Secondary Roads (sealed)
Townshend Island
Yeppoon
Rockhampton   Great Keppel Island
Keppel Bay
Curtis Island
Gladstone   Heron Island

Low tide reveals wonders of
Green Island's coral reef. Resort
islands off the Queensland coast
offer easy-going vacations that
revolve around the sea.

Divers discover an underwater coral world
miles from shore. Amphibians fly from
coast for reef exploring.

waters is Cairns, with its big boating complex. Townsville and Innisfail are well equipped for the sport, and several Great Barrier Reef resorts operate game-fishing launches. For more information on boat charters, contact the Queensland Government Travel Centre, 196 Adelaide Street, Brisbane 4000.

More than a dozen species of game fish flourish in reef waters: barracuda, black marlin, sailfish, wahoo, giant trevally, yellowfin tuna, dogtooth tuna, cobia, rainbow runner, barramundi, threadfin, Australian salmon, small tuna, and Spanish mackerel (kingfish).

Spanish mackerel increase in coastal waters between Gladstone and Mackay from April to June, and farther north between Townsville and Cairns from July to September, when sailfish also seem to peak. Giant black marlin (1,000 to 2,000 lbs.) begin to appear at Cairns in late August and September, continuing until early December. Barracuda season usually starts in August and peaks in December.

Diving. Getting down along the reef appeals to many divers. The water temperature is pleasant, and the underwater world is alive with tempting coral displays and multitudinous marine life. Island resorts often supply equipment, including air for tanks. In addition to island diveboats and day diveboats departing from the mainland, there are live-on-board diveboats for longer trips.

Boating on your own. All major ports on the Queensland coast, and many island resorts, offer vessels for charter. The largest number of boat rentals in northern Queensland are found between Shute Harbour and Cairns.

After a checkout of your sailing expertise and experience you can self-skipper a boat with a "bareboat" charter or participate in a skippered program.

The gateway cities

From Lizard Island in the north to the Capricorn Islands opposite Gladstone, a number of tropical island resorts provide bases for reef exploring. Access to the islands is via a series of coastal cities—first Cairns (northernmost gateway), then Townsville, Proserpine (rhyming with *porcupine*), Mackay (usually pronounced to rhyme with *eye*), Rockhampton, and Gladstone. These cities are reached by plane, train, and express coach service from Brisbane.

The busy port of Cairns

Cairns—itself a popular winter tourist resort, busy port, and commercial center—is the departure point for trips to Lizard and Green islands; for some interesting jaunts into tropical jungle country; for day cruises; for diving excursions; and for expeditions in search of the fighting deep-sea fish.

Around town. Cairns is a true tropical town with broad palm-sprinkled streets, stage-set architecture, and a dramatic seaside setting. Despite its location on the bay, the city has no beaches, but some of the world's greatest stretches of sand lie just north and south of town. Behind

the beaches a ring of sugar cane fields reaches to the steep mountain slopes. During crushing season (June to December) cane fires light up the night.

Lodging ranges from beach resorts just up the coast, to hotels and motels in town, and caravan parks. Dining spots are plentiful and, not surprisingly, much of the fare comes straight from the sea.

Most of the daytime action is outdoors. Down at the waterfront, the Hayles Cruises' catamaran departs mornings for a tour of Green Island and a trip to the Outer Reef.

During the 3 hours spent at the reef, passengers can go coral viewing in a semi-submersible vessel or go snorkeling from a special floating platform.

The Visitors' Information Centre (44 McLeod Street) offers a brochure describing historical sites in and around town. Especially interesting are the House of 10,000 Shells (a shell museum at 32 Abbott Street) and the Laroc coral jewelry factory (82 Aumuller Street).

A train ride to Kuranda. One of Australia's best, and most inexpensive, outings is the scenic rail excursion from Cairns to Kuranda. It took four years for hundreds of men wielding picks and shovels to hack a way through the lush jungle, build spans over deep gorges, and tunnel through rocky mountains to reach Kuranda in 1888. Each turn of the track unfolds a new view—the rugged splendor of Barron Gorge, Stoney Creek Falls, Barron Falls, and Victorian-style Kuranda railroad station with its profusion of tropical plants and flowers.

Trains depart Cairns at 8:30 A.M. and 9 A.M. daily, and return to Cairns at noon and 3 P.M.

The Atherton Tableland. Inland from Cairns lies the scenic Atherton Tableland, a rich volcanic area on the plateau of the Great Dividing Range. Many visitors consider it North Queensland's most spectacular area with tropical rain forests, volcanic lakes, and sparkling waterfalls.

Exploring the tableland is possible by rental car or coach, but perhaps the best way to get into the rain forest is by arranging a 1-day, four-wheel-drive safari. Safaris can be booked through Air Queensland or through the Queensland Government Travel Centre.

Up the coast. The Captain Cook Highway meanders north from Cairns to Port Douglas, less than an hour away. A good road by Queensland standards, the highway is given to unexpected loops and twists. A number of beautiful beaches with quiet resorts, caravan parks, and campgrounds line the coast.

From the quiet town of Port Douglas, the M.V. *Quicksilver* catamaran takes visitors to the reef for snorkeling, diving, and coral viewing in a semi-submersible vessel.

North of Port Douglas lies Cooktown—Australia's first British settlement, established by Captain Cook in 1770. Still farther north is the remote Cape York Peninsula. A road links Cooktown to Port Douglas, and four-wheel-drive safaris explore the area—but flying is still the best way to reach this historic town. Air Queensland in Cairns offers charters that include Cooktown; 5-day round-trip cruises from Cairns also stop here.

Green Island. Tropical plants flourish on this heavily wooded, 12-hectare/30-acre island that rises only 3 meters/10 feet above sea level. Low tide exposes miles of the reef for exploration. Glass-bottom boats and the portholes of Green Island's famous Underwater Coral Observatory also afford first-hand views of marine world wonders.

Anchored on the seabed in the midst of a living coral garden, the observatory is a steel-and-concrete chamber with 22 large portholes. If you're not a skin diver, this is a good way to enjoy the reef's underwater life. At Marineland Melanesia you'll find a crocodile pool, a 17-tank fish "arcade," a deep tank for large fish, and a coral grotto. There are also glass-bottom boat trips.

Green is one of the reef's true coral cays that has guest facilities. The year-round resort has 26 units, a restaurant, and a variety of water-sports options. You can reach Green Island from Cairns by high-speed catamaran (40 minutes) or launch (1½ hours).

Lizard Island. The most northerly resort in Queensland waters, Lizard lies northeast of Cooktown. Today a national park, Lizard was first explored by Captain Cook in 1770. Stranded inside the Outer Reef, Cook climbed Lizard's highest peak to find a break through which he could steer the *Endeavour* into deeper waters.

A coral reef surrounds the island; its waters teem with big game fish such as black marlin. Air Queensland provides service into Lizard daily from Cairns. The Lizard Island Lodge has 32 units. There's also a dining room and swimming pool. Activities include glass-bottom boat excursions, day cruises to the reef for snorkeling and diving, bush walks, fishing, water-skiing, tennis, sailing, windsurfing, and golf. The island has about two dozen isolated beaches.

Townsville, another gateway

Townsville is Queensland's third largest city and one of Australia's tropical centers. It is also the departure point for trips to Magnetic Island (reached by launch), Orpheus Island (reached by air and launch), Hinchinbrook Island (reached by launch via Cardwell and by air), and Dunk Island (reached by launch and air). Outer Reef cruises and fishing boat trips also depart from Townsville.

Magnetic Island. Almost a suburb, Magnetic is just off the coast near Townsville. Comfortable holiday accommodations are available at a number of resorts which nestle in secluded bays around the island.

Now a national park, the island is noted for its colorful tropical shrubs and groves of coconut palms, tamarinds, and mangoes. It is laced with hiking paths leading to the summit of Mount Cook with its far-reaching view.

Orpheus Island. A secluded, peaceful island, Orpheus belongs to the Palm Group near beautiful Hinchinbrook Channel, and lies south of huge Hinchinbrook Island near the Outer Reef. Accommodations are in 25 beachfront rooms including two separate cottages. The resort is designed for couples and small families. Access is by launch, seaplane, and helicopter.

Hinchinbrook Island. A mountainous island with beautiful palm-fringed bays and sandy beaches, Hinchinbrook is 26 km/16 miles from the mainland resort of Cardwell. It is a national park, one of the world's largest island parks. The resort, situated on its northernmost tip, offers bungalow accommodations. Launch service operates between Cardwell and the island and there's air service from Townsville. The island is a virtually unexplored wilderness with waterfalls and superb beaches. Elevated walkways lead through the mangroves at Missionary Bay.

Dunk Island. Like so many of the area's islands, Dunk was discovered and named by Captain Cook in 1770 during his famous voyage along Australia's east coast. Covering only 17 km/6½ square miles, Dunk still retains an unspoiled tropical beauty. Penetrating the heavy jungle foliage are miles of graded mountain tracks where you see numerous species of birds and giant butterflies. The island's shell-strewn beaches make it a beachcomber's dream.

Dunk Island's full-board resort has 138 rooms in bungalows and two-story complexes. Amenities include a restaurant, pools, tennis courts, golf course, and water-sports facilities. Guests can go horseback riding or take reef trips. You can reach Dunk by air from Townsville or Cairns, by launch from Clump Point (midway between the two towns), or by water taxi from South Mission Beach.

Proserpine and its island quartet

Proserpine is surrounded by acres of sugar cane fields. From here you catch a bus to Shute Harbour for the launches that transport you to Hayman, Daydream, South Molle, and Long islands. There's air service from Shute Harbour and Proserpine to Hayman and Daydream islands. To get to South Molle and Long islands, you can fly from Proserpine to Hamilton Island and take a launch.

Hayman Island. This well-known Great Barrier Reef resort has been recently remodeled and is now called the Ansett International Hotel, Hayman Island. It's open all year and provides cool, spacious accommodations in over 200 rooms including suites and penthouses, all situated around a beach lagoon. Island amenities include a filtered saltwater swimming lagoon, freshwater pools, marina, tennis courts, bowling green, health club, and dive shop.

When night comes, you can relax in quiet, attractive lounges or enjoy live entertainment including dance bands, cabaret performances, or special shows. The resort has several restaurants featuring a variety of cuisine.

Hayman Island is reached daily by the sleek boat, *Goddess*, from Shute Harbour or Hamilton Island. Ansett flies to Hamilton Island. There's also air service from Proserpine and Shute Harbour.

Daydream Island. This Whitsunday Group resort can be reached by daily launch from Shute Harbour or by air from Proserpine or Shute Harbour. There's also air service via Hamilton Island.

The buildings of the 100-room, two-story hotel curve around a huge, free-form swimming pool with its own island bar in the center. Each room has a panoramic view of the Whitsunday Passage. South Sea Island decor and entertainment highlight evening activities. The year-round resort features a badminton court, fishing, snorkeling, water-skiing, diving, tennis, sailing, windsurfing, and day cruises.

South Molle Island. Known for its carefree and relaxed atmosphere, South Molle nestles in a sheltered bay amid varied scenery—mountains, valleys, tropical gardens, and a sparkling series of beaches. This 405-hectare/1,000-acre island has 202 rooms.

Visitors have easy access to bush walks among lush forests with sparkling views of the Pacific. Free cruises and reef visits, aquaplaning, fishing, tennis, golf, and dancing are offered. Other island facilities include a dining room and four bars, a well-stocked store, a small arcade of shops, and even a store for divers which carries compressed air.

Long Island. This island's two small resorts, one at Happy Bay and the other at Palm Bay, offer activities to appeal to all ages—water-skiing, bush walking, tennis, fishing, and glass-bottom boat trips.

Long Island is reached by launch from Shute Harbour and by air from Proserpine to Hamilton Island with a connecting launch.

Mackay, base for cruises & islands

The attractive city of Mackay, with its wide, palm-shaded streets and tropical flower gardens, lies at the mouth of the Pioneer River. It is the airline embarkation point for trips to Brampton and Hamilton islands, and for two Whitsunday Passage cruises.

Brampton Island. One of the prettiest of the high-rise islands, this national park and wildlife sanctuary offers a view extending across the southern end of the Whitsunday Passage. Great stretches of palm-lined, white coral sands invite swimmers and sunbathers. Cruises can be arranged to other islands and the Outer Reef. In the evenings you can take in a movie, do a little dancing, or enjoy the entertainment.

Set in a coconut grove facing the beach, the modern all-year resort has 100 rooms. It is easy to reach by small plane or launch from Mackay.

Lindeman Island. Visitors to this mountainous national park can explore grassy hillsides, jungle gullies, and steep beach cliffs fringed with coral reefs. From Mount Oldfield, the view takes in more than 70 islands.

Guests keep busy with a selection of activities—bushwalking to deserted bays, watching flocks of multicolored parrots sweep over the groves, free cruises, shopping, golfing, picnicking, and coral viewing. Planes for flightseeing and launches for special cruises or big-game fishing are available at extra charge.

The 90-room resort has a large dining room, two cocktail lounges, a games room, dance floor, golf course, and swimming pool—all in a tropical setting a few minutes walk from the beach.

The Lindeman Aerial Service, operating daily on demand, flies between Lindeman and Hamilton Island, Shute Harbour, and Proserpine. Lindeman Aerial Service also conducts scenic flights of the area.

Hamilton Island. This large resort complex has an airstrip with facilities capable of handling both commercial and private jets. The resort's 381 rooms include condos, Polynesian-style bures, and hotel accommodations. Other facilities include restaurants, tennis courts, spas, saunas, a native animal park, underwater reef exhibit, and marina with full water-sports facilities. Hamilton also serves as a base for trips to the Outer Reef.

Rockhampton, for Keppel and cruises

Rockhampton, on the Tropic of Capricorn, is the departure point for trips to Great Keppel Island. Scenic flights to the reef also depart from Rockhampton.

Great Keppel Island. Situated 13 km/8 miles off the Queensland coast and 56 km/35 miles northeast of Rockhampton, Great Keppel attracts many overseas visitors.

The resort, located on a protected bay with an inviting, white sandy beach, is known for its host of activities including cruising, fishing, water-skiing, diving, windsurfing, snorkeling, golfing, playing tennis and squash, and dancing the night away in the island discotheque. Coral viewing is made easy in a glass-bottom boat or semi-submersible vessel. Accommodations include 160 motel-type units. Graded walks, leading to secluded bays and beaches, traverse the island.

Launches to Great Keppel depart Rosslyn Bay mornings and afternoons. Local flights to the island are also available from Rockhampton Airport.

Gladstone, gateway to Heron

About 483 km/300 rail miles north of Brisbane, Gladstone lies on the shores of Port Curtis, a near-perfect natural harbor. This fast-growing town, ranking among Australia's busiest cargo ports, is also the departure point for trips to Heron Island.

Heron Island. Surrounded by many miles of perhaps the best, most easily accessible coral beds of the entire reef area, this well-known, thickly wooded, low coral cay measures only 2 km/1¼ miles in circumference. Many varieties of birds nest in the island's pandanus groves and *pisonia* forest. They include noddy terns, herons, silver gulls, fairy terns, and the migratory mutton birds, which regularly return to the island in late October and leave exactly five months later.

From late October until April, giant turtles visit the island and lay their eggs in the warm coral sand. Within 10 weeks after the eggs are laid, the hatchlings emerge and head to the sea. Heron's Marine Biological Station displays many live specimens of colorful tropical fish and other marine life. The station's biologists have classified more than 1,150 varieties of fish and 200 varieties of coral in the vicinity.

Skin divers regularly meet at Heron. Special events include an annual Divers' Rally in June and July, and the Skin Divers' Festival each November. Experienced divers provide free instruction and guide outings to Heron, Wistari, and other adjacent coral reefs. Heron Island is considered to be one of the best dive spots in Australia.

Nondivers can test their fishing skills or go snorkeling. Other resort activities include a combined cruise and barbecue on a nearby uninhabited island, escorted bird watching, and low-tide reef walks.

Heron has 90 holiday units in one and two-story buildings facing the water. The facilities also include a dining room, bar and lounge, swimming pool, and dive shop.

Arrangements must be made in advance for the 30-minute scenic helicopter flight to Heron Island from Gladstone. There's also launch service from Gladstone.

BRISBANE

In subtropical Queensland, playground beaches & quiet highlands

More than half of Queensland lies above the Tropic of Capricorn. With a climate ranging from subtropical to tropical, this is Australia's vacation country.

From the urban center of Brisbane, Australia's third largest city and the state capital, the seaside resort towns of the Gold Coast stretch south to Coolangatta on the border of New South Wales. North of Brisbane, surfing beaches and fishing resorts edge the less-developed Sunshine Coast. Farther up, at the northeast corner of the state, are the undersea wonders of the Great Barrier Reef.

Balmy sea breezes, sandy beaches, and a lively resort life are the star attractions of the "Sunshine State." But swimming, sunning, and surfing are not all Queensland offers. On the north coast and along the river valleys to the south, dense tropical rain forests flourish, cleared in many places to provide space for pineapple and sugar cane plantations. Mountain resorts and national parks lie within easy reach of Brisbane. Not far inland, the Great Dividing Range stands sentinel over the entire length of the state. About 129 km/80 miles west of Brisbane, the western foothills of the range soften into the Darling Downs, 1.4 million hectares/3.5 million acres of rolling wheat and grazing lands where some of Australia's finest cattle, sheep, and race horses are bred. The Downs gradually merge into the plains, and still farther west, the land eventually dries out to become part of the great Australian outback.

In this chapter we cover the attractions of Brisbane and southern Queensland. For information about northern Queensland, including the Great Barrier Reef, see pages 110–117.

Brisbane, a city on the river

The busy port city of Brisbane is an ideal base from which to explore southern Queensland. A city of almost a million people, Brisbane spreads over both banks of the Brisbane River, 32 km/20 miles upstream from the river's outlet into Moreton Bay. The foothills of the Taylor and D'Aguilar ranges rise behind and a little west of the city. In their foothills, some of Australia's most beautiful homes are designed to take advantage of their view settings and tropical surroundings.

Gardens, parklands, and flowering trees border Brisbane's avenues. The river—trafficked by ferries, tugboats, freighters, ocean liners, and pleasure craft—winds through the city in deep, graceful curves. Six large bridges and eight ferry crossings link the north and south banks.

The city, just a few degrees south of the Tropic of Capricorn, has a subtropical climate. The best months to visit are from April through November, when the daytime temperatures range between 20°C/68°F and 27°C/80°F. Most of the rainfall comes during the summer months of December, January, and February. Temperatures then are very warm to hot, and humidity is high.

Getting your bearings

The center of Brisbane, bisected by Queen Street, occupies a peninsula bounded by the sea on one side and Brisbane River on the other. The main commercial streets follow a grid pattern. Streets running south to north have feminine names; those running west to east, masculine. The Parliament buildings and the Botanic Gardens nestle in a bend of the river at the tip of the peninsula.

At the south end of Queen Street, Victoria Bridge crosses the river to South Brisbane. The south river bank was chosen to be the site of Expo 88. The theme of this international exposition is "Leisure in the Age of Technology." It will be open from April 30 to October 30, 1988.

A helpful city map is available from the Queensland Government Travel Centre, 196 Adelaide Street. The National Trust, at 157 Ann Street, has a brochure detailing points of historic interest.

City sights

Like most state capitals, Brisbane has its share of fine parks, museums, dignified government and civic buildings, and monuments. You will see many of them on your downtown walking tour. Others are just a short bus or ferry ride away.

Architectural landmarks. City Hall is at Adelaide and Albert streets. This mammoth building on King George

Reflecting pool in Brisbane's Botanic Gardens mirrors contrasting architectural styles of Parliament House complex. Serene setting belies bustle of Queensland's capital city.

Square is one of Brisbane's showplaces. For a good overall view of the city and surrounding countryside, take the lift to the observation platform at the top of the clock tower. City Hall contains an impressive collection of paintings and historic treasures, and a grand organ said to be one of the finest in the Southern Hemisphere.

Parliament House, Alice and George streets, opened in 1868. This building is an imposing example of French Renaissance architecture. A newer annex now towers above the original structure.

The Observatory, Wickham Terrace, dates from 1829. Built by convict labor, it was designed to operate as a windmill, but the sails never worked so it was converted to a convict-manned treadmill.

John Oxley Memorial, an obelisk between Victoria and William Jolly bridges, marks the spot where Lt. John Oxley landed in 1823, establishing the site of Brisbane.

Newstead Park is the site of Brisbane's oldest residence, Newstead House, open Monday through Thursday from 11 A.M. to 3 P.M. and Sunday from 2 to 5. A memorial at Lyndon B. Johnson Place in the park was erected by the people of Queensland as a tribute to the United States. (During the Pacific crisis in World War II, General Douglas MacArthur made his base in Brisbane.)

Miegunyah, on Jordan Terrace in Bowen Hills, is a fine example of colonial architecture, memorializing Australia's pioneer women. Furnished in the manner of the late 1800s, it holds many relics of those early days. You can view the exhibit Tuesdays, Wednesdays, Saturdays, and Sundays from 10:30 A.M. to 4 P.M.

Early Street, 75 McIlwraith Avenue, Norman Park, re-creates a pioneer town. From 10 A.M. to 5 P.M. daily, visitors may inspect an old-time pub, a coach house, a settler's cottage, and an Aboriginal *gunyah* (a type of primitive shelter).

Museums and galleries. Queensland Art Gallery, M.I.M. Building, 160 Ann Street, houses a small but good collection of works by Australian contemporary painters. The gallery is open Monday through Saturday from 10 A.M. to 5 P.M. and Sundays from 2 to 5.

Visitors with a special interest in art may wish to visit the Ray Hughes Gallery, McInnes Galleries, the Town Gallery, and Philip Bacon Galleries as well.

Design Art Centre features pottery and applied arts as well as paintings and drawings. Jewelry, sculpture, and paintings by Australian and international artists are on view at New Central Galleries. The Potters' Gallery is also worth a visit. A colony of arts and crafts showplaces has grown among the old narrow streets of Spring Hill close to the city. The Queensland Government Travel Centre can provide a list of interesting places to visit on a stroll through the district.

The Queensland Cultural Centre, located on the south bank of the Brisbane River, is the hub of the state's cultural activities. The Performing Arts Centre and Art Gallery are currently open, with the State Museum and Library to be completed soon. The complex is open daily from 10 A.M. to 5 P.M., and until 8 P.M. on Wednesdays.

Gardens and parks. Botanic Gardens—20 hectares/50 acres of flowers, shrubs, and trees—borders the Brisbane River next to Parliament House. The gardens are open daily from sunrise to sunset.

New Farm Park, alongside the Brisbane River east of the city, is a favorite with flower lovers. Some 12,000 rose bushes bloom here from September through November.

(Continued on page 122)

Will your boomerang come back?

For decades, the Australian Aborigines used the boomerang for hunting and warfare. The Aborigines are believed to have developed the returning boomerang, but nonreturning boomerangs were used by hunters in other parts of the world as well. Even North American Indians used a form of nonreturning boomerang.

Today, Australia's returning boomerang has evolved into a plaything, and throwing it has become a sport. There's even a national boomerang throwing championship held annually in New South Wales.

During your travels in Australia you might have an opportunity to learn how to throw a boomerang, and the first thing you'll learn is that it's not as easy as it looks. Here are a few tips that might help make your returning boomerang come back as it's supposed to.

First, do your boomerang throwing in a clear, open area. Hold the boomerang vertically by one of its tips, with the flat side of it facing away from you. Bring your arm back behind your head and then throw the boomerang forward toward the horizon. The trick of a good throw is the snap you give the boomerang as you let it go after your arm is fully extended in front of you. This snap creates a spin that's necessary for the boomerang to gain lift. If there's too much lift, though, the boomerang will climb too quickly and eventually plummet to the ground—a good way to break a boomerang.

If you've thrown correctly, the boomerang will make a wide circle and then return to you in a horizontal position. As it nears you it may make several more small spins, or hover before it lands near your feet. A skilled boomerang thrower can send a boomerang into a 45-meter/50-yard-wide circle before it returns.

If you don't succeed the first time, keep practicing, remembering that it's the snap that counts.

You can purchase souvenir boomerangs throughout Australia, some of them decorated with Aboriginal designs. For a close-up look at how boomerangs are made, take a tour of the Hawes Boomerang Farm near Brisbane (see page 125).

Queensland

CORAL SEA

GREAT

Gulf of

Carpentaria

Cape

York

Peninsula

Cooktown

Mossman

Port Douglas

Atherton
Tableland

Kuranda

Cairns

Normanton

Innisfail

Ingham

BARRIER

SOUTH

Townsville

Camooweal

Charters Towers

PACIFIC

Mt. Isa

Cloncurry

Flinders

Hwy

Proserpine

REEF

Landsborough Hwy

Winton

Mackay

Boulia

Longreach

Clermont

Emerald

OCEAN

Capricorn

Hwy

Rockhampton

SIMPSON
DESERT
NATL.
PARK

Jundah

Gladstone

Windorah

Bundaberg

Fraser Island

Maryborough

Charleville

Warrego

Roma

Kingaroy

Gympie

Quilpie

Hwy

Thargomindah

Cunnamulla

BUNYA MTNS.
NATL. PARK

Sunshine Coast

St. George

Toowoomba

Ipswich

Brisbane

Goondiwindi

Warwick

Gold Coast

Kilometers
0   50   125

0   50   125
Miles

———— Principal Roads (sealed)
———— Secondary Roads (sealed)
- - - - Unsealed Roads

Sun worshippers *flock to the golden sands of Surfers Paradise, a large resort area on the Gold Coast.*

...Continued from page 120

In October and November, jacaranda and bougainvillea are in bloom. Red poinciana trees blossom in November and December.

Oasis Tourist Garden at Sunnybank is a much-enjoyed spot with landscaped gardens, trimmed lawns, aviaries, swimming pools, and a garden cafe.

Exhibition Grounds, Bowen Hills, annually hosts the Royal National Show (Queensland's equivalent of a state fair), usually beginning the second week of August. A highlight of the winter season, the fair attracts great crowds from surrounding districts.

Shopping suggestions

Brisbane's main shopping area is bounded by Elizabeth, Edward, Adelaide and George streets. Here you'll find arcades, specialty shops, boutiques, and major department stores. The main department stores, David Jones, Myer's, and Barry and Roberts, can be found on Queen Street. A traffic-free pedestrian mall stretches along Queen Street between Albert and Edward streets.

In the heart of Brisbane, next to City Hall, is City Plaza, an impressive complex of specialty shops and open-air cafes opening onto plazas and courtyards. Access to pedestrians is from George, Ann, and Adelaide streets.

Many gift shops specialize in souvenir items—rugs, garments, and bags made from hides and skins; curios from Queensland woods; and jewelry from local gemstones (rubies, sapphires, and opals). You'll find the best selection of native handicrafts and artifacts at Queensland Aboriginal Creations on George Street, open from 9 A.M. to 4:30 P.M. Monday through Friday.

Antique hunters will have a field day in Brisbane and its suburbs. Ian Still features a variety of Papua New Guinea and Oceania primitive art in addition to a mixed stock of antiques. More than 20 other dealers round out the antique scene in Brisbane. At the Brisbane Antique and Art Centre in Clayfield, 35 antique dealers have shops under one roof.

Entertainment

Though Brisbane is not a lively nighttime city, several theaters stage professional or amateur productions; rock, jazz, and folk groups are featured; and there are theater-restaurants and a few discos.

The S.G.I.O. Theatre on Turbot Street is the home of the Queensland State Theatre Company. Her Majesty's Theatre on Queen Street features professional artists, many from overseas. Amateur groups stage productions at the Brisbane Art Theatre, 250 Petrie Terrace; La Boite, 57 Hale Street; Rialto Theatre, West End; and Twelfth Night Theatre, 4 Cintra Road, Bowen Hills. The Festival Hall on Charlotte Street offers operas, concerts, and ballets featuring overseas and local stars. The Living Room, a theater-restaurant, presents a dinner show nightly Tuesdays through Saturdays.

In late September/early October, Brisbane takes on a carnival air during "Warana"—a week-long spring festival with parades, concerts, art shows, beauty contests, and other events.

Things to do outdoors

For a relaxing break from travel tensions, stroll through one of Brisbane's city parks. Several are described on pages 120 and 122. Near the city's center, Victoria Park extends over 78 hectares/193 acres, providing playing grounds for many sports. Included in the park are the Municipal Golf Links and the Centenary Swimming Pool, an Olympic-size pool open September through April.

Also in pleasant park settings are the swimming pools of the Acacia Tourist Garden and Oasis Tourist Garden in Sunnybank.

Brisbane's leading golf clubs usually permit visitors to play when introduced by a member. Some have reciprocal arrangements with overseas clubs. These championship courses are open to visitors: Brisbane Golf Club, Indooroopilly Golf Cluf, Cailes Golf Club, and Royal Queensland Golf Club. Public golf clubs, in addition to the one at Victoria Park, are Pacific and Redcliffe.

Major tennis matches are held at Milton, home of the Queensland Lawn Tennis Association. For information about where to play, contact the association.

Horse racing ranks as the number one spectator sport in Brisbane. The Stradbroke Handicap and Brisbane Cup in June and the Doomben Ten Thousand and Doomben Cup in July are the chief races. Meets are held at the Queensland Turf Club at Eagle Farm, and at Doomben (Albion Park), and Bundamba. Trotting races are held at Albion Park. Greyhounds race at Woolloongabba.

Major cricket matches are those between the Australian states for the Sheffield Shield. These matches, at Woolloongabba, are 4 days long, usually starting on a Friday or Saturday. The season runs from October to February.

Rugby matches are played at Lang Park.

Brisbane River sailors test their skills in frequent yacht races down the river and across Moreton Bay. For sun, surf, and sand, it's hard to top the beaches of the Sunshine Coast to the north and the Gold Coast to the south.

Excursions in Brisbane's environs

Many day, half-day, and extended tours and cruises operate from Brisbane. A sampling is given here. For folders and additional possibilities, visit the Queensland Government Travel Centre in Brisbane.

Mount Coot-tha Forest Park

From this oasis of tall eucalypts and native shrubs only 8 km/5 miles from the city center, you can look out over Brisbane and the surrounding countryside to Moreton Bay and sometimes as far as the Glasshouse Mountains, 80 km/50 miles away. Within the park are the Mount Coot-tha Botanic Gardens. More than 2,000 native and exotic plants are on view in its Tropical Display Dome. Also featured are a cactus garden, fragrance garden, and the Sir Thomas Brisbane Planetarium.

Lone Pine Koala Sanctuary

One of Brisbane's top attractions, this privately owned acreage on the banks of the Brisbane River was the first koala sanctuary established in Australia. Its koala colony of about 100 is the largest on public display anywhere.

Koalas breed freely here; the owners release their surplus stock each year to state forests and national parks in an effort to re-establish the koala in its natural environment. One group of Lone Pine koalas now resides in California's San Diego Zoo.

You can reach the sanctuary by car in 15 minutes. Bus tours include it, often with a stop at Mount Coot-tha for a view of the city. Launches travel upriver from Brisbane's Hayles Wharf to the sanctuary and back.

In the sanctuary, you can have your picture taken holding one of the cuddly koalas. You'll also meet kangaroos, wallabies, wombats, Tasmanian devils, dingoes, a platypus, and a fascinating assortment of native birds.

Moreton Bay district

After it passes through the city, the Brisbane River swings northeast and empties into Moreton Bay, a huge body of water sheltered by Moreton and Stradbroke islands. The protected waters of the bay are well known to Brisbane residents, who have camped, fished, gone crabbing, and enjoyed the bay's water sports for years.

Moreton Island, about 32 km/20 miles east of the mouth of the river, is 39 km/24 miles long and boasts the world's highest permanent sand dunes—Mount Tempest (279 meters/914 feet) and Storm Mountain (267 meters/875 feet). From Brisbane you can reach Moreton Island by launch or light aircraft (Tangalooma Air Taxis). You can visit the island's main resort, Tangalooma, on a day cruise. For those who wish to stay longer, the resort offers comfortable accommodations. Island activities include swimming, surfing, riding, sand-hill tobogganing, tennis, fishing, and skin diving.

Stradbroke Island, just south of Moreton Island, is really two islands. North and South Stradbroke stretch south for 61 km/38 miles—almost to Surfers Paradise. Launches, vehicular ferries, and light aircraft provide access to North Stradbroke Island and its sparkling white beaches, fresh-water lakes, wildlife sanctuary, and small resorts.

Other activity centers include Wellington Point, Cleveland, and Victoria Point resorts along the southern mainland shores of Moreton Bay, and Bribie and Bishop islands, both popular picnicking and camping spots. You can swim, sun-bathe, or fish at any of the many beaches and resorts along the Redcliffe Peninsula.

The essentials

A capsule version of what you need to know about getting to and around Brisbane, and enjoying your stay there.

Getting there. Brisbane is served by air, rail, and bus. For services to northern Queensland, see page 112.

Air. International service to Brisbane by Qantas and foreign-flag carriers. Domestic flights to Brisbane and Coolangatta (Gold Coast) by Ansett, Australian, East-West, and Air New South Wales from Sydney and other Australian cities. Connecting flights from Brisbane to other Queensland cities also available. Brisbane International Airport is 8 km/5 miles from town by bus or taxi.

Rail. *Brisbane Limited Express* to Brisbane from Sydney, one train in each direction daily, leaving late afternoon, arriving the next morning; trip takes about 15½ hours.

Bus. Daily service from Sydney to Brisbane with stops at intermediate coastal towns.

Accommodations. Among the many major hotels in the Brisbane area are Brisbane Parkroyal, Mayfair Crest, Gateway, Ramada Gazebo, Lennons Brisbane, Sheraton Brisbane, Hilton Brisbane, and Brisbane City Travelodge. Gold Coast hotels include the Conrad International Hotel and Jupiters Casino, Ramada Surfers Paradise, Holiday Inn, and Gold Coast International.

Food and drink. Wide range of ethnic restaurants in Brisbane and on Gold Coast. Local specialties: Queensland mudcrab, Moreton Bay bugs (a kind of crayfish, cooked and served in the shell), fresh seafood from the Great Barrier Reef, beef from central Queensland, tropical fruits in season. Local beers include Castlemaine.

Most restaurants are licensed to serve wine, ales, and spirits. You can take your own beverages to unlicensed restaurants (called BYO restaurants). You'll be charged a small corkage fee.

Getting around. City-operated buses operate throughout Brisbane. For a small fee, Day Rover Tickets allow unlimited bus travel on the day ticket is purchased. Private bus lines supplement the city system; there's train service to the suburbs. Ferry service is provided across the Brisbane River between the Creek Street Landing and Park Avenue in East Brisbane, and between the Botanic Gardens and Kangaroo Point.

Tours: Half-day and full-day tours of city and to Gold Coast (this page), Sunshine Coast (page 125), Mount Coot-tha and Lone Pine (page 123), Mount Tamborine (page 126), Toowoomba and Darling Downs (page 126), Noosa Heads (page 125), and Lamington National Park (page 126). River cruises on Brisbane River and to Moreton Bay and Lone Pine.

For more information. Queensland Government Travel Centre, 196 Adelaide Street, Brisbane 4000.

Surf & sand, a coastal journey

Brisbane is the gateway to Australia's vacation country—the golden beaches that edge the continent north and south of the city. In less than 2 hours, you can reach the sand, surf, and swinging resort life of the Gold Coast or the somewhat more subdued Sunshine Coast, Queensland's most popular family resort area.

The Gold Coast

More than 5 million pleasure-seekers flock to the beaches of the Gold Coast every year. This highly developed stretch of coastline is Australia's answer to Florida's Miami, Hawaii's Waikiki, and Europe's Riviera.

The Gold Coast begins at Southport, about 80 km/50 miles south of Brisbane, and curves south in a series of beaches and bays to Coolangatta. It comprises a long string of beach communities that are officially one city with one mayor.

The golden sands are backed by a ribbon of resort development culminating in the skyscrapers of Surfers Paradise. Inland from the Gold Coast Highway are canals and waterways where picnicking, fishing, and boating are popular. Farther afield, in the lofty MacPherson Range, is a mountainous hinterland of lush rain forests. (See Lamington National Park, page 126, and Mount Tamborine, page 126.)

You can reach the Gold Coast easily by road or plane. There's bus service from Brisbane (1½ hours), and there's daily air service to Coolangatta. Local buses travel the coast between resort areas.

The Gold Coast can be explored in a day excursion from Brisbane, but if you wish to spend more time, you'll find a full range of accommodations. The Queensland Government Tourist Bureau publishes a guide to them.

For those who tire of the surf and sand, there are golf courses, tennis and squash courts, greyhound and horse races, trail rides into the bush, and deep-sea fishing trips. Other manmade tourist attractions include marine life shows, a wildlife sanctuary, a bird sanctuary, an auto museum, and a zoo. Launch and paddle boat tours operate from Surfers Paradise along the Nerang River. There are coffee houses, night clubs, and discos. You can dine *al fresco* on meals prepared by Continental chefs or pick up fish and chips or a hamburger at a beachside stand.

Sea World occupies 20 hectares/50 acres on a finger of land called The Spit that juts north from Surfers Paradise. Half the area is a manmade lake system. Here you can enjoy the antics of dolphins and sea lions; see sharks being fed; pet turtles and dolphins; ride a paddle wheeler, miniature train, or helicopter; watch a water-ski show; and swim in a large salt-water pool. It's open daily, 9 A.M. to 5 P.M.

Nearby attractions, a short distance from Sea World, include Fishermans Wharf and Bird Life Park.

Fishermans Wharf, on Sea World Drive, is a waterfront complex of seafood restaurants, taverns, and shops specializing in sports and casual fashions. Water tours also depart from here.

Bird Life Park, next to Sea World, presents a special

selection of wildlife in a natural setting. The park has a free-flight aviary, plus kangaroos, and koalas. There are also shows, informative talks, and presentations about these animals of Australia, plus a special area where you can pet and hand-feed some of them. The park is open daily, 9 A.M. to 5 P.M.

Springbrook side trip. This lush plateau offers some of the hinterland's most beautiful scenery—pasturelands, gorges, rain forests, mountain streams, and waterfalls. To explore this lofty region, on a spur of the MacPherson Range above the coast, take the road to Mudgeeraba from Burleigh Heads or Broadbeach.

At Mudgeeraba, you can learn the art of boomerang throwing at Hawes Boomerang Farm. Boomerangs are made, displayed, and sold here. Visitors can watch exhibition throwing, receive instruction, and try their skills on a practice field. There are a boomerang museum, a boomerang-shaped lake (spanned by a 9-meter/30-foot model of the Sydney Harbour Bridge), and a manmade opal mine where visitors can try their luck at finding opal chips. The farm is open daily except Saturday.

Two national parks, Gwongorella and Warrie, have pleasant picnic areas and networks of graded trails leading to view points. In Gwongorella National Park, you can hike to the edge of Purlingbrook Falls and look down into the fern-filled gorge below. Canyon Lookout above Warrie National Park offers views out to the coast.

At Wunburra on the Springbrook Road, a link road branches into scenic Numinbah Valley, a long, rich valley that lies between the sheer face of the Springbrook spur and the densely wooded slopes of Lamington National Park.

Currumbin Bird Sanctuary is just south of Currumbin Creek. Large flocks of wild birds—mostly brilliantly colored lorikeets—fly into the sanctuary from the bush each day to be fed bread and honey on plates held by visitors. There are morning and afternoon feedings.

Chewing Gum Field Aircraft Museum, on Guineas Creek Road, 6 km/4 miles from Currumbin Bird Sanctuary, is dedicated to military memorabilia. Within a World War II hangar are an extensive collection of ex-service aircraft, plus guns, uniforms, models, and engines. The museum is open daily from 9 A.M. to 5 P.M.

Gilltrap's Yesteryear World at Kirra is a unique auto museum where visitors can not only see vintage and veteran cars displayed but also can observe some of them in action and even ride in them. Four hour-long shows are given daily. The museum is open daily from 9 A.M. to 5:30 P.M.

Natureland, on the New South Wales side of the border, is Australia's third largest zoo, with a fine collection of the usual zoo birds and animals. It is open daily from 9 A.M. to 5 P.M.

Captain Cook Memorial and Lighthouse, an imposing landmark on Point Danger, Coolangatta, commemorates Cook's discovery of the east coast of Australia. It contains the world's first laser lighthouse beam.

The Sunshine Coast

Moving north along the coast from Brisbane, sun lovers will discover a long chain of splendid surfing beaches, appropriately named the Sunshine Coast, stretching from Caloundra to Noosa Heads and beyond. Relatively undeveloped, this area offers quiet relaxation on uncrowded beaches—a restful complement to the commercialized atmosphere of the Gold Coast.

The Sunshine Coast (about 80 km/50 miles from Brisbane) is easily reached by car, bus, or train. Light planes fly into the airport at Maroochydore.

The largest resort is Caloundra (109 km/68 miles north of Brisbane). Other major resorts include Mooloolaba, Maroochydore, Coolum Beach, Peregian Beach, and Noosa Heads.

Though the choice of accommodations is considerably more limited than on the Gold Coast, the northern resort facilities are certainly comfortable—and, in some cases, luxurious.

The Glasshouse Mountains rise abruptly from near-level countryside a few miles west of Caloundra. Captain Cook named the striking trachyte pillars in 1770; he chose the name because he thought they resembled the glass furnaces of his native Yorkshire. Beerwah (an Aboriginal word meaning "up in the sky") looms the highest at 555 meters/1,823 feet.

Kondalilla National Park boasts an oddity—the curious "lung fish" (*Neoceratodus fosteri*), a living fossil that subsists in deep pools in the park. Kondalilla also offers a sparkling waterfall and 75 hectares/185 acres of lush tropical rain forests.

The Noosa Heads area has a reputation for exceptionally beautiful coastal scenery: Witches' Cauldron, Hell's Gates, Devil's Kitchen, and Paradise Caves are a few of the spots you won't want to miss. Sunshine Beach at Noosa Heads draws surfboard champions from all over the world. Noosa National Park is a rugged, scenic coastal area with trails and picnic sites.

North of Tewantin, tidal salt-water lakes and fresh-water Lake Cooloola provide good fishing and an opportunity to view black swans, cranes, and other waterfowl.

A ginger factory and a sugar cane train are interesting stops on the drive along the coast. The only ginger factory in the Southern Hemisphere operates at Buderim; visitors are welcome to tour the plant, where ginger products may be purchased. South of Nambour, at Sunshine Plantation, you can ride on a sugar cane train through plantings of pineapples, bananas, passion fruit, and avocados, and visit an adjacent macadamia nut processing plant.

Fraser Island

The waters of Hervey Bay are sheltered by 145-km/90-mile-long Fraser Island, the largest island off the Queensland coast. It is known for its sweeping beaches, good fishing, surfing, swimming, fresh-water lakes, flora and fauna reserves, and Aboriginal relics.

The main resort is the Polynesian-style Orchid Beach Village, facing the Pacific on the island's extreme northeastern tip. All of the village buildings follow a basic Samoan *fale* (thatched hut) architectural design, featuring natural timbers and Polynesian decor. Self-contained fales and hillside units with private bath, some air-conditioned, accommodate 73 guests. From some units, you enjoy a view of bushland gardens; from others, you look across the waters of Marloo Bay.

(Continued on page 126)

...*Continued from page 125*

There's direct air service to Fraser Island from Brisbane, and charter flights take off from Maryborough and Hervey Bay. Launches serve the island from Hervey Bay, and there's vehicular barge service from Inskip Point.

Other interesting side trips

If you have time for more excursions from Brisbane, or perhaps a side trip from the Gold Coast, these destinations are worth considering. Each has its own distinctive features. All can be sampled in a full day, but to explore the areas leisurely, you may want more time.

The Darling Downs

A checkerboard of farmlands due west of Brisbane, the Darling Downs comprises 69,948 square km/27,000 square miles of black soil plains. Here climate and topography combine with fertile soil to make one of the country's richest agricultural districts.

Three main routes open this scenic country to motorists. From Brisbane, the Warrego Highway leads northwest through Toowoomba to Oakey, Dalby, and the far western centers. Cunningham Highway goes over Cunningham's Gap to Warwick and continues west via Inglewood and Goondiwindi. The New England Highway starts at Yarraman and heads southwest through Toowoomba and Warwick to the state border.

Toowoomba, Queensland's largest inland settlement and the commercial center for the area, is perched at 610 meters/2,000 feet on the crest of the Great Dividing Range 129 km/80 miles west of Brisbane. It is the state's "Garden City." During its annual Carnival of Flowers in September, floral decorations enhance public buildings, and flower-decked floats are featured in a carnival parade.

Toowoomba's Lionel Lindsay Art Gallery, 27 Jellicoe Street, commemorates this Australian artist with many of his paintings, woodcuts, and etchings, and displays the works of other Australian artists.

At the corner of James and Water streets, the Cobb & Co. Museum contains another interesting Australiana collection, including relics of horse and buggy days. A well-landscaped historical garden next to the museum includes trees and shrubs from foreign lands.

Creative 92, at 92 Margaret Street, presents a comprehensive display of crafts, ceramics, and showings by Queensland artists.

For a good look at Toowoomba and views of the Darling Downs, follow the signed Blue Arrow Route, a scenic 52-km/32-mile drive through the city and along the escarpment of the MacPherson Range. It will take you to Mt. Kynoch and Mt. Lofty for panoramic views of the city, and past Redwood Park, a bird and animal sanctuary.

Don't miss the view from Picnic Point, a gigantic headland on the crest of the range. You look out over Table Top Mountain—an extinct volcano capped with a flat, grassy plateau and clad with trees—across the coastal lowlands to the majestic heights of the border ranges.

Warwick, second largest city on the Darling Downs, occupies a quiet setting 84 km/52 miles south of Toowoomba on the banks of the Condamine River. The first of Queensland's sheep flocks were bred here on the southern Downs, and three of the earliest sheep stations—South Toolburra, Canning Downs, and Rosenthal—are still in existence. Today some of Australia's finest race horses are bred in this region.

Pringle Cottage on Dragon Street, built in 1863, displays relics of pioneering days; it is open daily, afternoons only.

Mount Tamborine

A full-day tour south from Brisbane takes you to this popular mountain resort, through subtropical vine jungles, past waterfalls veiled in mist, and into the rich vegetation of the rain forest.

Here the trees grow tall, and their heavy top foliage provides filtered shade for creepers, palms, ferns, orchids, and lilies. Strange carrabeeb trees thrive in the rain forests. On the western slopes of the mountains, you can see prolific stands of macrozamia palm trees, a species of cycad dating back millions of years. Some individual trees at Tamborine are thought to be 1,000 years old.

Butterflies are bred at the Butterfly Farm on Long Road (open daily summer months only). A walk-through path into the netted enclosure gives visitors a close-up look.

For a nominal fee, you can fossick for gemstones at Jasper Farm, Wonga Wallen, upper Coomera; or at Thunderbird Park, Cedar Creek. Both are open daily.

Lamington National Park

Another favorite mountain resort area, Lamington National Park lies some 113 km/70 miles south of Brisbane amid the cloudy peaks of the rugged MacPherson Range. This is a land of awesome chasms, unexplored tablelands, forests of ancient Antarctic beech trees, and views stretching to the coast and south into New South Wales.

Many coastal streams have their origins in the park's mountains. At Moran's Falls, tons of sparkling water plunge into a deep gorge.

Masses of wildflowers bloom in the spring, and the park is alive with bird and animal life. On a hike you may glimpse the Rufus scrub bird (a ventriloquist) or the magnificently plumed male Albert lyrebird. Pademelons (small wallabies) and possums feed near the lodges in the mornings and evenings.

Two simple but comfortable guest houses offer accommodations within the park boundaries. O'Reilly's "Green Mountains" resort is situated on the western summit of the park. Binna Burra Lodge is near the northeastern boundary.

Hiking trails radiate from both lodges. Binna Burra Lodge offers guided hikes, rock climbing lessons, and horseback rides. A special feature at Binna Burra is the Senses Trail developed for the blind; a rope along the circular trail makes the route easy to follow, and signs in Braille help the hiker to experience the forest surroundings by means of touch, smell, and hearing.

Climate in this mountain region is mild, but visitors should be prepared for chilly evenings even in summer. The lodges are popular; book well ahead for holiday periods or long weekends.

Silhouetted against the light, koala and kangaroo pause briefly for a fast-shooting photographer.

INDEX

Sunset

New Zealand
TRAVEL GUIDE

By the Editors of Sunset Books
and Sunset Magazine

Lane Publishing Co. • Menlo Park, California

Book Editor: **Cornelia Fogle**

Design: **Cynthia Hanson**
Kathy Avanzino Barone

Illustrations: **Joe Seney**

Maps: **William Dunn & Joe Seney**

Photographers

Betty Crowell: 94. **Lynn Ferrin:** 11, 35.
Cornelia Fogle: 19, 27, 38, 75, 78, 103, 119.
Chris Gilbert: 3, 22, 62, 67, 83, 86, 111.
Libby Mills: 51. **Bruce Moss:** 54, 59, 91.
New Zealand Tourist Office: 6, 14, 30, 43, 46, 70, 106, 114. **Jim Rearden:** 122, 127. **Richard Rowan:** 98.

Cover: Clear waters of Lake Matheson mirror the snowy peaks of Mount Tasman (left) and Mount Cook (right) in Westland National Park. Photographed by Chris Gilbert.

Come with us . . .

to New Zealand, a land of rugged, scenic beauty and warm, hospitable people. Share with us a wealth of rewarding travel destinations and activities. And join with us as we explore and learn about a very special country and its people.

We deeply appreciate the many individuals and organizations in New Zealand who helped in the preparation of this book. In addition to the invaluable assistance of the New Zealand Tourist Office, especially Mike Damiano, we also gratefully acknowledge the information provided by tourism officials throughout the country.

And a special thank you to Fran Feldman for her careful copy editing of the manuscript.

Sunset Books
Editor, David E. Clark
Managing Editor, Elizabeth L. Hogan

Third printing July 1987

 Library of Congress Catalog Card Number: 84-80609. ISBN 0-376-06536-2. Lithographed in the United States.

CONTENTS

Cricket players dressed in traditional white garb bring a touch of England to Auckland Domain.

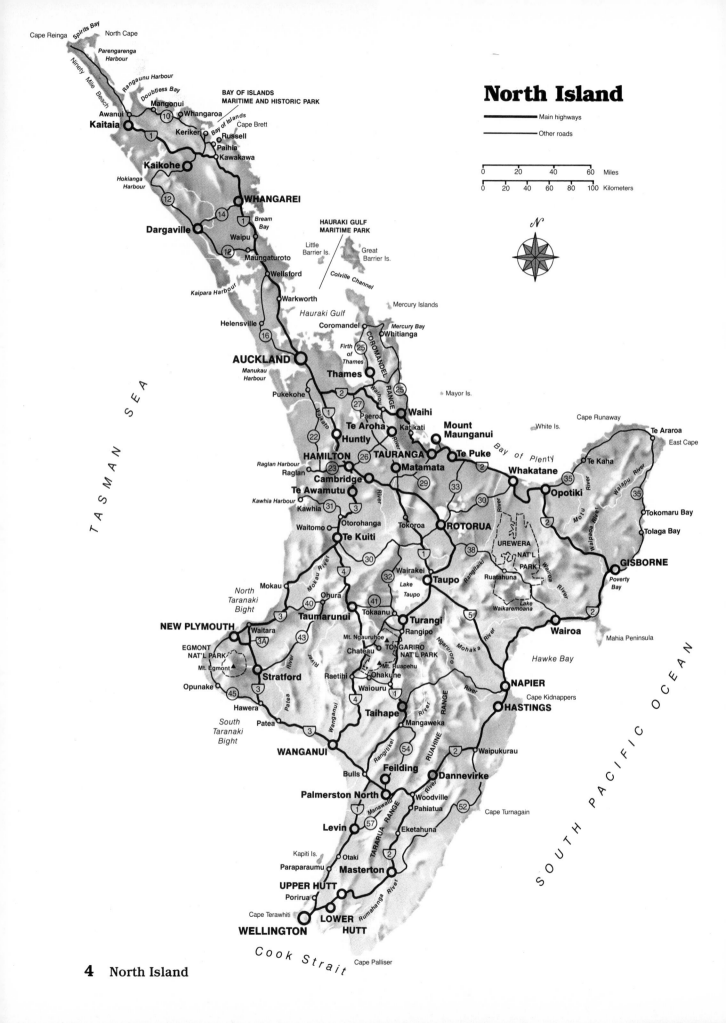

North Island

Main highways

Other roads

South Island

Main highways
Other roads

Miles: 0 20 40 60
Kilometers: 0 20 40 60 80 100

N

Cook Strait

TASMAN SEA

Farewell Spit
Golden Bay
Collingwood
Takaka
60
Karamea
ABEL TASMAN NAT'L PARK
Tasman Bay
MARLBOROUGH SOUNDS MARITIME PARK
Wangapeka Track
Motueka
61
Havelock
Nelson
6 1
Picton
Karamea Bight
Motupiko
Cloudy Bay
Westport
67
Kawatiri
Wairau River
Blenheim
Lake Grassmere
Buller River
Murchison
NELSON LAKES NAT'L PARK
Inangahua Junction
69
65
Clarence River
Punakaiki
Reefton
6
Grey River
Lewis Pass
Hanmer Springs
70
Kaikoura
Greymouth
7
Waiau
Kumara
Lake Brunner
7
Waiau
Hokitika
Taramakau River
Culverden
Waiau River
1
Ross
Arthur's Pass
Otira
ARTHUR'S PASS NAT'L PARK
Hurunui River
Arthur's Pass
7
SOUTHERN ALPS
Lake Coleridge
Waimakariri
Waipara
Franz Josef
Oxford
72
Rangiora
Pegasus Bay
Fox Glacier
Springfield
72
River
73
CHRISTCHURCH
Mt. Hutt
Darfield
Lyttelton
WESTLAND NAT'L PARK
Mt. Cook
MT. COOK NAT'L PARK
77
Rakaia
BANKS PENINSULA
75
Akaroa
Haast
Haast River
Rangitata River
Rakaia
River
Akaroa Harbour
Jackson Bay
Lake Tekapo
72
Haast Pass
Lake Pukaki
Lake Tekapo
1
Ashburton
MT. ASPIRING NAT'L PARK
Lake Ohau
Fairlie
79
Geraldine
Ahuriri River
6
Mt. Aspiring
Lake Hawea
8
Lake Benmore
Hakataramea River
8
Milford Sound
Hollyford Track
Lake Wanaka
Omarama
Timaru
Milford
Lindis Pass
Lake Aviemore
1
Routeburn Track
Wanaka
8
Lake Waitaki
Waimate
Homer Tunnel
Tarras
Otematata
Milford Track
QUEENSTOWN
Duntroon
Waitaki River
Cromwell
6
83
Oamaru
Doubtful Sound
Lake Te Anau
Clyde
Ranfurly
94
Lake Wakatipu
Alexandra
85
Sound
Kingston
8
Manuherikia River
Palmerston
Te Anau
Mataura River
Roxburgh
87
1
Lake Manapouri
Manapouri
6
Clutha
Taieri River
FIORDLAND NAT'L PARK
Mossburn
94
Lawrence
DUNEDIN
Lake Hauroko
Lumsden
Mosgiel
96
90
Tuatapere
Winton
96
Gore
Milton
Waiau River
99
6
1
Balclutha
INVERCARGILL
1
Foveaux Strait
92
Bluff
Oban
STEWART ISLAND

SOUTH PACIFIC OCEAN

INTRODUCING NEW ZEALAND

British heritage joins with Maori culture in this land of scenic wonder

Haere mai! Welcome to New Zealand!

Isolated by vast southern seas, New Zealand is a land of awesome scenic beauty—a spectacular coastline indented by tree-rimmed bays and inlets; magnificent glacial mountains upthrust above fiords, lakes, and streams; volcanoes towering above arid desert and subtropical forest. Its remote location has shaped its self-sufficient people.

Along with Australia, New Zealand is one of only two South Pacific countries peopled predominantly by immigrants of European origin. Coupled with its British heritage is New Zealand's Maori culture, which adds an underlying Polynesian graciousness to the country.

New Zealand is a young country with frontier vitality; the first British colonists arrived less than 150 years ago. Natural barriers—rugged mountain ranges and dense bush—confined early settlement largely to the coast, and today most major cities border the sea. Much of the land is sparsely populated and used mainly for farming and grazing. Meat, wool, and dairy products are the country's principal exports.

Outside the population centers is the real New Zealand, a land of clearly defined districts, each with a distinct character, molded by its landscape and its settlers.

The land and its people

New Zealand lies about 10,400 km/6,500 miles southwest of San Francisco, a similar distance south of Tokyo, and about 1,920 km/1,200 miles southeast of Sydney.

Jet boat skims along the Kawarau River near Queenstown on a golden autumn afternoon. Early snowfall dusts the Crown Range to the north.

New Zealand's two main islands extend about 1,600 km/1,000 miles along a diagonal fault line. To the west lies the Tasman Sea; to the east, the South Pacific Ocean. Narrow Cook Strait separates the two islands. Though relatively small in area, the country encompasses an amazing variety of geological and climatic conditions.

Both Auckland, its largest city, and Wellington, its capital, are situated on North Island. Important South Island cities are Christchurch and Dunedin.

Glaciers and volcanoes shaped the land

Dominating the topography is a magnificent snow-capped mountain range—the Southern Alps—extending some 650 km/400 miles along the western side of South Island. Often obscured by clouds, this mountain chain was probably the reason the Maoris called New Zealand *Aotearoa* — the long white cloud. From the high peaks, glaciers gouged out long, slender mountain lakes and coastal fiords.

Volcanic action shaped much of North Island; ash and lava showering over the central part of the island buried vast forests and dammed river valleys to create the Rotorua lakes. Two volcanoes are still active: Mount Ngauruhoe in Tongariro National Park and White Island in the Bay of Plenty. From Rotorua south to Taupo, thermal activity has created geysers, boiling pools, steam vents, and silica terraces.

Indenting the country's coastline are deep-water harbors, glacier-carved fiords, and "drowned" river valleys invaded by rising seas at the end of the Ice Age. Wooded headlands shelter curving bays and sandy beaches. Vast tracts of scenic wilderness have been preserved in ten national parks and three maritime parks.

As New Zealand's land forms vary, so do its rainfall patterns and climate. Prevailing westerlies drop most of

Tuning in to Kiwi conversation

Colorful expressions and breezy slang—some borrowed from their British and Australian cousins—brighten the conversation of most *Kiwis* (New Zealanders). Subtle humor, an independent tradition, and the outdoor life influence many of the words and phrases you'll hear.

For many men, social life revolves around the local pub, where they meet their *mates* (male friends) and *shout* (treat) a round of beer. Families may spend the weekend at a *bach* or *crib* (country cabin or house), go for a *tramp* (hike) on a *track* (trail) through the *bush* (woods, forest), or perhaps *hire* (rent) a *caravan* (camper or trailer) for their *holiday* (vacation).

Personal contacts. If you have a friend-of-a-friend to contact, find a *call box* (phone booth) and *ring up* (telephone) the *bloke* (fellow). If his wife invites you to their *flat* (apartment) for tea, check the time of the invitation; tea is not only a beverage, it's also the evening meal.

If you eavesdrop in a pub, you may hear a worker say he's *brassed off* (angry, frustrated) about his job, co-workers, or *screw* (salary). When you hear talk about a *hooker*, it's a rugby player they're discussing. If someone's called a *Pommie*, he's an Englishman; a *pakeha* is a person of European descent. You don't understand? Don't worry. It'll all *come right* (be O.K.).

On the road. If you drive a car during your travels, you'll put your luggage in the *boot* (trunk), clean your *windscreen* (windshield), stop for *petrol* (gasoline), and peer under the *bonnet* (hood) if you hear a strange noise.

For major problems, you may need to ring up a *breakdown truck* (tow truck), *locker* (locksmith), or *panel beater* (car body mechanic).

You'll drive on *sealed* (paved) and *metalled* (graded gravel or crushed rock) roads. Warning signs you'll encounter include the following: *collision corner* (dangerous intersection), *greasy if wet* (slippery if wet), *hump* (bump), *give way* (yield), *no exit* (dead end), *change down* (shift into low gear), *no overtaking* (no passing), *road works* (construction), *special care* (caution), and *uneven surface* (rough road).

Touring tips. When traveling by motorcoach, passengers take a break at the *wee-tea stop* (comfort stop); elsewhere, excuse yourself to *spend a penny*.

If you're motoring and get thirsty, stop for a *cuppa* (cup of tea or coffee), a *fizzy* (carbonated beverage), or—at the end of the day—even *spirits* (liquor). When you want to picnic, buy food supplies or ask your hotel to prepare a *cut lunch* (packed lunch) for you. Then, when you feel *peckish* (hungry), you can find a pleasant site beside the road or in a *domain* (park).

If you stay on a sheep station, you'll see flocks in the *paddocks* (fields). Shearers stop for a *smoko* (coffee break), then work *flat stick* (at maximum effort).

On back-country trips, it's customary to *boil the billy* (heat water in a small can over a campfire for tea). Trampers should take along some *sticky plaster* (adhesive tape) in case of blisters and a *torch* (flashlight) if it's an overnight trip. If someone tells you to *get cracking* or *rattle your dags*, they want you to hurry up. When the weather turns cool, pull on a *jersey* (pullover sweater). Try not to *grizzle* (complain) if it starts to rain. On the beach, you can stop to *natter* (chat) with a fellow *fossicker* (beachcomber).

You'll like New Zealand. Its people are *smashing* (terrific) and the country's a *beaut!* And we're not *having you on* (pulling your leg). Cheerio!

---

their moisture along the western slope of the high mountains. Depleted of moisture, dry winds fan over the warm eastern slope.

Temperatures are never excessively hot in summer nor uncomfortably cold in winter. Ranges are more extreme on South Island; here you'll find the wettest and driest regions of the country, as well as some of its warmest and coldest weather.

Seasons are reversed in the Southern Hemisphere.

Luxuriant forests and bright wildflowers

New Zealand's isolation and diverse geography and climate are reflected in its unique plants. Tree ferns and palms flourish in subtropical rain forest within sight of snow. Flowering trees and tiny alpine wildflowers bloom in colorful displays.

Native and introduced trees. In the northern region of North Island, kauri trees tower over lower-growing trees and shrubs. The crimson-blossoming pohutukawa tree—called "New Zealand's Christmas tree"—brightens the northeastern coast and other areas in December.

In luxuriant lowland forests, tall podocarps (conifers) such as rimu, totara, and kahikatea — all valuable commercial timber — rise above lower broadleaf trees. Among native varieties are tawa, miro, hinau, puriri, kohekohe, towai, and the red-flowering rata and rewarewa trees. Ferns and mosses thrive beneath the forest canopy.

Twining through the treetops are the scarlet-blooming rata vine and the clematis, with its fragrant, starry white flowers. In early spring, golden cascades of kowhai blossoms blanket river banks and open areas.

Beech forests abound in cooler mountain areas;

undergrowth is usually sparse. In areas where rainfall is heavy, such as Fiordland, trees may be festooned with beardlike mosses and scarlet-blooming mistletoe.

British colonists planted many European trees on their homesteads and along roads. In April, these trees produce glorious displays of autumn color, at its best in Canterbury and Otago. You may also see plantings of Monterey pine, Douglas fir, and even redwoods.

Other plants and wildflowers. In regions too dry to support forests, shrubby manuka often blankets entire hillsides with its starry white flowers. Tufted tussock grasses spread across much of South Island's high inland hill country.

Other distinctive plants you'll see are the silky, ivory-colored flowerheads of toetoe and the swordlike leaf clumps of New Zealand flax. The Maoris used tall dried toetoe stems for *tukutuku* paneling (page 48) and flax fiber for clothing, ropes, and baskets.

In late spring and early summer, alpine wildflowers — snow grounsel, mountain gentian, mountain buttercups, mountain daisies, and New Zealand edelweiss — put on a brief but colorful show. Lupine varieties brighten mountain slopes and coastal areas.

Forest wildflowers include kotukutuku (the pink-flowering native fuchsia) and flamboyant red kakabeak. More than 60 native orchid species grow in moist grasslands and perch on tree trunks and branches in the rain forests.

Unusual birds—but few animals

The New Zealand bush teems with native birds. Best known is the flightless kiwi, a wingless, tailless, nocturnal bird with grey brown plumage and a long, tapered bill. It has given its name to New Zealanders, who are called Kiwis the world over. Another flightless bird is the weka, a smaller relative of the kiwi.

Other birds you may spot in the bush are the bellbird, whose sweet song resembles the chime of silver bells; the tui, another songster recognized by a tuft of white feathers at its black throat; friendly bush robins and fantails; the tiny rifleman; the bright-eyed tomtit; and wood pigeons. The morepork, a small owl, is active after nightfall.

In wet, swampy places you'll often see the colorful pukeko, a long-legged swamp hen. Similar in appearance is the rare takahe, thought for many years to be extinct. Inhabiting South Island mountains is the shrill-voiced kea, a mountain parrot.

Shore and sea birds, such as penguins, petrels, shags, gannets, shearwaters, gulls, and terns, are abundant along the coast. You can visit a royal albatross colony east of Dunedin and a heron colony at Okarito Lagoon, north of Westland National Park.

New Zealand has no native animals. All of its wild animals are descendants of imported animals brought here for food, sport, fur, or as predators.

Europeans follow Maoris to New Zealand

New Zealand's earliest inhabitants—called "moa hunters"—were peaceful nomads who roamed the islands as early as 750 A.D., stalking the flightless moa birds for food. When and where they came from remain a mystery.

According to Maori tradition, Polynesian voyager Kupe sailed south about 950 A.D. from the legendary Maori homeland called Hawaiki, thought to be in eastern Polynesia, and discovered a land he called *Aotearoa*. Eventually, he returned to Hawaiki and passed on sailing instructions to the land of the long white cloud. Four centuries later, a number of canoes journeyed south to Aotearoa, guided by the sun and stars. It is from these ancestral canoes that most Maoris claim their descent.

The Maoris introduced tropical food plants, especially the kumara, a variety of sweet potato. They depended on fish and birds for meat. At the time the first Europeans arrived, most Maoris were living in the northern and central areas of North Island, where their agricultural society thrived in the warm climate. Intertribal battles were common.

Exploration and exploitation. Europeans had long speculated that a great unknown continent existed in the South Pacific before 1642, when Abel Tasman was dispatched by the Dutch East India Company in search of new trade opportunities. He sailed along the western coast of South Island, anchoring in Golden Bay near the northern tip. Several of his sailors were killed in a clash with Maoris, and Tasman departed without landing.

Captain James Cook sailed to the South Pacific on a British scientific expedition. Mission completed, he turned south in search of the unknown continent. On October 7, 1769, he sighted the eastern coast of North Island and landed 2 days later at Poverty Bay.

Sailing north along the coast, Cook passed in a storm the ship captained by French explorer Jean de Surville. During the next 6 months, Cook circumnavigated both islands, charting the coast and recording information on the flora and fauna and on the Maori people. After his report was published, New Zealand became known to the world. Cook returned on two more voyages, making his base at Ship Cove in Queen Charlotte Sound.

Interest in the South Pacific and its resources increased. In the 1790s, sealers arrived to slaughter seals by the thousands. A decade later, whalers seeking provisions began calling at the Bay of Islands, which soon became the center of European settlement. In the 1830s and '40s, whaling stations sprang up on bays all along the coast south to Foveaux Strait.

While sealers and whalers plundered the seas, timber traders were razing the great kauri forests. Mill settlements mushroomed along Northland harbors and rivers.

Maoris reeled under the impact of the sailors and traders, who brought contagious diseases and firearms that permanently altered Maori life. The missionaries who began arriving in the Bay of Islands in 1814 attempted to protect the Maori people from exploitation.

Annexation and settlement. The ravaging of the country's natural resources, threat of annexation by France, land speculation, and insistence by the impatient London-based New Zealand Company to colonize exerted pressure on the British to annex the country. Britain reluctantly decided to negotiate with Maori chieftains. On February 6, 1840, Captain William Hobson concluded the Treaty of Waitangi with leading Northland chiefs, and New Zealand became part of the British Empire (now Commonwealth). Maori land rights were protected, and Maoris were granted equal citizenship status with European settlers.

Once the treaty was signed, shiploads of Europeans—most of them British—began arriving to establish planned settlements on both islands. Sheepherders imported large flocks to graze on the vast grasslands. Misunderstandings inevitably arose between Maoris and European settlers over land purchases. In 1860, conflicts in Taranaki spread throughout much of North Island, and the Land Wars continued intermittently for 20 years.

Meanwhile, South Island was gripped by gold fever. After gold was discovered in Central Otago in 1861, the stampede was on. Able-bodied men deserted the towns for the diggings, and prospectors poured in by the thousands. Almost overnight, Dunedin became the country's richest and most influential city.

In the late 19th century, the introduction of refrigeration opened a new industry—supplying meat-hungry British markets with frozen lamb. Dairy herds yielded butter and cheese for export. Agriculture expanded as rivers were rechanneled to irrigate new areas.

New Zealand's government

An independent member of the British Commonwealth, New Zealand is governed by an elected, single-chamber Parliament modeled after Britain's House of Commons. Since 1865, Wellington has been the nation's capital.

Queen Elizabeth II is represented in New Zealand by her appointed Governor-General, who each year appears at the opening session of Parliament in full formal regalia to read the royal Speech-from-the-Throne that officially opens Parliament.

Parliament has one chamber, the House of Representatives, composed of 92 members (including four Maori legislators elected directly by Maori voters) elected for 3-year terms. The country has two main political parties, the National and Labour parties. The leader of the party winning a majority of seats in Parliament becomes the Prime Minister. Members of the Cabinet are selected from among the parliamentary membership of the winning party. Legislation is enacted or amended by a simple majority vote in Parliament.

Until World War II, New Zealand automatically followed Britain's lead in international affairs. Since that time, though, it has established close alliances with the United States and Australia and has taken a leadership role among the nations of Polynesia and the South Pacific.

Self-reliant, friendly people

Throughout its history, New Zealand has attracted people who wanted to make a fresh start. Self-reliant, hardworking, and independent, the Kiwi is an amiable, friendly companion.

About 90 percent of New Zealand's 3.2 million people are of British descent; Maoris make up about 9 percent of the population. Nearly three-quarters of the people live on North Island. *Pakeha* (persons of European descent) intermingle freely with Maoris, who have largely adopted the European life style while preserving their own traditions and culture.

Life here has a solid quality. Most people work a 5-day week. They treasure their weekends and actively pursue all kinds of sports and outdoor activities.

Traveling in New Zealand

Numerous international airlines — including the country's own Air New Zealand — serve Auckland International Airport. Flights from Australia and the South Pacific land in Wellington and Christchurch as well. Several steamship companies cruise between New Zealand and international ports.

Public transport links cities and towns

Getting around the country is a pleasure. Whether you travel by plane, train, motorcoach, car, or ferry, you'll appreciate New Zealand's comprehensive and dependable transportation network.

Air service. Air New Zealand, Mount Cook Line, Newmans Airways Ltd., and several small regional airlines provide scheduled flights between the country's main cities, provincial towns, and resort areas. Charter planes are based at many airports.

Trains. New Zealand Railways provides passenger rail service between the larger cities and towns on both islands. Fast, comfortable trains feature adjustable seats, smoking and non-smoking sections, buffet cars, and refreshment service.

North Island's main line runs between Auckland and Wellington, passing west of Tongariro National Park. Two express trains link the cities: the deluxe Silver Fern daylight train, which runs daily except Sunday, and the overnight Northerner, which operates daily.

On South Island, train routes branch out from Christchurch—south along the coast to Invercargill, west across Arthur's Pass to Greymouth, and north to Picton. The Southerner daylight express train links Christchurch, Dunedin, and Invercargill daily except Sunday.

Interisland ferries. Passenger/vehicular ferries steam across Cook Strait several times daily, providing sched-

Milford Track hikers cross a rushing stream on a metal suspension bridge. On organized trips, trekkers carry only personal gear.

uled service between Wellington, at the southern tip of North Island, and Picton, in South Island's Marlborough Sounds. The trip takes about 3 hours and 20 minutes.

Ferry service also links Bluff, at the southern tip of South Island, and Stewart Island.

Motorcoaches. Long-distance motorcoaches of Railways Road Services cover the country from Kaitaia, near the northern tip of North Island, to Invercargill, at the southern end of South Island. Scheduled service connects most of the country's places of scenic, historic, and cultural interest. Reservations are necessary on all Railways Road Services routes, but no seats are assigned; if you purchase your ticket 72 hours ahead, your seat is guaranteed. If you want a window seat, try to be near the head of the boarding line.

Mount Cook Line also operates a network of long-distance motorcoach lines on both islands, with brief stops in small towns along its routes. Newmans Coach Lines and H & H Travel Lines Ltd. also provide scheduled regional service.

Travel passes. Independent travelers should investigate the various travel passes available from Air New Zealand, New Zealand Railways, and Mount Cook Line. Check with your travel agent or the New Zealand Tourist Office (page 12) for information. All passes must be purchased prior to arrival in New Zealand, but no reservations can be made until after you arrive.

Tour packages— with a group or on your own

Many travelers appreciate the convenience of seeing New Zealand's highlights as part of a group. Your travel agent can provide brochures on a variety of tour packages, some covering the duration of your New Zealand visit and others just a portion. Tours range in length from 3 days to 3 weeks and depart throughout the year. Additional information is available from offices of international carriers flying to New Zealand.

If you prefer touring independently, ask about fly-drive or fly-coach touring plans. Offering a more flexible

Information for travelers

New Zealand government tourist offices are happy to provide visitors with general and specific travel information and to answer your inquiries, both before you go and after you arrive in New Zealand. Travelers planning an extended stay can obtain visas from the nearest New Zealand embassy or consulate.

While you're in New Zealand, contact visitor information centers in the large towns and resort areas for specific information on the locale you're touring.

Planning your trip. In North America, you'll find a New Zealand Tourist and Publicity Office in the following locations:

Los Angeles, CA 90024: Suite 1530, Tishman Building, 10960 Wilshire Boulevard

New York, NY 10111: Suite 530, 630 Fifth Avenue

San Francisco, CA 94104: Suite 810, Citicorp Center, 1 Sansome Street

Vancouver, B.C., Canada V7Y1B6: Suite 1260, IBM Tower, 701 West Georgia Street

U.S. citizens planning a visit longer than 30 days or Canadian citizens staying longer than 6 months can apply for a visa at the nearest embassy (in Washington or Ottawa) or consulate (same cities and buildings as the New Zealand Tourist Office).

Australian branches of the New Zealand Tourist Office are located in Brisbane, Melbourne, Perth, and Sydney.

London, Frankfurt, Tokyo, and Singapore also have branches of the New Zealand Tourist Office.

After you arrive. Once you land in New Zealand, the staff in the offices of the Government Tourist Bureau (G.T.B.), located in Auckland, Rotorua, Wellington, Christchurch, Dunedin, and Queenstown, can help you obtain accommodations throughout the country; they also make travel arrangements and provide tour information.

In cities and larger towns, check the local public relations offices (P.R.O.) and visitor centers for information on local attractions and special events.

In the main tourist centers, look for free tourist publications; these feature seasonal events and special attractions, restaurant listings, and shopping suggestions.

Motorists who belong to an automobile club can obtain motoring information, maps, accommodation guide books, and route-planning assistance at offices of the Automobile Association in larger towns. You'll need to present your home auto club membership card.

itinerary, most independent tour plans include international air fare and extend from 2 to 3 weeks or longer. Some plans include a hotel pass covering accommodations of your choice at listed hotels throughout the country. New Zealand operators also offer camping tours and youth hostel holidays.

After you arrive, you'll find many short fly-drive and fly-coach holidays available from Auckland and Christchurch to main tourist areas.

Traveling by car

If you enjoy touring leisurely, one of the best ways to see the countryside is by rental car or camper. For tips on driving in New Zealand, see page 56.

Major rental car companies include Mutual-Avis, Tasman-Hertz, and Budget. All three have branch offices and representatives in major towns and tourist areas throughout the country. Companies offer a variety of plans, including one-day rates, one-way hire, unlimited kilometer rates, fly-drive trips, and plans where a car awaits you at the wharf or railway station. Rental cars are not transported between the islands.

Campers or motor vans can be rented in Auckland, Wellington, and Christchurch. Vehicles come in several designs and accommodate up to 6 persons. Generally, campers are equipped with sleeping and limited cooking facilities, but no toilet or shower. (Most New Zealand campgrounds have communal kitchens and centralized shower and toilet facilities. For more on camping, see page 15.) Usually, you rent by the week; rates include unlimited mileage and insurance. Summer travelers should make rental arrangements well in advance.

In the main centers, you can arrange for a chauffeur-driven automobile, with a knowledgeable driver-guide to show you the sights.

Taxis and local bus service

Reliable and inexpensive public transportation makes sightseeing easy in the major cities. City bus service connects the central districts with outlying suburbs; Wellington also has electric commuter train service to its northern suburbs. Bus fares vary by the number of sections of the route traveled.

Taxis in cities and towns operate from taxi stands or on call. Rates vary throughout the country, but are normally charged on a per-kilometer basis, with extra charges for night and weekend trips and for extra luggage. You can arrange an hourly rate for sightseeing.

Enjoying your visit

In the cities and resort areas, you'll find tourist accommodations in all different price ranges. Facilities may be more limited in the countryside, but you'll find a warm welcome awaiting you wherever you go.

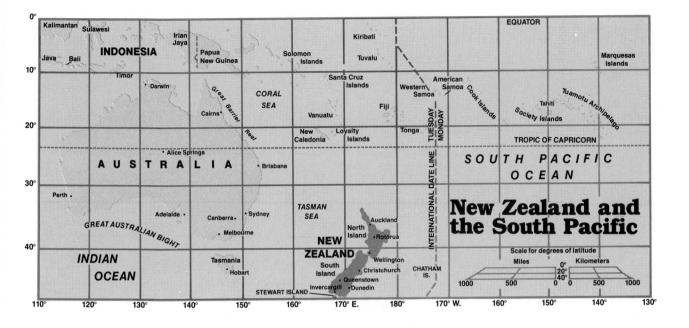

Hotels and motels

In recent years, numerous hotels, motor inns, and motels have been built in New Zealand, and many existing facilities have been upgraded. The cities offer choices ranging from modern high-rises to older, small hotels with a gracious charm. Country hotels are generally small, with friendly, old-fashioned atmosphere. Motels are situated throughout the country.

The main travel season extends from November through April. Peak demand occurs from mid-December through January and again during the Easter holidays, when New Zealanders take to the road; early reservations are recommended during these school vacation periods. Some hotels and motels apply a small surcharge for one-night stopovers. During the off-season, reduced rates may be available.

For current information on facilities and rates, consult your travel agent or the *New Zealand Accommodation Guide,* available from the New Zealand Tourist Office (page 12). In New Zealand, the Automobile Association publishes the *Accommodation and Camping Guide* for its members; it contains a detailed listing of hotels, motels, and motor camps.

Comfortable hotels. In addition to independent hotels, several chains maintain hotels throughout the country. The government-operated Tourist Hotel Corporation (THC) provides excellent resort accommodations on both islands. Other major operators include Hyatt Kingsgate, Sheraton, Travelodge, and Vacation hotels; Lion and Dominion Breweries (DB) also have hotels throughout the country. Older refurbished hotels make up the hostelries in the Establishment chain.

Rooms usually have tea and coffee-making facilities, telephone, and television. Some hotels provide daily newspapers, room refrigerators, and laundry facilities.

Hotels need licenses to be able to serve drinks on the premises. A hotel ranks as fully licensed (liquor can be sold to the public), tourist licensed (liquor available to hotel guests only), or unlicensed (no liquor sold).

Well-equipped motels. New Zealand's modern motels offer excellent value. Flag Inns and Best Western operate motels throughout the country, but most small motels are independently owned.

Motel flats provide fully furnished accommodations with kitchen facilities, refrigerator, cooking and dining utensils, and nearby laundry facilities.

Serviced motels are motorists' hotels with tea and coffee-making facilities but no kitchens. Breakfast is often available; larger motels have a restaurant on the premises.

Fishing lodges and golfing holidays

If you'd like to break your journey with several days of trout fishing or a few rounds of golf, you may want to seek out one of the special hostelries catering to your sport.

Some of the more expensive lodges are quite luxurious and take only a few guests. Others are comparable in price and comfort to an excellent first-class hotel; a few are extremely simple. For information, consult the *New Zealand Accommodation Guide.*

Your travel agent can help you arrange such a vacation. If you write to a hotel for a brochure, it's a good idea to enclose an international postal reply coupon to assure a prompt response.

Fishing lodges. Several North Island lodges offer fishing and hunting in a scenic or wilderness setting. Among those to consider are Solitude Lodge, perched on a peninsula near Rotorua overlooking Lake Tarawera; Waikato River Lodge, near Reporoa midway between Rotorua and Taupo; Huka Lodge, on the Waikato River north of Taupo;

Fattened Wairarapa lambs, bound for the freezing works, funnel through a loading chute at Pirinoa. Other flocks await their turn in the paddocks.

Tongariro Lodge, at the mouth of the Tongariro River near Turangi; and Wilderness Lodge, on the Ripia River in the mountain wilderness southeast of Taupo.

Deep-sea anglers might consider Kingfish Lodge Hotel, facing Whangaroa Harbour and accessible only by boat. Rustic cabins are available on Mayor Island, under the auspices of the Tauranga Big Game Fishing Club (P. O. Box 501, Tauranga).

If you're looking for a South Island retreat and are willing to put up with some inconveniences, try one of the fishing lodges or guest houses in the Marlborough Sounds (page 80); some are accessible only by boat or float plane from Picton. Another place fondly regarded by many Kiwis is family-run Mitchells, a fishing lodge on the shore of Lake Brunner on the West Coast.

Golfing holidays. Nearly 400 golf courses dot this small country, and many New Zealanders take to the links with enthusiasm.

In the Bay of Islands, you can walk to the excellent Waitangi course from the THC Waitangi Hotel. Built over-looking the island-studded bay, the course has a number of very good holes.

Near the trout-fishing center of Taupo, you can spend your daylight hours on the greens of the Wairakei International Course and your evenings enjoying the hospitality of the fine THC Wairakei Hotel.

Many excellent golf courses are located near cities and large towns. For more information about golfing in New Zealand, see page 16.

Home hospitality

A highlight for many travelers is spending a night or two in the home of a New Zealand family. You have your own room (and frequently, a private bath) and join the family for a leisurely home-cooked dinner, informal social activities, and a full breakfast. If you prefer, you can arrange bed-and-breakfast accommodation only, or lunches on request. Host families are scattered through-out both islands, in cities, in towns, and on farms. For more on farm visits, see page 124.

If you're looking for something more luxurious, con-sider one of the country's unusual dwellings that host a few paying guests. Overlooking Auckland's busy harbor is Ellerton Lodge, a restored colonial home in Devonport. Muriaroha is a gracious Rotorua home, filled with antiques and art and surrounded by gardens.

Your travel agent can make reservations for you through the New Zealand Tourist Office. In New Zea-land, stop at an office of the Government Tourist Bureau (page 12) or make arrangements directly through New Zealand Home Hospitality Ltd., P. O. Box 309, Nelson; phone (54) 85-727. Some regional organizations also arrange home stays; local tourist offices can provide more information. Usually, advance payment in full is re-quired, so only a voucher changes hands between you and your host.

Budget accommodations

You don't need a big budget to enjoy a New Zealand holiday. You'll find a wide range of moderately priced accommodations in small hotels and motels, guest houses, and cabins. Visitors can also stay in youth hostels or campgrounds.

Small hotels and guest houses. Moderate and low-priced licensed hotels offer clean rooms and good food without elaborate amenities. Guest houses and private hotels have no liquor licenses, and their rates vary according to their facilities. Rooms may or may not have a private bath, but most contain a sink and electric heater.

Youth hostels. The Youth Hostel Association offers its members an extensive chain of hostels throughout the country. Dormitory accommodation is available at moderate cost; you must provide your own sleeping bag. Communal cooking facilities are provided at each hostel, and stopovers are limited to 3 nights at any one place.

For information on membership and hostel locations, write the Youth Hostel Association of New Zealand, P.O. Box 436, Christchurch.

Campgrounds. During holiday periods, New Zealanders flock to the beaches and lakes, to the mountains, and to the country's national parks. Serving these travelers is a vast network of campgrounds, motor camps, and cabin and cottage accommodations. Many economy-minded overseas visitors have also discovered these facilities. It's a fine way to see the country and meet friendly Kiwi families.

Campgrounds are crowded during the December-January school holidays, but they're seldom full the rest of the year. Most campgrounds have a modern communal kitchen and dining room, laundry facilities, and centralized shower and toilet facilities. Some even offer a swimming pool, spa, children's play area, TV room, boat rentals, or barbecue facilities. You'll meet other campers easily; chatting and swapping experiences as you relax or do your chores are part of camping, New Zealand style.

General camping information is available from the New Zealand Tourist Office (page 12); detailed descriptions of campsites, motor camps, and cabins are provided in the Automobile Association's guide (page 13). Another helpful guide is the *Mobil Camping and Caravanning Guide;* look for it in New Zealand bookstores.

Eating and drinking, Kiwi style

In general, meals in New Zealand are substantial, no-frills affairs. But you can find continental finesse in both cooking and service in top city restaurants. Home entertaining is usually informal and hearty.

Food specialties. New Zealand lamb is world renowned and needs no introduction; you'll also find beef, pork, and poultry on restaurant menus. Venison and wild pork are available at restaurants specializing in wild game.

New Zealanders are very partial to what the Maoris call *kai-moana*—food from the sea—and it is superb. Rock lobster (crayfish) is most plentiful in spring and early summer. Tiny whitebait, netted in coastal rivers as they migrate upstream in the spring, are served in crisp, batter-fried fritters. Rock oysters are excellent, as are the succulent Bluff oysters scooped up from the chilly waters of Foveaux Strait. Scallops and mussels have distinctive yet delicate flavors. The rare toheroa usually goes into a rich soup; other creamy seafood soups feature the tuatua clam and the paua (abalone).

On restaurant menus you'll see a variety of ocean fish, including snapper, flounder, grouper, John Dory, and the sea perch called orange roughy. But if it's trout you want, you'll have to catch it yourself; trout fishing is strictly a sport, and none is caught commercially.

New Zealand fruits are superb in season, but you won't always find them on restaurant menus. In addition to familiar varieties, look for kiwifruit, passion fruit, feijoa, and tamarillo (tree tomato). The country's traditional dessert is pavlova, meringue with sliced fruit and whipped cream; it's best when prepared in New Zealand homes.

Among New Zealand cheeses you'll discover are a local blue vein, several types of cheddar, and others based on favorite international varieties.

In Rotorua, you can sample Maori-style cooking, with meat and vegetables cooked by steam in an underground oven (page 46).

Teas, lunch, and snacks. Morning and afternoon tea (or coffee) breaks are widely observed, both at home and at work. Along with your hot beverage you can enjoy scones, biscuits (cookies), thin sandwiches, or a "sweet."

In "takeaways," milk bars, coffee lounges, and other informal food centers, you can get a quick between-meals snack, such as fish and chips, thin sandwiches, or warm savories. Many hotels feature smorgasbord lunches with an array of hot dishes, cold meats, salads, and desserts.

Picnicking is a pleasant alternative when you're touring. Just be sure to plan ahead in areas such as the West Coast or Fiordland where facilities are widely scattered. You can pick up bread, cheese, fruit, and beverages for an informal repast; or, if you request it the previous night, your hotel may pack a lunch for you.

Beverages. Beer is the favorite drink, and spirits are also available. Among friends it's customary to take your turn "shouting" a round. Bars are open daily except Sunday, Christmas Day, and Good Friday. Licensed hotels serve drinks from 11 A.M. to 10 P.M. (to 11 on Saturday night) in bars, lounges, and licensed restaurants; guests staying in a licensed hotel can be served any time.

Licensed restaurants serve liquor, beer, and wine. Informal restaurants may be unlicensed (you can call ahead and inquire); if you want, you can bring your own wine and pay a modest corkage fee. Bottled wine, beer, and liquor are available in bottle shops.

Restaurant wine lists offer diners a growing selection of New Zealand table wines, as well as limited imports from Australia, the United States, and Europe. It's customary to pay the wine steward separately for wine and drinks.

Join the Kiwis in outdoor sports

Spurred on by the country's invigorating climate and inexpensive, easily available facilities, almost every New Zealander participates in one sport or another. On every fair-weather weekend, you'll see families heading for the beach, sailing in sheltered bays and harbors, and walking forest trails.

Many sports enthusiasts savor the tranquility of a favorite fishing stream or the camaraderie of play on the local golf course. Others seek the excitement of the racetrack or stadium, where they follow enthusiastically the fortunes of horse racing and team competition. Kiwis are renowned—not without reason—for their dedicated pursuit of "racing, rugby, and beer."

Visitors who join in outdoor activities gain special insight into the Kiwi life style. You can plan your travels to include hiking on one of New Zealand's scenic tracks (trails), skiing on its challenging slopes (page 52), or fishing in its clear lakes, streams, or offshore waters (pages 36 and 47). Pause for a while to watch a Saturday cricket match or a game of lawn bowls, or join the crowds cheering on a favorite horse or rugby team.

Golfers find challenging courses charging only modest fees; though weekends are busy, fairways are uncrowded mid-week. Motorized golf carts are not used, but you can rent a trundler (caddy cart) for a small fee. You'll find public and private courses throughout the country. Visiting members of overseas clubs are usually accorded guest privileges at private golf clubs; bring a letter of introduction from your home club secretary. You'll find more about the sport and a listing of some of the country's top courses in *Golf in New Zealand*, available from the New Zealand Tourist Office.

Tennis has thousands of enthusiasts—even some farms and sheep stations have a private court for family and guests. Visiting players can often arrange a tennis match with local players by contacting the regional secretaries of the New Zealand Lawn Tennis Association.

Evening entertainment

Much of the night life revolves around the hotels, where musicians entertain and bands play for dancing. Some towns have weekend cabaret entertainment.

Touring national and overseas artists visit the major centers, and local theater groups perform in the larger cities. Civic and university groups also offer music and drama. The New Zealand Symphony Orchestra, the Ballet, and the Opera Company tour on both islands. Maoris entertain in their traditional style in Rotorua.

For information on current entertainment, check local tourist publications and daily newspapers.

Shopping for New Zealand crafts

Shop craft centers and other stores for handcrafted articles and quality souvenirs. In country areas, it's fun to visit the general store—the local "sell everything" retailer.

Woolly sheepskins and lambskins—by-products of the export meat industry—are converted into rugs, car seat covers, toys, and wearing apparel. Other wool products include hand-knitted sweaters, weavings, car robes, and blankets (some in Maori designs). Suede clothing, leather goods, and opossum fur articles are also popular.

You'll see the work of New Zealand's excellent potters and woodworkers throughout the country. Native woods used singly or crafted in inlaid patterns are shaped into bowls, candleholders, trays, and other items.

New Zealand jade, called greenstone, is fashioned into traditional *tiki* pendants and contemporary jewelry. Iridescent paua shell is used handsomely in jewelry, trays, ashtrays, and boxes. Other pieces show off fine metalwork or New Zealand gemstones.

If you're interested in Maori culture, look for records of Maori music and Maori-carved wooden articles in traditional designs.

Festivals and annual events

Carnivals, festivals, flower shows, and sports events dot the New Zealand calendar. Summer is the busiest time, but you'll find activities in all seasons. Events mentioned below and those noted elsewhere are only a sampling of those you can attend. The New Zealand Tourist Office publishes an annual listing; you may find more events mentioned in local newspapers.

Spring (September through November) heralds the flower show season. Bulbs, rhododendrons, azaleas, and blossoming trees put on magnificent displays in botanic gardens. Alexandra salutes its commercial fruit industry with a September blossom festival. From October to April, lively and colorful A & P shows (page 123) are held at dozens of sites around the country.

In summer (December through February), many towns and resorts celebrate during the Christmas-New Year holidays with festivals, carnivals, regattas, parades, horse races, and other sports competitions. At Waitangi, an annual twilight ceremony on February 6 commemorates the signing of the Treaty of Waitangi in 1840.

Autumn (March through May) brings the Golden Shears sheep shearing competition in Masterton, Maori canoe races and other contests in Ngaruawahia, and the Highland Games in Hastings. National and international artists perform in Auckland's Festival of the Arts, in the Festival of Wellington, and in Christchurch's annual Arts Festival. Trout and game-fishing competitions are highlights of the autumn sports calendar.

In winter (June through August), Tauranga hosts a Citrus Festival and gathering of Scottish clans. Skiers take to the slopes, while ice skaters and curling enthusiasts head for South Island's frozen lakes and outdoor rinks.

Know before you go: tips for travelers

Documents, customs regulations, currency—this brief checklist will answer many of your questions as you prepare for your trip.

Entry/exit procedures. Passports are required of all overseas visitors except Australian citizens, and citizens of other Commonwealth countries who have been granted permanent residency in Australia and who are arriving directly from that country. Passports must be valid at least 6 months beyond the date the visitor intends leaving New Zealand.

Visas are not necessary for U.S. citizens (except American Samoans) staying 30 days or less, or for Canadian citizens visiting for 6 months or less. Visitors planning a longer stay can obtain visa application forms at U.S. consular offices in Washington, D.C., New York, Los Angeles, or San Francisco; or at Canadian offices in Ottawa or Vancouver.

Visitors do not need any inoculations to enter New Zealand unless they're arriving from South America or Asia.

All persons are required to complete passenger declaration forms on both arrival and departure. International air passengers pay a departure tax of NZ $2.

Customs. Visitors may bring in a limited amount of personal effects, which must be declared on entry and taken out of the country when the visitor leaves. Each adult may bring in duty-free six 750 ml bottles (4.5 liters total) of wine, one 1125 ml/40 oz. bottle of spirits, and 200 cigarettes (or up to 250 grams of tobacco or up to 50 cigars). Full details on customs limitations and restricted or prohibited imports may be obtained from the nearest New Zealand Government overseas representative.

Time. New Zealand is located just west of the International Date Line and has a single time zone—12 hours ahead of Greenwich Mean Time. Based on Standard Time, Auckland is 17 hours ahead of New York and 20 hours ahead of San Francisco. The country observes daylight-saving time from the last Sunday in October to the first Sunday in March; clocks are advanced 1 hour during this period.

Business hours and holidays. Offices and businesses are open on weekdays from 8 A.M. to 5 P.M.; post offices observe the same hours. Banking hours are from 10 A.M. to 4 P.M. Monday through Friday.

Shops and stores are usually open from 9 A.M. to 5:30 P.M. on weekdays (to 9 P.M. on late shopping nights). Many shops are open on Saturday morning.

Nationwide holidays include New Year's Day, Waitangi Day (February 6), Good Friday, Easter Monday, Anzac Day (April 25), Queen's Birthday (first Monday in June), Labour Day (fourth Monday in October), Christmas Day, and Boxing Day (December 26). Most attractions close on Good Friday and Christmas Day. Each province also celebrates an annual holiday.

Schools are closed from mid-December through the end of January (the main family holiday period), for 2 weeks in May, and again in August.

Currency. New Zealand operates on a decimal currency system based on dollar and cent denominations. A visitor may bring an unlimited amount of foreign currency and travelers checks into New Zealand, but government restrictions limit the transfer of New Zealand funds outside the country. Banks are located in all international transportation terminals and throughout the country.

Tipping. Employed persons in New Zealand do not depend on tips or gratuities for their income. You are not expected to tip for normal service; light tipping is done only for special service or attention. A 10 per cent tax on goods and services is added to applicable bills.

Medical and emergency facilities. Medical and hospital facilities provide a high standard of care. Hotels usually have a doctor on call for medical emergencies. Water is safe to drink, and there are no snakes or dangerous animals in the country.

In large towns, an emergency system (phone 111) brings immediate contact with police, fire, or ambulance service.

Climate. New Zealand lies in the temperate zone; its climate ranges from subtropical in the north to temperate in the south. Average midsummer temperatures range from 25° C/77° F in the Bay of Islands to 18° C/65° F in Invercargill. Average winter temperatures range from 15° C/59° F in the Bay of Islands to 8° C/46° F in Queenstown. Rainfall varies (it's heaviest on North Island and the West Coast of South Island), but rainy days are distributed throughout the year.

Seasons are reversed from those in the Northern Hemisphere. The busy summer holiday season extends from December to February; late spring and autumn are delightful times to travel in New Zealand.

Miscellaneous. Since New Zealand operates on the metric system, you'll find distances expressed in kilometers, elevations in meters, rainfall in millimeters, weights in grams and kilograms, and temperatures in Celsius.

Electrical current in New Zealand is 230 volts, 50 cycles AC. Most hotels and motels provide 110-volt AC sockets (20 watts) for electric razors only. Appliances that normally operate on a lower voltage require a converting transformer. Most New Zealand power sockets accept three-pin flat plugs (top two pins angled); you'll need a special adapter plug to use most appliances manufactured outside New Zealand.

NORTH ISLAND

Cities, rolling farm lands, volcanic peaks, fishing lakes, and a varied coast

More than 70 percent of New Zealand's 3.1 million people live on North Island. Auckland, the country's largest city, has a population of about 770,000. Wellington, the capital, is home to about 320,000 people. Outside the metropolitan areas are rolling farm lands dotted with grazing sheep and cattle, as well as widely spaced farm towns and coastal settlements. Major inland towns are Hamilton, Rotorua, Taupo, and Palmerston North. Other large towns lie near the coast.

Most of New Zealand's 280,000 Maoris live on North Island, primarily in the northern and eastern districts. Maori legends and customs are still strong here. As you travel around North Island, you'll become aware of the roles played by the missionaries, colonists, and farmers who developed and shaped this young country.

An island overview

Stretched out in the shape of an elongated diamond, North Island extends some 825 kilometers/515 miles from Cape Reinga in the north to Cape Palliser, southeast of Wellington, in the south. Narrow Cook Strait separates the island from neighboring South Island.

North Island's mountain backbone reaches from Wellington northeast to East Cape, a continuation of the alpine fault that created the Southern Alps on South Island. Isolated peaks and ranges mark the land.

Lake Taupo, the Rotorua lakes, and a trio of volcanoes mark the inland plateau. Volcanic activity has shaped this region: eruptions showered ash over the land, and lava flows dammed river valleys forming the Rotorua lakes. You'll see signs of geothermal activity throughout central North Island, from Tongariro National Park north to White Island in the Bay of Plenty.

From forested mountain watersheds, numerous rivers flow into the lakes or to the sea. During earlier years, many lowland rivers served as water highways for Maori canoes and coastal sailing ships. Longest of the nation's rivers is the Waikato, main source of North Island's hydroelectric power.

Along the coast, rugged capes and deep harbors add drama. Long, sandy beaches curving along many bays attract vacationing families, and pleasure boats cruise protected waters.

Only widely separated pockets remain of the vast forests that covered much of North Island when Captain James Cook sailed along these shores. In the early 1800s, kauri timber became the country's chief export; later, settlers cleared lands for farming. Today, fruits, vegetables, and many flowers thrive in North Island's rich soil and mild climate.

Exploitation marked the early years

According to tradition, ancestors of the country's Maori inhabitants sailing in canoes from Polynesia arrived in New Zealand in the 14th century.

Dutch navigator Abel Tasman skirted North Island's southwest coast in 1642, but no European set foot on New Zealand soil until Captain Cook and his party landed at Poverty Bay (near the present site of Gisborne) in 1769.

After accounts of Cook's discoveries were published, interest blossomed. Sealers and whalers roamed the southern seas; by the early 1800s, the Bay of Islands had become their major provisioning and repair base — and New Zealand's first European settlement.

Missionaries, who began arriving in 1814, established mission stations along the coast. Colonizing groups settled at Wellington, Wanganui, and New Plymouth, and timber speculators razed the extensive kauri

Grazing sheep roam the rolling green hills of the King Country southeast of Taumarunui. In New Zealand, sheep outnumber people 20 to 1.

forests. Trading and mill settlements mushroomed on harbors and along navigable rivers.

Maori tribes, who traditionally had battled among themselves, reeled under the impact of European development. To help keep the peace between land-hungry Europeans and the Maoris, the British Government reluctantly annexed New Zealand in 1840 when representatives of the British Crown and Maori chiefs signed the Treaty of Waitangi.

Misunderstandings and ill feeling soon arose over land purchases. In 1860, fighting erupted in Taranaki between Maori warriors and government troops and spread across the central part of North Island. Referred to as the Land Wars, the fighting continued for more than 20 years; it was not until formal peace was declared in 1881 that immigrants could expand into fertile new farmlands south of Auckland.

In the early years, population centered in the Bay of Islands. As settlement increased, the capital was moved southward—from the Bay of Islands to Auckland in 1840, and finally to Wellington in 1865.

Touring North Island

From the main tourist centers to remote, secluded beaches, North Island offers an array of intriguing destinations and activities. Both Auckland, New Zealand's largest city, and Wellington, its capital, are attractive, bustling cities situated on scenic deep-water harbors. Highlights in Rotorua include fascinating thermal attractions and a look at Maori life.

Three national parks and two maritime parks preserve areas of special beauty. Visitors enjoy alpine activities and bush walks in Egmont National Park. You can ski, hike, or explore the varied terrain at Tongariro Park's volcanic preserve. Urewera offers a pair of lovely lakes and trails through dense forest. In the Bay of Islands and the Hauraki Gulf, you cruise amid scattered islands.

If the sea attracts, you'll find busy summer resorts or quiet hideaways along the coasts of Northland, the Coromandel Peninsula, Bay of Plenty, East Cape, Hawke Bay, or along the Tasman Sea. Big-game fishing lures deep-water anglers to warm Pacific waters off Northland and the Bay of Plenty. To sample some of New Zealand's fabled trout fishing, head for Lake Taupo, the Rotorua lakes, or their tributary streams.

You can walk through kauri forests, visit mission stations and colonial dwellings, learn about Maori culture and pioneer history, gaze on thermal attractions, soak up the sun on coastal beaches, fly over active volcanoes, or go fishing or skin diving in the island-studded sea.

Excellent highways cut through the interior of the island and border both the Pacific and Tasman coasts.

Place names reveal a nation's heritage

New Zealand place names reflect the colorful heritage of its Maori people, the navigators and mountaineers who sailed its coastline and explored its mountains, and the settlers who colonized and developed the land.

Early explorers named places for themselves—Cook Strait, Tasman Sea, D'Urville Island, Haast Pass; members of their party—Young Nick's Head, Banks Peninsula; their patrons—Egmont; daily events—Cape Runaway, Cape Kidnappers, Cape Turnagain, Preservation Inlet, Cape Foulwind, Cape Farewell; or geographical landmarks—Bluff, Bay of Islands.

Settlers frequently honored heroes, such as Wellington, Marlborough, Nelson, Hamilton; illustrious statesmen or settlers, including Palmerston, Auckland, Fox, Russell, Lyttelton, Masterton; or their European origins—Norsewood, Balclutha, Dunedin, New Plymouth. Miners and sheepmen added colorful names such as Pigroot and Drybread.

Descriptive Maori names identify many settlements as well as geographical landmarks. These may reflect legendary happenings or actual events, or describe the appearance of the land. Among words often used in Maori place names are these:

Ahi (fire); *ao* (cloud); *ara* (path, road); *aroha* (love); *ata* (shadow); *atua* (god, demon); *awa* (valley, river); *haka* (dance); *hau* (wind); *hui* (assembly); *huka* (foam); *iti* (small); *iwi* (people, tribe); *kai* (food, eat); *keri* (dig); *kino* (bad); *ma* (white, clear); *ma* or *manga* (tributary, stream); *mata* (headland); *maunga* (mountain); *moana* (sea, lake); *motu* (island); *muri* (end); *nui* (big, plenty); *o* (of, the place of); *one* (sand, beach, mud).

Other words include *pa* (fortified village, stockade); *pae* (ridge, resting place); *pai* (good); *papa* (ground covered with vegetation, earth); *po* (night); *puke* (hill); *rangi* (sky); *rau* (many); *roa* (long, high); *roto* (lake); *rua* (cave, hollow, two); *tahi* (one, single); *tai* (coast, sea, tide); *tangi* (sorrow, mourning); *tapu* (forbidden, sacred); *te* (the); *tea* (white, clear); *wai* (water); *whanga* (bay, inlet); *whare* (house, hut); *whenua* (land, country).

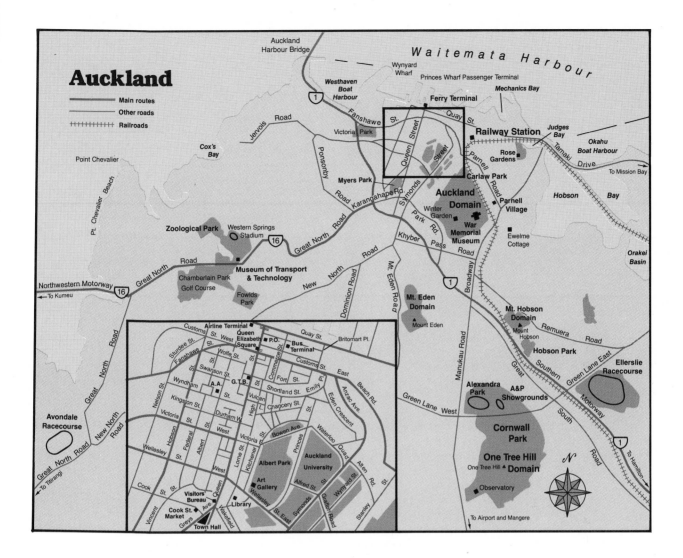

Auckland

Main routes
Other roads
Railroads

(Map of Auckland showing major streets, parks, and landmarks including Waitemata Harbour, Auckland Harbour Bridge, Westhaven Boat Harbour, Ferry Terminal, Railway Station, Auckland Domain, War Memorial Museum, Parnell Village, Mt. Eden Domain, Mt. Hobson Domain, Cornwall Park, One Tree Hill Domain, Ellerslie Racecourse, and the downtown inset map)

Highway 1 begins at Awanui, north of Kaitaia, and runs the length of the island through Auckland, Hamilton, and Taupo to Wellington. Highway 2 follows the eastern coast along the Bay of Plenty past Poverty Bay and Hawke Bay, then moves inland to its terminus in Wellington. Highway 3 skirts the west coast through the Taranaki and Wanganui regions. Other roads link the main routes and offer scenic alternatives for leisurely motoring.

Cosmopolitan Auckland

Sprawling across a narrow isthmus, Auckland and its far-flung suburbs separate two magnificent harbors.

To the east, at the city's downtown doorstep, lies sparkling Waitemata Harbour, guarded by Rangitoto Island; beyond spread the waters of the Hauraki Gulf and Pacific Ocean. West of the city, the shallow turquoise waters of Manukau Harbour funnel into the Tasman Sea. Protruding from Auckland's landscape are the cones of numerous extinct volcanoes, many of which were once fortified by Maori tribes. Northwest of the city rise the forested Waitakere Ranges.

New Zealand's largest city, Auckland contains nearly a quarter of the country's population. It's the country's commercial and industrial center, North Island's transportation hub, and the arrival point of most overseas visitors. Enhancing the city's cosmopolitan flavor are a large Maori community, immigrants from various European and Asian countries, and Pacific Islanders attracted by employment and educational opportunities.

New waterfront development and modern shopping and office complexes distinguish Auckland's downtown. In the older suburbs, restored Victorian buildings provide nostalgic contrast. The city's most striking manmade structure is the Harbour Bridge, arcing dramatically across Waitemata Harbour and linking the city with the fast-growing North Shore.

No one lives far from the water, and Auckland's balmy year-round climate (though often hot and humid in summer) encourages water-oriented recreation. On weekends, families flock to the beaches, and hundreds of yachts cruise the sheltered harbors and gulf waters.

Towers of Auckland's commercial district rise against a blue backdrop of Waitemata Harbour. Sailboats dot the water on weekends.

Unlike the country's three other main cities, Auckland was not settled by organized, closely knit colonizing groups. After Auckland became the country's capital in 1840, government officials, tradesmen, and laborers migrated here, but no immigrant ships arrived until 1842. To protect the young town from hostile Maori tribes to the south, four military settlements of the Royal New Zealand Fencible Corps were established on the isthmus at Onehunga, Panmure, Howick, and Otahuhu.

As Auckland's population increased, land-hungry settlers coveting the rich Maori lands to the south soon embroiled the province in the Land Wars. Auckland lost its role as capital in 1865 to Wellington, but commerce generated by the Thames gold fields in the late 1860s helped to revive the city's economy.

Today's wealth comes from development of Northland and Waikato farm lands and industrial expansion on the city's outskirts.

Getting settled in Auckland

Queen Street is downtown Auckland's main thoroughfare. From the Ferry Terminal on Quay Street to Karangahape Road, its route is lined with offices, stores, pedestrian malls, and shopping arcades.

Auckland offers a broad choice of entertainment. For current evening attractions and sporting events, check tourist publications, available at your hotel or from the Visitors' Bureau, or the daily newspapers.

City buses link the downtown district with most tourist destinations (page 24); bus information is also noted in some tourist publications.

Shopping. Serious shoppers will appreciate the city's impressive array of excellent stores and shops, many of them specializing in quality New Zealand crafts.

A leisurely walk through the main shopping district offers many places to pause. Queens Arcade, at the corner of Queen and Customs streets, houses a delightful collection of shops in a setting enhanced by natural light, plants, marble, and mirrors. At 22 Customs Street West, the renovated Old Auckland Customhouse has a new lease on life as a handsome shopping emporium. Shoppers can browse in an Edwardian atmosphere along Strand Arcade.

Shops are generally open from 9 A.M. to 5 or 5:30 P.M. on weekdays, and from 9:30 A.M. to noon on Saturday; some shops in the Downtown Airline Terminal are open daily. Queen Street shops stay open until 9 P.M. on Friday; Thursday is "late night" on Karangahape Road.

Just minutes from Queen Street, Victoria Park Markets re-creates the spontaneous atmosphere of a lively European village food and craft market; it is open daily from 6:30 A.M. to 11 P.M. in renovated buildings on Victoria Street West opposite the park. Near the Town Hall, the Cook Street Market bustles with shoppers on Friday from 9 A.M. to 9 P.M. and on Saturday from 10 A.M. to 4 P.M.

Some delightful shopping areas are located in the suburbs. In Parnell, Victorian buildings along Parnell Road have been transformed into boutiques and specialty shops. In Remuera, one of the city's oldest and most select suburbs, modern arcades vie with fascinating older stores to tempt passersby. Interesting shops dot Ponsonby, one of the long-established western suburbs. In the casual atmosphere of Karangahape Road, you'll find bargains, variety, and a glimpse of Polynesia.

Entertainment. For an evening out, Aucklanders and visitors alike can enjoy dinner and dancing, a cabaret show, musical acts, or a theater restaurant.

Most concerts and recitals take place at the Town Hall. Touring shows, ballet, and stage plays are presented at His Majesty's Theatre; local casts perform at the Mercury Theatre and several smaller theaters. Western Springs Stadium and the Auckland Showgrounds on Greenlane Road in Epsom host special events.

In addition to the City Art Gallery, which features the art of New Zealand, Auckland has numerous downtown and suburban galleries offering changing exhibitions.

Sports and special events. Horse racing takes place at Ellerslie Racecourse and Avondale Racecourse, and night trotting at Alexandra Park Raceway. Spectators can watch Rugby Union games and cricket test matches at Eden Park, Rugby League games at Carlaw Park in Parnell, soccer at Newmarket Park, and men's hockey at Hobson Park in Remuera. Basketball games and wrestling and boxing matches are held at the YMCA Stadium.

The beaches and bays of this city on the water attract thousands of bathers and boaters from November through March. Throughout the summer, yachts sail across harbor waters and amid the islands of the Hauraki Gulf. On the Monday nearest January 29, everyone heads for the Waitemata shore to watch the colorful Anniversary Day Yachting Regatta.

Largest of the country's A & P shows is the New Zealand Easter Show, held at the Auckland Showgrounds in Epsom. An annual event in July is the Auckland International Film Festival. Biennially in March, in even-numbered years, the Auckland Festival highlights all facets of the visual and performing arts.

On foot in downtown Auckland

Queen Street is Auckland's pulse — the district where people go to work, eat, shop, and walk. A leisurely walking tour along Queen Street from the waterfront to Town Hall and back through Albert Park will help you get acquainted with the city.

Between Quay and Customs streets, Queen Street is a pedestrian mall — Queen Elizabeth II Square, marked by a fountain and statues. A few blocks farther up the street, pause to enjoy the greenery and benches in Vulcan Lane; blacksmiths once plied their trade here.

At the Visitors' Bureau in Aotea Square, you can learn about inner city walks and obtain leaflets with maps showing a variety of suggested routes.

Town Hall. Topped by a clock tower, the 1911 Town Hall stands on Queen Street opposite Wakefield Street. A magnificent kauri slab, cut from a 3,000-year-old tree, dominates the foyer; kauri timber was used to panel the city council chamber. The building also houses a large auditorium and a concert hall.

Nearby is Myers Park, a secluded reserve known for its many grand Phoenix palms.

City Art Gallery. A 19th century building at the southwest corner of Albert Park (Kitchener Street and Wellesley Street East) is home for the country's most complete collection of New Zealand art, recording the entire history of European settlement in New Zealand. A modern collection includes representative works by living New Zealand artists. The art gallery is open from 10 A.M. to 4:30 P.M. on weekdays, to 8:30 P.M. on Friday, and from 1 to 5:30 P.M. on Saturday and Sunday.

Albert Park. This peaceful retreat — a lunchtime haven for city office workers — crowns a low hill a few minutes' walk east of Queen Street.

Students from the nearby University of Auckland relax on the lawns, and mothers bring children here to play. Beneath towering trees, a statue of Queen Victoria keeps a watchful eye on the park's fountain, flower beds, and floral clock. On summer Sundays, you can enjoy afternoon band concerts here.

Supreme Court. One of Auckland's first public buildings, this fine example of Gothic revival architecture was built in 1868 at the corner of Waterloo Quadrant and Anzac Avenue. Modeled after England's Warwick Castle, the turreted building is ornamented with stone gargoyles and likenesses of historic figures. Public galleries in the courtrooms are usually open to visitors.

Strolling along the waterfront

Wide and busy Quay Street skirts the downtown waterfront. Just steps from the shopping district, you can observe ocean-going ships maneuvering in and out of berths and watch yachts and other small boats sail across the broad harbor.

At the foot of Queen Street, the gracious old brick Ferry Terminal is a harbor landmark. From here, a small ferry chugs across Waitemata Harbour to Devonport on the North Shore. Launch trips to the Hauraki Gulf islands depart from nearby wharves, and passenger liners tie up at Princes Wharf. Amphibian planes leave from Mechanics Bay at the east end of the downtown waterfront.

Walking west along Quay Street, you'll see fishing boats moored in Freemans Bay. Early risers can catch the activity at the produce markets and seafood bazaar,

Auckland—the essentials

Auckland, New Zealand's largest city, lies between two large harbors. All transportation lines converge here, making it a popular departure point for excursions to all parts of North Island.

Getting there. Most overseas visitors arrive at Auckland International Airport, located at Mangere, about 20 km/13 miles south of the city center. Air service links Auckland with cities throughout New Zealand.

Auckland is the northern terminus of North Island rail service, and daily passenger trains connect the city with Wellington and intermediate points. A network of motorcoach routes links Auckland with North Island's larger towns and tourist destinations. Cruise ships dock at Princes Wharf on Quay Street.

Accommodations. Auckland visitors can choose from a full range of downtown and suburban accommodations.

Leading city hotels are the Sheraton-Auckland, on Symonds Street; Hyatt Kingsgate Auckland, at Waterloo Quadrant and Princes Street; the Regent of Auckland, at Albert and Swanson streets; Auckland City Travelodge, on Quay Street overlooking the harbor; South Pacific, corner of Queen Street and Customs Street East; and Town House, on Anzac Avenue adjacent to Constitution Hill Park.

Smaller, centrally located Auckland hotels include the Royal International, on Victoria Street West; DeBrett, at High and Shortland streets; and Grafton Oaks Courtesy Inn, on Grafton Road near the Domain.

Among the large suburban hotels are the White Heron Regency and Rose Park Hotel in Parnell, Vacation Hotel at One Tree Hill, and Mon Desir Motor Hotel in Takapuna on the North Shore. Near the airport, accommodations include the Auckland Airport Travelodge, Gateway Lodge, and Airport Inn. The suburbs also offer an excellent choice of motels, small private tourist hotels, and guest houses.

Hauraki Gulf accommodations are available on Pakatoa, Waiheke, and Great Barrier islands.

Food and drink. Auckland's cosmopolitan population is reflected in the variety and quality of its more than 200 restaurants. Choices range from elegant to informal settings in restaurants featuring New Zealand seafood and game, continental cuisine, or ethnic fare from many parts of the world. Some restaurants occupy historic buildings; others offer views rivaling the cuisine.

Getting around. Taxis are available at all terminals and on Customs Street West just off Queen Street, or ask your hotel porter to telephone for one. Rental car offices are located at the airport, downtown, or in the suburbs, but avoid city driving if you can—Auckland has one of the highest traffic-to-population ratios in the world.

Buses of the Auckland Regional Authority (ARA) and suburban companies provide public transport throughout the metropolitan area. You can obtain route information by phone (797-119) or from the Bus Place, 131 Hobson Street. Buses depart from several downtown points; the Downtown Bus Centre is located on Commerce Street behind the main post office. Shuttle buses transport passengers between the railway station and Karangahape Road via Queen Street and Greys Avenue (exact change required, varying by zone).

The ferry to Devonport, on the North Shore, departs from the Ferry Terminal on Quay Street. Launches to Hauraki Gulf islands also leave from the waterfront.

Several companies operate half-day and full-day sightseeing tours; longer excursions are also available. Flightseeing trips take off from Mechanics Bay.

Tourist information. The Auckland Visitors' Bureau, 299 Queen Street at Aotea Square, has information on attractions and walking routes; maps and guidebooks are also available. A Travellers' Information Centre at the airport aids incoming visitors and will book Auckland accommodations. To make travel arrangements, schedule tours, and reserve accommodations throughout New Zealand, visit the Government Tourist Bureau, 99 Queen Street. Motoring information is available to members at the Automobile Association office, 33 Wyndham Street.

---

tucked between Sturdee Street and the fishing boat basin. Auctioning starts at about 6 A.M. on weekdays and ends before 10 A.M.

Hilly parks and formal gardens

Numerous extinct volcanic cones jut above Auckland's flat landscape. Most were once fortified by Maori tribes, who terraced the slopes and strengthened their stockades with ditches, earthen ramparts, and wooden palisades. Today, sheep graze and children play on the grassy terraces. You can ride in comfort to these hilly summits for panoramic views over Auckland and its twin harbors.

Other parks and gardens scattered throughout the city present seasonal flower displays and other attractions.

Mount Eden. Auckland's highest point (196 meters/643 feet), Mount Eden offers the city's finest view—over the city and water to the distant Waitakere Ranges.

Eden Garden, on Omana Avenue off Mountain Road, is rich with native and exotic trees and shrubs.

One Tree Hill and Cornwall Park. Crowned by an obelisk, One Tree Hill is the city's most striking feature. This *pa*-terraced volcanic cone rises above Cornwall Park between Manukau Road and the Great South Road. In Cornwall Park is Acacia Cottage, Auckland's oldest surviving wooden building (1841).

Mount Albert. Located southwest of the downtown district, Mount Albert is reached via New North Road and Mount Albert Road. You can picnic in a grassy crater.

Alberton, a restored Victorian homestead built in 1862, is open daily at 100 Mount Albert Road. The scene of many parties, it was the social center of Mount Albert in colonial days and still contains many Victorian heirlooms. Indian-style towers and verandas were added to the house in the 1880s; other notable features include the ballroom, the kitchen, and a brick-lined well.

Other parks and gardens. Formal gardens at Ellerslie Racecourse attract visitors even on nonracing days.

Jellicoe Park, off Manukau Road in the southern borough of Onehunga, contains a military blockhouse built in 1860 to protect the settlement from anticipated Maori attacks. A small museum displaying colonial furnishings and other memorabilia is housed in a replica 1840s Fencible cottage; it's open on weekend afternoons.

Auckland Museum crowns a hill

Overlooking the city and Waitemata Harbour from a grassy hilltop in Auckland Domain, the outstanding Auckland War Memorial Museum contains a fascinating collection of exhibits on New Zealand and the Pacific Islands.

Dominating the museum's Maori Court is an impressive war canoe, handcarved about 1835 from a huge totara tree. Other Maori exhibits include tribal buildings, clothing, tools and weapons, personal ornaments, and historic portraits of tattooed chiefs and maidens.

Natural history exhibits show off New Zealand's native birds, trees and plants, sea life and shells, animals, geology, and paleontology. Other exhibits feature the peoples of the Pacific and articles from their daily life, decorative and applied art, and maritime and military memorabilia. Replicas of Queen Street shops of the 1860s line the museum's Centennial Street display. Planetarium shows are presented on Saturday and Sunday.

From the expansive Domain grounds surrounding the museum, you look across Waitemata Harbour to the North Shore. The Cenotaph in front of the museum honors those who served in two World Wars. Down the slope, near the kiosk and duck pond, tropical and subtropical plants flourish indoors in the Winter Gardens.

The museum is open Monday through Saturday from 10 A.M. to 5 P.M. (to 4:15 P.M. in winter), and on Sunday from 11 A.M. to 5 P.M. A free map guides you through the exhibits.

Skirting the harbor on Tamaki Drive

Bordering the city's downtown waterfront, this 11-km/7-mile scenic drive follows the shore of Waitemata Harbour through the eastern suburbs to St. Heliers Bay.

You'll pass Okahu Bay, a popular anchorage for pleasure boats. Farther on is Savage Memorial Park, honoring New Zealand's first Labour Prime Minister. From Bastion Point, site of wartime harbor fortifications, you can watch maritime activity.

At Mission Bay is the Melanesian Mission Museum, currently closed for reconstruction. Built of Rangitoto stone, it contains relics from the era of bishops Selwyn and Patterson (1842–71), as well as artifacts from Melanesia and the Solomon Islands. Night-lighted Trevor Moss Davis Memorial Fountain is a memorable feature of an evening drive along the harbor.

Mission Bay is a favorite with bathers, as are Kohimarama and St. Heliers. The sheltered beach at St. Heliers vies in size and popularity with Takapuna Beach on the North Shore.

Ponsonby's charming Renall Street

One of a network of narrow streets lacing the northern slopes of the Ponsonby district, northwest of the downtown area, Renall Street retains pleasing traces of the atmosphere and individuality that characterized 19th century Auckland. Preserved along this steep, slender street and forming an intimate community are about 20 wooden cottages, most originally occupied by artisans.

The compact houses sit primly on narrow lots, separate from, yet in harmony with, their neighbors. Verandas adorn the dwellings and picket fences add a unifying touch. Some cottages enjoy views of the harbor. Near the bottom of the angled street is Foresters' Hall, the site of community gatherings during Auckland's early years.

The Auckland City Council has designated Renall Street as a conservation area to ensure the preservation of the buildings. Privately owned and occupied, they're not open to the public. At the Visitors' Center in Aotea Square, you can obtain a leaflet describing some of the dwellings and the neighborhood's development.

Browsing in historic Parnell

One of Auckland's oldest districts has been imaginatively restored to create a lively shopping area that retains the charm of a small town. Within walking distance of the Parnell shopping district are several historic buildings and a handsome rose garden.

To avoid an uphill walk, begin your excursion above the Parnell shops. Seek out the distinctive buildings that appeal to you, then stroll down Parnell Road to enjoy the neighborhood's appeal.

Historic buildings. At the top of the slope, near Parnell Road and St. Stephen's Avenue, are Anglican church buildings associated with Bishop Selwyn, a missionary who arrived in 1842. "Selwyn churches" in the Auckland area are characterized by simple Gothic design, steep shingled roofs, exterior bracing timbers, and diamond-shaped leaded windows. St. Stephen's Chapel, built in

1857 as successor to an earlier chapel, is located off St. Stephen's Avenue at the end of Judge Street; many pioneers are buried in the churchyard. Spired and churchlike Selwyn Court was formerly the bishop's library.

Continuing south on Parnell Road, you'll pass St. Mary's Church, a Selwyn building completed in 1898 and notable for its excellent Gothic design.

On Ayr Street, two fine old 19th century dwellings are now open daily to the public. Kinder House, 2 Ayr Street, was built in 1857 as the home of Rev. Dr. John Kinder, a distinguished churchman and artist. Outside, roses bloom in a Victorian garden.

Shingle-roofed Ewelme Cottage at 14 Ayr Street is also set in a garden. Built in 1863-64 by the Rev. Vicesimus Lush, the kauri-wood dwelling housed his descendants for more than a century. The restored home, open daily, contains many of its original Victorian furnishings.

Parnell's shops. Rejuvenated Victorian dwellings and stores along Parnell Road now house boutiques, jewelry and craft shops, restaurants and food stores, antique furniture shops, and art galleries. Near the top of the hill, Parnell Village is a delightful complex of small shops.

Rose gardens. Hundreds of roses are in peak bloom from November to March in Sir Dove-Myer Robinson Park on Gladstone Road. Mature trees and native shrubs frame a view across Waitemata Harbour, and a walkway leads down to sheltered Judges Bay. Nearby is Parnell Baths, a large salt-water pool open from October to April.

Vintage cars and kiwis in Western Springs

In the Western Springs district, you can visit a transportation museum and pioneer village, and see kiwis in Auckland's zoo.

Pioneer transport. Mechanically minded visitors of all ages delight in the fascinating collection of vintage motor cars, steam locomotives, and aircraft at the Museum of Transport and Technology on the Great North Road, about 5 km/3 miles from central Auckland. The museum is open daily from 9 A.M. to 5 P.M.

An electric tram and a double-decker bus shuttle visitors around the grounds. One exhibit depicts the development of calculating machines, from the abacus to the computer. Other displays highlight agriculture, printing, and photography. Old buildings have been restored and assembled in Pioneer Village.

Zoological Park. Auckland's zoo is one of several places in the country where you can see the kiwi, a flightless nocturnal bird that occupies a special place in the hearts of New Zealanders. In the dim light of the zoo's kiwi house, you watch these unusual birds in a bush setting.

Animals, birds, reptiles, and fish are shown in near-natural settings. Three trails winding through the grounds link the exhibits and a children's zoo. Zoo hours are 9:30 A.M. to 5:30 P.M. daily.

Epsom's Highwic mansion

South of Auckland Domain in Epsom is Highwic, the elegant mansion of Alfred Buckland, a 19th-century Auckland business magnate and landowner. Buckland took over the property in 1862 and constructed the spacious dwelling to house his large family. After his death in 1903, his descendants maintained the property until 1978.

Built in the English manner, the house has vertical boarding, latticed casement windows, and steep slate roofs. Interior details include an elegant staircase, pointed Gothic panels on the doors, and fireplaces enhanced by marble mantels. Surrounded by lawns and gardens, the mansion manages to retain an aura of serenity and seclusion despite its proximity to industrial activity.

The house is open daily from 10:30 A.M. to noon and from 1 to 4 P.M.

New Zealand Heritage Park

Visitors can experience New Zealand's unique culture and life style in a new theme park in a southeastern suburb of Auckland. Just a 10-minute drive from downtown, the park is located off the Ellerslie-Panmure Highway on Harrison Road, about 1½ km/1 mile southeast of the Southern Motorway. It will be open daily from November through March, and from Wednesday through Sunday the rest of the year.

The park consists of three main sections: Natureworld, featuring native plants, a walk-through aviary, and trout pools; Agriworld, highlighting the importance of agriculture, with shearing and milking displays, farm animals, and other exhibits; and Cultureworld, presenting Maori entertainers, craftspeople, and audio visuals on the country's scenery and development. You can try your hand at Maori-style carving, milking a cow, or panning for gold.

Excursions from Auckland

The good beaches rimming the Auckland coast in all directions are a popular weekend destination for many. But other attractions beckon visitors, as well. On day trips from Auckland, you can explore the scattered islands of Hauraki Gulf Maritime Park, visit colonial Howick and rural Clevedon, ride a vintage train near Glenbrook, go wine tasting in the Henderson Valley, or tour the Hibiscus Coast north of Auckland.

Guided motorcoach excursions take visitors through the Auckland countryside; southeast to Coromandel, Waitomo, and Rotorua; and north to the Bay of Islands. Day cruises visit some of the Hauraki Gulf islands.

Flightseeing trips departing from Mechanics Bay on the Waitemata waterfront offer aerial views of the city, harbors, and gulf islands. Flights also serve Pakatoa, Waiheke, and Great Barrier islands.

Shopping is delightful in historic Parnell, where refurbished Victorians now house shops, boutiques, and restaurants.

The beach scene

On fair weather weekends, Aucklanders head for the nearby beaches and bays that provide much of the city's ambience. Most can be reached by public transportation.

Fine beaches abound on the North Shore, bordering Hauraki Gulf. West of Auckland is the more untamed, hilly expanse along the Tasman coast. Closer-in beaches include Okahu Bay, Mission Bay, and St. Heliers, and others southeast of Auckland on Tamaki Strait.

North Shore. From the Ferry Terminal on Quay Street, Devonport is just a short ferry ride across Waitemata Harbour. The town's sheltered shore is backed by a grassy picnic reserve.

Devonport's North Head, a recreation reserve within Hauraki Gulf Maritime Park, offers glorious views of the gulf. Entrance to the reserve is from Takaraunga Road.

Adults enjoy strolling along a water-level trail, while children explore abandoned tunnels and gun emplacements of a former military fort. In January, guides lead walking tours; for information, phone Auckland 771-899.

Takapuna is one of the district's most popular strands. Many homes border beaches along the East Coast Bays, a series of coastal resorts stretching from Milford north to Long Bay. More fine beaches rim the Whangaparaoa Peninsula and Hibiscus Coast near Orewa.

West coast beaches. Along the rugged Tasman coast, great sandy beaches sprawl at the foot of steep forested hills. From roads above the beaches, many trails wind through trees down to the sand. Surfcasters fish from the rocks, and picnickers and hikers roam the beach and bluffs. Ocean surfers ride the waves at Piha and Muriwai Beach; Karekare and Bethells Beach are also popular.

Boating holidays— by yacht, raft, or canoe

Sailing through island-studded waters or sleeping on a yacht anchored in a deserted bay is a dream vacation well within your reach. Increasingly popular in recent years, boating holidays offer a relaxing opportunity to explore another fascinating facet of New Zealand. In the maritime parks, it's the only way to really see the country.

If a more active vacation beckons, you can raft or canoe down scenic rivers. For information on operators and excursions, contact the New Zealand Tourist Office.

Yacht charters. You can explore the coastline and islands at your own pace when you charter a yacht through a commercial operator. You'll cruise leisurely across sheltered gulfs and bays, past verdant islands and golden sand beaches. You stop when you wish for a swim, a barbecue on a lonely stretch of beach, or a bit of fishing or snorkeling. Usually your boat provides accommodation as well as transportation.

Depending on your sailing skills, you can hire a yacht with skipper or arrange for a bareboat charter (without skipper). A boat with skipper is more expensive, but it's relatively hassle-free. The skipper will know where the best beaches and fishing spots are, and how to get the stove to work. Bareboat chartering means that you do your own sailing; your operator will teach you the essentials before you depart.

Most of the charter boats cruise the waters of Auckland's Hauraki Gulf, the Bay of Islands, Lake Taupo, and the Marlborough Sounds. Charter yachts also sail off the Coromandel coast, around the Mercury Bay-Mayor Island area, along the coast of Abel Tasman National Park north of Nelson, and on Lake TeAnau. For information on operators, contact the New Zealand Tourist Office or the New Zealand Charter Yacht and Launch Owners Association, P.O. Box 3730, Auckland.

The main boating season runs from November to Easter; you'll have the largest selection of boats in February and March, when New Zealand children are back in school after their midsummer holidays.

Cruising operators. If you prefer not to charter a boat but still want to enjoy a holiday afloat, you'll find several excursions where you can go along for the ride. You may even be able to learn the ropes and then practice by helping to handle the vessel.

In the Hauraki Gulf, Trans Tours Gray Line (P.O. Box 3812, Auckland) offers a 2-day cruise exploring the bays and rugged coastline of Great Barrier Island. Passengers are expected to help sail the schooner.

If you want to cruise in Fiordland waters, you can take a 3 or 6-day cruise operated by Fiordland Cruises Ltd. of Manapouri. Your boat is a 48-foot-long houseboat, specially designed for cruising the fiords; its shallow draft allows passengers to go ashore in areas that don't have wharf facilities.

Canoeing and rafting. Several commercial companies offer canoe or raft trips down New Zealand's scenic rivers. Canoe and kayak safaris range from a short trip on the Kawarau River to an extended excursion on the Wanganui River or Lake Tarawera.

Also available are rafting trips lasting anywhere from a half-day to 5 days; trips operate on a number of rivers on both islands. Your guide will know the course of the river, the history and geology of the area, and the best camping and fishing spots. For information on excursions, write to the New Zealand Tourist Office.

Hauraki Gulf Maritime Park

For a pleasant day's outing, explore Hauraki Gulf Maritime Park, just off Auckland's eastern coast. The park encompasses all or part of several dozen scattered islands, from the Poor Knights Islands northeast of Whangarei to the Aldermen Islands off the southern part of the Coromandel Peninsula.

On several islands, vacationers can enjoy walks, swimming, boating, and deep-sea fishing. Other islands, inhabited only by wildlife, are remote and hard to reach.

Blue Boat launches leave Auckland's waterfront on scheduled trips to several of the larger islands, including Rangitoto, Motutapu, and Motuihe; ferry service also links Auckland with Waiheke Island. Day cruises depart from the city waterfront for Pakatoa Island. North of Auckland, a ferry departs for Kawau Island daily at 10:30 A.M. from Sandspit, east of Warkworth. During peak holiday periods, additional cruises are available. For a longer trip, consider chartering a yacht.

Amphibian planes take off from Mechanics Bay in Auckland on regular flightseeing and charter trips.

Accommodations are available on Pakatoa, Waiheke, and Great Barrier islands. For more information about park activities, contact the Hauraki Gulf Maritime Park Board, P.O. Box 5249, Auckland 1 (phone Auckland 771-899).

Rangitoto Island. A landmark of Waitemata Harbour, Rangitoto's sloping cone stands sharply against the sky. A favorite picnic spot, the island is a short 40-minute launch trip from the city. A bus meets the boat and takes passengers on a tour. You'll find a tearoom and swimming pool at the wharf and a store and sandy beach at Islington Bay, near the causeway to Motutapu Island.

One of the few peaks not fortified by the Maoris, Rangitoto has little soil and no permanent source of water; yet vegetation thrives in apparently barren conditions. Walkers can stroll from the wharf to Wilson's Park, Flax Point Bridge, and McKenzie Bay. It's a steep 4-km/2½-mile climb to the summit, where you have unsurpassed views of the gulf and city.

Motutapu Island. Linked to Rangitoto by a causeway, this island is farmed by the Department of Lands and Survey. A walkway crosses the farm.

Motuihe Island. Less than an hour from Auckland by boat, Motuihe is a popular day outing. Sheltered picnic grounds, safe sandy beaches, and walking trails abound.

Waiheke Island. Largest of the islands, Waiheke is dotted with small farms. Its lovely bays and beaches attract boaters and anglers. Hotel and motel accommodations are available on the island, accessible by launch or amphibian plane.

Pakatoa Island. Reached by launch from Auckland, Pakatoa has been developed into a resort, open from August through June. The island's beaches and fine views are popular with honeymooners.

Great Barrier Island. Largest of the offshore islands, Great Barrier has a rugged coastline bordered with pohutukawa trees. Deep-sea fishing is a big attraction, with hapuka, kingfish, and snapper the major catches. Guest houses are located at some of the bays. Access is by chartered launch or amphibian plane.

Kawau Island. A summer haven for yachters, Kawau fascinates naturalists and those with a yen for history. A ranger is stationed at Two House Bay (phone Kawau 892).

In 1862, Sir George Grey, an early governor of New Zealand, purchased the island and built his home here. He transformed Kawau into a subtropical paradise of imported trees, plants, and animals. Governor Grey's Mansion House has been restored, and visitors see the house and gardens much as they were in Grey's time. Mansion House is open daily from 9:30 A.M. to 3:30 P.M. (3 P.M. on Friday). Wallabies and kookaburras still inhabit the bush. Cottages and mineshafts date from the 1830s and '40s, when copper and manganese were mined here.

Colonial history in Howick

Dairy farms surround the seaside town of Howick, a colonial settlement that's managed to retain some of its village atmosphere. Located 23 km/14 miles southeast of the city, Howick was the largest of the Fencible settlements (page 22) established in 1847 to defend settlers from possible Maori attack. Buses to Howick depart from Auckland's Downtown Bus Centre.

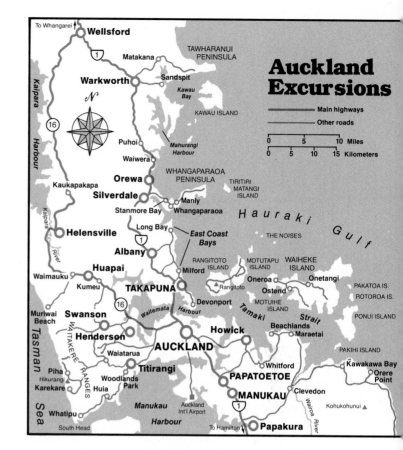

Nineteen colonial buildings from the 1840–1880 era are on display in Howick Colonial Village. Located in Lloyd Elsmore Park on Bells Road, off the main Pakuranga-Howick Highway, the village is open daily from 10 A.M. to 4 P.M. A small kauri plantation features trees and plant varieties popular in Victorian times, and an herb garden flourishes near the village pond.

Stockade Hill commands a view over the countryside and harbor. On Selwyn Road you'll see All Saints' Anglican Church, one of the distinctive "Selwyn churches" and the town's oldest building, dating from 1847. Near the beach is Shamrock Cottage; originally the Fencibles' canteen and later an inn, it's now a tearoom.

In the Garden of Memories on Uxbridge Street are more historic buildings; a small museum is open on Saturday and Sunday afternoons.

Golden beaches and rural villages

If you're driving, continue south to Whitford, then turn east and follow Maraetai Road to a chain of magnificent golden beaches that face Tamaki Strait.

In the village of Clevedon is the Clevedon Woolshed, a wool and craft shop that carries an extensive range of New Zealand products, including spinners' supplies, handspun yarns for weaving and knitting, and hand-crafted articles. Clevedon Country Explorers can arrange tours, farm visits, and demonstrations.

A regional botanic garden is located near Manukau.

Under full sail, yachts race in a strong breeze on Auckland's Waitemata Harbour. The Anniversary Day Regatta takes place here in late January.

A vintage railway

Southwest of Auckland, history buffs can ride on a vintage train and learn about the early settlement of the area.

South of Papakura, Highway 1 passes through fertile rolling farmlands as it ascends toward the Bombay Hills. Near Drury, turn west to Glenbrook and Waiuku.

On Sundays from October to June, locomotives and passenger cars from the early 1900s attract visitors to the Glenbrook Vintage Railway; you can board a train here for a nostalgic journey through the green farm lands.

Nearby Waiuku began as a portage settlement on the South Auckland trade route between Manukau Harbour and the Waikato River. During the 1860s, this area was the scene of conflicts between Maori warriors and settlers. The Waiuku Museum on King Street is open on weekend afternoons.

Market gardens near Pukekohe yield vegetables and fruit in abundance. For a splendid view, drive up Pukekohe Hill southwest of town; you'll gaze over the patchwork of gardens north across Manukau Harbour to Auckland and south to the mouth of the Waikato River.

Wine touring in the Henderson Valley

To become acquainted with New Zealand wines, spend a day touring and tasting in the Henderson Valley northwest of Auckland, heart of New Zealand's wine country. More than a dozen wineries are concentrated here, tucked into valleys at the foot of the Waitakere Ranges. Others are located a bit farther north near the towns of Kumeu, Huapai, and Waimauku.

Neat rows of vines sweep across the land, and huge fig trees cast welcome summer shade. The oldest vineyard in this region is Corbans, established in 1902 on its present site on Great North Road, just outside Henderson. Most of the wineries were established by Dalmatian settlers who originally came from Yugoslavia to work in Northland's kauri gumfields; many are still family operations, run by descendants of the founders.

Most wineries are open Monday through Saturday for tours and sampling. Often you'll talk to the winemakers themselves. Some tours include a winery stop; if you're touring independently, inquire at the Auckland Visitors' Bureau in Aotea Square for directions.

West of Henderson, the 50-km/30-mile Waitakere Scenic Drive follows the crest of the Waitakere Ranges, between Swanson and Titirangi. Bordered by lush tree ferns, the route affords spectacular views over Auckland and its two harbors. A side road leads to the Cascades reserve and Kauri Park. Signposted trails wind through native bush to waterfalls and stands of kauri trees.

Along the Hibiscus Coast

Bordering the Hauraki Gulf north of the Whangaparaoa Peninsula, the Hibiscus Coast is a favorite summer and weekend destination. You drive through rolling green farmlands to Orewa, a leading coastal resort and mecca for summer campers. Visitor attractions border the beach; ocean surfers frolic in the waters offshore.

Waiwera, about 48 km/29 miles north of Auckland, is noted for its hot mineral spring pools where bathers soak away aches and cares. Visitors can picnic nearby and hike in the surrounding woods. Just north of Waiwera is Wenderholm Regional Park, a beach and riverside reserve.

The farming community of Puhoi retains customs brought by Bohemian immigrants in 1862. Warkworth, on the Mahurangi River, is the site of a giant dishlike antenna linking New Zealand to the worldwide satellite telecommunications system. The Kawau Island ferry departs from nearby Sandspit.

Historic and scenic Northland

If you want to relax in scenic splendor and in a balmy climate, head north! Northland's tourist mecca is the lovely Bay of Islands, cradle of New Zealand's early European settlement. But the region offers far more.

You can picnic on sheltered bays rimmed with crimson-flowering pohutukawa trees, go deep-sea fishing or cruising among scattered islands, or walk along windswept beaches or amid towering ancient kauri trees.

Here you'll find links with explorers Tasman, Cook, and de Surville, as well as tales of Maori conflicts and bawdy whaling days. Anglican and Catholic missionaries set up mission stations here; other settlements thrived on the kauri timber and gum trades.

Whangarei, Northland's port city

The region's commercial and industrial hub is the thriving port city of Whangarei, on the eastern coast. Its sheltered, deep-water harbor has attracted a number of large industries, including the country's only oil refinery and first oil-fired power station.

During holiday periods, coach tours depart from Whangarei for the Tutukaka Coast, the Bay of Islands, and Cape Reinga. Scenic flights can also be arranged.

City attractions. Stop at the City Public Relations Office on Rust Avenue for a map and tourist literature. A 48-km/29-mile scenic drive begins here; it winds through business and residential areas and several parks. Savor the view over city, countryside, and harbor from the summit of Mount Parahaki, then continue east to the suburb of Onerahi.

As it flows along the city's eastern border, the Hatea River cuts through several fine parks, including Whangarei Falls, A. H. Reed Memorial Kauri Park, and Mair Park; here, the river broadens into a natural swimming pool. Trails wind through the forest, and picnic sites abound.

Amid the rose gardens in Whangarei's Cafler Park you'll find the Clapham Clock Museum, containing some 600 clocks of varying age, origin, and design.

On pleasant days, the tree-bordered Town Basin bustles with waterfront activity. You can hire a dinghy, charter a launch, or watch youngsters fish for "tiddlers" off the wharf. Water-skiers skim across the harbor, and families stroll and picnic on nearby beaches.

Whangarei Heads. For an enjoyable outing, take the 35-km/22-mile scenic drive along the harbor's north shore to Whangarei Heads and Ocean Beach. Along the way you'll pass the Parua Bay boat harbor, majestic Mount Manaia, and numerous picnicking, swimming, and fishing areas. A curious reef at Taurikura and the lonely stretch of beach north of Bream Head invite exploration.

Tutukaka Coast. Northeast of Whangarei, a string of beautiful bays and beaches indents the Pacific shore. Known as the Tutukaka Coast, it extends from Ngunguru some 13 km/8 miles north to Sandy Bay. The small resorts of Ngunguru, Tutukaka, and Matapouri offer accommodations for vacationers.

Pohutukawa trees border sandy beaches, where families spread picnic lunches and children splash in the waves. Pleasure boats anchor in sheltered harbors. Along the shore, fishermen surfcast from rocky peninsulas or along the beach at Woolley Bay. Surfers head for Sandy Bay. To reach Whale Bay's delightful cove, you follow a short trail through the woods.

At Tutukaka's marina, parties can charter deep-sea fishing launches for the day (all equipment provided) or arrange for sightseeing or skin-diving trips to the Poor Knights Islands about 19 km/12 miles offshore.

On a leisurely 80-km/50-mile loop, you can return to Whangarei through the Waro Limestone Reserve, where bare outcrops have eroded into unusual shapes and patterns, and the small farming town of Hikurangi.

West to kauri country

Provincial highways loop west from Highway 1 to Kaipara Harbour, Dargaville, the kauri parks, and remote Hokianga Harbour.

A century ago, ships of the kauri timber trade sailed the intricate Kaipara and Hokianga waterways, and small port and mill settlements sprang up along their shores. Today, pleasure boats cruise these lonely waters, and vacationers enjoy quiet holidays along the banks. Between the harbors, two kauri parks preserve portions of the forest that once covered much of North Island.

Kaipara Harbour. Southwest of Whangarei, the fingers of Kaipara Harbour probe deeply into the dairy lands. From the main north-south route, take Highway 12 west toward Maungaturoto. On the northern inlets you can picnic, swim, or camp at several beaches, including Pahi and Tinopai, both south of Paparoa. Numerous boat launching ramps testify to good harbor fishing.

At Matakohe, west of Paparoa, the fascinating Otamatea Kauri and Pioneer Museum chronicles the kauri era. Photographs depict the hard life of the bush-

Northland—the essentials

Tourists head for the lovely Bay of Islands for boating, big-game fishing, and other outdoor activities. Whangarei, at the head of a large, deep-water harbor, is the region's industrial and commercial center; Dargaville, near the west coast, is gateway to the kauri reserves. The center for excursions to the Far North is Kaitaia.

Getting there. From Auckland, direct flights on Mount Cook Line serve the Bay of Islands airport at Kerikeri, with connecting motorcoach service to Paihia. Air New Zealand flights link Auckland with Whangarei, on the east coast, and with Kaitaia, in the north.

Railways Road Services provides scheduled motorcoach service from Auckland to Whangarei, Kawakawa, Bay of Islands tourist centers, and Kaitaia. Buses also connect Auckland with Maungaturoto and Dargaville. Guided tours depart from Auckland for the Bay of Islands and other Northland attractions.

Accommodations. Leading resort in the Bay of Islands is the THC Waitangi Hotel, facing the bay at Waitangi; motel units are also available. In Paihia, you can choose from numerous large motels, such as the Autolodge Motor Inn, Busby Manor Motor Inn, Beachcomber, and Edgewater, as well as many smaller ones catering to family groups. Russell accommodations include the Duke of Marlborough Hotel and Commodore's Lodge, both facing the waterfront, and several smaller motels. You'll also find lodging in Kerikeri.

Elsewhere in Northland, Whangarei has a range of hotel and motel accommodations. In Kaitaia, you'll find the Northerner, Orana Motor Inn, Sierra Court Motel, and Kaitaia Hotel; many small motels are located along Highway 1 and at nearby Ahipara. In game-fishing ports, hostelries such as Kingfish Lodge in Whangaroa cater to anglers.

Getting around. Railways Road Services motorcoaches connect the larger towns and tourist centers. From Dargaville and Kawakawa, there's local service to Rawene, on the south shore of Hokianga Harbour; here, a vehicular ferry provides daytime service between Rawene and the north shore. Rental cars are available in Whangarei, Paihia, Kerikeri, and Kaitaia.

In the Bay of Islands, a passenger ferry links Paihia and Russell; vehicular ferries shuttle automobiles between Opua and Okiato. Motorcoach excursions depart from Paihia and Kaitaia for Cape Reinga and Ninety Mile Beach; local sightseeing trips on land or in the air are also available. Boat excursions leave from Paihia, Russell, and Kerikeri.

Tourist information. Visitors can obtain facts on local attractions and sightseeing tours at tourism offices in Whangarei, Paihia, Russell, Kaitaia, and Dargaville.

man, and you'll see some of the heavy equipment and tools they used in felling and milling the trees. A typical 19th century dwelling, built of kauri, contains hand-crafted kauri furniture and other period articles. Panels show the grain of various native woods, and you can study an outstanding collection of kauri gum.

Birdwatchers can head for Pouto, south of Dargaville near the tip of North Head, where waterfowl nest in shallow fresh-water lagoons.

Dargaville. Bordering the Wairoa River, Dargaville was a thriving port during the heyday of the kauri timber and gum trade. Today, it's a prosperous dairy center and the touring base for Northland's west coast.

Dargaville's museum features articles associated with the kauri industry, as well as local maritime relics; the collection is temporarily housed in the municipal building just north of the post office.

Bayly's Beach, just west of Dargaville, is a favorite summer recreation site and, in winter, a target for toheroa (clam) diggers. It's situated about midway along Northland's longest ocean beach, stretching some 109 km/ 68 miles from the mouth of Kaipara Harbour north to Maunganui Bluff. Side roads from Highway 12 provide access to this majestic coast at several points.

Near Maropiu, the three Kai Iwi lakes in Taharoa Domain attract trout anglers, sailors, and water-skiers.

Kauri parks. An extensive stand of kauri is preserved in Waipoua Kauri Forest, near the coast about 52 km/32 miles north of Dargaville. As you follow Highway 12 through the forest, towering trees loom above dense undergrowth. Short signposted trails lead through the bush to several of the oldest and tallest trees. In a small cottage museum at forest headquarters, you can see tools and other articles used by early kauri bushmen.

For those who want to linger, Trounson Kauri Park, located about 17 km/10 miles southeast of Highway 12 on the Donnelley's Crossing Road, has a campground and well-defined trails leading into the kauri grove, where you'll see young "rickers" as well as aged giants.

Hokianga Harbour. Carving a ragged inlet in the northwestern coast, Hokianga Harbour and its coastal tributaries jut deeply into sparsely populated farm lands. Omapere and Opononi, two small, unpretentious beach towns on the southern shore of the inlet, offer the quiet pleasures of boating, fishing, and exploring.

Two historic buildings on the southern shore are worth a detour. At Rawene is Clendon House, built in the late 1860s by James Clendon, the first United States consul in New Zealand; open daily, it contains many of his possessions. Farther east at Horeke is the 1838 Mangungu Mission House, the oldest Methodist mission building in the country; it's open Saturday through Wednesday. Hours at both buildings are 10 A.M. to noon and 2 to 4 P.M.

A vehicular ferry links Rawene with the Narrows, near Kohukohu on Hokianga Harbour's north coast; from Kohukohu, it's about an hour's drive to Kaitaia.

Highway 12 continues east through Kaikohe, a farming center and site of the outdoor Pioneer Village. Hot mineral baths await travelers at Ngawha Springs. You'll rejoin Highway 1 at Ohaeawai, north of Kawakawa.

The Bay of Islands

What makes the Bay of Islands special? For some visitors it's the scenery—broad vistas of sky and sea blended with wooded islands. For others it's the beaches, boating, and water sports. Some savor its historic sites. Yachters and anglers regard it as one of New Zealand's finest harbors and a top game-fishing area. Residents treasure its unhurried pace, its balmy climate, and its serenity.

Rich in legend and mystery, the Bay of Islands is a microcosm of early New Zealand history, with ties to the Maoris, whalers, missionaries, and early settlers. For decades this quiet pastoral district had few contacts with the outside world. Today, it's a popular holiday resort.

Tourist facilities and accommodations are concentrated at Paihia. Across the bay is Russell, one-time whaling port and now center of game-fishing activities, and headquarters for the Bay of Islands Maritime and Historic Park. Other historic sites include Waitangi (across the river from Paihia), Kerikeri, and Waimate North (pages 34–37). Farming and administrative center of the region is Kawakawa, south of the bay on Highway 1. Nearby is Waiomio Caves, a series of caverns with striking limestone formations and a glowworm gallery.

New Zealand's earliest settlements. The Bay of Islands has lured explorers for many centuries. According to Maori legend, the great Polynesian explorer Kupe visited the bay in the 10th century. Captain Cook, anchoring here in 1769, bestowed the simple name that captures its unpretentious charm. Three years later, the French explorer Marion du Fresne established a temporary base on Moturua Island.

In the early 1800s, sealers and whalers followed Cook's Pacific travels, anchoring in the harbor for ship repair and reprovisioning. An unruly settlement at Kororareka (now Russell) attracted assorted brigands and adventurers. Traders and colonists soon followed.

Next came the missionaries. Rev. Samuel Marsden and his party established an Anglican mission station at Rangihoua Bay in 1814; other missions followed at Kerikeri (1819), Paihia (1823), and Waimate North (1830). A Catholic mission was established at Kororareka in 1838.

By the early 1830s, most of New Zealand's white population had settled along the bay, and Britain appointed a British Resident, James Busby, to deal with problems caused by haphazard settlement. In 1840, Captain William Hobson arrived to negotiate with Maori chiefs. On February 6, 1840, British and Maori representatives signed the Treaty of Waitangi, proclaiming British sovereignty over New Zealand. Later that year the capital was moved south to Waitemata Harbour (Auckland), and the bay's era of influence was over.

The kauri: magnificent forest giant

Today, only a few pockets remain of the vast native kauri forests that once covered much of North Island. Now protected in reserves, these magnificent trees rival California's redwoods in age, height, and girth. Mature kauri trees (*Agathis australis*) can be as old as 2,000 years.

Kauri timber and kauri gum figure prominently in Northland's early settlement. Pioneer settlers cut the slow-growing trees at a rapid rate. The valuable timber became the country's first export—sought after for ships' masts and as a building material. Within a few decades, the vast forests were depleted.

As the timber trade declined, gumdiggers swarmed to Northland to "bleed" the remaining trees and dig the resinous kauri gum—used as a base in slow-drying hard varnishes—from the beds of buried prehistoric forests.

In the forest, the massive, ashen-trunked trees grow only in a few scattered groups, dwarfing smaller trees such as tawa, rimu, kahikatea, towai, and northern rata. They can reach 52 meters/170 feet in height with a maximum girth of 15 meters/50 feet. As the tree grows, its lower branches drop off naturally, yielding a tall, straight-grained, ash-colored trunk. In mature trees, the first branches appear high off the ground.

You can see kauri growing with other native trees in several forest reserves. Largest of these is Waipoua Kauri Forest, north of Dargaville on the west coast (page 32).

At Matakohe, west of Paparoa on Highway 12, the Otamatea Kauri and Pioneer Museum (page 31) focuses on the days when kauri was king. You'll also learn about the kauri timber and gumdigging industries at museums in Kaitaia, Dargaville, and Russell.

A maritime and historic park. Many island and mainland reserves and historic areas — extending from Whangaroa Harbour in the north to Whangaruru Harbour, south of Cape Brett—have been brought together in the Bay of Islands Maritime and Historic Park. Many historically significant sites, as well as scenic and recreational lands, are included within its boundaries. At the park visitor center on The Strand in Russell, you'll learn more about this delightful region and the feast of activities awaiting you: swimming, picnicking, fishing, boating, skin diving, camping, walks and hikes, scenic drives, charter boat trips, and visits to historical sites. Midsummer visitors can join in guided excursions.

Park information is available from the chief ranger in Russell (P.O. Box 134; phone Russell 685), from the ranger in Kerikeri (P.O. Box 128; phone Kerikeri 78-474), or from the information officer, Bay of Islands Maritime and Historic Park, P.O. Box 5249, Auckland (phone Auckland 771-899).

A fascinating water world. Sports enthusiasts from around the world come to fish these fabled waters, first popularized by American writer-fisherman Zane Grey in the 1920s. Other visitors skin-dive in the subtropical waters or cruise amidst the islands. The Bay of Islands is a favored port of call for large yachts and cruise ships.

More than a dozen game-fishing boats are available for charter, either for day or overnight trips. The main summer season extends from November through May and is climaxed by a major competition in early May.

Colorful subtropical fish glide through these clear seas, and corals and sponges thrive in the deeper water. Cape Brett is a favorite spot for divers; you can arrange for transportation and equipment in Paihia.

On the Paihia and Russell waterfronts, you can rent small boats by the day or week; charter boats are available at Opua and Russell (page 28).

Boat trips. To fully appreciate the beauty of this fabled, island-strewn bay, plan to cruise amid the wooded islets and explore the sparsely populated shore.

Best known of the boat excursions is the Cream Trip, named for a coastal launch route of the 1920s that collected cream and delivered mail and supplies to scattered dairy farms. You sail along the coast and among the islands; on some trips, you stop to deliver mail, newspapers, and freight to waiting islanders.

Another favorite is the launch or catamaran cruise to Cape Brett, where a lighthouse marks the bay entrance. You'll circle Piercy Island, cruise into Cathedral Cave, and pass through the Hole in the Rock. Schoolfish (which attract marlin) and dolphins abound in these waters.

During holiday periods, a replica of one of the early coastal steamers departs from Kerikeri for a trip on the Kerikeri Inlet (page 36).

Water taxi service links the resorts with the islands and more remote bays. You can arrange a trip to Moturua or Motukiekie Island, for example, and hike the trails that connect one beach to the next. After transporting your party to the site, the boat returns at a prearranged time. Take along a picnic and, if you like, fishing tackle or snorkeling equipment.

Paihia, busy harbor resort

Strung out along the waterfront, Paihia is the accommodations and excursion center for visitors to the Bay of Islands. The tourist information office is on Williams Road, across from the post office.

Busiest spot in town is the Paihia Pier, jutting into the bay at the end of Williams Road, where excursion launches, game-fishing boats, water taxis, and the passenger ferry jockey for position. In the nearby Maritime Building you can book tours and excursions, charter boats, and make other travel arrangements.

Motorcoach excursions depart daily from Paihia for Cape Reinga, the kauri forests, and other historic Northland destinations. You can arrange aerial sightseeing trips, also.

On the Paihia waterfront, a memorial church stands on the site of the original Paihia Mission Station. Nearby, a carved arch marks the entrance to the Ti Beach *marae*, where Maori chiefs and warriors camped before crossing the river to discuss and sign the Treaty of Waitangi.

Permanently moored near the Waitangi Bridge is the three-masted barque *Tui*. Now the Museum of Shipwrecks, it displays gold coins, jewelry, and other articles salvaged from Northland marine disasters.

Historic Waitangi

Across the river from Paihia, Waitangi National Reserve surrounds the historic Treaty House, symbol of New Zealand's birth as a nation. You can walk through the restored house and stroll beneath century-old trees on the spacious, well-kept grounds overlooking the Bay of Islands. The Treaty House is open daily from 9 A.M. to 5 P.M.

It was here, on the lawn in front of the house, that representatives of the British Government and Maori chiefs signed the Treaty of Waitangi on February 6, 1840. The Maori people voluntarily accepted British rule, New Zealand became part of the British Empire, and Maoris and Europeans were granted equal status as British subjects. Each year on February 6, an impressive evening ceremony commemorates the anniversary.

The Georgian-style Treaty House was built in 1833-34 by James Busby, after his appointment as British Resident. Wings were added to the original three-room dwelling in the 1870s. Inside, visitors find a small collection of Maori artifacts, paintings and photographs, and articles associated with the area's early settlement and the treaty signing. In front of the house, a tall flagstaff marks the signing site.

Nearby, the Waitangi *whare runanga* (meeting house) reflects traditional Maori craft skills. A gift to the nation from the Maori people during the 1940 centennial celebration, the building is unique in that its wall carvings are the work of many different North Island tribes.

Below the house, an open-air pavilion shelters a 36-meter/118-foot kauri war canoe. During the centennial festivities, 80 Maori warriors paddled the canoe from across the bay. A riverside trail begins here.

One of the country's finest 18-hole golf courses is nearby on Waitangi National Reserve, overlooking the bay.

Russell—whaling port to fishing center

Russell's tranquil waterfront belies the town's wild and bawdy origins as the whaling port of Kororareka. Beginning in the early 1800s, sealing and whaling ships anchored here. Despite the efforts of the missionaries, Kororareka was a lawless town, crowded with grog shops and Maori shipgirls who catered to the rough seafarers.

European traders and colonists soon followed, and by 1830 there was a sizable settlement. Soon after British control was established, conflict developed between British troops and disgruntled Maoris who resented white authority. Four times Chief Hone Heke chopped down the British flagstaff in an effort to rid his land of the newcomers. On the final attempt in 1845, his rampaging warriors also sacked the town.

Today, Russell is a peaceful retreat with an old-world charm—though it bustles in season with vacationers and sailors from the yachts and launches anchored offshore. Big-game fishing is the leading topic of conversation, and when word spreads of a major catch, crowds gather on the wharf for the weigh-in.

You can arrange for boat trips, water-skiing, big-game or line fishing, and charter boats here. A short sightseeing tour by mini-bus departs from the wharf.

Along The Strand. Buildings along The Strand — Russell's waterfront promenade—face the curve of a deep blue bay. At the Bay of Islands Maritime and Historic Park visitor center, you can get information about park activities.

Facing the wharf is the Duke of Marlborough Hotel, rebuilt for the fourth time in 1932. Nearby is the Police Station, originally the port's customs house, and at one time the courthouse and jail.

At the south end of The Strand is Pompallier House, built in 1841-42 to house the printing presses of the country's first Roman Catholic mission; the presses and other historic items are displayed inside. It's open daily from 10:30 A.M. to 12:30 P.M. and from 1:30 to 4:30 P.M.

At the end of the beach is a restored bungalow, built in 1853 by Captain James Reddy Clendon, the first American consul. Replicas of the Crown jewels of England are displayed in the Jewel House on The Strand.

Other attractions. New Zealand's oldest church is still in use at the corner of Church and Robertson streets. Built in 1835-36 by local settlers, Christ Church also served as courthouse and public hall. It still bears bullet holes and battle scars from the 1845 conflict; in the cemetery are the graves of those who died defending the settlement, as well as the remains of whalers, early settlers, and Maoris.

In Captain Cook Memorial Museum on York Street are relics of Kororareka and a seaworthy scale model (1/5 size) of Cook's barque H.M.S. *Endeavour.*

Overlooking the Bay of Islands, Waitangi Treaty House symbolizes New Zealand's birth as a nation. Maori and British officials signed an historic treaty here in 1840.

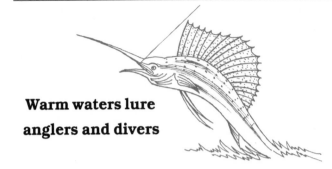

Warm waters lure anglers and divers

Anglers come from around the world to challenge the big, fighting game fish lurking in the warm Pacific coastal waters off North Island. Surf fishing is also popular here, as is snorkeling and scuba diving among the islands and reefs that border the long, irregular shore.

Big-game fishing. Along the coast from North Cape southeast to Cape Runaway, deep-sea anglers congregate in search of New Zealand's big-game fish: black and striped marlin, broadbill swordfish, shark (mako, thresher, hammerhead, and tiger), yellowtail (kingfish), and five species of tuna.

Activity centers in the Bay of Islands, but big-game fishing bases are also located at Whangaroa, Whangarei (Tutukaka), Whitianga (Mercury Bay), Tauranga (Mayor Island), and Whakatane (Whale and White islands). Though you can fish any time of year, you'll reel in the best catches from mid-January through April.

Since all the fishing bases are less than 200 miles from Auckland, anglers can enjoy a day of challenging fishing even if their time is limited. Charter boats, available in coastal resorts, provide equipment and tackle, and no license is required. For more information, contact the New Zealand Tourist Office.

Many visiting anglers join a local fishing club. A nominal membership fee entitles members to use club facilities, have their catches weighed and recorded, and partake of the general club conviviality.

Surf fishing. On weekends, you'll see surfcasters on just about every stretch of beach and rocky shoreline. Local camps and stores near the beach sell tackle and bait, and some rent equipment.

Surfcasting is popular during the summer, but some of the best fishing comes in the colder months of March to November. An annual contest on Ninety Mile Beach every January attracts hundreds of participants.

Underwater activities. Snorkelers and scuba divers also head for North Island's northeastern coast. Good diving areas lie offshore, from Three Kings Islands off the northernmost tip south to the Bay of Islands, Hauraki Gulf, Coromandel Peninsula, and Bay of Plenty.

The waters surrounding Poor Knights Islands, off the Tutukaka Coast east of Whangarei, are regarded as a marine sanctuary rich in exotic and colorful underwater life. Huge sponges and lacy corals cluster on vertical rock faces well below the surface. Reefs surrounding volcanic Mayor Island are also particularly lush.

Good South Island diving areas are located off the northern tip of the island, along stretches of the eastern and southwestern coasts, and around Stewart Island.

The best diving season is January to May, but many locals dive the year around. You'll need a wet suit in winter and for prolonged diving. Though winds sometimes make diving uncomfortable, divers don't need to worry about sharks.

Charter planes or boats transport divers from coastal towns to offshore islands and reefs. Some boats even provide gear, though you can rent or buy diving equipment in Auckland or in coastal towns. Paihia, in the Bay of Islands, has a thriving dive center.

Several dozen diving clubs are located throughout the country. All are affiliated with the New Zealand Underwater Association, P.O. Box 875, Auckland. Often club members serve as guides, though professional diving guides are also available. Some clubs organize excursions to popular diving areas.

For a splendid panorama, take the road to the summit of Maiki Hill (Flagstaff Hill). Swimmers can head for Long Beach, just across the peninsula facing Oneroa Bay.

Kerikeri for history, citrus, and crafts

Historic Kerikeri was founded as a mission station in 1819, second of the area's settlements established by the Church Missionary Society of London. Two of the country's oldest buildings, both open to visitors, overlook the head of Kerikeri Inlet. At high tide, pleasure boats sail up the inlet and anchor near the wharf.

Inland, tall hedgerows hide orchards of oranges and other citrus fruits. Other subtropical fruits grown here include kiwifruit, feijoas, passion fruit, and tamarillos.

In recent years, Kerikeri has attracted many artists and craftspeople, who display their work in local shops.

New Zealand's oldest surviving building is porticoed Kemp House, surrounded by an old-fashioned garden. Completed in 1822, it was part of the original settlement, and missionaries lived here until 1832, when it became the home of the Kemp family. Now operated by the New Zealand Historic Places Trust, it's open daily.

The two-story Stone Store, built in 1833, once housed Bishop Selwyn's library; now it contains a souvenir shop and a small museum of mission-related items.

The hillside across the river basin offers a fine view of the old buildings. You can also visit Rewa's Village, a replica of a pre-European unfortified Maori village.

During school holiday periods, you can explore Kerikeri Inlet aboard the M.V. *Ernest Kemp*, a replica of the shallow-draft steamers which operated along the coast in the early 1900s.

Several easy trails lead to destinations along the Kerikeri River. Ask for trail information and a map at the ranger station.

At Waimate North, a mission house

Inland from the Bay of Islands at Waimate North stands the Waimate Mission House, built in 1831-32 and the sole surviving building of a once-thriving mission farm. Of New Zealand's historic buildings, only Kemp House at Kerikeri is older.

Last of three similar late Georgian-style houses built in the mission's early years, the building is designed symmetrically around a central stairhall. In the 1870s, a gabled roof replaced the original hip roof and dormer windows. Period furniture and missionary items recall the early days. You can visit the house daily from 10 A.M. to 12:30 P.M. and from 1:30 to 4:30 P.M.

Nearby is the Church of St. John the Baptist, built in 1871. Its oak-shaded churchyard contains carved wooden grave markers unique to Northland.

Coastal route to the Far North

From the Bay of Islands, two roads head north to New Zealand's northern tip. Highway 1 follows a direct inland route to Kaitaia; Highway 10 skirts Whangaroa and Mangonui harbors and Doubtless Bay as it winds along the eastern coast. Narrow side roads branch off Highway 10 to coastal settlements and remote coves and beaches; mangrove trees grow in many tidal estuaries in this subtropical area.

Whangaroa Harbour. North of Kaeo, a road branches off to Whangaroa, where eroded volcanic pinnacles and steep timbered slopes enclose the calm harbor. Wooden houses with gabled roofs peek out from between the trees. Whangaroa attracts deep-water anglers who come here to fish the waters around the Cavalli Islands.

The only way to fully appreciate the inlet's scenic setting is by boat. From September through May, sightseeing cruises from Whangaroa follow the shoreline to the narrow-necked harbor entrance. Day trips and big-game fishing charters can be arranged.

A coastal road loops east from Whangaroa to fine ocean beaches at Wainui and Matauri bays.

Mangonui. Houses climb the rolling hills encircling attractive Mangonui Bay. In the early days, the harbor was the gateway to the Far North and served as a whaling base and mill port for ships engaged in the kauri trade.

Today, local fishing boats tie up at Mangonui's wharf. It also houses the Mangonui Sea Lab and Aquarium, which contains marine life found in local waters. Small boats anchor at Mill Bay. For a sweeping view over Mangonui and Doubtless Bay, take the road to the Rangikapiti *pa* site overlooking the harbor.

Doubtless Bay. According to Maori legend, the great Polynesian explorer Kupe landed at Taipa centuries before the "great migration" south from Hawaiki. In 1769, Captain Cook sailed past the entrance and named the bay; eight days later, French explorer de Surville anchored here and narrowly escaped being wrecked.

Splendid beaches along the shore attract families during holiday periods. Surfcasters and shell collectors enjoy Tokerau Beach; skin divers favor Matai Bay and Cape Karikari. Game fishing is excellent outside the entrance to the bay.

Kaitaia, hub of the "winterless north"

Shaped by decades of geographical and cultural isolation, the sparsely populated Far North retains an elusive quality that attracts an increasing number of visitors. Many residents are descendants of Dalmatian gumdiggers who stayed on to wrest a living from scrubby lands.

Tourist and commercial center of the Far North is Kaitaia, which was, in turn, a Maori village, an 1830s mission station, and a boom town for kauri gumdiggers. For today's visitors, it's the departure point for motorcoach trips to Cape Reinga and Ninety Mile Beach and for exciting safaris to remote beaches by expanded dune buggy. Scenic flights over the Northland countryside depart from Kaitaia Airport.

Stop first at the Far North Regional Museum on South Road (open daily) to obtain tourist information and learn more about the Far North.

Pride of the museum is its de Surville anchor, lost at the bottom of Doubtless Bay in 1769 and recovered for the museum in 1974. Photographs and artifacts recall pioneering days in the kauri forests, gumfields, and flax lands. You'll also see missionary relics, a large collection of kauri gum, and other excellent displays.

A 15-minute drive through dairy lands takes you to Ahipara, at the southern end of Ninety Mile Beach. From the hills sheltering the bay, you gaze northward along a magnificent sweep of sand.

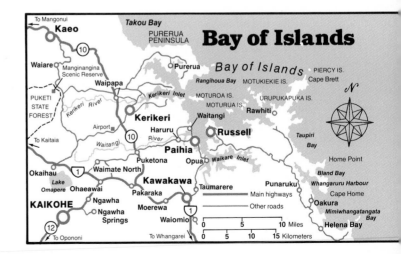

Neat houses on wooded slopes ring Mangonui Harbour, an inlet of Doubtless Bay. Mangonui began as a milling center and shipping port for the kauri timber trade.

For an adventurous day exploring windswept beaches and secluded coves, sign up for a trip by 38-seat dune buggy; it travels from Kaitaia to Wreck Bay, the gumfields, and wave-cut Reef Point.

North to Cape Reinga

From Kaitaia, a narrow road wends 116 km/72 miles north along the Aupouri Peninsula to Cape Reinga, popularly regarded as the country's northernmost point (cliffs on North Cape actually extend slightly farther north).

Motorcoach tours depart each morning from Kaitaia and Paihia for Cape Reinga, returning along the peninsula's Ninety Mile Beach. Depending on the time of high tide, the route may be reversed. Though the bus follows Te Paki Stream from the main road to the coast, quicksand in the stream bed makes this route unsafe for other vehicles.

At Houhora Heads, motorcoaches pause at the Wagener Museum, a collector's storehouse of exhibits ranging from natural history and Maori artifacts to old-time phonographs and washing machines in working order. Houhora, once the center of gumdigging activity, still boasts New Zealand's most northerly tavern.

Beach grasses and the young pine trees of Aupouri Forest are reclaiming some former gumfields and dunes. Near the peninsula's tip, the road winds through Te Paki Coastal Park before emerging at Cape Reinga.

Cape Reinga. A trail leads out to the cape's lonely lighthouse, perched 165 meters/541 feet above the waves. At night its light can be seen about 50 km/30 miles offshore. Below, two mighty bodies of water—the Pacific Ocean and Tasman Sea—collide in foamy combat. Views stretch west to Cape Maria van Diemen, first sighted by Tasman in 1642, and east across Spirits Bay toward North Cape.

Below the lighthouse, a twisted pohutukawa tree clings to the headland. According to Maori legend, the spirits of departing Maoris pass down its exposed roots into the sea on their underwater return voyage to legendary Hawaiki.

The northernmost of the New Zealand Walkways routes begins at Spirits Bay. It skirts the coastline around Cape Reinga and Cape Maria van Diemen; then for some 83 km/51 miles it follows the beach from Te Paki Stream south to Ahipara. Several camping and picnicking areas in the park are equipped with fireplaces, fresh water, and toilets; for information on park facilities, contact the ranger at Waitaki Landing, Private Bag, Kaitaia (phone Te Kao 521).

Ninety Mile Beach. The magnificent white sand stretches along the Tasman all the way to Ahipara. Surfcasters converge here during the New Year holiday to compete in a big surfcasting contest. As the bus speeds along the firm clean sand, it splashes through occasional streams and scatters flocks of skittish shore birds. Off season, you may have the entire coast to yourself.

The Waikato

Today, the lush green rolling hills south of Auckland bear few scars of the turbulent era over a century ago when this region was a battleground between land-hungry European settlers and Maori warriors seeking to protect their tribal grounds. The disputes began in the 1850s when settlers pushed southward seeking to buy — and later to confiscate — rich Maori lands in the Waikato. Misunderstandings arose between Maori and *pakeha*, and the Land Wars raged here for more than 20 years.

From Auckland, Highway 1 cuts southeast across the peaceful Waikato plains toward Hamilton. For much of the way, the route parallels the Waikato River, which gives its name to this broad area south of Auckland. The river, the country's longest, flows from Lake Taupo some 354 km/220 miles to meet the Tasman Sea south of Manukau Harbour. Main source of North Island's hydroelectric power, the Waikato is harnessed by a series of dams and power stations. Boaters and water-skiers enjoy the reservoir lakes behind the dams.

Busy Hamilton

Hamilton, hub of the Waikato plains and New Zealand's largest inland city, straddles the Waikato River about 138 km/85 miles south of Auckland. From its origin as a military settlement in 1864, Hamilton has grown into a busy farming, industrial, and agricultural research center.

Dubbed the fountain city, Hamilton is rich in parks and gardens. The main commercial and shopping district lies west of the river; Victoria Street is its principal thoroughfare. In the heart of the city is Garden Place, a landscaped pedestrian mall.

A 48-km/30-mile scenic drive begins at the Chief Post Office on Victoria Street. For information on city walks and local attractions, visit the Public Relations Office, in the Irvin & Stern Building on Barton Street.

Parks and gardens. Parks border both banks of the placid Waikato, which meanders through the city. On the western shore, strollers enjoy Ferrybank Park, where steamers and ferries docked in Hamilton's early years. Parana Park and Memorial Park rim the eastern bank.

Hamilton's largest and most popular park borders Lake Rotoroa (often called Hamilton Lake), an aquatic and recreational playground just southwest of the central district.

Floral displays take the spotlight in Rogers Rose Gardens and Hamilton Gardens. Jubilee Park preserves a remnant of the native forest that once covered this district.

Other attractions. The Waikato Art Museum, 150 London Street, features a Maori gallery dominated by a long war canoe and exhibits on the history of Hamilton and the Waikato district. It's open daily except Monday.

Centrally located in Boyes Park is the Founders' Theatre, opened in 1963. The Riverlea Performing Arts Centre is located southeast of Hamilton off Highway 1.

Northwest of the business district, Hilldale Zoo Park on Brymer Road has an extensive collection of animals and birds; you can visit daily from 9 A.M. to 5 P.M.

Swimmers will enjoy the impressive facilities of the indoor-outdoor Centennial Swimming Pool complex on Garnett Avenue. Nearby, racing fans watch some of New Zealand's best horses compete at the Te Rapa Racecourse. For trotting contests and greyhound racing, visit Claudelands Showgrounds, which also hosts the Waikato A & P Show and other annual events.

Touring the western Waikato

From Hamilton, you can venture north to a Maori village at Ngaruawahia and the Waingaro thermal baths, west to the coast at Raglan, south to an agricultural museum and the Waitomo Caves (page 40), and east to gracious Cambridge and horse-breeding country (page 41).

Ngaruawahia. The largest Maori *pa* in the country is at Ngaruawahia, 18 km/12 miles north of Hamilton at the junction of the Waikato and Waipa rivers. Home of the Maori king movement, Turangawaewae *marae* is the official residence of the present monarch, Queen Te Atairangikaahu. The best view of the buildings is from across the Waikato River. On Regatta Day in mid-March, Maori canoe races and other competitions take place here.

Waingaro. First known to the Maoris, this bubbling thermal spring 22 km/14 miles west of Ngaruawahia became a popular stagecoach stop on the Raglan road. Extensively developed in recent years, the baths offer sulphur-free waters in thermal pools, spa pools, and water slides.

Raglan. Normally quiet and peaceful, Raglan, situated 48 km/29 miles west of Hamilton, becomes a busy seaside resort during holiday periods. Anglers find excellent harbor and surf fishing here and, in season, whitebait in local streams. Surfers ride long, curling waves at Whale Bay.

Clydesdale Museum. Learn about New Zealand's agricultural pioneers at the country's largest agricultural museum, located at Mystery Creek, 16 km/10 miles south of Hamilton near the airport. You'll see implements used by pioneer farmers, examples of rooms in which they lived, and demonstrations of early farming methods. Historic buildings have been moved to the site, and the National Dairy Museum is located here.

Te Awamutu. Rose gardens bloom at the northern entrance to town. You can learn about regional history in the Te Awamutu Museum in the Civic Centre on Roche Street. Picnickers and boaters head for Lake Ngaroto north of town; trails in Pirongia Forest Park attract hikers.

Otorohanga. Farther south on Highway 3, Otorohanga is known for its bird park, where you can see kiwis and other native birds; it's open daily from 10 A.M. to 4 P.M.

Kawhia Harbour. Remote Kawhia, 60 km/37 miles west of Otorohanga on Highway 31, offers the timeless fascination of a remote settlement bypassed by main road and rail routes. Traders and missionaries arrived here in the 1830s. White settlers were ousted during the Land Wars, and the port never regained its early vigor.

In season, launches depart from Kawhia's wharf on harbor sightseeing trips. On Te Puia Beach, hot springs well up through the sands, and you can scoop out your own hot pool at low tide.

Exploring the Waitomo Caves

In the rugged hills south of Otorohanga, subterranean limestone outcroppings have been transformed into a

Waikato—the essentials

Hamilton is the hub of the Waikato and the touring center for exploring the district. To the south are the famous Waitomo Caves and the rugged King Country.

Getting there. Air New Zealand offers direct flights to Hamilton from Wellington, and commuter airlines link the Waikato with Auckland. The Northerner and Silver Fern trains serve Hamilton, Te Awamutu, Te Kuiti, and Taumarunui on the main Auckland-Wellington line. Railways Road Services motorcoaches provide daily service to Hamilton and other Waikato towns from Auckland, Rotorua, Taumarunui, and other towns.

Accommodations. Visitors can choose from a wide selection of motor inns, small hotels, and motels in Hamilton. At Waitomo Caves, the THC Waitomo Hotel offers gracious hospitality in a relaxed country setting. Small motels are available in country towns.

Getting around. Main line rail service and Railways Road Services motorcoaches link the main towns. Round-trip excursions operate daily from Auckland and Rotorua to the Waitomo Caves. Rental cars are available in Hamilton.

Tourist information. Travelers can obtain maps and local sightseeing information at visitor information offices in Hamilton, Cambridge, Matamata, Otorohanga, Paeroa, Te Aroha, and Te Awamutu.

series of spectacular caves. Three of these are open to visitors—the famous Waitomo Caves, renowned for their dramatic formations and a magical glowworm grotto.

You can visit the caves on a guided tour, conducted at regular intervals daily from 9 A.M. to 4:30 P.M.; wear walking shoes and bring a sweater.

Waitomo Cave. Highlight of the 45-minute tour is a boat ride, where you'll glide silently along an underground river in a flat-bottomed punt into a cavern spangled with the radiant blue green lights of thousands of tiny glowworms. You'll see some close up, their long, sticky "fishing lines" hanging to snare insects attracted by the lights.

Striking limestone formations include the famous Organ and the lofty chamber called the Cathedral.

Ruakuri and Aranui caves. Less frequently visited, these caves are about 3 km/2 miles beyond the Waitomo Cave entrance. They can be toured twice daily, in the morning or the afternoon; schedules are timed to coordinate with tours of the main cave.

Largest of the caves is Ruakuri, a fantastic complex of underground caverns resounding with the roar of a hidden waterfall. An underground river mysteriously appears and disappears in the cave.

Smallest and loveliest of the three caves is enchanting Aranui, noted for its delicate fluted limestone formations and unusual colorings.

Other attractions. Near the caves you can visit a replica Maori *pa* in Ohaki Maori village. Te Anga Road heads west to Mangapohue Natural Bridge, where a stream flows through a deep, narrow gorge and beneath a large limestone arch tunneled thousands of years ago by an underground river. At Marokopa Falls, the river plummets in a series of spectacular waterfalls. The road ends at the seaside fishing settlement of Marokopa, 48 km/29 miles from Waitomo.

The rugged King Country

It was not until formal peace was made in 1881, ending the Land Wars, that the government could extend its North Island rail line south to open up new farm lands. Highways 3 and 4 link the farming centers of the King Country with major markets. Te Kuiti, just south of the Waitomo turnoff, is a farming, mining, and timber town with a rich Maori heritage. Of special interest is the carved meeting house built in 1878 (ask permission before visiting). South of Te Kuiti, Highway 3 bends southwest, cutting through the scenic Awakino Gorge to the coast.

At Eight Mile Junction, Highway 4 veers southeast through the heart of the King Country to Taumarunui, a farming and timber center at the confluence of the Ongarue and upper Wanganui rivers. For generations, Maori canoes plied these inland waterways; today, canoeing parties still take to the scenic Wanganui River. From Taumarunui, highways lead east to Lake Taupo and south to Tongariro National Park.

Traveling in the eastern Waikato

East of Hamilton, highways crossing the plains toward the Kaimai Range pass through lush pasture land. Stud farms, where thoroughbred race horses are bred and trained, cluster around Cambridge and Matamata. South Waikato's prosperity is based on timber.

Cambridge. Both its name and its tranquil setting lend an English flavor to Cambridge, a river town on the Waikato 23 km/15 miles southeast of Hamilton. Giant trees, stately churches, and a village green add to the town's gracious charm. The Public Relations Office is in the public library on Victoria Street.

Visit the Cambridge Cultural Centre, just north of the town clock tower; then stop in Te Koutu Domain, where trees border an attractive lake. Southeast of town is Lake Karapiro, farthest downstream of the Waikato reservoirs and a favorite for water sports.

Putaruru. On Highway 1 just south of Putaruru, a timber museum is being developed. Plans call for a restored sawmill complete with forest tramway, historic buildings, and exhibits on the district's old timber mills.

Matamata. In Matamata, a historic area preserves Firth Tower, built about 1880 as a lookout and retreat in the event of an invasion by hostile Maoris; it's now a museum and art gallery.

Te Aroha. The area's mineral springs have spawned several spas and resorts, the best known of which is Te Aroha, a fashionable Victorian spa complete with quaint buildings. Public and private thermal pools are open daily. Marked trails lead through the woods, and a bus transports visitors to the summit of Mount Te Aroha.

Paeroa. Once a river port, today Paeroa is a farm town well known for its mineral-rich drinking water. On the Waihou River north of town, the Paeroa Maritime Park society operates several old river boats.

Coromandel Peninsula

Southeast of Auckland, the clawlike Coromandel Peninsula separates the Hauraki Gulf from the Bay of Plenty. Along its coast, the surf crashes against rocky cliffs and gently laps sandy crescents. Remnants of gold mining and kauri milling days still survive in its rugged interior.

Coastal roads border much of the shoreline; elsewhere, side roads lead down to the sea. Several winding mountain routes across the forested Coromandel Range link the western and eastern coasts.

The peninsula's population has fluctuated as wildly as its fortunes. Prospectors flocked here in the late 1860s in search of gold. Later, timber traders and gumdiggers razed the kauri forests and plundered the land; museums in larger towns recall this colorful era. In recent years,

many craftspeople have settled here to pursue their work.

The peninsula's isolation is part of its charm, but it limits touring options. Nearest airports are in Tauranga and Auckland. Railways Road Services coaches travel between Auckland and Thames, largest of the towns; from Thames, there's limited bus service to Coromandel and Whitianga. Rental cars are available in Thames.

Most accommodations are concentrated in Whitianga and in Whangamata, deep-sea fishing headquarters, but you'll find motels in Thames, Coromandel, and smaller towns as well. Tourist information offices are located in Thames and Tairua.

Along the western coast

Located about 120 km/75 miles southeast of Auckland, Thames is a convenient base for exploring the peninsula. Displays in the Thames Museum, at Brown and Cochrane streets, evoke the mining era.

Southeast of Thames, the Kauaeranga Valley road leads to pleasant riverside picnic sites and forest walks in Coromandel Forest Park. For trail information, stop at Forest Service headquarters, located alongside the river.

Farther north at Coromandel, memories linger of the 1867 gold rush that brought quick prosperity to the area. The road continues north to Long Bay, a popular picnicking and camping area; to Kennedy's Bay, a yachters' haven; and to secluded bays and beaches near the tip of the sparsely populated Colville Peninsula.

Slow but scenic Highway 25 winds from Coromandel high above Whangapoua Harbour and Mercury Bay to Whitianga. Narrow, winding Highway 309 is the direct route across the mountains; from it, a short, marked trail leads to a glade of giant kauri trees.

East coast attractions

The peaceful harbor town of Whitianga takes on a carnival atmosphere in summer as vacationers flock here for swimming and water-skiing, big-game fishing and surfcasting, gemstone hunting, and bush walking. A passenger ferry makes the short trip across the Narrows to Ferry Landing, where you can walk to several destinations.

From Whenuakite, side roads lead northeast to beautiful Hahei Beach and Hotwater Beach, where hot springs seep up through the sand. From Hahei, it's a 20-minute walk north over the bluff to Cathedral Cave, a magnificent sea-carved cavern between two coves.

Tairua and Pauanui are popular seaside resorts; diving and big-game fishing are favorite activities. You can also arrange guided hiking trips to learn more about the Coromandel's scenic attractions and birdlife. Busy Whangamata attracts surf swimmers and water-skiers. Offshore is Mayor Island, a major deep-sea fishing base.

Waihi, situated on the wooded southern slope of the Coromandel Range, flourished during the local gold rush. One of New Zealand's largest gold strikes was made here at the Martha Mine. Many of the town's buildings reflect an earlier era; you can learn about this period at the Waihi Museum, 50 Kenny Street.

Highway 2 swings inland toward Paeroa through the Karangahake Gorge, where mining settlements boomed—and subsequently vanished—in the late 19th century.

The Bay of Plenty

Gentle waves lap the golden sand beaches bordering the Bay of Plenty. The coastal towns of Tauranga, Mount Maunganui, and Whakatane are magnets for summer visitors who come here to relax on the beach, frolic in the surf, and go deep-sea fishing. Relaxing hot mineral springs and pools dot the area. Offshore is White Island, New Zealand's most active volcano. The Bay of Plenty earthquake in March 1987 had little effect on tourism.

Citrus and subtropical fruits thrive in the balmy climate. Timber from Kaingaroa State Forest is processed into paper and wood products in the mill town of Kawerau, at the foot of Mount Edgecumbe.

Tauranga: busy port and resort area

Sprawling along the shore of its harbor, Tauranga is a bustling agricultural and timber center, as well as a thriving summer resort. Across the water on the harbor's eastern shore is Mount Maunganui, a holiday town named for the peak rising above it.

Daytime passenger ferry service operates between Tauranga's Coronation Pier, at the east end of Wharf Street, and Mount Maunganui's Salisbury Wharf. You can arrange sightseeing and fishing excursions in both towns. The Tauranga tourist information office is located on The Strand, near Coronation Pier.

Missionaries established a station on the Te Papa Peninsula in 1835, but the settlement didn't begin to flourish until the 1860s when the military arrived. On a short walk you can visit Tauranga's mission house and walk around "The Camp," site of the military settlement on a cliff overlooking the harbor. An excellent open-air museum is located south of town.

Visitors and residents picnic and swim in Memorial Park, a waterfront beach bordering Devonport Road. City sports facilities are located in Tauranga Domain, west of Cameron Road.

Informal wine tasting is available daily except Sunday at Preston's Kiwifruit Winery on Belk Road, Tauranga. Unique to New Zealand, the fresh and fruity white wine available here is made from kiwifruit, grown in fields throughout the district.

Mission days. One of the country's oldest homes, the handsome old Te Papa mission house on Mission Street (now known as "The Elms") was built in the 1840s by Rev. Alfred N. Brown. Now filled with articles relating to the area's early history, the mission was a peaceful oasis during the troubled days of 1864-65, when Maoris and Government troops battled at Gate Pa and Te Ranga.

The elegant house faces a large garden shaded by spreading trees, including a pair of Norfolk pines that guided early sailors into port. The grounds are open Monday through Saturday, with guided tours at 2 P.M.

Robbins Park links two wooded knolls, one the site of the old mission burying ground and military cemetery off Mirrielees Road, and the other the location of the well-preserved earthworks of Monmouth Redoubt. Trees ring the old cemetery, with its monument and lichen-encrusted tombstones. At the southern end of the park, earthworks outline the redoubt, which housed soldiers and sheltered European women and children during the warfare.

Tauranga Historic Village. History comes alive at this open-air museum on 17th Avenue West. Open daily from 10 A.M. to 4 P.M., it portrays New Zealand town life around the turn of the century. Original and replica buildings typical of those used in early Bay of Plenty settlements have been erected here.

The small colonial town features shops, dwellings, a school, church, jail, post office, livery stable, and blacksmith shop. Other displays include a Maori village, and gold mining and sawmill exhibits. Visitors can ride in vintage vehicles or horse-drawn wagons. You'll also see the old steam tug *Taioma.*

Bay of Plenty—the essentials

Fine beaches, big-game fishing, thermal hot springs, and seaside resort activities draw vacationers to Tauranga, Whakatane, and neighboring coastal towns.

Getting there. Air New Zealand serves Tauranga and Whakatane from Auckland, Wellington, and other North Island towns. Railways Road Services motorcoaches link Auckland and Wellington with Tauranga and other Bay of Plenty towns.

Accommodations. Hotels and motels are concentrated in Tauranga and Mount Maunganui, but you can also stay in Whakatane, Ohope Beach, and Opotiki.

In Tauranga, accommodations include the Willow Park Motor Hotel, Tauranga Motel, Tauranga Motor Inn, and many small motels; in Mount Maunganui, the Westhaven Motor Lodge; in Te Puke, the Te Puke Country Lodge; and in Whakatane, the Motel Riviera.

Getting around. Limited bus service connects the resort towns, but you'll find a car handy for touring; rental cars are available in Tauranga and Whakatane.

Tourist information. For visitor information, check tourist offices in Tauranga (on The Strand) and in Whakatane (on Commerce Street).

Lawn bowlers, dressed in their "whites," compete on Rotorua's greens in front of handsome old Tudor Towers. Lawn bowling season lasts from October to Easter.

Day trips from Tauranga. Narrow-necked Tauranga Harbour, sheltered from the sea by Matakana Island, is marked by pleasant tidal beaches at Omokoroa and Pahoia and several developed hot mineral springs.

From October to March, you can join a short white-water rafting trip on the Wairoa River, about 15 km/9 miles from Tauranga.

East of Tauranga, Highway 2 veers inland to Te Puke, center of a thriving dairy and fruit-growing district. Farther east, a side road leads to the small coastal village of Maketu, where a cairn near the mouth of the Kaituna River marks the traditional landing site of the Arawa canoe, one of the ancestral canoes that transported Maoris to New Zealand in the 14th century.

Mount Maunganui's peak and beach

Across the harbor from Tauranga, Mount Maunganui's wooded peak rises 232 meters/761 feet above the bay. Allow about 1½ hours if you want to hike to the summit for a magnificent view along the coast.

A long, slim, sandy peninsula connects "The Mount" to the mainland. The resort of Mount Maunganui clusters at the base of the peak. A coastal road parallels the town's famous golden beach, which curves gently along the bay southeast to Papamoa Beach and beyond.

Two bay islands

From Tauranga and Mount Maunganui you can arrange excursions to Mayor Island, a big-game fishing center, and to White Island, an active volcano.

Big-game fishing. Mayor Island lies about 35 km/22 miles off the coast in waters teeming with yellowfin, mako shark, and other fish. Peak season extends from late December to early May. Charter fishing boats operate from Tauranga and Mount Maunganui.

Skin divers come here to view colorful marine life. The pohutukawa-bordered island has twin volcanic craters, each with a small lake. Hikers enjoy walks through the bush, where birdlife abounds.

An active volcano. New Zealand's most active volcano, White Island rises about 50 km/30 miles offshore at the northern end of the Taupo-Rotorua volcanic zone. The island regularly issues forth a billowing cloud of steam visible from the mainland.

Riddled with thermal activity, the volcanic island has boiling pools, steam and gas vents, and holes filled with sulphuric acid. The volcano erupts periodically, spewing lava and ash over the island. Flights offering a close look at the island from the air operate from Tauranga, Whakatane, Rotorua, and Taupo. The island is also accessible by launch from Tauranga.

Whakatane and the eastern bay

Located 100 km/62 miles southeast of Tauranga, the timber and farm town of Whakatane traces its origin to the landing of the Mataatua canoe, one of the ancestral canoes that brought Maoris to New Zealand in the 14th century. The town has its own waterfall, located behind the Commercial Hotel on Mataatua Street.

Big-game fishing trips depart from Whakatane, and scenic flights offer aerial views over White Island and the

Bay of Plenty district. Jet boat trips up the scenic Rangitaiki River depart from above Lake Matahina dam, south of Whakatane. A small museum, open daily, displays historic articles. Inquire at the Public Relations Office on Commerce Street about fishing, flightseeing, and jet boat excursions, as well as other attractions.

Ohope Beach. The long ocean beach of this seaside settlement east of Whakatane is lined with pohutukawa trees. A slim peninsula shelters Ohiwa Harbour, where anglers seek flounder and shellfish and water-skiers glide across the water. Skin divers cross the headland at the western end of the beach to Otarawairere Bay.

Rotorua—the essentials

In addition to luring visitors to its superb fishing lakes and thermal attractions, the resort of Rotorua also puts you in touch with Maori culture.

Getting there. Mount Cook Line, Air New Zealand, and Newmans Air link Rotorua with various North Island cities and tourist areas. All three also fly here from Christchurch and other South Island points. Railways Road Services motorcoaches serve Rotorua from many North Island cities and towns.

Accommodations. Large tourist hotels are located in town (Hyatt Kingsgate, Travelodge); near Whakarewarewa Thermal Reserve (THC Rotorua International, Sheraton); and along Fenton Street—Highway 5—connecting the two (Rotorua Hotel, Four Canoes Inn). Many smaller hotels and motels in the lake district also cater to visitors.

Travelers seeking a bit of luxury can try Muriaroha, on Old Taupo Road, where a few guests stay in a gracious home filled with antiques and art. Excellent fishing and a serene lakeside setting draw guests to Solitaire Lodge on Lake Tarawera; also popular with anglers are Lake Okataina Tourist Lodge and Lake Rotoiti Hotel.

Getting around. Half-day and full-day motorcoach excursions depart from the N.Z.R. Travel Centre on Amohau Street. The short tour covers city sights, the Agrodome, trout springs, and thermal attractions; longer trips travel to the Waitomo Caves and the Taupo district. Sightseeing flights over the lakes and thermal areas depart from Rotorua Airport, float plane trips from the Lake Rotorua waterfront. Other excursion choices include lake cruises and a four-wheel-drive trip up the slopes of Mount Tarawera.

Tourist information. For assistance with travel arrangements, tours, and accommodations throughout the country, stop at the Government Tourist Bureau at the corner of Fenton and Haupapa streets. Information on local tours is also available at the N.Z.R. Travel Centre. The Public Relations Office is on Haupapa Street.

Opotiki. Once a large Maori settlement, Opotiki is known for its martyr's church; it's also the starting point for a trip around the East Cape. Hukutaia Domain southwest of town offers pleasant walks in unspoiled forest. Rafting and jet boat trips on the Motu River depart from Opotiki.

Rotorua, a thermal resort

The resort of Rotorua curves along the southwestern shore of Lake Rotorua, largest of a cluster of tree-rimmed lakes at the northern end of North Island's volcanic plateau. To the east looms Mount Tarawera, split open by a violent volcanic eruption in 1886. For a view over the lake basin and plateau, drive northwest of town to the summit of Mount Ngongotaha.

Rotorua offers three exceptional attractions for visitors: an opportunity to learn about Maori culture, an intriguing variety of thermal activity, and some of the country's best trout fishing. A busy tourist area, Rotorua is the hub for numerous sightseeing excursions in every direction.

An important part of Rotorua's history and culture revolves around the Maoris who settled here. Ancestors of the present residents landed on the Bay of Plenty coast about 1340. Migrating inland, they established scattered villages on defensible hills, peninsulas, and islands. Violent battles between the warring Maori tribes were common.

After the Land Wars ended, the area's thermal attractions — including the famous Pink and White Terraces bordering Lake Rotomahana—began to draw an increasing number of visitors. And after Mount Tarawera's 1886 eruption, Rotorua flourished as a turn-of-the-century spa, highly regarded for the curative powers of its mineral waters.

Getting settled in Rotorua

Fenton Street is Rotorua's main north-south artery, linking the commercial district at the north end of town near the lakeshore with Whakarewarewa Thermal Reserve to the south. Stores and offices line both Fenton Street and perpendicular streets to the west.

East of the thoroughfare, on a peninsula jutting into Lake Rotorua, is Government Gardens, developed during the town's heyday as a Victorian thermal spa. Many of the city's sports facilities are concentrated here.

At the Government Tourist Bureau on Fenton Street, sports enthusiasts can obtain fishing and hunting information and hire a guide for a day of trout fishing. For big-game fishing, head for the Bay of Plenty, about an hour's drive north of Rotorua. Golfers can choose from several local courses. Watch out for a different kind of hazard at Arikikapakapa Golf Course—here, thermal vents dot the links with escaping steam. Horse racing events take place at Arawa Park.

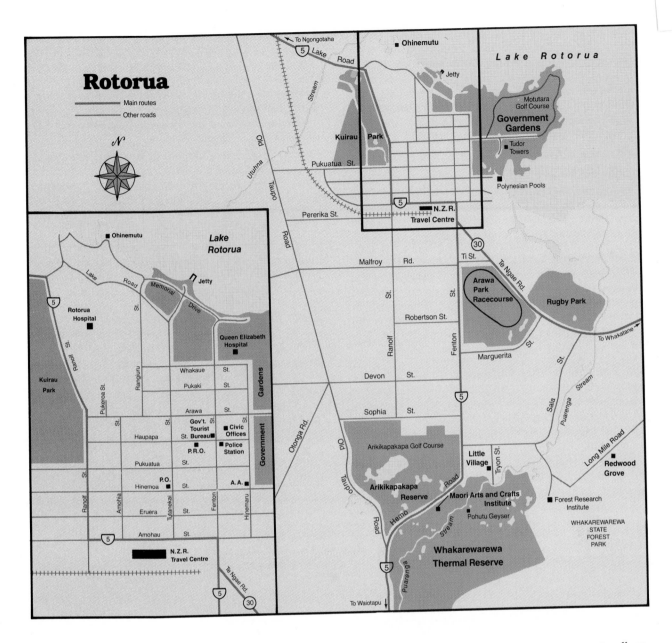

Walk through Government Gardens

Visitors to Government Gardens, a spacious peninsula park extending east from Hinemaru Street, are greeted by a distinctive Maori carving at the main Prince's Gate entrance on Arawa Street. Thermal attractions are interspersed amid the park's sports fields and flower beds.

From October to Easter, lawn bowlers, dressed in their proper "whites," compete in matches on the greens in front of the dignified old Tudor Towers building. Elsewhere, residents and visitors enjoy croquet, tennis, golf, roller-skating, or swimming. Indoor sports activities take place in the nearby sports and conference center.

One of New Zealand's most photographed buildings, the elegant Tudor Towers was built in 1906-07 as a bathhouse for people seeking the curative mineral and mud baths. Transferred to town ownership in 1963, the restored building now houses a museum, art gallery, licensed restaurant, and cabaret.

In the building's south wing, the Rotorua Museum features geological displays on the volcanic plateau, thermal activity, and the Tarawera eruption of 1886. Maori cultural exhibits contain family and tribal treasures contributed by local Maoris.

The city's art gallery, in the north wing, presents exhibits tracing the development of New Zealand painting and printmaking.

Relax in thermal waters

Developed as a spa, Rotorua for decades attracted visitors who came to "take the waters" to treat rheumatism and other ailments. Today's bathers enjoy these mineral-rich waters primarily for the feeling of well-being they bestow.

Many hotels and motels have pools for their guests, and there are large swimming pools in the Blue Baths in Government Gardens. At the Polynesian Pools, located at the east end of Hinemoa Street, you can relax in warm mineral waters or plunge into a thermal swimming pool. Private pools are available for those who prefer to soak *au naturel*. Pool hours are 9 A.M. to 10 P.M. daily.

Learning about the Maoris

Visitors who want to experience the Maori culture have many opportunities in Rotorua, including observing craftspeople at work, visiting Maori settlements, sampling Maori foods at a festive *hangi*, and enjoying programs of traditional songs and dances.

Maori Arts and Crafts Institute. Outside the main entrance to Whakarewarewa Thermal Reserve, at the south end of town, young Maori woodcarvers practice the skills taught to them by elder craftsmen. Women fashion skirts out of flax, make baskets, and demonstrate *taniko* weaving of bodices and headbands. Visitors are welcome on weekdays from 8:30 A.M. to 4:30 P.M.

Whakarewarewa Thermal Reserve. To take in one of Rotorua's top attractions, walk through the reserve with a Maori guide, or, if you prefer, stroll the paths at your own pace. The reserve is open daily from 8:30 A.M. to 4:30 P.M.

You'll see a model *pa* (Maori village), visit a kiwi house, then walk down through the thermal valley past bubbling mud pools, silica terraces, and vents of escaping steam. Periodically, Pohutu Geyser spurts high above the terraces.

At the lower end of the valley, you walk past Whakarewarewa village, where Maori residents use the hot pools for cooking, bathing, laundering, and heating.

Ohinemutu. Bordering Lake Rotorua northwest of town is the lakeside village of Ohinemutu. For generations, its residents have used the escaping steam and thermally heated water for daily activities.

Maori carvings and *tukutuku* panels decorate the interior of the Tudor-style St. Faith's Anglican Church, built in 1910. In the side chapel, a magnificent window depicts Christ wearing a chief's cloak of kiwi feathers. In the churchyard, tombs lie above ground because of thermal conditions.

Facing the church is a meeting house enhanced by traditional carvings. Some of the interior decoration dates from the early 1800s. Evening programs of Maori songs and dances are often presented here.

Maori food and entertainment. Rotorua's the place to attend a Maori *hangi*, a Polynesian feast traditionally steam-cooked in an underground pit. *Kai* (food) may include pork, lamb, chicken, seafood, marinated fish, venison, *kumara* (Maori sweet potato), salads, Maori bread, and fresh fruit.

After dinner, Maori entertainers serenade guests with traditional songs and perform Maori dances featuring twirling *poi* (balls on string) and the fierce *haka* (a posturing war dance).

The THC Rotorua International Hotel presents a traditional *hangi* every Sunday night throughout the year, and more often in summer. Food is cooked in an earthen

Excursion launch cruises past Lake Rotomahana's steaming cliffs. Fumaroles were created by the enormous volcanic eruption of nearby Mount Tarawera in 1886.

oven by natural steam. Hangi feasts and Maori entertainment are also presented at the Geyserland Motor Hotel, Sheraton-Rotorua Hotel, Travelodge Hotel, and Tudor Towers.

Programs of Maori songs and dances that chronicle events in tribal history and village life are presented at the Rotorua Maori Cultural Theatre, 18 Eruera Street, and at the Tamatekapua Meeting House in Ohinemutu.

Other city attractions

For a change of pace, take a walk through a grove of redwoods, shop for crafts, or visit Kuirau Park.

Whakarewarewa State Forest. Southeast of town, the tranquil trails of this forest park offer a relaxing break in sightseeing activity. Stop at the Forest Information Centre on Long Mile Road for a trail map.

A favorite destination is the Redwood Memorial Grove bordering Long Mile Road. Planted in 1901, the towering trees here are part of an experimental reforestation project begun after the Tarawera eruption devastated the area.

The large park extends from the Whakarewarewa Thermal Reserve and the Taupo highway east to the Blue and Green lakes. Other popular trails include the Blue Lake walk around the shoreline, a climb to the Tokorangi Pa site, and walks in the Green Lake Picnic Area.

Little Village. Near the exit from the Whakarewarewa Thermal Reserve, the Little Village on Tryon Street offers an intriguing collection of tourist and craft shops in a colonial village atmosphere. Often you'll see artisans at work on the premises.

Kuirau Park. Children will love Kuirau Park, located at Ranolf and Pukuatua streets; the park features the "Toot 'n' Whistle" miniature steam railway, a children's playground, an aquarium, sports fields, and an aquatic center. Walkways meander around the park's small lake, boiling mud pools, and large thermal fountain.

Excursions from Rotorua

Tourism is one of Rotorua's main industries, and a large number of excursions are available to visitors.

If thermal activity intrigues you, you can visit spouting geysers, steaming cliffs, boiling pools, and colorful silica terraces. Or cruise secluded lakes rimmed by native forest, walk down a thermal valley, explore a buried village, feed trout by hand, climb the side of a volcanic peak by four-wheel-drive vehicle, raft down a river, or take a flightseeing tour over lakes and valleys.

Aside from excursions to nearby attractions, one bus trip takes visitors south to Huka Falls, Wairakei, Lake Taupo, and Orakei Korako; another tour goes to Waitomo Caves. A 5-day hiking trek in Urewera National Park also departs from Rotorua (page 60).

Big fighting trout await the lure

Some of the world's best fresh-water fishing draws both casual and serious anglers to New Zealand's lakes and streams. In fact, if you want to eat trout here, you'll *have* to catch it yourself. Trout fishing is strictly a sport, with no trout grown or caught commercially. The hotel chef will cook your catch for you for breakfast or dinner.

Introduced late in the 19th century, rainbow and brown trout thrive in New Zealand's clear lakes and cold, fast-flowing rivers. Famed both for their size and tenacity, the trout can challenge the skills of even an expert angler. Yet each year, hundreds of visitors who have never fished before proudly display their catch.

You can fish throughout the year in the Rotorua and Taupo lake systems, but in most districts the season opens on the first Saturday in October and extends through April (in some districts through May or June). Most serious anglers try to avoid the January family vacation period.

On North Island lakes, trolling is popular during the warm summer months, but in autumn the action shifts to the mouths of lake tributaries as trout congregate prior to spawning runs. Most streams are for fly-fishing only.

Thousands of miles of uncrowded trout streams, along with excellent lake fishing in the Southern Lakes region, attract fly-fishing devotees to South Island. Brown trout predominate here, but rainbows and land-locked salmon also inhabit the lake systems. Salmon spawn in some of the east coast rivers, and South Westland has large runs of sea-run brown trout in spring and late summer. Whitebait migrate up many of the coastal rivers from September through November.

Your best insurance for a successful expedition is to hire a local professional fishing guide, available by the hour or day in all major fishing areas; the local tourist office can direct you to qualified guides and tell you where to obtain a fishing license. In addition to fishing know-how, guides usually supply the boat, all gear and tackle, and even transport to and from your hotel. Most guides charge a fixed price per party (up to three or four persons), depending on services and equipment required.

Dedicated anglers may want to spend a few days at a fishing lodge—or even plan an entire vacation around fishing. Several tour operators offer packaged itineraries that feature fishing; check with your travel agent or with international airlines flying to New Zealand. The New Zealand Tourist Office can provide general fishing information.

Maori legends and traditions reflect a unique culture

When European immigrants arrived in New Zealand in the early 19th century, they found the distinctive and well-established Maori culture. Hereditary warrior chiefs and powerful priests ruled the tribal society. History and traditions were passed down from father to son, mother to daughter, through legends, songs, and crafts.

Learning about the Maori culture is an integral part of the New Zealand experience. Many museums have fascinating exhibits of carved buildings, canoes, tools, ornaments, and garments.

At the Maori Arts and Crafts Institute in Rotorua, you can watch Maori woodcarvers at work; elsewhere in Rotorua, you can sample foods at a *hangi*, enjoy Maori entertainment, and learn about village life (page 46). In the Bay of Islands, the Waitangi meeting house (page 34) brings together carving styles of tribes from all parts of North Island. Maori communities are located throughout North Island, but visitors should ask permission before looking around a village.

To enrich your first-hand experiences, here is a description of some aspects of the Maori culture.

Myths and legends. Colorful, imaginative, and often touching legends, handed down from generation to generation, offer insights into how the early Maori viewed his world and accounted for the origin of the universe, the elements, and man.

Tales recount a time long ago when mountains fought and walked, their tears became streams and rivers, and men and gods spoke together. Many Maori legends explain distinctive landscape features. Other stories relate tales of heroism and endurance.

Before the arrival of the missionaries, Maoris had no written language. Oratory was regarded as an important art in passing on tribal history and culture.

Meeting house. Focal point of a Maori village is its open square (*marae*) and the traditional carved meeting house (*whare runanga*) facing it. Inside, symbolic carvings depict tribal ancestors and mythical figures.

The *poupou* (carved wall panels) record tribal history and legends. Woven *tukutuku* panels in geometric patterns usually separate the wooden carvings. Posts supporting the ridgepole are also carved. Patterned *kowhai-whai* designs painted in black, red, and white decorate the rafters.

Woodcarving. Intricately designed woodcarvings—stylized figures and grotesque birds, fish, and animals—depict stories of tribal events. Each tribe had its own distinct carving style.

Craftsmen preferred totara wood for carving. The distinctive color came from red ochre mixed with shark oil; iridescent paua shells were used for eyes. Distinctive motifs include curves and spiral designs, slanted eyes, and a three-fingered hand with backward-turned thumb. Figures were often depicted in warlike poses, eyes bulging and tongue outthrust in defiance.

Examples of the carver's art decorate not only meeting houses but also storehouses, gateways, and posts. In museums you'll see intricate carvings ornamenting articles used in daily life, such as war canoes, weapons, and musical instruments.

Greenstone. Valued by the Maoris for its hardness and beauty, greenstone (nephrite jade or bowenite) was carved into prized ornaments, tools, and weapons. Maori parties made difficult journeys through the mountains to certain West Coast valleys in search of the comparatively rare stone. New Zealand's good luck talisman is the *tiki*, a neck pendant carved in the form of a fetus. Several museums have fine greenstone collections.

Weaving. Women excelled in weaving flax and reeds into the *tukutuku* panels that decorate many meeting houses, dwellings, and churches. Among other women's crafts are basketry, *taniko* weaving of decorative bodices and headbands, and preparation of the flax *piupiu* kilts worn by both men and women.

Music and dance. Traditional Maori music includes a variety of chants and poetic songs expressing joy and sadness, welcome and farewell. Familiar melodies such as *Haere ra* ("Now is the hour") date from the 19th century. Simple nose and mouth flutes and trumpets of shell, bone, and wood sometimes accompany the singers; rhythm is supplied by stamping the feet, slapping the body, or tapping a piece of wood with a stick.

Most familiar of Maori dances is the spirited war dance (*haka pukana*), in which the performer engages in vigorous posture dancing as he grimaces, rolls his eyes, and thrusts out his tongue to frighten the enemy. New Zealand sports teams often perform it before international matches. Women entertain with the gentle *poi* dance, where they twirl raupo balls on string in time with music.

Tattooing. In traditional Maori society, tattooing was a form of adornment and status. A chief used his tattoo design (*moko*) as his signature. Males were liberally embellished with distinctive patterns on face and body as well as buttocks and thighs. Women were less heavily decorated, usually only on lips and chin. Tattooing was a long and painful process. A tiny bone chisel was used to make incisions according to a pattern, and soot was rubbed into the open wounds to provide coloring.

Most local sightseeing trips operate daily from December through April, less frequently the rest of the year. For information, inquire at the Government Tourist Bureau at the corner of Fenton and Haupapa streets.

Cruising on the lakes

Good roads provide access to most of the larger lakes. If you cruise their clear, tree-rimmed waters, you'll enjoy them even more.

Launch trips. Largest of the district's lakes is Rotorua, nearly circular in shape, with wooded Mokoia Island in its center. You board the launch at the jetty at the end of Tutanekai Street. After circling the island, the launch docks there and you have time for a short walk, and perhaps a quick swim in Hinemoa's Pool and a wish by the Arawa wishing rock. Trips leave Rotorua at 2 P.M. daily (additional trips in summer).

Renowned for its trout fishing, tree-bordered Lake Rotoiti is a favorite. Tourist facilities are concentrated at the western end of the lake. A launch trip on the lake departs from Okawa Bay Holiday Camp daily at 2 P.M.

You can also board a launch for a trip on Lake Tarawera, a tranquil retreat at the base of Mount Tarawera.

Fishing trips. Within a 16-km/10-mile radius of Rotorua are many good fishing lakes, and catches are legendary. At Lake Rotorua, for example, anglers catch rainbows weighing 2 to 4 pounds each. During the May to June spawning season, 9 to 10-pound rainbow trout are netted nearly every day at Lake Tarawera. A local guide can introduce you to some of the district's best fishing areas.

A circuit of Lake Rotorua

Trout springs, trained sheep, and redwood trees are only a few of the sights you'll see on a drive around the lake. Looming above the countryside northwest of Rotorua, Mount Ngongotaha looks out on a sweeping panorama toward the Bay of Plenty.

Trout springs. Clear, pure, cold water wells up from underground springs west of Rotorua. In several places, visitors can roam down fern-lined paths along clear trout streams and toss food to the fish. The springs are cool, woodsy retreats to visit on hot days.

You can stop at Paradise Valley Springs, west of Rotorua on the Valley Road; Rainbow and Fairy Springs, bordering Highway 5 west of the lake; or Taniwha Springs, near Awahou on the lake's northwestern shore. Rainbow and Fairy Springs has an animal park and nocturnal kiwi house. At Taniwha Springs there's a Maori *pa*.

The Agrodome. Nineteen trained champion rams, each representing a different New Zealand sheep breed, take the stage during a 1-hour pastoral show at the Agrodome, set in lush pasture land at Riverdale Park in Ngongotaha, west of Rotorua. Demonstrations of shearing and the maneuvers of sheep dogs help illustrate the story of wool,

one of New Zealand's most important products.

Shows are presented daily at 10:30 A.M. and 2:30 P.M., with extra performances during busy periods.

Hamurana Springs. A grove of lofty redwood trees shades Hamurana Springs, on the northern shore of the lake. You can rent a boat and paddle along the willow-bordered stream, watch trout in an upstream pool, feed tame deer, or golf on the nine-hole course.

Okere Falls. The clear green outflow of lakes Rotorua and Rotoiti surges and foams through a narrow rift, then plunges into a broad pool of the Kaituna River. Many an angler has caught a prize trout here. Rocky steps lead down the steep wooded slope to the foot of the falls and to caves where Maori women reportedly hid in time of war.

Spectacular views by land and air

Four-wheel-drive vehicles transport passengers on a half-day safari up the slope of Mount Tarawera, site of New Zealand's greatest volcanic eruption. From the brink of the crater, you peer into the deep, color-streaked chasm and gaze over an awesome panorama of lush forests and sparkling lakes.

One of the best views of the lakes and thermal attractions is from the air. Float planes lift off from Rotorua's lakefront jetty; helicopters and other aircraft leave from the Rotorua Airport on the eastern shore of the lake.

You can fly over the town of Rotorua and the lake district, Mount Tarawera's gaping volcanic chasm, and steaming geothermal areas. Longer flights circle volcanoes at White Island and Tongariro National Park.

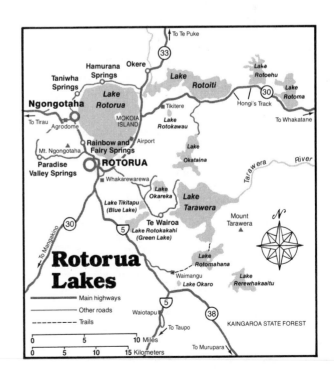

East to fishing lakes

Northeast of Rotorua, the Whakatane road (Highway 30) passes the thermal area of Tikitere and skirts the southern shore of three bush-rimmed fishing lakes — Rotoiti, Rotoehu, and Rotoma. A side road south of Rotoiti leads to unspoiled Lake Okataina.

The lakes figure prominently in local history as links in the Maori canoe route to Lake Rotorua. In 1823, Hongi

Volcanic plateau—the essentials

Trout fishing in Lake Taupo and its nearby rivers and streams, together with hiking and skiing in Tongariro National Park, are highlights for visitors to this region.

Getting there. Air New Zealand flights link Taupo with Auckland, Wellington, and other towns. New Zealand Railways' main line passes west of Lake Taupo and Tongariro National Park with stops in National Park and Ohakune. Railways Road Services motorcoaches travel from various North Island cities and towns to Taupo, Turangi, and Taihape.

Accommodations. Most visitors stay in or near Taupo or Tongariro National Park, though anglers range far afield. Among Taupo's many lakefront motels are the Ashley Court Motel, Lake Terrace Motel, Manuels Motor Inn, and Moana Reef Motel. North of Taupo at Wairakei is the comfortable THC Wairakei Hotel, noted for its excellent 18-hole golf course.

Several fishing lodges cater to trout anglers. These include the Waikato River Lodge near Reporoa; Huka Lodge, a historic fishing retreat on the Waikato River above Huka Falls; Wilderness Lodge, in the Kaimanawa wilderness southeast of Taupo; and Tongariro Lodge and small Bridge Fishing Lodge, both near the mouth of the Tongariro River at Turangi. Here you'll also find the DB Turangi Motor Hotel and several small motels.

Farther west at Tokaanu, the recently renovated THC Tokaanu offers an irresistible package for anglers— free accommodation if you don't catch a fish.

Tongariro National Park visitors can live in luxury at the renowned THC Chateau on Mount Ruapehu; nearby is the Ruapehu Skotel (skiers' hotel). Development of Turoa Skifield has brought many new accommodations west of the park, among them the Buttercup Alpine Resort and Drumlin Lodge Motel in National Park; and Sunbeam Ski Lodge and Venturelodge in Ohakune.

Getting around. Mount Cook Line motorcoaches travel between Wairakei and the Chateau, with stops at Taupo, Turangi, and Tokaanu. Rental cars are available in Taupo.

Tourist information. Visitor information centers are located at Taupo and Turangi. Park headquarters for Tongariro National Park is at Whakapapa Village on Mount Ruapehu (near the Chateau); ranger stations are situated in Ohakune and Turangi.

Hika and his warriors paddled across the lakes, portaging their heavy wooden canoes when necessary, on their way to attack the fortified Arawa settlement on Mokoia Island.

The district's most active thermal area, Tikitere is an inferno of sulphurous steam, boiling water, and bubbling mud. White pumice and golden sulphur combine to shape bizarre formations. Take the short bush walk through native trees and ferns to Kakahi Falls, where thermal waters cascade into an inviting pool.

A bush-bordered avenue south of Lake Rotoiti leads to lovely Lake Okataina. Totara trees and punga ferns shade the road, and *kotukutuku* (native fuchsia) brightens your way in late spring and early summer. Dense forest rims the lake. Okataina attracts people who enjoy peace and quiet — along with some of the area's best trout fishing.

Waimangu Valley—Lake Tarawera loop

Situated southeast of Rotorua are the steaming Waimangu Valley, lakes Rotomahana and Tarawera, and the buried village of Te Wairoa.

Half-day and full-day guided tours depart from the New Zealand Railways Travel Centre on Amohau Street. The shorter trip includes a tour of the valley, a launch cruise on Lake Rotomahana to the steaming cliffs, and transport back up the valley. Only travelers on the full-day tour make the entire loop.

Early on the morning of June 10, 1886, Mount Tarawera erupted in tremendous volcanic fury, awakening Aucklanders nearly 280 km/175 miles away. Splitting open from end to end, the volcano spewed forth a cubic mile of molten rock, boiling mud, and volcanic ash, which covered the countryside for miles around. Three villages were buried and more than 150 people died. The eruption destroyed Lake Rotomahana's famous Pink and White Terraces, fan-shaped silica staircases world-renowned for their beauty and shimmering colors. When the smoke cleared, Mount Tarawera was left with a gaping chasm and craters up to 210 meters/700 feet deep.

Evidence of the area's thermal activity abounds on the 4-km/2½-mile walk down the Waimangu Valley. Steam rises from the surface of the Waimangu Cauldron, a large thermal lake fed by subterranean boiling springs. Off the main path is Ruamoko's Throat, a turquoise lake rimmed by colorful cliffs. Your path down the valley follows a scalding stream. Near the lake, thermal waters fan over Warbrick Terrace, its silica deposits patterned with colorful algae.

At the bottom of the valley, you'll board a launch and cruise slowly past Lake Rotomahana's stratified cliffs, laced with steaming fumaroles.

Travelers on the full-day excursion disembark on the lake's northern shore and hike across the narrow saddle separating it from larger Lake Tarawera. Another launch waits at the Tarawera dock for a leisurely trip across the lake, where a bus picks up passengers and transports them on the final leg of the trip.

Before Mount Tarawera's eruption, Te Wairoa Village was the departure point for excursions to the terraces. Buried under 5 to 6 feet of volcanic mud, the village has been partially excavated. A self-guided walk links a museum and several structures. You can follow Te Wairoa Stream, Green Lake's outlet into Lake Tarawera, as it tumbles over Te Wairoa Falls.

On the way back to Rotorua you'll pass a pair of jewel-like lakes — Green Lake (Rotokakahi) and Blue Lake (Tikitapu). Off the main route is secluded Lake Okareka, a relaxing spot for a picnic, a swim, or a bit of fishing.

South to Waiotapu

Located 30 km/19 miles south of Rotorua near the Taupo road (Highway 5), Waiotapu is noted for the colorful silica surrounding its thermal attractions.

Lady Knox Geyser erupts daily at 10:15 A.M. Other attractions include the Artist's Palette silica terraces, tinged in delicate colors; lovely Bridal Veil Falls; and the shimmering Champagne Pool, which bubbles when sand is tossed into it.

Volcanic plateau

Dominating the center of North Island is a vast volcanic plateau, marked by Lake Taupo—North Island's largest lake—and a trio of active volcanoes in the heart of New Zealand's first national park.

Kiwis and visitors alike who love the outdoors come here for superb fishing, for water sports on Lake Taupo, and for hiking, climbing, and skiing in Tongariro National Park. Thermal energy is transformed into electricity at Wairakei's steaming geothermal bore field and at power stations along the Tongariro and Waikato rivers.

Silica terraces at Orakei Korako

Extensive silica deposits and a legendary cave draw visitors to Orakei Korako, 27 km/17 miles north of Wairakei. To reach the area, you board a jet boat and skim across the Waikato River where it flows into Lake Ohakuri.

Largest of New Zealand's silica terraces, the broad cascade called Great Golden Fleece extends along an ancient fault scarp. Above it is Artist's Palette, a large level basin riddled by dozens of small geysers and hot springs. Algae create color variations in the crusty silica deposits.

Tall tree ferns frame the entrance to Ruatapu (Aladdin's Cave) and filter sunlight to a small mirrorlike pool far below. For generations Maori women came here to bathe and beautify themselves.

Harnessing geothermal energy at Wairakei

Clouds of billowing steam greet travelers at Wairakei, located in the center of North Island's thermal belt. One of the world's foremost geothermal power projects,

Ranger-led group learns about Mount Ruapehu's rugged volcanic terrain on a summer nature walk in Tongariro National Park.

Winter fun on the slopes

When autumn weather turns chilly and snow begins to pile up on the high peaks, the thoughts of many Kiwis turn to winter sports. A great number take to the slopes—for alpine (downhill) skiing, for nordic (cross-country) ski touring, and in the Southern Alps, for glacier skiing, where ski-equipped planes and helicopters transport skiers to the high slopes.

Skiing. New Zealand's ski areas offer abundant powder snow, fine downhill runs, and uncrowded, timber-free slopes. Since seasons are reversed from those in the Northern Hemisphere, New Zealand's challenging slopes attract expert skiers from North America, Europe, and Japan. You'll find a relaxed, easy-going atmosphere and ample après-ski conviviality in the country's ski resorts. Though skiing can begin as early as May and extend into November, the season typically lasts from mid-July through October on North Island, and from early July through September on South Island. Several resorts feature ski package holidays, and major ski areas offer equipment rentals, ski schools, and public transport to the slopes.

Mount Ruapehu in Tongariro National Park is North Island's leading ski area. Well-established Whakapapa Skifield on the mountain's north-facing slopes is noted for spring skiing; the newly developed Turoa Skifield is on Ruapehu's southern slope.

Top resort sites on South Island are Coronet Peak, near Queenstown, and Mount Cook. South Island's most extensive skifield is Mount Hutt, located near Methven southwest of Christchurch.

Smaller areas include Rainbow Valley, in the St. Arnaud ranges near Nelson Lakes National Park; Porter Heights, off Arthur's Pass Road west of Christchurch; Mount Dobson, near Fairlie, and Tekapo, near Lake Tekapo, both in the vast Mackenzie Country; Lake Ohau, south of Mount Cook; and Treble Cone and Cardrona, both near Wanaka.

Mount Cook is the country's principal ski-touring and ski-mountaineering center. Ski-equipped planes and helicopters transport skiers to the high glaciers of the Southern Alps.

New Zealand has more than 60 ski clubs; just about every one operates huts in its particular area. Visitors can often arrange to stay in club bunk-style lodges and ski very economically. National administration of the ski clubs is handled by the New Zealand Ski Association, Inc. (P.O. Box 2213, Wellington 1).

Wairakei has attracted considerable attention since it began generating electricity in 1959. Visitors can learn about the project at the power plant's information office; guided tours are offered at the power stations.

Several thousand feet below the surface, hot volcanic rocks heat water to above-boiling temperatures. Deep bores intersecting this layer channel escaping steam to the surface, where hot water is extracted. "Dry" steam funnels through insulated mains to generating stations along the Waikato River. U-shaped loops in the pipes allow for expansion and contraction.

Inside the power stations, cold water pumped from the river condenses the steam; water is then returned to the river.

The upper Waikato River

Near Taupo, travelers satiated with thermal wonders can watch the powerful, yet placid Waikato River cascading over Huka Falls and Aratiatia Rapids.

About 5 km/3 miles north of Taupo, the Waikato suddenly funnels into a narrow chasm. Surging and foaming through the gorge, the roaring waters of Huka Falls catapult over a ledge into a wide, calm pool below. Though not high, Huka Falls is impressive in its raw power.

The Huka Falls loop road follows the river between Taupo and Wairakei. A trail parallels the river from Huka Falls downstream to Aratiatia Dam.

Aratiatia Rapids. Long regarded as one of the loveliest stretches of the Waikato Valley, Aratiatia represents a compromise between scenic beauty and the nation's power needs. At the head of the valley, a control dam holds back the Waikato, whose waters are channeled to a power station. Every afternoon from 2:30 to 4 the pent-up river is released to thunder down the deep, rocky ravine. To reach Aratiatia, turn east off Highway 5 north of Wairakei.

Huka Village. A North Island pioneer village has been re-created about 2 km/1 mile north of Taupo beside the Huka Falls Road. Pioneer buildings, moved here and restored, depict life during the era of the 1860s and '70s. Artisans demonstrate crafts of a bygone era. The village is open daily from 10 A.M. to 5 P.M.

Relaxing at Taupo

When you approach Taupo from the north on Highway 1, Lake Taupo's sparkling panorama spreads before you. Fed by dozens of streams, the lake fills a gigantic volcanic crater. Its only outlet is the Waikato River, which leaves the lake alongside the town of Taupo. In the distance rise the huddled peaks of Tongariro National Park.

The town dates from 1869, when an Armed Constabulary garrison was built here. Later, thermal activity attracted visitors. The town's growth spurted in the 1950s during construction of the Wairakei geothermal project.

At the Information Centre on Tongariro Street, you

can obtain maps and brochures, arrange local accommodations, and inquire about fishing and hunting trips, boat rentals, and flightseeing and coach excursions.

Fun on the lake. Pleasure boats and fishing launches anchor near the head of the river, upstream from the gates that control the lake's water level and regulate the flow of water downstream. You can rent small boats at the marina. Boat excursions leave from the wharf.

Though fishing is extremely popular, it's not the only activity on Lake Taupo. Water-skiers skim over lake waters along marked routes. Children splash in shallow water or paddle canoes just offshore. For a picnic by the lake, consider tree-bordered Acacia Bay, west of town.

Other diversions. You can soak away stiffness at thermal or heated fresh-water pools. If you'd rather swim in lake water, Waipahihi Hot Springs bubble from the lake bed along the northeastern shore (access off Lake Terrace).

South of the Napier turnoff, Waipahihi Botanical Reserve overlooks the lake at the end of Shepherd Road.

Back-country adventure. White-water rafting trips on the Tongariro and Mohaka rivers and hiking excursions in the Kaimanawa Mountains are organized by Kaimanawa Tours & Treks Ltd. (P.O. Box 321, Taupo). Trips depart from Taupo from mid-December through March.

Fabled lake and stream fishing

As Highway 5 skirts the eastern shore of Lake Taupo, it crosses a number of sparkling tributary streams flowing swiftly down from the Kaimanawa Mountains. Many anglers cast their lines near the mouths of these tributaries. Others prefer the waters of Lake Taupo or the famed trout pools of the snow-fed Tongariro River.

Just how good is the fishing? Wildlife authorities estimate that about 700 tons of trout are caught annually in Lake Taupo. Here, rainbows weigh in at 3½ to 6 pounds, and brown trout average more than 5 pounds.

Most of the main fishing streams, including the Tongariro River, enter the lake near its southern tip. River fishing is best here from April to August during the spawning runs. Streams flowing into the lake from the west can be reached only by boat.

The lake's southern shore

The town of Turangi owes its growth to construction of the nearby Tongariro hydroelectric power project and expansion of the district's farming and forest industries. Learn about local recreation, the power plant, and area history and geology at the Power Project Information Office, alongside Highway 41 at Turangi.

Nearby Tokaanu has a small thermal reserve with hot pools, boiling mud, geysers, and a small bathhouse. St. Paul's Anglican Church, decorated in Maori style with *tukutuku* panels and painted rafters, memorializes early missionaries.

A side road off Highway 41 leads to Waihi, a picturesque Maori village backed by a steep wooded cliff.

West of Turangi, the scenic Pihanga Saddle Road climbs to a viewpoint overlooking Lake Taupo and winds through luxuriant forest. About 10 km/6 miles southwest of Tokaanu, a signposted trail leads south from the road to Lake Rotopounamu, a small green lake nestled in a greenery-rimmed crater. A naturalist's delight, the 25-minute walk winds through forest abundant with ferns.

Just south of the road's intersection with Highway 47 stand the fortifications of Te Porere *pa*, site of the last major engagement of the Land Wars in 1869.

Volcanoes shape Tongariro National Park

South of Lake Taupo, three volcanic peaks loom above the plateau in a terrain unique in New Zealand. For generations, Maoris regarded these high mountains with awe, weaving legends about them. New Zealand's first national park, Tongariro is an unspoiled region shaped by eruption, glaciation, and erosion.

The park takes its name from the northernmost and lowest of the peaks, 1,968-meter/6,458-foot Tongariro, whose truncated crest is a maze of craters—some mildly active. A docile plume of smoke drifts from Ngauruhoe's symmetrical cone; every few years the 2,291-meter/7,515-foot volcano erupts spectacularly, belching lava and ash over its slopes. Highest of the three is 2,797-meter/9,175-foot Ruapehu, North Island's highest peak and foremost ski area. Snow-capped the year around, it has a simmering acid crater lake and small glaciers on its high slopes.

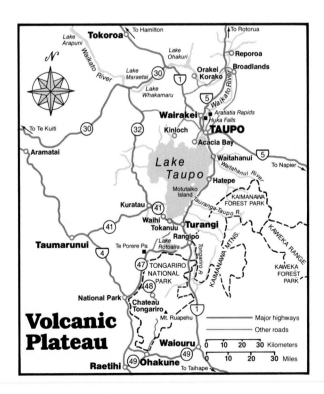

Mount Egmont's snowy cone, *partially shrouded by clouds, looms above Taranaki's dairy pastures. Hikers, climbers, and skiers enjoy the peak's wooded slopes.*

Among the park's most fascinating aspects are its varied terrain, vegetation, and birdlife. Wet lowland forests, lush with ferns and orchids, on Ruapehu's southwestern slope contrast dramatically with tussock grasslands, wildflower-sprinkled alpine rock gardens, and stark volcanic formations at higher elevations. More than 500 native plant species have been identified in the park.

Year-round fun at Tongariro

Center of park activity is Whakapapa Village on Mount Ruapehu. Skiers flock here in winter, hikers and climbers in summer.

At park headquarters, open daily from 8 A.M. to 5 P.M., you learn about the park's geology and volcanic activity, history, plants, and birdlife. You can also obtain trail information and check the weather forecast. In summer, rangers conduct nature walks, climbing excursions, and illustrated programs. They also arrange for climbing guides, hunting permits, and use of mountain huts.

You can also obtain park information by contacting the chief ranger (Park Headquarters, Mount Ruapehu; phone Ruapehu 814). Ranger stations are located at Ohakune, on the Mountain Road (phone Ohakune 578), and at Turangi (phone Turangi 8520).

Skiing on Mount Ruapehu. Whakapapa Skifield, on Ruapehu's north slope, is one of New Zealand's oldest established ski areas. From Whakapapa Village, the Bruce Road climbs about 7 km/4 miles to the ski area. Rental equipment and ski holiday packages are available.

Recently developed on Ruapehu's southwestern flank is Turoa Skifield, which boasts the highest vertical lift in Australasia (720 meters/2,360 feet). You can obtain information on Turoa skiing in Ohakune; ski buses transport skiers from town to Turoa. At the skifield, T-bars and triple chair lifts offer access to uncluttered, challenging slopes where skiing lasts until November.

Walks and hikes. Summer visitors venturing forth on foot to explore the park can follow any of several short walks beginning near Whakapapa Village. Trails cut through varied terrain—beech and fern forests, golden tussock, boggy areas, and alpine meadows. From Highway 47 it's a steep, uphill tramp to Ketetahi Hot Springs, but a soak in the warm waters below the springs rejuvenates tired muscles.

Several fine walks begin along the Ohakune Road; consider the Mangawhero Forest Walk through a pocket of lush subtropical rain forest or the bush walk to Waitonga Falls, the park's highest waterfall.

Longer hikes lead to the Tongariro Craters and to Mount Ruapehu's hot acid lake, surrounded by ice and snow. A round-the-mountain tramp curves from the Chateau to the Ohakune Mountain Road.

The Mount Ruapehu Alpine Walk, a 5-day guided trek above the timberline with accommodations in mountain huts, explores this fascinating country. Hikers make a high traverse around the mountain, with side trips to small glaciers and to Ruapehu's crater lake. Groups depart from Ohakune weekly from mid-December to early February, weather permitting. Information is available from Venturetreks Ltd., P. O. Box 3839, Auckland.

Ohakune Mountain Road. Motorists can drive up Ohakune Mountain Road, which climbs from the town of Ohakune straight up Ruapehu's southwestern flank.

Ascending, you traverse a cross section of the park's varying climate and vegetation zones—from lowland rimu forest through silver and mountain beech into high tussock shrublands to the alpine gravel fields at road's end. You can picnic beside the Mangawhero River as it falls over the edge of old lava flows. Ask at park headquarters for a descriptive leaflet of the road.

Across the Rangipo Desert

One of North Island's most unusual drives crosses the desolate, windswept Rangipo Desert just east of the park. From Turangi 63 km/39 miles south to Waiouru, Highway 1 is known as Desert Road. Generations of Maori travelers hurried across the forbidding plains, not daring to stop or look at the sacred mountains for fear of antagonizing the gods, who might punish them with storms of snow and ice.

Dry, cold winds sweep down from snowy Mount Ruapehu, and only sparse and stunted plants survive in the harsh climate. Sculptured by wind and frost, road cuttings expose the region's layered volcanic deposits.

On Highway 1 south of Waiouru, the Queen Elizabeth II Army Memorial Museum chronicles New Zealand's military history—from the Maori Land Wars to the present—with exhibits of weapons, uniforms, photographs, paintings, and personal memorabilia. The museum is open daily from 9 A.M. to 4:30 P.M.

Continuing south, Highway 1 passes through the railway town of Taihape and follows the Rangitikei River southwest through white-walled gorges. Several forest reserves are located near Hunterville, in the heart of the district's farm lands. Highway 1 meets the west coast road (Highway 3) at Bulls, another agricultural center.

Exploring the western coast

From the King Country, Highway 3 veers southwest through the wooded Awakino River gorge to the coast. A trio of small fishing settlements—Awakino, Mokau, and Tongaporutu — marks the mouths of coastal rivers.

New Plymouth, the hub of rich Taranaki farm lands, is a city of splendid parks and gardens, and the gateway to mountain recreation in Egmont National Park.

The coastal highway continues southeast to Wanganui, at the mouth of the Wanganui River, and through the Rangitikei and Manawatu farming districts to Wellington.

Taranaki—land of dairy farms

Renowned for its lush pastures, Taranaki is often called the "garden of New Zealand." Solitary Mount Egmont, its snowy cone looming above the surrounding green fields and dairy farms, dominates the province.

Western coast—the essentials

Taranaki's largest town, New Plymouth, is the starting point for visiting Egmont National Park and exploring the Taranaki countryside. Farther south is Wanganui, where travelers embark on trips up the Wanganui River.

Getting there. Air New Zealand flights serve both New Plymouth and Wanganui. Newmans Coach Lines travels from Auckland, via Waitomo and Hamilton, to New Plymouth. Railways Road Services provides service from Wellington north to Wanganui and New Plymouth.

Accommodations. On the west coast, hotels and motels are concentrated in New Plymouth and Wanganui, though you'll also find accommodations in smaller towns.

Largest of New Plymouth's many hostelries is the Plymouth Hotel; others include the Autolodge, Devon Motor Lodge, and Westown Motor Hotel, all centrally located, and DB Bell Block Hotel, near the airport.

Mountain guest houses offer simple but friendly family-style accommodation for Egmont National Park visitors. Dawson Falls Tourist Lodge perches on Mount Egmont's southeast slope, and Stratford Mountain House occupies a site on the east flank. At North Egmont, visitors can stay at a camp house with bunks and stove, or at huts on some of the hiking trails (contact the chief ranger for information). Motels are located in towns along Highway 3 east of Egmont.

Among Wanganui's leading hotels and motels are Avenue Motor Inn and Bryvern Motor Inn, both a few blocks north of the business district, and Hurley's Grand Hotel, in the center of town.

Getting around. Railways Road Services motorcoaches travel between New Plymouth and Wellington, with stops at Stratford, Hawera, Patea, Wanganui, and other towns. Rental cars are available in New Plymouth and Wanganui. Wanganui River trips depart from Wanganui, Pipiriki, and Taumarunui.

Tourist information. Visitor information centers are located in New Plymouth, Hawera, and Wanganui. The main Egmont National Park visitor center is at North Egmont, near Egmont Village.

Exploring the countryside by car

One of the best ways to see new Zealand is to rent a car and head for the country, where you can explore out-of-the-way places at your leisure. Outside the metropolitan areas, traffic is usually light; in rural districts, you'll occasionally run into a flock of sheep or herd of cattle being prodded along the road to pasture.

Rental cars are available in cities and larger towns. Visitors from the United States, Canada, Australia, and the United Kingdom may hire a car by presenting a current driver's license. A variety of fly-drive touring programs are available for travelers, or you can plan your own itinerary or weekend excursion.

The New Zealand Automobile Association offers reciprocal membership privileges to members of other national automobile touring clubs; bring your membership card. At A.A. offices in the major cities, you can obtain maps, comprehensive motoring information, and accommodation and camping guides. District A.A. offices are located in many large towns.

You'll drive on the left side of the road in New Zealand. The speed limit is 80 kph/50 mph on the open road, 50 kph/30 mph (or as posted) in built-up areas. As you travel, yellow A.A. signposts direct you to points of interest.

Roads are sealed (bitumen surfaced) or metalled (graded gravel, usually all-weather). Country roads have improved considerably in recent years, but city drivers may find some unfamiliar conditions.

Use care and common sense on narrow roads, keeping left and driving at country speeds. Resist the impulse to brake suddenly on graveled roads, since it's easy to skid. Corrugations form in sandy road surfaces despite regular grading, so drive slowly and learn to spot ridges in advance. On narrow bridges, traffic in one direction has the right-of-way; oncoming traffic yields.

In rural areas, you may meet stock on the roads, particularly in early morning and late afternoon. Usually, the farmer will direct his dogs to make a path through the group for you. Move slowly but steadily; don't toot your horn or rev your engine unnecessarily. If the herd is moving toward you, it's simplest just to stop and let them move past. When you're driving after dark, stay alert; animals occasionally wander onto the roads.

New Zealand observes the right-hand rule: unless otherwise controlled by traffic signs or lights, you give way to all traffic on your right (unless you're on a main highway). When turning, you give way to *all* traffic. Use of seat belts is compulsory.

The A.A. booklet *Motoring in New Zealand*, available from the New Zealand Tourist Office or A.A. offices, contains helpful information for motorists.

A historic Maori battleground, Taranaki was invaded many times by fierce tribes from the north and was the scene of the first major battles in the Land Wars. Hostilities spread through the central part of North Island and lasted until 1881. In Waitara, the meeting house at Manukorihi Pa contains outstanding examples of characteristic Taranaki carvings and *tukutuku* work.

In the early 1960s, natural gas was discovered at Kapuni, south of Mount Egmont, and in 1969, offshore drilling rigs began tapping the vast Maui natural gas field off the coast. Natural gas from Taranaki fields now supplies most of North Island and a number of petrochemical industries.

Lush parks enhance New Plymouth

Located about midway between Auckland and Wellington, New Plymouth is Taranaki's only large town. Famous for its outstanding parks and gardens, the town is an important agricultural center, as well as the mainland point for development of the offshore natural gas deposits. The Port Taranaki complex serves coastal and overseas shipping.

Settlers from the British counties of Devon and Cornwall laid out the New Zealand Company's colonizing settlement in 1841. Devon Street (Highway 3) marks the town's main commercial area, and superb parks and gardens lie only minutes away from the central district.

Stop at the Public Relations Office, 81 Liardet Street, for information on city and regional attractions, scenic drives, and other excursions.

City parks. The city's jewel is Pukekura Park, often called the country's most outstanding city park. Just a 10-minute walk up Liardet Street from downtown, it has footpaths winding around two manmade lakes and through the wooded reserve. Azaleas, rhododendrons, and other spring flowering plants put on a spectacular show here from September through November. Rare ferns flourish in the Fernery, and begonias, orchids, and fuchsias bloom in the Begonia House. From the tea kiosk, visitors can enjoy a fine view of Mount Egmont. During summer and holiday periods, rowboats crowd the upper lake.

Adjoining Pukekura Park is Brooklands, a park occupying the wooded site of a pioneer homestead. Native pines ring the Bowl of Brooklands, a natural amphitheater that accommodates up to 19,000 people. During the annual Festival of the Pines in January and February, spectators sit on the grass to enjoy music, dance, and drama under the stars.

Taranaki Museum. Noted for its Maori and colonial collections, the Taranaki Museum, at the corner of Brougham and King streets, is open afternoons only. It has an excellent Maori collection and an Early Colonists' exhibition portraying living conditions in Taranaki's early days.

Other city attractions. Several buildings recall the town's early years. Near Brooklands Park on Brooklands Drive stands The Gables, last of four cottage hospitals built in New Plymouth in the 1840s. Small and simple Hurworth, built in 1856, has been restored by the New Zealand Historic Places Trust; located at 548 Carrington Road, it contains mementos of the family of Sir Harry Atkinson, four times Prime Minister of New Zealand.

Govett-Brewster Art Gallery on Queen Street has a collection of contemporary art from New Zealand and other Pacific countries; it also presents changing exhibits.

For a view over the city and port, follow the scenic drive west to Moturoa Lookout. Inland, Mount Egmont's snowy peak juts above Taranaki pasture lands.

Taranaki excursions

For a different look at Taranaki's abundance, explore some of the region's natural attractions. On two easy side trips from New Plymouth, visitors can hike through remote areas of central North Island and savor the outdoors in Egmont National Park.

Lake Mangamahoe. Located 10 km/7 miles south of New Plymouth off Highway 3, Lake Mangamahoe is famed for its magnificent view — the snow-capped cone of Mount Egmont mirrored in the greenery-framed lake. For the best reflections, come in early morning and drive to the far end of the lake.

Pukeiti Rhododendron Trust. Some 800 varieties of rhododendrons, along with many alpine, bog, and woodland plants, thrive in this large, internationally known private garden about 24 km/15 miles south of New Plymouth. Reached by Upper Carrington Road, the reserve is open the year around, but peak blooming season is from September to November. Grassy paths and forest trails wind through the valley.

A look at Egmont National Park

Loneliest and loveliest of North Island's peaks, Mount Egmont was sighted and named by Captain James Cook in 1770. An almost perfect cone, it dominates the Taranaki Peninsula. Egmont National Park encompasses the mountaintop and its densely wooded slopes, popular with climbers and hikers in summer and with skiers in

winter. Mountain guest houses offer simple but cozy family-style accommodations for visitors.

Learn about the park and its activities at the excellent North Egmont Visitor Centre, near Egmont Village, open daily from 9 A.M. to 5 P.M. More park exhibits are located in the Dawson Falls Display Centre on the southeast slope. You can also get park information from the Public Relations offices in New Plymouth and Hawera, or by contacting the park's chief ranger (P.O. Box 43, New Plymouth; phone 80-829).

Mount Egmont's tranquil appearance masks a dormant volcano that last erupted over 200 years ago. Great variations in rainfall and altitude (from sea level to 2,518 meters/8,260 feet), coupled with the mountain's isolation from other high peaks, have endowed it with an unusually varied flora, including a number of plants unique to Egmont.

Nature walks and picnic areas are located near facility areas at North Egmont, East Egmont, and Dawson Falls. In good weather, the climb to the summit isn't difficult, but weather conditions can change rapidly. In summer, you can join a guided excursion. On clear days, hikers gaze inland to the peaks of Tongariro National Park and over undulating dairy lands to the sea.

To reach the park, take Highway 3 southeast from New Plymouth toward Hawera. Roads penetrate the park from Egmont Village in the north, from Stratford in the east, and from Kaponga in the southeast.

Friendly Wanganui

Beyond Egmont, Highway 3 continues southeast through a belt of farming communities — bordering the south Taranaki coast. You'll pass the remains of several historic Maori fortifications.

At the mouth of the Wanganui River is the large town of Wanganui, nestled in a broad curve along the river's west bank. Attractive parks, a well-planned central district, and an outstanding regional museum make Wanganui an inviting stop for travelers. It's also a departure point for boat trips up the Wanganui River.

Wanganui's cultural center is attractive Queen's Park, occupying the site of an early stockade east of Victoria Avenue. Here you'll find the Wanganui Regional Museum, the Sarjeant Art Gallery, a memorial hall complex and conference center, and the public library. Nearby is Cooks Gardens, the town's sports center.

For information about city sightseeing, boat trips, walking tours, and other activities, stop at the Information Centre (Hospitality Wanganui Inc.) beside the City Council Chambers at Guyton and St. Hill streets.

Wanganui Regional Museum. A Maori-style entry invites visitors into the country's largest regional museum. Its outstanding Maori collection is displayed around a 22-meter/72-foot war canoe once paddled by Maori tribesmen on the Wanganui River. You can also see natural history exhibits and a replica settler's cottage.

Jet boats skim the wild rivers

Jet boats were developed in New Zealand for navigating the country's shallow rivers. Fast, versatile, and highly maneuverable, they add a thrilling dimension to New Zealand sightseeing and provide convenient transportation to remote recreation areas.

The jet-propulsion motor that powers the boat was designed by the late Bill Hamilton, a New Zealand farmer with an engineering background and an ability to improvise. His North Canterbury sheep station covered wild and desolate high country, much of it accessible only by traveling up the fast, rock-strewn rivers that raced down from the icy Southern Alps. He wanted access to this remote country, not only to muster his stock but also to open up the magnificent, untamed hunting and fishing country that otherwise took days to reach on foot or horseback.

The powerful jet boat engine Hamilton devised sucks up water beneath the hull of the craft and spits it out behind; this gives the boat the required thrust, as well as enables it to perform at full speed in as little as 10 centimeters/4 inches of water.

Today, on many of the world's wild rivers, Hamilton jet boats skim through white-water rapids, avoiding midstream boulders and sheer canyon walls often by just a deft turn of the wheel.

Located at the entrance to Queen's Park at Watt Street and Maria Place, the museum is open on weekdays from 9:30 A.M. to 4:30 P.M., and on weekends and holidays from 1 to 5 P.M.

Sarjeant Art Gallery. Visitors enjoy changing exhibitions and displays from the gallery's permanent collection of 19th and 20th century British and New Zealand paintings. The gallery's domed building is located in Queen's Park above the Veterans' Steps. Hours are Monday from noon to 4:30 P.M., Tuesday through Friday from 10 A.M. to 4:30 P.M., and weekends and holidays from 1 to 4:30 P.M.

Durie Hill lookout. For a splendid view of the town and surrounding countryside, cross the river on the City Bridge, at the end of Victoria Avenue. From Anzac Parade at the bridge, pedestrians walk through a tunnel to the hill elevator, a commuter service for hilltop residents. For the best views, climb the spiral stairway to the top of the elevator building or ascend the nearby Durie Hill Memorial Tower, a city landmark. Motorists drive up Portal Street to reach the summit.

Parks. Wanganui's floral showplace and favorite picnic spot is serene and lovely Virginia Lake, surrounded by attractive residential areas north of the city on St. John's Hill. Highway 3 skirts the lake's southern shore. You can walk around the lake or through the woods, feed the waterfowl, visit the walk-through aviary, or enjoy flower displays in the Winter Gardens.

An imaginative children's playground and several picnic areas attract families to Kowhai Park, beside the river on Anzac Parade by the Dublin Street Bridge.

Other attractions. At Holly Lodge Estate, a colonial homestead, visitors can sample local wines, browse in a craft shop, and view displays in a small museum. From the lodge jetty, jet boat trips depart daily at 10 A.M. and 2 P.M. up the Wanganui River to Hipango Park. To reach the estate, take Somme Parade along the river.

Southeast of the Wanganui River in Putiki, St. Paul's Memorial Church is an outstanding example of Maori craftsmanship. Carvings, *tukutuku* panels, and painted rafters decorate the interior. From Wanganui, cross the river on the Cobham Bridge (Highway 3); turn left at the first street (Wikitoria Road) and left again on Anaua Street.

The beach at Castlecliff, west of town, attracts swimmers. Walkers can explore Bushy Park Homestead and bush reserve at Kai-Iwi, northwest of Wanganui.

Up the Wanganui River

Maori canoes and flat-bottomed river steamers once plied this historic waterway, which links the rugged interior of North Island with the west coast. Flowing down from Mount Tongariro, the Wanganui is one of New Zealand's longest and most beautiful waterways.

The most scenic stretch of the river is above Pipiriki; this section is accessible only by jet boat, canoe, and trail. For much of the way, the upper river winds between steep, fern-draped banks and tumbles over some 240 rapids. Below Pipiriki, the lower river is generally placid and bordered by willows.

Wanganui River Road. Close by the river is Wanganui River Road, which follows a winding route above the river northwest to Pipiriki, then turns east to meet Highway 4 at Raetihi, southwest of Tongariro National Park.

Several of the riverside settlements began as mission stations, their original names transliterated into Maori equivalents. Most travelers stop at Matahiwi to see the historic water-powered Kawana Flour Mill, built in 1854. At Pipiriki, the Colonial House Information Centre and Museum is open daily in summer from 10 A.M. to 5 P.M., at other times on request at the ranger's house.

Excursions. Jet boat operators in Pipiriki and Taumarunui transport sightseers and hikers deep into the Wanganui country, and several canoe operators offer guided trips during the summer. Information on the Wanganui River reserves is available from the senior ranger (Pipiriki, RD 6, Wanganui; phone Raetihi 4631).

On the East Cape Road *between Te Kaha and Waihau Bay, a tiny Anglican church overlooks the reef at Raukokore. Norfolk pines tower above the burial ground.*

From Wanganui, jet boat excursions explore the lower river some 32 km/20 miles upstream to Hipango Park. In summer, the riverboat M.V. *Waireka* also operates on the lower river. Mini-bus tours take sightseers from Wanganui to Pipiriki on weekdays during the tourist season. Information on excursions is available from the Information Centre in Wanganui.

The Wanganui River Walk, operated by Venturetreks Ltd. (P.O. Box 3839, Auckland), is a 4-day escorted hiking trek into this country. Departing from Ohakune from December through February, the excursion includes transportation and all camping equipment. Camps are set up each night, and hikers carry only personal gear.

Along the eastern coast

From Opotiki on the Bay of Plenty, motorists can follow Highway 35 as it twists around the rugged, heavily forested East Cape or take Highway 2, which runs southeast across the base of the cape. The routes meet again at Poverty Bay, and Highway 2 continues south along the coast.

Two mountain highways cut inland to central tourist areas. From Wairoa, Highway 38 heads northwest through Urewera National Park and Kaingaroa State Forest to Rotorua. Highway 5 follows a historic Maori track and stagecoach route northwest from Napier to Taupo.

Around the East Cape

Cut off by wooded mountains from the rest of North Island, sparsely populated East Cape clings to the leisurely pace of an earlier era. Pohutukawa trees border curving bays and deserted, log-strewn beaches.

To explore the cape, follow the coastal road (Highway 35) from Opotiki. The route closely borders the Bay of Plenty northeast to Cape Runaway, then loops around past New Zealand's most easterly point and continues south, briefly touching the shore at Tokomaru and Tolaga bays before reaching Gisborne.

Captain Cook sailed along the East Cape shore in 1769 and anchored at Tolaga Bay to take on water and wood. In the 1830s, whalers operated along this scenic coast, but the cape's isolated location discouraged European settlement. East Cape traditionally has had a sizable Maori population; you can see excellent examples of Maori carving and art decoration in churches and meeting houses in Te Kaha, Hicks Bay, Tikitiki, and Ruatoria.

Along the coast road, you'll pass Te Kaha, set in an attractive cove, and Hicks Bay, a popular campground. Te Araroa is known as New Zealand's most easterly village. Hot mineral springs are located at Te Puia. South of Tokomaru Bay, a short side road leads travelers to a magnificent stretch of beach and a coastal trail through Anaura Bay Scenic Reserve. Attractive Tolaga Bay offers good swimming and fishing; it's an easy walk to Cook's Cove, with its lookout points over the sheltered bay.

Eastern coast—the essentials

The winding shoreline road (Highway 35) skirts the East Cape shore between Opotiki and Gisborne. The more direct route is Highway 2, which cuts across the base of the cape and continues south past Poverty Bay and Hawke Bay. Tourist towns along the route are Gisborne, on Poverty Bay; the busy seaside resort of Napier; and Hastings, a fruit-growing and winemaking center.

Getting there. Air New Zealand flights serve Gisborne and Napier from Auckland and Wellington. New Zealand Railways provides daily train service between Wellington and Gisborne, with stops at larger towns. Motorcoach service by Mount Cook Line and Railways Road Services links the east coast centers with Auckland, Hamilton, Rotorua, and other towns; Newmans Coach Lines operates on the Wellington-Napier route.

Accommodations. Simple accommodations are available in some of the scattered East Cape settlements, among them Waihau Bay, Hicks Bay, Te Araroa, Ruatoria, Te Puia, and Tolaga Bay. Gisborne accommodations include the Sandown Park Motor Hotel, DB Gisborne Hotel, Teal Motor Lodge, Blue Pacific Beachfront Motel, and Orange Grove Motel. Urewera National Park visitors stay in motel, cabin, and camping facilities at Waikaremoana and Ruatahuna.

In Napier, centrally located accommodations include Napier Travel Inn, Tennyson Motor Inn, and the refurbished Masonic Establishment Hotel. Modern motels are clustered along Kennedy Road in the suburb of Pirimai and along Highway 2 north of town. In Hastings, there's a wide choice, including the Angus Inn, Mayfair Hotel, and Elmore Lodge Motel. In Havelock North, the DB Te Mata Hotel and several small motels serve travelers.

Getting around. Railways Road Services motorcoaches provide scheduled service from Gisborne around East Cape to Opotiki (Bay of Plenty), and stop at Napier and Hastings on longer runs. Mount Cook Line coaches operate local service between Gisborne and Napier. Rental cars are available in Gisborne, Napier, and Hastings.

Tourist information. Obtain sightseeing suggestions at Public Relations Offices in Gisborne (209 Grey Street), Napier (on Marine Parade near the Colonnade), and Hastings (on Russell Street North). In Urewera National Park, tourist information is available at Aniwaniwa.

Gisborne—Captain Cook's landing site

Bordering the shore of Poverty Bay, prosperous Gisborne belies the name bestowed by Captain Cook. His party came ashore at Kaiti Beach, near the mouth of the Turanganui River, on October 9, 1769, the first Europeans to land on New Zealand soil. A monument on Kaiti Beach Road marks Cook's landing site.

From a lookout atop Kaiti Hill, you have a splendid view over the city, harbor, and surrounding river valleys. Nearby is Cook Memorial Observatory.

For information on local activities, visit the Public Relations Office at 209 Grey Street. A regional museum and arts center is located on Stout Street. In summer, bathers enjoy Waikanae Beach, near the center of town at the end of Grey Street. Other good swimming beaches extend north of Gisborne from Wainui to Whangara.

Urewera National Park

Dense virgin forests cover the rugged Urewera ranges west of Gisborne. Following an old Maori route, Highway 38 branches inland from Highway 2 at Wairoa; it proceeds northwest through mountains and valleys to remote Urewera National Park and its sparkling gem, Lake Waikaremoana.

You can enjoy the park's scenery from the highway, but if possible, allow time for at least a short walk through the dense forest. At park headquarters at Aniwaniwa, visitors can obtain trail information, see exhibits, and purchase fishing licenses and shooting permits. In summer, rangers conduct field trips and nature programs. Park information is also available from the chief ranger (Waikaremoana, Private Bag, Wairoa; phone Tuai 803) or from rangers in Murupara (west of the park on Highway 38) or Taneatua (north of the park on Highway 2).

Walks range from a few minutes' stroll to nearby waterfalls to a 5-day tramp around the lake. Near the park visitor center, short trails lead to lovely Bridal Veil, Aniwaniwa, and Papakorito falls. A half-day excursion traverses beech forest and ferny glades to Lake Waikareiti. Huts are maintained on longer trails.

Many trout anglers cast near Mokau Landing, an inlet on Lake Waikaremoana's north shore. Water-sports enthusiasts come here for swimming, boating, and water-skiing. Picnickers enjoy Rosie Bay, south of park headquarters.

From November through March, Te Rehuwai Safaris (Ruatahuna, Private Bag, Rotorua) operates a 5-day Urewera adventure trek through Maori lands and the national park. Led by Maori guides well versed in local history and forest lore, the group departs from Ruatahuna (on Highway 38) and hikes about 30 km/19 miles down the Whakatane River Valley. Groups sleep in tents and cook meals over an open fire. All equipment is provided; trekkers carry only their personal effects.

Napier, lively seaside resort

One of North Island's prettiest towns, Napier is the main holiday and commercial center of the Hawke's Bay district, a region of sheep farms, fruit orchards, and vineyards. Along Napier's rocky beach runs a long esplanade bordered with tall Norfolk pines and an array of recreation facilities and activities.

Above the Marine Parade, white houses dot the slope of Bluff Hill above the blue waters of the bay. Most of

Napier's buildings were rebuilt after a 1931 earthquake and fire destroyed the town.

The Public Relations Office, on Marine Parade just south of the Colonnade, provides information on activities and a street map outlining the city's scenic drive.

Marine Parade. Most of Napier's attractions face this pine-bordered oceanfront avenue. Thousands of tiny lights festoon the trees during the summer holidays.

At the south end of the Parade is the handsome Hawke's Bay Aquarium, housing an 86,000-gallon salt-water oceanarium filled with an impressive display of marine life, a wave-action tank and tidal pool, New Zealand fish swimming in a fresh-water stream, and tanks displaying many kinds of marine life and imported fresh-water tropical fish. On the top floor you can see large turtles and native tuatara lizards.

Performing daily at Marineland of New Zealand, also on Marine Parade, are trained marine animals — dolphins, leopard seals, penguins, and sea lions.

You can see New Zealand's famous kiwis, wekas, opossums, and other night-roaming birds and animals at the Nocturnal Wildlife Centre; feeding time is 2:30 P.M.

Other seaside attractions include the Sunken Gardens, built on rubble from the 1931 earthquake; a boating lake; midget racing cars; outdoor roller-skating rink; putt-putt golf; outdoor salt-water pool (open in summer only); floral clock; and children's play areas. The Pania statue stands near the fountain. On alternate summer Saturdays, craftspeople set up stalls near the sound shell.

Bluff Hill. For viewpoints over Hawke's Bay, follow the city's scenic drive to a pair of overlooks atop Bluff Hill. At the top of Lighthouse Road, you look down on the harbor, where cranes load cargo onto freighters bound for overseas ports. A streetside platform beside Clyde Road offers another view over the town and tree-lined waterfront south to Cape Kidnappers.

Other attractions. Across Marine Parade opposite the Colonnade, you'll find the Lilliput Village and Railway. Miniature trains circle a model village populated by tiny animated figures engaged in daily chores and play.

The Hawke's Bay Museum and Art Gallery on Herschell Street features exhibits on the 1931 earthquake, Maori displays dating from the moa hunter era, artifacts of the region, and changing art exhibitions.

Napier's Botanical Gardens spill down the slopes of Hospital Hill. Trees give way to formal gardens, an aviary, and an outdoor amphitheater where open-air concerts are staged. Roses bloom in Kennedy Park.

Small boats anchor in the Iron Pot, an Ahuriri district inlet named by early whalers. Acres of lowlands, upthrust here during the earthquake, have been reclaimed.

Local sightseeing tours take in many Hawke's Bay attractions; on specialized tours, visitors can see rural homesteads, watch craftspeople at work, or spend a day fishing.

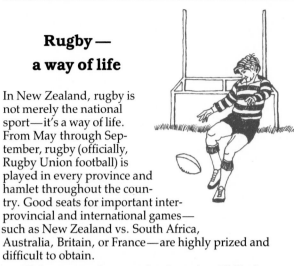

Rugby — a way of life

In New Zealand, rugby is not merely the national sport—it's a way of life. From May through September, rugby (officially, Rugby Union football) is played in every province and hamlet throughout the country. Good seats for important interprovincial and international games— such as New Zealand vs. South Africa, Australia, Britain, or France—are highly prized and difficult to obtain.

To be a team player on the champion All Blacks (so-called because of the color of their uniforms) is the ambition of every boy from the first time he handles the oval ball. Boys begin playing rugby, a completely amateur sport, at the age of seven and often continue into adult life.

Rugby has much in common with American football. Each side attempts to carry a blown-up pigskin over the goal line or kick it through the goal posts with more consistency than the opposition. Unlike football, though, rugby players don't wear heavy padding, and action is continuous. Play does not halt until someone scores, the ball goes out of bounds, or a rule is broken. Each side has eight forwards and seven backs, and every man on the field can run, pass (laterally or backward), and kick. When tackled, the man with the ball must let go once he is pulled down.

You can learn more about the history of the sport of Rugby Union at the National Rugby Museum, located at Grey and Carroll streets in Palmerston North. Open afternoons only, the museum exhibits clothing, photographs, badges, programs, and other memorabilia from the game's early years.

Safari trip to a gannet sanctuary

Getting there is half the fun when you travel to the world's only mainland gannet colony at the tip of Cape Kidnappers. Usually, the birds breed only on isolated islands.

The large sea birds, white with a golden crown and black-tipped feathers, return here in late July. Chicks hatch in late November and December. The best period to visit is from November to March, when migration begins.

Gannet Safaris operates four-wheel-drive vehicles from Summerlee Station on an overland route through gorges, along river beds, and atop cliffs to reach the remote sanctuary. Burden's Beach Safaris features a trip by tractor-drawn trailer from Te Awanga along beach and cliffs. At low tide, you can also reach the colony by a beach route.

Behind the commercial district, tidy houses climb the green hills surrounding Wellington's harbor. Numerous city walks offer splendid views.

Tread the Hawke's Bay wine trail

Vineyards thrive in the sunny Mediterranean climate of Hawke's Bay, second largest of the country's wine-producing areas. Wineries welcome visitors Monday through Saturday for informal tasting; a leaflet with map showing the locations of the wineries is available at tourist offices in Napier and Hastings.

After a mission station was established here in 1851, the French missionaries planted vineyards and soon began producing wine for church and table use. About 1,400 acres of vineyards now cover the sunny slopes and plains around Napier, Hastings, and Havelock North.

Commercial production began here in 1896; New Zealand's oldest winery is Te Mata Estate Winery on Te Mata Road, Havelock North, where visitors see historic buildings and displays on early winemaking in the region. Vidal Wine Producers in Hastings features a vineyard wine bar and wine museum. Some wineries offer guided or self-conducted tours.

Hastings—the country's fruit basket

Orchards and market gardens surround Hastings, a city of parks and gardens on the Heretaunga Plains. Often called "the fruit bowl of New Zealand," it is renowned for its productive orchards—apple, peach, pear, plum, nectarine, and other fruits. Though food-processing factories can and freeze most of the harvest, farmers still sell produce directly to the public at roadside stalls.

The tourist information office faces Russell Street North a half-block from the post office. Ask for a scenic drive folder routing motorists to the area's highlights.

Bagpipes herald the Highland Games in Hastings on Easter weekend. National and provincial champions meet here to compete in piping, drumming, dancing, and athletic events.

Parks. The city's best-known landmark is Fantasyland, a community playground for the young at heart in Windsor Park, east of the business district. Built around a fanciful storybook castle, the imaginative play equipment depicts children's storybook characters. A train chugs around the playground, and rental boats bob on the lake.

Cornwall Park is noted for its trees, superb formal flower gardens, and small aviary. In Frimley Park, you can picnic beneath rare trees, enjoy the rose gardens, and swim in the nearby aquatic center. A mile-long canopy of oak trees, especially lovely in autumn, graces Oak Avenue, northwest of the city off Omahu Road.

Havelock North. This choice residential area spreads along hilly slopes southeast of Hastings.

For the finest view of the Hawke's Bay district, follow Te Mata Peak Road 6 km/4 miles up to the mountain's summit. Your view extends over the region's orchards, gardens, vineyards, rivers, towns, and coast. Before leaving the peak, amble down one of the wooded nature trails in Te Mata Park.

Through the Wairarapa farm lands

South of Hastings, Highway 2 veers inland through rolling pastures and small farm towns toward Wellington. In the 1870s, Scandinavian settlers carved Norsewood, Dannevirke, and Eketahuna out of the vast totara forest then covering the region.

At Woodville, Highway 3 branches west through the magnificent Manawatu Gorge and the town of Palmerston North, noted for its agricultural research and as the home of Massey University. Several parks border the river.

From its headwaters in the Ruahine Range, the Manawatu slices westward through the mountainous spine of North Island and into the Tasman Sea. Built in the 1870s, the road through the scenic Manawatu Gorge was a difficult construction feat; at times, workers were suspended from the clifftops by ropes.

Pahiatua, on Highway 2 south of Woodville, marks the northern end of the rugged Tararua Range.

Rare native birds breed in captivity at the Mount Bruce Native Bird Reserve, 24 km/15 miles north of Masterton. Visitors can watch takahe, kakapo, kiwi, pukeko, and other birds daily from 10 A.M. to 4 P.M., except during the October to mid-December breeding period.

Heart of the Wairarapa farming district is Masterton, about 100 km/62 miles north of Wellington. The world's fastest shearers compete here each March at the Golden Shears International Sheep Shearing Contest.

The highway continues south through dairy and sheep-fattening farms and market gardens to Carterton, Greytown, and Featherston. Roads lead west from the highway to the edge of Tararua Forest Park.

Wellington, the capital city

Wooded hills curve like a green amphitheater around Wellington's sparkling harbor, giving New Zealand's capital city its character and charm. From atop Mount Victoria and other lofty viewpoints, your gaze sweeps over a magnificent vista with ever-changing moods.

Located at the southwestern tip of North Island, Wellington is the country's second largest city. Forested peninsulas and shipping wharves jut into the harbor. In the heart of the city, commercial and government buildings rim the waterfront; the curving thoroughfares of Lambton and Thorndon quays mark the city's original shoreline. Nostalgic Victorian buildings mingle pleasantly with more modern structures. Above the business district, dwellings cling precariously to the steep slopes.

Wellington was the first settlement organized by the London-based New Zealand Company. In 1840, shiploads of settlers sailed into Port Nicholson's sheltered waters. When the seat of government was transferred from Auckland to Wellington in 1865, the permanent character of the young town was determined.

Wellington's changeable marine climate is generally free from extremes of heat and cold. Bracing winds that funnel through Cook Strait clear the air and add zest to daily life. A nearby geologic fault subjects the city to occasional earthquakes.

Getting settled in Wellington

Heart of Wellington's shopping district is Lambton Quay, which winds through the middle of the commercial district. Featherston Street is the city's financial center. Transportation facilities are located north of the business center: the railway station borders Thorndon Quay; interisland ferries tie up at the terminal on Aotea Quay.

Shopping. Shops, boutiques, and department stores flank a mile-long thoroughfare extending from Lambton Quay south along Willis and Manners streets to Courtenay Place. Another lively district is The Oaks complex, a pedestrian shopping mall on Cuba and Manners streets. Downtown stores are generally open on weekdays from 9 A.M. to 5:30 P.M. and on Friday evening until 9 P.M.

Entertainment and the arts. Wellington is the home of both the New Zealand Symphony and the national ballet company; in addition, it supports numerous amateur drama and music groups. Much of Wellington's after-dark musical entertainment centers around the city's hotels and drinking establishments. Current attractions are listed in Wellington tourist publications and the daily newspapers.

New Zealand and overseas artists perform at the Town Hall. Plays are presented by the Downstage Theatre repertory group, the Circa Theatre, and the Wellington Repertory Theatre. The Wellington Operatic Society offers musical productions. In summer, the symphony plays a series of promenade concerts, and music groups perform in the Botanic Gardens sound shell.

The art scene is also flourishing, with many galleries and several craft markets showcasing the work of the country's artists and craftspeople.

Sports. Horse racing fans head north of the city to Trentham Racecourse in Upper Hutt; trotting events take place at Hutt Park Raceway in Petone. Rugby Union games are held at Athletic Park, Rugby League at Rugby League Park, soccer and cricket matches at Basin Reserve. Championship tennis matches are played at Central Park, and you can watch bowls and croquet at Kelburn Park. Golfers find several fine courses in and near the city; the seaside links at Paraparaumu, a 45-minute drive north of the city, rank among the country's top courses.

Oriental Bay's boat harbor is the center of yachting activities; in summer, you often see yachting and rowing races on the harbor. Swimmers can choose salt or fresh water, beach or pool, surf or calm harbor waters. No matter what the weather, swimmers enjoy Freyberg Pool off Oriental Parade. On warm, sunny days, crowds flock to the beach fronting Oriental Parade, near the heart of the city. Surfers head for the Miramar Peninsula.

Wellington—the essentials

New Zealand's capital city, Wellington curves around a scenic harbor at the southwestern tip of North Island. Nearby towns and beaches along the Tasman coast are favorite weekend destinations.

Getting there. Air New Zealand flights serve Wellington Airport, about 8 km/5 miles southeast of the city, from cities and larger towns on both islands. Wellington Railway Station on Waterloo Quay is the southern terminus for North Island rail service. Motorcoaches of Railways Road Services, Mount Cook Line, and Newmans Coach Lines also converge on the capital. Interisland ferries travel several times daily between Picton, on South Island, and Wellington's Aotea Quay terminal. Cruise liners moor at the Overseas Passenger Terminal during Wellington stopovers.

Accommodations. Largest of Wellington's downtown hotels is the James Cook, towering above the business district from its hillside site on The Terrace. New hotels commanding fine views over the city and harbor are the luxurious Parkroyal, at the eastern end of Oriental Parade, and the Terrace Regency, tucked away in a quiet part of The Terrace. Older downtown hotels include the St. George, De Brett, and Waterloo.

Among other modern, centrally located hotels are the Abel Tasman Courtesy Inn at Willis and Dixon streets, and the Wellington Travelodge and Town House Motor Inn, both near the Overseas Passenger Terminal.

Travelers who prefer to stay outside the central district can lodge at the Sharella Motor Inn, on Glenmore Street near the entrance to the Botanic Gardens, or the Shaw Savill Lodge, in suburban Kilbirnie near the airport.

Food and drink. Wellington offers a pleasant choice of elegant or informal restaurants. Reservations are recommended, especially on weekends. Several of the capital's best-known restaurants specialize in French cuisine; others feature Italian dishes or New Zealand specialties, such as seafood and game. For special atmosphere, consider Plimmer House, an elegant restaurant in a lovely old Victorian house, and Windows on Wellington, noted for its panoramic views over the city and harbor.

Getting around. Taxi stands are located at all terminals and at several downtown locations. Airport buses provide 20-minute shuttle service between the central district and the airport. Trolley and diesel buses of the Wellington City Transport Department fan out to the city's residential areas; for information, phone 856-579. Most bus lines begin at the railway station (platform 9) or on Courtenay Place and run along Lambton Quay at some point. The Kelburn cable car travels between Lambton Quay and Kelburn at 10-minute intervals.

Electrified suburban trains depart from the railway station for Hutt Valley towns and west coast settlements as far north as Paekakariki. Rental cars are available in downtown Wellington, at the airport and ferry terminal, and in Lower Hutt.

A city sightseeing tour departs daily at 2 P.M. from the Public Relations Office on Mercer Street. Weekend full-day excursions take visitors to Otaki and west coast beaches along the Golden Coast, and to Palliser Bay and the south Wairarapa coast.

Tourist information. Sightseeing suggestions and information on local walking tours and scenic drives are available at the Public Relations Office at Mercer and Victoria streets (phone 735-063). Travel accommodations and arrangements throughout the country are handled by the Government Tourist Bureau, a block away at 27-31 Mercer Street. Automobile club members can obtain motoring information and maps at the Automobile Association office at 166 Willis Street.

Savor harbor views

Arterial roads and suburban streets wind up, down, and around the city's hills, and spectacular views are only minutes away from downtown.

For the best view, make your way to the top of Mount Victoria. Below you, the city and its hills encircle the sparkling harbor. Your panorama extends north to the Hutt Valley, to the eastern bays backed by the Rimutaka Range, and south across the harbor and Cook Strait.

The quickest and easiest route to a magnificent view is aboard one of the bright red cable cars that climb from Lambton Quay to Kelburn. Board at the lower terminal on Cable Car Lane, off Lambton Quay opposite Grey Street. In 3½ minutes, the electrically operated cars ascend high above city traffic. Several interesting walks begin near the upper terminal and wind down through the Botanic Gardens and interesting neighborhoods to Lambton Quay.

The best water-level viewpoint of the harbor is from the Massey Memorial on the top of Point Halswell, about 11 km/7 miles from the city center. It's a favorite stop on the City Marine Drive that skirts the harbor.

On foot in Wellington

Despite its steep hills, you can explore much of the city on foot. Stairways and footpaths climb Wellington's slopes. Buses and the Kelburn cable car take you to more distant destinations.

Along the waterfront. As you walk along Wellington's waterfront, you may see ships docking at downtown wharves and Cook Strait ferries steaming across the harbor. From the Wellington Boat Harbour, look up at the pastel wooden houses clinging to the hills above Oriental Bay.

At Queens Wharf on Jervois Quay, tour the Maritime Museum in the fine old Wellington Harbour Board building. You'll see models and relics of ships that have sailed these waters, as well as historic charts, journals, photographs, and other articles chronicling the port's history. Visitors are welcome on weekdays from 10 A.M. to 4 P.M. and on Saturday from 2 to 5 P.M.

The commercial center. In Wellington's early years, Lambton and Thorndon quays bordered the waterfront. A series of sidewalk plaques mark the original shoreline. Settlers began reclaiming land as early as 1852, and today, much of the business district is built on reclaimed land.

You'll enjoy exploring Lambton Quay, the city's shopping thoroughfare, and its side streets. Higher on the hills, new office buildings and apartment towers indicate a building boom along The Terrace.

Few streets link Lambton Quay with the upper level commercial and residential areas. One shortcut is the Plimmer Steps, a pedestrian stairway connecting Lambton Quay (near Hunter Street) with Boulcott Street. An elevator runs between The Terrace, just north of the James Cook Hotel, and Lambton Quay.

Civic center. South of the shopping district is Wellington's Town Hall and the new Michael Fowler Centre, a multipurpose concert and conference center completed in 1983; its main entrance is on Wakefield Street. Across Mercer Street, the Rotary Garden Court with its handsome conservatory is a popular picnic spot for nearby office workers.

The Wellington Public Library, 8-18 Mercer Street, has a New Zealand room and a newspaper reading room where you can find domestic and international papers. The Golden Bay Planetarium, behind the library on Harris Street, offers programs on weekend afternoons.

Hillside walks. Several enjoyable walking routes begin near the upper terminal of the Kelburn cable car (page 64). Map brochures, available at the Public Relations Office, Mercer and Victoria streets, guide your way.

It's a pleasant downhill stroll through the Wellington Botanic Gardens, a large hillside reserve. In spring, azaleas, camellias, rhododendrons, and bulbs blossom forth in a spectacular display. Roses bloom from November to April in formal plantings in the Lady Norwood Rose Garden. Indoor flowering plants and ferns are on view daily in the Begonia House. On Sunday and on summer evenings band concerts are presented in the sound shell. Near the Rose Garden, you can board bus number 12 to return to downtown.

Just below the Botanic Gardens is historic Thorndon, one of Wellington's most charming districts. Though many of the city's older wooden dwellings have fallen victim to the motorway that cuts a broad swath along the hills, you'll still find delightful cottages and other buildings dating from the 1870s along Ascot Street, Tinakori Road, and terraces branching off it. The *Thorndon Walk* leaflet guides you along the way.

Weekend wanderings for city visitors

New Zealanders treasure their weekends. Most shops, offices, and services operate on a limited schedule or close completely on Saturday and Sunday, and city streets empty as Kiwis head for home, country, or shore.

The savvy traveler plans ahead. To learn about special events and other activities, check local newspapers and tourist officials. If you want to rent a car, reserve ahead (the earlier the better) and arrange a pick-up time. Travelers planning a weekend excursion using public transportation should confirm the time schedule in advance.

Explore on foot. If you've just arrived, get acquainted with the downtown district, walk along the waterfront, or follow paths through hillside forest parks. Join local families in admiring the flowers or listening to a band concert in the botanic gardens.

Take a boat ride. In most cities and tourist areas, you can board a harbor launch, ferry, jet boat, lake cruiser, or other boat for an afternoon on the water.

Visit a museum. Learn about New Zealand natural history, Maori culture, and the colonial days. Inspect vintage vehicles and even take a ride in one at a transportation museum.

Head for the beach. Soak up the sun, watch boats, swim, or surf in the waves. Take along a picnic and spread it out on the sand.

Watch a sports event. Saturday is sports day in New Zealand. Go to the races or attend a rugby match.

Join the animals. Visit the zoo. See a kiwi bird and other native—and introduced—birds and animals.

Visit the library. If the weather is gloomy, catch up on home news in the library's newspaper reading room or browse through the New Zealand book collection.

Another route is the *Town and Gown Walk,* which starts near the upper Kelburn terminal and cuts down through the hillside campus of Victoria University along Salamanca Road.

Government Centre—heart of the nation

One part of Wellington belongs to all New Zealanders: the country's political center. It crowns a knoll near the north end of Lambton Quay, where it intersects with Bowen and Molesworth streets.

Horse racing — a popular spectator sport

Some of the world's top thoroughbred horses are raised in New Zealand, where the breeding and racing of horses is big business. Spectators flock to racetracks throughout the country, and a Saturday or holiday spent at the races will bring you in close contact with a crowd of enthusiastic Kiwis.

Most of the important gallop racing meets take place at North Island tracks, including Ellerslie and Avondale (Auckland), Te Rapa (Hamilton), Trentham (Wellington), Awapuni (Palmerston North), and Hastings (Hastings). Among main South Island tracks are Riccarton in Christchurch and Wingatui in Dunedin.

Major harness racing tracks include Alexandra Park and Epsom in Auckland, Hutt Park in Wellington, Addington in Christchurch, and Forbury Park in Dunedin. Many races take place at night under floodlights.

Admission prices vary, depending on whether you buy an inside or outside enclosure. Inside is similar to reserved grandstand seating; outside is comparable to general admission.

Parliament Buildings. Dignified Parliament House, completed in 1922, and the lighter Gothic architecture of the 1897 General Assembly Library contrast dramatically with the new circular Executive Wing (commonly called "the Beehive"), opened by Queen Elizabeth in 1977. New Zealand materials, especially native woods and Takaka marble, were used liberally in their construction.

The buildings are not open to casual sightseers, but you can join a conducted tour of the public areas. Tours depart from the main reception desk at regular intervals; information is available from the Chief Messenger's Office (phone 749-199). Parliamentary procedures, modeled after those of Britain's Parliament, are explained. If Parliament is in session (usually from May through October), you can watch the proceedings from the visitors' gallery.

Other buildings. At Museum and Bowen streets behind the Parliament Buildings is Broadcasting House, center of the Broadcasting Corporation of New Zealand.

Facing Lambton Quay opposite the Cenotaph are the Government Buildings, a marvelous example of Wellington's early architecture. Constructed on reclaimed land in 1876, the 152-room wooden building converts traditional 19th century stone architecture into timbered Italianate style.

Open on weekdays, the buildings of the Law Courts on Ballance Street house three levels of New Zealand's legal hierarchy — the Magistrate's Court, the Supreme Court, and the Court of Appeals.

Reminders of the Victorian era

In older sections of the city, Victorian dwellings and other historic buildings provide nostalgic contrast to more modern structures. Gabled houses climb the hills, their brass doorknockers and tall bay windows adding touches of 19th century elegance.

Old St. Paul's Church. Just a short walk from the Parliament Buildings, Wellington's renowned old Anglican church is a Mulgrave Street landmark. Built in 1866, it adapted traditional Victorian Gothic architecture to colonial conditions and native woods. Inside, stained glass windows and brass plates provide a valuable century-long record of its parishioners.

Supplanted by a new cathedral in 1966, the church has been restored as a tranquil setting for cultural events. It's open to the public Monday through Saturday from 10 A.M. to 4:30 P.M. and on Sunday from 1:30 to 4:30 P.M.

Early houses. Among former dwellings still in use are the Plimmer House, an 1870s gem on Boulcott Street, now a fashionable restaurant; and the stately, turreted Williams residence at 53 Hobson Street, incorporated into Queen Margaret College. Antrim House, an ornate Edwardian town house at 63 Boulcott Street, is headquarters for the New Zealand Historic Places Trust.

Colonial Cottage Museum, 68 Nairn Street, is housed in a cottage built in the 1850s. Restored and furnished with period articles, it recalls the life of the city's pioneers. Museum hours are 10 A.M. to 4 P.M. Wednesday through Friday and noon to 4 P.M. on Saturday and Sunday.

National Museum and Art Gallery

Overlooking the city and harbor, the National Museum and National Art Gallery share a handsome building on Buckle Street. A large tower in front of the museum contains a carillon and the Hall of Memories, the national war memorial. To reach the site, take bus number 1 or 3 from the railway station to Basin Reserve and walk 2 blocks west.

The museum is noted for its fascinating Maori collection, which concentrates on articles from Taranaki and central North Island. Highlight of the colonial section is an early Wellington dwelling furnished in 1840s style. Relics from Captain Cook's voyages are also on display.

The National Art Gallery shows works by New Zealand and overseas artists and puts on special exhibitions.

Something for everyone

Depending on your interests, attractions ranging from historic manuscripts to collections of native plants and flowers invite your perusal.

Domed "Beehive," housing executive offices of Parliament, is a new Wellington landmark. Its modern lines contrast with older Parliament House.

Alexander Turnbull Library. Visitors as well as scholars come here to see the original signed parchment sheets of the Treaty of Waitangi, as well as changing displays from the library's fascinating collections. The library is celebrated for its valuable books and manuscripts, as well as its historic maps, charts, and pictures relating to New Zealand history and Pacific exploration. Located at 44 The Terrace (2nd floor), the library is open on weekdays from 10:30 A.M. to 5 P.M. and on Saturday from 9 A.M. to noon.

City Art Gallery. Located at 65 Victoria Street, the gallery sponsors a series of stimulating exhibitions. It's open on weekdays and on Saturday and Sunday afternoons.

Katherine Mansfield Memorial Park. This shaded garden on Fitzherbert Street, off Hobson Street just east of the motorway, honors New Zealand's most acclaimed writer of short stories (her real name was Kathleen Beauchamp). Many of her best-known works are set in Wellington. Her birthplace still stands at 25 Tinakori Road.

Native plant garden. New Zealand's most complete collection of native flora has been assembled at the Otari Open-Air Plant Museum in the northwest suburb of Wilton. Paths through formal areas lead into a sheltered, wooded valley where visitors can picnic. To reach the garden, located off Wilton Road, take bus 14 from the city.

Castle Collection of Musical Instruments. Also located in the Newtown district, this private working collection contains several hundred early and unusual instruments from all over the world. Tours are by prior arrangement only (at least a week in advance). The collection is housed at 27 Colombo Street (phone 898-296).

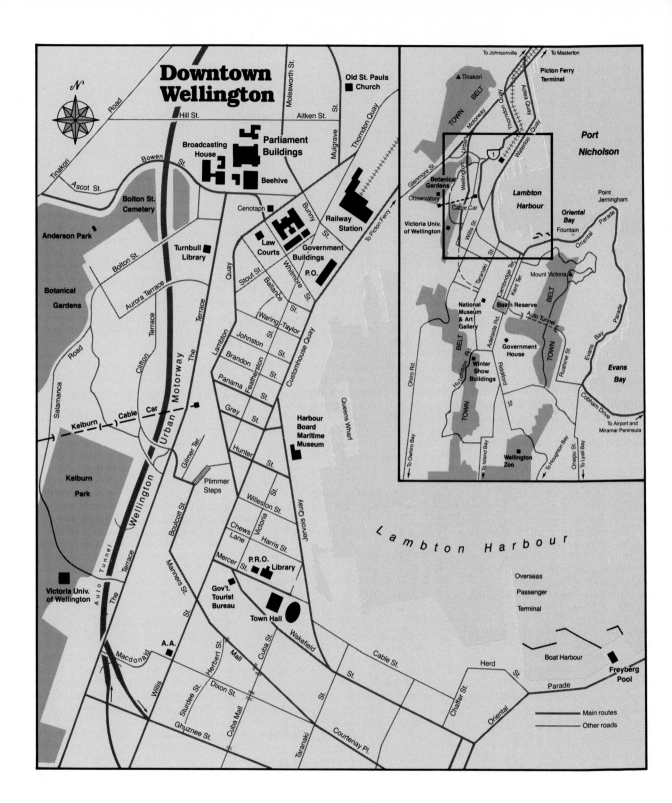

Wellington Zoo. Located about 4 km/2½ miles south of the city center, the zoo is open daily from 8:30 A.M. to 5 P.M. (Hours at the kiwi house are 10 A.M. to 4 P.M.) Leopards and tigers are fed in midafternoon. On weekend and holiday afternoons, you can board a miniature train for a ride around the zoo's pond. To reach the zoo, take bus 11 from the railway station to Newtown Park.

Excursions from Wellington

City sightseeing tours depart daily at 2 P.M. from the Public Relations Office on Mercer Street. You can take a scenic flight or a harbor cruise, or, if the day is pleasant, board a ferry for a trip across Cook Strait to Picton.

The City Marine Drive offers a look at suburban beaches east and south of the city. To the north, you can explore the Hutt Valley, the Golden Coast, or the Eastern Bays. On weekends, motorcoach tours travel to beach towns along the Tasman, and to rugged Cape Palliser.

Discover suburban beaches

From the city center, the 39-km/24-mile City Marine Drive follows the harbor shore to nearby beaches. The route skirts Oriental and Evans bays on the inner harbor, then loops around the Miramar Peninsula past a series of attractive bays. Along the way you'll pass moored pleasure boats, fine swimming beaches, and surfing areas.

On the northern tip of Miramar Peninsula, the Massey Memorial offers picnic tables and a fine view of the harbor. Along the peninsula's eastern shore, the road curves past a series of inviting beaches at Scorching, Karaka, and Worser bays. Outer harbor beaches at Lyall and Island bays attract hardy swimmers and surfers. Island Bay is home for a small fishing fleet.

The Hutt Valley and beyond

Hemmed in between hills, the Hutt Valley towns sprawl along Highway 2 over alluvial plains bordering the Hutt River. In Petone, the Settlers' Museum on the Esplanade commemorates the first landing of settlers in Port Nicholson. Lower Hutt is a center of scientific and industrial research. Railroad fans flock to the Silverstream Railway on Sunday afternoon. Farther north in Upper Hutt is Trentham Racecourse.

Hikers enjoy the rugged hills of Tararua Forest Park, an hour's drive north of the capital, where trails wind through the bush and along streams. Access routes to the vast reserve are signposted off the main highways.

Along the Golden Coast

North of Wellington, Highway 1 connects coastal towns along the Tasman shore from Plimmerton north to Otaki. Suburban trains link the capital with the larger beach towns, and Saturday shopping draws many weekend visitors to this region, dubbed the "Golden Coast." Many Wellingtonians have built beach cottages or retirement homes here.

If you're a fan of vintage vehicles, three museums await you here. At Paekakariki, the Engine Shed museum recalls the era of steam locomotives; the collection is open to visitors on Saturday. Trams, trolley buses, and an old-time fire engine await you in the Wellington Tramway Museum in Paekakariki's Queen Elizabeth Park, open on weekends and holidays; you can also picnic and swim in the park. Classic cars take the spotlight at the Southward Car Museum, open daily in Otaihanga, just northwest of Paraparaumu.

Otaki, 74 km/46 miles north of Wellington, has one of the country's finest Maori churches. Its plain exterior gives little hint of the outstanding interior.

The Eastern Bays

A pleasant excursion follows the harbor northeast through Petone to prime residential suburbs bordering the Eastern Bays. By bus, it's a 40-minute ride from the Wellington railway station to Eastbourne.

The road passes a series of sheltered beaches bordering Lowry, York, Mahina, and Days bays before reaching Eastbourne. Houses spill down the steep wooded slopes, and some hill dwellers have installed private cable cars to transport them between street and home. From Kowhai Street in Eastbourne, a signposted trail climbs over a hilly ridge with good harbor views and down to a peaceful valley at Butterfly Creek.

Rugged Cape Palliser

Cape Palliser, the rocky, storm-wracked southern tip of North Island, has been the scene of many shipwrecks. Crowning a hill is the Cape Palliser Lighthouse, linked by a long flight of steps with the keeper's dwelling below. Visitors can enjoy surfcasting here and can view seals at a nearby seal colony.

Home hospitality

New Zealanders enjoy meeting overseas visitors, and they believe hospitality begins at home. You'll enjoy sharing the relaxed life style of these friendly, hospitable people, exchanging ideas without a language barrier, and learning about daily life in a different land.

In some areas, residents who want to meet visitors join voluntary hospitality programs; they may extend an invitation for tea and an hour or two of conversation, or they may offer to guide you around their town. Learn about these programs through local tourist offices.

Throughout the country, families in towns and on farms open their homes to visitors on a paying guest basis. Several organizations can arrange host family accommodations; for information, contact the New Zealand Tourist Office or local tourist offices. Though many host families are located near major cities, there are host families scattered all over both islands.

If you have a special interest or hobby, you may be able to meet Kiwis with similar interests. Visitors who belong to international service organizations can often link up with members of local chapters in New Zealand's larger towns. If trout fishing is your idea of a perfect vacation, you can stay with a New Zealand angler host and fish the lakes and streams of Rotorua, Taupo, or South Island; for information, write to Club Pacific, 790 27th Avenue, San Francisco, CA 94121.

SOUTH ISLAND

The icy Southern Alps tower above rain forest, sea, and glacial lakes

On sparsely populated South Island, lofty mountains flanked by icy glaciers set the scenic tone. Adding to the visual drama are subtropical rain forests, coastal fiords of awesome beauty, vast grazing lands, deep alpine lakes bordered by thick forests, windswept headlands, and sunny beaches. The island proudly carries the imprint of the hardworking 19th century colonists, sheepmen, and prospectors who scouted and tamed this splendid and diverse land.

South Island's variety of natural scenery, climate, and vegetation is matched by seasonal changes more distinct than those on North Island. Springtime fruit blossoms give way to the ripe fields of summer. Colorful foliage brightens the autumn landscape. In winter, snow blankets much of the interior.

About 28 percent of New Zealand's 3.1 million people live on South Island. With a population of about 850,000, the entire island supports a population barely larger than that of Auckland, the country's largest city. Most settlements border the eastern coast.

An island overview

Separated from its sister island by narrow Cook Strait, elongated South Island stretches southwest some 800 km/500 miles. A diagonal geologic fault, rising abruptly from the western coast to create the magnificent mountain chain called the Southern Alps, divides the island for most of its length.

Thousands of years ago massive glaciers covered much of the island. Grinding down the valleys, they sculpted the mountains, sheared rocky cliffs, carved deep

Glowing autumn color brightens roads and river valleys north of Queenstown in late April; early snow already dusts the summit of Coronet Peak.

grooves in the southwestern coast, and gouged out long, slim lakes.

Immigrants transformed the land

Captain James Cook circumnavigated the islands and mapped the coast in 1769-70. Sealers and whalers established shore stations in the early decades of the 19th century. Finally, European colonists, who began arriving in earnest during the 1840s, founded settlements at Akaroa in 1840, Nelson in 1841, Dunedin in 1848, and, finally, Christchurch in 1850.

The English and Scottish colonists, transforming the virgin landscape, plotted neat townsites and planted thousands of trees. They erected sturdy buildings to house their churches, schools, and governmental bodies and reserved parklands for the enjoyment of succeeding generations.

While the Maori land wars raged across North Island, Australian sheepmen opened up South Island's hilly interior. Discoveries of gold in Central Otago in 1861 were followed shortly by rich new finds on the West Coast, accelerating the exploration and settlement of these remote regions.

That pioneer spirit never quite died—a strong streak of hardy individualism persists today.

Sparsely settled South Island is still the home of many proud descendants of pioneer stock, hospitable hard-working farm families who share the conviviality of country gatherings, as well as the problems of flood, drought, snow, stock losses, and isolation.

Lush forest and grassy plains

Luxuriant greenery descends to the blue Tasman Sea along the wet and wild western coast. Moisture-laden clouds drop more than 200 inches of rain annually as they sweep in from the sea and strike the steep barrier of the Southern Alps.

Along the northwest coast, the towns of Westport, Greymouth, and Hokitika were born during gold rush days. Farther south is Westland National Park, where Franz Josef and Fox glaciers descend steeply toward the sea, and the virtually untouched, fiord-indented southwest coast.

On the drier east side of the mountains, a vast network of waterways drains the alpine snowfields, hilly grasslands, broad plains, and coastal valleys. More than half of the island's population is concentrated along the Pacific coast near Christchurch and Dunedin and in the smaller towns of Timaru and Oamaru.

Other sizable towns are Invercargill, on the south coast, and Nelson and Blenheim, near the island's northern tip. South Island's leading resort is Queenstown, hub of the southern lakes district.

Scenic highways follow historic routes

Modern highways hug the coastline and cut across the mountains to link the island's eastern and western settlements. Highway 1, bordering the east coast from Picton to Bluff, passes through major cities and towns. Highway 6 cuts from Blenheim through Nelson and the Buller Gorge to Westport and down the western coast.

Centuries ago, Maoris seeking West Coast greenstone discovered riverside routes through the mountains. Today, scenic transalpine highways follow these traditional routes. The Lewis Pass Road (Highway 7) links Waipara and Greymouth. Arthur's Pass Road (Highway 73) winds through the high country from Christchurch to Kumara Junction, north of Hokitika. Highway 6, which cuts across Haast Pass from Wanaka, provides a southern route to Westland National Park.

Other main highways thrust deeply into the provinces of Canterbury and Otago and cut through the valleys of Fiordland to Milford Sound.

South Island's highlights

Beyond the cities, travelers find attractions in rich variety. Seven national parks and a maritime park preserve outstanding scenic areas of South Island for public enjoyment. On the north coast are historic Abel Tasman National Park and the delightful waterways of Marlborough Sounds Maritime Park. Nelson Lakes National Park contains a pair of slender, beech-fringed glacial lakes.

Straddling the snowy crest of the Southern Alps are four national parks—Arthur's Pass, Mount Cook, Westland, and Mount Aspiring—attracting climbers, hikers, and others who love the alpine country. Vast and varied Fiordland National Park offers awesome mountains, dense forests, tranquil lakes, and majestic fiords.

Many travelers enjoy the Queenstown district and the southern lakes, Nelson's sunny beaches, unspoiled Stewart Island, and the sleepy old mining towns of Central Otago.

Activities include fishing for trout and salmon; visiting coal mines, historic museums, or bird sanctuaries; walking on a glacier or through fern-filled rain forest; staying overnight with a farm family; dining on local scallops, crayfish, oysters, or venison; and exploring the island's remote districts on foot or horseback or by jet boat, sightseeing plane, or four-wheel-drive vehicle.

Christchurch on the Avon

Nestled at the base of the hilly Banks Peninsula, New Zealand's third largest city faces inland toward a broad panorama—the flat Canterbury Plains backed by the snowy Southern Alps. South Island's largest city, Christchurch is the busy yet relaxed capital of the province of Canterbury.

Though known for its peaceful ambience and unhurried pace, Christchurch is a city that gets things done. It has one of the country's busiest and most modern airports, a handsome town hall bordering the Avon River, and an outstanding sports complex developed for the 1974 Commonwealth Games. A new shopping mall on Cashel and High streets attracts downtown shoppers.

The Canterbury settlement was the last and most successful of the mid-19th century colonizing ventures. Four shiploads of hand-picked English colonists arrived at Lyttelton in 1850 and made a historic trek across the Port Hills to found Christchurch. Surveyors laid out the town in a grid pattern, its dignified order broken only by the serpentine course of the Avon River.

Enjoying Christchurch

Occupying a spacious square in the heart of the city is Christchurch Cathedral, a reminder of the important role the Church of England played in the settlement of Canterbury. Major arteries radiate from Cathedral Square.

Often called "New Zealand's most English city," Christchurch retains many features established by its Anglican settlers. Shaded by overhanging trees, the Avon River meanders through the city, adding a note of gracious, old-world charm. Still in daily use are many stately Gothic buildings, constructed by early civic leaders to house the settlement's religious, educational, governmental, and cultural institutions.

Parks soften the city's rectangular layout, and home gardens blaze with color from spring through autumn. You'll probably see uniformed students cycling along city streets or waiting for city buses. A special Christchurch touch: baby strollers hook a ride on the front of the buses, a convenience reflecting the city's relaxed pace.

Shopping. Christchurch's main shopping district clusters around Cathedral Square. Nearby shopping arcades such as Chancery Lane and New Regent Street offer shops and a relaxed atmosphere. A two-story shopping center links Hereford and Cashel streets near High Street, and a pedestrian mall—the Triangle Centre—connects High and Cashel streets.

Shops are generally open from 9 A.M. to 5:30 P.M. on weekdays and until 9 on Friday evening. The city mall and most suburban malls are also open on Saturday morning but closed on Sunday. In Riccarton, stores stay open late on Thursday night. New Brighton shops are closed on Monday; on Saturday they're open until 9 P.M.

Entertainment. Most ballet and theater performances, concerts, and touring shows take place at the city's handsome Town Hall. Plays are presented in the Court Theatre at the Arts Centre of Christchurch.

Major hotels and many restaurants offer live entertainment and dancing in the evening, particularly on Friday and Saturday. If you'd like to meet a local family, you can make arrangements through the Information Centre or the Government Tourist Bureau.

Sports and special events. In the Christchurch area, you can play golf, go river or surf fishing, and ski from May through November at Mount Hutt.

You can see some of the country's top horses in action here at two of the country's finest tracks. Light-harness racing (trotting) takes place at Addington Raceway; racing and steeplechase events are held at Riccarton Racecourse. Racing events highlight November's Carnival Week celebration. Premier classic on the racing calendar is the New Zealand Cup; the companion New Zealand Trotting Cup race takes place at Addington. The Canterbury Agricultural & Pastoral Show is also held during Carnival Week.

Other annual events include the New Zealand Grand National in August and the Easter Cup Carnival meetings in autumn. From late February to mid-March, the annual Christchurch Festival offers a program of floral displays, art shows, sporting events, and other activities.

Christchurch—the essentials

Christchurch, South Island's largest city, is also the hub of the island's transportation system. Air, rail, and motorcoach lines link Canterbury's capital with all parts of the island, as well as with more distant destinations.

Getting there. Passengers arriving by plane disembark at Christchurch International Airport, only 10 km/7 miles northwest of Cathedral Square.

Travelers who have made the interisland ferry crossing from Wellington to Picton continue by rail south to Christchurch. Other trains link Dunedin and Invercargill in the south and Greymouth on the west coast with Christchurch. The railway station is on Moorhouse Avenue.

Long-distance buses of Railways Road Services, Mount Cook Line, Newmans Coach Lines, and H & H Travel Lines connect all areas of South Island with Christchurch. Cruise liners anchor at Lyttelton, south of Christchurch.

Accommodations. Christchurch has dozens of hotels and motels, located in the central business district, in the suburbs, and near the airport.

Major downtown hotels include the high-rise Noah's Hotel and the older Clarendon Hotel (both overlooking the Avon River a block from Cathedral Square), and the Hyatt Kingsgate, on Colombo Street facing Victoria Square. Among the smaller downtown hotels are the refurbished 1884 United Service Hotel, facing Cathedral Square, and Coker's Hotel on Manchester Street. For a centrally located motor hotel, try the Avon Motor Lodge, Latimer Motor Lodge, or Avon Park Hotel, among others.

Accommodations near the airport include the Christchurch Travelodge, Commodore Motor Inn, and Hotel Russley. Among other leading hotels are the Chateau Regency on Deans Avenue, Shirley Lodge Motor Hotel on Marshland Road, Canterbury Inn in Riccarton, DB Redwood Court Hotel on Main North Road, Autolodge on Papanui Road, and Gainsborough Motor Lodge on Bealey Avenue.

Restaurants. In Christchurch and its surroundings, you can choose from restaurants offering continental dining, ethnic specialties, home-style cooking, or grilled meat and seafood specialties. Dinner reservations are advisable at leading restaurants, especially on weekends.

Getting around. Taxis are available at Cathedral Square and at all transportation terminals. Bright red city buses depart from Cathedral Square for city and suburban points; for route information, inquire at the kiosk in front of the cathedral.

Several companies operate half-day and full-day sightseeing tours. Some depart daily the year around; others are scheduled only on certain days or during the main October-to-April tourist period. Tours feature Christchurch attractions, the Port Hills and Lyttelton (page 78), Akaroa and the Banks Peninsula (page 79), Erewhon Park (page 101), and other destinations.

Tourist information. For city maps, local sightseeing tours, and information on points of interest in the Christchurch area, stop at the Canterbury Information Centre, 75 Worcester Street (corner of Oxford Terrace).

Travel arrangements, tour information, and accommodation reservations are handled by the Government Tourist Bureau, located in the Government Life Building facing Cathedral Square. For motoring information, visit the Automobile Association office, 210 Hereford Street.

On foot in Christchurch

Christchurch is a walker's city—compact, level, and varied. Begin your stroll at Cathedral Square, the city's bustling center. Along your route you'll get a close look at distinctive old and new buildings. You can linger along the Avon, sample outstanding parks and gardens, and visit some of the city's stimulating cultural centers.

Cathedral Square. Heart of the city is Cathedral Square, now a tiled pedestrian plaza softened by trees and flower-filled containers. Shoppers pause to rest on benches, office workers purchase fruit and flowers from pushcart vendors, and noontime entertainers amuse the lunch crowd.

Buildings around the perimeter of the square include not only sleek, high-rise office buildings but also elegant older structures—the main post office (built 1877-79), the *Press* newspaper building, and several vintage hotels. A statue honors John Robert Godley, called "the founder of Canterbury."

Christchurch Cathedral is the finest Gothic-style church in the Dominion and the spiritual center of this essentially Anglican city. Built of stone quarried in the Port Hills, it reflects the courage, vision, and dedication of the early settlers who began construction in 1864, only a few years after they arrived. Inside, memorial tablets and

Looking south to Antarctica

No city has stronger or more enduring ties with the icy southern continent of Antarctica than Christchurch. During the early days of exploration, Lyttelton was the port of departure for Antarctic expeditions. Beside the Avon River, a statue of Captain Robert Falcon Scott, the English explorer who lost his life returning from the South Pole in 1912, is a daily reminder of these hazardous explorations.

You can view an outstanding collection of relics, records, and equipment from both early and recent explorations in the Hall of Antarctic Discovery in the Canterbury Museum (page 76).

Today, a dozen countries are engaged in scientific research on the southern continent. Christchurch International Airport is the supply base and communications center for Operation Deep Freeze, the nonmilitary U.S. scientific study at McMurdo Sound.

windows record the origins of the town and Canterbury province. If you feel energetic, you can climb the 133 steps up through the bell tower to observation balconies overlooking the city. The cathedral spire towers more than 63 meters/207 feet above the square.

Victoria Square. Two blocks north of the cathedral is Victoria Square, departure point for some sightseeing tours. The Bowker Fountain provides a graceful backdrop for a sturdy statue of Captain Cook, and a replica of Queen Victoria keeps an eye on passing traffic.

Town Hall. A block beyond Victoria Square and bordered by the Avon River is Christchurch's striking glass and marble Town Hall. Opened in 1972, it's the center for civic and cultural activities, performing arts events, and meetings and conferences. Events are presented in the main auditorium or in the smaller 1,000-seat theater.

Guided tours leave the main lobby at frequent intervals on weekdays and on Saturday and Sunday afternoons. Tickets for theater and ballet performances, concerts, and other attractions are handled by the Town Hall booking office. A restaurant overlooks the placid river, Victoria Square, and the Ferrier Fountain.

Provincial Government Buildings. Follow the Avon upstream along Oxford Terrace. Near the river at Armagh and Durham streets, you'll see the stone tower and wooden extensions of the Canterbury Provincial Government Buildings, one of the most intriguing structures in the country. Seat of Canterbury's government from 1859 to 1876, the Provincial Council Chamber is open on weekdays from 9 A.M. to 4 P.M.; guided tours are available on Sunday afternoon at 2 and 3 P.M.

The chamber, on the Durham Street side near the river, was built in 1865 of local stone and native timber. Almost churchlike in appearance, the neo-Gothic chamber has a magnificent gilded and painted barrel-vaulted ceiling, mosaic wall panels, and stained glass windows. Balcony seats once accommodated the public.

During Canterbury's early years, the chamber was the scene of many lively debates and historic decisions. Provincial architect Benjamin Mountfort designed the complex, as well as many of Canterbury's other historic public buildings.

Along the river. Rimmed by grassy, tree-shaded banks and spanned by graceful stone bridges, the winding Avon provides a tranquil corridor skirting the center of the city. Couples stroll the riverside walkways, office workers eat their lunches on the lawn, and children feed the ducks. For a leaflet describing points of interest along the river, stop at the Information Centre, 75 Worcester Street.

Across Worcester Street is a statue of Captain Robert Falcon Scott, the famous Antarctic explorer. At Cashel Street you pass the Bridge of Remembrance, a war memorial. Continuing along Oxford Terrace, you see the distinctive wooden St. Michael's and All Angels Anglican Church, built in 1872.

Shaded by overhanging trees, the Avon River flows languidly through
Christchurch's Botanic Gardens. Water lures boaters; grassy slopes beckon picnickers.

Boating on the Avon

It's pleasant to walk along the river, but the best way to
enjoy the Avon's charm is by boat. You can hire a canoe,
pedal boat, or rowboat any day at Antigua Boatsheds,
facing the shallow river on Cambridge Terrace near
Rolleston Avenue.

You step off the sloping wooden dock and lower
yourself into your craft, then leisurely venture upstream
under drooping willows past the Botanic Gardens and
Hagley Park. In spring, you glide beneath blossoming
trees; in autumn, golden leaves cast reflections in the
water. Your fellow paddlers range from preteens to grand-
parents. On sunny weekends, picnicking families relax
along the grassy bank and watch the passing parade.

A city of parks and gardens

The English colonists who settled Christchurch transformed the "flat, treeless, featureless" site of the 1850s by
landscaping their young town with European trees and
grasslands and by setting aside vast areas as public parkland. Today, pocket parks dot residential areas, and city
gardeners groom their plots in competition for annual
best-garden and best-street awards.

Botanic Gardens. A few minutes' walk from Cathedral
Square takes you to the Botanic Gardens, a 75-acre reserve
encircled by a deep bend of the Avon. Here you'll find
mature trees gathered from all parts of the world (many
are labeled), a rose garden, water gardens, and splendid
seasonal flower displays. In late spring, the woodlands
are bright with daffodils, azaleas, and rhododendrons.
Tropical and flowering plants are displayed under glass.

On fine afternoons from noon to 4 P.M., you can
climb aboard an electric cart—called the "Toast Rack"—
for a tour of the gardens. Snacks and a smorgasbord
lunch are available in the tea kiosk.

Hagley Park. Across the Avon from the Botanic Gardens
is Hagley Park, a 450-acre playground for the city's
cyclists, dog walkers, golfers, joggers, horseback riders,
and model yachting enthusiasts. Often, there's a game
of cricket, soccer, or rugby in progress, or you may
see competitors engaged in croquet, lawn bowling, tennis, or other sports. A fitness course is located in North
Hagley Park.

North of Harper Avenue is Millbrook Reserve, noted
for its azalea and rhododendron displays.

Deans Bush (Riccarton House). Situated west of Hagley
Park and north of Riccarton Road, this modest reserve
contains the only remaining stand of native swamp forest
originally found on these treeless plains. On the property
are Riccarton House, the Deans family homestead for
some 90 years (now used for receptions), and Deans Cottage, a tiny plains homestead built in 1843 and preserved
as a small museum.

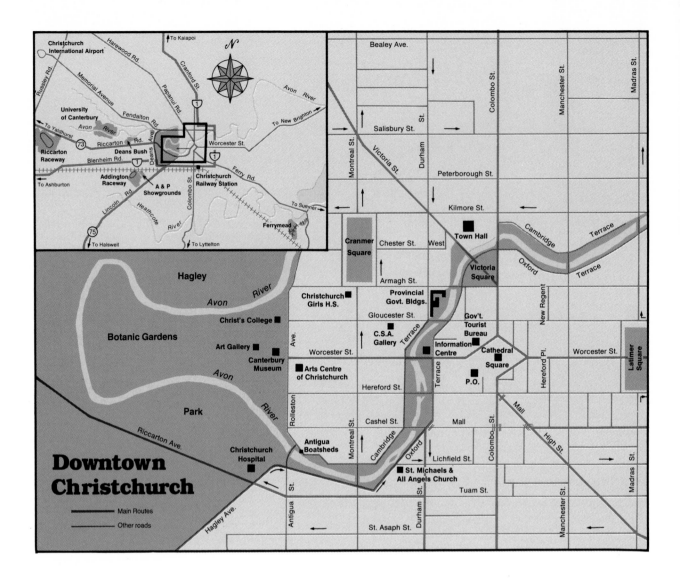

Fascinating Canterbury Museum

For many visitors, the city's most absorbing attraction is Canterbury Museum, a treasure house of Canterbury and New Zealand lore. One of the finest museums in the Southern Hemisphere, the museum is located on Rolleston Avenue. Hours are Monday through Saturday from 10 A.M. to 4:30 P.M. and Sunday from 2 to 4:30 P.M.

The museum's Hall of Antarctic Discovery contains a fascinating collection of articles used by Antarctic explorers. Personal effects, clothing, survival equipment, and diaries from the heroic era of exploration (1900 to 1917) give insights into Antarctic hardship, exhilaration, and tragedy. Modern thermal clothing and mechanized equipment contrast vividly with the historic artifacts. Additional exhibits offer information on Antarctic geology, fossils, and penguins, and on life beneath the sea.

In the Pacific Hall, you'll learn about the three voyages of Captain James Cook and see mementos collected during his travels. A 14-meter/47-foot-long war canoe dominates the exhibits on the Maori culture.

A replica Christchurch street typical of colonial days (1850s to mid-1870s) shows well-stocked shops patterned after actual businesses of the era. Other colonial displays include a three-room cob house containing costumed figures and a Cobb & Co. stagecoach.

A lively interest in arts and crafts

The activities of Christchurch's artistic community focus around the busy Arts Centre and excellent art galleries.

Arts Centre of Christchurch. When the University of Canterbury moved to a new campus in 1975, its historic townsite was presented to the people of Christchurch. The handsome stone buildings at Rolleston Avenue and Worcester Street have gained a new lease on life serving as the home of more than 60 local artistic, cultural, educational, and community organizations.

Visitors are welcome to stroll through the center's spacious quadrangles and cloisters. On weekdays from 8:30 A.M. to 5 P.M., you can stop at the Arts Centre Information Office in the Clock Tower for a descriptive leaflet and information on special events.

Artists, craftspeople, musicians, and dancers maintain studios and rehearsal space in the old neo-Gothic buildings. Cultural clubs and community service organizations meet here. A resident company performs plays in the 230-seat Court Theatre and in the more intimate 70-seat Studio Theatre. Ballet programs are presented by the Southern Ballet, and the former gymnasium has become a movie theater. Students learn new techniques in a theater workshop, and a youth orchestra rehearses here on Saturday mornings.

Visitors can watch skilled artisans at work and purchase their crafts at the Cornerstone Pottery and the Craft Workshop. Original prints and drawings by New Zealand artists are displayed in the Gingko Gallery. On Saturdays from October to March, artists and craftspeople offer their wares at an outdoor market under the trees.

You can visit the small basement laboratory, now a museum, where famed nuclear physicist Ernest Rutherford conducted his first scientific experiments in 1893-94 (apply at the reception office in the Clock Tower).

Robert McDougall Art Gallery. Located behind the Canterbury Museum facing the Botanic Gardens, this gallery houses the city's collection of early and contemporary Australasian and European paintings, sculpture, pottery, and weaving. Special exhibitions are presented throughout the year. The gallery is open daily (closed on Saturday and Sunday mornings).

Canterbury Society of Arts. You can view changing exhibitions of contemporary New Zealand art, as well as art from other countries, at the C.S.A. Gallery at 66 Gloucester Street. Other events include musical recitals, films, and photographic evening programs. Open daily, the gallery is closed on Saturday and Sunday mornings.

Other points of interest

If time permits, you may want to visit a pair of transport museums, some of the province's educational institutions, or Christchurch's seaside suburbs.

Transport museums. Still in the development stages, Ferrymead Historic Park and Transport Museum strives to recapture the pioneering atmosphere of early Christchurch. Volunteers have restored many early vehicles to working order; visitors can enjoy rides through the site on weekends. Replicas of colonial shops and houses recreate a community of the Edwardian era. Located on Bridle Path Road south of the Heathcote River, Ferrymead is open daily from 10 A.M. to 4 P.M.

At Yaldhurst, 12 km/7 miles from Christchurch on the Main West Road, the Yaldhurst Transport Museum features horse-drawn vehicles, dating from 1810, and other historic transport. The museum is open from 10 A.M. to 5 P.M. daily from September through May, weekends and holidays only during the winter.

Educational institutions. Reminiscent of an English public school, the gray stone buildings of Christ's College are grouped around a grassy quadrangle north of the Canterbury Museum bordering Rolleston Avenue.

You'll often see uniformed schoolboys cycling along city streets or competing in sports in nearby Hagley Park.

In 1975 the University of Canterbury, noted for its School of Engineering, moved from its town site to a spacious new campus in the western suburb of Ilam. Visitors are welcome to stroll the landscaped grounds.

Lincoln College (Canterbury Agricultural College) lies 21 km/13 miles southwest of the city near the village of Lincoln. Surrounded by acres of model farmland, it trains young farmers and supervises research in agriculture and animal husbandry. Founded in 1873, the college was one of the world's first schools of agriculture. It has been an important factor in Canterbury's agricultural growth and prosperity.

Bicycling around Christchurch

You'll see Christchurch in fresh perspective if you explore the city by bicycle. Level streets, a compact central area, and the vast greensward of Hagley Park offer incentives for wheeling around the city. You'll enjoy the fun and freedom of pedaling at your own pace, savoring the fresh air and scenery, and you'll have plenty of company —many students, office workers, shoppers, and business people bicycle to and from school, work, and other activities.

You can rent leisure bikes, 10-speed touring bikes, or tandems by the hour, day, or week. Two shops rent bikes: Rent-A-Bike, N.Z. Ltd., in the Avon Carpark Building, 82 Worcester Street; and Penny Farthing Cycle Shop, 17 Victoria Street. A refundable deposit is required; damage and theft insurance is optional and available at extra charge. Ask for city and touring maps.

You can explore the city easily in a few hours. Many roads have bicycle lanes. A favorite destination of cyclists is Hagley Park, where paved paths wind across green parklands and along the Avon. If country touring is your hobby, rent a 10-speed touring bike, equipped with carrier bags, and pedal off to the Banks Peninsula, Canterbury Plains, or other destinations.

Cyclists keep to the left of traffic, even on bicycle paths in the park. You're not permitted to ride on sidewalks or footpaths along the Avon River in the downtown area.

Gothic-style cathedral, begun by Canterbury settlers in 1864, dominates Cathedral Square. Lofty observation balconies offer a fine city view.

Seaside suburbs. Christchurch has its own coastal suburbs. New Brighton, traditionally known for its Saturday shopping, has a long beach bordering the Pacific. The Queen Elizabeth II Park complex, site of the 1974 Commonwealth Games, contains swimming pools, water slides, squash courts, and an all-weather athletic track.

South of the Avon-Heathcote Estuary is Sumner. Its esplanade curves past Cave Rock and along Sumner Bay. You can take the steep road over the bluff and descend to Taylor's Mistake, a pleasant sheltered beach, or climb to Evans Pass and the Summit Road.

Orana Wildlife Park. New Zealand's first drive-through wild animal park, open daily, is located near the airport on McLeans Island Road. Lions are a big attraction, but the park also includes tigers, camels, water buffaloes, Barbary sheep, kangaroos, and many exotic birds.

Canterbury excursions

If you prefer to see Christchurch and its surrounding area on a guided excursion, you'll find several tour companies ready to show you the sights. Since not all tours operate the year around, be sure to check at the Canterbury Information Centre, the Government Tourist Bureau, or other travel agencies for information on available excursions.

Visitors who want to explore the area on their own can head southeast across the Port Hills to Lyttelton or make a loop around the Banks Peninsula. To the north you'll find the scenic Kaikoura Coast and Hanmer Springs, a spa in the forest. Routes take motorists west across the Southern Alps or south over the Canterbury Plains.

Walkers will want to ask about the Christchurch area's excellent network of trails, many of them part of the N.Z. Walkways system. Trails winding through the Port Hills offer hikers spectacular views of the city, harbor, plains, and mountains.

Superb views from the Summit Road

Winding high above the city along the crest of the Port Hills, the Summit Road offers magnificent vistas northward over Christchurch and checkered plains to the snow-capped Southern Alps, eastward over Lyttelton and its harbor encased in the crater of an extinct volcano.

From the seaside community of Sumner, you climb to Evans Pass to meet the Summit Road as it snakes for 26 km/16 miles along the hills overlooking Lyttelton Harbour some 300 meters/1,000 feet below. A southern section continues from Dyers Pass Road (at the Sign of the Kiwi teahouse) along the western side of the harbor to Gebbies Pass.

Lyttelton. South Island's leading port, Lyttelton is connected with Christchurch by road and rail tunnels. Wooden houses cling to the steep streets above the harbor. Along the waterfront, cargo handlers service docked freighters, and weekend yachtsmen ready their boats for sailing the sheltered bays. Commuter launch service links Lyttelton and Diamond Harbour on weekdays, and launch cruises leave Lyttelton every afternoon.

A quartet of 19th century churches adds historic interest. On Saturday and Sunday afternoons you can see displays on the historic port and its ships at Lyttelton's museum, centrally located on Gladstone Quay.

The Canterbury Pilgrims who came ashore at Lyttelton in 1850 followed a zigzag bridle path across the Port Hills to found their colony on the plains. Today, walkers still enjoy the old Bridle Path trail, and hundreds make a nostalgic trek between Lyttelton and Christchurch annually on the Sunday nearest December 16.

Roadhouses. Along the route are three old stone roadhouses offering shelter to travelers. Best known is the Sign of the Takahe, overlooking the city from the Cashmere Hills. Modeled after a medieval baronial manor, this showplace has richly ornamented ceilings, wood carvings, intricate stonework, and colorful murals. You can stop for a meal or tea here.

Light refreshments are also available at the Sign of the Kiwi, located on Coronation Hill at the junction of Summit and Dyers Pass roads. The third roadhouse—the Sign of the Bellbird—serves no refreshments.

Akaroa and the Banks Peninsula

Set apart both geographically and geologically from the rest of Canterbury, the Banks Peninsula offers a relaxing retreat about 1½ hours southeast of Christchurch. Contrasting dramatically with the placid Canterbury Plains, the peninsula was formed by two extinct volcanoes whose collapsed craters now hold the splendid natural harbors of Lyttelton and Akaroa.

The road to Akaroa. From Christchurch, Highway 75 heads south through farming country to the peninsula. Lake Ellesmere, a shallow coastal lagoon, supports great flocks of waterfowl. The narrow, winding road snakes through the peninsula's green and golden hills past farmhouses and cottages tucked into folded valleys.

Cutting deeply into the eroded old volcanic cones are narrow bays, some of them used in the 1830s by whaling parties. From the main route, steep side roads lead down to these unpeopled inlets—Port Levy's protected harbor, Pigeon Bay and its campground, and Little Akaloa with its unusual church embellished with Maori-style carvings. At Barry's Bay, visitors can watch the traditional cheesemaking process at Settlers Farmhouse Cheese Factory.

Other roads lead to Okains Bay, known for its beach and museum; Le Bons Bay and its sports ground; and Peraki's historic whaling site.

Akaroa—village with a French flavor. New Zealand's first French settlers landed at Akaroa in 1840—nearly a

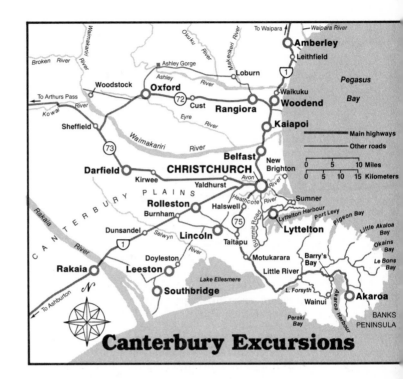

Canterbury Excursions

decade before the colonial settlements at Dunedin and Christchurch—and the village keeps alive its Gallic heritage. Located 84 km/52 miles from Christchurch, New Zealand's most English city, Akaroa is a popular spot for midsummer and weekend holidays. Accommodations are available at Akaroa Village Resort and at several small motels and hotels. You'll enjoy the village's unique charm more if you visit on a weekday or out of season.

Along the waterfront you'll see whalers' pots and the early customs house, but to sample Akaroa's real charm, stroll along the side streets above the harbor. Spreading trees shade wooden Victorian cottages, and decorative fences enclose flourishing gardens of subtropical flowers. Attractive small churches invite worshippers. One of the settlement's earliest buildings is the Langlois-Eteveneaux House and Museum; the two-room cottage is furnished in 1840s style. Open from 1:30 to 5 P.M. daily, it also houses the town's information center.

From the waterfront, you can walk up wooded glades to the surrounding hills for views over the town and harbor.

Exploring North Canterbury

From Christchurch, Highway 1 curves north, paralleling the coast and cutting across the rolling hills and lush river valleys of North Canterbury. Side roads lead to coastal beaches bordering Pegasus Bay.

An all-day loop from Christchurch takes you through farmlands to the dramatic gorges of the Ashley and Waimakariri rivers. You'll find pleasant picnic and swimming areas along both rivers. In season, there's good salmon and trout fishing. If you're interested in a raft trip

Marlborough—the essentials

Located on South Island's northeastern tip, the province of Marlborough is a favorite destination of boaters, thanks to the web of waterways—called "the sounds"—dotting its northern end. Picton, at the head of Queen Charlotte Sound, is Marlborough's main port and the hub of vacation activity in the area. The administrative center is Blenheim, 29 km/18 miles inland.

Getting there. From North Island, you can take a 30-minute flight from Wellington across Cook Strait to Blenheim, but the most satisfying approach is by ship. Interisland ferries make the 3½-hour crossing between Wellington and Picton several times daily.

Newmans Coach Lines link Marlborough's main towns with Nelson and Christchurch. Rail service connects Picton with Christchurch and intermediate towns daily except Sunday.

Accommodations. Most vacationers headquarter near the water. Prime holiday season in this sunny region extends from November through April; make peak season reservations well in advance.

In Picton, the Picton Motor Inn, Harbour View Motel, and several smaller motels overlook marine activity; the DB Terminus Hotel is near the waterfront. Other motels are situated near the central district or along Waikawa Road, east of the harbor. Blenheim's leading downtown hotels are the Autolodge Motor Inn and the DB Criterion; the town also has a number of good motels. Simple motel units are available at Havelock.

Rustic lodges and guest houses are nestled along secluded bays throughout the Sounds; some are accessible only by boat or float plane (inquire about access when you're making reservations). Among these waterside accommodations are Gem Resort and Punga Cove Holiday Resort, both bordering Queen Charlotte Sound; Furneaux Lodge Holiday Resort on Endeavour Inlet; and the Portage Hotel on Kenepuru Sound. There's a campground at Momorangi Bay and numerous informal camping areas at various bays throughout the Sounds.

Getting around. Motorcoaches link the region's larger towns. Rental cars are available at Picton Ferry Terminal and in Blenheim. On Picton's London Quay, several operators offer launch sightseeing excursions on Queen Charlotte Sound. You can also arrange for water taxi service and fishing expeditions. Mail boat trips depart from both Picton and Havelock (page 82).

In Picton you can arrange for scenic flights over the Sounds and for sightseeing trips by minicoach.

Tourist information. For ideas on what to see and do in Marlborough, inquire at the Public Relations Office, facing Market Square, in Blenheim. For information on Marlborough Sounds Maritime Park, contact the chief ranger in Blenheim or stop at the ranger station in Havelock.

or jet boat excursion up the Waimakariri River, inquire at one of the tourist information offices in Christchurch.

At Waipara, Highway 7 branches inland toward Hanmer Springs. Anglers find good fishing in the Hurunui and Waiau rivers. Highway 7 continues across Lewis Pass (page 96) to the West Coast (page 87).

Forest walks at Hanmer Springs

South Island's principal thermal resort, Hanmer blossomed as a spa in the late 19th century. Today visitors come not only to bathe in the hot springs but also to enjoy crisp mountain air and forest walks. An easy 1½ to 2-hour drive north of Christchurch, Hanmer sits on a high plateau ringed by mountain spurs of the Southern Alps. Forestry workers here tend one of the country's largest and most varied tree plantations.

In town, the thermal pools of Queen Mary Hospital are open daily; bring your bathing suit and a towel.

Walkers and hikers can take Jollie's Pass Road from the center of town to Hanmer Forest Park. At the trail information center, ask for a descriptive leaflet with a map of the trails, which vary from easy nature walks to strenuous day-long treks. In autumn, the woods are bright with color. For views over the forest and Waiau Plain, take the zigzag trail from Conical Hill Road to the summit.

Recreation opportunities abound in the Hanmer district. Tennis courts, a golf course, and a putting green are within walking distance of town. From Hanmer, you can arrange for horseback trips through the countryside and for expeditions into the rugged hill country by four-wheel-drive vehicle. Anglers find good fishing in nearby rivers, boaters enjoy Tennyson and Horseshoe lakes, and skiers head for nearby Amuri Skifield.

The Kaikoura coast

Scenery ranging from verdant farmlands to spectacular panoramas awaits travelers following the coastal road—Highway 1—between Christchurch and Picton.

South of Cheviot you can visit and picnic at Cheviot Hills domain, now a scenic reserve. You'll see the homestead and some buildings of the vast Cheviot Hills run, one of the earliest Canterbury sheep stations. At Hundalee you cross the Conway River, marking the Canterbury-Marlborough boundary, then descend through the hills to meet the sea at Oaro.

For nearly 100 km/60 miles north of Oaro, Highway 1 hugs the rock-strewn Pacific shore. Ever-changing seascapes, impressive views of rugged inland mountains, and the small resort town of Kaikoura are highlights. Seaside camping and picnicking areas are busy in summer.

Take the time to drive to the tip of Kaikoura Peninsula for a memorable panorama of village and sea backed by the snow-draped Seaward Kaikoura Range. A fishing fleet operates out of Kaikoura, where local crayfish are packed for export. The coastal town draws many surf-fishing enthusiasts and skin divers.

Marlborough Sounds

Narrow, watery fingers deeply indent the lush green Marlborough coastline at the northeastern tip of South Island. Called "the Sounds," these drowned coastal river valleys create more than 1,000 km/600 miles of shoreline, a delightful maze of sheltered waterways, inviting bays and coves, and wooded peninsulas sloping steeply to the sea. Pleasure craft now sail the waters first explored by Captain James Cook more than 200 years ago.

For a perfect introduction to Marlborough's waterside attractions and leisurely pace, plan to arrive aboard one of the interisland ferries that link Wellington and Picton. After crossing Cook Strait, you'll cruise majestically up Tory Channel into Queen Charlotte Sound, past densely forested hills and scattered settlements, to the vacation center of Picton.

Picton, the busy deep-water port

Recreational activity in the Sounds focuses on Picton, the small but bustling ferry port at the head of Queen Charlotte Sound. Pleasure boats and sightseeing launches cluster along the waterfront, and interisland ferries steam in and out of port.

Bordering Picton's foreshore is London Quay, where you can arrange for sightseeing trips or water taxi service, inspect local crafts, and observe waterfront activity. A small museum recalls the whaling era with displays of equipment and artifacts.

Vacationing families come to Picton to play in the sun—swim, fish, water-ski, hike—or to explore the endless waterways by boat. For a pleasant stroll, cross the humpbacked bridge arching above the marina and follow the path along the harbor shore to Bob's Bay, a sheltered cove where you can swim and picnic.

Sightseeing excursions. Tour operators along London Quay offer a wide variety of trips by boat, plane, or minicoach.

On a launch trip of Queen Charlotte Sound you'll be treated to spectacular scenery, close-up views of isolated vacation houses, and commentary on the region's fascinating history and unusual way of life. Many tours pause at the site of the shipwrecked *Edwin Fox* and at Double Cove, where tame fish swim to the surface when food is thrown to them.

On a longer trip you can picnic at Kumutoto Bay or Ship Cove, near the mouth of the sound, where Captain Cook's ships anchored in the 1770s. Queen Charlotte Sound was one of his favorite Pacific anchorages—he paused here on five separate occasions during his explorations.

You can also arrange for sightseeing trips by minicoach to Nelson and Port Underwood and along Queen Charlotte Drive. Flights departing from Picton offer grand, bird's-eye views of the Sounds.

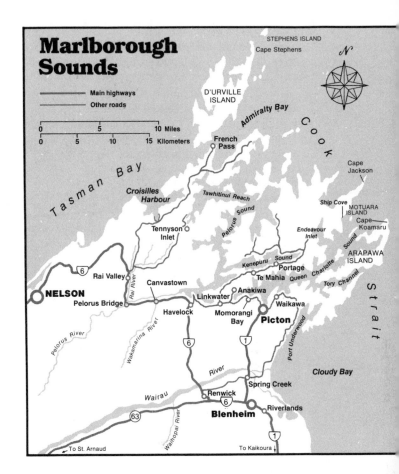

Beautiful drives. From Picton, scenic roads branch west along Queen Charlotte Sound and northeast to Waikawa and Port Underwood.

Closely following the shore of Grove Arm, Queen Charlotte Drive climbs to headland viewpoints, then dips to waterside to meet bays and coves. Side roads lead to the Cobham Outward Bound School at Anakiwa and to settlements bordering Kenepuru Sound. Allow about an hour for the leisurely drive through Moenui to Havelock.

Waikawa Road passes Picton's marina, then continues northeast toward Waikawa. Take the marked side road to Victoria Domain for a lovely view. Anchored boats bob on the sheltered waters of Waikawa Bay. A winding road continues across the saddle between Queen Charlotte Sound and Port Underwood, the center of feverish whaling activity in the late 1820s. Whaling ships from many countries operated in these waters.

Marlborough Sounds Maritime Park

A watery playground for vacationing Kiwis and other visitors, the park features sheltered tidal waters and myriad bays and coves backed by native bush. More than 100 separate reserves, interspersed with farmland and private vacation homes, make up the park.

Rich in history as well as scenery, some reserves recall Maori or pre-Maori occupation; others are linked with early European explorers, such as James Cook and Dumont d'Urville, or 19th century whalers. Still other reserves—particularly islands in the Sounds and Cook Strait—are breeding grounds for birds and animals.

Picton, facing Queen Charlotte Sound, and Havelock, at the head of Pelorus Sound, are departure points for launch trips to shore and island reserves. Though the park is best explored by water, roads lead to some recreational areas, and a float-plane service operates out of Picton. In addition to sightseeing cruises, you can arrange charter excursions and fishing trips in Picton; you can also hire small boats with outboard motors for exploring on your own.

Some reserves in the park offer good picnicking and camping sites, as well as trails for bush walking (some are accessible only by boat). Largest of the reserves is Tennyson Inlet, reached from Highway 6 by road from Rai Valley; here you'll find dense forests and varied birdlife.

Permits are required for camping, shooting, and visiting protected wildlife reserves. For information on permits, hiking trails, or other features of the park, contact the chief ranger in Blenheim (P.O. Box 97; phone Blenheim 86079) or the ranger station in Havelock (phone Havelock 159).

Sailing and fishing in Marlborough

If you're a sailing enthusiast, consider chartering a boat for a few days' cruising on the Sounds (page 28). You can explore the unspoiled shore, anchoring in secluded bays and coves for picnicking, swimming, and hiking on nearby trails. A popular destination of many sailors is beautiful Kenepuru Sound, a landlocked waterway branching off Pelorus Sound.

Anglers are attracted to the Sounds' sheltered waters, which abound with cod, terakihi, snapper, garfish, grouper, and kahawai. Along Marlborough's east coast, surfcasters concentrate in the area between Kaikoura and Cape Koamaru.

For fly-fishing, head inland for the Rai and Pelorus rivers. Brown trout are also abundant in the Wairau and Opawa rivers and in Spring Creek. In summer, salmon migrate up the lower reaches of the Wairau River.

Blenheim, the business center

A tidy town of parks and gardens surrounded by vineyards and farmlands, Blenheim lies 29 km/18 miles inland. With a population of 18,000, it's Marlborough's largest town, as well as its administrative and agricultural center. Focal point of the business district is triangular Market Place, featuring a filigreed band rotunda. Tourist information is available at the nearby Public Relations Office.

A walk through town. From Market Place, walk a block west on High Street to Seymour Square, colorful with seasonal flower displays. In the park you'll see the town's

Hitch a ride aboard the mail boat

For a unique view of life in the Sounds, take a trip aboard one of the boats that delivers mail and supplies to remote waterside settlements and that provides transportation for residents in those outlying areas.

You'll clamber aboard a launch piled high with mailbags, newspapers, boxes and bags of foodstuffs, hardware, and farm equipment—rolls of fencing wire, perhaps, or a shiny shovel tagged for its new owner. If rain threatens, a tarpaulin is tied over the cargo.

Your fellow passengers may be residents returning to their homes, campers stopping for a few days at one of the scenic reserves, anglers who will be dropped off at a remote site and picked up on the return journey, or student travelers stopping at the Havelock youth hostel.

The launch cruises mile after mile of unspoiled waterways, past countless coves and bays where lush greenery slopes down to the waterline. Occasionally, the boat may nose up to the bank to deposit or reclaim a party of campers or fishing enthusiasts. You'll pass scenic and wildlife reserves; if you have binoculars, bring them along to watch native birds.

Since many families living on outlying homesteads get "out" infrequently, the mail boat is their major link with the outside world. As you approach each destination, you'll see at least one person—often an entire family and a dog or two—eagerly awaiting your arrival. If no dock is available or the tide is low, a couple of children or an adult will row out to meet the boat, exchange greetings with the crew, and collect groceries and mail.

On most weekday mornings, you can board a mail boat in Havelock for a day-long trip on Pelorus or Kenepuru sounds. Trips on Queen Charlotte Sound depart from Picton. The Marlborough Public Relations Office in Blenheim has information on mail boat trips. Telephone the day before—Havelock 42-276 or Picton 175—to check departure time and reserve space. You can also enjoy a mail boat trip in the Bay of Islands (page 33).

Plan to arrive at the wharf early in the morning and bring your lunch. Dress warmly; you may want to carry rain gear if the weather is changeable.

memorial fountain and stone clock tower. Just across the street are the public library and the modern circular council chambers.

Other pleasant places to explore include Riverside Park, with its footbridges spanning a stream, and Pollard Park, a favorite for its rose gardens, sports grounds, and flower-bordered walkways along a creek.

Nearby attractions. Southwest of town on New Renwick Road, Brayshaw Museum Park contains a miniature railway, vintage machinery and vehicles, and other displays.

Riverlands cob cottage, a restored, mud-walled pioneer house built around 1860, is located about 5 km/3 miles southeast of Blenheim on Highway 1. A cobblestone path leads to the small cottage-museum, now refurbished with period household articles and costumed figures in colonial dress.

West of Blenheim you'll pass vast vineyards; Montana Vineyards opened its Riverlands Winery here in 1977.

Marlborough has its own skifield at Rainbow Valley, southwest of Blenheim; the ski season extends from June through late October.

Over the mountains to Nelson

West of Havelock, Highway 6 winds through the dairy country of the Pelorus and Rai valleys, across forested mountains, and down the Whangamoa Valley into Nelson province.

Along the highway at Havelock, an old bush logging engine outside a former church marks the local museum. Mussels are grown commercially in Pelorus Sound near Havelock; a small fishing fleet moors at the head of the sound. At Canvastown, a roadside display of 1860s mining equipment from the gold fields up the Wakamarina River evokes the mining activity that was concentrated upstream at Deep Creek.

Allow time to wander through a pocket of virgin bush at Pelorus Bridge Scenic Reserve. A short, self-guided nature trail called the Totara Walk identifies many of the native ferns and trees—rimu, miro, tawa, kamahi, a giant totara—and leads down to a swimming hole in the Pelorus River.

You can pick up picnic supplies in Rai Valley.

Nelson and the Sunshine Coast

One of the earliest settlements of the colonizing New Zealand Company, Nelson has its roots deep in the soil. Apples, kiwifruit, hops, and tobacco dominate the broad agricultural patchwork of the Waimea Plains and Motueka Valley.

Both Nelson province and its largest city — also named Nelson — honor Britain's great naval hero, and you'll see additional reminders of the region's links with

Vacation homes at Moenui overlook sheltered coves of Pelorus Sound. Scenic Marlborough waterways and wooded reserves attract boaters and hikers.

sailors of various periods and nations. Other sizable provincial towns include Motueka, Takaka, and—on the West Coast—Westport. Two national parks, Abel Tasman and Nelson Lakes, preserve areas of scenic beauty.

Sunny, relaxing Nelson

Facing a sheltered harbor and encircled by wooded mountains at the head of Tasman Bay, Nelson is one of the country's oldest cities; colonists settled here in 1841. The city's lively interest in the arts indicates that more than agriculture thrives in the delightful climate here.

Dominating the town's skyline on Church Hill is the towering Christ Church Cathedral, built of local Takaka marble. Open daily, the Anglican church contains many historic relics of the area.

Nelson—the essentials

Its sunny weather and sheltered coastline lure many visitors to Nelson. Two national parks—Abel Tasman and Nelson Lakes—preserve dramatic areas of rugged seacoast and glacial lakes.

Getting there. Air service links Nelson with Christchurch, Wellington, and Auckland. Newmans Coach Lines connect Nelson with Christchurch (via Blenheim or Lewis Pass), Picton, and Greymouth.

Accommodations. The province's only large city is Nelson; its main downtown hotels are the DB Rutherford and the DB Nelson. Numerous motels near Tahunanui Beach cater to vacationing families. Lodging is difficult to find during warm weather periods; many Kiwis book a year ahead for the school holidays in late December and January.

Modest accommodations (primarily small motels) are located in Motueka, Takaka, and Collingwood; along the coast you'll find beach campgrounds. At Nelson Lakes, simple accommodations, as well as camping areas, are available at St. Arnaud and Rotoroa.

Getting around. You can hire taxis in Nelson. Newmans Coach Lines has service to Picton, Blenheim, and Takaka. If you prefer exploring on your own, rental cars are available in Nelson.

Half-day tours take in Nelson's major attractions or head north through farmland to Motueka and Kaiteriteri.

Tourist information. Stop at the Nelson Public Relations Office, corner of Trafalgar and Halifax streets, for information on the city and province. To learn about activities in Abel Tasman National Park, visit the information office in Takaka (open only during the summer holidays) or contact the ranger in Motueka. Headquarters for Nelson Lakes National Park is in St. Arnaud; a ranger station is located at Lake Rotoroa.

Popular viewpoints for enjoying the panorama of city and bay are Cleveland Terrace and Princes Drive, two features of the city tour. Industrial and recreational waterfront activity is concentrated around Port Nelson, north of the business center near the entrance to Nelson Haven. Farther south is the magnificent white sweep of Tahunanui Beach.

A downtown stroll. For a look at Nelson's central district, begin your walk at the city's traditional meeting place, the church steps leading down to Trafalgar Street. The city's main downtown artery, Trafalgar bisects the business district and crosses the tree-lined Maitai River.

Queens Gardens offers a sylvan oasis about a 10-minute walk east of Trafalgar Street (on either Hardy or Bridge Street). Nearby, in an 1898 building on Bridge Street, the Suter Art Gallery contains one of the country's best small collections (open daily except Monday from 10:30 A.M. to 4:30 P.M.; open daily during school holiday periods).

Spreading trees shade the close-in sports grounds of the Botanical Reserve at the east end of Hardy Street. One of the favorite city walks is the 30-minute climb up 147-meter/483-foot Botanical Hill, where you're rewarded with a panoramic view of the city, port, and Maitai Valley.

Glimpses of the past. Nelson's early residents left a rich legacy of opulent houses and horticultural treasures. Many of the European trees they brought and planted have now grown to impressive maturity.

Just a few minutes south of Church Hill, the city-owned Melrose mansion reflects the Victorian architecture of the 1880s. Located in spacious grounds at Brougham and Trafalgar streets, it's used for a wide range of community activities.

Bishop's School, located on Nile Street East (next door to Marsden House), was established in 1844 and served as a school for almost 90 years. Now restored by the New Zealand Historic Places Trust, it's open daily from 10:30 A.M. to noon and 1 to 4 P.M.

At 108 Collingwood Street, you can savor the serenity of an old-world herb garden surrounding a century-old home. Lavender Hill Herb Garden is open on weekdays and Saturday morning.

Isel Park, 3 km/2 miles south of town, is the setting for Isel House and the Nelson Provincial Museum. Thomas Marsden, one of the original settlers of the New Zealand Company, built his two-story stone and timbered homestead in 1886 and surrounded it with a 12-acre garden planted with trees from around the world. The antique-filled house, located off Main Road in Stoke, is open on weekend afternoons (also Tuesday and Thursday in January).

Behind Isel House, the Nelson Provincial Museum contains exhibits depicting local maritime history and the early days of the colony. Museum hours are 10 A.M. to 4 P.M. Tuesday through Friday (also Monday in January), 2 to 4 P.M. on weekends.

Not far away—on Nayland Road in Stoke—is Broad-green, a restored 1855 cob house flanked by tree-shaded lawns and a large rose garden. Modeled after a Devonshire farmhouse, the two-story house has thick walls made of packed earth originally dug from the cellar. Refurnished with period furniture, Broadgreen is open to visitors on weekends from 2 to 4:30 P.M. (also on Tuesday and Thursday during school holiday periods) or by appointment.

Walking trails. If you'd enjoy exploring the area on foot, stop at the Public Relations Office for information on local walks and trails. Your choices range from a city historic walk to longer treks into the nearby hills. The Dun Line Walkway, part of the countryside network, follows the scenic route of New Zealand's first railway line.

North along Tasman Bay

Below Richmond, Highway 60 branches northwest along the shore of Tasman Bay. Blossoming apple and pear orchards brighten the countryside in October. The coastal road (via Mapua and Ruby Bay) cuts through the heart of the apple district. In season you'll pass roadside stalls piled high with produce. Collectors find interesting sea-shells along the shore of Ruby Bay.

Near Motueka, wire-hung hopfields and bright green fields of tobacco mark the center of New Zealand's hop and tobacco-growing industries. Fishing boats oper-ating from Port Motueka land scallops and oysters from August to early November. North of Riwaka, a short side road branches off to Kaiteriteri, a sheltered bay bordered by a curve of beach. Boat trips along the coast (page 87) depart from Kaiteriteri.

Inland routes. From Motueka, Highway 61 follows a sleepy river route south through the Motueka Valley farming country to meet Highway 6 at Kohatu.

Another road heads southeast from Motueka up the Moutere River. Lower Moutere is the site of the River-side Community, a family-operated commune founded by pacifists during World War II. Upper Moutere, settled by German immigrants in the 1840s, retains a faint Bavarian aura.

Takaka Hill. Northwest of Motueka, a side road leads inland from Highway 60 at the base of the hill to a wooded picnic site near the source of the Riwaka River. Often, you'll see anglers dipping their lines here.

As the highway curves and climbs Takaka Hill, pull off the road to take in the panorama of the Motueka Valley and Tasman Bay.

Marble quarried on Takaka Hill (also called Marble Mountain) was used in the construction of some of New Zealand's most imposing buildings, including Nelson's cathedral and Wellington's Parliament Buildings. Near the summit you'll notice strange marble outcroppings and unusual funnel-shaped rock basins. In summer you can see the delicate formations inside Ngarua Caves, near the top of Takaka Hill.

Craft shopping in Nelson

Attracted by Nel-son's sunny climate and superb scenery, artists and craftspeople have flocked to the area, giving the city claim to the title of New Zealand's crafts center. Excellent clay in the district has drawn potters for many years; more than 60 now have studios in the Nelson area. They've been joined by weavers, silversmiths, woodworkers, dollmakers, and artisans who create in glass and fabric. Many of them welcome visitors by appointment. But the best way to see the variety of handiwork available is to visit the city's craft shops, exhibitions, and craft fairs.

To follow Nelson's arts and crafts trail, stop first at the Nelson Public Relations Office, at the corner of Trafalgar and Halifax streets. Here you can pick up a guide to craftspeople all over the province who in-vite visitors; it also lists the shops and galleries that specialize in the arts of the region.

In Nelson, numerous galleries exhibit work by local artists. One—the South Street Gallery, near the cathe-dral—displays pieces rustically in one of Nelson's his-toric 19th century cottages. Some craftspeople showcase their wares in the town's cooperative stores. Chez Eelco, a coffeehouse and gallery on Trafalgar Street at the foot of the cathedral steps, is a favorite gathering place with changing exhibitions by local painters, potters, weavers, and photographers.

On Friday and Saturday, you can browse through assorted crafts at the Market Bazaar, an indoor market at 109 Hardy Street.

Takaka Valley. Continuing north, the highway twists down the mountain's steep northern slope to the dairy country of the Takaka River Valley. Until this road was completed, Golden Bay was relatively isolated from the rest of the province.

Tame eels in the Anatoki River are fed daily (10 to 11 A.M. and 3 to 5 P.M.), weather permitting, from the end of August to early May. To reach Anatoki, turn west off Highway 60 just south of Takaka.

Northwest of Takaka is Waikoropupu (Pupu) Springs, where an estimated 266 millions gallons of pure cold water flow from fresh-water springs each day. The road to the springs leaves Highway 60 north of Takaka.

Abel Tasman National Park

New Zealand's smallest national park honors the country's first *pakeha* visitor, Dutch explorer Abel Tasman, who sailed these waters in 1642. A memorial overlooking Ligar Bay commemorates the site where he anchored.

The town of Takaka contains several motels and motor camps, convenient for visitors making a day trip into Abel Tasman National Park. You'll find the park information office in Takaka (open daily during the summer holidays); there's a visitor center at Totaranui Beach.

Park information is available from the chief ranger in Takaka (P.O. Box 53; phone Takaka 58026) or from the ranger in Motueka (phone Motueka 78110).

Takaka to the coast. The 33-km/20-mile route from Takaka to the beach at Totaranui is the only access road into the park. Along the way you'll spot good beaches at Pohara, Ligar Bay, and Tata. Adjacent to Pohara Beach are a campground and recreational facilities.

The first 11 km/7 miles of the road from Takaka to the park are paved, but the surfacing ends at Tata Beach. The winding, graded road (not recommended for vans) soon begins to climb into the forested hills. Spreading tree ferns rising above you shade the road; streams cascade down gullies toward the bay. Trails wind through the park's primeval rain forest and along the shore.

At Totaranui, bush-covered headlands frame the golden sand beach and deep blue bay. Here you'll find a small campground and the visitor center, which features displays on the park's vegetation, sea and land birds, and other natural features.

Guided treks. Three and four-day group treks depart from Motueka from the beginning of February to mid-December. Winter days in this area are usually calm, crisp, and clear.

After a short coach trip to Kaiteriteri, the group boards a launch and cruises north along the coast to Tonga Bay, where the first day's walk begins. Heavy packs are left on board the launch. After tea, hikers turn south and follow the shore to a lodge at Torrent Bay, where hot showers and comfortable beds await them. Next day, guides offer a choice of shorter walks or other activities—fishing, boating, or snorkeling. (Four-day trekkers spend another day at the lodge.) On the final day, the group hikes down the coast to Marahau and returns to Motueka by coach. The trips are operated by Abel Tasman National Park Enterprises, Green Tree Road, R.D. 3, Motueka, Nelson.

Golden sands and clear waters draw vacationers to the sheltered beach at Kaiteriteri. Summer boat trips cruise north from here along the Abel Tasman park coast.

Day cruises. From late December through March, launch trips depart from Kaiteriteri daily at 10 A.M. for a scenic 6-hour cruise along the coast. The launch makes brief stops at several bays to deliver supplies to campers and isolated cottages; tides permitting, it also journeys up the forest-rimmed Falls River. During a 2½-hour stopover at Torrent Bay, you have a chance to explore a small corner of the park.

Tramping through luxuriant bush

Many backpackers have discovered the Heaphy (Hee-fee) Track, a one-time prospectors' trail cutting across the grassy downs and subtropical valleys of northwest Nelson province.

Beginning southwest of Collingwood (via Bainham), the 72-km/45-mile trail climbs through rimu and beech forest and then descends through the red tussock country of the Gouland Downs to the fern-filled valley of the Heaphy River. Here you'll find not only luxuriant stands of nikau palms but also giant sandflies—insect repellent is a "must" for hikers.

The magnificent final section of the track follows the bush-bordered seacoast south to end at the Kohaihai River north of Karamea. Hikers can arrange taxi service at both ends of the trail.

Tramping groups generally take from 4 to 6 days to make the trek, staying overnight in trail huts along the route. Most hikers prefer the months of February and March, after the summer rains. But be prepared for all kinds of weather in this region—it receives up to 200 inches of rain annually.

Experienced trampers who prefer a more challenging and less popular route seek out the Wangapeka Track, another miners' trail south of the Heaphy. It goes westward from Wangapeka through mountains and river valleys to end south of Karamea near Te Namu.

Check with New Zealand Forest Service rangers in Nelson or Takaka for current information on track conditions before setting out on either trek.

Collingwood and the northern tip

From Collingwood you can arrange four-wheel-drive trips to Farewell Spit and other off-road destinations near South Island's northern tip. Collingwood Safari Tours organizes daily trips from mid-December to early February. The rest of the year, trips leave only on Wednesday; groups can make special arrangements for other times.

Heading for the beach? You'll find safe swimming and easy boat launching at Paton's Rock and alluring shells and colored pebbles at Parapara; both are south of Collingwood. Surfcasting, swimming, a campground, and a store are to be found farther north at Pakawau. On the north coast near Cape Farewell, Wharariki Beach offers wave-cut rock formations, a seal colony, and sea birds.

For an inland summer destination, drive southwest through the rich dairy land of the Aorere River Valley to see limestone formations and glowworms in Te Anaroa Caves (open during the summer holidays). Take along picnic supplies—including some Collingwood Cheddar cheese—for lunch beside the river.

Nelson Lakes National Park

In the southern part of the province, dark beech-covered mountains rise steeply from the water to enclose a pair of slender glacial lakes—jewel-like Rotoiti and Rotoroa—in Nelson Lakes National Park. Recently increased in size, the park extends south from Highway 63 to the rocky crags of the Spenser Mountains and east to the St. Arnaud Range. Nelson Lakes includes the northern part of the great alpine fault that dominates South Island.

Two routes lead to the park. From Blenheim and Renwick, Highway 63 heads up the Wairau Valley to Nelson Lakes. From Nelson, you travel south on Highway 6 to Kawatiri Junction, then turn east and follow the Buller River upstream.

Swimming, boating, water-skiing, and picnicking attract many visitors to Lake Rotoiti. More isolated Lake Rotoroa draws anglers, hunters, and hikers. In winter, skiers flock here to enjoy the fine runs on Mount Robert.

Along the Buller River

Lake Rotoiti's outflow becomes the Buller River, the principal river on the West Coast. For most of its route, the Buller churns through a steep, wooded gorge — one of New Zealand's most beautiful river drives.

Murchison, near the junction of highways 6 and 65, serves both nearby farmers and travelers. Originally a gold mining settlement, Murchison has been rebuilt since 1929, when it stood near the epicenter of a devastating earthquake. Exhibits from the earthquake and the town's mining days fill the local museum. Maruia Falls, about 22 km/14 miles south on Highway 65, was created when the earthquake changed the course of the Maruia River.

About 14 km/9 miles west of Murchison, Highway 6 crosses the line of the Murchison earthquake fault. Look for evidence of land displacement across the river. At Inangahua Junction, Highway 69 branches south to Reefton; Highway 6 continues through the scenic Lower Buller Gorge to Westport. Evergreens, beech, and ferns blanket the slopes of the gorge.

The West Coast

When New Zealanders refer to "The Coast," they're talking about the wild, wet West Coast of South Island, a slim strip of land hemmed in between the jagged peaks of the Southern Alps and the rough waters of the Tasman Sea. Highway 6 follows the shore for most of its length.

Though Maoris traveled here over difficult mountain routes in search of greenstone, early European visitors found few attractions. Only the lure of gold could stimulate migration to this long-isolated region.

In the mid-1860s, prospectors swarmed to the Coast. Boom towns appeared overnight, and fortunes were won and lost by hard-working, hard-drinking miners. The West Coast's main towns — Westport, Greymouth, and Hokitika — date from gold rush days, when supply ships anchored near the mouths of the larger coastal rivers to trade with the miners. Travelers lured by the magnificent scenery of the area began arriving in the late 19th century.

Averaging only about 50 km/30 miles in width, the narrow coastal strip offers great variety in geography, climate, and terrain. Lofty peaks, snow covered the year around, tower along the spine of the Southern Alps. Icy glacial fingers inch slowly down the alpine valleys, terminating at relatively low elevations only a short distance from the sea. Luxuriant native rain forest covers the lower slopes. Since coastal weather tends to be unpredictable, always be prepared for rain.

Renowned for their friendliness and hospitality, today's "Coasters" reflect the lively spirit and camaraderie of gold rush days. No group represents this fun-loving region better than the colorfully dressed Kokatahi Miners Band, a musical aggregation whose travels and outrageous exploits are well documented in coastal folklore.

West Coast — the essentials

The main towns along this rugged coastline are Westport, Greymouth, and Hokitika. Primary lure for travelers is spectacular Westland National Park; another favorite attraction is Shantytown, a replica mining town south of Greymouth.

Getting there. Most visitors travel to the West Coast by rental car or motorcoach, but air and rail service is also available. Air New Zealand serves Westport and Hokitika from Christchurch and Wellington. New Zealand Railways trains link Christchurch and Greymouth via Arthur's Pass. Newmans Coach Lines provides service between Nelson and Greymouth. Railways Road Services motorcoaches travel from Christchurch to Westport and Greymouth, between Westport and Fox Glacier, and from the glaciers area via Haast Pass to Queenstown.

Accommodations. Though many travelers stay in Westport, Greymouth, or near the glaciers, modest accommodations and camping areas are available in smaller towns as well.

Westport has a number of hotels (largest is the DB Westport) and motels. In Greymouth, Revington's is a comfortable older hotel in the center of town. Other accommodations include the DB Greymouth Hotel, Ashley Motel and Motor Inn, King's Motor Hotel, and numerous small motels. Hokitika also offers both hotel and motel rooms. Fishing enthusiasts enjoy Mitchells Hotel at Mitchells, 47 km/29 miles southeast of Greymouth on the shore of Lake Brunner.

Activity in the glaciers area centers around the excellent THC Franz Josef Hotel and the Westland Motor Inn at Franz Josef, and the Vacation and Fox Glacier hotels at Fox Glacier. Motel accommodations and motor camps are also available. The DB Haast Hotel is at the western end of scenic Haast Pass.

Getting around. Rental cars and taxis are available at Westport, Greymouth, and Hokitika. Flightseeing trips, glacier walks, and other alpine excursions can be arranged at both Franz Josef and Fox Glacier.

Tourist information. For specific information on West Coast attractions, inquire at local information offices in Greymouth and Hokitika. Visitor centers in Westland National Park are located at Franz Josef and Fox Glacier.

Westport, coal shipping center

Though gold brought prosperity to Westport, coal — "black gold" — has sustained it. Bituminous coal mining began in the Paparoa Range in the 1870s. Westport, located at the mouth of the Buller River, continues as the country's major coal shipping port. Large freighters anchor at riverside wharves to load coal, timber, and cement.

Along the main street, intricately detailed ironwork decorates the pillars and façades of vintage buildings. City parks include Victoria Square, a grassy gathering spot near the center of town, and Westport Domain, a section of subtropical bush at the upper end of Palmerston Street.

Coaltown Trust. Housed in a converted brewery at the upper end of Queen Street, this community museum highlights the area's coal mining industry. Open daily from 9 A.M. to 4:30 P.M., it includes a simulated coal mine, displays of old-time mining equipment and artifacts, and a model of the famed Denniston Incline coal conveyor. Other exhibits depict the area's pioneering and transportation history and the early New Zealand brewing industry.

To Cape Foulwind. From the Buller bridge, a road runs west from Highway 6 past the airport and Carters Beach (a popular swimming and sunning spot) to Cape Foulwind. Topped by a lighthouse, the headland is New Zealand's closest land point to Australia.

Farther south at dune-backed Tauranga Bay, low tide uncovers fascinating tidepools. Walk up the headland at the north end of the beach for a look at the seal colony just offshore.

Visit a coal mine. If you want to learn more about the local coal mining industry, you can arrange to visit an operating coal mine. For information, stop at the Mines Department office in Westport.

One of the most renowned coal towns was Denniston, once a settlement of 2,000 but now a virtual ghost town. To reach the site, about 25 km/16 miles northeast of Westport, take Highway 67 north to Waimangaroa and veer off on the twisting road that climbs eastward into the Paparoa Range. From here the famed Denniston Incline conveyed millions of tons of coal from the mine bins some 600 meters/2,000 feet to the railway below. Acclaimed as an engineering feat when it was established in 1880, the Incline operated until the late 1960s. Now coal from several underground mines is trucked to Waimangaroa and then transported by rail.

Farther north at Granity, also a Buller coal center, another mining road climbs past Millerton's burning mine to the hilly site of Stockton. Here an 8-km/5-mile-long aerial cableway carries coal from Stockton's open cast mine down to Ngakawau.

Karamea and the "winterless north"

From Westport, Highway 67 heads north along the coast toward the remote community of Karamea, an isolated dairy center about 98 km/60 miles north of Westport. Cradled between the mountains and the sea, the district is known for its mild climate; subtropical fruits flourish here.

Along the route to this "winterless north," you can hunt for gemstones, go surfcasting along the beach, or enjoy short walks through the bush. North of Ngakawau you'll pass between steep hills and the sea, then turn inland across the Mokihinui River to wind slowly through thick forests atop Karamea Bluff. Stop at the top for a memorable panoramic view. Short trails lead to a giant matai tree and to tiny Lake Hanlan.

If time permits, continue about 15 km/9 miles north of Karamea to the road's end at the Kohaihai River. Cross the footbridge there and walk part of the spectacular coastal section of the Heaphy Track.

Gold rush memories and scenic grandeur

South of Westport, Highway 6 curves southwest across Addisons Flat; little remains of the gold diggings that once lured thousands of miners here.

In Charleston, the European Hotel keeps the gold rush era alive with its collection of photographs and mining relics. Charleston's tiny roadside post office serves an extensive area of the Coast.

After climbing into the hills south of Charleston, the highway hugs the shore as it cuts through some of the wildest shoreline scenery in New Zealand. Subtropical greenery blankets the slopes of the craggy coastline to the very edge of the Tasman Sea. Large nikau palms, tree ferns, flax, and hebe species border the exposed coast; just inland rise rimu, miro, beech, and rata trees. Bush birds include the bellbird, tomtit, and weka.

The stratified Punakaiki Pancake Rocks, one of the Coast's best-known features, jut into the sea on Dolomite Point about midway between Westport and Greymouth

Coping with sandflies

In many wet lowland areas, "getting away from it all" means walking straight into the domain of the sandfly.

During his May, 1773, sojourn at Dusky Sound on the southwest coast, Captain James Cook noted in his log that sandflies were "so numerous and . . . so troublesome that they exceed everything of the kind that I have ever met with." The tiny pests are still with us today.

Thriving in moist and humid regions up to 3,000 feet in elevation, these silent and persistent insects appear when the air is calm, particularly at dawn, dusk, or before rain. The small, black sandflies are least belligerent in hot sunshine, in cold weather, or during strong winds or heavy rain.

Only the females bite. In many people these bites set up a series of reactions, often resulting in an allergy to subsequent bites. Vulnerable hikers rely on a powerful insect repellent or vitamin B_1 tablets to discourage the flies from biting. Antihistamine drugs minimize side effects from the bites.

(page 94). Centuries of surf action at this spot have tunneled out rocky grottoes, surge pools, and blow holes beneath the thinly layered limestone headland. On clear days you can see the Southern Alps from here. At the visitor center across the highway in Punakaiki, you'll find tourist facilities and displays explaining features of this geologic anomaly. A modern campground is nearby, and trails lead into the bush and along the coast.

Greymouth, gateway to Shantytown

The largest town on the West Coast is Greymouth, hub of a coal and timber-producing district and the western terminus of Highway 7. Like most other coastal communities, it flourished during the 1860s gold rush. Today, visitors flock to nearby Shantytown, a replica gold mining town. For local tourist information, stop at the West Coast Public Relations Office in the Regent Theatre.

The Grey River carves a broad valley—known as The Gap—through coastal limestone to the sea. On clear days you can gaze eastward to a snowy panorama of the high peaks of the Southern Alps; the best view is from the south breakwater. Another memorable vista is from King

Domain; the steep track starts from Mount Street (leave your car in Smith Street if you're driving) and climbs to several lookouts.

During the spring whitebait season, you may see local anglers netting for the tiny transparent fish in the Grey River and other West Coast streams. Tuna boats call at Greymouth from January to May.

You can see wild game in a natural setting at Hunting and Safari (N.Z.) Ltd.'s wildlife park at Paroa, south of Greymouth; it's open daily.

Highway 73, the Arthur's Pass Road across the mountains (page 96), reaches the coast south of Greymouth.

Coal miners' train. You can board the Rewanui coal miners' train weekdays at 12:30 P.M. at Greymouth's Riverside Station for a ride into the Paparoa hills to an operating underground coal mine. Ask at the ticket office for the Rewanui Miners' Train brochure; it includes a map of the area.

The train travels northeast to Runanga and Dunollie, then climbs steep Seven Mile Canyon to Rewanui. During the short stopover, you'll have time to poke around the mine buildings, coal bins, and conveyor belts of the Liverpool Mine. The train arrives back in Greymouth about 3:05 P.M. (2:35 P.M. on Friday).

Shantytown. Popular Shantytown offers a glimpse of life in a West Coast gold mining town of the 1860s. Set amid native bush 13 km/8 miles southeast of Greymouth, it's open daily from 8:30 A.M. to 5 P.M.

A century-old church, general store, hotel-saloon, and typical shops line the main street. A few buildings have been moved here from other sites; others are reproductions of earlier structures. Among the sights you'll see are an 1837 printing press, an excellent gemstone display, vintage vehicles and equipment, and a replica Chinese den containing articles used by these early miners.

You can climb aboard a stagecoach for a tour of the grounds or ride through the bush on the Kaitangata steam railway. A short trail leads to the gold sluicing area, where you can pan for gold.

West Coast gold country

Discoveries of gold along West Coast streams triggered a massive rush as prospectors of all nationalities flocked to the Coast. Full-fledged towns—complete with hotels, banks, bars, and shops—sprang up almost overnight. In late 1864 only 800 people had settled here, but a year later the population had boomed to 16,000. By the end of 1866, some 50,000 miners had arrived in search of riches.

Miners struck gold in such places as Blackball and Moonlight. In the Ngahere region, Nelson Creek, Red Jacks, and Notown were all thriving gold sites. But the boom collapsed almost as suddenly as it had begun. After the rush to Addisons Flat in May 1867, most prospectors moved on to the new Coromandel gold fields, though mining continued in Westland on a sizable scale until the

mid-1880s. And all activity is still not over—the Kaniere electric-powered dredge continues to recover gold from the Taramakau River.

For information and brochures on side trips from Greymouth to former mining centers, inquire at the Public Relations Office in Greymouth. Forest Service rangers in Hokitika and Totara Flat (on Highway 7 southwest of Ikamatua) can also provide information.

Grey Valley. An enjoyable loop trip from Greymouth follows the north bank road up the Grey River to Blackball, continues on to the timber and rail center of Ikamatua, and returns to the coast on Highway 7.

Coal miners still live in Blackball, where you'll see the old mine's dilapidated outbuildings. Several roads and trails—including the Croesus and Moonlight tracks—head into the Paparoa Range from Blackball. On Highway 7 near Ngahere, roads and trails border the creeks where miners panned for gold a century ago. Waiuta, in the hills southeast of Hukarere, was productive as recently as 1950.

Lake Brunner. Another inland destination is Lake Brunner, a favorite of anglers, yachters, and hikers. There's a picnic area at Moana on the northern shore (accessible from Highway 7). Mitchells, on the southern shore, is a fishing and boating center and the departure point for bush walks. The road to Mitchells veers north from Highway 73 at Kumara and follows part of the old 1865 miners' route through the Greenstone Valley. In Kumara you can examine historic items in the Holy Trinity Anglican Church; built by gold miners, the church has been in continuous use since 1878.

Hokitika for greenstone

Boisterous "capital of the gold fields" in the lively 1860s, today Hokitika is Westland's administrative center and headquarters of the greenstone processing industry. Tourist information is available at 29 Weld Street.

Mining displays and early photographs at the West Coast Historical Museum on lower Tancred Street recall gold rush days. Exhibits include scale models of a gold dredge and a mining shaft. Museum hours are 9:30 A.M. to 4:30 P.M. weekdays, 2 to 4:30 P.M. weekends.

Northeast of town on the airport road, a plane table identifies more than 50 peaks visible in a panorama of the Southern Alps. For a closer look, scenic flights are available.

Crafts. Early Maoris obtained highly prized jade, called greenstone, from the nearby Arahura Valley; from it they carved their weapons, cutting tools, and personal ornaments. Modern craftsmen fashion the hard stone into jewelry, *hei-tiki* pendants, and other decorative objects. On weekdays you can watch greenstone carvers working at two Hokitika factories — Westland Greenstone Company on Tancred Street and Hokitika Jade Company Ltd., 110 Revell Street.

Ski-equipped planes land skiers on an icy glacier after an exhilarating trip over the rugged peaks of the Southern Alps. Nonskiers experience similar thrills on flightseeing trips.

Visitors can also watch glassblowers demonstrate their craft on weekdays at Hokitika Free Form Glass Co., Ltd., 130 Revell Street.

Excursions. At the Blue Spur Gold Mine, about 5 km/3 miles east of Hokitika, you can visit a working gold sluicing operation, pan for gold, and even enter some of the mine shafts and tunnels. The mine is open daily.

Lake Kaniere — one of Westland's loveliest — often mirrors a view of forested hills backed by the snow-topped Southern Alps. Located 18 km/12 miles southeast of Hokitika, the lake is popular for boating, swimming, and water-skiing. Yachting and speed boat regattas ruffle the waters on summer weekends.

Back country explorers and trampers can follow the Hokitika River upstream via Kokatahi and Kowhitirangi. For trail information, check with the Forest Service ranger in Hokitika.

South to the glaciers

From Hokitika, Highway 6 crosses the Hokitika River on a long combined road/rail bridge and curves inland up the valley. Franz Josef lies 147 km/91 miles southwest, Fox Glacier another 25 km/16 miles beyond.

Lake Mahinapua, west of the highway a few kilome-

ters south of Hokitika, attracts picnickers and yachters. You can walk in (30 minutes) from the highway or follow a loop road and approach the lake from the west through a tunnel of lush greenery. Ross, a former gold town located south of the turnoff for the lake, is noted for the cherry trees that flower along its main street each spring.

From the Waitaha River south to Lake Ianthe, you wend your way through a forest corridor of tall rimu, lush ferns, and other dense bush. West of Lake Wahapo, a signposted road forks 13 km/8 miles to the coastal settlement of Okarito. From September to February, a white heron colony nests at Okarito Lagoon.

Westland National Park

On the western slope of the Southern Alps, some of New Zealand's most spectacular alpine country has been set aside in Westland National Park. Most visitors focus on Franz Josef and Fox glaciers, a pair of broad, icy tongues that push steeply down from permanent snowfields to within a few kilometers of the sea. And there's more—the park's rain forests, lakes, and coursing rivers, all backed by the range of snow-clad peaks, are equally captivating.

Accommodations and tourist facilities are concentrated in the communities of Franz Josef and Fox Glacier. Park visitor centers feature exhibits on park geology, bot-

Hiking and climbing amid superb scenery

Whether you enjoy a quiet stroll along a short nature trail or go in for strenuous hiking through mountain wilderness, you'll find New Zealand's network of trails one of the country's special treats. Dedicated hikers (called "trampers" in New Zealand) and mountaineers head for the verdant bush and alpine parks, but even the casual walker can enjoy many rewarding short routes.

Many trails are suitable for walkers wearing street shoes; other paths require sturdy walking shoes or hiking boots. Sandy sections of some trails may be soggy after a heavy rain.

New Zealand Walkways. From Cape Reinga in the north to Invercargill in the south, trails offer access to the countryside for Kiwis and visitors alike. Frequently located near urban centers, many of the trails are part of the New Zealand Walkways project, an ambitious and imaginative network of routes. Designed for the walker rather than for the serious backpacker, the trails traverse the scenic areas of the country. In length, they range from an hour's easy walk to a strenuous full-day excursion.

Local tourist offices can provide trail information—and often a descriptive leaflet with a map of the route.

Bush walks. Many of the best short forest walks wind through scenic reserves and national parks. Trees are identified on some nature trails. At park visitor centers, you can study exhibits on local trees, flowers, and birds; park officials can suggest special points of interest and provide trail information. Elsewhere, inquire at Forest Service offices and local tourist centers.

Longer treks. Best known of the longer hikes is the famed Milford Track (page 119), a challenging tramp through South Island's Fiordland National Park; it begins at the head of Lake Te Anau and ends at Milford Sound. Not far away, the Routeburn Track (page 115) traverses the impressive alpine country of Mount Aspiring and Fiordland national parks. A third face of Fiordland National Park may be seen on the low-level river route through the Hollyford Valley (page 118) to Martins Bay.

At the northern end of South Island, the Heaphy and Wangapeka tracks (page 87) wind through native forest and tussock to the lush greenery of the West Coast.

North Island routes range from a coastal trek around Cape Reinga and down Ninety Mile Beach (page 39) to wilderness trails into the Wanganui country (page 57).

Backpackers should check in with the nearest Forest Service ranger before departing to obtain the latest information on weather and track conditions.

Group excursions. Organized group trips on the Milford, Routeburn, and Hollyford routes allow hikers to travel into isolated areas with only lightweight packs. Lodging and meals are provided in huts along the route, and each hiker carries only personal gear in a backpack.

Less strenuous is the South Island excursion that takes hikers from Motueka, northwest of Nelson, into Abel Tasman National Park (page 86); accommodations are provided in a waterfront lodge on Torrent Bay.

Group trips also probe the untamed areas in the central part of North Island. Maori guides lead 5-day tramping adventures into the Urewera country southeast of Rotorua (page 60).

Venturetreks (P.O. Box 3839, Auckland) organizes 5-day guided excursions in the Wanganui Valley (the Wanganui River Walk, page 59), and in the wilderness of Kaimanawa and Kaweka state forest parks east of Tongariro National Park (the Kaimanawa Wilderness Walk, page 53), and the Alpine Walk around Tongariro National Park (page 55).

Mountaineering. New Zealand's high peaks attract experienced mountaineers, and some—such as Sir Edmund Hillary—have won worldwide fame. In the Southern Alps, more than a dozen peaks top 3,050 meters/10,000 feet; highest of all is Mount Cook.

Major climbing areas on South Island lie along the slopes of the Southern Alps. Mount Cook and Westland national parks flank the range's main divide and offer superb alpine scenery. Other high peaks in Mount Aspiring, Arthur's Pass, and Fiordland national parks lure mountaineering enthusiasts.

North Island's mountains are lower than those of South Island, and the major peaks are either extinct or mildly active volcanoes.

Equipment and information. You can purchase or rent equipment for serious hiking and mountaineering in the main towns and alpine resort hotels.

Write to the New Zealand Tourist Office for the brochure *New Zealand Tramping and Mountaineering.* For more specific information, inquire at the park headquarters of each national park or at outdoor clubs. Hikers and trampers can contact the New Zealand Federation of Mountain Clubs, P.O. Box 1604, Wellington. For mountain-climbing information, write to the New Zealand Alpine Club, P.O. Box 41038, Eastbourne, Wellington.

any, and wildlife. You can obtain trail information and park publications at the visitor centers or from the chief ranger in Franz Josef (P.O. Box 14; phone Franz Josef 727) or the ranger in Fox Glacier (P.O. Box 9; phone Fox Glacier 807).

Walking on a glacier. Hikers in good physical condition can join one of the guided glacier excursions departing daily from Franz Josef and from Fox Glacier. Walking on the glacial ice involves fairly strenuous hiking over terminal moraine and ice. Guides outfit participants with well-oiled boots, heavy socks, and—in rainy weather—knee-length slickers. Do not attempt to hike on the ice without proper equipment. A 2½-hour guided trip departs at 9:30 A.M. and 2 P.M. from Fox Glacier.

Popular heli-hike excursions take off from Franz Josef Airfield. During the summer season, visitors can choose either a half-day or a full-day trip. The rest of the year, heli-hike excursions operate on demand, weather permitting. A helicopter takes passengers up the glacier, where the aircraft lands; guides then escort groups of outfitted hikers down the ice. You'll see pinnacle blue ice, crevasses, and ice caves. The full-day trip takes participants up to Victoria Falls under the glacier's main ice fall.

On sunny days, it's essential to protect your eyes and skin against glare from the snow. For comfort on the walk, plan to have both hands free.

Occasionally, you may hear the sound of grinding and cracking ice; it's a sign that the glacier is inching forward under tremendous pressure from the vast ice field above.

Flying through the Alps. Many travelers consider a flightseeing trip through the snowy peaks of the Southern Alps one of the most exciting and memorable experiences of their trip.

Ski-equipped Mount Cook Line planes depart frequently during periods of good weather from airports at Franz Josef and at Fox Glacier. Because demand is great, sign up as soon as you arrive so you won't be disappointed. On most flights, the pilot lands the small plane on a glacial snowfield so passengers can walk on the ice, take photographs, and throw a snowball or two. On longer trips, you fly over the divide and down the Tasman Glacier on the eastern slope of the Alps.

Guided alpine trips. Mountaineering courses and excursions into the Southern Alps are conducted from November to mid-March by Alpine Guides–Westland (P.O. Box 38, Fox Glacier). Winter mountaineering and ice-climbing training and a number of alpine ski tours are scheduled from June through October.

A pause at Franz Josef

Named by explorer Julius von Haast in 1865 for the emperor of his native Austria-Hungary, Franz Josef is the shorter and steeper of the two glaciers; it descends the western slope of the Southern Alps some 11 km/7 miles to terminate about 300 meters/980 feet above sea level.

If you approach from the north, you'll get your first view of the glacier from across Lake Mapourika. Another vista comes as you cross Tatare Bridge north of town. Closer views loom above the THC Franz Josef Hotel

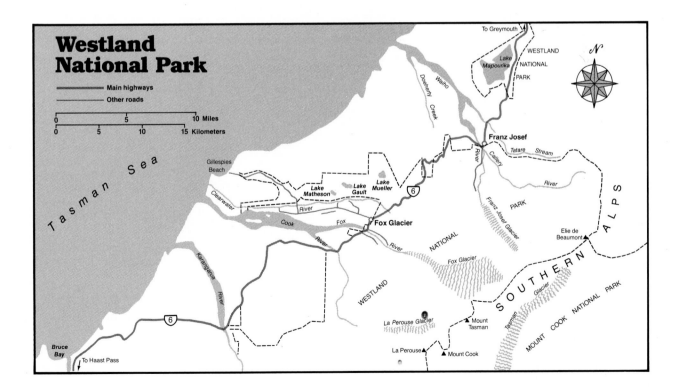

grounds and from Glacier Road, which branches off Highway 6 just south of the Waiho River.

After you've stopped at the park visitor center, be sure to visit nearby St. James' Church to see the alpine view framed in the chancel window.

If you have time for only one walk, take the Terrace Track through the rain forest to historic Callery Gorge, stop at the warm springs, and return along the Waiho River. A booklet, available at the visitor center, describes natural features and points out traces remaining from gold mining days on the Waiho.

From Glacier Road, a 5-minute walk leads to Peters Pool, a "kettle" lake with a glacier reflection. You can continue on the Douglas Track past the swing bridge over the Waiho, then return through bush and moraine areas to the road.

Fox Glacier's walks and views

The curvy, 24-km/15-mile route from Franz Josef to Fox Glacier winds over spur ranges before descending into the broad valley known as the Cook River Flats. The cozy

settlement of Fox Glacier is headquarters for excursions into the southern part of the park. The glacier was named for Sir William Fox, one-time premier of New Zealand.

Stop at the visitor center to see its exhibits of park plants, birds, and geology and for printed information on trails and other park features.

Bush walks. Trails offer enjoyable hikes through luxuriant bush, spectacular views of snowy peaks and tree-rimmed lakes, and a close look at evidence of the glacier's advance and retreat. Leaflets available at the visitor center describe points of interest and help you identify trailside plants.

The walk to Lake Matheson is delightful any time of day, but the classic panorama—Mount Cook and Mount Tasman reflected in the lake's dark waters—is most striking at sunrise, when the first rays streak the clouds and strike the snowy peaks. It's an easy 30-minute walk to the lake and about another 30 minutes on a rock trail to the "view of views" at the far end of the lake. The Lake Gault trail branches north from the Matheson trail.

Just south of the township, the Minnehaha Track is a

Thin layers of limestone create the Pancake Rocks at Punakaiki. Lush greenery, grottoes, blowholes, and a visitor center lure travelers to this coastal curiosity.

20-minute loop from the highway through the bush to the edge of the quiet Minnehaha stream. Several other tracks begin along the South Approach Road (Glacier View Road) south of the river.

If Westland mists lift, some of the most inspiring glacier views come along the steep switchback track up Cone Rock. In less than an hour, you'll climb some 300 meters/980 feet above the Fox River for a grandstand view of the large glacier. After a rain, though, handholds are slick, and you'll dodge one waterfall after another.

A shorter and less strenuous track, also offering splendid views, leads to the Fox Chalet Lookout.

The effects of the glacier's advance and retreat are particularly noticeable on the Moraine Walk through the Fox Valley. Along the way you see forests of varying ages, terminal moraines marking the glacier's advance in earlier centuries, and erratic boulders pushed along by the ice.

Other attractions. You'll discover breathtaking vistas of Fox Glacier and the high peaks from several viewpoints. One of the best is from the Clearwater River bridge on the road to Gillespies Beach. From the South Approach Road, you see the glacier framed by trees, and there's a good view of Mount Tasman from the Fox River bridge.

After dark, you can walk to the glowworm grotto signposted just south of town. Here, glowing iridescent green lights attract night-flying insects. (For more on glowworms, see page 40.)

Gillespies Beach, west of Fox Glacier, was once an isolated gold mining settlement. Gorse now covers the old tailings behind the dunes. Captivating coastal scenery and alpine views await visitors.

If you plan to hike north to the seal colony (1 to 1½ hours round trip), check first at the park visitor center, since part of the beach route is passable only at low tide. An alternate path takes you inland over sections of the old miners' road.

Down the South Westland coast

From Fox Glacier, Highway 6 continues 118 km/73 miles south to Haast Junction. Forest lines much of the route; in summer, white plumes of toe toe, scarlet-blooming rata, and yellow gorse add accents of color.

You can picnic beside the sea at Bruce Bay, where the road briefly skirts the coast before turning inland, or farther south at Lake Paringa or Lake Moeraki, both good fishing lakes. Just north of the Moeraki River bridge, a short side road leads to the start of the Munro Track, a 40-minute walk to the beach through a forest thick with large tree ferns and native fuchsia.

The highway meets the coast again at Knights Point, where a windy viewpoint high above the sea offers vistas of bush-covered headlands, golden sand beaches, and jagged offshore rocks.

About 5 km/3 miles south of Knights Point, you can walk to the beach along Ship Creek; remains of shipwrecks are sometimes visible below the bridge at low tide.

Lonely road to Jackson Bay

After crossing the Haast River bridge, longest of New Zealand's single lane bridges, most motorists turn inland on Highway 6 to cross Haast Pass, 64 km/40 miles distant. A hardy few continue along the coast toward Haast township and Jackson Bay. Experienced trampers head up the Okuru River into Mount Aspiring National Park.

Just south of the Arawata River bridge, a signposted, unpaved side road leads 4 km/2 miles to the start of the Ellery Track. The 45-minute forest walk beside the outlet stream brings you to secluded Lake Ellery.

Jackson Bay, 48 km/29 miles below Haast Junction, provided a sheltered anchorage for early whalers and sealers. The bay was also the site of one of Westland's most isolated early settlements.

Across rugged Haast Pass

Originally an old Maori route to the West Coast, Haast Pass, at 563 meters/1,847 feet, links the West Coast with the Southern Lakes district and forms the boundary between Westland and Otago.

Geologist-explorer Julius von Haast crossed the pass in 1863 and named the route after himself. In the late 1800s and early 1900s, pack horses carried supplies across the pass to isolated West Coast settlers. Cattle had to be driven up the coast or over the tortuous Haast Pass track, freight came and went by ship, and radio and later aircraft provided the primary means of communication. Not until 1960 did completion of the Wanaka-Haast route end a century of virtual isolation for the people of Haast.

Snow seldom closes the highway, but rainfall is abundant. All too often for visitors, clouds obscure the scenery. Waterfalls pour from hanging valleys into the glacier-cut gorges of the Haast and Makarora rivers.

Camping areas, picnic tables, and rest rooms are located at several roadside points, but you may have to share facilities with aggressive sandflies.

West of the divide. Silver beech trees populate the wet forests on the western slope of the mountains. Southeast of the Pleasant Flat picnic area, a short track leads to Thunder Creek Falls. At the Gates of Haast, the clear, pale blue waters of the Haast River foam over immense boulders wedged into the narrow gorge. The old bridle trail used by prospectors, cattle drovers, and other early travelers parallels the highway near the pass.

Eastern slope. Mountain beech predominates on the drier eastern side of Haast Pass. You descend on an unpaved road along the Makarora River through the northern part of Mount Aspiring National Park. Side roads lead to high-country sheep stations.

The highway cuts through brown tussock lands to skirt the northeastern shore of Lake Wanaka, then angles across The Neck—where the ancient Hawea and Wanaka glaciers met to gouge out the lake beds—and continues south along Lake Hawea to Wanaka.

The Southern Alps

Often shrouded in clouds, the magnificent peaks of the Southern Alps form New Zealand's snow-capped backbone. Towering majestically above western rain forest and eastern plain, they extend some 650 km/400 miles along the western edge of South Island.

Few roads cut through the high alpine valleys. At the northern end, Highway 6 links Nelson and Westport through the Buller River Gorge (page 87); it recrosses the Alps near the southern end through Haast Pass (see page 95). The Milford Road (page 118) links Te Anau and Milford Sound.

In the central part of the range, highways follow old Maori greenstone routes through Lewis Pass and Arthur's Pass to the West Coast.

Lewis Pass Road

Constructed during the Depression of the 1930s, the Lewis Pass Road (Highway 7) begins at Waipara, north of Christchurch, and passes south of Hanmer Springs. Canterbury farmlands give way to rolling golden foothills and beech forests as you follow the Waiau Valley northwest across 864-meter/2,840-foot Lewis Pass. The road then descends through rugged greenery to the West Coast.

At Maruia Springs, just west of Lewis Pass, you can swim in hot pools in an alpine setting. East of Reefton, the Blacks Point Museum — housed in a wooden former church — displays local mining memorabilia. The highway follows the Grey River toward the sea and meets the West Coast highway at Greymouth.

Across Arthur's Pass

Shortest, steepest, and most spectacular of the routes across the Southern Alps, Arthur's Pass Road (Highway 73) is the main link between Canterbury and Westland. Construction of the route began in 1855, boosted by the efforts of Christchurch businessmen seeking to direct the flow of gold from West Coast mines through the Canterbury capital.

From the Canterbury Plains, the road climbs into the mountains and curves around Craigieburn State Forest Park. In winter, inhabitants of Christchurch and the surrounding area enjoy tobogganing at Porters Pass, ice skating at nearby Lake Lyndon, and skiing at Porters Heights and Temple Basin skifield.

Headquarters for Arthur's Pass National Park is located in Arthur's Pass township, just east of the 922-meter/3,029-foot summit.

West of the divide, the highway descends steeply to the railway settlement of Otira; no vans are permitted on the Arthur's Pass-Otira section of the road. At the settlement of Jacksons, a wayside tavern recalls its early years as a stagecoach inn before the rail line was pushed through the mountains; historic photographs evoke this colorful period. The road continues down the Taramakau Valley to meet Highway 6 near Kumara.

A bird's-eye view of nature's wonders

One of the most thrilling adventures for visitors in this air-minded nation is flightseeing—sightseeing by small airplane. These maneuverable, low-flying aircraft have opened up remote and rugged parts of New Zealand formerly inaccessible to most travelers. From the air, New Zealand's fabled scenery takes on a dramatic new perspective.

In most of the country's main tourist centers you can climb aboard a single or twin-engine plane, float plane, or helicopter for a bird's-eye view of the region's lakes, mountains, fiords, or coastline. Photographers will find the most expansive views from the seats beside or immediately behind the pilot.

Perhaps the most spectacular trip is the flight through the rugged white wonderland of the Southern Alps. Ski-equipped planes leave from Mount Cook, Franz Josef, and Fox Glacier. You thread through snowy peaks, fly over gaping crevasses, and then land briefly on one of the high snowfields.

In Rotorua, Taupo, and the southern lakes district, you soar above bush-rimmed lakes. Gaping volcanic craters and steaming geothermal valleys assume new dimensions from the air. Flights from Queenstown and Te Anau take you over Fiordland's dense bush and above hikers' huts along the Milford Track.

For an aerial view of bush-covered headlands bordering an azure sea, consider a flight over the Marlborough Sounds waterways (from Picton) or the Bay of Islands (from Paihia). Above Auckland you look down on Waitemata Harbour and the islands of the Hauraki Gulf. From Kaitaia, fly along Ninety Mile Beach to Cape Reinga—and see Northland's kauri gum fields and mangrove swamps, as well.

Arthur's Pass National Park

Spanning both slopes of the Southern Alps, the park encompasses a broad cross section of alpine flora. Mountain beech forest predominates on the eastern slope, and dense forest covers the western side. Waterfalls tumble from glacier-cut valleys. Alpine wildflowers bloom from mid-November through February; the brilliant crimson flowers of the rata turn the mountainsides ablaze with color. Above the tree line, the scenery is cold and severe. In winter, snow blankets the slopes.

Park activities are concentrated in Arthur's Pass township, about 154 km/95 miles northwest of Christchurch. At park headquarters here, you'll see exhibits depicting the history of the park and the difficult construction of the road and railway. You'll also see one of the old Cobb & Co. stagecoaches that transported passengers and freight across the rugged route before the completion of the Otira tunnel in 1923. Other displays identify local plants and birds. Evening programs are presented here in summer.

Descriptive leaflets are available for several of the park's trails. Popular routes include the Dobson Nature Walk and trails to Bridal Veil Falls, Devil's Punchbowl, and Bealey Valley. All-day climbs lead up nearby peaks, where you can often spot novice rock climbers learning mountaineering skills.

Near the highway summit, a memorial honors Arthur Dobson, the surveyor-engineer who discovered the pass in 1864.

Magnificent Mount Cook

Travelers approach Mount Cook either by air — over the green and golden patchwork farms of the Canterbury Plains — or by road across the tussock-covered hills of the Mackenzie Country or Lindis Pass. On the western horizon, the snow-draped Southern Alps rise majestically.

The heart of this spectacular alpine country — extending some 65 km/40 miles along the eastern slope — has been protected in Mount Cook National Park. Renowned for its craggy beauty, it's a magnet for mountaineers who pit their climbing and skiing skills against its challenging peaks and glaciers. Less energetic visitors are attracted by the park's alpine scenery, its wildflowers and wildlife, and its network of trails. Visitor facilities and accommodations are located in Mount Cook village.

Lofty peaks. Smallest of South Island's four major alpine preserves, Mount Cook National Park encompasses the highest peaks of the Southern Alps. More than 140 mountains rise above 2,100 meters/7,000 feet. Of these, over a dozen top 3,050 meters/10,000 feet. Looming above them all is the range's mighty monarch, the highest peak in Australasia. The Maoris called it *Aorangi* (the cloud piercer). Later explorers named the 3,763-meter/12,349-foot peak in honor of Captain James Cook, first European to set foot on New Zealand soil.

Largest of the park's glaciers is the Tasman, 29 km/

Southern Alps — the essentials

Though Mount Cook National Park attracts the most visitors, you can also experience and enjoy the rugged alpine country in Arthur's Pass and Mount Aspiring national parks. For information on Nelson Lakes National Park, at the northern end of the Alps, see page 87; Westland National Park, located on the western slope of the mountains, is described on page 91.

Getting there. Paved roads penetrate each of the parks. Newmans Air and Mount Cook Line planes and motorcoaches provide transportation to Mount Cook from Christchurch, Queenstown, and other towns. Travelers can reach Arthur's Pass township by train or by Railways Road Services motorcoaches from Christchurch or Greymouth. To reach Mount Aspiring National Park, most visitors travel by air or motorcoach to Queenstown, then continue on to the park by bus or car.

Accommodations. Advance reservations are essential at these remote sites. At Mount Cook, many visitors stay at The Hermitage, one of New Zealand's fine THC hotels, or at Glencoe Lodge; motel flats, chalet units, and a youth hostel are also located in the village. Informal camping is available near Glentanner Park. At Arthur's Pass, motels, a youth hostel, and other accommodations are available in Arthur's Pass township; the park has no formal camping areas. Mount Aspiring visitors stay in hotels, motels, and motor camps in Queenstown, Wanaka, or smaller towns. Mountain huts (for hikers and climbers) are scattered throughout the parks; information on huts and camping regulations is available from each park's chief ranger.

Getting around. At Mount Cook, visitors can arrange for flightseeing trips, coach excursions, rafting trips, and ski-mountaineering expeditions. Guided walks and nature programs are scheduled in summer. Rental car agencies are located in larger towns outside the parks.

Tourist information. A factual guide on all national parks is available from the New Zealand Tourist Office. Park visitor centers are in Mount Cook village, Arthur's Pass township, and Wanaka (for Mount Aspiring National Park). Also serving Mount Aspiring visitors are ranger stations (open weekdays only) at Glenorchy in the Dart Valley and at Makarora on the Haast Pass Road (Highway 6).

18 miles long and up to 3 km/2 miles wide. Other main glaciers include the Mueller and Hooker, both within relatively easy walking distance of park headquarters, and the more distant Murchison and Godley glaciers.

Alpine flora and fauna. Botanists have identified more than 300 species of native plants in the park; labels identify many trees and shrubs along park trails. Small alpine plants flower in high rock crevices. Wildflowers bloom from October to January; best known is the mountain buttercup (often mistakenly called the Mount Cook lily). In December, lupines stretch in a colorful midsummer carpet on the slopes below The Hermitage.

Native birds, including the inquisitive and raucous kea (mountain parrot), inhabit the forests, river beds, and rocky crags. Introduced animals — thar, chamois, and deer — browse in alpine and subalpine scrublands.

Enjoying your visit to Mount Cook

This splendid alpine park attracts people who love the mountains — both vacationers who come primarily to enjoy the scenery and mountaineers who expend their energies striving for the heights.

Allow time to pause and let the mountains enfold you in their beauty and serenity. Listen to the bird songs, let the sun's heat warm your body, watch Mount Cook's sharp peak turn to glowing pink and purple in the sun's waning rays. On an after-dinner walk, enjoy the moonlight on the snow or gaze at a multitude of stars.

Obviously, all that snow and ice doesn't arrive in the sunshine. When rain clouds settle over the mountains, far too many visitors succumb to the cozy lure of the fireplace. Even on threatening days you can stop at the visitor center and walk some of the shorter trails.

Blending in with its alpine backdrop, the steeply roofed visitor center, located just below The Hermitage, is the park's administrative headquarters and major source of information (P.O. Box 5, Mount Cook; phone Mount Cook 819). Photographs, relief maps, and other displays add to your knowledge of the park's history, terrain, plants, and wildlife. You can ask about park trails and guide services or check road conditions or the weather forecast. During holiday periods, park rangers conduct nature walks and evening programs.

At The Hermitage or Glencoe Lodge, you can arrange for sightseeing flights or guided excursions.

Sightseeing flights. One of the "don't miss" experiences in New Zealand is a flight by ski-plane over the icy peaks and glaciers of the Southern Alps. Weather conditions permitting, ski-equipped aircraft operate from the Mount Cook Airport. Helicopter trips depart from the Glentanner Park Helipad.

Within a few minutes after takeoff, your small plane is flying above the gleaming slopes, saw-edged ridges, and jumbled icefalls to the head of Tasman Glacier. If your flight includes a snowfield landing, the pilot lowers the plane's retractable skis, and the craft skims to a gentle stop on the granular ice. You step out onto terrain once accessible only to experienced mountaineers.

Snowy peaks of the Southern Alps tower above Lake Tekapo. Small stone church honors the pioneers who homesteaded the remote Mackenzie Country.

Hiking park trails. Even if clouds move in to obscure the mountains, you can get out and walk some of the paths fanning out from park headquarters. As long as you dress for it and watch for worsening conditions, a brisk hike can be invigorating—even in wet weather.

At the visitor center, you can obtain printed trail information on several of the walks. Boots, heavy socks, and other equipment can be rented at The Hermitage.

The Governor's Bush trail begins below Glencoe Bridge and loops through silver beech forest behind the post office. Even shorter is the Bowen Bush trail, a 10-minute walk on the knoll south of Glencoe Stream. It offers a view up the Hooker Valley to Mount Cook.

Longer hikes take you into the mountains. The Kea Point Nature Walk begins in front of The Hermitage and ends with a view of Mueller Glacier. In summer, hikers favor the Sealy Tarns trail, which leads to small mountain lakes where you can swim. The track to Red Tarns and Mount Sebastopol begins behind Glencoe Lodge.

Other trails lead up the Hooker Valley. The main route forks off the Kea Point path, crosses the Hooker River on a pair of swing bridges, and continues to the lower edge of the Hooker Glacier; experienced mountaineers and guided parties continue up to Hooker Hut and Copland Pass. Beginning at the Ball Hut Road bridge, the Wakefield Track runs along the Hooker River and follows the trail used by parties traveling to the Tasman Glacier in the early 1900s. Short trails lead from Ball Hut Road to Blue Lakes and to a viewpoint of Wakefield Falls.

Tasman Glacier trip. Each morning and afternoon a bus departs from The Hermitage for the 2½-hour trip up rocky, single-lane Ball Hut Road to a viewpoint of the Tasman Glacier and the surrounding peaks.

Rafting on the Tasman River. For a different kind of wilderness experience, consider a raft trip down the Tasman River, the runoff of the Tasman Glacier. On the 3-hour trip, you'll enjoy fine views of the glacier, bounce through rapids, and stop for billy tea and biscuits.

Alpine climbs. Though climbers began arriving at Mount Cook in the 1880s, the peak was not conquered until 1894. Mount Cook National Park encompasses one of the world's most challenging moutaineering areas, where ardent mountaineers find a wealth of demanding climbs. At least one experienced climber should accompany each party, and groups should always notify a park ranger of climbing plans before starting out.

You can arrange for climbing instruction and guide service at The Hermitage, where equipment is available for hire or purchase. The mountaineering school operates from November through March. Full-day guided trips to Hochstetter Icefall, Hooker Hut, Mueller Hut, and other destinations can be arranged. On overnight trips, mountaineers stay in alpine huts.

Skiing the high country. Ski-equipped planes and helicopters allow experienced alpine skiers accompanied by guides to enjoy the pristine white slopes of the glaciers and high snowfields. Generally, skiing is excellent from July to October.

In recent years ski-touring and ski-mountaineering have become popular; groups bunk overnight at high-country huts. At The Hermitage, visitors can rent equipment, arrange for instruction, or hire an alpine guide.

Mount Aspiring National Park

Southernmost of South Island's alpine preserves, Mount Aspiring National Park encompasses the high slopes on both sides of the divide between the Haast and Te Anau-Milford highways. Its highest and most magnificent peak is 3,035-meter/9,957-foot Mount Aspiring.

A mountaineer's park, Mount Aspiring draws hikers and climbers who probe its remote river valleys and ascend through beech forest to rugged, glaciated peaks. Numerous alpine huts offer shelter from variable mountain weather.

Cutting across the northern end of the park, Highway 6 offers hikers access to the Wilkin Valley and other tributaries of the Haast and Makarora rivers. From Wanaka, motorists can follow a lonely road (unpaved beyond Glendhu Bay) up the scenic Matukituki Valley to the park boundary for views of Rob Roy Glacier, Mount Avalanche, and Mount Aspiring's pyramid-shaped peak. To reach the Dart, Rees, and Routeburn valleys, follow the Glenorchy road from Queenstown.

Park information is available at the visitor center in Wanaka; or contact the chief ranger (P.O. Box 93; phone Wanaka 7660). At the center you can check the current status of trails and weather, as well as view displays on the park's flora, fauna, and history. Ranger stations are open weekdays only at Makarora (on Highway 6, the Haast Pass Road) and at Glenorchy (near the head of Lake Wakatipu).

Exploring South Canterbury

From Christchurch, Highway 1 stretches across the checkerboard farmlands and sheep pastures of the Canterbury Plains and turns south toward the coastal resort of Timaru, a touring base for exploring the region. Highway 72 veers farther inland, passing through the Rakaia Gorge to Geraldine and on into the lonely hills of the Mackenzie Country; it's hard to surpass this route for scenic variety.

Bordered on the south by the Waitaki River and on the west by the imposing Southern Alps, South Canterbury is a land of contrasts. Inland from the coastal beaches, you'll see spacious farmlands, the rolling tussock-covered hills of the Mackenzie Country, and the glacier-gouged Tekapo, Pukaki, and Ohau lakes. Trees planted by English settlers more than a century ago border roads and shade stately homesteads. On the southern boundary, the Waitaki River is marked by a series of massive hydroelectric dams and reservoirs.

Anglers come to South Canterbury for the plentiful trout in the lakes and streams, for the hefty (to 30 lbs.) quinnat salmon migrating up the Rangitata and Opihi rivers in late summer, and for the salt-water fish north and south of Caroline Bay. In winter, skiing and ice skating claim the sports spotlight.

The Canterbury Plains

From Christchurch, the flat Canterbury Plains extend inland to the foothills of the Southern Alps. Viewed from above, the plains form a vast rural patchwork of green and gold farmlands, criss-crossed by country roads and cut by broad rivers. The plains are New Zealand's granary, a rich agricultural region renowned for its wheat, wool, and livestock. Sheep and cattle farms abound. More than a century ago, Australian sheepmen began grazing their flocks on the open plains, and today Canterbury lamb has a worldwide reputation. On the big, isolated sheep stations in the high country, sheep are raised for wool, rather than for meat.

South Canterbury—the essentials

South of Christchurch, farming centers such as Ashburton and Geraldine dot the rich Canterbury Plains. Visitors can relax at the popular beach resort of Timaru, then head inland to explore the lonely Mackenzie Country and the austere but beautiful Waitaki lakes.

Getting there. Christchurch International Airport is the terminus of most flights, though Timaru has a small airfield. From Christchurch, New Zealand Railways and Railways Road Services provide daily train and motorcoach service to main towns along the South Canterbury and Otago coasts. Mount Cook Line motorcoaches serve inland towns between Christchurch and Queenstown (including Geraldine, Twizel, and Cromwell) and also between Timaru and Mount Cook.

Accommodations. Timaru has numerous hotels and motels. Elsewhere in the region, overnight facilities are limited and often modest. You'll find accommodations in Methven, Ashburton, Geraldine, Fairlie, Lake Tekapo, Twizel, and at Lake Ohau. Many farm families welcome overnight visitors (page 124).

Getting around. Motorcoaches provide daily service between the larger towns (see above). Rental cars are available in Christchurch, Timaru, and Ashburton. From Christchurch, you can take a day-long excursion to Erewhon Park.

Tourist information. Canterbury touring information is available at Christchurch tourist offices (page 73). Timaru also has a local Public Relations Office at 7 The Terrace.

The main route across the plains is Highway 1, which crosses the Rakaia River on the country's longest bridge. Massive trees shade the brick buildings of Ashburton, the district's farming center. Anglers fish the Rakaia, Ashburton, and Rangitata rivers for salmon and sea-run trout.

Other routes from Christchurch head west across the plains to Windwhistle, gateway to the Rakaia Gorge and Canterbury lakes. Gouged out by long-departed glaciers, these mountain lakes attract local sports enthusiasts. Lake Coleridge is popular for fishing and boating. In winter, tiny Lake Ida freezes to become a natural outdoor ice rink. There's skiing at Mount Hutt and in the Craigieburn Mountains.

One of New Zealand's best ski areas, Mount Hutt is only 104 km/65 miles from Christchurch. From its slopes, skiers enjoy panoramic views over the Canterbury Plains. Skiing begins in May and continues through November. Whether you're a beginner or an expert, you'll find runs suitable for your level of ability. Rental equipment and ski school lessons are available at the area. Advanced skiers can arrange for guided helicopter skiing in the surrounding basins. There's transportation to the resort from Methven and Christchurch.

Methven, 84 km/52 miles from Christchurch, is a fast-growing resort town serving the Mount Hutt skifield; it's also a base for mountaineering, fishing, and other back-country activities. Jet boat and raft trips travel through the scenic gorge of the nearby Rakaia River.

Timaru, a holiday town

Located midway between Christchurch and Dunedin, the coastal town of Timaru is one of South Island's most popular seaside resorts. An easy, 160-km/100-mile drive across sheep-covered plains southwest of Christchurch, Timaru is a departure point for exploring the spectacular highlands of the Waitaki-Mackenzie Basin.

Built on gently sloping hills facing Caroline Bay, Timaru attracts visitors the year around with its mild climate, fine tourist and conference facilities, and protected beach.

A long breakwater shelters Timaru's artificial harbor, the only port between the Banks Peninsula and Oamaru. Center of a large farming region, Timaru is a major shipping port for the province's grain and meat, as well as home port for a fishing fleet. North of the breakwater, fine sand has accumulated at the old whaling cove of Caroline Bay to form a sweeping beach. Thousands flock here for Timaru's annual New Year's beach carnival.

Laid out by rival surveyors, Timaru has an irregular street grid. Winding Stafford Street follows an old bullock track near the waterfront. Local bluestone was used in the construction of many buildings.

You can stroll along the Centennial Park Walkway, which parallels a stream through the park, or visit the Botanic Gardens bordering Queen Street. Part of the city's scenic drive winds through the gardens; inquire at the Public Relations Office, 7 The Terrace, for a map showing the route. Fine paintings and touring exhibitions are housed in the Aigantighe Art Gallery, 49 Wai-iti Road. At the South Canterbury Historical Museum on Perth Street, you can learn about local history and port development.

In the countryside, more than 200 wild animals roam the rolling hills at Hadlow Game Park. Temuka, just north of Timaru, is known for its earthenware pottery and good fishing streams.

Highway 8 heads up the Tengawai River toward Fairlie. Along the way, stop at Pleasant Point to see a restored steam locomotive and railway museum. In the village of Cave, the old stone Church of St. David is a hand-built memorial to Mackenzie Country pioneers.

Waimate, south of Timaru on the slopes of the Hunters Hills, is the center of a varied agricultural district.

Autumn color in Geraldine

Located inland at the edge of rolling downs, Geraldine once supplied isolated sheep stations. Today it serves a flourishing agricultural district. English settlers planted trees in profusion here—not the pines of the plains, but elm, larch, oak, poplar, ash, and willow. In autumn, the golden foliage is a feast for the eyes. You can picnic beside the Waihi River, which flows through town. From Geraldine Downs behind town, the panorama extends over mountains, across tree-studded plains, and along the coast from the Port Hills south to Waimate.

River gorges. North of Geraldine, roads follow the Orari, Waihi, and Hae Hae Te Moana rivers to historic buildings, riverside picnic areas, and hiking trails.

At Orari Gorge Station, the New Zealand Historic Trust has restored the original homestead buildings. Both Waihi Gorge and Te Moana Gorge have fine recreation sites, and you can swim in the Waihi River. In Pleasant Valley you pass rustic St. Anne's Anglican Church, built in 1862 of pit-sawn native timber. Horses can be rented for saddle trips up the Waihi Gorge. In Woodbury, the slate-roofed, Norman-style St. Thomas' Anglican Church contains carved oak furniture and memorial tablets.

Up the Rangitata. North of Geraldine is Peel Forest park, a pocket reserve of native bush favored for its easy walks, waterfalls, and abundant birdlife. Families picnic and camp here, and anglers fish the Rangitata River. A short distance beyond Peel Forest stand the historic buildings of Mount Peel Station.

West of the coastal hills lies another world, one where treeless expanses of greyish brown tussock extend to the rugged slopes of the Southern Alps. An unpaved road, fording tributary streams, continues another 46 km/ 29 miles beyond to the isolated station of Mesopotamia. This remote sheep run inspired pioneer runholder Samuel Butler to write the classic 19th century satirical novel *Erewhon*, in which he describes the utter loneliness of the rolling tussock country and the dwarfing vastness of mountains and plain.

North of the Rangitata River is Erewhon Park, accessible from Highway 72 at Mount Somers; it caters to

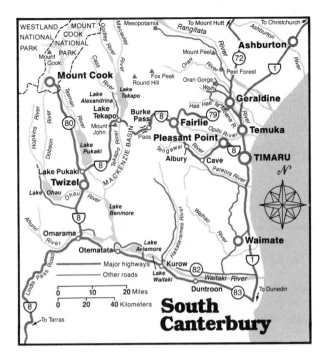

visitors who enjoy the outdoors. Anglers, climbers, hunters, and horseback riders enjoy this remote country in summer; skiers and ice skaters come here in winter.

The lonely Mackenzie Country

This great upland plain first came to general notice in 1855 with the capture of James McKenzie, a Scottish rustler who discovered it while spiriting away sheep stolen from the lowlands. Though sparsely populated, the remote back country supports vast pastoral runs with thousands of hardy sheep.

Set in rolling, tree-dotted downs, Fairlie is gateway to the Mackenzie Country. About 5 km/3 miles northeast is Strathaven Clydesdale Stud, where working teams pull horse-drawn farm implements in much the same way as was done in pioneer days. Fairlie's historical and transport museums offer an interesting look at the past. The Mackenzie Country Carnival is a big event during the Christmas-New Year holidays.

From Fairlie you follow the Opihi River upstream, climbing through a wooded valley to Burke Pass.

As you enter the Mackenzie Country, the transformation is abrupt and total. Spread before you is a vast, shimmering sea of tussock grasslands merging into a distant purple wall of snow-capped peaks. Sunlight glints off the light blue waters of glacier-fed lakes. You'll want to breathe deeply and enjoy the pure air.

The Mackenzie Basin provides access to the high mountains, and its lakes feed the upper Waitaki hydroelectric power project.

The Waitaki lakes. Fed by melting glaciers and snow, the milky turquoise Waitaki lakes occupy the lower ends of glaciated valleys in the shadow of the Southern Alps. Walled in by moraines, these austerely beautiful lakes feed the great Waitaki River.

Lake Tekapo. On still days, Tekapo is a vast mirror reflecting the majestic mountain panorama. Acres of wild lupines in brilliant shades of bluish purple, pink, and yellow brighten the lake shore in summer. During bad weather, savage alpine winds churn the lake into a maelstrom and slice across the exposed hills.

Silhouetted against the mountains, the solitary little Church of the Good Shepherd conveys the isolation and endurance of the Mackenzie Country pioneers in whose memory it was erected. Inside, a large window above the altar frames a splendid view of lake and mountains.

Farther along the shore, a bronze collie monument honors the devoted and hard-working sheep dogs. Atop Mount John are an observatory and a U.S. satellite tracking station.

West of Tekapo, smaller Alexandrina and McGregor lakes offer good trout fishing, swimming, and camping.

Lake Pukaki. Fed by the Tasman River, icy Pukaki points north toward Mount Cook. The scene is a paradox of wild beauty and forbidding solitude—the pale blue lake and golden tussock contrasting with the snow-capped Alps, purpling in the western shadow. The road to Mount Cook National Park follows the western shore of the long lake.

Lake Ohau. Anglers, hikers, boaters, and skiers enjoy this beautiful back-country region. Unpaved roads closely follow Lake Ohau's shore, and trails lead into the nearby beech forest.

The Waitaki Valley

Marking the boundary between Canterbury and Otago, the broad Waitaki River drains the high snowfields of the Southern Alps. Rivers flowing from the Waitaki lakes meet in the Mackenzie uplands above Benmore Dam. A series of dams and canals store and redirect lake waters to the project's power generating stations. As the Waitaki River flows eastward, it broadens into three manmade lakes — Benmore, Aviemore, and Waitaki — and then meets the ocean north of Oamaru.

A side road from Highway 83 leads to an observation area overlooking Lake Benmore, the largest of New Zealand's manmade lakes. The giant 110-meter/360-foot-high Benmore Dam created a vast reservoir bordered by some 110 km/68 miles of shoreline. Power boats and waterskiers cut white swaths, and sailboats glide across the water. Fishing is good, and in summer, visitors can take sightseeing boat trips. Below the dam, a sheltered recreation area attracts picnickers and swimmers.

Farther east, a scenic 19-km/12-mile road loops north from Otematata around Lake Aviemore. Here extensive tree planting and landscaping have softened the harsh effects of construction.

Early wandering hunters and fishermen drew pictures on the rock walls of the Waitaki Gorge; many are now submerged beneath the lakes, but some Maori rock drawings are visible beneath a large limestone bluff just west of Duntroon (signposted over a stile).

Omarama, Otematata, and Kurow are centers for anglers who come to fish in the lakes and in some of South Island's best trout streams. In late summer, migrating quinnat salmon are caught below Waitaki Dam. Omarama also attracts glider pilots, who gather here in summer to take advantage of the area's favorable air currents.

From Omarama, the Lindis Pass Road (Highway 8) follows an old Maori trail south and links the Waitaki Valley with Central Otago. Stretching over the lonely hills are vast sheep stations, some in operation for more than a century.

Gracious, dignified Dunedin

Spread over the hills at the head of one of the country's loveliest harbors, Dunedin was envisioned by its Scottish founders as the "Edinburgh of the South." The Presbyterian settlement was colonized by settlers who landed at Port Chalmers in 1848.

After gold was discovered in Central Otago in the 1860s, the tiny frontier colony thrived. Prosperity ushered in a golden era in architecture, culture, and industry. Dunedin soon became the wealthiest and most influential town in Victorian New Zealand — the model for the rest of the country.

A gracious and dignified city, Dunedin has a special charm. Its Scottish heritage is evoked in its street names and in the sturdy appeal of its handsome stone buildings. You'll find the country's only kiltmaker and whisky distillery here, and a statue of Scottish poet Robert Burns overlooks downtown activity from the Octagon, a small grassy park in the heart of the city.

Getting settled in Dunedin

Dunedin is a planned city, its streets and suburbs fanning out from the Octagon. Bisecting this downtown oasis is Dunedin's main thoroughfare, named George Street north of the park, Princes Street to the south. Most of the major downtown stores, banks, hotels, and restaurants are concentrated along or near this street. Stuart Street branches at right angles from the main street.

You'll find restaurants in the larger hotels and motor inns and others specializing in English, Italian, or continental cuisine scattered throughout the city. For an experience a little out of the ordinary, dine in an atmosphere reminiscent of a turn-of-the-century railway station at Carnarvon Station, housed in the historic Prince of Wales Hotel, 474 Princes Street. Vintage train carriages and equipment combined with handsome architectural features from one of the city's early mansions recall Dunedin's golden age.

Gothic clock tower rises above the slate-roofed bluestone buildings of the University of Otago. The country's first university moved to this site in 1878.

Most evening entertainment revolves around the hotels. Concerts are presented at Town Hall, and visiting artists perform at the Regent Theatre.

A walk around town

If you enjoy exploring a city on foot, you'll like Dunedin's compact central district. In an hour or two, you can stroll many of the downtown streets, enjoy a few of the city's parks and architectural gems, and absorb a bit of Dunedin's history. Ask for leaflets that indicate points of interest.

Many fine Victorian buildings give the city its distinctive character and recall the era when Dunedin was the most important settlement in the country. In older parts of the city, houses reflect the Scottish heritage of its early settlers.

The Octagon. Heart of the city is the grassy Octagon, where you stand beneath aging trees and survey the passing scene alongside the statue of Scotland's bard, Robert Burns. Shoppers pause here to chat, and office workers eat lunch on the grass on pleasant days.

Facing the park are the impressive St. Paul's Cathedral, the Municipal Chambers with its adjacent Town Hall, and the Regent and Fortune theaters. Daily at 12:30, 6, 7:30, and 9 P.M., the Star Fountain puts on a colorful display utilizing water jets, music, and lighting effects.

First Church. Walk east down Stuart Street, detouring a block south on Moray Place for a look at the First Church of Otago. One of the country's finest churches, it was designed by R. A. Lawson, architect of many of Dunedin's most distinctive buildings, and dedicated in 1873. Interior features include a lovely rose window and imaginative plant and animal motifs carved in Oamaru stone.

Railway station. Returning to Stuart Street, continue east past the Law Courts to Dunedin's elegant old railway station, built in 1904. Its facade features granite pillars supporting an arched colonnade, and heraldic lions ornament the copper-lined tower. A delightful touch is the New Zealand Railways' motif (NZR) used with abandon — etched in glass, patterned in mosaic floor tile, even created in stained glass (in the second-floor windows depicting a smoke-belching train).

Early Settlers' Museum. Follow Anzac Avenue south to the Early Settlers' Museum, noteworthy for its collection of vintage vehicles (steam locomotives, a cable car, a Cobb & Co. stagecoach, and Dunedin's first fire engine), old paintings and photographs, and relics of whaling and mining days. The museum is open weekdays from 9 A.M. to 5 P.M., Saturday from 10:30 A.M. to 4 P.M., and Sunday from 1:30 to 4:30 P.M.

Angle a block south on Cumberland Street past Queens Gardens, a tranquil island in a sea of traffic. Then walk west on Rattray Street to the ornate Gothic Cargill Monument at Princes Street.

Dunedin — the essentials

Dunedin is the country's fourth largest city and the capital of Otago, the largest province. A commercial and manufacturing center, a busy port, and a transportation hub, Dunedin is the gateway to Central Otago and the Southern Lakes district.

Getting there. Air New Zealand and Mount Cook Line planes land at Dunedin's attractive airport, located 29 km/18 miles southwest of the city near Mosgiel. Trains and Railways Road Services motorcoaches provide service to Dunedin from the larger east coast towns between Christchurch and Invercargill. Other motorcoaches link Dunedin with inland towns, including Alexandra, Cromwell, Wanaka, Queenstown, and Te Anau.

Accommodations. Downtown accommodations within walking distance of the Octagon include the Town House, City Hotel, Southern Cross, and DB Wain's Hotel. Cherry Court Lodge enjoys a garden setting a few blocks north of the park, and Leisure Lodge borders the Leith waterway near the Botanic Gardens. Pacific Park Motor Inn overlooks the Town Belt and harbor. The Shoreline Motor Hotel is located in south Dunedin. At Larnach Castle on the Otago Peninsula, the stables have been converted to overnight accommodations.

On the North Otago coast, Oamaru has many hotels and motels; small motels are scattered along the coast.

Getting around. A bus tour of the city and Otago Peninsula departs daily at 1:45 P.M. in front of the Government Tourist Bureau. Taxis and chauffeur-driven cars are available in Dunedin for local transport and touring. You can rent cars in Dunedin or Oamaru.

Tourist information. Stop at the office of the Otago Council Inc., 119 Princes Street, for information about Dunedin and Otago province. For travel reservations and tour information, visit the Government Tourist Bureau, 131 Princes Street. Local tourist information is also available in Oamaru.

Classic buildings. Some of the city's well-designed 19th century buildings are still in use in the stock exchange area. Many are constructed of Port Chalmers or Oamaru stone and include interior furnishings of native and imported woods.

Among buildings of special note are these on Princes Street: the 1874 Lawson-designed A.N.Z. Bank, built in classical Greek style; DB Wain's Hotel, built in 1878 and embellished with carvings above its street-level bay windows; and the 1883 Bank of New Zealand, noted for its fine ceiling in the banking hall. Another century-old building is St. Matthews Church on Stafford Street; it contains a rebuilt 1880 organ.

To return to the Octagon, return to Princes Street and walk north for several blocks.

Dunedin's hilly green belt

To fully appreciate Dunedin's harbor setting, head for the hills. Framed between rugged peninsulas, narrow Otago Harbour cuts inland. At its head, Dunedin's buildings rim the water and climb the encircling hills.

Dunedin's planners reserved a band of greenery — called the Town Belt — on the higher slopes of the hills facing the harbor. Queens Drive, a 7-km/4-mile scenic road winding through this wooded retreat, offers motorists and walkers a succession of magnificent vistas.

Favorite close-in viewpoints include Unity Park, Bracken's Lookout (Northern Cemetery), and Southern Cemetery. For sweeping panoramas of Dunedin, the harbor, and the Otago Peninsula, head north of the city to Signal Hill or Mount Cargill.

One of the city walks (map brochure available) takes you through part of the reserve. It starts near Queen and Regent streets and follows Queens Drive north through Prospect Park and the Woodhaugh Gardens.

Other Dunedin highlights

Dunedin's handsome architecture not only delights the eye but also provides tangible evidence of the prosperity and talent that enriched the burgeoning town during the late 19th century. It was then that wealthy residents began assembling some of the country's outstanding collections of art and historical items.

Otago Museum. One of the finest museums in the country, the Otago is noted for its Pacific collections of Oceanian art, Polynesian and Melanesian cultural displays, marine life and maritime exhibits, and fine arts collections. In Maori Hall, you'll see a reconstructed meeting house and storehouse, along with exhibits of Maori wearing apparel, tools, carvings, and greenstone articles. The adjacent Hocken Library is a repository of historic New Zealand books, manuscripts, maps, photographs, and art.

Located at 419 Great King Street, the museum is open weekdays from 9 A.M. to 4:30 P.M., Saturday from 10:30 A.M. to 4:30 P.M., and Sunday from 1:30 to 4:30 P.M.

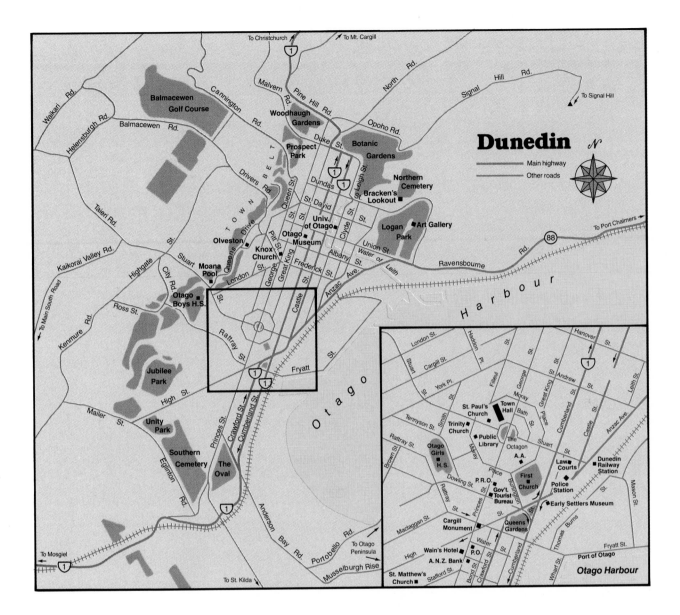

Botanic Gardens. Established in 1868, this north Dunedin showplace is lovely in any season but at its best in spring when the rhododendrons and azaleas bloom in profusion and daffodils pop out of the lawn. Colorful autumn foliage brightens the upper area during April. The main entrance to the gardens is at Pine Hill Road and Great King Street; walking paths wend through the gardens.

Art Gallery. Located in Logan Park, the gallery is noted for the Smythe Collection of watercolors, paintings by Frances Hodgkins, and frequent special exhibitions. The museum is open weekdays and Saturday and Sunday afternoons.

University of Otago. New Zealand's first university was founded in 1869; it moved to its present site 9 years later. Walk through the stone archway and the quadrangle and

savor the old stone buildings, the mature trees, and a placid stream called the Water of Leith. About 7,000 students attend school here.

Olveston. Built for a wealthy and well-traveled Dunedin businessman and bequeathed to the city by his daughter, this 35-room mansion depicts a bygone era of gracious living. The Jacobean-style house, completed in 1906, stands on a landscaped acre and is sheltered by tall trees. A showplace of Edwardian grandeur, the house contains antique furniture, paintings, and elegant household articles shipped here from all parts of the world.

Located at 42 Royal Terrace (at the corner of Cobden Street off Queens Drive), the building is open daily for guided tours.

The beach scene. Sunworshipers head for St. Clair and St. Kilda, two beach communities south of Dunedin. You

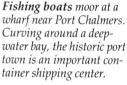

Fishing boats moor at a wharf near Port Chalmers. Curving around a deep-water bay, the historic port town is an important container shipping center.

can watch surfers ride the waves, play a round of golf, swim in a heated salt-water pool, or follow the horses at Forbury Park Raceway.

From St. Kilda, a short, scenic drive cuts across the sand dunes to a lookout at Lawyers Head.

Day trips from Dunedin

Short excursions from Dunedin offer visitors a look at the hilly Otago Peninsula with its numerous attractions, the deep-water harbor at Port Chalmers, and the North Otago coast.

The Otago Peninsula loop

Northeast of Dunedin, the hilly Otago Peninsula offers a delightful rural excursion. Small settlements and week-end cottages dot the harbor's sheltered slopes, in contrast to the wild and lonely beauty of the Pacific side. Dry stone walls, tinted with moss and lichen, lace the peninsula. Sea birds abound, not only the famous royal albatross but also shags, yellow-eyed penguins, godwits, and oystercatchers.

Take the Portobello Road along the harbor, then return along the high road that follows the crest of the peninsula hills to take in panoramic views of the rugged coastline and secluded bays.

Glenfalloch Gardens. Nestled in a fold in the hills above the harbor, this 27-acre woodland garden reflects a century of loving care. The original 1871 homestead still stands. Now owned by the Otago Peninsula Trust, the garden peaks in spring when primroses bloom under English oaks and azaleas and rhododendrons burst forth with color. Bush walks lead up the glen; a small stream trickles down the hill to the harbor.

Larnach Castle. Set in 35 acres of trees and gardens and crowning a wooded hill, this sumptuous residence was built in the 1870s by Dunedin banker W. J. N. Larnach for his first wife, a French heiress.

Building the hilltop mansion far from town was an audacious project. Designed in Scotland, the 43-room neo-Gothic castle took 3 years to build, another 12 to complete the handsome interior. Master craftsmen were brought here from around the world, as were materials—marble and Venetian glass from Italy, tiles from England, woods from many countries. The 40,000-square-foot house required 46 household servants to maintain. Larnach added the 3,000-square-foot ballroom as a 21st birthday present for his favorite daughter.

Furnished in the grand manner, the house is open daily to visitors. After completing your self-guided tour of the interior, take the spiral stone stairway up to the battlements for a commanding panorama from Dunedin across the harbor to the headlands and open coast. Before leaving, stroll through the gardens and visit the dungeons (used by Larnach for storing firewood). The castle's brick-paved stables have been converted to accommodations.

Harborside attractions. The Portobello Marine Biological Station occupies a site facing Otago Harbour. Part of the University of Otago, it maintains a variety of marine life in tanks and pools.

Otakou—corrupted by early whalers to Otago—was the site of an ancient Maori settlement from which the province took its name. A plaque near the water marks the location of the 1830s whaling station. Behind the Otakou Maori Church, built in 1940 to replace an earlier structure, are a small museum and a cemetery. Three important South Island Maori chiefs are buried here.

Albatross colony. The world's largest sea bird — the royal albatross — breeds in a mainland colony at Taiaroa Head at the northern tip of the Otago Peninsula. Adult birds have a wing span up to 3½ meters/11 feet long. During high winds, you sometimes see the giant birds circling above their nesting grounds.

The birds begin to arrive at Taiaroa in early spring. At the beginning of November they build their nests; each female lays a single white egg about 13 centimeters/ 5 inches in diameter. Males and females share charge of the egg during incubation. Chicks hatch in January.

By prior arrangement, small groups may visit the colony from late November through September; best months for viewing are December to May. Inquiries and reservations are handled by the Government Tourist Bureau in Dunedin.

On the peninsula's southeast coast, yellow-eyed penguins come ashore to nest at Penguin Place, and seals bask on a rocky isle just offshore. Access is from Taiaroa Head.

Port Chalmers, Otago's seafaring town

Otago's first settlers arrived by sea, landing at Port Chalmers in 1848. The town faces a sheltered, deep-water bay on Otago Harbour's northern shore about 14 km/9 miles northeast of Dunedin.

Thousands of fortune hunters debarked here in the 1860s on their way to the gold fields. New Zealand's first export cargo of frozen meat was shipped from Port Chalmers in 1882. Antarctic explorers Scott, Shackleton, and Byrd called here on their expeditions to the southern continent.

Today, Port Chalmers's prosperity rests on its modern wharf and container shipping facilities.

Overlooking the town is St. Iona's Presbyterian Church, its spire-topped stone clock tower commanding the skyline. On the headland dominating the harbor stand a restored flagstaff — erected in 1862 to regulate harbor traffic—and a lookout.

Dotting the old seafaring town are numerous 19th century buildings, many of them constructed of Port Chalmers stone. At 55 Harrington Street is Stonehenge, best preserved of four remaining stone houses built in the 1880s. Holy Trinity Church, dating from the mid-1870s, has a hammer-beamed ceiling, stone walls, and an unusual organ. St. Mary's Star of the Sea Church opened in 1878; its interior reflects the town's link with the sea.

The local fishing fleet anchors at Careys Bay, just north of Port Chalmers. At low tide the rotting hulks of several old sailing ships become visible just off the shore of Deborah Bay. The coastal road continues to Aramoana, where vacation homes face an ocean beach; flocks of sea birds feed here.

Along the Otago coast

North of Dunedin, Highway 1 parallels the coast for 125 km/78 miles to Oamaru. Swimming off sandy beaches, river and surf fishing, and other water-related activities draw visitors to the many small beach communities along the coast. Near Oamaru, notice the use of the local white stone in buildings, bridges, walls, and chimneys.

North of Waitati, a coastal road skirting the shore of Waikouaiti Bay offers marvelous vistas and ocean beaches. The pleasant seaside village of Karitane is a holiday retreat for Dunedin families, who come here to swim in the river and ocean, fish, go boating, and frolic on the sandy beach. Near the flagstaff is the homestead of Sir Truby King, a medical reformer who founded the Plunket Society, an organization dedicated to educating mothers in the care of infants.

Otago's oldest European settlement (dating from 1840) and an early port, Waikouaiti today attracts visitors to its sandy beach and coastal bird sanctuary. The settlement has several old churches, and local historic artifacts are displayed in a roadside museum. At Palmerston, Highway 85 (known as The Pigroot) heads inland to Central Otago. Farther north, sea birds congregate on the rocks at Shag Point.

A landmark of the Otago coast, the Moeraki boulders are a geological curiosity. Strewn on the sand along Katiki Beach and north of the fishing village of Moeraki, the spherical, gray rocks weigh several tons each and extend up to 4 meters/13 feet in diameter. Geologists say they were formed on the sea floor millions of years ago when lime salts accumulated around a center core.

The white stone city of Oamaru

North Otago's thriving commercial center is Oamaru, noted for its wide, tree-lined streets and many handsome stone buildings. Built of the local creamy white limestone (quarried at Weston), they give the town its special appearance and unity.

From the war monument in the center of town, walk south along Thames Street to admire the classic stone buildings — among them Brydone Hotel (1880), Waitaki County Council Chambers (1882), Borough Council Offices (1880), courthouse (1883), post office (1884), National Bank (1870), and Bank of New South Wales (1884). The two banks were designed by R. A. Lawson, architect of Dunedin's First Church. Even earlier buildings line waterfront streets.

Public gardens off Severn Street provide a pleasant urban retreat, and on the city outskirts, country lanes cut through large market gardens.

For a view of Oamaru and the surrounding country, take Tyne Street south to Tamar and turn uphill to the lookout reserve.

Golden days in Central Otago

Sun-baked in summer and numbingly cold in winter, "Central" is a grand and desolate region of craggy ranges, stark ravines, fruit orchards, and tawny tracts of wind-rippled tussock stretching toward the distant horizon. Sleepy old mining towns and abandoned stone cottages drowse in the golden sun beneath brilliant blue skies.

Sheep runholders who opened up this parched hinterland in the late 1850s earned their wealth by enduring lonely isolation and hardship. A few years later, prospectors established the first settlements; colorful names bestowed during mining days still identify many towns, hills, and gullies.

Settlers transformed the once-barren landscape by planting trees along river banks and roadways and in windbreaks; in April, travelers delight in the vibrant displays of autumn color visible in the area today.

More recently, dams on major rivers and a network of irrigation channels have made farming feasible and added hydroelectric power. Development is currently underway in the Clutha Valley.

Up the Clutha River

About 60 km/37 miles southwest of Dunedin near Milton, Highway 8 branches off the east coast road and cuts northwest into the bare, brown, and beautiful hills of Central Otago — gold country.

Lawrence. Poplars and birch trees line the highway as you approach Lawrence, a once-raw mining town that has grown old gracefully. Its Victorian buildings reflect its history — prosperity followed by gradual decline. Lawrence lies at the convergence of two gold-bearing streams: Gabriels Gully, where Gabriel Read discovered gold in May, 1861, triggering the Otago gold rush; and Wetherston, also the scene of feverish activity.

Roxburgh. Commercial fruit orchards and a massive hydroelectric power dam dominate Roxburgh's site. Most of the peaches, apricots, apples, and strawberries harvested here are airlifted to northern markets. Sea-

Central Otago—the essentials

You can make a 2-day loop trip from Dunedin into Central Otago, or sample the country briefly as you travel between Dunedin and Queenstown.

Getting there. Railways Road Services motorcoaches provide scheduled service to Clutha Valley towns on routes between Dunedin and Queenstown or Wanaka; you can also travel from Dunedin to Cromwell on the Mosgiel-Taieri Valley-Ranfurly route. Mount Cook Line buses stop in Cromwell on the Queenstown-Christchurch run, and Mount Cook planes link Alexandra with Dunedin and Queenstown.

Accommodations. In Alexandra, the region's major town, you can stay in the DB Golden Central Hotel or in one of several small motels. Cromwell, center of the Clutha Valley hydroelectric project, and Clyde also offer a choice of accommodations. Overnight facilities are available in Ranfurly and Roxburgh.

Getting around. Scheduled motorcoach service offers a glimpse of the country, but you'll need a car to do any exploring. Rental cars are available in Dunedin, Queenstown, Wanaka, and Alexandra.

Tourist information. Stop at Dunedin (page 104) or Queenstown (page 112) tourist offices before you depart. There's also an information center in Cromwell.

sonal pickers converge on the town at harvest time, and "pick-your-own" orchards attract Otago families on weekends. Coal mining at Coal Creek and sheep farming are also important.

Alexandra, hub of Central Otago

Prospectors rushed here after gold was discovered in 1862, but for many years Alexandra was outshone by its twin town of Dunstan (now called Clyde). Gold dredging gave the town a new lease on life in the 1890s.

Today, Alexandra is the hub of a prosperous fruit-growing district. Apricots, peaches, nectarines, plums, cherries, apples, and pears are shipped all over the country. Alexandra's spring blossom festival is a major event. In April, deciduous trees are ablaze with autumn colors.

The small Bodkin Museum, southeast of Pioneer Park on Thomson Street, is open on weekday afternoons. Here you'll see interesting gold mining exhibits, including articles used by Chinese miners.

Near Alexandra, side roads lead up many old gold mining gullies, some now planted with fruit trees. Anglers and water-sports enthusiasts head for trout-stocked reservoirs. In winter, local families enjoy ice skating and curling on the frozen lakes behind Idaburn and Lower Manorburn dams.

North of town, giant Roxburgh Dam holds back the waters of the Clutha River. Behind the dam, a narrow lake extends far upriver; it's a boaters' favorite.

The Cromwell Gorge

Upriver from Alexandra, the Clutha and its tributaries drain the great glacier-carved valleys containing lakes Wanaka, Hawea, and Wakatipu. Joined by the Kawarau River at Cromwell, the Clutha funnels into the rocky Cromwell Gorge. For nearly 20 km/12 miles the deep river flows steadily onward between steep, barren slopes, relieved only occasionally by an orchard.

The character of the Upper Clutha basin is undergoing a major change. Construction has begun on the first of several hydroelectric dams planned for the region. When completed in 1987, the dam at Clyde will create a large lake — to be called Lake Dunstan — that will flood the scenic Cromwell Gorge and widen out above Cromwell. Other dams will be constructed upstream on the Clutha and on the Kawarau rivers.

Clyde. Once a boisterous mining town called Dunstan, the settlement of Clyde still has many of its old stone buildings, constructed with rock quarried during road building through the Cromwell Gorge. Mining memorabilia are on display in Goldfields Museum, located in the 1864 stone courthouse on Blyth Street.

Cromwell. Perched above the junction of the swift-flowing Clutha and Kawarau rivers, Cromwell is the center of the construction project. Completion of the Clyde dam will turn Cromwell into a lakeside town; part of its commercial center will be relocated. The information cen-

ter on Melrose Terrace offers a fascinating look at Cromwell's past—photographs from mining days and artifacts unearthed by project archeologists—as well as details of the region's future as Clutha Valley development unfolds.

From December to May, you can learn about mining methods and equipment—from simple gold pan to massive quartz stamper and dredging machinery — at The Goldminer on Main Street. A walk along the Kawarau River begins in the garden by the bridge.

From Cromwell you can visit several deserted gold towns, marked by abandoned stone buildings, piles of waste rock, and scattered trees. Highway 8 follows the Clutha north to Lowburn and Bendigo. South of Cromwell, unpaved roads lead to Bannockburn and old mining sites in the Carrick Range.

Golden ghosts of the Maniototo

To reach the Maniototo Plains head north from Alexandra up the Manuherikia Valley. Settlements are small and scattered. Side roads lead to sheep stations — some stocked since the 1860s—and old mining sites in the foothills of the Dunstan Mountains and Raggedy Range.

Off the main road are St. Bathans and Naseby, both former gold mining centers and worth a detour. About halfway between Alexandra and the coast is Ranfurly, a farming center and the largest town (population 1,000) on the Maniototo Plains. Highway 85 continues east across The Pigroot, a well-worn route to the gold fields.

St. Bathans. A string of tired Victorian buildings, anchored by the Vulcan Hotel, descends the settlement's sloping street. After the miners left, the excavated valley flooded to form Blue Lake. Years of hydraulic mining created the high, fluted cliffs surrounding the deep pool. Nearby Vinegar Hill and Cambrians also saw extensive mining activity.

Naseby. One of the most attractive of the mining towns, Naseby has a peaceful, unhurried charm. Trees shade most of its streets. Some buildings, including the 1863 Ancient Briton Hotel, are built of sun-dried brick. The Maniototo Early Settlers' Museum has memorabilia of mining days and early curling contests, as well as an outdoor display of vintage vehicles. In summer, Naseby is popular with campers; in winter, visitors come here to ice skate and enjoy the Scottish sport of curling.

Northeast of Naseby, the narrow and unpaved Dansey Pass route twists across the Kakanui Mountains to the Waitaki Valley. Heaped tailings and ragged cliffs identify the Kyeburn diggings. The Dansey Pass Hotel, built in the 1880s, provides refreshments and accommodations for travelers in this lonely region.

Ranfurly. No ghost town, Ranfurly is Maniototo's administrative and supply center. It lies in the heart of a vast inland plain broken only by occasional clumps of pines and poplars. South of Ranfurly are isolated stations and scattered farming settlements, some—such as Hamiltons and Patearoa—dating from mining days. The paved road ends at Patearoa, but a gravel route continues to Paerau (formerly called Styx), where you'll see buildings from the early 1860s. Styx was an overnight coach stop on the Old Dunstan Road at the Taieri River crossing.

Over The Pigroot. East of Ranfurly, Highway 85 is known as The Pigroot, an old coach road that linked Palmerston with the Otago gold fields. Vast, lonely expanses of golden tussock stretch toward distant mountains, and a few rough roads lead off to abandoned digging sites and deserted roadside inns.

Across the Taieri Plain

Before The Pigroot stage road to the gold fields opened in the mid 1860s, miners followed the Old Dunstan Road. Highway 87 parallels part of this historic route west from Dunedin.

Mosgiel district. Colonists who settled on the fertile Taieri Plain prospered during the gold rush by supplying provisions for the miners. With their proceeds the settlers built large homesteads and developed farms where they improved stock breeds and pioneered new farming methods.

Many colonial buildings of the 1860s and 1870s are still in use in Taieri farms and communities. The country's oldest woolen factory, operating in Mosgiel since 1871, was the first major industry on the Taieri Plain. The handsome East Taieri Church is another one of R. A. Lawson's many splendid designs; built in 1869, the brick and stone church is elaborate by Presbyterian standards. The 1877 manse and cemetery are nearby.

Outram. Gold seekers forded the Taieri River at Outram; today, you'll find an attractive riverside picnic area here. Taieri Historic Park features colonial buildings, moved here from other sites. In the town itself are a number of restored 19th century buildings.

The road north. West of Outram, traffic to the gold fields took the hilly Old Dunstan Road. Highway 87 follows the prospectors' route northwest to Clarks Junction; from here the rugged miners' track branches off to climb steeply over the mountains to Paerau (Styx) and other former digging sites.

Highway 87 continues north to Middlemarch, tucked in a valley below the Rock and Pillar mountains, then follows the Taieri River toward Kyeburn. In Macraes Flat, 19 km/12 miles southeast of Hyde, sturdy old Stanley's Hotel still serves thirsty travelers as it has since gold mining days.

Scenic Queenstown

Queenstown, South Island's principal resort, is the hub of the Southern Lakes District, a popular recreation area. Visitors come to Queenstown the year around to enjoy its lake and mountain scenery, exhilarating climate, changing seasons, and varied surroundings.

Born as a canvas town during the Otago gold rush, Queenstown prospered as miners uncovered rich finds in the Arrow, Shotover, and Kawarau rivers. When the easily won gold was gone, most of the prospectors moved on to the new West Coast gold fields, and sheepmen staked out the grassy slopes for vast high-country stations.

Close by are the southern lakes, filling deep troughs scooped out by ancient glaciers. From lakes Hawea and Wanaka in the north to Fiordland's beautiful Te Anau and Manapouri, these tranquil, water-filled valleys lure water-sports enthusiasts and anglers. Another favorite lakeside resort is Wanaka, located at the southern end of Lake Wanaka.

Getting settled in Queenstown

Backed by steep mountains, Queenstown nestles in a curve of Lake Wakatipu at the head of a small, horseshoe-shaped bay. Because it's so compact, Queenstown is a perfect walkers' town; most attractions are near the lake.

Evening activity centers around Queenstown's numerous hotels, which often feature music, dancing, or cabaret entertainment during peak seasons. In winter, après-ski activity is lively in local hotels and pubs.

Since outdoor activities dominate life in Queenstown, most restaurants are relatively casual and specialize in hearty food and generous portions. Tourist or hotel staff can direct you to a variety of restaurants.

For dinner with a view, take the gondola to the restaurant at Skyline Chalet on Bob's Peak and enjoy sunset views over the lake and mountains. If you're seeking historic atmosphere along with your food, consider the elegant Packers' Arms, just north of Arthur's Point; it's housed in a stone-walled inn that first served miners during the 1860s gold rush. For a more informal evening, you can dine in a former miner's cottage at Roaring Meg's, 57 Shotover Street.

A stroll around town

Tourist activity centers around the mall at the foot of Ballarat Street, a busy and colorful block where you'll find information and tour-booking agencies, major stores, and several of the town's historic buildings. Eichardt's Hotel, at the foot of the street facing the lake, began serving thirsty travelers in 1871.

Perpendicular to the mall, Marine Parade borders the waterfront. You board the hydrofoil or Kawarau jet boat at the small pier, where children toss bread to tame trout and greedy ducks swimming below. Along the gravelly shore, benches shaded by weeping willows invite you to pause and enjoy the scenery and lake activity.

Lake Wakatipu. Shaped like an elongated S, Lake Wakatipu fills a deep and narrow 83-km/52-mile-long glacial trough. Rugged mountains rise abruptly around its shore. Third largest of New Zealand's lakes, it's noted for its seiche action—a rhythmic oscillation in water level that rises and recedes as much as 13 centimeters/5 inches within 4 or 5 minutes. Scientists say the oscillation is due to mountain-funneled winds or changes in atmospheric pressure. Maori legend claims the motion is caused by the heartbeat of a giant at the bottom of the lake.

Lakeside parks. You'll enjoy a stroll through Government Gardens, a wooded park on a peninsula jutting into the lake and separating Queenstown Bay from Frankton Arm. A small stone bridge arches across the park's lawn-bordered pond. You can watch lawn bowlers in summer. St. Omer Park offers a grassy lakeside promenade along the bay beyond the steamer wharf.

City attractions. Upstairs in the Shotover Arcade on Beach Street, the Sound & Light Museum presents a 30-minute audio-visual show re-creating the sights and sounds of Queenstown in the 1860s.

Vintage touring and racing cars, motorcycles, and pioneer aircraft—all in working order—are on exhibit at the Queenstown Motor Museum on Brecon Street, just below the gondola terminal. The museum is open daily.

Grand old lady of Lake Wakatipu is the coal-burning Earnslaw, *last of the steamship fleet that once cruised the lake. Trips depart from Queenstown from late October to mid-May.*

Queenstown district—the essentials

Water sports, fishing, and back-country trips attract summer vacationers; in winter, skiing is the main lure. Since Queenstown is popular with visitors throughout the year, travelers are wise to make advance reservations, particularly during the school holidays (page 17), on long weekends, or during the ski season.

Getting there. Mount Cook Line flights link Queenstown's airport with most of the country's large cities and major resorts, and Mount Cook motorcoaches travel daily between Christchurch and Queenstown. Railways Road Services motorcoaches offer scheduled service to Queenstown from Dunedin, from Milford and Te Anau, from Invercargill, and from the West Coast glacier area via Wanaka.

Accommodations. Major Queenstown hotels include the Travelodge, on Beach Street near the steamer wharf; Lakeland Resort Inn, a 10-minute walk from town on the Lake Esplanade; Country Lodge on Fernhill Road; and Hyatt Kingsgate on Frankton Road. Smaller hotels include the Vacation (O'Connells), Wakatipu, and Mountaineer Establishment, all centrally located; and Hotel Esplanade, terraced above the water facing Frankton Arm. Among many excellent motels are the A-Line Motor Inn and the Ambassador, Lakeside, and Modern motels. Arrowtown has several small motels.

Accommodations at Wanaka include the fine THC Wanaka Hotel overlooking the lake, as well as numerous motels. A pleasant campground borders Lake Wanaka at Glendhu Bay.

Getting around. Numerous excursions departing from Queenstown invite visitors to explore the countryside by bus, plane, or four-wheel-drive vehicle, on horseback, or on foot. Rental cars are available in Queenstown and Wanaka.

Tourist information. You can make travel and accommodation reservations at the Government Tourist Bureau, 49 Shotover Street. Information on tours and excursions is available at booking offices facing the Mall at the foot of Ballarat Street. For information on Mount Aspiring National Park, stop at the park's visitor center in Wanaka.

Panoramic viewpoints and walks

The steep slopes rising from the lake offer spectacular views of Queenstown, Lake Wakatipu, and the sawtooth peaks of The Remarkables along the eastern shore.

Take a gondola ride up Bob's Peak in a four-seat bubble car to the Skyline Restaurant and adjoining tearoom, housed in a glass-walled mountainside chalet perched high above the lake. To reach another popular

viewpoint, start at Deer Park Heights, a game reserve near Frankton (page 115). The chair lift ride to the summit of Coronet Peak provides a splendid view over the river basin, Crown Range, and other towering peaks.

If you want some exercise as well, take the trail up Queenstown Hill behind town or the longer trek up Ben Lomond. Other tracks lead up river valleys to old mining sites. Tourist officials can suggest routes you'll enjoy.

Excursions from Queenstown

Using Queenstown as your touring base, you can explore this historic district by boat, plane, motorcoach, four-wheel-drive vehicle, gondola, chair lift—even by horseback. Your main problem may be deciding what to do first among the bewildering array of activities.

Popular excursions fill rapidly, so book early. Some tours are seasonal; others require a minimum number of participants. You can obtain current tour information and make reservations at booking offices bordering the Mall at the foot of Ballarat Street.

Sightseeing by bus and plane

After you've explored Queenstown on foot, it's time to venture farther afield.

Half-day bus excursions depart from Queenstown for Coronet Peak, Skippers Canyon, Arrowtown, Waterfall Park, Deer Park Heights, and Goldfields Town. A full-day trip follows the lake road from Queenstown to Glenorchy and on to the Routeburn Valley.

For another full-day sightseeing trip, you can depart from Queenstown on the early Railways Road Services bus, travel through farming country to Te Anau, continue on the Milford Road to Milford, have lunch and take a launch trip on Milford Sound, and return to Te Anau by dinner time (or continue back to Queenstown, if you prefer).

Scenic flights departing from Queenstown's airport fly over Lake Wakatipu and the rugged mountainous country to the west. On a round-trip flight to Milford Sound, you pass over the Milford Track and experience eye-level views of Sutherland Falls and snowy peaks. Helicopter flights range from short trips over Queenstown to an excursion into the high peaks of The Remarkables.

Boat trips galore

You can cruise Lake Wakatipu on a sturdy old steamship, speed across the water on a hydrofoil, skim through scenic river gorges in a jet boat, float leisurely with the current aboard a raft, glide silently in a canoe, or charter a boat for a few hours of fishing.

Lake steamer. The grand old lady of the lake is the T.S.S. *Earnslaw,* a white-painted, coal-burning steamship that

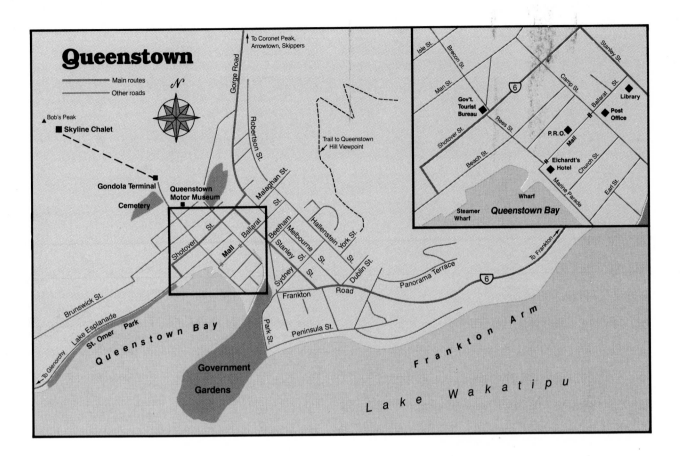

made her debut on Lake Wakatipu in 1912. Last of the steamship fleet that once plied the lake, she makes morning and afternoon cruises to Mount Nicholas Station and a lunch cruise up Frankton Arm from late October to mid-May. A dinner cruise is added in summer.

Jet boat trips. Several Queenstown operators offer an array of exciting trips on Otago's historic gold-bearing rivers. You can shoot white-water rapids through the narrow canyon of the Shotover River or skim the waters of the Kawarau River through the Kawarau Gorge. One excursion combines jet boat travel on both rivers.

If you crave even more excitement, you can choose an outing combining a jet boat ride with helicopter sightseeing, river rafting, or a hydrofoil trip.

Hydrofoil. Departing from the wharf at the foot of the mall, the 17-passenger hydrofoil *Meteor III* takes passengers on a one-hour, 40-km/25-mile cruise on Lake Wakatipu. Speeding along smoothly on its foils with its hull above the water, the boat passes lakeside sheep stations and mountain scenery in the upper reaches of the lake. During school holiday periods, shorter trips depart at frequent intervals.

Raft and canoe trips. From September through May, you can raft down the Shotover or Kawarau rivers on trips ranging in length from 2 hours to a full day. Or you can paddle your own canoe on a 3-hour safari down the

Kawarau. Without noise or fuel fumes, you float downstream past pine-studded cliffs and grazing livestock as you savor views of the valley and distant mountains. Overnight rafting trips on more remote rivers are also available (page 114).

Fishing expeditions. If fishing is your passion, you can charter a boat and guide for a few hours or a full day of trolling on Lake Wakatipu or fly-fishing on one of the local rivers. All equipment is provided by the guide.

Exploring the rugged back country

Four-wheel-drive vehicles provide access to some of the district's scenic and unspoiled valleys. You can raft down remote rivers or ride horseback to old mining areas.

Skippers Canyon. Best known of the back-country excursions is the trip up historic Skippers Canyon. The narrow, single-lane road snakes high above the Shotover River, where a century ago miners panned for gold. Rock monoliths jut above the craggy terrain. Intense sun scorches the parched valley in summer; biting winds and snow ravage the gullies in winter.

You'll see stretches of the pack horse trail to the Upper Shotover gold fields and part of the narrow road built by Chinese workers, who were lowered over the cliff to hammer out the route. Occasionally, you pass the dilapidated remains of a long-abandoned building.

Slender poplar trees in brilliant gold rim Lake Hayes. In autumn, you'll see foliage displays around Queenstown, Arrowtown, and Wanaka.

Other day trips. From Queenstown you can also arrange excursions by four-wheel-drive vehicle to Moke Lake, the ghost towns of Macetown and Sefferton, and up the Rees and Dart river valleys. Most trips stop for billy tea (brewed in a can over an open fire); day-long trips include lunch.

Trail riding. Escorted trips on horseback follow trails used by miners more than a century ago. On half-day and full-day excursions, you ride up the Shotover Gorge and —on longer journeys—into the Moke Valley to the site of Sefferton. Other trips traverse the Wakatipu farmlands.

Hiking and rafting excursions. Danes Back Country Experiences (P.O. Box 230, Queenstown) offers longer outback safaris that explore the remote valleys of the Upper Shotover, Matukituki, Hunter, Dart, Rees, and Landsborough rivers. Operated between October and April, the trips range from 2 to 5 days in length. Participants are transported into the valleys by four-wheel-drive vehicle or helicopter, then continue on foot or by raft. Groups camp in tents and cook over open fires.

See a cattle show

A good opportunity to learn about New Zealand's beef and dairy industry is at the Cattledrome 7 km/4 miles north of Queenstown. Shows are held daily at 9:30 A.M. and 2:15 P.M. at the exhibition center on Skippers Road. You'll see trained pedigreed cattle walk to their places on stage and watch cows being milked with glass milking machines. You can even try your own hand at milking.

Coronet Peak—for skiing and scenery

In winter, Queenstown turns into an alpine skiers' paradise. The challenging terrain of Coronet Peak, an easy 19 km/12 miles north of Queenstown, offers excellent skiing from mid-June until October.

Facilities at Coronet Peak are among the best in Australasia. A double chair lift transports skiers from the cafeteria-restaurant at 1,140 meters/3,800 feet to the 1,650-meter/5,400-foot summit. A triple chair lift provides access to the expert slopes, and other lifts take novice skiers to learners' areas. One fine days, you'll see many skiers soaking up the sun from the restaurant deck.

Coronet Peak has a ski shop and ski school; you can rent skis, boots, and poles in town or at the ski area. Skiers find ample accommodations and plenty of après-ski activity in Queenstown; during ski season, regular coach service operates between Queenstown and the ski area.

In summer, sightseers take the chair lift to the summit station, then climb to a glassed-in viewpoint for a breathtaking panorama over the Lake Wakatipu region and the Southern Alps. On chilly days, army greatcoats help ward off the biting wind during your ride.

A new warm-weather attraction is Cresta Run, a 600-meter/1,800-foot stainless steel toboggan run. Adventurous riders maneuver one or two-passenger toboggans down the curving slide beneath the chair lift.

Mining memories linger in Arrowtown

The 20-km/12-mile trip to Arrowtown is a diverting one. Memories of gold rush days come to mind as you cross the Shotover River and pass rebuilt 1860s inns still serving travelers. Side roads lead to Skippers Canyon and Coronet Peak. As you drive through the peaceful Wharehuanui Valley, you may meet a herd of cattle ambling along the road.

Mellow old Arrowtown has a lively past. After gold was discovered in the Arrow River, a midwinter flood in 1863 wiped out the riverside canvas town. Permanent stone and wooden buildings were built on higher ground; many have been converted into shops. A former bank, thickwalled and barred, houses the mining and pioneer memorabilia of the Lakes District Centennial Museum.

Century-old sycamores form a shady canopy over upper Buckingham Street and its wooden cottages. You'll find the empty Arrowtown jail off Cardigan Street. If you stroll the upper streets, you'll discover old stone buildings mortared with river sand, dry rock fences, attractive village churches, and clapboard houses with pillared porches and ornamental ironwork.

Gravestones in the cemetery record poignant tales of early death—miners who drowned in floods, children "too gentle for this bustling world." You can picnic along the river or under the willows by Bush Creek.

Horseback treks depart from Arrowtown on half-day excursions up the Arrow River; full-day trips continue on to Macetown.

Return to Queenstown past Lake Hayes, its glassy surface reflecting the pastoral countryside and mountain backdrop. Poplar trees ringing the lake turn brilliant gold in autumn.

Along Frankton Arm

East of Queenstown, Highway 6 skirts Frankton Arm, outlet of the Kawarau River into Lake Wakatipu. A small zoological garden borders the river near its outlet. The Kelvin Peninsula marks the arm's southern shore.

Located 3 km/2 miles east of town on the Frankton road, Goldfields Town seeks to re-create life in a mid-19th century mining village. Typical gold rush buildings are furnished in period style. Outside displays feature mining equipment and old vehicles.

One of the best views of the lake district comes from a private game reserve atop Deer Park Heights on the peninsula. Plan ahead — to enter the reserve you'll need to purchase a token at the Queenstown Public Relations Office or at small grocery stores in Frankton.

From Frankton, the road to Deer Park Heights climbs to a viewpoint high above Frankton Arm. On the drive you'll see several kinds of deer, as well as thar, chamois, mountain goats, and wapiti (elk), roaming the grassy park. From the summit you look down on Queenstown, nestling in its own bay, and mountains rising steeply around the rim of Wakatipu's waters. Coronet Peak looms high over pastoral valleys and several small lakes.

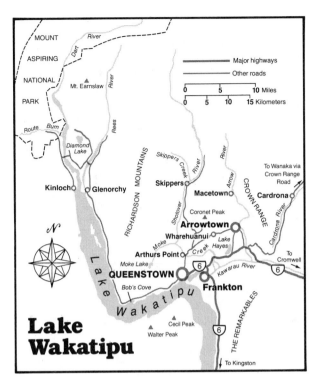

Visit a sheep station

You can combine a cruise on Lake Wakatipu with a visit to a high-country sheep and cattle station. Located on the far shore of the lake and inaccessible by road, the isolated stations are reached from Queenstown by station launch or the steamship *Earnslaw*.

Homesteaded during the 1880s, the stations now cater to day visitors from Queenstown. Homestead buildings have been restored or rebuilt and furnished with articles of historic interest. Visitors learn about the station's past and current farming activities, enjoy tea (or a meal on longer trips), tour some of the early buildings, and watch demonstrations of shearing and wool spinning. You'll also see sheep dogs at work.

Trips operate the year around to Cecil Peak Station (overnight accommodations also available) and Walter Peak Station; launches transport visitors from Queenstown Wharf. Visitors to Mount Nicholas Station board the *Earnslaw* for the trip across the lake; this excursion operates from late October to mid-May.

Hiking the Routeburn Track

Queenstown is the departure point for hikers following the Routeburn Track, a 40-km/25-mile alpine trail winding through the magnificent country of Mount Aspiring and Fiordland national parks. The trail cuts along river valleys and through untouched beech forest, past cascading waterfalls and saucerlike alpine tarns, and across a challenging 1,280-meter/4,200-foot mountain pass. Portions of the trail are exposed and can be dangerous in bad weather. Huts provide overnight shelter for hikers.

The track is usually open from mid-November to late April, though snow may still cover parts of the trail early in the season.

You can hike the trail independently or with a guided group from either end—beginning at road's end north of Kinloch or from the Divide on the Milford Road near the Hollyford junction. You can arrange to connect with hiking trips on the Milford or Hollyford tracks.

For those who prefer not to carry a heavy pack, Routeburn Walk Ltd. (P.O. Box 271, Queenstown) conducts 4-day guided excursions over the trail. Hikers carry only their personal gear; all food, utensils, and sleeping equipment are provided. Parties are small — usually 12 hikers and 2 guides. Huts at Routeburn Falls and Lake Mackenzie are complete with down sleeping bags, mattresses, and hot showers.

The Wanaka country

Many travelers know Wanaka only as a brief stopover on the Haast Pass route linking the West Coast with Otago and South Canterbury destinations. Other visitors linger to indulge in the lake resort's amenities and sports facilities. Wanaka draws water-sports buffs who come to boat, swim, water-ski, and fish on long and narrow Lake Wanaka, neighboring Lake Hawea, and their tributaries.

Wanaka. Clustered at the southeastern end of Lake Wanaka, the resort faces glacier-molded hills. For an overview, walk from the business district to the lookout above town, in front of the white war memorial. Outside town, the 3D Maze of intricate passageways is a popular family attraction.

In season, you can arrange for lake sightseeing and fishing trips, raft trips on the Clutha River, and scenic flights. Rental bicycles, boats, and fishing equipment are available. At the Gin and Raspberry Stables in the Cardrona Valley, you can rent horses for day or overnight treks through the historic gold fields.

In summer, Wanaka is the departure point for hikers heading into Mount Aspiring National Park (page 99). Winter visitors head for the ski fields at Treble Cone and Cardrona, and for heli-skiing in the Harris and Richardson mountains.

Day excursions. Short drives lead to sheltered Albert Bay, pleasant for a picnic and afternoon swim, and to Glendhu Bay and West Wanaka, center of water-sports activities. Willows and poplars along the lakeshore form an attractive golden border in autumn. Hiking trails lead up Mount Iron and Mount Roy.

Lake Hawea is a favorite of anglers for its rainbow trout and landlocked salmon. Many boat owners come here in summer to escape Wanaka's crowds. Small vacation homes hug the cliffs above the shoreline.

Crown Range Road. A scenic alternative to Highway 6 from Wanaka to Queenstown is Crown Range Road (Highway 89), an unpaved 70-km/44-mile route (closed in winter). Not recommended for nervous drivers, the road wends south from Wanaka through the Cardrona Valley, passes Cardrona's sagging old hotel, and continues to the summit of the Crown Range. From the crest you survey the entire Wakatipu Valley. The road then plunges in zigzag curves to the valley, where it crosses the Arrow River and meets Highway 6 northeast of Queenstown.

All aboard the Kingston Flyer

Every summer a shrill whistle and the hiss of escaping steam herald the approach of the Kingston Flyer, New Zealand's vintage steam train, as it chugs leisurely through the wooded hills and farm country south of Lake Wakatipu. Children wave as the train passes scattered homes and villages, and grazing sheep scurry in alarm as the smoke-belching engine nears.

Beginning in the 1880s and continuing for many years, express passenger trains transporting tourists to scenic Lake Wakatipu and its surrounding mountains provided fast service between Gore and Kingston via Lumsden. A few years ago a pair of the old coal-fired locomotives and some of the historic dark green carriages were brought out of retirement, carefully restored, and redecorated to 1920s elegance.

You can choose your seat in the combined first-class car and guard's van, the "birdcage" or gallery carriage, the refreshment car, or the passenger carriages. Brasswork gleams and woodwork is varnished to high luster. Match-striker plates, ornate luggage-rack brackets, and gas lamps add a nostalgic touch. The traditional spittoons have been removed, though, and in some carriages horsehair seats have been replaced with foam-padded vinyl. You can buy light refreshments and souvenirs in the refreshment car.

From October to mid-May, the Kingston Flyer makes three round trips daily between Kingston and Fairlight. Each one-way trip takes about 25 minutes.

Rugged, remote Fiordland

New Zealand's largest and most remote national park, Fiordland encompasses the entire southwestern corner of South Island. Incredibly beautiful and wild, the region is an intriguing combination of rugged mountain ranges, dense rain forest, solitary alpine lakes, sparkling rivers, and splashing waterfalls. Majestic fiords indent its western coast. Much of Fiordland is virtually unexplored wilderness, still inhabited by such rare birds as the takahe and kakapo.

Sports enthusiasts come here for boating, hiking and climbing, fishing for trout and salmon, and hunting deer and wapiti. You can arrange for fishing or hunting guides. and for float planes to transport your party to one of the remote lakes. Many visitors enjoy scenic flights and launch trips; others join hiking groups on the Milford, Hollyford, or Routeburn tracks.

Te Anau, gateway to Fiordland

Largest of the southern lakes is Lake Te Anau, which marks Fiordland's eastern boundary for some 60 km/38 miles. Its three long fingers probe deeply into the park's thickly wooded mountains. Near the lake's southern end is the town of Te Anau, gateway to this wilderness country and base for excursions south to Lake Manapouri and Doubtful Sound and north to Milford.

From Te Anau, visitors can cruise on the lake, visit a glowworm cave, or go flightseeing. If you prefer more leisurely pursuits, you can rent a bicycle, stroll along the lake shore, or enjoy a day of fishing or golf. Arrangements can be made in town for guided back-country fishing or hunting trips. To see some of Fiordland's rare birds, including the takahe, visit Te Anau's wildlife park.

Te Ana-au Caves. Launches make regular trips the year around from Te Anau to the glowworm caves. Located about 16 km/10 miles north of Te Anau on the far side of the lake, the site can be reached only by boat.

Maoris probably discovered and named this "Cave of Rushing Water," but it was not rediscovered until 1948. Geologically young, it's known as a "living cave," since the limestone cavern is still being eroded. A powerful underground stream cascading from Lake Orbell continues to hollow out the limestone cliffs of the Murchison Mountains.

A short boat ride takes you into the cavern, where lighted walkways guide you past frothing waterfalls and limestone formations. A punt transports visitors along the cave's underground river into the glowworm grotto.

Boat trips. Jet boat and rafting trips depart from Te Anau for the Upper Waiau River. You can enjoy white-water thrills on the jet boat excursion, drift leisurely down Fiordland's largest river aboard a raft, or even combine the two.

Fiordland—the essentials

Spectacular scenery and outdoor activities attract visitors to this corner of New Zealand. You'll find few commercial diversions here. The region's most accessible destinations are majestic Milford Sound and the lakes of Te Anau and Manapouri.

Getting there. Mount Cook Line planes connect Te Anau with major South Island cities and resorts; flights operate on demand, weather permitting, between Queenstown and Milford, less often between Te Anau and Milford. Railways Road Services buses travel to Te Anau from Dunedin, Queenstown, and Invercargill, and provide daily service to Milford from Queenstown and Te Anau.

Accommodations. Te Anau, headquarters for most Fiordland excursions, offers a variety of accommodations, including the THC Te Anau Hotel, Vacation Hotel, and Campbell Autolodge (all facing the lake), Fiordland Motor Lodge, and Luxmore Inn. At Manapouri, most motorists stay at the DB Manapouri Motor Inn.

On the Milford Road, accommodations are available at the Te Anau Downs Motor Lodge at Te Anau Downs, 27 km/17 miles from Te Anau, and at Cascade Lodge at Cascade Creek. Campsites with fireplaces and toilets are located along the Milford Road. Facilities at Milford are limited to the THC Hotel Milford, facing the sound, and the Milford hostel, used mainly by Milford Track hikers.

Getting around. Scheduled motorcoach service links the main destinations. Scenic Fiordland flights depart from Te Anau; anglers and hunters can charter float planes for trips to remote lakes and fiords. Weather permitting, small planes fly between Queenstown and Milford and between Te Anau and Milford, offering a spectacular aerial view of the lush and rugged country. Many Milford visitors travel one way by road, the other by air.

Boat trips and other excursions depart from Te Anau, Manapouri, and Milford. Rental cars are available in Te Anau for independent exploring.

Tourist information. Details on excursions are available from Fiordland Travel Ltd. or Mount Cook Travel Bureau in Te Anau. For information on Fiordland National Park campsites, trails, and activities, contact park headquarters in Te Anau.

From November to early April you can take a trip to the head of Lake Te Anau. A motorcoach delivers visitors to Te Anau Downs; the trip continues aboard a launch to Glade House, start of the Milford Track. You return later in the day by the same route.

It's possible to arrange launch or water taxi trips from Te Anau to such lakeside destinations as Gorge Falls, on the lake's south fiord, or Brod Bay (for swimming, picnicking, a nature walk, or a hike up Mount Luxmore). Yacht charters can be arranged for one-day or overnight trips exploring Lake Te Anau's fiords, bays, and islands.

Flightseeing excursions. Several carriers operate scenic flights over this rugged countryside by float plane, land-based aircraft, or helicopter. You fly above the lakes and rivers, through uninhabited valleys, and over thick forests and hidden waterways to the western fiord country. Helicopters transport hikers and skiers to Mount Luxmore.

Float plane and helicopter trips depart from the Te Anau lakefront; other flightseeing excursions leave from the Te Anau/Manapouri Airport.

Aerial views of Fiordland National Park, its splendid scenery, and the recovery of live deer by helicopter are shown in an audio-visual program at the Fiordland Flights Theatre, 90 Te Anau Terrace.

Fishing and hunting trips. Experienced guides are available for one-day or longer fishing and hunting trips into Fiordland National Park. Permits, available at park headquarters in Te Anau, are required to hunt in the park. Chartered float planes transport anglers and hunters to remote sites.

Fiordland National Park

Less than 15,000 years ago this region was locked in thick ice. Glaciers sculpted the land on a larger-than-life scale, gouging out long, narrow lakes, carving out coastal fiords, and shearing high mountain valleys. Captain James Cook sailed along the coast in 1770 and returned here in 1773, putting in at several fiords and anchoring at Dusky Sound for rest and ship repair.

The best of Fiordland lies off the roads, to be experienced in solitude, on foot or by boat. The region's appeal is not only in its awesome beauty but also in its isolation and challenging terrain.

Park headquarters is in the town of Te Anau (P.O. Box 29, Te Anau; phone Te Anau 819); the visitor center is open daily. Permits for backpackers planning an independent trek on the Milford Track (page 119) are available here.

At the visitor center you'll learn about park wildlife, accessible attractions, and current activities. Nature programs are scheduled in summer. You can also get current information here on road, trail, and weather conditions.

By air to Milford

You can reach Milford by air over the rugged Fiordland wilderness, through mountain valleys along the Milford Road, or on foot along the Milford Track. Each approach offers an unforgettable experience.

The flight over Fiordland to Milford Sound gives travelers a thrilling perspective of this rugged and remote region. It's a good idea to book space ahead, especially in summer.

In Queenstown or Te Anau, you board a small plane for an aerial look at Fiordland's mountains, forests, and waterways. You fly over the route of the Milford Track, gazing down on hikers' huts along the trail, past 580-meter/1,904-foot Sutherland Falls plunging in a spectacular triple cataract from Lake Quill's glacier-carved basin, then down the Arthur Valley to land at Milford's small airstrip.

After a brief stop, your plane returns by a different route, soaring high for a bird's-eye view of world-famous Milford Sound, then flying between crinkled icy peaks and down alpine gorges that broaden into river plains.

The memorable Milford Road

If you travel from Te Anau to Milford by car or bus, you'll follow the 119-km/74-mile Milford Road (Highway 94), an alpine route cutting through some of New Zealand's most untouched country. The route is maintained in good condition; a section about 20 km/12 miles long—from Cascade Creek over the Divide to Marian Corner—is graded gravel. During bad weather, the road may be closed temporarily due to snow, ice, or flooding. You can get current road information and a leaflet describing roadside points of interest at Fiordland National Park headquarters.

If you're driving, plan to leave early so you can have a leisurely trip. Allow at least 2½ hours for the journey to Milford—more if you want to stop or make side trips. By late morning, fast-moving buses speeding along the route raise clouds of dust on the unpaved parts of the road. Camping vans and trailers are not permitted beyond Cascade Creek.

The Eglinton Valley. From Te Anau you follow the shore of Lake Te Anau north to Te Anau Downs, then veer up the broad wooded valley of the Eglinton River, popular for fly-fishing. Beech-covered mountains frame a view of distant peaks, and colorful lupines brighten the valley floor in summer. You'll find picnicking and camping sites scattered throughout the valley.

You pass the tiny Mirror Lakes, where photographers capture mountain reflections in calm weather, before arriving at Cascade Creek, the only travelers' oasis (rustic accommodations, meals, gasoline) between Lake Te Anau and Milford. If you want to stretch your legs, take the short self-guided nature walk that begins across the creek from the lodge.

Continuing past lakes Gunn, Fergus, and Lochie, you cross the Divide, the lowest pass (534 meters/1,752 feet) in the Southern Alps. From here hikers depart for Lake Howden and the Routeburn and Greenstone tracks to Lake Wakatipu.

Down the Hollyford Valley. A side road follows the Hollyford River, a sparkling stream that empties into the Tasman Sea at Martins Bay. About 8 km/5 miles from the highway at Gunns Camp, a small museum displays a fascinating collection of mementos, old photographs, and yellowed clippings on various aspects of Fiordland lore

Float plane lands on Milford Sound, rippling the mirrored reflection of Mitre Peak. Visitors can fly over the fiord or cruise past waterfalls all the way to open sea.

— ill-fated settlements, legendary local characters, shipwrecks and plane crashes, early Milford Track hikers, the construction of the Homer Tunnel.

From late October to mid-April, guided groups take the Hollyford Valley Walk from road's end to Martins Bay. You hike the first 14 km/9 miles, then travel by jet boat about 38 km/23 miles down the lower river and across Lake McKerrow. Groups bunk in comfortable riverside lodges. At Martins Bay you can visit a seal colony, see sites of pioneer settlements, or go fishing or beachcombing. Participants on the 4-day trip depart on a scenic flight terminating at Milford Sound. On the 5-day excursion, hikers retrace the valley route by jet boat and on foot. For more information, contact Hollyford Tourist & Travel Co. Ltd., P.O. Box 216, Invercargill.

Through the Homer Tunnel. Mountains crowd closer as you climb toward the Homer Tunnel, a rough-hewn bore piercing the Darran Range. Sharp-eyed travelers can spot signs of glacial activity and avalanches.

Formerly restricted to one-lane travel, the tunnel is now open to two-way traffic. Turnouts at both ends of the tunnel allow motorists to pause and enjoy the scenery. Walks lead from parking areas through natural alpine gardens, where wildflowers bloom in December and January.

Cleddau Valley. West of the tunnel, the switchback road descends the steep upper Cleddau Valley. Sheer walls rise from the valley floor; after a rain, the cliffs are curtained by waterfalls. About 7 km/4 miles below the tunnel, a signposted trail leads to the Chasm. Take the 5-minute walk through beech forest to a railed platform overlooking the turbulent Cleddau River as it thunders through a narrow rocky gorge and drops in frenzied cascades on its route to the sea.

"The finest walk in the world"

Hikers find the Milford Track more than just a scenic adventure — it's a total experience. Thousands have traversed this wilderness trail between Lake Te Anau and Milford Sound. Yet each feels a sense of achievement gazing down from the summit of Mackinnon Pass or catching the first glimpse of awesome Sutherland Falls.

Trampers experience many of the same challenges the pioneer Milford hikers did in the 1890s — rivers to be crossed, a mountain pass to be conquered, the caprices of rain and weather to be endured. Yet today's walkers take

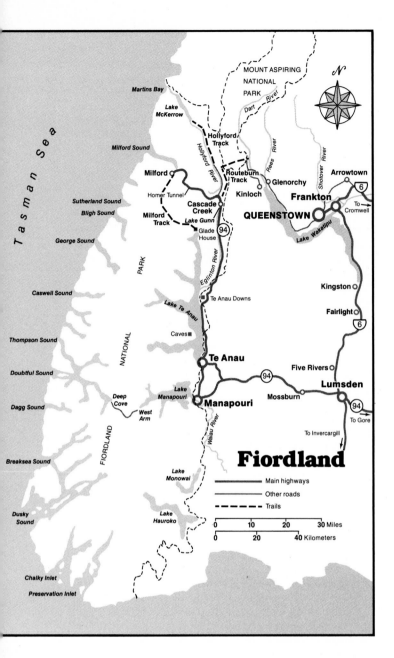

Fiordland

Main highways
Other roads
Trails

| 0 | 10 | 20 | 30 Miles |

| 0 | 20 | 40 Kilometers |

Organized group trips. From mid-November through March, parties depart Te Anau three times a week (daily in midsummer) on the 53-km/33-mile tramp to Milford Sound. Along the route hikers stay in huts equipped with bunks, electricity, hot showers, and toilet facilities. Meals are provided.

You must book space months in advance (through the New Zealand Tourist Office) for these popular 5-day excursions. Hikers carry only clothing and personal articles needed on the trail; "city clothes" are sent ahead.

Along the Milford Track. Hikers depart from Te Anau by motorcoach, then cross Lake Te Anau by launch to reach Glade House, start of the trail.

Though it is "good going," the trail is challenging even in fine weather, for you must ford numerous streams and cross a 1,067-meter/3,500-foot alpine pass. In bad weather, it's a difficult and demanding route, even for experienced, physically fit hikers.

The trail is divided into three sections; hikers do a section a day at their own pace. From Glade House the route climbs through native beech forest along the Clinton River to Pompolona Hut. Next day comes the most challenging part of the trip: a steep climb through open alpine country to Mackinnon Pass, followed by a switchback descent to Quintin Hut. From here, a trail leads to the bottom of famous Sutherland Falls. On the final day of hiking, you follow the Arthur River downstream, skirting Lake Ada, to Sandfly Point, where a launch transports hikers the final step across Milford Sound. The trip ends after lunch the following day at Milford.

The grandeur of Milford Sound

Milford Sound leaves an indelible impression in the memories of many travelers. Far from any population center, it's a destination renowned solely for its beauty.

From the head of the fiord, one of New Zealand's classic views unfolds before you. Steep granite peaks, wooded on their lower slopes, frame the glacier-carved inlet and cast mirrored reflections on its dark, calm waters. Dominating the scene is the triangular pinnacle of mile-high Mitre Peak, Milford's landmark. Along the sheer cliffs, several waterfalls tumble more than 150 meters/500 feet into the sheltered sound. Only a few moored boats and a scattering of buildings at the head of the sound break the unity of mountains, forest, and water.

The grandeur of Milford's unspoiled setting is best appreciated from the water. Launches depart from the Milford wharf several times daily on 1 and 2-hour cruises; if you have time, take the longer trip—it goes all the way to the open sea. You'll glide past Mitre Peak and glacier-topped Mount Pembroke. Spray blows over you as the boat noses close to Stirling and Bowen falls. Often, you'll spot a seal or two basking on sun-warmed rocks.

Overnight visitors can experience Milford's quiet moods. In early morning, shafts of sunlight pierce the mist to illuminate Mitre Peak. At day's end, pastel sunset

for granted comforts beyond the dreams of those early tourists, one of whom called this footpath through Fiordland "the finest walk in the world."

You can hike the track independently, packing all your equipment and supplies, or join a group and carry only personal items. Trail access is controlled by Fiordland National Park headquarters in Te Anau (P.O. Box 29, Te Anau; phone Te Anau 819). Since only a limited number of independent hikers (called "freedom walkers") are permitted on the Milford Track, advance reservations are necessary. Because of variable weather and trail conditions, only experienced hikers with proper equipment are allowed on the trail. All hikers walk the track in one direction—from Lake Te Anau to Milford Sound.

tints streak the cloud-strewn sky. In any season, passing clouds can bring drenching rainstorms, which create dozens of new waterfalls.

Information on walks is available at the hotel reception desk. The Bowen Falls trail begins near the wharf and follows the shore along the cliff face; wear a raincoat or waterproof parka. The Lookout Track starts behind the hotel. A 5-minute climb gives you a view over the hotel to the water. Beyond this point, you'll need agility and sturdy footwear to clamber over exposed roots and rocks on the slippery slopes.

Island-studded Lake Manapouri

Many New Zealanders consider Manapouri, south of Te Anau, the most beautiful lake in the entire country. Thick forests border its meandering shoreline, and some 30 bush-clad islets stud its expanse of blue. Flanking the lake on three sides are high mountains, their snow-tipped peaks mirrored in lake waters.

Boat excursions depart from Pearl Harbour on the Waiau River. You also can rent a rowboat or arrange for water taxi service here. A favorite destination for a beach picnic is Stockyard Cove, one of the lake's loveliest bays, where you can walk through conifer forest.

From Manapouri you can take a half-day trip to the power station at West Arm, or a full-day excursion that continues on to Doubtful Sound for a cruise on this unspoiled fiord. Trips operate daily from late August to mid-May, three times weekly in winter.

Manapouri Power Station. To visit the power station, visitors cross the lake to West Arm, where a bus whisks them down a steep, spiraling tunnel to the powerhouse, 213 meters/700 feet below ground. Hewn from solid rock, it houses seven turbines, each driving a powerful generator. Water from the lake enters vertical penstocks, plunges through the turbines, and then is channeled through a 10-km/6-mile-long tailrace tunnel for release into the sea at Doubtful Sound, located on the other side of the mountains. The station furnishes power for the aluminum smelter at Bluff.

On to Doubtful Sound. Construction of the power station opened up some of New Zealand's most spectacular scenery. Visitors can now see at close hand virtually untouched country.

From the power station, travelers board a motorcoach and ride on an upgraded construction road over 671-meter/2,200-foot Wilmot Pass to Deep Cove on Doubtful Sound.

Here you board a launch for a 2-hour cruise on Doubtful Sound, one of the region's most majestic fiords. Noted by Captain James Cook (as Doubtful Harbour) in 1770, it is 10 times larger than Milford Sound. As you cruise into Hall Arm, you'll gaze at vertical cliffs thrusting high into the sky. Mighty waterfalls plunge over the sheer rock faces. In fine weather, mountains and greenery are reflected in the protected waters of the fiord.

On foot in Fiordland

Fiordland's tracks offer opportunities for hikers to escape urban pressures and enjoy the special qualities of this intriguing area.

The types of country you can traverse here vary greatly, but the tramps have much in common. Routeburn concentrates on the high country (above sandfly level); Milford ranges from open alpine terrain to lush rain-forest valleys; Hollyford is a low-level river track. Their proximity and complementary nature make it possible to combine two—or all three—walks on an extended hiking vacation.

A hiker's adventure. Hiking the Milford or Routeburn track is a tramping adventure, not a tourist excursion. The trip can be difficult for the inexperienced or out-of-condition hiker; sections of the trail are demanding and strenuous, particularly in foul weather.

On the trail you enter a remote world almost untouched by man. Dwarfed by gigantic mountains, you follow a twisting track through dense forest, across alpine grasslands, along swift-flowing rivers, and past cascading waterfalls. Naturalists delight in the varied flowers, trees, ferns, and shrubs. Tumbling streams glint in the sun like molten silver, and only the liquid trill of a forest songbird or the shrill call of a kea breaks the quiet.

You cross the deeper streams on suspension bridges or large fallen trees; smaller streams are forded. Be prepared for wet weather; a short rainstorm can suddenly deepen creeks and create dozens of new waterfalls.

Along with your trail companions you'll carry a "cut lunch" and share "scroggin," a high-energy mix of nuts, raisins, and ginger, and hot "billy tea" brewed from the water of snow-fed streams. Evenings are a time for the comfortable camaraderie of shared experiences.

Keep your pack light. If you're joining one of the group trips, you'll receive a recommended packing list. Each hiker carries personal gear; you can rent a backpack, but your own will probably be more comfortable.

One hiker's formula: "Be prepared for bad weather, carry a minimum amount of clothing, and be very fit." You'll want a waterproof hooded jacket and comfortable footwear. Lightweight boots (well broken in), worn with two pairs of woolen socks, provide shock absorption and traction. A complete change of warm clothing and underwear is essential insurance against a downpour.

Miscellaneous equipment includes a small flashlight, adhesive tape, sunglasses, and insect repellent. Milford hikers can purchase evening refreshments and small items at hut shops.

Exploring Southland

Though whalers roved the southern seas as early as the 1840s and pastoral runholders had claimed most of Southland's grazing lands by the 1860s, real settlement got a late start in this region. During the Otago gold rush, most Southland residents prospered only indirectly by providing food and other supplies for the miners.

Southland's future lay in less spectacular but more enduring assets — primarily its rich grasslands, but also its timber and coal reserves. Wool and meat are exported from here to markets around the world; dairy products add their share to Southland's wealth. Mills began to ship timber to Dunedin in the 1860s, and coal has been mined in the Ohai-Nightcaps district since 1880.

Though legally Southland has no provincial standing, its boundaries cover the southernmost part of South Island, skimming the south shore of Lake Wakatipu and stretching from the east coast to the western fiords. Off the South Island "mainland" is unspoiled Stewart Island.

Roaming the interior

Between Lake Wakatipu and the south coast, only scattered small farm towns break the open plains. Sheep and cattle munch on the rich grasslands; they'll provide wool and meat for the export market. Deer farming is an increasingly important industry. Anglers come here to enjoy well-stocked trout streams, among them the Aparima, Oreti, and Mataura rivers.

From the junction town of Lumsden, highways radiate in all directions — north to Queenstown, west to Te Anau and Milford Sound, south to Invercargill, and east to Gore and Balclutha. Near Mossburn to the west, red deer browse in the tussock and manuka at the West Dome Deer Ranch.

Coal mines. West of Winton, rich deposits of coal in the foothills above Ohai and Nightcaps have been mined for nearly a century. Coal from underground and open-cast mines fuels many Southland industries. For more information stop at the state Coal Mines Office in Ohai.

Southern Fiordland. Lying near the Waiau River in limestone cave country, Clifden is the gateway to Lake Hauroko and southern Fiordland. At the Fiordland National Park ranger station in Clifden you can obtain trail information and hunting permits.

One of the park's southernmost lakes, Hauroko occupies a wild and beautiful bush setting. There's a camping area near the park boundary. Trails beginning near road's end follow the lake shore and lead into the park. Remains of a Maori burial cave have been discovered on Mary Island.

Timber country. Tuatapere, a timber town in the Waiau Valley, is the principal lumber milling center for Otago and Southland markets. Anglers come here to fish for trout and salmon. You can picnic or camp in a wooded park on the riverbank. On New Year's Day, axmen from around the country converge here to compete in wood-chopping contests.

Country driving offers the unexpected. Here, drivers meet a flock of sheep on the road. Sheep dog (at far right) maneuvers strays with the rest of the group.

Hokonui Hills. Southland's second largest town is Gore, surrounded by lush rolling pastures and fields of grain. West and south of Gore are the Hokonui Hills, for decades synonymous with illicit whisky. The Scottish sheepmen who settled this district brought with them knowledge of whisky distilling, as well as a taste for the brew. Until World War II, moonshiners and Customs officials engaged in a continuous battle of wits over the stills.

South of Gore, at the foot of the hills, Dolamore Park has a pleasant, forest-rimmed picnic area and trails winding through the bush. The Mataura Plain farther south is cattle and dairy country; its main centers are Mataura, Edendale, and Wyndham.

The southeast coast

From Balclutha, center of the rich South Otago sheep farming area, Highway 92 follows a slow and winding coastal route southwest to Invercargill. Side roads turn off to unspoiled beaches and seaside points of interest, some best observed at low tide. An unpaved stretch of roadway cuts through nature reserves where trees and ferns spill down to the sea.

South of Balclutha, you can follow a scenic coastal road to Port Molyneux, where you'll enjoy a magnificent view. Kaka Point is a favorite family vacation retreat just north of the lighthouse at Nugget Point.

In Owaka, farming center of the Catlins district, the small Catlins Historical Society Museum on Waikawa Road contains displays on whaling, early industry and transport, and other facets of the region's colorful history.

South of Owaka, side roads lead to Jacks Bay Blowhole, impressive at high tide and in stormy weather, and to Penguin Bay, where in late afternoon penguins come ashore to nest in the bush. An easy walk through beech forest takes you to Purakaunui Falls, where a stream cascades over a series of broad terraces. Farther south, Tautuku Beach is a superb sandy strand backed by trees.

Southeast of Chaslands, a steep trail leads down to Waipati Beach and the Cathedral Caves. Accessible only at low tide, the interconnected, high-ceilinged sea caves cut far back into the cliffs. Check tide times before exploring and take a flashlight if you plan to venture into the caves.

Visible at low tide, Curio Bay fossil forest contains the petrified logs of a subtropical forest, buried by volcanic ash millions of years ago. When the land mass re-emerged from the sea, waves cut the sandstone to reveal the petrified stumps and broken logs.

At the east end of Toetoes Bay, hidden reefs extend beyond the Waipapa Point lighthouse to mark the eastern entrance to Foveaux Strait.

Invercargill, Southland's market center

Thriving economic center of Southland, Invercargill spreads across the open plains along the New River estuary. The city shares Dunedin's Scottish origins. Broad

A & P shows— a warm look at rural life

Enjoy a festive glimpse of New Zealand's rural life style by attending one of the Agricultural & Pastoral Society shows held in farming communities throughout the country. Most take place on Saturdays from October through March. Tourist information offices, local newspapers, and word-of-mouth alert you to upcoming shows.

The smaller A & P shows are the most fun. From outlying farms and ranches, families bring their prize livestock, produce, and handmade crafts to the show grounds. Activities are informal, and the whole family participates.

Early in the day, most men congregate near the livestock exhibits, where they stand in small groups discussing the merits of different breeds of sheep and cattle. Youngsters nervously groom their animals before the livestock judging and riding events. In the exhibit building, women arrange their preserved and baked goods, sewing and knitting projects, garden produce, and cut flowers. Children's art work is displayed on the walls.

Sheep dog trials and horse-jumping events are afternoon highlights. Burly wood choppers and skillful sheep shearers have their own competitions. Food vendors, amusement rides, and displays of new farm equipment vie for attention. Children scamper about trying to see everything at once.

Later, thirsty participants may gather at a local pub to rehash the day's events.

streets—many named for Scottish rivers—and numerous parks mark its level site.

Invercargill was a busy river port during the late 1850s and 1860s, but during later decades Bluff gradually gained dominance as the principal coastal shipping port. Today, Invercargill is New Zealand's eighth largest city and the market center for the surrounding district. Ringing the city are massive freezing works that prepare fat Southland lambs for world markets.

Lovely parks enhance Invercargill's appeal. The city's showplace is Queens Park, a large reserve north of the business district. Its magnificent gardens flourish in Southland's equable climate. In season you'll enjoy extensive displays of irises, rhododendrons, and roses. Tropical plants thrive under glass in the Winter Garden. Nearby, sleek bronze animal statues rim the shallow children's pool. Sunday concerts attract families in summer.

Stay with a farm family

Spending a night or two with a hospitable farm family is a wonderful way to meet New Zealanders. Throughout the country, congenial families open their homes to visitors who want to sample the friendliness of farm life or just relax for a few days in a rural setting. Other than during the main holiday periods, arrangements can usually be made on short notice.

A farm visit offers a relaxing change from the usual hotel room and fast-paced touring itinerary. In addition to getting acquainted with a friendly Kiwi family, you also get a first-hand look at the backbone of the country's economy. Some stations have been farmed for more than 100 years.

Usually you stay in a cozy guest room in the family homestead (frequently, though not always, with private bath) and eat hearty, country-style meals with the family. During informal evenings at home, you share conversation with your host family. Most families take only a few guests at a time to keep the experience on a personal level.

If you like, you can join in farm chores and watch sheep dogs go through their paces. Perhaps you'll want to lend a hand with the mustering, join the haying crew, learn to operate a spinning wheel, observe sheep shearers at work, or ride along with your host to the local stock sale.

If you prefer, you can use the farm as a base for touring or just relax on the veranda.

Other activities vary by station—often you can ride horseback around the farm, fish for trout in a nearby stream, go swimming, hunt for deer in the hills, or picnic out in the countryside.

Accommodations range from farms just a few miles from main roads and country towns to high-country stations off the beaten track. If you're traveling by public transport, your host family can usually meet you at the nearest sizable town.

You can obtain details on individual farms and arrange for accommodations at offices of the Government Tourist Bureau in major New Zealand cities (page 12). Of the organizations promoting farm visits, the largest is Farm Holidays Ltd., P.O. Box 1436, Wellington; they also have reservation centers in Auckland and Christchurch.

Sports fields include an 18-hole golf course, hockey and cricket grounds, lawn bowling and croquet greens, and tennis and squash courts.

Near the southern boundary of Queens Park, the Southland Centennial Museum and Art Gallery contains excellent displays on the region's Maori culture and natural history, as well as collections of whaling and pioneer relics and Victoriana.

The City Art Gallery is located in Anderson Park, about 7 km/4 miles north of Invercargill. Works by early and contemporary New Zealand artists hang in the former home of Sir Robert Anderson, whose family gave the city the house and its well-tended gardens and surrounding bush.

Other parklands lie south of the main shopping district, where greenery lines Otepuni Creek as it flows through the city, and near the city's northern boundary. Here, Thomsons Bush, an 85-acre scenic reserve of native trees, borders the upper Waihopai River; in summer, you can rent canoes and paddle along the quiet stream.

Horse racing is presented at Southland Racecourse, on the city's eastern boundary, throughout the year.

Along Foveaux Strait

The protected waterways and coastal beaches lining Foveaux Strait are Southland's playground. Just west of Invercargill, weekend boaters race, row, and water-ski on the long, straight stretches of the Oreti River and New River estuaries, and anglers cast for trout. Yachts and power boats cruise the strait and its sheltered bays.

Beaches border Foveaux Strait from the estuary west to Riverton. On warm weekends and during long summer twilights, local families converge on Oreti Beach west of Invercargill. Toheroas are taken from the beach during the short winter clamming season.

Riverton exudes the mellow charm of an unpretentious seaside resort; families come here on holiday, particularly during the New Year carnival period. Fishing boats and pleasure craft moor along the estuary's south shore. Flanking the seaside road to Howells Point are The Rocks, a local landmark. Farther west on Highway 99, the village of Colac Bay faces the strait and Centre Island.

Bluff and the southern tip

Built on a natural harbor, Bluff is Southland's seafaring town. The port is a major meat and wool exporting center. Storage tanks and coolstores rim the sheltered inlet. Ferry service links Bluff with Stewart Island.

Across the water on Tiwai Point gleam the silver buildings of the large Comalco aluminum smelter. Oxygen is extracted from aluminum oxide shipped here from Queensland, Australia, and the molten aluminum is cast; some is alloyed with other metals before being exported. The Manapouri power project (page 121), developed in conjunction with the smelter, provides the massive amounts of electricity needed for the process.

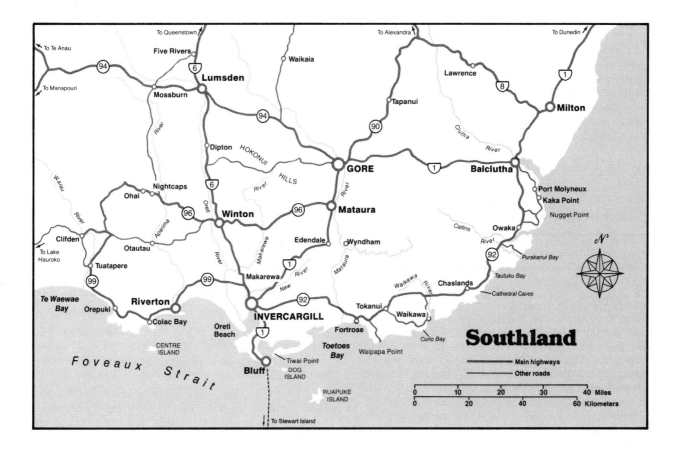

Bluff is home port of a large commercial fishing fleet, including the sturdy boats that dredge Foveaux Strait for the succulent Bluff oysters. The country's oyster lovers anxiously await the opening of the March-to-August season; the shellfish are air freighted from here to all parts of New Zealand.

Houses cover the low slopes of Old Man Bluff, the hill that gave the town its name. Turn uphill by the post office and follow the road to the summit, where a wind-swept panorama over Bluff Harbour and the town, sprawling Southland plains, and Foveaux Strait islands opens before you.

Highway 1 ends at Stirling Point lookout, where a signpost gives kilometer distances to various worldwide points. A walking track begins at road's end; the 2½-hour Foveaux Walk follows the coast as it winds around the bush-covered bluff toward the island's southern tip. It gives fine views across Foveaux Strait to Stewart Island.

Unspoiled Stewart Island

Separated from South Island by the waters of Foveaux Strait, Stewart Island is less a destination than a way of life. For residents and visitors alike, its attractions lie in its virtually untouched beauty, glowing skies, and unhurried pace. Time is unimportant; only the tide governs daily activities. You'll find few cars, few roads, and little tourist development here. Most of the island is a nature reserve, rich in birdlife.

Since warm currents sweep eastward through Foveaux Strait, the island, about 32 km/20 miles from the mainland, enjoys a mild — if frequently wet — climate despite its southerly latitude; temperatures are seldom very high or very low. But on the southern tip, raw icy blasts sweep north from the Antarctic. Year-round rainfall provides most of the island's water supply. Brilliant dawns and sunsets streak these southern skies, and occasionally the aurora australis — the "southern lights" — adds special radiance.

Visitors come in all seasons, but most prefer the summer months, when the whole island is alive with native birds and the scent of flowers perfumes the air. But even in winter the skies retain their glow, and coastal waters lure fishing enthusiasts.

First impressions

Mountainous and heavily forested, Stewart Island is roughly triangular in shape, and about 60 km/40 miles long and 30 km/20 miles wide. Steep, wooded promontories rise sharply from the clear waters. Many fine harbors and beach-rimmed coves indent its irregular shoreline. Off the coast lie numerous islets, including the Mutton-bird (Titi) Islands off the southwest cape, where Maoris traditionally collect many young birds each autumn.

Stewart Island's only sizable settlement is Halfmoon Bay (also called Oban), a fishing settlement bordering a scenic bay. Low buildings ringing the bright blue water blend into the wooded hills behind. Sheltered from westerly winds by the island's forested ranges, the tranquil village basks in the sun. Only a tiny stretch of the northern coast has been touched by roads and habitation.

Southland—the essentials

At the country's southern tip, Invercargill is the region's commercial center and largest town. South of Bluff, across Foveaux Strait, is unspoiled Stewart Island, a popular summer destination.

Getting there. Air New Zealand flights land at Invercargill's airport, about a 5-minute drive west of the business district. The Southerner train and Railways Road Services motorcoaches provide regular service to Invercargill from Christchurch, Dunedin, and other east coast towns. Motorcoaches also link Invercargill with the lake resorts of Te Anau and Queenstown.

Stewart Island, about 32 km/20 miles from the mainland, is a 15-minute flight from Invercargill or a 2½-hour ferry trip from Bluff.

Accommodations. Most travelers stay in Invercargill, where accommodations include the centrally located Kelvin Hotel, the gracious older Grand Hotel, Don Lodge Motor Hotel, and Ascot Park Hotel/Motel. You'll also find many smaller hotels and motels in town. Anglers on fishing forays to Southland rivers may want to make Gore their headquarters. Bluff's small hotels cater to travelers taking the Stewart Island ferry.

On Stewart Island, you'll find simple but comfortable accommodations at the South Seas Hotel, the world's most southerly pub; the small Rakiura Motel; and well-equipped camping vans at Ferndale Caravan Park. Cabins and campsites are available at Horseshoe Bay. There's also a youth hostel on the island. Summer accommodations on Stewart Island must be booked months ahead.

Getting around. Trains and motorcoaches stop in Milton, Balclutha, and Gore on east coast routes; buses also serve the inland towns of Winton and Lumsden on routes to the lake resorts. Anglers and hunters can charter float planes for trips to remote lakes. Taxis and rental cars are available in Invercargill.

On Stewart Island, visitors can take a short coach tour of the main settlement and nearby attractions; in summer, a launch trip operates to Ulva Island.

Tourist information. Visitors can obtain local information at the office of the Southland Progress League, Oreti House, 120 Esk Street, Invercargill.

The island has about 450 permanent residents; many are descendants of European whalers who intermarried with the island's Maori inhabitants. They ride their fishing boats westward into the heavy swells in search of the crayfish and cod that provide the residents' main source of income.

Most visitors come for just the day; to experience the island's special appeal, though, plan to stay for several days. A mini-bus transports visitors on a short tour of the northern hills and bush-fringed bays.

Stewart Island Museum, on Ayr Street near the shore, contains a fascinating collection of relics from the island's past, when whaling, sealing, and timber milling were the main industries. You'll also see exhibits of island plants and birds.

Exploring the island

To enjoy Stewart Island's special attractions, you'll want to explore its coastline and forest reserves.

Cruising the coast. In summer, regular launch trips operate for fishing and sightseeing. You can also charter a launch for a day of cruising; inquire at the general store on the waterfront or check the notice board outside.

Only a thin strip of land divides Halfmoon Bay from Paterson Inlet, the large, landlocked harbor on the northeastern side of the island. Wooded to the water's edge, the inlet is a favorite of sailboats and other pleasure craft. You can cruise into Price's Inlet — perhaps stopping to see relics of a Norwegian whaling base at Surveyors Bay—or venture farther up Paterson's southwest arm.

Enchanting Ulva Island, near the inlet entrance, is a popular stopping point. Its sandy beaches are ideal for a picnic; trails wind through unspoiled forest, and birdlife abounds. Nearby Native Island was the site of a Maori settlement.

Hiking island trails. Numerous walking tracks hug the coastline and cut through the bush. Shellhounds head for Ringaringa Beach, about a mile from Halfmoon Bay, or for Horseshoe Bay. Other easy walks lead to Garden Mound or Lee Bay; day-hike destinations include Butterfield Beach, Golden Bay, Thule, and the lighthouse.

Ambitious hikers enjoy the walking tracks in some of the more remote and wild parts of the island. Forest Service huts offer overnight shelter on the longer routes; you bring your own food and equipment and replace the firewood you use.

The island has a wealth of unique native plants and rare birds. Rimu, rata, miro, and totara trees stretch skyward from the mossy floor. All birdlife is protected; you may see tuis, parakeets, bellbirds, kakas, and perhaps a rare weka or kiwi searching for insects in the dense undergrowth. Deer also roam the island.

Information on island trails is available at the Forest Service information center at Halfmoon Bay. A light waterproof jacket and sturdy footwear come in handy any time of year.

Index

Maori entertainers perform in Rotorua, where visitors can tour Maori villages, learn about their crafts, and sample foods at a hangi *feast*.

Islands of the
SOUTH PACIFIC

By the Editors of
Sunset Books and
Sunset Magazine

Lane Publishing Co.
Menlo Park, California

Cascade *of snowy feathers marks lesser bird of paradise, one of many colorful species brightening Papua New Guinea's tropical forests.*

Acknowledgments

We are grateful to the many people and organizations that helped in the preparation of this travel guide. We wish to acknowledge the assistance and cooperation of the editorial staff of *Pacific Travel News,* especially Phyllis Elving, James Gebbie, Jane Keator, and Victoria Wolcott.

For assistance on individual countries, we thank the following:

American Samoa: The Office of Tourism, especially Vaeotagaloa Maaka Nua. **Cook Islands:** Cook Islands Tourist Authority, especially Ian Fogelberg; and Anne DeWolfe, Air New Zealand, Los Angeles. **Easter Island:** LAN-Chile Airlines. **Fiji:** Fiji Visitors Bureau, especially Sitiveni Yaqona; and John and Joan Holmes, Holmes Associates. **Kiribati:** Broadcasting and Publications Division, Chief Minister's Office; and N.P. Jones, Manager, Otintai Hotel. **Lord Howe Island:** Lord Howe Island Tourist Center. **Micronesia:** Guam Visitors Bureau, especially Martin Pray; Marianas Visitors Bureau, especially J. M. Guerrero; Economic Development Division, Trust Territory of the Pacific; Mike Ashman, Pacific Area Travel Association, San Francisco; and Tom Talamini, Daily and Associates, San Francisco. **Nauru:** Office of Consulate General of Nauru, San Francisco, especially Carlton Skinner. **New Caledonia:** Office du Tourism, especially Bruno Tabuteau. **Vanuatu (New Hebrides):** Tourist Information Bureau, especially Joe Mulders. **Norfolk Island:** Norfolk Island Tourist Board; and Australian Tourist Commission, New York. **Papua New Guinea:** Office of Tourism, especially David Bamford; and Peter Barter, Melanesian Tourist Services. **Solomon Islands:** Solomon Islands Tourist Authority, especially Bara Buchanan; C.B. Grey, Air Niugini; and Jack Banley, Guadalcanal Travel Service. **Tahiti and French Polynesia:** Tahiti Tourist Development Board, especially Patrick Picard-Robson; Charlotte Hyde and Loretta Iannalfo, Transportation Consultants International, Los Angeles. **Tonga:** Tonga Visitors Bureau; especially Semisi Taumoepeau; and Charlotte Hyde and Loretta Iannalfo, Transportation Consultants International, Los Angeles. **Tuvalu:** Office of Ministry of Commerce and Natural Resources. **Western Samoa:** Western Samoa Visitors Bureau, especially Vensel Margraff.

Research and Text: Joan Erickson
Supervising Editor: Cornelia Fogle

Special Consultant: Frederic M. Rea
  Editor & Publisher, Pacific Travel News

Design and Illustrations: Joe Seney

Cover: Over-the-water thatch hotel bungalows on Tahiti stand silhouetted against vibrant colors of South Seas sunset. Photographed by Morton Beebe.

Sunset Books
  Editor, David E. Clark
  Managing Editor, Elizabeth L. Hogan

Fourth printing July 1987

Contents

ISLANDS OF THE SOUTH PACIFIC

Mention the South Seas, and myriad enchanting tropical images float through your mind. Picture yourself strolling along a palm-shaded, white sand beach beside a lagoon so dazzling blue it hurts your eyes. Pause in the mist below a cascading waterfall, then plunge into its greenery-rimmed pool for a swim. Saunter down a curving path bordered by lush plants laden with blooms. At sunset, linger to enjoy the glowing skies as they fade into twilight. Everywhere you are greeted by friendly people whose relaxed life style you sometimes envy.

Immortalized in song and art, in poetry and prose, the islands of the Pacific have lured travelers for generations. Today, you can explore these islands yourself to experience their bewitching allure and beauty.

Three Regions

Strewn across the sun-warmed waters of the vast Pacific—the earth's largest ocean—lie thousands of tropical islands whose charms have been recounted by generations of travelers. Scattered between the Tropic of Cancer and the Tropic of Capricorn, these islands generally are divided into three regions—Polynesia, Melanesia, and Micronesia.

Nesia means island. Polynesia translates as *many islands,* an apt description of the numerous islands bounded within the Polynesian triangle. Melanesia means *black islands,* a name derived from the darkness of island vegetation or the dusky skin tones of the region's inhabitants. Micronesia, or *small islands,* concisely describes the diminutive islands in this Pacific area.

Mountain peaks, coral atolls

Island topography varies within Polynesia, Melanesia, and Micronesia. You'll find mountainous volcanic islands with craggy, towering peaks, deep valleys, broad plains, and rushing streams, contrasted with low patches of coral with a few palm trees and no running water.

High islands. The high islands are exposed summits of partially submerged volcanoes. Some thrust numerous jagged peaks out of the sea; others are no more than lumps of rock. Most of the high, volcanic islands are drained by rushing rivers that tumble into dramatic waterfalls or empty into broad flatland swamps. Protective coral reefs usually surround at least part of the island.

Low islands. These are coral reefs or atolls built by coral polyps. Ring or horseshoe shaped, most of them enclose salt-water lagoons. Some low islands are nearly submerged; others are uplifted coral masses.

Colorful flora, interesting fauna

The rich fertile soil of the high islands supports the most abundant tropical vegetation, but you'll find fascinating plant life on most of the Pacific islands.

A host of brilliant blossoms brighten the islands—fragrant frangipani and plumeria, cascading flamboyants, multihued orchids, and carpets of bougainvillea. The people of these tropical lands adorn themselves with flowers, tucking blooms in their hair and wearing floral leis around their necks.

The islanders enjoy the fruits of island plants such as breadfruit and mangoes, and weave the leaves of the pandanus into fine mats and baskets as well as walls for their thatch-roofed houses. The coconut palm provides both food and building materials.

In addition to fascinating tropical flora, the Pacific has interesting wildlife. Of particular note are tropical birds such as the multicolored birds of paradise in Papua New Guinea and New Caledonia's *cagou* bird, a rare flightless bird that barks like a dog.

Marine life, of special interest to snorkelers and scuba divers, features multihued coral gardens and a dazzling array of colorful tropical fish.

Island People

You'll also find variety in the peoples of Polynesia, Melanesia, and Micronesia. Each island group has its distinctive physical characteristics, languages, social systems, and dress. Yet all Pacific peoples have one thing in common—the sea. The sun, winds, tides, and dependence on the ocean for food influence their attitudes and ways of life.

Early migration

The people of Polynesia—brown skinned with straight hair—live within the archipelagoes of a vast triangle extending from Hawaii southwest to New Zealand and eastward to Easter Island. Melanesia's people—dark skinned with curly hair—occupy islands on the western fringe of the South Pacific. On the small Micronesian islands in the northwest Pacific, you'll find a variety of brown-skinned people with Malaysian and Polynesian traits.

Ancestors of these island people migrated to the different regions from Asia by way of the Malay Peninsula. The first to migrate were the Melanesians, who may have settled in New Guinea as early as 8000 B.C. Next to arrive were the Micronesians. Carbon dating indicates the Marianas were inhabited by 1500 B.C. The final group to migrate were the Polynesians. These skilled navigators journeyed the farthest, settling as far east as Easter Island, as far south as New Zealand, and as far north as Hawaii.

Europeans discover the Pacific islands

The Pacific migration had ended several centuries before the first European laid eyes on the Pacific Ocean.

In 1513, Vasco Nuñez de Balboa sighted the Pacific after hacking his way through the jungle of Panama's isthmus. Naming his discovery the Great South Sea, he claimed all the land touching it for Spain. Little did he know that the body of water covered one-third of the earth's surface—181 million square km/70 million square miles. Ferdinand Magellan learned of the Pacific's vastness in 1521 when he sailed across the ocean for 3 months without seeing land until he discovered Guam.

The 17th and 18th centuries brought more European explorers. Most notable was Captain James Cook who charted Tahiti, the Marquesas, Vanuatu (New Hebrides), New Caledonia, Easter Island, the Cooks, Tonga, Fiji, Norfolk, and Niue. Other seamen to explore the Pacific included Captain Samuel Wallis, Louis Antoine de Bougainville, Jean La Perouse, Abel Tasman, Captain William Bligh, Fletcher Christian, Pedro de Quiros, and Alvaro de Mendaña.

These first travelers returned to Europe with tales of their discoveries. The explorers' reports excited adventurers who sailed to the area. Traders wanted the precious sandalwood that grew in abundance on the islands. Others sought men to work as slave labor in distant sugar cane fields. The missionaries arrived full of zeal to save the souls of the errant natives who wore minimal clothing, sang and danced with abandon, and lived a carefree existence.

Finally, foreign governments asserted their influence and rule on the Pacific islands. These foreign powers introduced their foods, apparel, and architecture. Only in recent years have many Pacific island countries achieved the right to self-government.

Life today in the Pacific

After generations of relative isolation, today's Pacific islanders must cope with more rapid change. Airplanes and ships bring the modern world to them quickly—a modern world to which it is sometimes difficult to adjust. Some old customs fade as new ideas are accepted. Yet amid this change many islanders strive to maintain traditional practices.

Communal life style. Most islanders still live a communal existence in small villages. To satisfy their needs they harvest vegetables from their gardens and fish from the nearby sea. They spend their free time weaving mats, making tapa, or socializing. Evenings are filled with songs and dances that have been passed down for generations. The family unit is still important in village life, and chiefs are respected.

Modern civilization has made some impact on these village people. Instead of walking or riding horses, islanders now prefer to travel around on motorscooters. Many canoes are motorized, and meals are sometimes supplemented with canned foods from the local store.

Getting together. The jet age has helped Pacific Island people learn of each other. Every 3 years athletes from all over the western Pacific area compete in the South Pacific Games, an island Olympics. Every 4 years an Arts Festival is held, attracting performers from many Pacific islands.

Visiting the Pacific

Today's visitors to Polynesia, Melanesia, and Micronesia can choose from a wide variety of experiences ranging from the very primitive to the modern.

You can enjoy a touch of French sophistication while shopping in the boutiques of Nouméa, New Caledonia, or Papeete, Tahiti. The latest stereo equipment is offered for sale in duty-free shops in Suva, Fiji, and Agana, Guam. If you want an interesting shopping experience, rise early and stroll through the public market. Here you'll mingle with islanders in native dress.

When you leave the town to venture into the countryside, you'll see villages of thatch-roofed huts and white-steepled churches. Here, too, are remnants of early island culture—*maraes* (temples) in Tahiti, the Ha'amonga Trilithon in Tonga, and *latte* stones in the Marianas.

Traditional customs remain

Primitive rituals and traditions still exist in parts of the Pacific. On Pentecost Island in Vanuatu (New Hebrides), men dive once a year from tall towers with nothing to break their fall but vines wrapped around their ankles. They believe this tradition ensures a good harvest.

The Highlanders of Papua New Guinea paint their faces in bright colors and don elaborate headdresses made of bird of paradise feathers to participate in sing sings where they perform ancient chants and dances.

A time and place to relax

The islands of the Pacific offer you not only the experiences of interesting sights and cultural events, but also a warm and relaxing tropical climate and unhurried pace. Water sports provide the most popular form of recreation. Beautiful beaches and calm, clear lagoons are abundant throughout the Pacific.

Modern resorts or thatch bungalows

In accommodations, the Pacific islands offer something for everyone. You can stay at modern resorts like The Fijian in Fiji, Maeva Beach in Tahiti, or various high rises along Tumon Bay near Agana, Guam.

Perhaps you prefer a "get-away-from-it-all" refuge; if so, you might choose an over-the-water thatch bungalow on Bora Bora or a simple hut at an island retreat like Toberua Island in Fiji. Nostalgia seekers will enjoy the colonial ambiance of Suva's Grand Pacific Hotel or Aggie Grey's hostelry in Apia, Western Samoa.

Cosmopolitan dining experiences

Throughout the Pacific, you'll find island restaurants offering French, Chinese, Italian, Indian, and other international dishes. At a native feast you can sample local foods such as chicken, fish, and pork that have been wrapped in banana leaves and baked slowly on hot stones in an underground oven. Raw fish marinated in lime juice and coconut milk is a popular item in nearly every Pacific island country.

Following the feast, local performers dressed in colorful native costumes will entertain you with traditional music and dances.

Traveling to Pacific islands

Travelers can reach the islands of the Pacific from virtually any direction: from Honolulu and the U.S. west coast, from Australia and New Zealand, from the Orient, from Southeast Asia, and from Chile.

Major airlines serving the South Pacific include Continental, Pan American, Air New Zealand, Qantas, UTA French Airlines, Japan Air Lines, Cathay Pacific, Philippine Airlines, CP Air, Braniff, and LAN-Chile. Regional carriers like Air Pacific, Air Micronesia, Air Niugini, Polynesian Airlines, Air Nauru, and South Pacific Island Airways operate regular service between Pacific islands. Some also link Australia, New Zealand, and the United States with Pacific points.

Sea transportation. Cruise ships departing from United States, Australia, and New Zealand ports stop at several islands during South Pacific voyages. Cargo/passenger lines carrying a limited number of passengers also call at South Seas ports and destinations in Micronesia.

Tours. A number of organized tours include islands in the Pacific. From the United States, Tahiti and Fiji can both be stopovers on excursions to Australia and New Zealand. Other tour operators feature the islands of French Polynesia or arrange for visitors to live part of the time with local villagers. Special interest packages focus on Micronesia for scuba diving and on Tahiti for yachting holidays.

Destinations, length of stay, and special features vary with each package. Many include accommodations, land arrangements, entertainment, and even local feasts.

Ask an expert. Since South Pacific travel offers such a wide array of destinations and choices of accommodations and transportation, prospective travelers should seek the advice of a knowledgeable travel agent to help plan the trip.

Peoples of the Pacific *share a love of flowers, bright colors, and traditional music and dance.* **Above:** *Trio of young Polynesian women fashion blooms into floral crowns.* **Top right:** *Musician entertains visitors with Melanesian melodies.* **Bottom right:** *Colorful headband adorns Micronesian performer.*

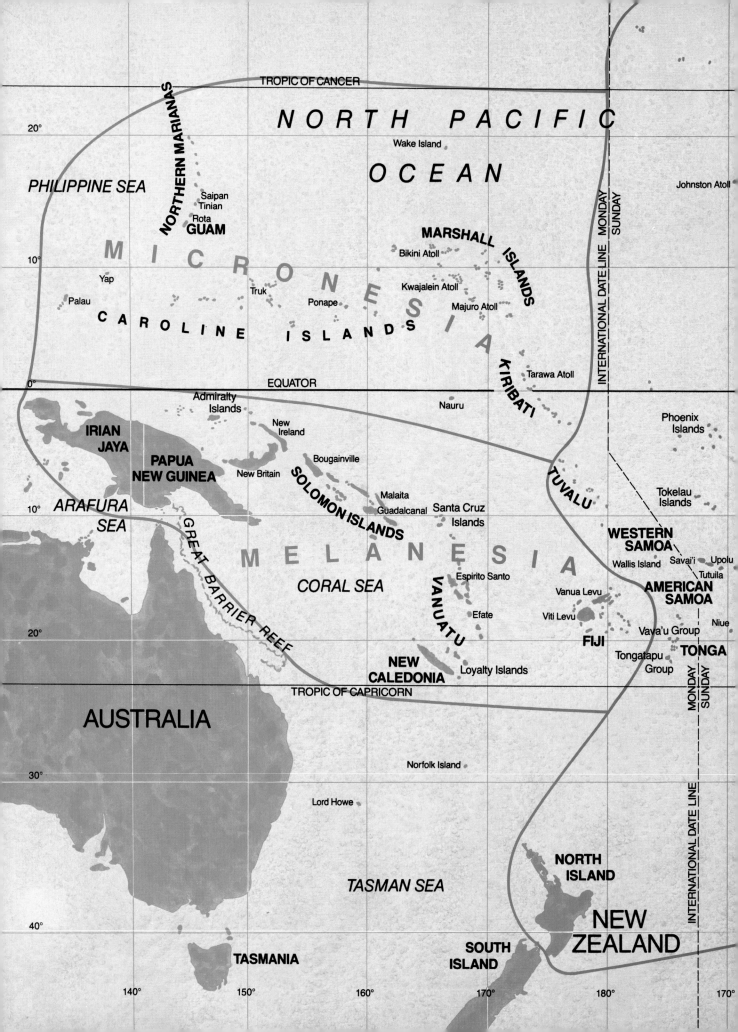

TROPIC OF CANCER

20°

NORTH PACIFIC

PHILIPPINE SEA

OCEAN

Wake Island

Johnston Atoll

NORTHERN MARIANAS

Saipan
Tinian
Rota
GUAM

MARSHALL ISLANDS

10°

Bikini Atoll

M I C R O N E S I A

Yap

Truk

Kwajalein Atoll

Palau

Ponape

Majuro Atoll

C A R O L I N E   I S L A N D S

KIRIBATI

INTERNATIONAL DATE LINE

MONDAY
SUNDAY

Tarawa Atoll

0°

EQUATOR

Admiralty
Islands

Nauru

Phoenix
Islands

**IRIAN
JAYA**

New
Ireland

**PAPUA
NEW GUINEA**

Bougainville

New Britain

SOLOMON ISLANDS

TUVALU

Tokelau
Islands

10°

*ARAFURA
SEA*

Malaita

Guadalcanal

Santa Cruz
Islands

**WESTERN
SAMOA**

Savai'i

Upolu

M E L A N E S I A

Wallis Island

Tutuila

GREAT BARRIER REEF

CORAL SEA

VANUATU

Espirito Santo

Vanua Levu

**AMERICAN
SAMOA**

20°

Efate

Viti Levu

Niue

Vava'u Group

**NEW
CALEDONIA**

Loyalty Islands

FIJI

Tongatapu
Group

TONGA

MONDAY
SUNDAY

TROPIC OF CAPRICORN

AUSTRALIA

Norfolk Island

30°

Lord Howe

**NORTH
ISLAND**

TASMAN SEA

INTERNATIONAL DATE LINE

40°

**SOUTH
ISLAND**

**NEW
ZEALAND**

TASMANIA

140°   150°   160°   170°   180°   170°

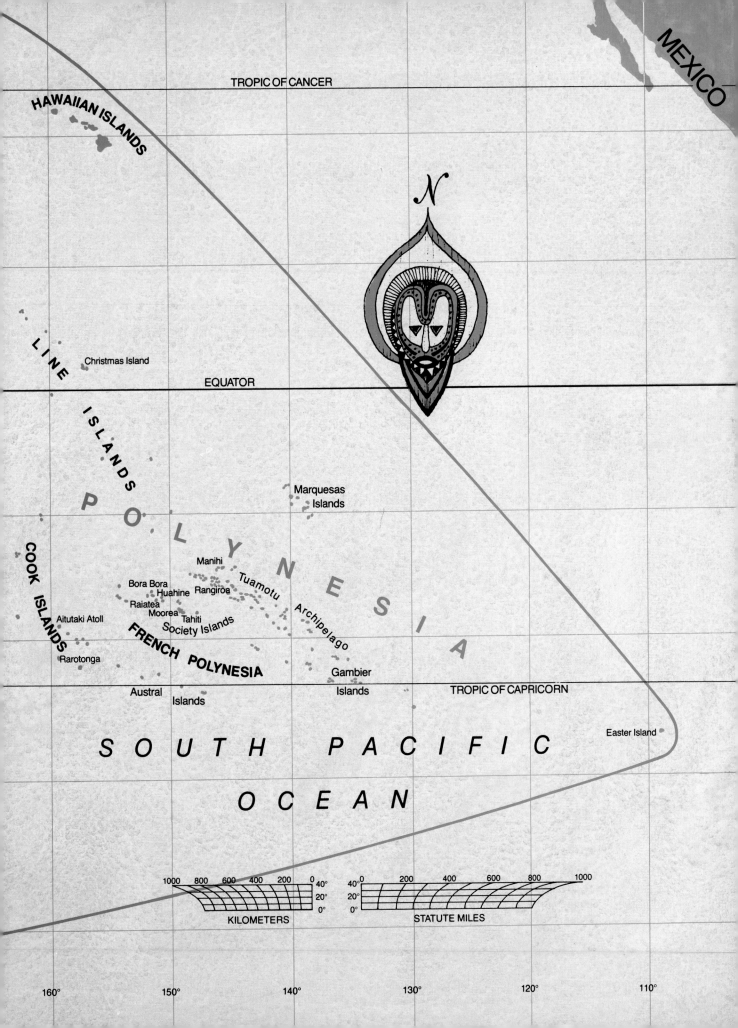

MEXICO

TROPIC OF CANCER

HAWAIIAN ISLANDS

N

LINE ISLANDS

Christmas Island

EQUATOR

P O L Y N E S I A

Marquesas
Islands

Manihi

COOK ISLANDS

Bora Bora
Huahine Rangiroa
Raiatea
Aitutaki Atoll   Moorea Tahiti
Society Islands

Tuamotu

Archipelago

Rarotonga

FRENCH POLYNESIA

Gambier

Austral   Islands
Islands

TROPIC OF CAPRICORN

Easter Island

S O U T H   P A C I F I C

O C E A N

1000 800 600 400 200   0 40°
                              20°
                               0°
KILOMETERS

40° 0
20°
 0°   200   400   600   800   1000
STATUTE MILES

160°   150°   140°   130°   120°   110°

POLYNESIA

Tahiti and French Polynesia, The Samoas, Tonga, Cook Islands

When people yearn for the romantic South Seas and deserted tropical isles, they usually think first of Polynesia—a word that has become synonymous with a carefree way of life. Since European mariners discovered these islands more than 200 years ago, adventurers, missionaries, traders, writers, painters, and other travelers have been lured by Polynesia's charms—its smiling brown-skinned people, balmy trade winds, palm-trimmed beaches, and unbelievably blue lagoons sheltered by coral reefs.

The word Polynesia means "many islands." These island groups lie scattered across the Pacific Ocean within a vast triangle, stretching from Hawaii southwest approximately 8,000 km/5,000 miles to New Zealand, and a similar distance southeast from Hawaii to Easter Island—an area covering some 39 million square km/15 million square miles.

Inside the Polynesian triangle, you'll find Tahiti, American and Western Samoa, Tonga, the Cooks, and smaller island groups. Living under different governments and in diverse surroundings, the Polynesian people share similar languages and a common heritage and physical appearance—brown eyes, straight hair, and golden-brown skin.

Pacific Migrations

Long before the first European explorers dared to sail beyond the horizon of a world many felt was flat, double-hulled Polynesian canoes plied the waters of the Pacific Ocean. Today archeologists, anthropologists, and linguists are just beginning to unravel the amazing story of these first brave migrations into the unknown. Countless theories exist regarding the path of these early Polynesian migrations.

First explorations

Many scientists believe that the first Polynesians sailed from Asia's South China coast sometime after 2000 B.C. Some authorities think they came in two separate migrations by way of the Malay Peninsula, stopping at various Melanesian and Micronesian islands on their journey. They continued on to Tonga and the Samoas, where they remained for several thousand years before venturing farther eastward. During this period of relative isolation, Polynesian islanders developed their languages, physique, and culture.

Samoans disagree with this theory. In Samoa no legends have been handed down recounting the arrival of the first Samoans or telling of an ancient homeland. Therefore, many Samoans believe that their islands have been populated since the dawn of history. According to this theory, all Polynesians descend from the first Samoans.

Voyages of discovery

Sometime around the birth of Christ, Polynesians once more climbed into their double-hulled canoes and sailed eastward in search of new islands. These migrations continued for another 1,000 years.

Their first stop was probably the Marquesas in French Polynesia. From here, some scientists theorize they journeyed southeast to Easter Island around A.D. 400. Other sailing canoes headed northward toward Hawaii and south to other islands in French Polynesia. From Raiatea, Polynesians continued south to New Zealand and also made a second trip to Hawaii.

By the time the first Europeans arrived in the Pacific

Island fishermen *toss float-rimmed net into shallow lagoon waters near Bora Bora's shore. Traditional ways persist in outer islands.*

in the 16th century, the Polynesian migrations had ended. The Polynesians had explored and colonized nearly all the islands in the Polynesian triangle.

Why did they migrate?

There are as many theories about the reasons for the early migrations as there are about the routes they took. In the past, some scientists believed that the voyages were accidental. They thought the Polynesians were blown off course while traveling between neighboring islands, and that they then drifted for days until sighting land.

However, today many scientists think the trips were intentional. Women, children, animals, and plant cuttings always accompanied the men on these journeys. In most cases canoes were sailed upwind and against the currents.

Many reasons are possible for departure on the long voyages. One theory is that a group defeated in war had to leave its territory to avoid being killed or enslaved.

Another reason might have been lack of food because of overcrowding. Only limited amounts of food could be grown on many of the smaller islands, and when the population increased, food became scarce, forcing groups to leave in search of new islands to settle on.

Sometimes, wars were fought over agricultural land and lagoon fishing rights. The losing group had to leave the island or starve to death.

Navigating unknown seas

These early Polynesian adventurers were skilled navigators. In their sailing canoes they traveled thousands of miles across treacherous, uncharted waters. On these voyages they discovered hundreds of tiny islands that were mere specks in the giant Pacific Ocean.

They made these epic journeys in large twin-hulled canoes. Built up to 30 meters/100 feet long, these canoes could accommodate 60 or more people plus pigs, dogs, fowl, coconuts, and tuber crop cuttings. The large platform linking the twin hulls held both people and supplies. In the center of this platform, a thatch hut provided shelter from sun and rain.

The canoes were powered by paddlers and by pandanus mat sails. The Polynesian navigators observed the stars and the sea. They studied crisscrossing wave patterns generated by distant islands, observed the direction birds flew when returning to land in the evening, and sighted clouds forming over distant land.

European Influences

When the first European explorers arrived in Polynesia, they were greeted by descendants of the ancient Polynesians. Following the traditions of their forefathers, these people lived in harmony with the wind, sea, and sun. They worshipped the gods of their ancestors and recalled legends in song and poetry. As a people they were fierce in battle and gentle in love.

When the European adventurers returned home, they recounted wondrous tales of a tropical paradise—lush green, mountainous islands rich in scenic beauty and gracious people. Soon other travelers arrived. Some stayed, and left a lasting impression on Polynesia.

The missionaries brought Christianity, and soon the Polynesian gods and idols were forsaken. Islanders adopted European dress, and European-style houses were built. From the foreigners who eventually ruled most of the islands, the Polynesians acquired new languages, new food, and new customs.

Polynesia Today

Modern Polynesia is changing. Many of these island countries have been governed by foreign powers which have left a cultural impact. International visitors require facilities and bring new ideas. But despite the influences of the outside world, most Polynesians still retain many of the traditions and customs of their ancestors.

As you travel through Polynesia, you'll discover the charms that have long lured visitors to the islands—beautiful scenery and gracious people who are proud of their heritage.

French Polynesia, a fabled paradise

Anyone seeking a tropical island paradise might well pause here—and wonder whether there's need to look farther. Since its discovery by 18th century European explorers, French Polynesia (Tahiti and its sister islands) has been the destination of countless wanderers, writers, and painters.

When you visit French Polynesia, you'll understand why these islands have become legendary. Green mountains rise to lofty, cloud-piercing peaks. Clear aquamarine lagoons lap white sand shores. Cascading waterfalls plunge into deep, sparkling pools. Aromatic flowering shrubs and trees add color to lush tropical forests.

French Polynesia is a delightful blend of cultures. You'll hear both French and Tahitian spoken. On the streets, smiling pareu-wrapped women pass beret-hatted men carrying long loaves of French bread. They'll both shop in Chinese-owned stores. One night you can enjoy a French dinner by candlelight, the next afternoon Tahitian delicacies traditionally cooked in an earth oven.

Tahiti. Of all the islands in French Polynesia, Tahiti has been the most influenced by modern western civilization. Here, you'll find most of the major resort hotels, the international airport, and rush hour traffic in Papeete rivaling that of large metropolitan cities.

But on Tahiti you can also visit a museum honoring artist Paul Gauguin, who produced some of his best work in the islands. You can visit the site where Captain Cook landed, see the tombs of Polynesian royalty, and view interesting *maraes* (ancient Polynesian temples). Perhaps best of all, you can relax and enjoy Tahiti's beaches, lagoons, and waterfalls.

Outer islands. To experience the French Polynesia of yesteryear, take a trip to the outer islands. Here you'll find a few small resorts and a quiet way of life that has changed little over the years.

Sitting in a beachside bungalow, you'll be aware of silence broken only by the lapping of waves and the rustle of palm fronds caressed by trade winds. At dawn you may be awakened by a noisy rooster eager for the day to begin. After a breakfast of fresh fruit, stroll leisurely down the one main street of a lazy, sunbaked island town, or perhaps bicycle down a dirt road uncluttered by traffic.

Each outer island has its own special magic. Moorea offers you spectacular views of Cook's Bay and Tahiti. On Bora Bora (considered by some to be the most beautiful island in the world), you may want to spend hours snorkeling in a large lagoon filled with spectacular coral formations and brilliantly colored fish. The maraes of Raiatea and Huahine recall a time when Polynesian gods and idols were worshipped. Venturing to Rangiroa or Manihi, you'll experience life on an atoll where land barely rises above the crashing waves of the sea.

Relaxed life style. Wherever you travel in French Polynesia, you'll be intrigued by the people. Proud and happy, they live a relaxed life, generally ignoring the rushed pace of the intruding outside world. They love to sing and dance and revel, and these parties can go on for days.

This relaxed pace, combined with the beauty of the landscape, makes French Polynesia a refuge where you can unwind and escape from urban pressures.

The Samoas, land of tradition

Like other islands in the South Pacific, American and Western Samoa offer visitors a warm climate cooled by the trade winds; volcanic greenery-clad mountains; plummeting waterfalls; unpeopled beaches; and inviting lagoons.

The Samoan people are dignified protectors of their Polynesian heritage. You'll find that these islands—considered by many the cradle of the Polynesian race—are rich today in ancient Polynesian myths, ceremonies, and customs.

Since American Samoa became a United States territory, American institutions and features have gradually filtered into these islands. Yet beneath the thin western overlay, American Samoa still clings to its Samoan traditions.

Fa'a Samoa. Wherever you travel in the Samoas, you'll experience *fa'a Samoa*—the Samoan Way. Tradition plays an important part in Samoan life.

One of the charms of the Samoas is their villages. In both countries clusters of thatch-roofed *fales* dot sandy island shores.

The basic unit of the village community is still the *aiga* (family). A complex hierarchy of chiefs still governs these families and villages.

Each village has at least one imposing church. The Samoans are very proud of their churches, and they pursue Christianity with fervor.

Hospitable people. You'll find the village people warm and friendly. Hospitality is part of *fa'a Samoa*. Robert Louis Stevenson, whom the Samoans affectionately named "Tusitala" (teller of tales), spent his final years here. Margaret Mead, at age 27, arrived in Samoa in 1925 to spend a year studying adolescent girls in a primitive society. Both wrote of the Samoans with love and respect.

Tonga, a Polynesian kingdom

Located just west of the International Date Line, Tonga is the first country in the world to greet each new day.

At first glance, Tonga's scattered island groups resemble most other South Pacific island countries, but they differ in one important way. Tonga is a constitutional monarchy—the last remaining Polynesian kingdom. King Taufa'ahau Tupou IV traces his ancestry to ancient ruling chiefs whose names have been preserved in art and legend. He resides in an elegant Victorian Royal Palace that dates from 1867; it is topped by a stately cupola.

A friendly land. After meeting the people of Tonga, Captain Cook named the country "The Friendly Islands." These gentle people live a traditional way of life in a country rich with ancient history.

Touring Tongatapu, Tonga's main island, you'll see centuries-old ruins of archeological interest. The massive upright coral slabs of Ha'amonga Trilithon, thought to be a kind of South Pacific Stonehenge, were erected around A.D. 1200. Scientists believe the trilithon was used as a seasonal calendar by Tonga's early inhabitants. The nearby terraced tombs known as Langi are the final resting place for royalty dating back to A.D. 950.

Natural beauty. Of equal fascination is Tonga's natural beauty. The country has its full share of coral reefs, clear blue skies, sandy beaches, and inviting atolls.

On Tongatapu, you can watch spouting water jet high into the air at the Houma Blow Holes. In the Vava'u Group, the Port of Refuge is reached by a 13-km/8-mile fiordlike passage—one of the most beautiful waterways in the South Pacific.

The Cook Islands, unspoiled and friendly

Long isolated from major travel routes, the Cook Islands have preserved much of the romance and charm of old Polynesia. Life in these islands moves at a slow, pleasant pace. Most people still farm the land and fish the seas for their basic foods. This peaceful existence offers a welcome relief from the complex demands of modern society.

The main island of Rarotonga is only 34 km/21 miles in circumference, small enough to explore thoroughly at a leisurely pace. You'll enjoy meeting the people of the Cook Islands, who smile, wave, and converse easily with visitors. (Bilingual, they speak both English and Maori.) They will welcome you to their country as a guest, not a tourist.

The friendly people of the Cooks will entertain you with their harmonious church choirs, fantastic drumbeats, and dance performances acclaimed as some of the best in the South Pacific. If relaxation is your goal, you will be pleased to find beautiful unspoiled beaches and lagoons.

TAHITI & FRENCH POLYNESIA

The islands of French Polynesia (Tahiti and its sister islands) have long been acclaimed as the most beautiful in the South Pacific. Explorers Samuel Wallis, Louis Antoine de Bougainville, and James Cook described them in their journals, and Paul Gauguin painted them on canvas.

What are the lures of fabled Tahiti and her neighboring islands? Spectacular mountains plunge into an ocean reflecting every shade of blue. Tropical rain forests teem with brilliant flowering shrubs and trees. Deserted beaches and quiet lagoons lure you to stroll and swim undisturbed. Colorful markets offer an opportunity to mingle with the local people. In candlelit restaurants you can dine on French-inspired specialties.

The atmosphere of French Polynesia blends French sophistication and Polynesian gaiety. The people love to laugh and sing; they approach life with a joyous spirit. As you pause on French Polynesia's shores, relax, and enjoy what many visitors consider to be paradise.

Four Island Groups

The 130 islands of French Polynesia lie in the South Pacific about midway between Australia and the United States. Divided into four groups, these islands encompass an ocean area about the size of western Europe.

Best known of these groups is the Society Islands, consisting of the Windward group (Tahiti, Moorea, Meheitia, Tetiaroa, and Maiao) and the Leeward group (Huahine, Raiatea, Tahaa, Bora Bora, and Maupiti). Other island groups include the Tuamotu Archipelago (including the Gambier Islands), the Austral Islands, and the Marquesas Islands.

Volcanic islands, coral atolls

Geographically, French Polynesia has two types of islands—high islands that are volcanic in origin and low islands that are coral atolls. All the island groups except the Tuamotus have high islands.

Steep, jagged mountains with plummeting waterfalls characterize the high islands. With narrow coastal strips forming the shoreline, most of the islands (except the Marquesas) are protected by an encircling coral reef.

On the low islands, a thin ring of coral surrounds a lagoon with no mountainous island center. Standing on one of these atolls, you hear the ocean waves crashing against the outer shore behind you while you gaze at a quiet, blue-green lagoon.

Island flora. Flowers abound in the rich volcanic soil of the high islands. The sweet, heady scent of tiare-tahiti (Tahitian gardenia) and frangipani fills the warm, tropical air. You'll delight in seeing red, yellow, and orange flamboyants in cascading clusters; delicate multihued orchids; colorful carpets of bougainvillea; and brilliant red poinsettias.

A variety of trees and shrubs thrive in the humid climate and rich soil of the high islands. They include *fei* (wild bananas), *mape* (Tahitian chestnut), pandanus, coconut, breadfruit, mango, casuarina, and tree fern.

In contrast the calcareous, dry soil of the low islands produces little vegetation beyond a few coconut palms and some pandanus and breadfruit trees. Few flowers grow on these islands.

Underwater life. Aquatic life teems in the numerous temperate lagoons of French Polynesia. Exploring these waters, you'll discover a fairyland of multishaped corals and rainbow-colored fish. Parrotfish, bonitos, lobsters, crabs, clams, bass, and groupers all thrive in these waters.

Lovely shells such as conch, cone, cowrie, and triton can be found in lagoon and reef areas. Shells have become an integral part of Tahitian life. Shell necklaces are a traditional farewell gift.

Wildlife. French Polynesia has no dangerous or poisonous animals. Many of its animals—including pigs, dogs, and chickens— were brought to the islands in outriggers by migrating Polynesians. Coconut rats and lizards were stowaways on these first voyages. Europeans later introduced horses, cows, cats, and turkeys.

Discovered by the English and the French

Captain Samuel Wallis, an Englishman, had been at sea for 8 months searching for Terra Australis Incognita when he and his crew accidentally came upon the island of Tahiti in June 1767. Anchoring the H.M.S. *Dolphin* in Matavai Bay off the peninsula now called Point Venus, he claimed Tahiti for England, naming it King George III Island.

Also searching for Terra Australis Incognita, French explorer Louis Antoine de Bougainville anchored off Tahiti in April 1768. Unaware of Wallis's visit, Bougainville claimed the island for France, calling it Nouvelle Cythère—New Island of Love. Bougainville's botanist named the scarlet and violet, paperlike flowers he saw on the island "bougainvillea" after his captain.

A year later Lieutenant James Cook, commanding the H.M.S. *Endeavor*, was directed to take an astronomer to the South Pacific to view the planet Venus as it crossed the disk of the sun. Upon Wallis's suggestion, Cook chose King George III Island as the observation point, building a fort on Point Venus.

During Cook's 3-month stay, he recorded information

Brilliantly costumed *entertainers break into pulsating rhythm of the* tamure, *Tahiti's famed native dance. Native songs and dances highlight Polynesian feast entertainment.*

Verdant *tropical islands provide scenic vistas for yachters who sail annually to French Polynesia, anchoring in protected waters.*

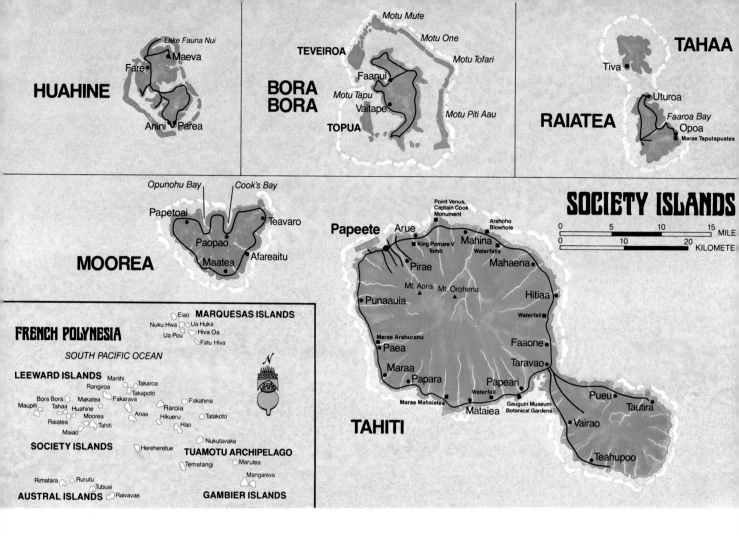

about native customs, manners, religion, and law, and charted Tahiti's coastline. After leaving Tahiti in July 1769, Cook discovered Huahine, Raiatea, Tahaa, and Bora Bora. He named these islands the Society Islands because of their contiguous location. Cook returned to Tahiti in 1773, 1774, and 1777 during further exploratory voyages.

Hearing tales of Tahiti's Garden of Eden, a variety of adventurers flocked to the islands in the years that followed. In March 1797, a large group from the London Missionary Society landed on Tahiti, but they soon found that converting the fun-loving Polynesians to a puritanical life was not easy—it took them 15 years to win their first convert.

During the first half of the 19th century, the islands were torn by wars brought about largely by rival Protestant and Catholic missionaries and their supporting governments (England and France). Tahiti became a French protectorate in 1846 during the reign of Queen Pomare IV. In 1880 King Pomare V made a gift of his kingdom to France, ending the century-old Pomare dynasty.

The country's status changed from colony to territory in 1957, and it became known as French Polynesia. Recently it has been granted internal autonomy. A 7-member council and a local Territorial Assembly of 30 elected members govern the country's internal matters. A High Commissioner, appointed by France, oversees external affairs.

French Polynesia's People

With a culture that blends its ancient Polynesian beginnings with more than 200 years of contact with the outside world, French Polynesian society is a dynamic one. Its population of 137,000 is a composite of 77 percent Polynesian, 14 percent European, and 9 percent Asian (mainly Chinese).

Easygoing people

The indigenous Tahitians are a fun-loving people who believe that life should be lived in the pursuit of happiness. Their easygoing philosophy is summed up in their phrase *aita pea pea*—a kind of happy "Who cares?"

Sharing a love of singing, Tahitians join together in song on almost any occasion. It's not unusual to see several youths sitting along the roadside, strumming their guitars and singing. You'll hear both traditional folk songs and the latest American and European hits—all sung in Tahitian.

They also love to dance. Whether dancing in Papeete's smoke-filled bars or at a village feast, they never seem to tire or become bored with it. One of the best known traditional dances is the *ori-tahiti* or *tamure*. To the accompaniment of wooden drums, the female performs tantalizing, fast-moving hip motions while the male executes equally rapid knee movements.

Urban and rural life styles

Life styles in French Polynesia range from the busy activity of urban Papeete to the relaxed pace of lightly populated rural areas, especially on islands other than Tahiti. Westernization intrudes more slowly on these outer islands than on Tahiti.

Papeete's citizens work for businesses, factories, the government, and the tourist industry. They live in modern homes built of wood and concrete. At the local supermarket they can purchase not only staples but also imported items such as French cheeses and wines. Judging from the traffic on Papeete's main thoroughfares, it appears that nearly everyone owns a motorbike or automobile.

Elsewhere on Tahiti—and especially on the outer islands—you still find vestiges of a slower paced, more traditional life style. But even on these outer islands, western civilization has made inroads.

You'll still see some *fares*—Tahitian dwellings with thatch roofs. However, many have been replaced with houses of concrete block—painted in bright colors of yellow, orange, red, green, and blue—topped by corrugated metal roofs. Cooking is now done inside on a butane stove, not in the *ahimaa,* the traditional hole-in-the-ground oven heated with hot stones.

Villagers still grow their own root crops, fruits, and coconuts. They fish with traps, nets, and harpoons, but night fishing is now done by *mori gaz* (pressure lamps) rather than by torch. Today's diet is supplemented with canned corned beef from the village store.

Walking, outrigger canoes, and horses remain popular forms of transportation, but both motorscooters and motorboats are beginning to infiltrate the outer islands.

Western dress. Tahitians have adopted an informal western style of dress. (Traditional grass skirts appear only on special occasions.) Men wear brightly patterned shirts and shorts or slacks; women don colorful, flower-printed dresses. The *pareu,* a wraparound garment made in a bright *pareo* print fabric, is worn by both men and women. The Tahitians love their flowers—they wear floral leis and *couronnes* (flower crowns) both on special occasions and just for the fun of it.

Speak Tahitian. French and Tahitian are the country's official languages. Tourist industry employees and some shopkeepers also speak English. (If you want to learn more about the Tahitian language, see page 19.)

Religion important. Religious worship plays an important part in the Tahitian daily life. Women don their finest dresses and broad-brimmed straw hats, and men their best suits, to go to church. People sometimes attend services several times a week, participating enthusiastically in a capella congregational hymn singing and in *himene* (trained choir).

More than half of the French Polynesian people are Protestants. There are also a number of Catholics and a few Mormons, Seventh-Day Adventists, Jehovah's Witnesses, and Buddhists.

Copra is prime export. French Polynesia's main agricultural product is copra. Vanilla and coffee add

CAPTAIN COOK
He Mapped the Pacific

Of all the explorers who sailed the Pacific following Magellan's voyage in the early 1500s, the man who traveled the farthest and left the most lasting impression was Captain James Cook. Entering the British navy as a common seaman in 1755, he later became one of England's most renowned explorers.

Between 1768 and 1779, he made three voyages totaling almost nine years. Cook touched nearly every island group in the South Pacific: Easter, the Marquesas, Tahiti, the Cooks, Tonga, Fiji, New Caledonia, Norfolk, Niue, Hawaii, New Hebrides, and Pitcairn. In addition, he charted 2,000 miles of Australia's east coast, circumnavigated and charted New Zealand, charted the west coast of North America, and was the first European to cross the Antarctic Circle.

Today, some 200 years later, Cook is still a name to be reckoned with in the South Pacific. You'll find numerous geographical points named for him—islands, straits, mountains, coves, headlands, and streams.

In addition to all his accomplishments, Cook was known as a kind and gentle person, a considerate commander, and a courteous and understanding student of the native inhabitants of the lands he discovered. Ironically, he met his death in his 50th year (1779) at the hands of Hawaiians at Kealakekua Bay, Hawaii. He was killed during a fracas that followed the theft of one of his small boats.

To the lords of the Admiralty, he had been a source of amazement: a man who overcame "the social handicap of lowly birth" to rise to the rank of Post Captain in the Royal Navy.

Greenery *brightens Papeete's business district, where modern structures housing shops, offices, restaurants have sprouted among older wooden buildings.*

Thatch-roofed *bungalows provide resort accommodations in tropical garden or seaside setting. At Hotel Bali Hai Moorea, guests relax on decks built over lagoon.*

SAY IT IN TAHITIAN
A Pronouncing Primer

French is Tahiti's main language, but most Polynesian residents speak Tahitian.

You'd have to be quite a linguist to learn enough Tahitian to carry on a whole conversation, but you can learn some basics of pronunciation and a few common phrases. If you do, it will make your visit more meaningful, and Tahitians will be pleased with your attempt to use their language.

The Tahitian alphabet has only 13 letters with 5 vowels (a, e, i, o, u) and 8 consonants (f, h, m, n, p, r, t, v).

First, let's tackle vowel pronunciation. More emphasis is placed on pronouncing the vowels in Tahitian than in English.

- *a*—pronounced as in *father*
- *e*—usually pronounced as *a* in *may*, but sometimes as a shorter *eh* sound.
- *i*—pronounced as *e* in *be*
- *o*—pronounced as *o* in *go*
- *u*—pronounced as *u* in *dude*

Each syllable in Tahitian ends with a vowel. Each vowel, when following another vowel, should be pronounced as a separate syllable. Frequently three vowels will be grouped together, in which case all three should be distinctly pronounced. An example is *Faaa* (the international airport)—pronounced "Fah-*ah*-ah."

In general, Tahitian words are accented on the next-to-last syllable, except when an apostrophe separates the final vowel from the vowel preceding it. Then both vowels are given equal emphasis. For example, *mataura'a* (meaning custom) is pronounced "mah-tah-oo-*rah*-ah."

Tahitian consonants are pronounced the same as in English.

Now for a few words and phrases:

Hello—*"Ia-ora'na"* (ee-ah-oh-*rah*-nah)
How are you?—*"Maita'i oe"* (Mah-ee-*tah-ee* oh-ay)
I am fine—*"Maita'i vau"* (mah-ee-*tah-ee* vah-oo)
Thank you very much—*"Mauruuru roa"* (mah-oo-roo-*oo*-roo *roh*-ah)
Goodbye—*"Parahi"* (pah-*rah*-hee)
To your health—*"Manuia"* (Mah-noo-*ee*-ah)
Please repeat—*"Tapiti"* (Tah-*pee*-tee).

Now go back and practice saying Papeete (Pah-peh-*ay*-tay) a few more times, and it will all come naturally.

---

some revenue. On atolls like those of the Tuamotu Archipelago, mother-of-pearl and pearl-bearing oysters provide much of the income.

The country has a few small factories producing palm oil, soap, ice cream, corned beef, soft drinks, and beer. The tourist industry is also an important source of income.

A sports loving country

The Tahitian people have always loved sports. Ancient Polynesians were avid sports fans enjoying competitions in foot races, wrestling, boxing, javelin throwing, and archery. Today, other sports have been added. There are stadiums on Tahiti and some of the outer islands.

Soccer is the number one spectator sport. Enthusiastic fans gather in a number of locations every Saturday and Sunday during the season (January–July) to watch district teams compete, and the rivalry is keen. Occasional games are played against visiting international teams from New Caledonia, New Hebrides, New Zealand, France, and Chile.

Horse racing has also become a popular sport. From April through November, races take place on the first Sunday of each month at the track in Pirae (5 km/ 3 miles from Papeete). Many of the jockeys race Tahitian style—bareback, wearing only a brightly colored pareu and crown of flowers. Spectators come not only to watch the races and do a little betting, but also to catch up on local news and drink some beer.

Other spectator sports include archery, bicycle races, boxing, outrigger canoe and sailboat races, volleyball, and various track events. If you are in French Polynesia during the July Bastille Day celebrations, you'll see a number of festive events including outrigger canoe races, bicycle races, and javelin throwing contests.

Planning Your Trip

For some prospective visitors, this tropical paradise may seem far away. However, Papeete on the island of Tahiti lies just 6,612 km/4,109 miles southwest of Los Angeles; 5,311 km/3,300 miles northeast of Sydney, and 4,094 km/ 2,544 miles northeast of Auckland.

Papeete can be easily reached by direct or connecting flights of major Pacific international and regional airlines. Planes land at Faaa International Airport, just 5 km/3 miles southwest of Papeete. Transport to hotels is by taxi or Le Truck (the public bus).

(Continued on page 20)

Several passenger liners cruising the Pacific dock at the quay in central Papeete. A few also stop at Bora Bora and Moorea.

Getting around French Polynesia

Once you have arrived in Papeete, you can explore both Tahiti and the outer islands by rental vehicle or public transportation.

The larger tourist hotels on Tahiti are located at least 8 km/5 miles from downtown Papeete. Taxis are relatively expensive, and their rates double between 11 P.M. and 5 A.M. The cheapest—and most colorful—form of island transport on Tahiti is Le Truck (see page 25).

Taxis are also available on the outer islands. However, they don't run after 5 P.M. unless previous arrangements have been made. Most hotels have airport shuttle service. Le Truck service is limited. For around-the-island exploration, your best mode of transportation on outer islands is a rental motorbike, jeep, or car.

Plane travel. From Tahiti, the fastest way to visit the outer islands is by air. Air Polynésie, the local airline, flies regularly from Papeete to Moorea, Huahine, Raiatea, Bora Bora, Maupiti, and the remote islands (the Marquesas, Australs, and Tuamotu Archipelago).

Air Tahiti flies between Papeete and Moorea in an "air bridge" shuttle service daily between dawn and dusk (approximately 6 A.M. to 6 P.M.). Planes depart from Faaa International Airport every 5 to 15 minutes, or whenever there is a planeload of passengers. Reservations are not necessary.

Cruising. American Hawaii Cruises offers 7-day interisland cruises aboard the *Liberté,* departing each Saturday year round from Papeete. Exploration Holidays and Cruises' *Majestic Tahiti Explorer* departs on Sundays on 7-day cruises; 3 and 4-day trips are also available.

Interisland boats. Daily interisland boat service links Papeete with Moorea. Copra boats and schooners provide regular scheduled service from Papeete to Huahine, Raiatea, and Bora Bora. These boats also make unscheduled trips to the Marquesas, the Austral Islands, and the Tuamotu Archipelago. Tahiti visitors can board the freighter *Aranui* for leisurely 14-day trips to the Marquesas Islands; trips depart about once a month.

Rental vehicles. If you prefer to explore the islands on your own, you can rent a car or jeep, or you can hire a car and English-speaking driver. Rental cars are available on Tahiti and many of the outer islands. To rent a car you must be 21 years old and have a valid driver's license. Traffic keeps to the right. Many hotels have bicycles available for use by their guests.

Taking a tour. Tour operators offer a variety of excursions around French Polynesia's many islands. Check with your hotel or a local travel agency for information on bus or flightseeing tours and boat rides.

Accommodations, Tahitian-style

French Polynesia's favorite form of resort hotel architecture is the *fare,* the Tahitian-style, thatch-roofed bungalow. Both modern and comfortable, these bungalows usually are situated in a tropical garden setting near the beach or overlooking a lagoon. All the resort hotels on Tahiti's outer islands have this type of architecture, and most are small—about 50 rooms.

On Tahiti you'll find larger, several-story resort hotels (some also offering bungalow accommodations) as well as a few small bungalow-type hotels. According to the French Polynesian building code, no hotel can be higher than the tallest coconut palm tree—a ruling that has produced some interesting architecture. The Hotel Tahara'a near Papeete could be termed a "downrise," since its seven stories stretch down the side of a steep cliff. The lobby is on the top floor.

Most of the hotels on Tahiti are within a few miles northeast or southwest of Papeete, though a few are located downtown on the waterfront. You'll also find comfortable resort hotels on Moorea, Bora Bora, Raiatea, Huahine, Rangiroa, and Manihi.

Less expensive, family-style accommodations with housekeeping facilities are also available on many of French Polynesia's main islands. In the more remote areas where there are no hotels, you can arrange to stay with a local family; these accommodations may be spartan.

For information on staying with a family or for a list of hotels and their rates, write to the Tahiti Tourist Development Board, B.P. 65, Papeete.

You will find it easier to get accommodations during the low seasons—April to June and September to November. During peak seasons, there is a hotel room shortage. It is especially important to book rooms on the outer islands ahead of time all year, since these islands have only a few hotels.

Dining and entertainment

Dining in French Polynesia can be an exciting experience. All the resort hotels have at least one restaurant, and you'll also find excellent dining at various French, Italian, Chinese, and Vietnamese restaurants outside the hotels, especially on Tahiti. You can savor French soufflé Grand Marnier, Chinese sweet and sour pork, or Tahitian *ei'a ota* (raw fish marinated in lime juice, and smothered with coconut milk, tomatoes, and hard-cooked egg).

For French dining on Tahiti, try Le Bélvèdere, high in the mountains overlooking the Papeete Harbor (complimentary hotel pickup); and L'Auberge Landaise and Acajou, both on the waterfront in Papeete. For seafood try Baie des Pecheurs near the Maeva Beach Hotel in Punaauia. A la Soupe Chinoise on Rue Paul Gauguin and Jade Palace on Rue Jeanne d'Arc in Papeete feature Chinese specialties. La Pizzeria on the Papeete waterfront serves pizza. Note that many restaurants are closed on Sundays.

Desiring a brief respite while exploring Papeete, you can stop at a *salon de thé* for a reviving cup of coffee or tea and a pastry. These casual snack shops open around 6 A.M. and close about 6 P.M. If you're hungry, try one of their minipizzas, quiches, or pâtés. Favorite *salons de thé* include Hilaire on Rue General de Gaulle; Le Pam Pam on Place Notre-Dame; and La Marquisienne on Rue Colette.

Resort hotels on Tahiti and the outer islands feature barbecues or buffet-style dinners with Tahitian specialties at least once a week.

The tamaaraa. One of the best ways to sample Tahitian foods and enjoy Tahitian entertainment is to attend a *tamaaraa*—a Tahitian feast. The traditional Polynesian meal is followed by Tahitian music and group dances. Tamaaraas are offered at a number of hotels on Moorea. A package trip from Papeete to the feast includes transportation and sightseeing.

Much of the food for the tamaaraa is cooked in an *ahimaa*—an underground earthen oven. The menu usually consists of pig, fish, breadfruit, and bananas. To this basic list may be added chicken, fish, taro, fresh fruit, and Tahitian *poe*. Poe is a dessert made of papayas, taros, pumpkin, manioc, or bananas with sugar, vanilla, and coconut milk.

Following this lavish meal—traditionally eaten with the fingers—guests are entertained by grass-skirted Tahitians who perform harmonious songs and pulsating dances. Don't be surprised if you are invited to learn the hip-jolting *tamure*.

Other entertainment. Many hotels schedule Tahitian entertainment several times a week and music for dancing nightly. Papeete has several discotheques.

Shopping in Papeete

Visitors discover some of the best shopping opportunities in Papeete. Small shops are scattered around

FESTIVAL TIME

Perhaps the best known of French Polynesia's enthusiastic celebrations is Bastille Day. However, the Tahitians' love for revelry is not restricted to this celebration. You can see numerous other festivals throughout the year.

January—April

New Year's Day. On January 1, Tahitians all over the country gather with their families and friends for singing, dancing, and guitar playing.

Chinese New Year. French Polynesia's Chinese community celebrates this traditional holiday in late January or early February with legendary dances and fireworks.

Coronation Ball. In March, Tane Tahitian—handsomest Tahitian of the Year—is selected in Papeete. A ball follows.

Miss Bora Bora Contest. A contest winner is selected and crowned at the end of April on Bora Bora.

May—August

Annual "Maire" Day. Exhibitions of ferns are on display in Papeete in May. There is a ball at day's end.

Miss Moorea Contest. A winner is selected and crowned on Moorea in early June.

Miss Tahiti and Miss Tiurai Contest. In early July, Tahiti's prettiest girl of the year—who will represent the country of French Polynesia in all international beauty events—is selected. Also chosen is her local representative, who reigns over the Bastille Day celebrations.

Bastille Day. This celebration of France's independence officially lasts one week beginning July 14. However, the merriment of this event—called La Fête by the French and Tiurai by the Polynesians—sometimes continues for another 2 weeks.

There's a carnival atmosphere day and night with games, contests, and dances at the fair grounds near Papeete. You'll see bareback horse races, fruit carrier races, javelin throwing contests, canoe races, and singing and dancing contests. Celebrations are also held on Raiatea, Tahaa, Huahine, and Bora Bora.

Night of the Guitar and Ute. In August, local musicians compete in playing guitar French Polynesian-style and in performing the *Ute* (satirical improvisation songs) on Tahiti.

September—December

Te Vahine e te Tiare (the Woman and the Flower). Tahitian women dress up for this floral theme ball at the beginning of September on Tahiti.

Old Tahiti Ball. Near the beginning of October, participants dress up in costumes of a bygone era to attend this ball on Tahiti.

All Saints Day. Cemeteries (particularly in Papeete, Faaa, Arue, and Punaauia on Tahiti) are illuminated with candles on November 1. There are religious services and hymn singing.

Thousand Flowers Contest and Pareu Day. Prizes are given for exhibitions of French Polynesian flowers at a ball in November in Papeete. Attendees wear pareu dress.

Tiare Tahiti (National Flower) Day. Tiare flowers are distributed to everyone on the streets of Papeete, in the hotels, and on departing planes. Arriving passengers receive a *hei* (Tahitian wreath). The Tiare Ball is held in the evening.

New Year's Eve. The Papeete waterfront is illuminated on December 31. Competitors run through the Papeete streets in the "Cross de la Saint Sylvestre."

the town, and you'll find several shopping centers as well as Marché Papeete, the municipal market.

One of the most attractive local handicrafts is pareo cloth, a brightly colored, handblocked fabric. Tahitians use a variety of pareo fabrics to make curtains, bedspreads, shirts, dresses, bathing suits, scarfs, and ties. If you can't find what you want ready-made, a tailor or dressmaker can quickly make it for you. (Note: Some pareo cloth is imported from Japan.)

Other handmade Tahitian items include shell garlands, costume jewelry made of black and gold lip-pearl shells, woven hats and Marquesan woodcarvings.

You can shop Monday through Friday from 7:30 to 11:30 A.M. and 2 to 5 P.M., and Saturdays from 7:30 to 11 A.M.

Recreational opportunities

Not surprisingly, recreational activities focus on the water. Inviting warm, tropical lagoons and bays surround islands trimmed by beautiful sand beaches. Resort hotels cater to water sports; equipment is available for fishing, snorkeling, scuba diving, sailing, canoeing, water-skiing, and glass-bottomed boat touring. In addition, several local companies have equipped fishing boats, diving boats, and sailboats available for charter for day trips as well as for longer excursions.

Fishing. Deep-sea fishing in French Polynesia gained worldwide prominence in the 1930s when Zane Grey hooked record and near-record game fish in the area. The sport remains popular today. Big game fish you can catch include black marlin, sailfish, mahi mahi (dolphin), wahoo, ocean bonito, barracuda, red snapper, and red bass. Peak season is November through April.

Fully equipped deep-sea fishing boats are available for hire in Tahiti, Moorea, Raiatea, Bora Bora, Rangiroa, Huahine, and Manihi. The Haura Club in Papeete, an affiliate of the International Game Fish Association, can provide further fishing information; write them at P.O. Box 582, Papeete. Visiting fishermen may use the club's scales and the service of the weighmaster. The club is located on Route de l'Ouest.

Trout fishermen can fish in mountain streams for Tahitian trout, called *nato*. You also might want to seek out a Tahitian for a lesson in night lagoon fishing.

Scuba diving. Warm waters, fantastic coral formations, and an abundance of colorful tropical fish lure many divers to French Polynesia. Good diving locations exist off Tahiti, Huahine, Raiatea, Bora Bora, and Rangiroa. Although diving is possible all year, conditions are best between June and September.

Many resort hotels have diving equipment and boats available for hire. You can also rent diving equipment through several sports operators in Papeete—Tahiti Aquatique at the Maeva Beach Hotel, Tahiti Actinautic at the Beachcomber Hotel, and Marina Lotus in Papeete.

Swimming and surfing. In addition to your hotel pool, you can swim in quiet lagoons or beautiful mountain rivers and pools. Papeete's municipal, olympic-size, swimming pool is just a 10-minute walk south from town center along the waterfront.

Surfing is as popular a sport today as it was when Captain Cook landed in the 1700s. Good surfing spots on Tahiti include the north coast near Arue, the beaches in the Papenoo district, and the west coast around Paea and Papara.

Hiking. Hikers learn early that the islands' mountainous interiors are rugged (however beguiling they may appear) and warrant the help of a guide. Inquire at your hotel for guide information. For details on mountain climbing, write Club Alpin, B.P. 65, Papeete.

Horseback riding. Rent a horse to journey into the island valleys or to gallop along a deserted beach. You can rent horses from Club Equestre de Tahiti at the race course in Pirae. Horses are also available for hire on Moorea at Les Tipaniers Hotel and Hotel Moorea Village, and on Huahine at the Centre de Tourisme Equestre.

Tennis. On Tahiti, tennis players will find courts at the Fautaua Stadium, 2 km/1 mile northeast of Papeete, and at Hotel Tahara'a, Maeva Beach Hotel, Tahiti Beachcomber Hotel, Climat de France Tahiti, and Te Puna Bel Air Hotel. On Moorea, there are tennis courts at the Hotel Bali Hai Moorea, Hotel Moorea Village, Captain Cook Beach Hotel, Kia Ora Village, and Club Bali Hai. There are also tennis courts at resorts on Bora Bora and Huahine. Rackets are sometimes hard to come by, so it's best to bring your own.

Golf. Atimaono Golf Course, 45 km/28 miles southeast of Papeete, is the country's only 18-hole course.

Tahiti, the Main Island

Tahiti—French Polynesia's principal island—covers 1,041 square km/402 square miles. Figure 8 in shape, it somewhat resembles a floating sea turtle with a protruding head. The larger part is called Tahiti-Nui, the smaller section Tahiti-Iti.

About 70 percent of French Polynesia's 136,000 people live on Tahiti, either in Papeete (the country's capital) or along the island's narrow coastal shelf. The interior of the island—practically uninhabited—is an area of jagged peaks and deep gorges. Tahiti's highest peak is 2,231-meter/7,321-foot Mount Orohena.

A fringe of foam marks the coral reef encircling the island. The reef protects the lagoons and beaches; it strikes a dividing line between the indigo of the deep ocean and the lighter shades of blue and green in the lagoons. Occasional breaks in the reef allow boats and ships to sail through.

Tahiti is the visitor's main gateway to French Polynesia. Here, you experience the bustle of Papeete with its numerous restaurants and comfortable hotels. You can visit a colorful public market or ride into the countryside to see a *marae* (ancient temple) or a museum devoted to Gauguin. If you prefer, you can spend the day lying on a beach or beside your pool.

Getting acquainted with Papeete

Papeete, French Polynesia's capital and only city (56,000 population), lies on a busy, crescent-shaped harbor on the northwest coast of Tahiti. Arriving in

Bora Bora woman *weaves mat of dried palm fronds. Local shops display array of woven hats, mats, baskets.*

Sleepy *South Seas atmosphere pervades Uturoa, largest town on Raiatea. Lush greenery rises behind rusting corrugated iron roofs.*

the country by either air or sea, you will stop first in Papeete.

The town's business district—a conglomeration of modern concrete structures and brightly painted wooden buildings—rambles along the waterfront in a several block strip. Narrow streets dotted with iron-roofed houses drift back from this central district. Where these side streets end, lush green foothills rise toward jagged mountain peaks half hidden in the clouds.

Like many towns suffering growing pains, Papeete has a traffic problem. It seems as though nearly everyone in Papeete owns either a car, motorbike, motor-scooter, or truck. During morning and evening rush hours, they converge on Papeete's narrow streets, creating one noisy traffic jam.

You'll see Papeete best on foot, beginning at the waterfront. Most town activity centers on or near the street rimming the harbor. This street, Boulevard Pomaré, is really a series of *quais,* starting on the southwest with Quai de l'Uranie, merging into Quai Bir-Hakeim, then Quai du Commerce, and lastly Quai Gallieni.

Papeete's waterfront has changed in recent years. The rim road, once a hodgepodge of old shacks and souvenir shops, is now a wide and attractive boulevard, divided by a grass strip and edged with sidewalks. Where old warehouses once stood, handsome new buildings have been built. The once-celebrated Quinn's—most famous bar in the South Pacific—has been replaced by a new shopping center. The area known as "Quinn's block" disappeared in December 1975, when a fire destroyed most of it.

An important part of waterfront color still remains. On Quai Bir-Hakeim, you can stroll by the yachts that tie up at the edge of the sidewalk. On their sterns you see markers reading like a roll call of world ports. Nearby, large passenger liners from all over the world still dock at the wharf on Quai du Commerce.

On the land side of the quais, people gather at sidewalk cafes to sip coffee and observe the passing scene. Supermarkets, department stores, Chinese shops, and shipping and airline offices are sandwiched between these eating establishments. You'll find more stores a block or two inland from the quais.

As you stroll along the waterfront, stop at the Tahiti Tourist Development Board in the Fare Manihini building on Quai du Commerce (near the ships' passenger terminal), or the Syndicat d'Initiative in Vaima Shopping Center to pick up maps and brochures on sightseeing, shopping, hotels, and restaurants.

Marché Papeete. Just a block inland from Boulevard Pomaré on Rue Halles (between Rue Cardella and Rue du 22 Sept. 1914), you'll find Papeete's open-air, roofed municipal market. Visit this colorful marketplace early. Activity begins around 5 A.M. daily when the first bus-loads of Le Truck passengers arrive. Soon the market is alive with a babble of voices, a blending of Tahitian and French. Items for sale include neatly strung colorful fish; pyramids of papayas, watermelons, and mangoes; fragrant rows of flowers; baskets of tomatoes, onions, and long skinny cucumbers; buckets of clams and oysters; and rows of woven hats, baskets, mats, and shell jewelry.

One of the best times to visit the market is Sunday —the principal market day when many of Papeete's housewives do their week's shopping. Tahitians come to town from villages all around the island to sell their products. They travel to Papeete on Saturday, sleep at the market overnight, and get up at dawn Sunday to sell their wares. The market closes at 8:30 A.M. on Sundays. During the week it stays open until 5:30 P.M.

Government Center. The French Polynesian government buildings are located a block off Boulevard Pomaré along Avenue Bruat. Flanking the avenue are the executive and judicial offices of the Territory; to the east on a parklike expanse is the Territorial Assembly building. Behind the government buildings, you'll see the High Commissioner's residence with its interesting five-gabled roof.

Glass-bottomed boat ride. One way to see underwater life without getting wet is to take a tour of the lagoon in a glass-bottomed boat. The daily 2-hour trip departs from the Maeva Beach and Tahiti Beachcomber hotels.

Excursions to other islands. From Papeete, you can take a helicopter flightseeing trip that will give you a bird's-eye view of Tahiti and neighboring Moorea.

Cruises to French Polynesia's other islands, with comfortable shipboard accommodations, are offered by Exploration Cruise Lines. Trips vary in length, the shortest being 4 days/3 nights. Ports of call can include Raiatea, Bora Bora, Tahaa, Huahine, and Moorea. You fly to French Polynesia and pick up your cruise ship there.

Lagoonarium de Tahiti. About 13 km/8 miles southwest of Papeete, near the Maeva Beach and Beachcomber hotels, you can see more of French Polynesia's underwater life at the Lagoonarium de Tahiti. This underwater observatory provides viewing windows where visitors see coral gardens and reef and ocean fish. The Lagoonarium's restaurant features regular performances by a Tahitian dance troupe who arrive by double-hulled canoe.

Musée de Tahiti. Near the Lagoonarium, you'll find the Museum of Tahiti and the Islands. Formerly located in downtown Papeete, this museum now occupies the site of a former *marae* (Tahitian temple) in Punaruu, 16 km/10 miles southwest of town. Operated by the Societé des Etudes Océaniennes (Society of Oceanic Studies), the museum contains many archeological and ethnological artifacts of Polynesia as well as a display of the area's flora and fauna. The museum library features historical information about missionary times in Polynesia.

Where to stay. In the Papeete area you'll find comfortable hotels both downtown and along the beachfront northeast and southwest of town.

Downtown hotels include the KonTiki, Tahiti, Royal Papeete, Ibis Papeete, and Matavai. Northeast of town you can stay at several beach resorts—Hotel Royal Tahitien, Princesse Heiata, Hotel Tahara'a, and Hotel Tetiaroa. Resorts southwest of Papeete include the Tahiti Beachcomber, Te Puna Bel Air, Maeva Beach, and Climat de France Tahiti. Best Western Hotel Tahita is located on the opposite coast, south of Taravao.

After the sun goes down. Nearly every hotel in the Papeete area has a nightclub with nightly dancing. Tahitian entertainment is presented at least once a week by many of the larger hotels.

You'll find discos at the Maeva Beach Hotel and Royal

LE TRUCK
It's Fun and Inexpensive

You might glimpse Le Truck for the first time as it bounces along the main road past your Tahiti hotel. Or perhaps you'll notice one parked in front of Papeete's municipal market. These brightly painted, open-sided, covered buses—the islanders' basic form of public transportation—can also be the answer to your transportation needs on Tahiti. You'll find a few Les Trucks on some of the outer islands. They offer an inexpensive way of touring.

To catch Le Truck, flag it down on the main road in front of your hotel. On Tahiti, you can board one at Papeete's municipal market, the start and finish for Le Truck service on the main island. Make sure the vehicle is heading in the direction you want to go.

Your fellow passengers include young Tahitian girls in brightly colored dresses, wide-eyed school children, housewives with baskets of vegetables and squawking chickens, and an occasional fisherman who ties his strings of fish on the ladder at the back. Teetering atop your vehicle in the baggage rack might be a dented milk can, a wash tub, and baskets of produce.

On your trip you'll soon learn that there is no set schedule. Your bus might detour down a narrow road to drop someone off in front of his house. Perhaps a guitar-playing youth will strike a chord, and soon everyone in the bus will be singing. Or if everyone becomes thirsty, the trip will be interrupted for a refreshment stop.

You experience Tahitian life first-hand on Le Truck. It's fun to try—even if you only have time for a short trip.

Papeete Hotel as well as a number of lively nightspots in town. Papeete travel agencies offer after-dark tours stopping at some of these places.

Touring Tahiti

To discover Tahiti's quiet, tropical charms, take a trip along the 116-km/72-mile Route de Ceinture—the Belt Road. This paved route circles Tahiti-Nui, the larger portion of the island. Side roads branch off Belt Road

to wind down the north and south coasts of Tahiti-Iti, the smaller portion of the island.

Driving along the coast, you'll pass black sand beaches, outcrops of lava rock, mountains that soar into the clouds, and deep valleys with plummeting waterfalls. Of note are the three waterfalls in Faaruumai Valley (just south of Arahoho Blowhole); the Cascade de Vaiharuru on the Faatautia River (south of Hitiaa); and Vaipahi Falls (west of Papeari).

Every few kilometers, you see a native village with

churches, a school, and charming houses painted in bright pastel colors. You'll be constantly reminded of Tahiti's lush, flowering beauty. Flamboyant trees display limbs laden with red color; gigantic blooms in reds, oranges, and pinks decorate towering hibiscus; and pink cassia send down showers of pale pink petals. Malay apple trees mix with banana, papaya, avocado, and breadfruit trees.

If you leave no later than 9 A.M. from Papeete, you can make the journey around Tahiti-Nui in a day. This will give you plenty of time to stop at points of interest, go for a swim, and have a picnic or long lunch at a pleasant restaurant such as the Restaurant Musée Gauguin near the museum.

If you wish to see some of Tahiti-Iti as well, try to allow at least 2 days for a leisurely trip. You can stay at the Puunui Beach and Hill Resort on Tahiti-Iti. The resort has an aquatic center and beach.

You can make the trip independently by rental car or motorbike. Guided tours travel around Tahiti-Nui daily from Papeete, or you can hire a car and guide-driver for a personal tour.

Try to avoid making your island trip on Sunday. On this day, many local inhabitants take to the road in sports cars, minibuses, Les Trucks, motorbikes, and bicycles.

Following the island road eastward from Papeete, you'll pass the following points of interest.

Tomb of Pomare V. Tahiti's last monarch is buried at Arue, 4 km/2 miles from Papeete. The tomb, constructed of coral from a nearby lagoon, is topped by an unusually shaped urn similar to a Grecian funeral urn. Some people feel that it resembles a bottle of Benedictine, one of the king's favorite alcoholic beverages.

Point Venus. A lighthouse now stands on the headland where Lieutenant James Cook and his expedition observed the transit of Venus in 1769. Nearby, a monument honors the 18th century European explorers who anchored in Matavai Bay and came ashore here— Samuel Wallis, Louis Antoine de Bougainville, and James Cook. In the Musée de la Découverte (Museum of Discovery), you'll see lifelike wax figures of the three explorers and the Tahitian monarchs who greeted them. The museum also houses a fine collection of artifacts, engravings, maps, and other memorabilia.

Point Venus is about 13 km/8 miles from Papeete. A sign marks the side road leading to the point.

Blowhole of Arahoho. About 22 km/14 miles northeast of Papeete, you'll come to this geologic phenomenon. Ocean waves surge through a natural formation in basalt rock, sending up jets of water that sometimes splash onto the road.

Monument to Bougainville. In Hitiaa, 39 km/24 miles from Papeete, a bronze sign marks the bay where Louis Antoine de Bougainville first anchored upon his arrival in 1768.

Side trip to Tahiti-Iti. In the Taravao area, you can branch off Belt Road for a trip to villages along Tahiti-Iti's north or south coast. Roads wind along each coast for about 18 km/11 miles. From the north coast route, a side road leads to a plateau view point over Tahiti-Nui.

Gauguin Museum. Back on the Belt Road near Papeari, you come to Musée Gauguin. Set in a spacious garden,

Tahitian youths *prepare vegetables for a* tamaaraa, *a traditional feast. Guests eat meal with fingers, then watch native entertainers perform traditional songs and dances.*

this museum is a series of rooms open to the tropical breezes. Only two original Gauguin paintings and one original sculpture are housed in this museum—a memorial to Gauguin and his work. Most of his art work now belongs to art collectors around the world.

Instead, the museum recreates the triumphs and tragedy of this great artist through the use of photographs, maps, reproductions, and other graphic devices. The museum is open daily from 9 A.M. to 5 P.M.

Gauguin arrived in Tahiti in 1891 at the age of 42. For 2 years he lived in Mataiea on Tahiti-Nui's southern coast. After a sojourn in France, he returned to French

Polynesia, settling first at Punaauia on Tahiti's west coast, then moving to Atuona in the Marquesas where he spent the last 8 years of his life. He died at the age of 54, penniless and unrecognized. Today much of the world knows Gauguin's work. He used bold colors to vividly depict the Tahitian people and their land.

Botanical Garden. Adjacent to the museum is a botanical preserve created by American botanist Harrison Smith. In this garden, you'll discover an impressive collection of trees, shrubs, and flowers representing nonindigenous tropical vegetation of French Polynesia. Meandering paths lead past towering trees, stands of bamboo, and lovely flower beds. A couple of tortoises in the garden love to have their heads scratched.

The gardens are open daily from 10 A.M. to 5 P.M.

Maraes. You'll find two *maraes* on Tahiti-Nui's west coast southwest of Papeete—Marae Mahaiatea (35 km/ 22 miles from town) and Marae Arahurahu in Paea (19 km/12 miles from Papeete). During ancient times *maraes* were Polynesian open-air temples of worship. Constructed of several tiers of stone or coral, the temple stood at one end of a rectangular courtyard.

Marae Arahurahu has been restored by the Society of Oceanic Studies. Marae Mahaiatea lies in ruin.

Maraa cave. The largest cave on the island is located on the coast between Marae Mahaiatea and Marae Arahurahu. Water drips constantly from the ceiling of the fern-covered grotto into a dark, cold lake. A short trail (marked by a sign) leads from the road to the mouth of the cave.

Exploring the Outer Islands

To discover the Polynesia of your dreams, you must travel to the outer islands. Here you'll see rugged, emerald green mountains towering above unbelievably clear lagoons; fishermen paddling outrigger canoes and pareu-wrapped women strolling along the road (scenes reminiscent of the Polynesia depicted by Melville, Gauguin, and Michener).

Luring travelers to the outer islands are beautiful beaches, lagoons ideal for snorkeling, and a pace of life that needs no clock.

Moorea, for a slower pace

As you gaze across the bay from Papeete at sunset, the jagged peaks of Moorea—silhouetted against a brilliant red-orange sky—will beckon you. Heed the call and take a short 17-km/11-mile trip to Moorea's shores. You'll be rewarded with tranquil beauty and a pace of life much slower than Papeete's.

By air, it's only a 7-minute flight from Papeete's Faaa Airport to Moorea's airport near Temae, on the northeast side of the island. Numerous flights operate daily during daylight hours. From Papeete's waterfront, highspeed launches make the 50-minute trip daily to Moorea. (To enjoy the scenery, take the boat trip at least one way. Morning—before the seas get rough—is the best time for boat trips.)

If you prefer, you can travel to Moorea with a group. Local operators offer 1 to 3-day trips from Papeete. (Day tours to Moorea go one way by air, the other by boat.)

Island tour. One of the best ways to see tiny Moorea —only 220 square km/85 square miles—is to travel along the coast road that circles the island. Most of Moorea's 6,000 people live in villages along the narrow coastal shelf. Behind their tin-roofed, wooden houses, mountains covered in lush vegetation soar skyward.

On this route, you'll catch glimpses of Polynesian life—children fishing from a bridge, women in bright-colored pareus riding bicycles or motorscooters, and skinny loaves of French bread sticking out of wooden mailboxes. In the villages, fascinating Chinese stores carry everything from pareo prints to fresh fruits, canned vegetables, plastic dishpans, and bicycle tires.

If you don't have the time for the entire 53-km/33-mile circuit, take a shorter journey along the north coast. Here you'll find a good sampling of interesting villages, spectacular volcanic peaks, beautiful beaches, and two fiordlike bays—Opunohu and Cook's.

In Papetoai, on the north coast near the western shore of Opunohu Bay, you'll discover an octagonal church. Built in 1829 by missionaries, it is the oldest European structure still being used in the South Pacific. You also may want to see the Catholic church in Paopao on Cook's Bay; an impressive mural by Pierre Heyman decorates the area above the altar.

At the head of Opunohu Bay, a winding side road leaves the shore route and climbs into the hills. In Opunohu Valley, you see several *maraes* (ancient Polynesian temples) that have been restored under the guidance of archeologists from Hawaii's Bishop Museum. From the Belvédère lookout point, you'll see both Opunohu and Cook's bays cutting into the north coast.

You can travel the island by rental car, jeep, motorbike, or bicycle. Bus tours and lagoon excursions are available. Even if you're traveling with a group, spend a little time exploring at your own leisurely pace. Relax and enjoy a beach picnic or visit one of the local villages.

The island also has taxis, irregular Le Truck service, and limited airport shuttle service from hotels.

Where to stay. Most of Moorea's hotels—built as thatch-roofed bungalows—are located facing the beach along the island's west and north coasts. You can choose from Club-Mediterranée Moorea, Les Tipaniers, Moorea Village, and Captain Cook Beach Hotel (on the west coast); Moorea Lagoon (on the peninsula between Opunohu and Cook's bays); Club Bali Hai, Ibis Moorea, and Kaveka Village (on Cook's Bay); Bali Hai Moorea (east of Cook's Bay); and Kia Ora Moorea (on the east coast).

After the sun goes down. Several of Moorea's hotels feature Tahitian music nightly. *Tamaaraas* (Tahitian feasts and dancing) are held at most of Moorea's hotels on a weekly basis. Among interesting nightspots on the island are the Kia Ora's disco on a converted copra schooner and the One Chicken Inn in Paopao. At the inn, you experience a real raucous Polynesian Saturday night party with the locals.

All the major hotels have restaurants. In addition, visitors enjoy the Manava on Cook's Bay, Chez Michou near the Bali Hai, and Temae at the airport.

Bora Bora, the "most beautiful" island

Perhaps the most acclaimed of the French Polynesian isles, Bora Bora has long been known for its beauty. For some travelers, including writer James Michener, it's the most beautiful island in the world.

To find out if you agree, go and see for yourself. From Papeete, nonstop daily flights take only 50 minutes. (Schooners sail weekly from Papeete to Bora Bora.)

A relatively small island, Bora Bora is home to about 2,600 people. Its topography is dominated by craggy mountains that loom dramatically above the turquoise green lagoon surrounding the island. One of the loveliest lagoons in French Polynesia, it is nearly enclosed by a barrier reef dotted with tiny *motus* (islets). Bora Bora's airstrip sits on one of these islets—Motu Mute. A launch ferries passengers across the shimmering lagoon to the main island.

You can make the round trip to Bora Bora from Papeete in one day if you don't mind crowding in several hours of travel. Or you can relax on Bora Bora for several days, enjoying the island's beauty and leisurely pace. Local operators offer 1, 2, and 3-day tours from Papeete.

Touring the island. A 27-km/17-mile unpaved road circles the island. You can take a bus tour or make the trip by taxi, rental car or jeep, motorbike, or bicycle. There's also irregular Le Truck service.

Traveling along the lagoon's edge, you'll pass groves of coconut palms and tiny villages hugging the shoreline. You might also see the ruins of *maraes*—the island has about 40 of them.

Vaitape contains the tomb of French navigator Alain Gerbault, who circled the globe alone in a small boat in the 1920s. Vaitape is the administrative center for the island.

After you've toured the island, you can take an excursion in an outrigger canoe, picnic on a motu, join a round-the-island boat trip, or view the lagoon's coral gardens and fascinating marine life from a glass-bottomed boat. Your hotel can provide information on these activities.

Where to stay. A number of Bora Bora hotels offer guests comfortable bungalow-style accommodations—Hotel Bora Bora, Club-Mediterranée-Noa Noa (an extension of Club Med Moorea), Sofitel Marara, Marina Hotel, Oa Oa Hotel, Hotel Matira, Yacht Club de Bora Bora, and the Bora Bora Bungalows.

Huahine, two islands at high tide

Growing in popularity as a tourist destination is Huahine, 177 km/110 miles northwest of Papeete. Fourteen 50-minute flights weekly link Papeete with the Huahine airport on the western edge of Lake Fauna Nui. A schooner also travels weekly to Huahine.

At high water, Huahine is really two islands—Huahine-Nui in the north and Huahine-Iti in the south—divided by a strait connected by a bridge. Each island has a mountain—710 meter/2,331 foot Mount Turi on Huahine-Nui and 456 meter/1,495 foot Mount Moufene on Huahine-Iti. A barrier reef protects the island sections.

Nor far from the airport on Huahine-Nui, you can visit Maeva Village, built at a point where Lake Fauna Nui joins a lagoon. Maeva's houses sit on stilts over the water. A century-old system of fish traps is still used near the village. (The island's people make their living by fishing and farming.)

You'll find numerous ancient maraes in the Lake Fauna Nui district. At one time, all district chiefs lived side by side in this area and worshipped in their own maraes. Recent archeological discoveries indicate that Huahine has been populated for at least 1,100 years.

The island's principal town is Fare on Huahine-Nui's west coast. Reminiscent of a frontier town, Fare has aging colonial-style wooden buildings lining its tree-shaded waterfront street.

The unpaved main road connects villages on Huahine-Nui with villages on Huahine-Iti. Island transportation for visitors includes rental cars, rental bicycles, and taxis. Le Truck service is irregular. Visitors can also join island tours by taxi and bus or go sightseeing in a native canoe or motorboat.

The Hotel Bali Hai Huahine and the Huahine Beach Hotel are the island's only tourist hotels. You can also stay in one of several small modest hotels, or arrange to stay with a local family.

Raiatea, the second largest island

Second only in size to Tahiti (288 square km/179 square miles), the large island of Raiatea lies 220 km/137 miles northwest of Papeete. About 9,900 people live on Raiatea. To the north, the neighboring island of Tahaa shares a barrier reef and lagoon with Raiatea. A narrow 3-km/2-mile-wide channel separates the two islands.

Raiatea is thought to be the site of one of the first ancient Polynesian settlements. From here Polynesians sailed northward to populate the Hawaiian Islands and southwest to form the Maori colonies in New Zealand.

From Papeete, planes fly daily to the Raiatea airport near Uturoa. The flight takes about 45 minutes. Schooners sail weekly from Papeete to Raiatea. To reach Tahaa, you must travel from Raiatea by boat.

On Raiatea you can explore by car, bicycle, or taxi. Local bus and boat tours are available, and there is some Le Truck service. A road follows the shoreline from Opoa on the east coast northward around the island to Fetuna on the southwest coast.

Uturoa. This main village sits on Raiatea's northeast tip. With a population of 2,500, Uturoa is French Polynesia's second largest town. Several interesting Chinese stores on the main street are crowded with merchandise—pareo prints, handmade baskets, native carvings, and island necessities such as groceries and motorbikes.

If you come to Uturoa on Wednesday, Friday, or Sunday, be sure to visit the lively public market near the pier. People from Raiatea and Tahaa travel by boat and Le Truck to sell their produce. Fish, fruit, vegetables, pigs, ducks, and chickens are all for sale in the marketplace.

Opoa. On the east coast about 30 km/19 miles south of Uturoa, Opoa was the religious center of the Society Islands in pre-European times. On a point of land east of the village, you'll find Marae Taputapuatea. Restored in 1968, this temple was once one of the most important maraes in the South Pacific—the ancient seat of knowledge and religion.

Faaroa River. Be sure to take a boat tour up the Faaroa River while you're on Raiatea. (The river is 13 km/8 miles northwest of Opoa.) From this river, the original Maoris sailed for New Zealand. The ancient homeland of the Maoris is now overgrown with tropical vegetation.

Trip to Tahaa. Tours to Tahaa depart from the Hotel Bali Hai Raiatea, located southeast of Uturoa. The boat trip to the island takes about 40 minutes. The first stop is Tiva, a small village, where passengers visit Chief Tavana's home. The chief has a shark aquarium, a turtle pool, and a museum of sea relics.

Firewalking. The ceremony of firewalking, *Umu-ti*, on Raiatea dates from early times. Today, it is performed on the grounds of the Hotel Bali Hai Raiatea. Villagers from Apoiti re-create the ancient rite of walking barefoot across white-hot stones.

Where to stay. Raiatea's only tourist-style hotel is the Bali Hai Raiatea, less than 2 km/1 mile southeast of Uturoa. There are also several small hotels with modest rooms on Raiatea and Tahaa.

Remote Polynesian retreats

Several islands in the more remote areas of French Polynesia—such as the Tuamotus, Marquesas, Australs, and Gambiers—can be reached by plane or boat from Papeete. However, most of these islands remain basically undeveloped without hotels. Accommodations can be arranged with island families.

Two islands in the Tuamotu group, northeast of Tahiti, offer hotels—the Kia Ora Village, Rangiroa Village, and Village Sans Souci on Rangiroa and Kaina Village on Manihi. Both of these islands are atolls—thin strips of sand dotted with coconut palms. On one side of the narrow beach is the pounding surf, on the other a quiet lagoon. These islands offer peaceful surroundings, miles of beach, and your choice of water activities.

Know Before You Go

The following practical information can help you plan your trip to French Polynesia.

Entry/exit procedures. For stays of less than 30 days, you will need a valid passport and an onward travel ticket. Longer stays require a visa.

Visitors coming from Fiji and the Samoas must have all baggage (except hand luggage) fumigated upon arrival. Taking about 2 hours, the fumigation is required to protect French Polynesia's coconut trees from pests found on other South Pacific islands. Visitors may wish to carry clothing and toilet articles for the first night's stay in hand luggage.

Only travelers arriving from an infected area need vaccinations against small pox, yellow fever, and cholera.

There is no airport departure tax.

Customs. In addition to personal belongings, you can bring in 400 cigarettes, 100 cigars, or 500 grams/1 pound of tobacco; and 1 litre/quart of spirits. Amateur photographers are allowed 2 still cameras with 10 rolls of unexposed film, and 1 movie camera with 10 rolls of unexposed film.

Currency. The French Pacific Franc (CFP)—Coins include denominations of 1, 2, 5, 10, 20, 50, and 100, and notes include denominations of 500, 1000, and 5000.

Tipping. Tipping is not customary in French Polynesia. It is against the Tahitian idea of hospitality.

Time. French Polynesia is GMT (Greenwich mean time) −10. For example, when it is 1 P.M. Saturday in Papeete, it is 3 P.M. Saturday in San Francisco; 11 A.M. Sunday in Auckland; and 9 A.M. Sunday in Sydney.

Weather and what to wear. French Polynesia has a tropical climate cooled by trade winds. Travelers who visit during the cool, dry season from March through November, enjoy temperatures averaging 23°C/73°F. During the warm moist season—December through February—you can expect 13 to 18 days of rain a month, and temperatures can reach 30°C/86°F.

Casual lightweight attire is the key to proper dress in French Polynesia. Even in the evening, men can wear just slacks and a shirt. Ties and jackets aren't required in restaurants. Women often wear casual, long dresses to dinner.

Other items you'll want to pack include an umbrella or plastic raincoat, a sweater or jacket for cool evenings, sunglasses and suntan lotion, mosquito repellent, and tennis shoes or plastic beach shoes for coral reef exploring.

For more information. For further information on French Polynesia, write to the Tahiti Tourist Board, B.P. 65, Papeete.

In the United States you can contact the Tahiti Tourist Board at 2330 Westwood Boulevard, Suite 200, Los Angeles, CA 90064.

Residents of Australia and New Zealand can write the Tahiti Tourist Board, 12 Castlereagh Street, Sydney, New South Wales 2000, Australia. In Great Britain write the Tahiti Tourist Board, 178 Piccadilly, London W1V OAL, England.

THE SAMOAS

The Samoas—American and Western—are considered the heart of Polynesia. Early Polynesians sailed from here to populate other Pacific islands.

Today, these two politically separate countries share the world's largest full-blooded Polynesian population and a strong belief in tradition. After a short time in the Samoas, you'll learn how much *fa'a Samoa*—the Samoan Way—is valued.

Much of the charm of the Samoas lies in the simple village life and the friendly people. Passing thatch-roofed *fales* (open-air dwellings), you see village chiefs sitting cross-legged on woven grass mats, solving problems unhurriedly and with great dignity. The women sit placidly stringing shells on fishline for *ula sisis* (shell leis) and weaving baskets made of pandanus leaves. Smiling children come running to meet you, and villagers welcome you with the cheery Samoan greeting, *"Talofa."* Hospitality is an important part of fa'a Samoa.

In addition to the friendly Samoan people, you'll find a striking landscape—soaring volcanic mountain peaks, rugged coastlines, calm lagoons and white sandy beaches, and tropical rain forests rich in flowering plants.

The Heart of Polynesia

The 16 islands of the Samoan group cluster near the heart of Polynesia.(Western Samoa is about 4,205 km/ 2,613 miles southwest of Hawaii and 2,897 km/1,800 miles northeast of New Zealand.) Stretching some 402 km/250 miles across the South Pacific, this chain of islands is divided into two political units—the U.S. Territory of American Samoa and the independent country of Western Samoa.

At the eastern end of the Samoan chain, the seven islands of American Samoa cover a land area of 197 square km/76 square miles. The country's capital, Pago Pago, is located on the main island of Tutuila. Other islands include Aunu'u, the Manu'a group (Ta'u, Olosega, and Ofu), Swains, and Rose. Uninhabited Rose Island is a wildlife sanctuary.

Western Samoa lies about 129 km/80 miles northwest of American Samoa. Its nine islands comprise a land area of 3,031 square km/1,100 square miles. A narrow strait separates the country's two main islands—Savai'i and Upolu. Savai'i is the westernmost and largest island in the Samoan group. Western Samoa's capital, Apia, is located on Upolu. The country's other islands include Manono and Apolima, located in the strait between Upolu and Savai'i, and five uninhabited islands within or near the reef surrounding Upolu.

Lush, volcanic isles

Most of the islands in both American and Western Samoa are high islands of volcanic origin. Jungle-clad mountains rise abruptly from the sea, jagged peaks stretch toward the sky, and fiordlike bays cut deeply into narrow valleys. Rivers cut through the dense forests, plunging down steep cliffs into inviting pools. Along the narrow coastline, beaches rim blue-green lagoons protected by coral reefs.

Island flora. Tropical plants thrive in the volcanic soil. Rain forests rich in banyan trees, ferns, and vine creepers cover much of the islands. Blossoming hibiscus, ginger, frangipani, gardenias, and orchids add splashes of color to the dark greenery.

Wildlife. Over 50 species of birds inhabit the Samoas. They include tooth-billed pigeons, Samoan fantails, Samoan broadbills, reef herons, and fruit doves. Field rats, lizards, and flying foxes (a type of bat) also roam the islands. Domesticated animals include beef and dairy cattle, pigs, and poultry.

Cradle of Polynesia

Scientists say the first Polynesians migrated from Southeast Asia to Samoa long before the birth of Christ. From Savai'i, the cradle of Polynesia, the race spread to other islands in the Pacific.

Dutch navigator Jacob Roggeveen was the first European to sight the islands in 1722. More than 40 years later, Louis Antoine de Bougainville visited the Samoas, which he named the Navigator Islands. Next came La Perouse in 1787. Little information about the Samoas reached the outside world until 1830, when John Williams of the London Missionary Society arrived.

By the mid-19th century Britain, Germany, and the United States began to show commercial interest in the Samoas and sent representative consuls to the islands. Augmenting the Samoan tribal strife already existing during this period, fierce rivalry developed between the competing countries. This power struggle almost resulted in war.

Finally, in 1899 a treaty was drawn up giving the Eastern Samoan islands to the United States and the Western Samoas to Germany. Britain withdrew, having territorial rights elsewhere in the Pacific.

As a territory, American Samoa was administered by the U.S. Navy for the first half of the 20th century. When the naval base was closed in 1951, administration was transferred to the U.S. Department of the Interior.

After World War I, the League of Nations mandated Western Samoa to New Zealand. Following World War II, the country became a Trusteeship Territory, still administered by New Zealand. After a period of self-

(Continued on page 33)

Cruise ship *anchors in deep water of Pago Pago Bay. Steep, forested mountains rim fiordlike harbor, considered one of the Pacific's most spectacular. Tramway offers 6-minute ride above port to summit of Mount Alava.*

Dressed *in bright red lava-lavas, men join in tug of war during holiday festivities in American Samoa.*

PACIFIC ARCHITECTURE
It's Eclectic

FIJIAN BURE

SAMOAN FALE

PALAU MEN'S HOUSE

NEW CALEDONIA HUT

Take heavy lengths of timber cut from a coconut tree and lash them together to make a sturdy frame. Add walls made of woven niaouli bark or bamboo. Top it all off with a high-pitched roof of palm leaves or grass thatch, and you've created a traditional Pacific island home.

Built from the materials of the earth, it's a simple abode, designed mainly to protect its inhabitants from sun and rain. The steeply pitched roof allows warm air to rise, providing natural air conditioning. Most activities take place outside in the balmy tropical breezes.

Many of today's Pacific islanders choose to live in modern houses built of concrete blocks or wood topped by corrugated metal roofs. But traveling through the countryside, you'll still see traditional homes.

The architecture of these huts may vary from country to country and even from region to region. In the Samoas for example, the thatch-roofed homes are round with open sides that allow for maximum natural air conditioning. Although some of the huts in New Caledonia and Papua New Guinea are also round, they have low sides and more steeply pitched conical roofs.

Europeans introduced the rectangular shape to Pacific island architecture; you'll find examples of this type in Fiji. A-frame architecture is used in the men's council houses of Palau and Yap and in the *haus tambaran* (spirit house) style of Papua New Guinea.

The variety of hut shapes and construction materials adds an interesting facet to your Pacific island explorations.

government in the 1950s, Western Samoa finally achieved independence on January 1, 1962.

American Samoa's government today. American Samoa is an unincorporated territory of the United States administered by the Department of the Interior. American Samoans have free access to the United States but are not U.S. citizens.

Until recently, the territory's governor was appointed by the Department of the Interior, but he is now elected by the people. The territory has a bicameral legislature, the *Fono,* consisting of a House of Representatives elected by universal adult suffrage and a Senate elected by the *matais* (chiefs) in accordance with Samoan custom.

Government in Western Samoa today. Western Samoa is a constitutional monarchy. The country's constitution—its supreme law—provides for a head of state, prime minister, legislature, and judiciary.

The present head of state, Malietoa Tanumafili II, will rule for life. Succeeding heads of state will be elected every 5 years by the Legislative Assembly. According to tradition, the monarch is chosen from the Four Royal Sons or families.

The matais of Western Samoa, numbering over 10,000, elect 45 members of the Legislative Assembly. Two other members are elected by universal adult suffrage.

Executive governmental matters are carried out by a prime minister, elected by the Legislative Assembly with the approval of the head of state.

The Samoan People

The world's largest full-blooded Polynesian population resides in the Samoas. Nearly 90 percent of the Samoas' 185,000 people are Polynesian. The other 10 percent include Asians, Americans, Europeans, Australians, and New Zealanders.

Western Samoa's population numbers 155,000, most of whom live on Upolu. The majority of American Samoa's 30,000 residents call Tutuila home.

Fa'a Samoa, the Samoan Way

The Samoans are friendly, generous, modest, and fun-loving. Proud of their heritage and customs, they work to preserve them. In Samoan conversation you'll often hear the expression *fa'a Samoa*—the Samoan Way. Adhering to tradition, the people have managed to withstand many outside influences, at the same time adapting foreign ideas to their way of life.

Extended family. Despite western influences, the basic unit of the village community remains the *aiga* (extended family), a group consisting of blood relatives, in-laws, and adopted members. Traditionally, people must place the extended family before themselves; and no family member should go in need.

Chiefs. The family members of each aiga elect a *matai* (chief) as head of the family. In return for services rendered and money contributed by family members, he represents them in village affairs, takes responsibility for their protection and well-being, and acts as trustee for family lands and property.

Above the family chiefs is a hierarchy of chiefs. Each of these chiefs has his own talking chiefs who act as his orators. Custom requires that frequent speeches be made. The talking chiefs know the correct language and the ranks and titles of people being addressed.

In the Samoas, titles are hereditary only to a degree. Every energetic and capable young man can aspire to a title someday. At present there are more than 8,000 Samoan chiefs of varying ranks.

Life in the Samoas

Most Samoans reside in villages. Western Samoans remain relatively traditional in their life styles, whereas American Samoans have adopted some new ideas. Traditional customs still exist in both countries.

Many Western Samoans still live in traditional *fales*—elliptical, open-sided houses set in a semicircle around a grassy village green. Topping each fale is a thatch (or corrugated metal) roof supported by a circle of pillars. Woven mat blinds are lowered for protection against rain and wind. On the floor of the fale is a raised platform of coral, topped with smooth pebbles and covered by mats. Modern fales contain some furniture.

American Samoans have adopted western-style fales, rectangular in shape and built of concrete blocks with corrugated metal roofs. The dwellings have pastel-colored walls and large, louvered windows. You also see some traditional fales.

Dress. Samoan men prefer *lava-lavas*—bright, knee-length wraparound skirts—worn with or without shirts. Samoan women wear dresses, skirts and blouses, or the more traditional *puletasi* (tunic and long skirt).

Religion. In both American and Western Samoa, religion plays an important role in the lives of the people. You'll see numerous imposing, elaborately designed churches here. Every village, no matter how small, has at least one steepled church.

In addition to two Sunday services, families gather in their homes early each evening for 10 to 15 minutes of prayer. Visitors should not walk through a village or enter a fale during this prayer time.

Most Samoans are Protestant, though there are some Roman Catholics and Mormons.

Language. English is the official business language of the Samoas. You'll find Samoan spoken widely in both countries.

The Samoan language is closely related to other Polynesian tongues. In pronouncing words, note that the Samoan "g" is equivalent to the English "ng." For example, Pago Pago is pronounced "Pango Pango."

Economic mainstays

Unlike many South Pacific countries, American Samoa does not rely mainly on copra for economic support. The country's thriving fish industry produces such items as canned fish, pet food, and fish meal. Economic development in American Samoa is encouraged through U.S. federal appropriations.

In contrast, Western Samoa's economy depends on

FESTIVAL TIME

Both American and Western Samoa offer a variety of special events that visitors can enjoy.

January—April

Cricket Season. In both American and Western Samoa, cricket season runs from January to April. You can see matches in Pago Pago and Apia.

Rugby Season. March through June you can enjoy rugby matches in Apia and in the villages of Western Samoa.

Flag Day. American Samoa's biggest holiday is Flag Day, April 17. Parades, singing, dancing, longboat races, and numerous other events herald the first rais-

ing of the American flag in the territory.

Anzac Day. On April 25 Western Samoa observes this day in commemoration of the casualties of war.

May—August

Independence Day. Western Samoa's biggest event is Independence Day, celebrated the first three consecutive working days in June. You'll see dance performances, sports events, feasting, and longboat and horse races in Apia.

Samoa International Golf Tournament. Western Samoa holds this annual tournament

in August at the Royal Samoa Golf Club in Fagali'i.

September—December

White Sunday. On the second Sunday in October, American and Western Samoan children are honored. Special plays are presented at churches, and children dressed in new Sunday whites take the honored seats at family feasts.

Palolo scooping. Sometime between October and early November the coral worms, called *palolo,* float up from the reefs in both Samoas. Thousands of islanders wade out and enthusiastically scoop up the "caviar of the Pacific."

---

three agricultural crops—coconuts, cocoa, and bananas. Other exports include lumber, fruits, and vegetables.

Tourism is becoming an important industry in both countries.

Cricket, Samoan-style

The most popular sport in both American and Western Samoa is cricket—Samoan-style. Throughout the year Samoans play the game on village greens. Unlike traditional British cricket which has 11 team members, Samoan cricket can include the whole community— 50 to 100 men, women, and children. Children too young to play practice by using coconut fronds instead of wooden bats.

Other competitive sports enjoyed by the Samoans include boxing, rugby, American football, basketball, volleyball, and tennis. You can watch lawn bowling throughout the year at the Apia Bowling Club, next door to the Tusitala Hotel in Apia.

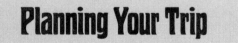

Planning Your Trip

The islands of American and Western Samoa lie south of the equator and east of the International Dateline.

Neighboring countries include both Fiji and Tonga.

Both American and Western Samoa are easily reached by air. International flights land in American Samoa at Pago Pago's Tafuna Airport (11 km/7 miles southwest of town center) and at Western Samoa's Faleolo Airport (37 km/23 miles west of Apia). Buses and taxis provide transportation into town from both airports.

Two local carriers—Polynesian Airlines and South Pacific Island Airways—provide daily service linking Pago Pago and Apia. The flight takes about 30 minutes.

Pago Pago and Apia are ports of call for a number of passenger and passenger/cargo lines sailing the South Pacific. In American Samoa passengers disembark at the main dock in the central part of busy Fagatogo, just southwest of Pago Pago. Ships arriving at Apia, Western Samoa, dock directly across the waterfront road from Aggie Grey's Hotel.

For information on local transportation, see page 37 (American Samoa) and page 40 (Western Samoa).

Where to stay

In the Samoas, you can choose to stay in a large, modern hotel, a simple bungalow or small motel, or a tent. Most of the hotels and motels have dining rooms, cocktail lounges, and coffee and tea making facilities.

American Samoa has only one large hotel—the Pago Pago Rainmaker. Western Samoa's major hotels are Aggie Grey's, a South Pacific landmark, and the Tusitala.

For more information on accommodations in American Samoa, see page 37; Western Samoa information will be found on page 40.

Flanked by village elders, *Samoan chief's daughter solemnly prepares kava in large wooden bowl for guests. During welcoming ceremony, guests sit cross-legged on mats, each drinking a cup of kava in single gulp.*

Fia fia, the Samoan feast

One of the best ways to experience both traditional Samoan food and entertainment is to attend a *fia fia*—a Samoan feast. In both American and Western Samoa, the fia fia is an important part of island life; no special occasion passes without a feast to honor it.

The fare. At a *fia fia*, you'll find an exotic array of Samoan dishes. Many of the items are baked in an *umu* (Samoan oven), where food wrapped in banana leaves cooks slowly over hot stones. From these ovens come fish, chicken, and a variety of tropical fruits and vegetables.

Other island specialties include suckling pig (cooked on a spit or in an umu), barbecued chicken, pigeon, crab, *masi* (biscuits made from grated, fermented breadfruit), and *ota* (raw fish marinated with chili, pepper, or garlic).

If you are in the Samoas in October or early November, you can sample the South Seas version of caviar—*palolo*. These coral worms—considered a local delicacy—wiggle out of the reef just once a year.

Kava ceremony. While the food is cooking, you might be fortunate enough to participate in a kava ceremony. At a village fia fia, this is performed by the village chiefs in the guest fale where you sit cross-legged (Samoan-style) on a matted floor. The kava—made from dried, pulverized pepper plant root mixed with water—will be solemnly prepared before you in a large wooden bowl, usually by a chief's daughter. One by one each guest is handed a cup of kava, which should be drunk in a single gulp. The kava ceremony is an important ritual of Samoan hospitality.

The entertainment. Following the kava ceremony, while you dine, Samoans in traditional dress perform ancient songs and dances.

Etiquette, Samoan-style. If you participate in a village fia fia, you should follow certain Samoan rules of etiquette.

• Before drinking a cup of kava, first tip a little liquid from the cup onto the ground immediately in front of you, at the same time saying *"Manuia."*

• Don't walk across the mats in the fale; instead, circle around the edge of them as you approach your host. Never speak to anyone seated in the fale while you are standing. Address the chief from a sitting position.

• When you sit, cross your legs in front of you, or fold them behind you. It is considered rude to stretch out your legs and feet in front of you.

• Before eating, wait for grace to be said.

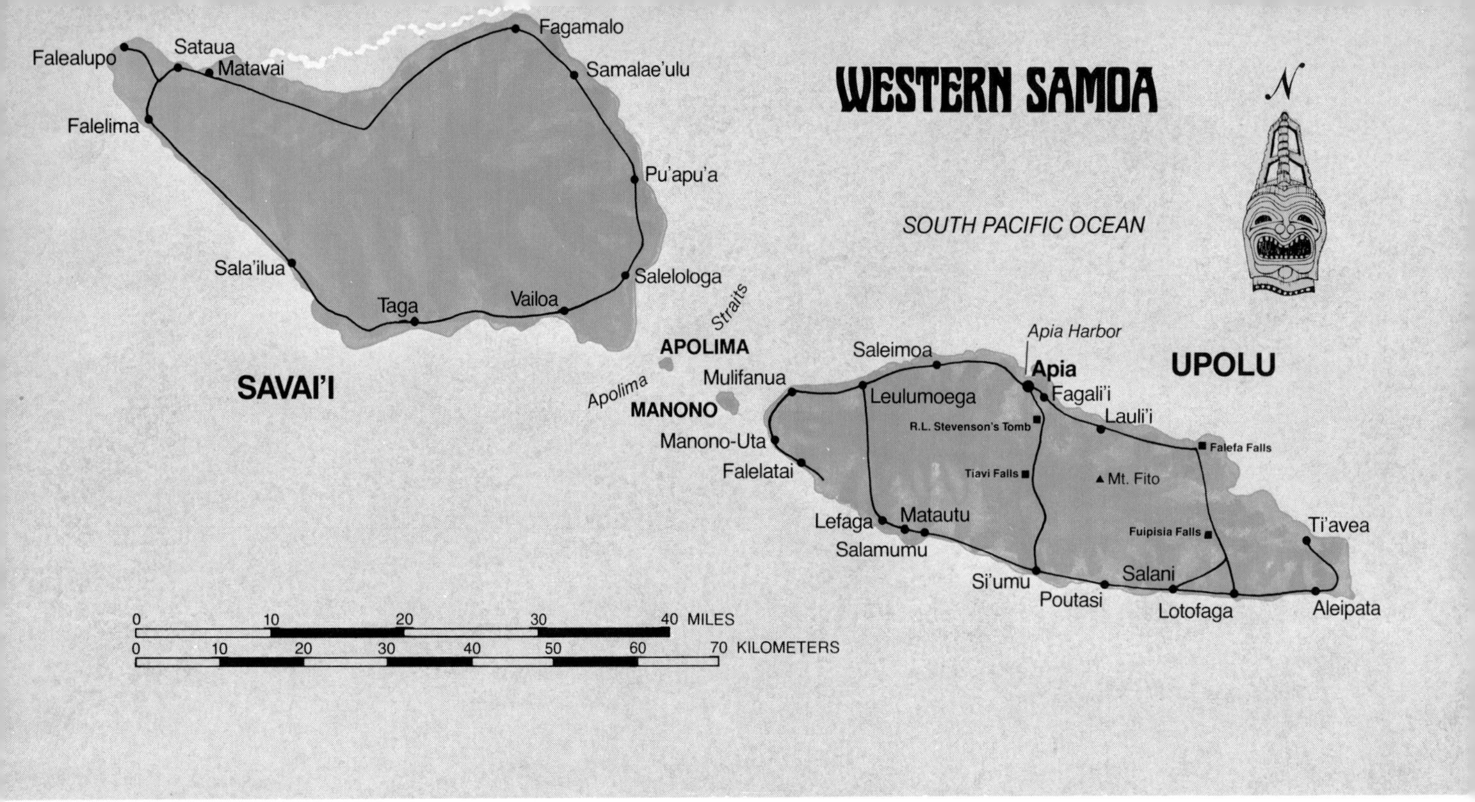
WESTERN SAMOA
N
SOUTH PACIFIC OCEAN
Falealupo
Sataua
Matavai
Fagamalo
Samalae'ulu
Falelima
Pu'apu'a
Sala'ilua
Salelologa
Taga
Vailoa
Apolima Straits
APOLIMA
SAVAI'I
Apolima
MANONO
Mulifanua
Manono-Uta
Falelatai
Saleimoa
Apia Harbor
Apia
Fagali'i
UPOLU
Leulumoega
R.L. Stevenson's Tomb
Lauli'i
Falefa Falls
Tiavi Falls
Mt. Fito
Lefaga
Matautu
Salamumu
Fuipisia Falls
Ti'avea
Si'umu
Salani
Poutasi
Lotofaga
Aleipata
0 10 20 30 40 MILES
0 10 20 30 40 50 60 70 KILOMETERS

Shopping for Samoan specialties

Travelers can shop for interesting handicrafts in both American and Western Samoa. Many visitors select attractive Samoan woven products such as double-woven floor mats, plaited place mats, baskets, and woven purses. Samoan women are highly skilled in weaving.

Other local craft items include hand-painted fabric, tapa cloth, lava-lavas and puletasis, woodcarvings, and shell jewelry.

Most stores in American Samoa are open Monday to Friday from 8 A.M. to 5 P.M. and on Saturday from 8 to 1. In Western Samoa, you can shop from 8 A.M. to 4:30 P.M. weekdays and from 8 to 12:30 on Saturday. During the week, stores are closed at lunch (noon to 1:30 P.M.). In both countries most stores are closed on Sundays and public holidays.

Recreational opportunities

As in many areas of the South Pacific, the climate and waters of the Samoas encourage water sport activities. Both countries have a number of good beaches where you can go swimming or surfing.

Scuba and skin diving. Scuba and skin divers will be delighted with the clear waters around American Samoa, where visibility averages 30 meters/100 feet. Good diving spots include Taema Banks about 3 km/2 miles outside of Pago Pago Bay and Nafuna Bank 2 km/1 mile off Aunu'u Island. For information on diving and snorkeling in American Samoa, inquire at your hotel or at the Office of Tourism in Pago Pago.

In Western Samoan waters, scuba and skin divers report visibility up to 152 meters/500 feet. Good diving spots on Upolu include the lagoons at Lauli'i and Luatuanu'u. You can rent snorkeling and diving equipment at Aggie Grey's Hotel and the Hotel Tusitala in Apia.

Fishing. In the waters off American and Western Samoa, fishing prospects are topnotch. Catches include marlin, tuna, wahoo, mahi mahi, sailfish, and broadbill. For more information, check with your hotel.

Golf. In American Samoa golfers enjoy the 9-hole course near Pago Pago's Tafuna Airport. Western Samoa visitors can play the Royal Samoa Golf Club's 18-hole course at Fagali'i, about 5 km/3 miles east of Apia on Upolu. Visitors can make arrangements to play through the club secretary.

Tennis. If tennis is your game, you can wield your racket in American Samoa at a number of courts in and around Pago Pago. You'll find courts in Pago Pago Park and Tafuna.

In Western Samoa you can play tennis on grass, asphalt, and concrete courts in and around Apia.

First Stop, American Samoa

For many visitors, the first stop will be Tutuila—American Samoa's major island. Here, cloud-topped mountains rise steeply from placid lagoons; row after straight row of coconut palms wave in the breeze; and tiny villages cluster on white sand beaches.

Near the island's center, Pago Pago Bay thrusts a fiordlike arm deep into the land, nearly bisecting 10-km/

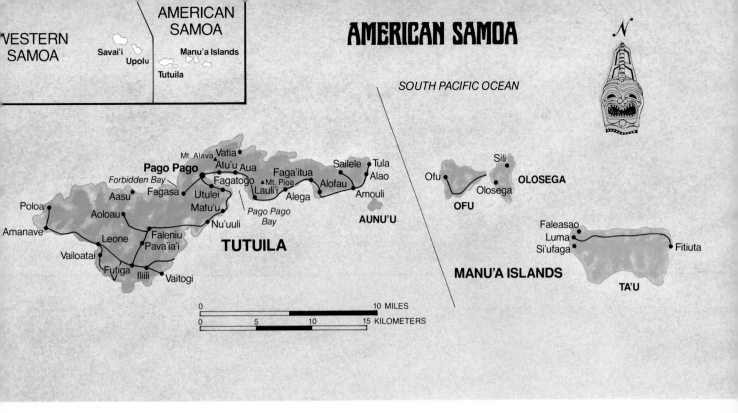

6-mile wide, 29-km/18-mile long Tutuila. One of the world's most spectacular tropical island harbors, Pago Pago Bay was formed centuries ago when the seaward wall of a great crater collapsed, allowing water to enter the steep-sided, lushly green volcano.

Getting around American Samoa

Visitors usually spend most of their time exploring the shore of Pago Pago Bay and touring the rest of Tutuila Island. Nearly 80 km/50 miles of paved road curve along the island's south shore. Some north shore villages are reached by side roads branching off this main road.

Taxis are plentiful on Tutuila; they come in all shapes, sizes, and colors. If you want to rent a car, bring along a current driver's license. Traffic keeps to the right.

An inexpensive method of local transportation is the open-air bus. Passengers can travel from one end of Tutuila to the other for less than a dollar. Although buses run frequently to the villages east and west of Pago Pago, they don't follow a precise timetable or a prescribed route but go where the passengers want them to go. Don't expect specified bus stops. When you want to board a bus, flag it down and tell the driver where you want to be let off. There is little bus service after 5 P.M. and none on Sundays or holidays.

Boat service. Adventurous travelers can explore the islands by cargo boat. Used primarily to transport freight between the islands, they also carry passengers.

Cargo boats make the 129-km/80-mile trip from Pago Pago to Apia, Western Samoa, several times a week. There's also once-a-week boat service to the Manu'a group from Pago Pago.

Once weekly, a government boat makes a full-day trip around Tutuila from Pago Pago, dropping off school supplies. Stops include the small, offshore island of Aunu'u and villages along the north shore.

Air travel. In addition to regular daily air service between Pago Pago and Apia, daily flights on South Pacific Island Airways and Manu'a Air Transport also serve the Manu'a Islands.

Island tours. Local operators offer a variety of tours around Pago Pago, to other villages on Tutuila, and to the Manu'a group.

Accommodations are limited

American Samoa has only one large hotel—the 188-room Pago Pago Rainmaker, located on a peninsula jutting into Pago Pago Bay. With buildings designed to resemble traditional Samoan fales, the hotel sits on the site of the old Navy Goat Island Club. It was named after the old Rainmaker Hotel made famous in Somerset Maugham's short story, "Rain."

On a smaller scale with only 8 rooms is the Apiolefaga Inn in the downtown area.

The government has recently opened a campground at Aoa on Tutuila's northeast coast. Here, vacationers can stay in a tent or Samoan-style fale. There's a Samoan guest fale on Ta'u in the Manu'a group.

Dining in American Samoa

Hungry travelers find variety ranging from authentic Samoan foods to American hamburgers at the Pago Pago Rainmaker Hotel. At least once a week the hotel offers a Mongolian barbecue, where guests select desired meat, vegetables, and sauces which the chef cooks.

For a special treat attend a fia fia, a Samoan feast. The feasts are presented regularly at the Rainmaker Hotel. Local tour operators also sponsor group trips to fia fias in nearby villages.

Soli's Restaurant has a Polynesian floor show several nights a week. Nightclub tours are available.

Samoan girls *splash in pool at waterfall's base near Apia. Visitors traveling Upolu's coastal or cross-island roads discover numerous inviting spots to picnic or swim.*

South Pacific landmark, *Aggie Grey's gained fame as World War II gathering place for Seabees and sailors. Aggie still presides at Apia hotel, which attracts a cosmopolitan crowd.*

Exploring the Pago Pago area

Pago Pago (pronounced "Pango Pango") is one of several small villages situated along the narrow shore of beautiful Pago Pago Bay. Here you'll find most of the shops, ship docks, and business and government buildings of American Samoa. At the southwest edge are the Pago Pago Rainmaker Hotel and the adjacent villages of Fagatogo (pronounced "Fangatongo") and Utulei. In fact, Fagatogo is really the capital of American Samoa. However, because of the fame of Pago Pago Bay, Pago Pago is used collectively to refer to several villages.

Jagged, bush-covered mountains ring the harbor, ascending abruptly from the coast. Across the harbor from the Pago Pago district, Mount Pioa looms from a height of 524 meters/1,718 feet. Called "The Rainmaker" by the Samoans, this massive bulk of volcanic rock attracts moisture-filled clouds around its summit, bringing Pago Pago more than its fair share of rain.

Visitors find the Pago Pago area an unhurried, restful place to visit. Shops offering a miscellany of merchandise line the main streets. Residential sections sprawl up the hills, and footpaths continue from dead-end roads to the entrances of houses. Almost every block has its place of worship.

Below are some of the sights to visit in the Pago Pago area.

Tramway ride. One of the first things most visitors enjoy is the 6-minute aerial tramway ride to the top of Mount Alava. It operates daily from 8 A.M. to 4 P.M. except during strong winds. The best times to take the ride are early morning and late afternoon.

Boarding the tram car at Solo Hill (a short distance from the Pago Pago Rainmaker Hotel), you'll cross the harbor and ascend 488 meters/1,600 feet to the mountaintop.

On a clear day, you can see Pago Pago township, the harbor, Western Samoa's islands to the northwest, and the Manu'a group to the east. The tramway was built in 1965 to transport personnel and heavy equipment during construction of a television transmitting tower on Mount Alava.

Government House. As you leave Solo Hill on your tram ride, you pass over the rooftop of Government House. For more than 70 years, this two-story white, wooden mansion has served as the home of the territory's chief executives.

Television Center. In Utulei, across the road from the Pago Pago Rainmaker, visitors can tour the Michael J. Kirwan Educational Television Center. Heart of the educational television system established by former Governor H. Rex Lee, the center produces lessons for American Samoa's elementary and secondary school students. In the evenings, station programs educate and entertain adults.

Guided tours are held Monday to Friday between 2 and 5 P.M.

Jean M. Haydon Museum. Named after the wife of former Governor John M. Haydon, this museum contains an impressive assortment of Samoan artifacts and ancient handicraft items.

Located in downtown Fagatogo next to the fire station, the museum is housed in the old post office—an early 20th-century building dating from the U.S.

Navy years. You can visit the museum weekdays from 8 A.M. to 4 P.M. and Saturdays between 9 and noon.

Sadie Thompson territory. If you've read Somerset Maugham's story, "Rain," you'll want to see the site where the author reputedly gathered material for his famous tale. The former boarding house, now the **Max Haleck Store #3,** is located on Fagatogo's main road past the marketplace.

Other sights. Another Fagatogo point of interest is the Fono building, home of the territory's legislature. Its architecture combines traditional fale construction and modern materials. In front of the Fono building is the *malae* (village green), where traditional games, singing, and dancing take place on special occasions.

East of the malae, the town market attracts villagers from outlying areas who come to sell taros, yams, bananas, and vegetables. Across the street from the market, you'll see the High Court, a stately, two-story white building reminiscent of a southern U.S. mansion. It has been designated a historical monument.

Touring Tutuila

Outside of Pago Pago, the island offers green tropical forests, waterfalls, rivers, beautiful coastal and mountain scenery, charming villages, and friendly villagers.

You can see much of the island by taking the main road west or east from Pago Pago, skirting the island's inhabited southern and western coasts. Tutuila's rugged northern coast has few villages.

To the west. West of Pago Pago you'll find a number of interesting villages and some beautiful scenery.

Along the coast near Vailoatai you'll discover black lava cliffs and spectacular blowholes. Farther west, stop at Leone—American Samoa's second largest town and former capital.

You can observe the making of Samoan handicrafts at several villages along the way. Inland at Aoloau, see how Samoan plants are used for food, traditional medicines, housing, and utensils. In Amanave, near Tutuila's western tip, villagers demonstrate weaving and woodcarving.

To the east. East from Pago Pago, the road winds along the rocky coastline past thatch fales, pastel western-style houses, churches, and wrecks of old fishing vessels half sunk in the surf. The road ends 26 km/16 miles east of Pago Pago at Tula village.

The north coast. From central Pago Pago, travelers reach the north coast on a road that cuts snakelike across Fagasa Pass to the north side of Tutuila. From a roadside lookout point, you see Pago Pago Valley in one direction and Forbidden Bay in the other.

American Samoa's other islands

Visitors who seek a glimpse of untouched American Samoa can visit islands in the Manu'a group (Ta'u, Olosega, and Ofu). Located about 129 km/80 miles east of Tutuila, they can be reached by daily flights, weekly Inter-Island Transport boat service, and day or overnight tours. It was on the island of Ta'u that anthropologist Margaret Mead in 1925 gathered material for her classic book, *Coming of Age in Samoa.*

Visiting Western Samoa

The charm of Western Samoa lies in its relative lack of development. Your first exposure comes on the 32-km/20-mile drive from Upolu's Faleolo Airport into Apia. Considered one of the most beautiful routes in the South Pacific, it passes lagoons bordered by leaning palm trees and numerous villages with impressive churches and traditional thatch-roofed fales.

Most of the country's residents live in small villages on the main islands of Upolu and Savai'i, and on the smaller islands of Manono and Apolima. Only 20 percent of the country's people live in Apia, the capital.

Getting around Western Samoa

You can explore Upolu on your own or join an organized tour. Roads follow the island shore and cross it to link major points of interest.

Numerous taxis are available at moderate rates for exploration around town. Local, wooden-seated buses offer an inexpensive way to see the island of Upolu.

If you choose to tour the island independently, you can rent a car in Apia from several different firms. Motorscooters are also available for hire. On presentation of your driver's license at the police department, you will be issued a Western Samoa license for a fee of five *tala* (the Western Samoa dollar). The local license is required by law before you can rent a vehicle.

Transportation on Savai'i is limited to coastal village bus service. The island has no rental cars or taxis. Tour operators in Apia offer both sea and air tours to Savai'i and a boat tour to tiny Manono.

Boat travel. The *Limulimutau,* a passenger/vehicle ferry, sails daily at 6 A.M. from the Mulifanua Wharf on western Upolu. After unloading at the Salelologa Wharf on Savai'i, the boat returns across the channel at 9 A.M. Taking about 1½ hours each way, the trip provides a good view of Upolu, Savai'i, and the smaller islands of Manono and Apolima.

Local flights. Polynesian Airlines and South Pacific Island Airways provide regular service between Apia's Faleolo Airport on Upolu and Pago Pago's Tofuna Airport in American Samoa.

Hotel with a history

Most famous of Western Samoa's hotels is Aggie Grey's —a South Pacific landmark frequented over the years by countless writers, film stars, poets, and adventurers.

Aggie, the energetic owner-founder of the hotel, is believed to be the model for the character of Bloody Mary in James Michener's book, *Tales of the South Pacific.* She began her business career in 1919 by opening a bar called the Cosmopolitan Club on the site of the current hotel.

With 115 modern rooms, the hotel today sits in a tropical garden setting just across the road from the ocean, a short distance from downtown Apia.

Samoan architecture has been adapted in the design of Apia's only other large hotel—the 96-room Tusitala. The hotel is situated across the road from the harbor within walking distance of town center.

Small hotels in the Apia area include the Harbor Light Hotel, Tiafu Hotel (in town center on the beach), Nauru Hotels Operations (fronting the ocean overlooking the harbor and mountains), and Vaiala Beach Cottages (also on the beach).

On the island of Savai'i, visitors stay at the Savai'ian Guest Fales to experience traditional, open-air Samoan living. Tour operators can arrange for an overnight stay on Savai'i.

Dining in Western Samoa

In Apia, the Hotel Tusitala, Aggie Grey's Hotel, Nauru Hotels Operations, Tiafu Hotel, Tusitala Hotel, and Vaiala Beach Cottages all have restaurants.

Fia fias (Samoan feasts with Samoan entertainment) are held regularly at Aggie Grey's Hotel and the Hotel Tusitala. The Tiafu Hotel has Polynesian floor shows. Local operators also sponsor group trips to nearby village fia fias.

Apia, the capital

Perched on the north coast of Upolu, Apia is reminiscent of an old South Seas port during early trading days. Colonial-style wooden buildings and churches straggle along the tree-shaded main street—Beach Road—that curves around the harbor.

From Apia, you can visit several nearby sights.

Mulinu'u. Just a 5-minute drive around Apia Harbor to its western tip brings you to Mulinu'u, the location of *Fale Fono* (Parliament House); the *malae* (village green) where national celebrations are held; Land and Title Courts; and Independence Monument. You'll also see Tiafau, the traditional burial ground for Samoan royalty.

Vailima. Located 5 km/3 miles inland from Apia, the former home of Robert Louis Stevenson is the current residence of Western Samoa's head of state. The gracious, serene-looking house is approached by a driveway flanked on both sides by handsome old teak trees. The grounds are open to the public. However, in order to visit the grounds passes must be obtained from the Prime Minister's Department. Visitors aren't permitted inside the house.

Directly above Vailima is Mount Vaea. At its summit is Stevenson's tomb with the words of his immortal "Requiem" carved on it. A rugged switchback trail ascends 152 meters/500 feet to the top. This hike—recommended only for the fit—is best made early in the day before temperatures get too hot.

Upolu, miles of unspoiled scenery

Any trip on the island of Upolu passes through mile after mile of unspoiled landscape. You can travel around the island skirting the north and south coasts or cut across the island on several roads. Pause, if you like, at villages and plantations (coconut, cocoa, and coffee); and stop for a swim or picnic at inviting waterfalls, pools, and beaches.

Waterfalls. Traveling 29 km/18 miles east of Apia, you'll come to Falefa Falls tumbling into a deep, verdant valley. Turning south, the road climbs to Mafa Pass where you'll enjoy a breathtaking view of the shoreline. Descending past Fuipisia Falls, you enter the Aleipata district on the southeast coast, an area known for sandy beaches and quiet lagoons.

Lefaga. If you take the road leading south from Apia, you'll cut across the central part of the island past Tiavi Falls. At Si'umu turn west along the coast. Stop at Salamumu—considered one of the most attractive collections of thatch fales in Western Samoa—then continue on to Lefaga. The American movie *Return to Paradise* was filmed here in 1952.

Western Samoa's other islands

Across the narrow Apolima Strait from Upolu, you can visit Savai'i. From here, Polynesians sailed the ocean to colonize other Pacific islands.

The largest island in the Samoas, Savai'i is even less westernized than Upolu. Visitors stay in open-air guest fales or small hotels. The island can be reached by ferry service.

A 30-minute boat trip from Manono-Uta on the western end of Upolu transports passengers to Manono Island in the Apolima Straits. Since there are no cars on the island, you can stroll at a leisurely pace enjoying white sandy beaches and coconut palms.

Know Before You Go

The following practical information will help you plan your trip to the Samoas.

Entry/exit procedures. If you are a United States citizen entering American Samoa, you will need only proof of citizenship. Non-U.S. citizens need passports, An onward travel ticket is also required. No visas are required for stays up to 30 days. For longer stays an entry permit is required.

Visitors to Western Samoa will need valid passports and onward travel tickets. No visas are required for stays up to 30 days. For longer stays visas can be obtained from New Zealand and British consular offices or from the Immigration Division of the Prime Minister's Department in Apia.

Both Samoas require smallpox and yellow fever inoculations for travelers arriving from an infected area. (Note: Since health requirements change from time to time, check with your local public health department before leaving on your trip.)

American Samoa has no airport departure tax. In Western Samoa you will pay WS $20 when you depart by air.

Customs. Visitors to both countries must make a written declaration upon arrival. You may bring in duty free 1 bottle of liquor, 1 carton of cigarettes, 50 cigars, and 1½ pounds of tobacco.

Currency. In American Samoa, the currency is the U.S. dollar.

Western Samoan currency is the tala (WS $). Coins are sene—100 sene equals 1 tala.

Tipping. Tipping is neither customary nor expected in either American or Western Samoa.

Time. Both American and Western Samoa are GMT (Greenwich mean time) −11. For example, when it is 1 P.M. Saturday in the Samoas it's 4 P.M. Saturday in San Francisco; noon Sunday in Auckland; and 10 A.M. Sunday in Sydney.

Weather and what to wear. American and Western Samoa enjoy a tropical climate. American Samoa gets more rain than its neighbor, with over 500 cm/200 inches per year in Pago Pago. Western Samoa's average is 282.5 cm/113 inches.

The best time to visit either country is winter—June through October. During the Samoan summer months, downpours can last days at a time. Humidity stays at about 85 percent all year, but the trade winds cool the air between May and November. The average temperature is around 27°C/80°F.

Lightweight, informal attire is appropriate all year in the Samoas. However, women should not wear shorts in town, at church services, or at village feasts. Useful items to pack include sunglasses, suntan lotion, a rain hat, and rubber soled beach shoes.

For more information. For further information on the Samoas, write to the Department of Tourism, P.O. Box 862, Apia, Western Samoa; and American Samoa Office of Tourism, P.O. Box 1147, Pago Pago, American Samoa 96799.

TONGA

Tonga, situated just west of the International Date Line, is the first country to greet each new day.

At first glance, Tonga may seem similar to other South Pacific island groups, but it has one unique difference: Tonga is a constitutional monarchy—the last remaining Polynesian kingdom. In past centuries, many Pacific islands—including Tahiti, the Samoas, and the Cooks—were ruled by royalty. Today, the only remaining South Pacific monarch is Tonga's King Taufa'ahau Tupou IV.

Tonga's attractions feature the South Pacific charms of coral reefs, clear blue skies, and inviting atolls. Its gentle people maintain a traditional way of life that has changed little in more than 10 centuries.

As you travel in Tonga, you'll get to know these people. You'll watch them gracefully perform traditional dances, admire their handicraft skills used in making tapa and woven mats, enjoy their foods at bounteous Tongan feasts, and mingle with them in villages and public markets. You'll soon understand why Captain Cook called Tonga "The Friendly Islands."

Many Islands, Little Land

Tonga's 170 islands lie in a 426-km/265-mile-long archipelago just west of the International Date Line. Nuku'alofa, the country's capital, is a 2-hour flight southeast of Suva, Fiji, and a 1½-hour flight southwest of Apia, Western Samoa. Tonga lies 3,219 km/2,000 miles northeast of Sydney, Australia, and 1,770 km/1,100 miles northeast of Auckland.

The islands divide naturally into three groups—Tongatapu in the south, Ha'apai in the center, and Vava'u in the north. Tonga's land area totals only 697 square km/269 square miles. Only 45 of Tonga's islands are inhabited; more than 75 percent of the population lives on Tongatapu, the main island.

High and low islands

Tonga is a contrast of hilly volcanic islands and nearly flat coral formations. Highest point is the 1,125-meter/

3,690-foot extinct volcanic cone on the island of Kao, in the western part of the Ha'apai Group. The neighboring island of Tofua has an active volcano. Nearly all the other islands in the Ha'apai Group are flat.

Tongatapu—only 82 meters/270 feet above sea level—possesses no distinctive hills and no running streams. In contrast, rolling hills mark the neighboring island of Eua. The northern Vava'u Group is also hilly and forested.

Discovered by the Dutch

Two Dutch navigators, Willem Schouten and Jakob Lemaire, were the first Europeans to visit Tonga in 1616, followed by Abel Tasman, who arrived in the islands in 1643. Others followed—Captain Samuel Wallis in 1767; Captain James Cook in 1773, 1774, and 1777; and Captain William Bligh in 1789. (The famous mutiny on the *Bounty* occurred in Tongan waters.)

Missionaries from the London Missionary Society arrived in Tonga in 1797, but things didn't go favorably for them. Two years later several were killed in a civil war, and others fled to Sydney. More missionaries arrived in the 1820s and by midcentury, despite continuing civil war, they had converted most Tongans to Christianity.

The warfare that had wracked the country for a half century finally ended in 1845 when the victor, George Tupou I, became king. He introduced a constitutional form of government and land reforms that are still in effect. Political and social stability exists largely because of his decisions.

Today, the kingdom of Tonga is ruled by a direct descendant of King George, King Taufa'ahau Tupou IV, who became king in 1965 following the death of Queen Salote Tupou. The royal family traces its descent from ancient ruling chiefs whose names are preserved in Tongan art and legends.

For 70 years—from 1900 to 1970—Tonga operated under the protection of Great Britain as a British Protected State. The country became fully independent in 1970.

Tonga's People

According to archeologists, the Tongan islands have been inhabited since the 5th century B.C. Most of Tonga's 90,000 people are Polynesian, descendants of the first inhabitants. (There are also a few other Pacific Islanders and Europeans.)

You'll find the people of Tonga warmhearted, friendly, and eager to show you their country. Though Tongan is the official language, many people also speak English.

A simple life style

For the most part Tongans live a simple existence, taking what they need from the land and the sea. Congregating in scattered seashore villages of several hundred people, they live in traditional oval-ended, thatch-roofed fales

Royal standard *flies atop red-roofed cupola of Royal Palace in Nuku'alofa. Victorian decoration and second-story veranda enhance white wood home of Tonga's monarch. Well-kept grounds surround palace.*

Copra, *mainstay of island economy, dries on mats in sun. Dried meat is shipped to crushing mill where oil is extracted. Village dwelling combines thatch roof with wood walls and louvered windows.*

or houses built of local timber or concrete block. Some of these modern structures have thatch roofs while others are topped with corrugated iron.

Bound to the traditions of their ancestors, the people have preserved customs, legends, and archeological treasures. Royal traditions still triumph, for the king symbolizes Tonga's proud independence. Tongans have great respect for their king, his nobles, and the great hereditary chain of chiefs existing within the country's social structure.

Dress. Tongan respect for customs is reflected in their attire. Most Tongans dress in traditional wraparound *valas* (skirts)—long for women, short for men.

Finely woven mats, called *ta'ovala,* are worn over these around the waist. (Women sometimes wear a *kiekie,* a highly decorative waistband, instead of the mat.) These mats—held on by a *kafa* (belt) of woven coconut fiber—indicate respect for elders and the royal family. No well-dressed Tongan would consider attending an important occasion without wearing a ta'ovala. Though some mats are tattered beyond belief, the treasured heirlooms are still worn for very special functions.

As you travel in Tonga, you'll see many people dressed in black. Tongans believe that the black of mourning should be worn for many months after a relative's death, and Tongan families are very large.

Land. In Tonga, all land is the property of the crown. The system of land distribution designed by King George Tupou I is unique. At age 16, each male Tongan may request a parcel of farmland (called an *'api*) and a village site on which to build a house.

Economy. Agriculture dominates the Tongan economy. Major exports are bananas, copra, and desiccated coconuts. Other crops—harvested primarily for local consumption—include pineapples, watermelons, tomatoes, taro, and yams. Tongans catch fish for their dinner tables and raise a few cows, some poultry, and a large number of pigs. These pigs are in great demand for festive occasions. As many as 8,000 pigs have been roasted for a single feast attended by thousands of people.

Between July and October some Tongans supplement their income by whale hunting. Tonga is one of the few places in the world where men still hunt the humpback whale using small boats and harpoons. Although the number of whales killed is small, the profit for the whaler can be great. Almost every morsel of whale—including the skin and blubber—is sold as food.

Religion. Tongans devote Sundays to church going and relaxation. Observance of the Sabbath is even written into Tonga's constitution: "The Sabbath Day shall be sacred in Tonga forever and it shall not be lawful to do work or play games or trade on the Sabbath. Any agreement made or documents witnessed on this day shall be counted void and not recognized by the Government." Anyone who disobeys this law can be fined T$10 or be sentenced to up to 3 months of hard labor for nonpayment of the fine.

In recent decades this law has been stretched enough so that taxi drivers can transport passengers to and from ships and planes, and hotels can be operated.

Many Tongans belong to the State Church (a Tongan version of the Wesleyan Methodist). Other local denominations include the Free Church of Tonga, Roman Catholic Church, Mormon Church, Seventh-Day Adventist Church, and Anglican Church. If you're in Tonga on a Sunday, you may enjoy attending a church service where you'll be rewarded with harmonized hymn singing. Afterwards, you might be invited to join a Sunday feast.

Love for sports

Tongans share a boundless enthusiasm for sports—so much so, in fact, that at one time when cricket was popular, the government put a curb on it by issuing a regulation prohibiting play except at certain hours on designated days. Rugby union and soccer matches also generate a lot of interest. Other popular spectator sports include basketball, tennis, track and field events, boxing, and sumo wrestling. Major sports events are held at the sports grounds in Nuku'alofa.

Tongans also enjoy several indigenous games. One game, *lafo,* is similar to bowls except that it is played with round wooden disks made from coconut shells instead of bowls. Another favorite is a juggling game called *hiko.* Young girls juggle up to six candlenuts or oranges at one time while singing or reciting special rhymes in archaic words.

Planning Your Trip

Tonga's proximity to Fiji and the Samoas makes it feasible to combine a visit to Tonga with travel to these other South Pacific islands.

Regularly scheduled direct flights link Tonga with Fiji, Western Samoa, American Samoa, New Zealand, and the United States. Planes land at Fua'amotu Airport on Tongatapu, the country's main island. Taxis and buses transport passengers on the 21-km/13-mile trip into Nuku'alofa, the capital.

Cruise ships and cargo/passenger liners call at Tongan ports on South Pacific excursions. At Nuku'alofa, ships dock within a few blocks of the business district. Some ships also stop at Neiafu on Vava'u.

Traveling around Tonga

Nuku'alofa visitors can choose from several forms of transport. Most interesting, perhaps, is the *ve'etolu*—a colorful three-wheeled, open-sided taxi. Regular taxis are also plentiful. Taxi fares should be agreed upon in advance. If you and a friend would like to explore the town aboard a two seat, three-wheeled bicycle, you can rent one at the International Dateline Hotel.

A rental car offers a good way to see the island of Tongatapu independently. Visiting drivers need a Tongan driver's license, obtained by showing a current domestic license and paying a small fee at the Police Traffic Department in Nuku'alofa. Traffic keeps to the left in Tonga. Outside Nuku'alofa, pigs and other livestock are occasional road hazards.

Tongatapu also has public bus service. On Sundays public transportation is limited to vehicles taking visitors to and from the airport or wharf.

Outer island transportation is limited.

Air service. South Pacific Island Airways and Tonga Air provide regularly scheduled air service linking Tongatapu with Eua, the Ha'apai Group, and Vava'u.

Boat service. To sail from Nuku'alofa to Ha'apai and Vava'u, you can board an interisland boat. A shorter trip—just 3½ hours—goes south to Eua, second largest island in the Tongatapu group. Check boat schedules carefully—they can change on short notice because of

TAPA MAKING
It's a Lengthy Process

Tap, tap, tap—it's a sound you'll hear from morning till night in villages throughout Tonga. It's the rhythm of tapa beating, one of the first steps in the making of tapa.

The lengthy process of tapa making begins when the inner bark is stripped from cut sections of the paper mulberry tree. This inner bark is then soaked and pounded with a wooden mallet on a special wooden log. The single, pounded sheets are glued together with arrowroot or tapioca to form a larger piece. (Single tapa cloths can average 23 meters/75 feet in length.)

The women villagers then lay this cloth atop special relief design tablets that have been attached to a long convex board. They rub natural dyes in brown tones onto the tapa, making the raised designs underneath appear on the cloth. After the tapa has dried, the women outline the brownish designs by hand with black dye.

Tapa making is a community project in Tonga. Women gather in their homes or at village tapa houses to help each other.

Tongans use large quantities of tapa for wall hangings, sheets, blankets, room partitions, and dance costumes. Lengths of tapa are a traditional gift for a birth, death, or marriage.

weather or local commitments. No boats operate on Sundays.

Tours. Tongatapu excursions explore Nuku'alofa and the island of Tongatapu. Other tours feature glass-bottomed boat rides, evening feasts on the beach, and picnic excursions to nearby islets. Visitors can also travel to both Eua and Vava'u.

Varied accommodations

In Tonga accommodations range from resort hotels to simple guest houses. Most have dining rooms.

On Tongatapu most accommodations are located in or near Nuku'alofa. Largest (76 rooms) is the first class International Dateline Hotel, located near town center facing the harbor. Travelers who prefer smaller hotels can choose from a number of possibilities including the Moana Hotel, Beach House Hotel, Way In Motel, Joe's Tropicana Hotel, Captain Cook Vacation Apartments, Nukuma'anu Motel, Friendly Islander Motel, Good Samaritan Inn, or Ramanlal Motel. A half-hour's boat ride from Nuku'alofa is modest Fafa Island Resort, where thatched bungalows are set amid palm trees.

Tonga's only other first class hotel is the Paradise International Hotel in Neiafu on Vava'u. With 33 Tongan-style bungalows, this resort is within a short walk of town and overlooks the beautiful harbor. Other Vava'u accommodations include several guest houses.

Eua has one small hotel, the Leipu Lodge. In the Ha'apai Group, there are guest house accommodations, or visitors can arrange to stay in a village. Check with the Tonga Visitors Bureau in Nuku'alofa.

Feasting in Tonga

Tongans are known throughout the South Pacific for the amount and variety of foods offered at their feasts. *Polas*—long trays made from plaited coconut fronds—sag under the weight of some 30 different types of food including suckling pig, fish, crayfish, beef, octopus, vegetables, and fruits. Many of these delicacies are baked in an *umu,* an underground oven, while the suckling pig is roasted on a spit over an open fire.

Coconut cream is the basic sauce for many Tongan dishes. Favorite foods you might want to sample include *'ota iki'*—marinated raw fish in a coconut cream, lemon, onion, and herb marinade; and *lu pulu*—meat and onions marinated in coconut milk, wrapped in taro leaves, and baked in an umu. If you'd like to attend a Tongan feast, check with your hotel for information.

After-dinner entertainment. Usually singing and dancing follow a Tongan feast. The dancing is both reserved and graceful. In contrast to Tahitian dancing, which emphasizes hip movements, Tongan dancing features hand and foot movements. The dancers relate the story in song as they perform, dressed in colorful costumes of tapa cloth and leaves, their bodies glistening with scented coconut oil.

In addition to feast entertainment, programs of Tongan dancing are presented regularly at several Tongatapu hotels, including the International Dateline Hotel and also at Oholei Beach.

Other dining possibilities. You can also try various restaurants in the Nuku'alofa area including the restaurant at the International Dateline Hotel. For excellent seafood try the Sea View Restaurant near the palace or the Good Samaritan Inn at Kolovai Beach. On Vava'u the Paradise International Hotel has a restaurant featuring a variety of cuisines.

Local brew. While in Tonga, try *otai*—a fresh fruit punch, and *kava*—a brew made from the root of a pepper plant. Besides performing kava ceremonies on all formal

Interisland boats *transport freight and passengers–and often domestic animals and livestock–between islands. Longer trips cruise across open sea.*

occasions, Tongans also gather informally to drink kava and exchange gossip.

Shopping for handicrafts

Tonga ranks as one of the best marketplaces in the South Pacific for well-made traditional handicrafts. Among the specialties are tapa cloth (see page 45) and finely woven mats and baskets. The giant woven Ali Baba baskets make excellent laundry containers. Other high quality goods include trays, fans, turtle shell ornaments, and woodcarvings.

Parades, singing, elaborate feasts, and contests highlight many of Tonga's celebrations. Below are a few that might enrich your stay in Tonga.

January—April

Good Friday and Easter Sunday. You can hear magnificent choral singing in churches throughout Tonga during this time.

Anzac Day. On April 25, military parades are held by Tongans to honor the soldiers killed during war.

May—August

Birthday of H.R.H. Prince Tupouto'a. Military parades herald the birth of the crown prince on May 4.

Opening of Parliament. A colorful ceremony—including a 21-gun salute—marks the opening of Parliament in early June.

Emancipation Day. On June 4 Tongans celebrate their unity under one king (King George I) and their union with the Commonwealth in 1970.

Birthday of King Taufa'ahau Tupou IV. On July 4, parades, religious ceremonies, and feasts celebrate the king's birthday.

September—December

Royal Agricultural Show. King Taufa'ahau Tupou IV visits all the island groups in September or October to attend shows displaying produce. Horse races, chariot races, and coconut tree climbing contests are added events.

Music Festival. In December instrumental groups, choirs, and soloists compete in Nuku'alofa.

King Tupou I Day. The king is honored on December 4.

Available in small shops throughout Nuku'alofa, handicraft items are also sold at the Langa Fonua Women's Institute on Taufa'ahua Road in Nuku'alofa and at the Talamahu Market. When cruise ships are in port, you can buy handicrafts in Fa'onelua Gardens next door to the Tonga Visitors Bureau. Langa Fonua also has a small shop in Neiafu on Vava'u.

If you have a stamp collector in the family, stop at the philatelic section of the Treasury Department on Vuna Road. Here you'll find Tonga's uniquely shaped stamps that rank among the most unusual in the world.

You can buy duty-free items such as cameras, radios, jewelry, and perfumes at the International Dateline Hotel and the Fua'amotu airport. The Tonga Broadcasting Commission's shop in Nuku'alofa sells a variety of radio and sound equipment.

Shops in Tonga are open Monday through Friday from 8 A.M. to 5 P.M., and on Saturday, 8 A.M. to noon. All stores are closed on Sunday.

Recreational activities

Tonga's abundant white sand beaches and reef-protected lagoons offer plentiful swimming and snorkeling opportunities. Tongatapu's best beaches include Oholei, Ha'amalo, Ha'atafu, Monotapu, Laulea, 'Utukehe, Fahefa, and Fua'amotu. Nearly all the beaches in the Ha'apai Group are good. On Vava'u favorites are Keitahi, Talau Fanga, and Toula.

Skin and scuba diving. Divers will enjoy Tonga's underwater delights including fan black coral, drop-offs, caves, deep reefs, and sunken ships. For diving information, contact the Tonga Dive Club through the Tonga Visitors Bureau. The club has its own compressor, boat, and a limited number of tanks.

Fishing. Your hotel can provide information on deep-sea fishing excursions. Charter boats are available for hire, and catches include barracuda, tuna, marlin, and sailfish.

Boating. You can hire a boat for an hour or a day to go water-skiing, diving, fishing, or cruising to an offshore islet for a picnic. Check with your hotel for boat rental information.

Other sports. Other recreational possibilities include horseback riding, bicycling, and hiking. Inquire at your hotel for information on equipment and destinations.

Tennis players find courts at the International Dateline Hotel on Tongatapu and the Paradise International Hotel on Vava'u. There's a 9-hole golf course at Manamoui Racecourse, which is located 8 km/5 miles from Nuku'alofa.

Visiting Tongatapu

Located at the southern end of the Tongan archipelago, the Tongatapu Group consists of two large islands—Tongatapu and Eua—plus several smaller ones. Most heavily populated of the Tongan islands, Tongatapu is the largest island in the archipelago.

On Tongatapu's northern shore you'll find Nuku'alofa, the country's capital and major port of entry. After exploring the city, you can tour the island of Tongatapu, travel to nearby Eua island, and arrange to visit Tonga's other island groups to the north.

Nuku'alofa, the capital

Sprawling along the sea and backed by a lagoon, Nuku-'alofa is a commercial town of white-frame, picket-fenced houses.

Nuku'alofa's small size (30,000 people) makes it easy to explore on foot. Vuna Road, a wide thoroughfare skirting the waterfront, is the center of activity. At one end of the road you'll find the Royal Palace, at the other end, the Yacht Club. Along the road between these points are the public market, the town *malae* (meeting place), the Tonga Visitors Bureau, and numerous hotels. At a right angle to Vuna Road is Taufa'ahau Road where you'll find markets, small shops, general stores, pool-rooms, cinemas, transportation offices, government buildings, and churches.

The Royal Palace. Overlooking the sea and Nuku-'alofa's waterfront, the Royal Palace stands in immaculately kept grounds bright with tropical flowers and shrubs. Norfolk pines surround the two-story white-frame Victorian structure with its distinctive red roof, wide verandas, and stately cupola. Built in 1867, the palace remains unchanged except for the addition of the veranda in 1882.

Although it is not open to the public, you can view the palace easily over the surrounding low coral wall.

The Royal Chapel. The royal family worships in the chapel adjacent to the palace. Visitors may attend church services on Sunday evenings. The coronations of King George Tupou II, Queen Salote, and Tonga's present king took place here. All weddings and baptisms of royalty also occur in this chapel.

The chapel, prefabricated in New Zealand, was assembled here in 1882.

Royal Tombs. Elevated above the ground, the Royal Tombs are situated near the center of town on the estate of Tonga's first king, George Tupou I. He and Queen Salote are both entombed here.

Talamahu Market. Three blocks east of the Royal Palace, you can stroll around Tonga's major fruit and vegetable market. Farmers gather here to sell their produce—pineapples, watermelons, oranges, papayas, and a variety of vegetables. Handicraft items are also available for sale at the market.

Fa'onelua Tropical Gardens. Here you can see a model Tongan village and tour the gardens which feature more than 100 varieties of hibiscus as well as other flora indigenous to the South Pacific.

Touring the island

Heading east or west from Nuku'alofa, you drive through many Tongan villages, travel deep into banana and coconut plantations, and pass white sand beaches. In either direction, you'll find plenty of interesting places to explore.

To the east. One of your first stops east of Nuku'alofa will be Captain Cook's landing place just west of Mu'a. A monument marks the spot where Cook came ashore in 1773.

Northeast of Mu'a you'll come to the Langi—terraced tombs of ancient kings dating from around A.D. 1200.

Large blocks of coral stone about 4 meters/12 feet high face the 4-sided mounds.

Ten km/6 miles northeast of the tombs is a stone monument called the Ha'amonga Trilithon. Erected around A.D. 1200, it consists of two great uprights—5 meter/16-foot high coral slabs—topped by a horizontal connecting stone or lintel about 6 meters/19 feet long.

For years experts thought the trilithon was a gateway to a royal compound. However, recent observations by the present king have led to the theory that the trilithon probably was used as a seasonal calendar. Notches carved in the lintel point directly to the rising sun on the longest and shortest days of the year.

If you travel 19 km/12 miles southeast from Nuku-'alofa, you can see one of the island's most scenic spots—Hufangalupe, "The Pigeons' Doorway." This area, along the southern coast of Tongatapu, offers several dramatic features: sea churning through a natural bridge, cliffs towering above the shore, a beguiling beach lying at the base of the cliffs. To reach this beach, follow a steep trail carved into the cliffs.

To the west. On the western side of Tongatapu, you'll see several more interesting attractions.

At Houma, 14 km/9 miles southwest of Nuku'alofa, waves provide a spectacular show, especially at high tide. Along this area's rocky terraced shoreline, the ocean surges through holes in the coral rock, creating water spouts up to 18 meters/60 feet high. The Tongans call this stretch of coastline *Mapu'a Vaea*, the chief's whistle, for the whistling noise the waves make as they shoot up through the blowholes.

Hundreds of flying foxes (a type of fruit bat) hang chattering from tree branches in Kolovai, 18 km/11 miles northwest of Nuku'alofa. At night they leave to forage for food, returning at dawn to roost once more. Tongan legend claims the bats are descendants of bats presented as a gift from a Samoan princess to an ancient Tongan navigator. Sacred to the Tongans and protected by custom, these bats can be hunted only by members of the royal family.

You also can tour the Dessicated Coconut Factory at Havelu (3 km/2 miles south of Nuku'alofa) to see how the coconuts are husked and the meat processed.

Eua, a delightful contrast

The island of Eua, located just 40 km/25 miles southeast of Nuku'alofa, offers a delightful contrast to its larger island neighbor. Visitors can enjoy one day or several days exploring this 88 square km/34 square mile island of rolling hills, dense forests, and high cliffs.

Eua's attractions are many. You'll want to visit Hafu Pool, a small, crystal-clear pond surrounded by hibiscus bushes and other tropical plants. On a walk through the island's forests, you'll hear—and perhaps glimpse—the chattering and screeching blue-crowned lories and red-breasted musk parrots.

Journeying to the southern part of Eua, you'll come to Matalanga'a Maui, a natural bridge cut by the surging sea. A short distance away are the cliffs of Lakufa'anga, dropping 107 meters/350 feet to the shore. Often you can see turtles in the sea at the base of these cliffs.

Transportation on Eua is limited—you can travel by foot, horseback, or rental jeep.

Other Island Groups

North of Tongatapu, you can visit two strikingly different island groups. The Vava'u Group, at the northern tip of the Tongan Kingdom, is a group of hilly, verdant islands.

South of the Vava'u Group is the Ha'apai Group, a cluster of low islands that barely peak above the sea. The highest points on these islands are the palm trees lining sandy shores.

Seeing Vava'u

Located 274 km/170 miles north of Tongatapu, the 34 islands of the Vava'u Group cover a land area of about 117 square km/45 square miles. With a population of 15,000, Vava'u is the largest island in the group and the main tourist center. Many of the tiny, densely forested islands in the group remain uninhabited.

Neiafu, the group's capital, nestles into a hillside overlooking one of the most beautiful ports in the South Pacific—the Port of Refuge. Arriving by boat, you'll sail up a 13-km/8-mile channel to the fiordlike harbor entrance.

While in Neiafu, you'll want to take a short boat trip to Swallows' Cave. Sunlight streams through an opening in the cathedral-like chamber creating multicolored splendor. In autumn, the cave is a sanctuary for thousands of swallows.

Skin divers might enjoy a visit to Mariner's Cave. Legend relates that this drowned grotto provided refuge for a young chief and his beloved long ago when feuds rocked Tongan families.

Traveling to the Ha'apai Group

The line of islands in the Ha'apai Group lies 161 km/100 miles north of Nuku'alofa, midway between Tongatapu and Vava'u.

Few visitors journey to the Ha'apai Group. Accommodations are limited to a guest house and villagers' homes (check with the Tonga Visitors Bureau in Nuku'alofa for information). Those travelers who do come here discover islands blessed with deserted beaches and an atmosphere of unbelievable peace and tranquility.

The charming town of Pangai, the group's capital on Lifuka, was once the seat of the Royal Family. Captain James Cook anchored off the coast near the town in 1777 on his third visit to Tonga. Today, Pangai is the headquarters of the kingdom's fishing industry. The island group's airport is located at the north end of Lifuka, a short distance from Pangai.

Know Before You Go

The following practical information will help you plan your trip.

Entry/exit procedures. Visitors to Tonga staying 30 days or less need only a valid passport, a confirmed onward ticket, and adequate funds for their stay.

Visitors need a smallpox vaccination and inoculation against yellow fever only if they have been in an infected area prior to their arrival in Tonga. (Note: Since health requirements change from time to time, check with your local public health department before leaving on your trip.)

Departing international air passengers pay an airport departure tax of T $5, payable only in local currency.

Currency. The Tongan currency is the Tongan dollar or *pa'anga* (T $). The coin is the seniti—100 seniti equals 1 pa'anga or Tongan dollar.

Tipping. Tipping is neither customary nor encouraged.

Time. Tonga is 13 hours ahead of Greenwich mean time. When it is noon Saturday in Nuku'alofa, it is 11 A.M. Saturday in Auckland, 9 A.M. Saturday in Sydney, and 3 P.M. Friday in Los Angeles.

Weather and what to wear. The climate on Tonga is surprisingly cool for the tropics. Temperatures range from lows just over 21.2°C/70°F between May and October to highs around 32°C/90°F in December and January. The humid, rainy season (summer) runs from December to April.

You'll be most comfortable in casual, lightweight attire. Short shorts and bathing suits are fine for the beach but are frowned upon in villages. Tongan law prohibits any person appearing in a public place without a shirt.

Articles you'll want to pack include a sweater or stole for evenings during the cooler months, a lightweight raincoat and umbrella for the rainy season, sunglasses, suntan lotion, and beach shoes for reef walking.

For more information. You can get additional information on Tonga by writing the Tonga Visitors Bureau, Box 37, Nuku'alofa. In Australia, write 61 Cross St., Double Bay, NSW 2028.

COOK ISLANDS

❀ ❀ ❀ ❀ ❀ ❀ ❀ ❀ ❀ ❀ ❀

For years isolated from major tourist routes, the Cook Islands offer the visitor untouched beauty and a peaceful way of life. Here you'll stroll along beaches edged with swaying palms and swim in warm lagoons protected by coral reefs. But most of all, you'll enjoy the warm and hospitable people of the Cook Islands.

Fifteen Scattered Islands

Located near the center of the Polynesian triangle, the Cook Islands include 15 specks of land scattered across 2,202,073 square km/850,000 square miles of the South Pacific. Their closest neighbor, French Polynesia—lies over 1,126 km/700 miles to the east. New Zealand is some 3,059 km/1,900 miles southwest and Fiji is about 2,414 km/1,500 miles west.

Totaling a mere 241 square km/93 square miles in area, the islands divide naturally into two groups. The eight islands of the southern Cooks include the tourist destinations of Rarotonga and Aitutaki. All of the southern Cooks are volcanic islands, except for Manuae and Tukutea, which are coral atolls. The seven islands of the northern group are all low lying, remote atolls.

Named after Captain Cook

Spaniard Alvaro de Mendaña was the first European explorer to venture into Cook Island waters. In 1595 he sighted Pukapuka in the northern Cooks. His countryman Pedro Quiros discovered Rakahanga 10 years later.

During the 1770s Captain James Cook charted five more islands, and eventually the island group was named after him. In 1789, Fletcher Christian and fellow mutineers of the *Bounty* wandered into the southern Cooks, anchoring off Rarotonga to barter for food.

Missionaries soon followed. Arriving in 1823, John Williams and other members of the London Missionary Society soon converted most of the islanders.

The Cook Islands became a British Protectorate in 1888, and in 1901 they were annexed by New Zealand. Political changes began in 1947 that finally led to the country's internal independence in 1965.

The Cook Islanders

Over 96 percent of the 18,130 Cook Island residents are Maori (Polynesian); most of the remaining 4 percent are European.

Many of the Cook Island Maoris trace their ancestry to the country's early settlers, who arrived by canoe from the Society Islands between A.D. 600 and 800. According to Cook Island legend, the Maoris sailed from Rarotonga to colonize New Zealand. Strong similarities in language, traditions, and customs exist between the two Maori groups.

A simple life

Many Cook Islanders enjoy a gentle, quiet pace of life. They live in houses built of coral lime and concrete block, clustered in villages along coastal areas. They respect the traditions of their ancestors, believe in the extended family, and owe allegiance to their tribal chief.

Religion. The church plays an important role in the lives of Cook Islanders. There are Sunday services and several religious holidays. Visitors are welcome to attend services and enjoy hymn singing.

Economy. Agriculture is the mainstay of the Cook Island economy. People grow fruits and vegetables not only for their own consumption but also for export.

Island festivities

A love of sports and music is reflected in the Cook Islanders' special events and festivals. Many include sports activities and dancing and singing contests.

Bareback horse races are held about every 6 weeks on Muri Beach. However, there's no guarantee that the ponies will finish the race. Some stop running at the halfway point and others detour into the ocean for a swim.

The Cook Islanders also enjoy lawn bowling, tennis, sailing, rugby, netball, and cricket.

Planning Your Trip

Few travelers visited the Cook Islands until 1973, when the international airport capable of handling big jets was completed. Before that time, international transportation relied on passenger ships and flying boats.

Now travelers fly to the Cook Islands from New Zealand, Tahiti, Fiji, Nauru, and American and Western

Pineapple *and citrus fruits thrive in rich volcanic soil of southern Cooks. Avarua factory processes juice for export.*

Children *dressed in bright costumes gather to perform religious plays outdoors on Gospel Day, October 26.*

Samoa. You'll arrive on Rarotonga, the country's main island. The airport is just a 5-km/3-mile drive west of Avarua, the capital. Most hotels provide airport shuttle service and a few taxis are available.

Both cruise and passenger/cargo ships stop in the Cook Islands on South Pacific voyages. Since the Avarua harbor can't accommodate large ships, passengers can be ferried by launch to the downtown wharf.

Traveling around the Cooks

The islands of Rarotonga and Aitutaki are the two main tourist destinations in the Cook Islands. Regular scheduled air service by Cook Islands Airways and Air Rarotonga links the two islands.

Small interisland cargo vessels provide service when needed to outer islands in the northern and southern Cooks. Used mainly by the local people, these vessels have limited passenger accommodations.

Sightseeing on your own. On Rarotonga, there's circle-island minibus service. Transportation is limited on Aitutaki. If you want to tour the islands independently, rent a bicycle, car, or motorscooter—the Cook Islanders' favorite form of transportation. Traffic moves on the left in the Cook Islands.

Tours. On Rarotonga, you can take a variety of interesting tours. There are flightseeing trips, lagoon cruises, and trips by power-drawn buggy. Aitutaki also has a number of different tours.

Where to stay in the Cooks

With 150 rooms, the Rarotongan—8 km/5 miles south of the international airport—is the country's only large, international-class resort hotel.

Rarotonga's other hotels and motels are small (3 to 40

rooms) but comfortable. They include Are Renga Motel, Arorangi Lodge, Beach Hotel, Edgewater Resort, KiiKii Motel, Lagoon Lodges, Little Polynesian, Mangaia Lodge, Moana Beach Lodge, Onemaru Motel, Palm Grove Lodges, Puaikura Reef Lodges, Punamaia Motel, Tamure Resort, Tiare Village Motel, and Raina Village Motel. On Aitutaki, try the Aitutaki Resort or Rapae Cottage Hotel. On Aitu Island, 130 miles southeast of Aitutaki, Atiu Motel is the only facility.

Since accommodations are limited in the Cooks, visitors must have confirmed reservations prior to arrival. Camping is prohibited in the Cook Islands.

Dining and entertainment

One of the best ways to see Cook Islands entertainment and sample local foods is to attend a special island night. These are held regularly at the Rarotongan.

In addition to the above-mentioned restaurants, you may want to try the Vai Ma in Tikikaveka, the Kumete in Avarua, and the Outrigger in Arorangi.

Shop for handicrafts

You'll find examples of Cook Island crafts for sale at the Women's Federation Handcraft Shop in Avarua. You can select from carved wooden bowls; shell jewelry; woven straw baskets, hats, and mats; and ukuleles made from coconut shells. The intricate, brightly colored designs of the *Tivaevae* (bedspreads) are painstakingly hand sewn, then appliquéd.

Most stores are open from 7:30 A.M. to 3:30 P.M. Monday to Friday and from 7:30 to 11:30 A.M. Saturday. Some village stores near entertainment centers stay open in the evenings. Bargaining is not customary.

Recreational activities

You can enjoy both water sports and land sports in the Cook Islands. Reef walking is popular on the reef surrounding Rarotonga. If you're interested, join a guided tour to learn about the reef marine life.

For a closer look at aquatic creatures, go skin diving, scuba diving, or snorkeling in the lagoons of Rarotonga and Aitutaki. Snorkeling equipment and some diving equipment are available for rent. Inquire at your hotel.

Fishermen can contact the Cook Island Tourist Authority in central Avarua for information on deep-sea fishing. Catches include tuna and marlin.

Land sports include golf and tennis. You can golf at the Rarotonga Golf Club at Nikao and at a course near the airport on Aitutaki. The Rarotongan and the Edgewater Resort have tennis courts.

Seeing the Cook Islands

During your visit, you will spend most of your time on Rarotonga Island. Many travelers consider this mountainous island one of the most spectacular in the South

Pacific. A tiny piece of land—only 67 square km/26 square miles—it has 12 peaks over 305 meters/1,000 feet.

The smaller island of Aitutaki is a less mountainous island. Only an hour's flight from Rarotonga, it has a beautiful 10-km/6-mile-wide lagoon dotted with islets.

Touring Rarotonga

The country's capital of Avarua—located on Rarotonga's north shore—is the place to begin your exploration. Over a third of Rarotonga's population of 9,800 lives in the Avarua area.

Avarua sights. The Avarua area offers several historic sights to explore. The old Mission House—built in 1847 to house the headquarters of the London Missionary Society in the Cooks—is being restored and serves as a Church Museum. Many of the first missionaries are buried in the churchyard of the nearby Cook Islands Christian Church.

You'll also want to visit the busy wharf area. All fishing boats and interisland traders arrive and depart from here. Laden with flowers, whole families gather on the dock to greet or bid farewell to friends and relatives traveling on the interisland boats.

Circling Rarotonga. Venturing beyond Avarua, you can take the 32-km/20-mile road (Ara Tapu) skirting the perimeter of Rarotonga. On this road travelers see beaches, lagoons, villages nearly hidden among coconut palms, flowering trees and bushes, and towering mountain peaks covered in vegetation. You'll see fishermen out on the reef, children riding ponies along the beach, and men working in taro patches. Be sure to stop at Ngatangiia Harbor. From here, legend states, one of the last great Polynesian migrations sailed for New Zealand.

Historical road. Inland from the main road, you can still travel on sections of Ara Metua, a road built over 1,000 years ago. Cook Island legend says that this coral block road—now potholed and overgrown by vegetation in places—was engineered by a powerful warrior king named Toi about A.D. 900.

Trip to Aitutaki

The island of Aitutaki is located 224 km/139 miles north of Rarotonga. With a population of 2,500, Aitutaki is even more tranquil than its sister island.

Aitutaki achieved recognition in the 1950s when Tasman Empire Airway's (now Air New Zealand) Coral Route flying boat service used the island of Akaiami in Aitutaki's large lagoon as a refueling base. This was the first time that an uninhabited island had been visited by an international airline.

Know Before You Go

The information below will help you plan your trip to the Cooks.

Entry/exit procedures. If you are staying in the Cook Islands 31 days or less, you won't need a visa, just a valid passport and onward ticket.

Baggage of arriving passengers from Fiji, Western Samoa, and Hawaii is no longer fumigated, speeding up immigration arrival procedures.

Smallpox vaccinations are required if you're arriving from an infected area. (Note: Since health requirements can change, it's advisable to check with your public health department before your trip.)

There is no airport departure tax.

Customs. Visitors may bring in duty-free personal effects plus 200 cigarettes, 50 cigars, or a half pound of tobacco; 1 quart of wine and 1 quart of spirits; and 2 still cameras or 1 still and 1 movie camera.

Currency. New Zealand dollars. Coins are 1, 2, 5, 20, and 50 cents. Notes are 1, 2, 5, 10, 20, 50, and 100 dollars.

Tipping. There is no tipping.

Time. The Cook Islands are 10½ hours behind Greenwich Mean Time. When it is noon Saturday in Avarua, it is 2:30 P.M. Saturday in Los Angeles; 8:30 A.M. Sunday in Sydney; and 10:30 A.M. Sunday in Auckland.

Weather and what to wear. The Cook Islands have a warm tropical climate tempered by the trade winds. The cool season runs from May to October with temperatures averaging 25 °C/77 °F. During the warmer, wetter months (December to March), temperatures average 28 °C/82 °F.

Visitors dress in casual resort wear all year. If you plan to attend a church service, remember that Cook Islanders dress up for church. Women visitors should plan to wear a dress and men long trousers and a dress shirt. You'll need beach shoes for reef walking.

For more information. Your best source of information is the Cook Islands Tourist Authority, P.O. Box 14, Rarotonga, Cook Islands.

In Australia, you can write Walshes World, P.O. Box R177, Sydney, NSW 2000. In New Zealand, write P.O. Box 3647, Auckland, New Zealand.

Another good source of information in North America, the United Kingdom, and Australia is any Air New Zealand office.

MELANESIA

Fiji, New Caledonia, Vanuatu, Papua New Guinea, Solomons

Situated between the equator and the Tropic of Capricorn, the Melanesian islands include the countries of Fiji, New Caledonia, Vanuatu (New Hebrides), Papua New Guinea, and the Solomon Islands.

The word Melanesia is derived from a Greek word meaning "black islands." Seafaring explorers may have given this name because of the dark-skinned inhabitants. Or they may have chosen the word to describe the jungle covered mountainous islands that appeared dark and forbidding from a distance.

The islands of Melanesia offer far more than dark vine-entangled jungles. Visitors can walk through rain forests rich in exotic tropical flowers and birds, ride across grassy plateaus dotted with grazing cattle, travel to primitive river villages by comfortable riverboat, swim in turquoise lagoons, or hike to mountaintops to enjoy wide-ranging views.

The Melanesian People

The people of these fascinating islands are as diverse as their landscape. Physically, they range from small and stocky types to medium or tall. Skin tones vary from deep brown to blue black. Most have wiry, curly hair. You'll see some traces of Polynesian and Micronesian ancestry; both of these groups stopped briefly on some Melanesian islands during their Pacific explorations.

The Melanesian migration

Scientists believe that the Melanesian islands were inhabited long before the first Polynesians explored the Pacific Ocean. They believe that at the end of the last glacial period, nomadic tribes migrated from the freezing forests of Asia south through the warm Malay peninsula, finally settling in New Guinea. Carbon dating of artifacts indicates that New Guinea was inhabited as early as 8000 B.C. Unlike the Polynesians, the Melanesians have no legends telling of migration from a homeland.

Over the years, additional tribes migrated into the area. These latecomers were physically larger than their predecessors, causing the first nomadic clans to retreat into the remote interior mountain regions.

Creation of separate cultures

The ruggedness of the land isolated many individual tribes and clans, who developed their own languages, traditions, and cultures that still exist today. Each clan or tribe held itself apart from the others. All strangers were suspect and automatically considered enemies.

These feelings made war between the clans and tribes inevitable. Elaborate preparations for war and fighting were part of normal village life. When a person from one tribe was killed by a member of another, a "payback" war or killing was customary. Some rituals demanded human sacrifice, and cannibalism was common in some areas.

Arrival of White Men

The first white men to land on Melanesian islands—mainly explorers—quickly discovered that the people of

Hideaway retreats *such as Fiji's Mana Island offer carefree relaxation on palm-fringed beaches. Overnight guests stay in thatched cottages.*

Melanesia were less friendly than their Polynesian neighbors.

The Melanesians were highly suspicious of these light-skinned people who had oddly shaped heads (hats) and removable skin (clothing). Many tribesmen feared that these white men could only be the evil spirits of their ancestors. They felt these evil spirits must be driven away with bows and arrows and spears. When the white men responded to the attacks not with spears but with magic sticks that smoked and killed (guns), the natives knew for certain that these evil spirits had supernatural powers.

The explorers who survived fled back to their homelands, spreading tales of the hostility and cannibalism existing in the dark islands. This news kept many travelers from visiting Melanesia.

The lure of money

Some adventurers ignored the stories of bloodthirsty savages because of the lure of money. Sandalwood traders had learned that the Melanesian islands were rich in sandalwood, so they talked the natives into helping them cut down the trees. Later, some traders destroyed entire villages, killing all the people before sailing away. Others exchanged firearms for sandalwood. The natives learned to use these "magic sticks" on each other, and massive warfare ensued, resulting inevitably in the deaths of many islanders.

Another money-hungry group of white men arrived in the Melanesian islands during this period. Not interested in the riches of the land, these "blackbirders" wanted the people for use as slave labor on South Pacific sugar cane plantations. Thousands of young Melanesian men were sold by their chiefs in exchange for guns—or simply shanghaied away from their villages and shipped off to a strange land. Many of them never saw their island homes again.

Christianity arrives

Inspired by success in the Polynesian islands, missionaries ventured into Melanesia to spread the Christian word, but they didn't always receive a cordial welcome. After continued hardship and many deaths, they finally began to make inroads, converting many Melanesians to Christianity.

However, in some remote areas today, there are tribes that still cling to traditional practices and ancestor worship.

Foreign rule

As more missionaries and other foreign settlers began to arrive in the Melanesian islands, they began to demand protection from their own governments.

One by one, the Melanesian islands came under foreign rule. Great Britain claimed the Solomons and Fiji. France began to govern New Caledonia. The Dutch and the British divided Papua New Guinea (later Australia took over), and Britain and France shared the responsibility of ruling the New Hebrides with a condominium form of government.

Today, the Melanesian countries are again gaining their independence from outside control. Fiji, Papua New Guinea, and the Solomons are all independent nations. Recently the New Hebrides gained their independence and changed their name to Vanuatu.

World War II influences

In the early 1940s, war came to many Melanesian islands. Natives who had known little about the world outside their primitive villages were suddenly exposed to modern technology. People from across the sea brought in a bewildering array of military equipment—airplanes, tanks, bombs, battleships, kerosene lamps, tents, and radios.

Many of the Melanesians, so recently removed from the Stone Age, fought bravely beside the Allied soldiers to drive the Japanese invaders from their land during World War II.

Melanesia Today

Today the Melanesian countries are struggling to enter the modern technological world while maintaining the customs, crafts, and culture of their ancestors. Visitors traveling to these countries see a sharp contrast in life styles between modern concrete towns congested with motor vehicles and the peaceful, thatch hut villages in the countryside where the only traffic moves by foot or horse.

In your travels, you'll experience the influences of foreign rule on the architecture in the towns, the restaurant food, and the language. You'll also learn of the Melanesian people's cultural heritage reflected in their crafts, their dances, their music, their architecture, and their dress.

One important element has changed since early explorers set foot on Melanesian soil. Unlike the reception accorded some of these first visitors, you will be welcomed as a friend, not an evil spirit or enemy. Everywhere you travel, Melanesian smiles will greet you.

Today Melanesia is a place where traces of the Stone Age and modern society live side by side.

Fiji, a friendly country

You can't help liking Fiji. From the moment you arrive by plane or ship, the friendliness of its people warms you like the waters of the South Seas. Dignified Fijians smile and greet you with *"Bula"* (hello)—not just once but repeatedly. Travelers enjoy a standing invitation to play or relax in modern towns, thatch hut villages, or on sandy beaches.

Towns and villages. In Suva, Fiji's capital, you stroll streets lined with aging, colonial-style wood buildings and modern concrete high rises. In the public market, you'll mingle with sari-clad Indians and sulu-wrapped Fijians. Visitors find a fascinating combination of ethnic groups in Fiji.

Outside the relative sophistication of Suva, you discover traditional villages of thatch-roofed *bures* (huts) where the people cling to the ways of their ancestors. Villagers don't need clocks or watches—they live a sun-and-tides existence geared to their fishing and agricultural economy.

Beach resorts. After you've explored Fiji's towns and villages, you can relax on its beaches. Scattered along the southern shore of Viti Levu, you'll find numerous Coral Coast resorts where visitors enjoy a variety of recreational activities ranging from water sports to golf and tennis.

If you yearn for a brief Robinson Crusoe existence, take a short boat trip to any of several offshore hideaway islands. Here you can stay in a thatch bure with the beach and clear blue lagoon just a few steps from your door.

Fijian culture. The Fijian people retain many traditions of their ancestors. You'll discover some of them as you view the ritualistic preparation of *yaqona* (a ceremonial drink made from a pepper plant root) and enjoy dances and songs at a *meke* (Fijian celebration). At a firewalking ceremony, visitors watch in amazement as barefooted Fijian men walk across white-hot rocks without getting burned.

New Caledonia, a touch of France

New Caledonia has been a possession of France since 1853. For more than a century, French influences have created a touch of France in the South Pacific.

Nouméa. These French influences are most prevalent in the country's capital, Nouméa, sometimes affectionately called the Paris of the Pacific. Here you'll find French boutiques, old houses with "gingerbread" iron grillwork, sidewalk cafes offering French dishes and wines, and bakeries selling long, crusty loaves of French bread.

Beyond Nouméa. Outside the capital, you can explore the other attractions of Grande Terre (the main island) plus some of New Caledonia's offshore islands. You'll see villages of thatch huts and smiling Melanesian women bedecked in colorful Mother Hubbards (loose fitting dresses). A trip to the Isle of Pines offers vistas of haunting beauty—short-branched pine trees; incredibly white, velvet-soft beaches; and shimmering lagoons of brilliant turquoise.

The French call New Caledonia "L'Île de Lumière," the Island of Light. After you have strolled its beautiful beaches, explored its lush mountain valleys, and swum in its sparkling sea, you'll agree.

Vanuatu, land of primitive rituals

In some ways, the Vanuatu (New Hebrides) islands seem more distant and foreign than any of the other island groups in the South Pacific. The visitor finds offbeat travel experiences in these islands, where volcanoes smoke and erupt and the people still perform primitive rituals.

Men on Pentecost Island still dive headfirst from high platforms—restrained only by vines around their ankles—in a century-old ritual. Other people of Vanuatu cling to the belief that "John Frum" will eventually send them cargos of riches from across the sea; their red, wooden crosses dot the countryside and villages of Tanna Island.

World War II touched these islands, and the rusting scrap of military debris remains. Luganville on Espirito Santo was one of the key staging areas for U.S. troops advancing on the Solomon Islands.

Papua New Guinea, a multicultured country

More than 700 languages and 700 different cultures exist in Papua New Guinea—a place where primitive traditions retain a strong appeal. Many tribes have emerged only recently from a dominant Stone Age culture. Hidden among Papua New Guinea's isolated plateaus and secluded valleys are areas where tribespeople remain untouched by the 20th century, living just as their ancestors did.

Meeting the people. Touring, especially in the Highlands, is a fascinating experience. On ceremonial occasions, tribesmen adorn themselves in unusual costumes; each tribe has a distinctive personality. Here you'll find wig men, top-heavy with huge elaborate bull-horn hats of woven human hair; mud men, grotesque in baked earthen masks, their bodies caked with mud; and basket men, encased from head to foot in cones of wicker. Other tribal men and women paint their faces and bodies in brilliant reds, blues, and yellows and adorn their heads with large headdresses made of colorful bird of paradise feathers.

In contrast to the Highlands, you can cruise along the Sepik River, meeting people who live in stilt houses and fear the crocodiles lurking nearby. The primitive art of these people is renowned as some of the best in the South Pacific.

Seeing the land. Papua New Guinea offers a varied landscape ranging from soaring mountain peaks—sometimes topped with snow—to mist-shrouded, alpine meadows; white, sandy beaches; vine-entangled jungles; and mangrove swamps.

You can visit Port Moresby, the country's capital, or travel out to Rabaul on New Britain. Rabaul, the Japanese center of operations in the southwest Pacific in World War II, has been completely rebuilt since it was destroyed during the war.

The Solomons, World War II battleground

Many World War II veterans who fought in the South Pacific will never forget the Solomon Islands. Places like Guadalcanal, Bloody Ridge, Iron Bottom Sound, and the "Slot" all recall memories of the fierce battles that were fought here.

Guadalcanal marked the point where U.S. Marines succeeded in stalling the formidable Japanese military offense, changing the course of the war in the Pacific. On the tiny island of Olasana (now known as Plum Pudding Island), John F. Kennedy and 10 other survivors of PT-109 were marooned.

As you tour the Solomons today, you travel past rusting war remains and military battlegrounds. You can meet Solomon Islanders who live in stilt house villages and barter with money made from shells.

FIJI

Volcanic mountains, navigable rivers

Volcanic mountain ranges span Fiji's larger islands in a northeast-southwest line. Heavy rains—up to 3,048 mm/120 inches per year—fall on the eastern, windward side of these mountains, producing dense, dark green, tropical forests. Yellow green, rolling grasslands and sugar cane fields border the islands' western, leeward side where rainfall is only half as much.

Many navigable rivers and small streams drain the mountain ranges. Local people ply these waterways in punts and motorized launches, visiting nearby villages and going to market. One of the largest navigable rivers is the Rewa, located on Viti Levu east of Suva.

Countless palm-lined beaches border turquoise lagoons. Offshore, coral lies in broken patches and fringing reefs. Largest of Fiji's coral reefs is the 193 km/120 mile Great Sea Reef north of Viti Levu. Colorful coral and marine life inhabit the lagoon and reef areas.

Exotic flowers—among them poinciana, bougainvillea, hibiscus, frangipani, and orchids—bloom profusely in the warm, tropical sun. Abundant fruits such as breadfruits, mangoes, and bananas provide an important part of the Fijian diet.

Wildlife includes flying foxes (a type of bat), lizards, and several types of snakes—all nonpoisonous. One of the islands' more prevalent mammals is the mongoose, introduced in the 19th century to eliminate the burgeoning mice and rat population. Instead, the ferretlike animal developed a fondness for villagers' poultry and has become a pest.

A Pacific crossroads

Fiji has long been a Pacific crossroads. Archeologists believe the Fiji Islands were inhabited as early as 1500 B.C. Migrating Polynesians presumably stopped here on early journeys to Tonga and Samoa.

The first recorded European discovery of the Fiji Islands was made by Abel Tasman in 1643. His stories of cannibalism and treacherous coral reefs kept explorers away from Fiji until 1774, when Captain James Cook briefly sailed through the southern islands. Fifteen years later, Captain William Bligh (of *Mutiny on the Bounty* fame) reported barely escaping pursuing cannibals when he ventured into the area.

But the profitable lure of sandalwood and *bêche-de-mer* (sea cucumber, a marine animal consumed mainly by the Chinese) finally drew traders and sailors to the Fiji Islands in the early 19th century. These adventurers introduced European firearms which the native tribes began to use against each other. Fierce intertribal warfare and increased cannibalism plagued the country for the next 40 years.

During this period the first missionaries came to these "cannibal isles." They helped to abolish the practice of cannibalism and transcribed the Fijian language into writing.

Fiji didn't become unified and relatively peaceful until the mid-19th century, when a tribal chief of Bau, Ratu Cakobau, assumed leadership. However, Cakobau found himself unable to resolve all of the country's secular and religious problems. In 1858 he offered the islands to Great Britain, but his offer was refused. He next offered the islands to the United States, but since

"Bula!" You'll hear this friendly Fijian hello often as you explore these tropical islands. Smiling strangers greet you warmly on city streets and wave on rural roads. Little wonder visitors from all parts of the world consider Fiji one of the South Pacific's most hospitable countries.

In Fiji (locally pronounced "Fe-*gee*"), visitors discover a fascinating population representing many ethnic groups—in addition to Fijians, you'll see Indians, Chinese, and Europeans as well as other South Pacific islanders. Strolling the streets of Suva, Fiji's capital, you pass turbaned Sikhs, sari-clad Indian women, and Fijians wrapped in skirtlike *sulus*.

Beyond the bustle of Suva's urban communities, villagers live much as their ancestors did generations ago—a sun-and-tides existence geared to their agricultural and fishing economy. They dwell in thatch-roofed houses and cling to the old communal life style.

Beyond the villages and urban centers, Fiji offers golden sandy beaches and beautiful blue lagoons.

A Tropical Archipelago

Situated just west of the 180th meridian south of the equator, the Fiji Islands are approximately 2,736 km/1,700 miles northeast of Sydney, 1,770 km/1,100 miles north of Auckland, and 9,012 km/5,600 miles southwest of Los Angeles.

How many islands comprise the Fiji archipelago? Estimates range from 300 to 500, depending on whether you count every little coral atoll (many of them underwater at high tide) or only the large atolls and islands. Of these, only about 100 are inhabited.

Viti Levu, the largest island, covers about 10,363 square km/4,000 square miles—over half of Fiji's land area. Fiji's main towns dot the Viti Levu coast at Suva, Lautoka, and Nadi.

A short distance northeast of Viti Levu is its smaller sister island, Vanua Levu. Other lesser islands and island groups include Taveuni, Ovalau, Vatulele, Beqa, the Laus, the Mamanucas, and the Yasawas.

Tropical islands *off Viti Levu attract visitors for day excursions or longer stays. Resorts like Plantation Village feature white sand beaches, water sports, simple accommodations, buffet meals.*

Costumed Fijian entertainers, *their soot-painted faces grimacing in mock fierceness, brandish spears to accompaniment of loud, forceful chants. Tribal warriors formerly performed intimidating war dance preceding battle.*

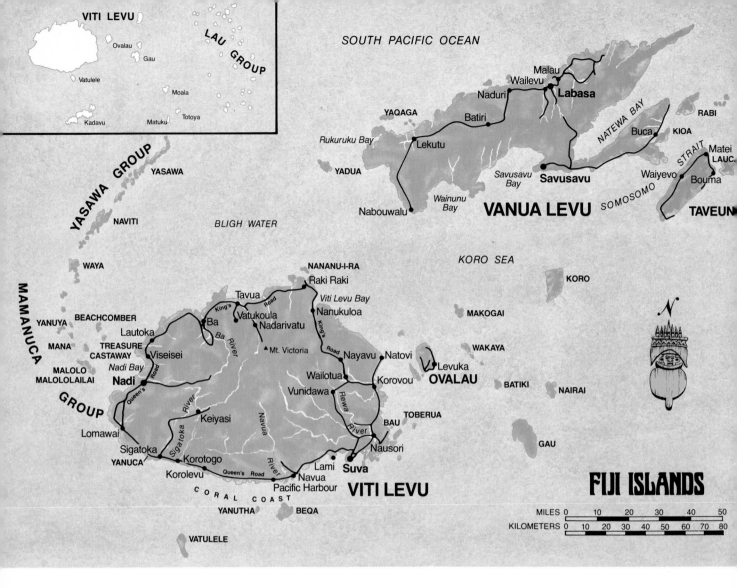

that country was engaged in its Civil War, this offer was ignored. Britain finally accepted a second offer, and, under a Deed of Cession, Fiji was annexed as a British Crown Colony on October 10, 1874.

Nearly a century later, Fiji achieved full independence. On October 10, 1970, the country became a member of the British Commonwealth with Dominion status.

Today Fiji has an elected House of Representatives, an appointed Senate, a Prime Minister, and a Governor-General representing the British Crown. King Cakobau's war club has now become the mace of the Fijian legislature.

Fiji's People

The people of Fiji provide an interesting contrast of cultures. Of the 586,000 people, nearly 259,000 are Fijian and 292,000 Indian. Most of the remaining 35,000 inhabitants are of Chinese or European ancestry or are from other South Pacific islands.

Village and rural life

The tall, handsome, easygoing Fijians are mainly Melanesian, with a trace of Polynesian ancestry. Most of them live in small, rural villages in thatch-roofed *bures*—small walled huts constructed from natural materials such as grass, dry leaves, bamboo, and reeds. They participate in a communal life style where rewards and obligations are shared equally, and all activity is governed by a chief. Even those who work in town feel a continuing obligation to their village and contribute financially when they can.

Fijian villagers grow yams, taros, *cassava* (tapioca), *kumalas* (sweet potatoes), and other vegetables and fruits in their gardens. Crops not consumed are sold or used for trade.

Missionaries—particularly Methodist—left a lasting mark on village life, and the church still plays an important role in community activities.

Many Fijian men and women wear the traditional *sulu,* a wrap-type skirt. Men's sulus are calf-length and worn with western-style shirts or flowered, loose-fitting tops called *bula* shirts. Women wear ankle-length sulus (they feel their legs should not be exposed—a vestige of missionary influence) with long tops.

The Indian influence

Indians originally were brought to Fiji from India as indentured servants in the early days of British colonial rule. European settlers imported them to work the sugar plantations—a job the Fijians didn't want.

Descendants of these indentured servants who remained in Fiji have prospered. They dominate Fiji's town life as merchants and professional people.

Some still work on or manage sugar cane plantations. However, over 85 percent of Fiji's land is community property, owned by the native Fijians and administered by the Native Lands Trust Board.

Many of these island-born Indians—some of them third generation—have never been to India, yet they observe traditional customs and religious beliefs. Hinduism is the predominant religion of the Indians; Moslems and Sikhs are also represented. Unlike India, Fiji has no caste system.

You can identify Indian settlements by their brightly painted, multicolored wooden houses. Many Indian women still wear flowing silk saris, but most Indian men choose western-style dress.

Sugar, copra, and a little gold

Sugar leads the list of Fiji's agricultural exports. Large processing plants are located in Lautoka and Ba (on Viti Levu) and Labasa (on Vanua Levu). Other exports include copra and a little gold.

In recent years tourism has become an increasingly important source of revenue.

Sporting enthusiasts

Fijians love athletic competition, either as spectators or participants. Rugby, soccer, hockey, cricket, boxing, and wrestling all arouse fervent enthusiasm. Various Fiji teams compete both locally and internationally. They have played in the United Kingdom, Canada, Australia, and New Zealand.

Competitions in skin diving, deep-sea and river fishing, swimming, lawn bowling, bicycling, yachting, and power boating are also popular.

Planning Your Trip

Since the days of canoe exploration, Fiji has been at the hub of South Pacific travel. Today, it lies on an important route between North America and Australia and New Zealand. Several international airlines and various cruise ships and cargo/passenger liners stop in Fiji.

When you arrive, you'll land on Fiji's main island

YAQONA
It's a Drink of Welcome

In Fiji as well as other South Pacific islands, the ceremonial drinking of *yaqona* serves as a symbol of welcome, an expression of hospitality and friendship. Outside Fiji, the drink might be called *kava*, or perhaps *ava* or *sakau*.

Although preparation may differ slightly from country to country, the drink is made primarily from powdered pepper plant roots blended with water. Many travelers who taste the liquid for the first time claim it tastes like what it looks like—muddy water. However, those who have acquired a taste for the cloudy mixture find it refreshing. After several bowls, the nonalcoholic drink can produce a slightly numb tongue and lips.

A solemn, stylized ritual—requiring total silence on the part of the honored guests—accompanies the ceremonial preparation and drinking of yaqona in Fiji. As a guest, you sit cross-legged in front of a large *tanoa* (wooden bowl with legs) to witness the preparation of the drink. Words are chanted and the *lali* (wooden drum) sounded. When the yaqona is the right consistency, your portion is served in a half coconut shell *bilo* (cup). You clap once, accept the bowl in both hands and down it in a single draught while your host claps three times. Both you and your host then clap three more times and your host shouts *"maca"* (meaning "it is drained").

At various hotels, the yaqona ceremony precedes an evening of native dancing and feasting. It is also held before a Fijian firewalking demonstration.

Venerable *Grand Pacific Hotel, built in 1914, adds colonial accent to Suva's Victoria Parade. Locally called the GPH, hotel exudes languid South Seas atmosphere. Lobby accents include ceiling fans and rattan chairs.*

Shaded *by parasols from tropical sun, Indian women draped in saris display vegetables for sale in Suva market near King's Wharf. Early morning is busiest time.*

FIJIAN PRONOUNCING PRIMER...

Mind Your Bs and Qs

In the Fijian language, there's more to the printed word than meets the eye. Take for instance, the town name—Nadi. It's pronounced "*Nan*-dee." Or the island of Beqa, home of the firewalkers. It's pronounced "M*beng*-ga." Sigatoka is pronounced "*Sing*-a-toka." Cakobau Road, "Tha-*komb*-au" Road.

Keeping track of these added consonants can boggle the mind of the visitor who'd like to pronounce his bs and qs and other consonants correctly while he's in Fiji. You even hesitate saying *bula* (hello), wondering whether it shouldn't come out sounding something like "mboula." (It should.)

Actually there are just five consonants in the Fijian language that take special treatment. Fix in your mind the pronunciations of b, c, d, g, and q and you'll have an easier time. If you memorize the following rules and words, they'll help you in your Fiji travels:

- B is pronounced "mb"; the "m" is almost a silent murmur. Try saying "M*ba*" (Ba) and "M*bau*" (Bau).
- C is pronounced "th." Try saying "Ma-ma-*nu*-thas" (Mamanucas) and "Ya-*nu*-tha" (Yanuca).
- D is pronounced "nd." Try saying "*Nan*-dee" (Nadi).
- G is pronounced "ng." Try saying "*Sing*-a-toka" (Sigatoka).
- Q is pronounced "ng-g." Try saying "M*beng*-ga" (Beqa).

Now that you've mastered a little of the Fijian language, remember that as you drink a cup of *yaqona* (Fiji's national drink) someday you'll be telling a friend about a drink called "yang-*gona*."

---

of Viti Levu—at Suva Harbour if you come by ship, Nadi International Airport if by plane. (Some South Pacific flights land at Nausori Airport near Suva.)

Getting around Fiji

Air Pacific, Fiji Air, Island Air, Sunflower Airlines, and Turtle Airways all provide transportation within the Fiji Islands. Regularly scheduled flights link the main towns on Viti Levu and the other islands, and there is also service to resorts on Viti Levu's Coral Coast and Nadi Bay resorts.

If you have the time to explore the countryside beyond Fiji's towns and resorts, you can take a coach or rent a car. Coaches allow passengers to enjoy the scenery without worrying about the curving road ahead. If you prefer to travel at a more relaxed pace and don't mind tackling dusty (sometimes muddy) roads, drive yourself.

Taxicabs are plentiful in Viti Levu's main towns. They also operate on Vanua Levu, Taveuni, and in Levuka on Ovalau. Drivers are well informed and rates are moderate. Taxis are metered in town. However, for trips of more than 16 km/10 miles, driver and passenger should mutually agree on the fare before departure.

In Suva, Lautoka, and Levuka on Ovalau you can take a local bus around town.

Traveling by bus. Island buses—without air conditioning—provide regular service between main towns on Viti Levu, Vanua Levu, and Taveuni. For a short trip, these commuter buses provide a colorful experience. Buses have no glass windows; instead, canvas blinds are raised during dry (dusty) weather and unfurled when it rains. Accompanying you and your fellow passengers may be live chickens and freshly caught fish.

On Viti Levu, an air-conditioned coach follows the Queen's Road between Suva and Nadi International Airport, stopping at all the major hotels.

Driving in Fiji. Fiji has 3,138 km/1,950 miles of public roads, yet outside the towns, very few of them are paved. The unpaved roads are narrow, winding, and bumpy. Dusty during the dry season, they become muddy and subject to flash floods during rainstorms.

Following British tradition, traffic moves on the left side of the road. Visitors who plan to drive will need a valid driver's license issued by their own country.

If you are renting a car to drive long distances over unpaved roads, check to see that the car's tires (including the spare) are in good condition. Repair shops are infrequent.

Rental car agencies are located in Nadi, Suva, Lautoka, Pacific Harbour, Sigatoka, and Labasa (on Vanua Levu).

The traveler who enjoys the freedom of motoring —but who doesn't want to drive—can hire a chauffeur-driven car.

Cruising. If you have a leisurely itinerary, consider interisland cargo vessels as another way of seeing Fiji's islands. The boats make more-or-less regular stops at most of the inhabited islands, where they leave supplies, pick up copra, and take on an occasional passenger.

Don't expect luxurious accommodations, since these ships are designed for hauling cargo. Your schedule must be flexible, because weather, cargo loading, and related conditions affect departure times.

Posh resorts or simple bures

Fiji's accommodations suit a range of tastes and pocketbooks. You can stay in a convenient downtown hotel or try one of several elegant beach resorts complete with tennis and golf. If total escape is what you're looking for, you can settle into a simple but comfortable thatch or tile-roofed country *bure* (a small bungalow with steeply peaked roof and louvered windows). Additional choices include budget-priced, family-oriented housekeeping units; inexpensive guest houses with breakfast included in the price; and large luxurious condominiums, each with a private swimming pool.

Most accommodations include coffee and tea-making facilities in each room, so you can enjoy a "cuppa" any time. Some rooms contain small refrigerators.

Accommodations can be found on Viti Levu, Vanua Levu, Ovalau, the Mamanuca Group, and Taveuni. Information on the types of accommodations available in each area can be found under specific destinations.

Fiji's tourist season peaks in May, August, and from mid-December through mid-January. Reservations for this holiday period are sometimes made a year in advance.

Eating—Fiji-style

Fiji's wide range of ethnic cuisines offers some new experiences in dining. Stone-roasted suckling pig, spicy Indian curries, and Chinese noodles are just three of the items from which to choose. Hotel restaurants provide the best places to enjoy these dishes, though some local restaurants feature Chinese, Indian, British, and American foods.

Island fare. Local specialties include a variety of fish, fresh from the ocean and well prepared. A favorite Fijian first course is *kokoda*—chopped raw fish, onions, and coconut milk (*lolo*).

Lolo—milk obtained from grating and straining fresh coconut—is an ingredient in many Fijian dishes. It is used to flavor anything from a fish specialty like kokoda to the simple *dalo* (vegetablelike taro root).

In Fiji you'll find an abundance of tropical fruits such as mangoes, oranges, *paw paws* (papayas), bananas, pineapples, and coconuts. Other local desserts include tapioca, British-type puddings, and ice cream.

Many hotels hold buffet-style feasts and barbecues featuring Fijian-type foods at least once a week. Tasty specialties include crab, shrimp, oysters, fish, suckling pig, *kumalas* (sweet potatoes), several types of yams, baked bananas, and Indian curries. Some items may be cooked traditionally—wrapped in banana leaves and baked in a *lovo* (earth oven) for several hours.

Buffet-style meals are very popular in Fiji for both lunch and dinner—and sometimes even for breakfast.

The country's traditional drink is *yaqona,* made from pepper plant roots. A ritualistic ceremony accompanies the preparation and drinking of this liquid (see page 61). One of the most popular beverages is locally brewed Fiji beer. All wines and liquors are imported.

Flashing spears and joyful song. Feasts (also called *magitis*) held at the hotels often include a *meke*—a Fijian celebration in song and dance. To the beat of the *deruas* (thick bamboo lengths) and *lali* (hollow log drums), costumed Fijians perform generations-old dances and songs.

Tall, muscular, grass-skirted men—their faces painted with soot—leap toward you, brandishing spears or clubs.

Their flashing eyes and loud, forceful chants remind you that this was once a war dance performed before battle.

On a gentler note, the women—attired in floor-length *masi* (Fijian tapa cloth) garments—sing of domestic village life and the planting of crops. Much of their dance movements are performed seated, their hands moving gracefully to tell the story. When they stand, they sway in a kind of slow hula, their hands still the prominent feature of their dance.

During a meke, you might be invited to join the Fijians in the *taralala*. In this popular dance, partners move side by side, their arms about one another. They take several quick steps forward and several back in time to the music.

A shopper's paradise

Shops in Fiji offer everything from modern Japanese stereo equipment to traditional Fijian woodcarvings—sometimes sold side by side in the same store.

Before buying, try to do some comparison pricing. Some storekeepers have fixed prices; others like to bargain. Bargaining is common in the public markets. The prices are in Fijian dollars (see page 73).

Most shops are open weekdays from 8 A.M. to 4:30 P.M. (until 5 on Fridays) and from 8 to 12:30 on Saturdays. When cruise ships stop at Lautoka or Suva on Saturday afternoons and Sundays, duty-free shops in the area will open 1 hour after docking and remain open for 4 hours.

Duty-free shopping. Fiji is noted for good shopping values. Items you can buy include radios, cameras, projectors, stereo equipment, watches, French perfume, tape recorders, and diamonds.

Suva is the most popular duty-free shopping area because of its large number of stores. However, you can also shop in Nadi, Lautoka, and Sigatoka.

Fijian and Indian products. Locally made crafts and Indian products vie for your attention in many stores. Handwoven mats and baskets, shell jewelry, colorful sulus and flowered bula shirts, woodcarvings, *masi* (Fijian tapa cloth), and pottery head the list of Fijian craft items. Indian imports include bright silk saris and shiny brassware.

Public markets. Don't miss browsing through at least one public market. Tables laden with fresh fruits and vegetables are intermingled with bins of exotic Indian spices. The marketplace buzzes with excitement—conversation, punctuated with laughter, is carried on in Indian, Fijian, and English.

Though other towns have public markets, the best known is in Suva near King's Wharf. The most colorful time at any public market is early morning on Friday or Saturday when the place abounds with activity.

A South Pacific playground

Visitors to Fiji can choose from a multitude of recreational activities.

Fiji's many calm lagoons are a perfect playground for sailing, canoeing, coral viewing, snorkeling, skin diving, and fishing. You can collect shells on miles of deserted beaches or set off on a trek across a coral reef at low tide.

At the resort hotels, you can participate in archery, horseback riding, tennis, volleyball, ping pong, badminton, golf, or lawn bowling.

Skin and scuba diving. Divers won't be disappointed in Fiji. Major reefs provide a wide range of waters— shallow areas inside the lagoons for snorkelers and spear fishermen, deep waters outside the reefs for skin and scuba divers.

Around the larger islands, waters are the clearest during the cool, dry months from June through October. Scuba diving and snorkeling are possible the year around, but during the rainy season, rivers discharge muddy water into the surrounding sea.

You can find good diving spots at Astrolabe Lagoon (a 6-hour boat trip south of Suva); Argo Reef in the Lau Islands; Beqa Island waters (a 1-hour boat trip from Suva); Taveuni's Rainbow Reef; Mamanuca Group waters, especially around Mana Island (near Lautoka); and the Queen's Road coast between Suva and Nadi.

You can charter diving boats with scuba tanks at Mana Island, Suva, and Taveuni. Masks, snorkels, and flippers can be rented at most beach hotels.

Scubahire, with facilities at the Tradewinds Hotel marina in Suva, offers a complete selection of diving equipment for rent or sale. They also give diving instruction.

It is illegal to use spear guns fired with cartridges in Fiji waters unless you are a member of a spear fishing group and have received special permission from the Fiji police. (Police will only exempt equipment brought in for temporary use.) In an effort to protect marine life, diving organizations in Fiji actively discourage the use of spear guns.

Fishing. Fishermen will revel in Fiji's year-round fishing season. Most black marlin and sailfish strike between October and April; peak season occurs in January and February. Yellow-fin tuna are plentiful from December to June. Billfish, dolphin, barracuda, bonito, walu, and wahoo are caught throughout the year.

You can hire deep-sea fishing boats at a number of Fijian resorts. In Nadi, boats are available for hire at the Regent of Fiji. You can also go deep-sea fishing from off-shore island resorts near Lautoka, from resorts along Viti Levu's Coral Coast, or from Taveuni's Castaway Taveuni. In Suva, deep-sea fishing boats are available for hire at the Tradewinds Hotel.

At some hotels you can rent smaller boats by the hour for lagoon fishing. If you stay on shore, you can

FESTIVAL TIME

Fiji's varied cultural background and the people's lively interest in sports provide Fiji with an active calendar. Below are a few events that will add to your Fiji visit.

January—April

New Year's Day. Fireworks, floral decorations, and festivities herald "Vakatawase" (the welcoming of the new year) on the first Monday in January.

Easter. Good Friday to Easter Monday activities include the Annual Easter Cricket Tournament in Suva and the Annual Easter Sports Meeting (track events) in Levuka.

Rugby. Early April marks the beginning of rugby season in Suva, where matches are held every Saturday through October at Albert and Buckhurst parks.

May—August

Queen Elizabeth's birthday. The queen's official birthday is celebrated on the Monday closest to June 14.

South Pacific Bowling Carnival. In June, lawn bowlers from Fiji, Australia, and New Zealand compete in this 10-day event in Suva.

Bula Festival. In mid-July, Nadi hosts this weeklong event, including floats, processions, and the crowning of a Bula Queen.

Hibiscus Festival. Late August marks one of Suva's most lively events. The week of activities features Fijian, Chinese, Indian, and Polynesian entertainment, as well as sports events, youth rallies, a fashion show, baby shows, and a parade.

Indian firewalking. People of the East Indian community hold this solemn religious ritual once a year between June and August at various locations in Fiji. The biggest firewalking event takes place in August on Howell Road in Suva.

September—December

Suva Orchid and Horticultural Show. Tropical plants and flowers are displayed at this September event in Suva.

Cricket. Early October marks the opening of the cricket season throughout Fiji. The season ends in March.

Fiji Day. On the Monday closest to October 10, Fiji's independence from Great Britain is heralded.

Diwali Festival. In late October or early November, Fiji's Indian population celebrates the Hindu New Year. Houses, porches, and paths come alive with twinkling lanterns and candles.

Prince Charles's birthday. The prince's birthday is celebrated on the Monday closest to November 14.

Christmas Day. Fijians honor this day with feasts, special church services, and Christmas programs.

enjoy fishing along the shallow flats, estuaries, and mangrove streams for salmon, cod, and mangrove snapper. Freshwater streams and rivers yield *ika droka* (jungle perch), trout, and bass.

No fishing licenses are required.

Yachting. Yachtsmen who are accredited members of overseas yacht and power boat clubs are welcome at the Royal Suva Yacht Club. Yachts and cruisers are available for charter by the day or for longer periods in both Suva and Lautoka.

Shell collecting. Several easily accessible areas just off Viti Levu offer a great variety of specimens for avid shell collectors. The Coral Coast is noted for gold cowries, while the area off Queen's Road between Navua and Suva is known for cowries and mitres. Be wary of cone shells in these areas—some are poisonous. The area around Suva is also a shell collector's paradise. Natewa Bay, off the east coast of Vanua Levu, is another area worth exploring.

Governmental restrictions prohibit taking triton shells out of the country.

Golf. If you plan to golf, you'll find numerous courses, many on Viti Levu and one on Vanua Levu. You can play on 18-hole courses in Suva at the Fiji Golf Club or at Pacific Harbour Resort's championship course on Viti Levu's Coral Coast. Nine-hole courses are located on Viti Levu, at Nadi, Lautoka, Nausori, Ba, Vatukoula, and Penang. Vanua Levu's one course is at Labasa.

Resorts with putting greens, driving ranges, or 9-hole courses include The Fijian, Reef Hotel, Dominion International Hotel, Regent of Fiji, Hyatt Regency, Naviti Beach Resort, Turtle Island Lodge, Fiji Mocambo, Skylodge Hotel, Hotel Tanoa, Man Friday Resort, and Castaway Taveuni.

Tennis. Visitors who enjoy a game of tennis will find courts at the Suva Lawn Tennis Club in Albert Park, just across from the Grand Pacific Hotel. Fiji has 12 lawn tennis clubs whose seasons run from May to late November (before the rains start). Check with your hotel to arrange an introduction with a club official. Players are required to wear white attire. Albert Park also has Municipal Courts (hard court). John Newcombe's South Pacific Tennis Ranch (next to the Regent of Fiji) has both grass courts and paved, all-weather, flood-lit courts.

You'll find tennis courts at some of Fiji's resorts also including the Fiji Mocambo, The Fijian, Reef, Naviti, Korolevu Beach, Hyatt Regency, Castaway Island, Club Naitasi, Castaway Gateway, Skylodge, Tanoa, Castaway Taveuni, and Plantation Island.

Exploring Viti Levu

Viti Levu, Fiji's main island, occupies more than half the land mass of the Fiji Islands. Volcanic in origin, the oval island possesses several navigable rivers. Many of its mountains rise above 914 meters/3,000 feet.

On the western side of the island, broad plains of sugar cane and grasslands stretch upward from the coast toward the densely wooded peaks. Junglelike tropical forests replace the grasslands on the island's wet east side.

Nearly 70 percent of Fiji's population live on Viti Levu. Main towns include Suva, the capital, on the island's southeast coast, and Nadi and Lautoka on the west coast.

Most visitors to Fiji spend most of their time on Viti Levu, where they enjoy duty-free shopping, miles of beaches and blue bays, and an array of recreational activities. Excursions depart from major towns to nearby offshore island retreats.

Nadi-Lautoka area

Situated on Viti Levu's west coast in the heart of lush sugar cane country, the Nadi-Lautoka area offers a composite of Fiji's scenic attractions. For many visitors —en route to other South Pacific destinations—it is their only glimpse of Fiji.

Miles of cane fields surround peaceful villages of thatch-roofed huts and Indian settlements of brightly painted, wooden houses. In Nadi and Lautoka you'll find opportunities to shop, or you can relax at nearby resorts.

A definite plus for this area is its climate. Because it's located on the leeward, "dry" side of the island, the average annual rainfall is only about 1524 mm/60 inches. (The Suva area gets nearly twice this much.)

Nadi. Fiji's main airline gateway, Nadi is a town of 23,000 located 6 km/4 miles southwest of Nadi International Airport.

Strolling down the one main street of Nadi Town (as it is affectionately known), you'll mingle with shoppers from nearby sugar plantations. Duty-free shops flank the thoroughfare, their bold signs luring prospective buyers. Along the side streets you'll discover thatch-roofed huts and wooden houses topped by rusting tin roofs. Cows and horses quietly graze in adjoining fields.

Lautoka. Fiji's second largest town, Lautoka is 32 km/ 20 miles north of Nadi. Primarily a port and sugar mill community, Lautoka has a population of 22,000. A number of ships—many of them passenger liners—dock here annually.

If you have only a short time in Lautoka, explore one of its tree-lined streets. On Vitogo Parade, the main street, you'll find both department stores and duty-free shops.

Another stop might be the local market, on Naviti and Vakabale streets, where you'll see an enticing variety of tropical fruits and vegetables. At Churchill Park on Verona Street, sports fans can watch local groups lawn bowl or play cricket, rugby, or soccer in season.

Discovering sugar cane country. During crushing season—May to December—you can see how sugar cane is processed at the South Pacific Sugar Mill near the outskirts of Lautoka. Phone ahead for reservations for the guided tours, which depart daily except Tuesday and Sunday. The mill tour leads you through each step of the processing—from cane crushing and the forcing out of juice to the purifying and refining of sugar.

Sugar cane fields abound near both Nadi and Lautoka. On a short drive, you're apt to see patches of sugar cane in varying shades of green. The darker cane is new growth; as it matures it grows lighter.

The harvested cane is loaded on small railroad cars and hauled to nearby sugar mills. You'll see tracks of the narrow-gauge sugar train weaving in and out of the plantations.

Nearby excursions. The village of Viseisei, located midway between Nadi and Lautoka, is the site where ancient Fijians supposedly first landed. The chief and leader of the migration is considered the legendary ancestor of the tribes of northwest Viti Levu.

Offshore island cruises. Both Nadi and Lautoka are embarkation points for cruises to Fiji's outer islands (see page 72).

Where to stay. More than a dozen hotels in the Nadi-Lautoka area offer visitors comfortable accommodations with restaurants, swimming pools, and a variety of recreational activities.

You can stay right next to the Nadi International Airport at the Castaway Gateway Hotel; or 5 to 10 minutes away at the Dominion International, Fiji Mocambo, Westgate Hotel, Nadi Airport TraveLodge, Hotel Tanoa, or Skylodge Hotel. Fifteen minutes from the airport is the Regent of Fiji beach resort.

In Lautoka, travelers can stay at the Cathay Hotel and the Lautoka Hotel.

After the sun goes down. Many hotels have special island nights with buffet dinners and Fijian song and dance. The Fiji Mocambo and the Regent of Fiji have weekly Fijian firewalking demonstrations.

Suva, Fiji's capital

Fiji's major city is Suva, located on Viti Levu's southeast coast 209 km/130 miles east of Nadi. The town's peninsula site facing a natural harbor made it an excellent choice for Fiji's capital, which was moved here from Levuka in 1882. Today, Suva is the country's main port, accommodating ships of all sizes from throughout the world.

Backed by lush, dark green hills of the Suva-Rewa Range, much of the town's waterfront is built on land

Indian woman *greets acquaintance outside Chinese general store at Savusavu, where merchandise ranges from hardware and dishes to groceries and soccer balls. Village residents meet here to exchange island news and gossip.*

reclaimed from tangled mangrove swamps. This waterfront district and intersecting streets provide the hub for much of Suva's activity.

The town's center is a conglomeration of British colonial-style and modern architecture. Wooden, two-story, arcaded buildings—their upper levels decorated with sagging verandas—intermingle with more recently built utilitarian concrete structures. Spreading up the hills from the waterfront, the residential area features gracious, colonial-style homes set in gardens rich with tropical flowers and spreading shade trees.

A multiracial settlement of 64,000, Suva is populated by Fijians, Indians, Europeans, Chinese, and other South Pacific islanders. You'll notice the contrast of cultures as you stroll the busy town streets—passing sulu-clad Fijians, Indian women in beautifully elaborate saris, and Tongans in *lava-lavas* (wrapped skirts similar to Fijian sulus) with plaited straw sashes.

Many people carry umbrellas, since Suva is located on the "wet" side of Viti Levu. Brief thundering downpours, South Seas style, are not unusual.

Getting there and getting around. The fastest way to travel to Suva from Nadi is by air, landing at Nausori Airport 23 km/14 miles north of town. International flights from other South Pacific islands also land at Nausori.

For a more scenic trip, you can follow the coast road from Nadi to Suva. The bus trip takes at least 6 hours. If you drive, you'll want to make a slower journey—2 days perhaps.

Some passenger liners cruising the South Pacific make brief stops at Suva.

In addition to taxis, you may want to ride one of Suva's commuter buses—a great way to see the town on a limited budget. The circular route through the city takes only 45 minutes. Buses depart from the bus station, located next to the public market near King's Wharf.

Strolling Victoria Parade. Despite the possibility of showers, Suva is an excellent town to explore on foot. Many of the main points of interest are located on Victoria Parade and its extension, Queen Elizabeth Drive.

Beginning your stroll south of Cakobau Road on tree-shaded Queen Elizabeth Drive, you glimpse Government House—home of the Governor-General—on a hillside surrounded by landscaped grounds. A stern military sentry—clad in a red jacket and white sulu—stands guard in front of the pillared gate. The Changing of the Guard that occurs here once a month is reminiscent of the parade and pomp at Buckingham Palace.

North of Government House is Thurston Gardens, Suva's botanical park lush with flowering plants, shade trees, and green lawns. Objects reflecting 3,000 years of Fijian history are exhibited at the Fiji Museum in the middle of this garden. The museum has fine displays of Melanesian artifacts, objects from Fiji's maritime era, and reminders of cannibal days. The museum is open daily except Saturdays.

Albert Park, across Cakobau Road from Thurston Gardens, became the "First Pacific International Airport" in 1928 when Sir Charles Kingsford-Smith landed his *Southern Cross* here on the first transpacific flight from California to Australia. Today, sports-loving Fijians use the park for rugby, soccer, hockey, and cricket.

The venerable Grand Pacific Hotel, built in 1914, faces Albert Park on the seaward side of Victoria Parade. As you enter the lobby with its stately columns, giant ceiling fans, and high-backed rattan chairs, you will be reminded of Fiji's colonial past when the hotel was the fashionable place to stay.

Immediately behind the hotel, you'll often see Fijians standing waist deep in the harbor netting fish.

Suva's wharves. One other stop on your walk might be the Prince's Landing-King's Wharf area just north of Suva's shopping district bordering Usher Street. Tying up here are international passenger liners and cargo ships; work-worn, interisland copra boats; local Fijian commuter vessels; and glass-bottomed tourist boats. Many a cruise ship passenger vividly remembers the colorful greeting and marching serenade of the Royal Fiji Police Band or Royal Military Forces Band. In their navy blue shirts or red jackets and white sulus, the bandsmen briskly perform on the dock.

Shopping around. You'll find good browsing in the heart of Suva's business district at the northern end of Victoria Parade and on nearby side streets bordering Nubukalou Creek.

Lining the streets are boutiques selling locally manufactured resort wear; tour and airline offices; shops featuring Mikimoto pearls and French perfume; department stores; and camera, radio, and stereo dealers. Everywhere sign-burdened shops proclaim they have "duty-free" goods. Between Thomson Street and Renwick Road is Cumming Street—a narrow, block-long lane lined with these shops.

Another Suva shopping adventure is the City Market on Usher Street. Located near the heart of wharf and port activity, the market dazzles the senses with its array of fruits, vegetables, fish, and flowers.

Handicrafts such as masi cloth, woven mats, baskets, shells, jewelry, and woodcarvings can be purchased nearby at the handicraft center on Stinson Parade. Other shops featuring handicrafts include Fiji Museum's gift shop in Thurston Gardens, The Cottage on Ellery Street, and the Fijian Women's Society Handicraft Center, about 5 km/3 miles from town in Mabua.

Other Suva sights. Suva Aquarium, located in the Old Town Hall in downtown Suva, contains a large oceanarium featuring sharks, rays, turtles, moray eels, and other sea life. Still other tanks feature marine life from Fiji's lakes and coastal waters. The aquarium is open daily from 8 A.M. to 7 P.M.

The hills above Suva's waterfront are resplendent with tropical flowers and shrubbery in a residential setting. Explore the streets on your own or take a tour of several private gardens.

The Bay of Islands, a short distance north of town, provides a peaceful contrast from Suva's busy harbor. Pleasure craft lie quietly moored in a blue bay dotted with tiny green isles.

Cruising Suva's harbor. Glass-bottomed boats ply the coral-ringed harbor, then cruise to an outer island for a day of swimming and sunning. Evening island cruises include a dinner and Fijian entertainment. Most cruises depart from Stinson Parade jetty.

Orchid Island-Fiji on Display. Fijian life, both past and present, is represented at this exhibit. Located 11 km/7 miles west of Suva on Queen's Road, it features

FIREWALKING

A Mystifying Ceremony

The hushed audience stares in wonder as the Beqa Islanders use long poles to casually toss aside the burning logs. Chanting "O-vulo-vulo" as they work, they reveal a circular firewalking pit of white-hot rocks that have been heating beneath the pile of burning timbers for 6 hours.

With the pit finally readied, the *Bete* (leader) shouts "Vuto-O" and the barefoot firewalkers enter the arena.

Dressed in colorful skirts of dyed pandanus leaves and frangipani leis, they calmly step single file into the pit. Standing momentarily on the glowing rocks, they smile, wave at the audience, and shout "Bula." Their faces show no pain as they walk around the pit.

Following the ceremony, the firewalkers proudly display their feet to the audience. There are no signs of burns.

Firewalking, or *Vilavilairevo* as the Fijians call it (literally meaning "jumping into the oven"), has been practiced by the Sawau tribe of Beqa Island for generations. According to legend, firewalking began when a Sawau warrior, Tui-na-iviqa-lita, promised a famous storyteller that he would give him whatever he caught while fishing. He caught an eel which transformed itself into a spirit god. Pleading to be set free, the spirit god offered in exchange the gift of immunity to fire. To prove the validity of his gift, the spirit god built a fire pit, leaped onto the white-hot stones, and commanded Tui to follow. Tui did so and was unharmed.

Today the islanders believe the Bete is a direct descendant of Tui-na-iviqa-lita. He and his tribesmen have inherited Tui's ability to walk on fire. For 2 weeks before a ceremony, all firewalkers must adhere to two rules—separation from their wives, and no eating of coconut.

Firewalking ceremonies are held several times a month on Viti Levu at hotels in Suva, Nadi, and along the Coral Coast. Check locally for dates.

The East Indians who have settled on Fiji also have a firewalking custom. Traditionally an annual ritual during a religious festival, it is based on different concepts and is conspicuously different from that of the Beqa Islanders.

a model Fijian village and pagan temple *(bure-kalou)*. Orchid Island, connected to the village by a bridge, includes displays of native flora and fauna.

You'll see museum bures, including one containing a detailed portrayal of Fiji's history; a handicraft center; and Fijian entertainment.

The exhibit is open daily except Sunday.

Visiting other villages. You can journey to several other Fijian villages in the Suva area.

Marau Model Village, located 10 minutes from Suva in Tamavua, is an authentic replica of an early Fijian native village showing its way of life and handicrafts. It is open daily except Sunday.

Local operators offer tours to nearby villages by both bus and boat. Adventurous travelers can take 6 and 8-day trips into the interior by foot, horse, and boat.

Royal home. Bau, former island fortress home of King Cakobau and his royal tribesmen, lies just off Viti Levu's east coast northeast of Suva. Visitors travel to Bau by launch. Permission for visiting Bau must be obtained from the Fijian Affairs Board on Victoria Parade in Suva.

(Continued on page 71)

Rowboat transports villagers *from interisland ferry to Taveuni shore. Sailing daily from Buca Bay on Vanua Levu, ferry carries passengers, produce, copra, and domestic animals. International Date Line once split island into two time zones.*

When cannibalism was practiced, the tiny island—connected to Viti Levu at low tide by a narrow, coral causeway—harbored over 3,000 people armed with 100 war canoes. Although the island's population has diminished to about 400 and war canoes are a thing of the past, Bau is still home of Fiji's highest chiefs.

Bau's major sights are the Cakobau Memorial Church, a council house, and an ancient tree peppered with notches—each notch said to be the record of a villager who met his fate in the oven of an old-time cannibal chief.

Where to stay. Downtown Suva offers a wide range of modern hotels for travelers, including the Suva TraveLodge, Suva Courtesy Inn, and Southern Cross. Several apartment hotels are also available. The venerable Grand Pacific Hotel appeals to nostalgia buffs seeking South Seas colonial atmosphere.

A short distance from town are the President Resort Hotel overlooking the harbor and the Tradewinds Hotel facing the Bay of Islands.

After the sun goes down. Many local hotels feature a special weekly buffet dinner or barbecue. The Tradewinds Hotel has a Fijian firewalking show on a regular basis.

Levuka, Fiji's original capital

To glimpse a bit of Fiji's frontier past, take the day excursion from Suva to Levuka on Ovalau.

Raucous sailors, traders, whalers, plantation owners, and beachcombers once reeled through the streets of Levuka in pursuit of adventure at any of a multitude of wine and grog shops. Today Levuka is a sleepy fishing village—its brawling port days just a memory.

Until 1882 Levuka was Fiji's capital and main port, harboring many wooden sailing ships. After the capital was moved to Suva, its harbor soon became the country's major port.

Levuka today. The town drowses on a narrow shelf of land with little room to expand—even if it wanted to. The steep crags and mountain mass of volcanic Ovalau rise abruptly just behind the town. Part of the residential area struggles up the mountainside, its streets no more than flights of stairs. For a rewarding view, climb the 199 steps to Mission Hill, site of an 1837 Methodist mission.

Relics of the past survive in this quaint coastal town. A sprinkling of old, iron-roofed, wooden buildings line the crescent-shaped, main street fronting the harbor. Traces of missionary influence are still apparent in the town's aging churches, convent, and mission house. Visit the town hall to see photographs of early Levuka.

Just outside of town, a monument marks the spot where King Cakobau signed the Deed of Cession with the British. A stone marker commemorates Fiji's independence from Britain. Nearby is a large native bure, still used for Fijian chief tribal meetings.

The town's main industry is the Pacific Fishing Company—a tuna canning operation. Call if you'd like to tour the premises.

Getting there. You can reach tiny Ovalau (the island is only 13 km/8 miles by 11 km/7 miles) daily on Fiji Air flights from Suva's Nausori Airport. The 20-minute scenic trip passes over several smaller islands on the way. From the Ovalau airport it's a 21 km/13 mile trip to Levuka. Besides scheduled service, a special day tour departs from Suva for Ovalau on Fiji Air.

You can also reach Ovalau by launch from Natovi, a 2-hour bus trip north of Suva. The daily boat trip takes another 2½ hours.

Where to stay. Reminiscent of yesteryear, Levuka's homey accommodations feature ceiling fans, beaded curtains, wicker furniture, and an unpretentious atmosphere. Visitors can stay at the Royal Hotel.

Circling Viti Levu

A 531 km/330 mile road—longest in Fiji—circles the island of Viti Levu. One portion of it—Queen's Road—skirts the western and southern coast between Lautoka and Suva. King's Road continues inland from Suva up the eastern part of the island and along the northern coast to Lautoka.

Part of Queen's Road is now paved, but all of King's Road remains unpaved though graded. Unpaved roads can be bumpy and muddy when it rains. A more leisurely trip on either road will include an overnight stop along the way.

If you don't wish to drive, you can hire a car and driver or take a bus. Air-conditioned buses operate daily between Nadi and Suva on Queen's Road, stopping at several resorts along the way. Sunflower Airlines provides service between Nadi and Pacific Harbour and Air Coral Coast flies between Nadi and Korolevu and Malololailai Island. Non-air-conditioned buses travel King's Road daily. A local tour operator offers a 5-day, circle-island tour, departing Nadi on Monday and returning on Friday.

If you decide to make the journey by road, the resorts and scenery you'll see on the journey make the trip worthwhile.

Queen's Road. Winding along the palm-fringed coastline on Queen's Road, you'll pass deserted beaches and blue lagoons. Villages of thatch-roofed huts stand in forest clearings. As you pass, villagers will stop their activities to smile, wave, and shout "Bula." If you stop, don't be surprised if you're invited to visit the village.

One of the most popular sections of Queen's Road is the 97 km/60 mile Coral Coast stretching from Yanuca Island to Pacific Harbour. Sprinkled along this section of road are numerous resorts, both large and small, offering accommodations ranging from luxurious villas —each with individual swimming pools—to modest bure-style bungalows.

Major hotels along the Coral Coast—The Fijian, Reef, Naviti, Korolevu Beach, Paradise Point, Crow's Nest, Hyatt Regency, and Man Friday—operate as resorts with pools, boats, tennis courts, and water sports. Some have golf courses. One resort, the Pacific Harbour development, not only offers accommodations, but also has a cultural center featuring Fijian crafts, entertainment by Fiji's National Dance Theatre, and a colonial-style marketplace for shopping.

Many of the hotels are departure points for day tours to local villages, cruises to nearby islands, or a Navua River trip.

Firewalking (see page 69) is the greatest nighttime

attraction at Coral Coast resorts. Hotels featuring this entertainment include the Pacific Harbour Resort, The Fijian, Naviti Resort, Hyatt Regency, and Korolevu Beach. All the major hotels in this area have a buffet dinner or barbecue and *meke* (Fijian entertainment) at least once a week.

King's Road. To discover a more primitive part of Viti Levu, take the drive between Suva and Nadi by way of King's Road. Traversing the eastern interior and northern coast, this route is for the more adventurous traveler. None of the narrow, winding road is paved.

Again you will experience the beauty of the Fijian countryside. The eastern "wet" side of the island is thick with bamboo, banana trees, ropelike vines, and hibiscus. As you travel westward along the northern coast, waving sugar cane fields appear.

For an interesting side trip, leave King's Road at Tavua on the north coast and head 11 km/7 miles inland to Vatukoula, site of a working gold mine. Guided tours of the Emperor Gold Mine can be arranged by contacting the supervisor at the mining company office 24 hours in advance.

Small hotels, located in villages along King's Road, include the Tailevu Hotel, Raki Raki Hotel, Tavua Hotel, and the New Ba Hotel.

Romantic getaways

Island hideaways and long leisurely cruises through quiet tropical waters characterize the Fiji experience.

Island retreats. No journey to Fiji is complete without a day trip to an island hideaway off Viti Levu. Several tiny island resorts—renowned for their palm-lined beaches and coral-rimmed lagoons—can be reached by a short cruise or flight. You'll have most of the day free to relax and enjoy the beach and water.

If you want more time, stay several days. Accommodations range from bures (cottages), many of them family-size, to bunk-bedded dormitories. In addition to lavish buffet-style meals, several resorts present Fijian entertainment.

Island hideaways off Viti Levu's west coast possess such intriguing names as Castaway, Beachcomber, Treasure, Plantation Village, Dick's Place, Mana, Club Naitasi, and Navini Island. Further north in the Yasawas is Turtle Island. Many of these islands can be reached on organized day boat trips from The Regent of Fiji (for Nadi Bay resorts) or from the Lautoka area. Connecting boat service also links some of the island resorts. There's air service to Malololailai as well as seaplane service to other islands.

Visitors to the Suva area can relax at Toberua Island Resort. Launches sail daily from Nakelo Landing, 29 km/18 miles east of Suva. The 1-hour cruise takes you 8 km/5 miles down the Rewa River past villages before entering the ocean.

One added attraction at Toberua—besides its tropical setting and numerous water sports—is a monthly fish drive. Villagers from neighboring islands gather to demonstrate this ancient art of catching fish. Guests take a launch to a nearby reef to watch the villagers, and perhaps join in, as the scare line is spread in a circle; the water pounded amidst excited yells; and the frightened fish caught.

Cruising. Another kind of Fiji-type escapism can be enjoyed on a 3-day cruise through the Yasawa Group northwest of Viti Levu. Blue Lagoon Cruises offers daily departures from Lautoka. Seafarer Cruises, whose itinerary includes the Yasawas and the Mamanuca Group, sails from Lautoka on Wednesdays and Saturdays.

Blue Lagoon Cruises also operates 7-day cruises into the Yasawas aboard the *Yasawa Princess*.

On all these cruises you travel on motorized ships with comfortable accommodations and conveniences. On a cruise, you leave the hectic world behind as you sail leisurely through a blue sea to palm-studded islands sparsely dotted with thatched hut villages. There's time to bask on a deserted white sand beach, snorkel in pristine waters, and bargain with friendly villagers for shell leis and local crafts. Each night you dock at a different island lagoon. Your evening entertainment may include a Fijian feast and lively Fijian dancing.

Reservations should be made well in advance for all these cruises. For Blue Lagoon cruise reservations, write P.O. Box 54, Lautoka, and for Seafarer Cruises, write P.O. Box 364, Lautoka.

Fiji's Other Islands

Many visitors miss relatively undeveloped Vanua Levu and Taveuni—two of Fiji's other islands. The charm of these islands lies in their unspoiled beauty, friendly people, and gentle pace of life.

Vanua Levu, second largest island

Located northeast of Viti Levu is Fiji's second largest island, Vanua Levu. About half the size of the main island, Vanua Levu covers an area of about 5,544 square km/2,140 square miles. Volcanic mountains, thermal hot springs, waterfalls, sugar cane fields, and copra plantations landscape this island. Savusavu and Labasa are Vanua Levu's two main centers.

Most visitors arrive by air. Regularly scheduled flights serve the towns of Labasa and Savusavu and the nearby island of Taveuni from both Nadi Airport and Suva's Nausori Airport. The three centers are also connected by regular air service.

Blue Lagoon Cruises' *Salamanda* sails weekly from Lautoka to Labasa. Even though it serves primarily as a round-trip passenger cruise with cargo deliveries and tourist visits to remote villages, one-way passage can be arranged. Regular interisland cargo vessels also stop at Vanua Levu.

Taxi service is available on the island and fares are reasonable. If arrangements are made ahead, a tour can be included in the taxi ride. Rental cars are available only in Labasa, but Vanua Levu has very few roads, and most of them (except in town) are unpaved.

Savusavu. Surrounded by copra plantations, the small harbor town of Savusavu sits on Vanua Levu's southern coast. Peaceful tropical beauty is its main attraction.

From Savusavu you can enjoy long scenic drives through the countryside, visit local villages, and cruise to a nearby, uninhabited island.

Visitors can stay at Scotts-Savu Savu overlooking an island-studded bay, hilly peninsula, and downtown Savusavu.

Namale Plantation combines a working copra plantation and hideaway tropical paradise located on a bay headland only 10 km/6 miles from Savusavu. Surrounded by the plantation, bures nestle in a garden setting of brilliant, tropical flowers. Beautiful beaches and lagoons can be found nearby.

Labasa. Situated on a river on Vanua Levu's north coast and surrounded by sugar cane fields, Labasa is a bustling, sun-baked town. Its predominantly Indian population works as cane farmers, shopkeepers, lawyers, and accountants.

Things to explore in and around Labasa include the colorful public market, sugar mill, hot spring, floating island, waterfalls, and nearby villages.

While in Labasa, you can stay at the Hotel Takia.

Taveuni, the garden isle

Renowned for its lush vegetation, many streams, and a plummeting waterfall, Taveuni is known as the "Garden of Fiji." Just 42 km/26 miles long and 11 km/7 miles wide, it ranks third in size in the Fiji island group.

Copra is the mainstay of the Taveuni economy, although cotton, coffee, sugar, arrowroot, and cinchona have all been grown in the past. Tropical trees, flowering shrubs, fruits, and vegetable gardens all compete for space on this verdant isle.

From Buca Bay on Vanua Levu, you can board the ferry to Taveuni daily—sharing your ride with local villagers, produce, copra, and perhaps a few roosters. Or you can fly from Nadi, Savusavu, or Suva to Taveuni's Matei Airstrip. Taxis provide island transportation.

One gravel road extends the length of the island along the northwest coast's beaches. Along this route you might see women, waist deep in ponds, fishing with nets for their evening meals.

Midway down the island road, a sign reads "180th Meridian, International Date Line, Where One Can Stand With One Foot In Yesterday and One Foot In Today." The 180th meridian normally marks adjustment of time from one day to the next. Once, Taveuni was split into two time zones—the eastern half of the island was one full day (23 hours) behind the western half. To resolve the obvious problem, the Date Line was adjusted so all of Fiji falls on the west side of it. However, the sign remains. The Taveuni International Hotel is a good center for island excursions.

Two miles—a 10-minute boat ride—from Taveuni, the Qamea Beach Club has opened on Qamea Island. It features water sports, game fishing, and fine beaches.

Know Before You Go

The following are some practical details to help you in planning your trip to Fiji.

Entry/exit procedures. You will need a passport valid for 6 months after your departure date from Fiji and an onward travel ticket. Nationals of most countries don't need a visa. Upon your arrival, you will receive a 30-day visitors permit, which may be extended for up to 6 months.

If you are arriving from an infected area, you need cholera, yellow fever, and smallpox inoculations.

When you leave Fiji by air, you will pay a F $5 airport departure tax in local currency.

Customs. Visitors are allowed to bring in duty-free personal effects, including 200 cigarettes, 25 cigars, or a half pound of tobacco; one quart of liquor; and F$20 worth of new merchandise.

Currency. The Fijian dollar. Denominations of coins are 1, 2, 5, 10, 20, 50, and notes—1, 2, 5, 10, 20.

Tipping. Heavy tipping is not expected in Fiji. Visitors are requested to tip only when they wish to reward particularly good service.

Time. Fiji is GMT (Greenwich mean time) +12. For example, when it is noon Sunday in Suva, it is 4 P.M. Saturday in San Francisco, noon Sunday in Auckland, and 10 A.M. Sunday in Sydney.

Weather and what to wear. Fiji's "cool" season extends from May to November with temperatures rarely below 16°C/60°F. The hot rainy months include December through April when temperatures can reach nearly 32°C/90°F.

You can dress in casual resort wear the year around in Fiji, though it is not considered appropriate for women to wear shorts in town. Useful items for you to pack include an umbrella, a lightweight sweater, and sunglasses. Bring tennis or beach shoes to wear when swimming in coral-infested areas.

For more information. Your best source of travel information is the Fiji Visitors Bureau. You can contact the bureau in Fiji at P.O. Box 92, Suva. In North America, write the Fiji Visitors Bureau at 6151 W. Century Blvd., Suite 524, Los Angeles, 90045. In Australia, Fiji Visitors Bureau offices are located at 38 Martin Place, Sydney, NSW 2000. The New Zealand address is P.O. Box 1179, Auckland 1.

NEW CALEDONIA

New Caledonia lingers in the memory long after you have taken a last look at Grande Terre and its small offshore islands.

You remember the haunting beauty of the Isle of Pines, renowned for its short-branched pine trees, white, velvet-soft beaches, and abundant wild orchids; Amédée Island, a mere sand spit in the sea topped by a lighthouse built in the time of Napoleon III; Nouméa, noted for its atmosphere of *la vie française,* its excellent restaurants and stylish boutiques; and the remote reaches making up the rest of New Caledonia, where neat, well-tended Melanesian villages peek out from forest clearings.

More than the sights, you remember the people—smiling Melanesian women bedecked in colorful Mother Hubbards, children on the roadside waving hello, and hospitable French innkeepers offering home cooking.

Grande Terre and Other Islands

The cigar-shaped island of New Caledonia—402 km/250 miles long and 48 km/30 miles wide—lies halfway between Fiji and Australia. Scientists believe it was once part of an ancient land mass linked to Australia.

Scattered around the main island are New Caledonia's small island dependencies. They include Ouvéa, Lifou, and Maré (the Loyalty group) situated off the east coast; the Isle of Pines and Ouen Island to the south; and the Belep group to the north.

Called "Grande Terre" by the locals, the main island of New Caledonia is rich in minerals, tropical plants, and white sand beaches. The island (also known as the "mainland") is divided geographically by the Chaîne Centrale. This mountain range—scarred by nickel mining—runs the length of Grande Terre, creating two distinct climatic and geographic regions. Blessed by heavy rains, the east coast boasts rich plant life and large rivers that plummet through mountainous countryside to the ocean. In contrast, the "dry" west coast appears savannalike with broad, grassy plains ideal for cattle ranching. Two major peaks of the Chaîne Centrale are Mount Panié and Mount Humboldt.

Unique plants and wildlife

Nearly 2,000 species of plant life have been found in New Caledonia, many of them unique to these islands. Of particular note are the *niaouli* (native gum trees), plentiful along Grande Terre's west coast; and the *Araucaria cookii,* an unusual looking species of pine on the Isle of Pines.

The call of the country's rare *cagou* bird might fool you—it sounds like a young dog barking. The gray-plumed cagou is a flightless running bird similar to New Zealand's kiwi. Unfortunately, the cagou faces extinction because it can't run as fast as its predators which, ironically, include the canine population.

A Captain Cook discovery

New Caledonia remained virtually undiscovered until 1768, when French navigator Louis de Bougainville noted the island in his ship's log as he sailed south from the New Hebrides. However, it wasn't until 1774 that Captain James Cook actually discovered and landed on the island on his way to New Zealand. Because its pine-clad ridges reminded Cook of Scotland (called Caledonia in ancient times), he named his discovery New Caledonia.

During the late 18th and early 19th centuries, various navigators, explorers, missionaries, traders, and runaway seamen sailed to New Caledonia's shores. Although it seemed likely that Great Britain would annex the island, France did it first in 1853, when soldiers were sent in to protect French missionaries who had occasionally been attacked by cannibalistic tribes.

From 1864 to 1897 New Caledonia served as a French penal colony. Long-term political prisoners and convicts were deported from France to the colony. During World War II, New Caledonia served as an important Allied military base.

Today, New Caledonia is a French Overseas Territory with internal economic control. It is administered by a High Commissioner, assisted by a 7-member Government Council elected by a Territorial Assembly. However, at press time in early 1985, the nation is embroiled in a political conflict over the extent of future independence of the nation.

The New Caledonians

Of the 135,000 people that inhabit New Caledonia, only 55,000 are Melanesians. The country has a sizable European population—about 52,500—many of them descendants of 19th century settlers. Other residents have immigrated here from Wallis, Tahiti, Indonesia, Vietnam, and other areas.

Melanesian with a French influence

When the first explorers journeyed through these islands, the indigenous Melanesian population numbered 50,000 to 70,000. Living in small tribal groups,

Shady pedestrians' haven *in bustling Nouméa, Place de Cocotiers contains bright yellow benches where townspeople pause to converse and watch passersby. Greenery and flowering plants brighten city streets.*

French influence *permeates all phases of New Caledonian life. Officers in tropical white uniforms participate in awards ceremony.*

the dark-skinned, curly-haired natives existed on subsistence agriculture and fishing.

Village life today. Most of the Melanesian people today dwell in small villages scattered through the islands. Existence is still eked from the land and the sea.

In the villages, thatch-roofed dwellings cluster around a large square carpeted with well-kept lawn. Many of the rounded, beehive-shaped, windowless abodes have been replaced by rectangular windowed structures.

City life. In Nouméa, the country's major city, the population of 60,000 is predominantly French. Smaller numbers of Tahitians, Indonesians, Vietnamese, Vanuatuans (New Hebrideans), Martiniquais, and New Caledonian Melanesians are also represented. Old French colonial cottages and modern, government-built housing projects provide living accommodations.

The reigning economic force in Nouméa is not agriculture, it's nickel. Société le Nickel, the French nickel mining company, employs many Nouméans.

Dress. New Caledonian dress reflects both native and French influences. On the streets of Nouméa you'll see barefoot native women chatting in missionary-inspired

Mother Hubbards—loose fitting, lace trimmed, floral print or solid color dresses. Other women pass them adorned in the latest Parisian fashions purchased from local boutiques.

Countryside attire leans to traditional Mother Hubbards. Men wear *sulus*, wrap-type skirts.

Language and religion. French, New Caledonia's official language, is spoken everywhere. Though a knowledge of the language is helpful, visitors get along quite easily with English in Nouméa and the resort areas. Few people in the countryside understand or speak English. They mainly speak Melanesian or French. Most islanders are Catholics or Protestants.

Cricket and other diversions

New Caledonians have enthusiastically adopted many games and sports introduced by the 19th century European settlers.

One such sport, English cricket, takes on a different look when played in New Caledonia. (See the special feature on page 77.)

The French game of *pétanque* has also become a part of New Caledonian life. Similar to English bowls, it is played with baseball-size metal balls which players toss across a dirt game area. On weekends and public holidays Nouméan men play pétanque in the Place de Cocotiers or near the waterfront.

Other popular sports include horse racing (early August to the end of September), soccer and rugby (October to April), judo, and track and field events.

Mineral exports dominate the economy

Minerals—primarily nickel—dominate New Caledonia's export trade. The country contains one of the world's largest reserves of nickel oxide ore.

The two main agricultural exports are coffee and copra. Crops grown for local use include yams, taros, mangoes, maize, sweet potatoes, rice, and bananas. Other New Caledonian products such as meat and saltwater fish are also consumed locally. Food production in New Caledonia has not matched the country's demands, so much of the country's food must be imported, contributing to the high cost of living.

Planning Your Trip

New Caledonia is located midway between Fiji and Australia in the southwest Pacific Ocean. Its closest neighbor is Vanuatu (New Hebrides), 536 km/333 miles northeast of Nouméa.

Several international air carriers and passenger ship lines stop in the country. Visitors arrive on Grande Terre, the main island of New Caledonia. Air passengers land at Tontouta International Airport about 51 km/ 32 miles northwest of Nouméa, the country's capital and largest city. At the airport you'll find bus, taxi, and airport limousine service into town. Ship passengers dock at the wharf in Nouméa.

Getting around New Caledonia

Visitor transportation runs the gamut from Nouméa's local blue buses to regularly scheduled air service to main island towns and island dependencies.

Driving in New Caledonia. Rental cars are available in Nouméa at Tontouta Airport. You'll need a valid driver's license and passport to obtain a temporary driving permit. Minimum age for rental is 25.

Traffic moves on the right side of the road. Refrain from honking your horn in Nouméa; this privilege is reserved for wedding parties.

Traveling by bus. An inexpensive way to explore Nouméa and its nearby suburbs is to hop on a local blue bus. You can board one at Gare Routière, near Baie de la Moselle.

Taking a taxi. Traveling by taxi in New Caledonia is relatively expensive. Expect to pay an extra charge for

LADIES' CRICKET
In Mother Hubbards

"That's cricket?" might be the question raised by Englishmen upon viewing New Caledonia's version for the first time. Although it differs from the more sedate game played back home, the shouting, riotous matches are ladies' cricket, New Caledonian-style. The game has been played here since it was introduced by the missionaries.

Watching a match, you'll see that the ladies take this competitive sport seriously. It also provides an entertaining show.

The bat, for instance, is as big as an oversize loaf of French bread. Each team sports its own "uniform": loose Mother Hubbard dresses made from the same color material. Usually each player wears a twisted ribbon or scarf headdress in the same color as the uniform.

Bare feet are *de rigueur,* and they pound up and down the field to the noise of flat-sounding whistles, blown by both the referee and lady spectators. From the sidelines come shouts of advice or encouragement—from husbands, boyfriends, offspring, relatives, and friends.

Action takes place on school grounds, at local cricket fields, or in vacant lots, usually on Saturday mornings during the winter months, July to April.

Gleaming *white sands and clear waters lure visitors to Isle of Pines. One-time prison home to 19th century French exiles, island is now quiet retreat.*

service after 7 P.M. on weekdays and on Saturday afternoons, Sundays, and public holidays.

Flying. Air Calédonie provides frequent domestic air service from Nouméa to outlying towns on Grande Terre and to the Isle of Pines, Ouen Island, Belep Islands, and the Loyalty group. All local flights leave from Magenta Airport, located within the Nouméa city limits.

Cruising. If you're traveling on a leisurely schedule, you can journey to the outer islands on a small trading vessel—the local villagers' mode of interisland transportation. Schedules are often irregular. Check with the Harbor Authority office in Nouméa for current information.

Resort hotels, wayside bungalows

Most of New Caledonia's accommodations are located in the Nouméa area. Resort beach hotels (Chateau Royale—Club Mediterranée, Isle de France TraveLodge, Hotel Le Lagon, Mocambo, Nouméa Beach, Le Nouvata, Hotel Le Surf) lure visitors to the Anse Vata/Baie des Citrons areas (15 minutes south of downtown).

In downtown Nouméa, you'll discover several modest hotels offering comfortable accommodations, including La Perouse Hotel, Nouméa Village Hotel, and Hotel de Paris. The downtown hotels might not front the ocean, but their rates are lower than the beachfront resorts.

At towns and villages on the east and west coasts of Grande Terre (and on several outer islands, as well), small casual hotels and an occasional *relais* (country inn) provide comfortable overnight stopping points.

Make reservations for accommodations well in advance of your visit. The peak tourist season comes in January; August is the least crowded month to visit.

Mini-meals to native feasts

Dining in New Caledonia is a gastronomic adventure. New Caledonians love to eat—and so will you upon discovering the variety of tempting offerings available.

In Nouméa you can sample French, Cantonese, Mandarin, Vietnamese, Indian, Tahitian, Indonesian, and Spanish cuisine. If you prefer a mini-meal, stop at one of numerous snack bars and fancy pâtisseries. Better yet, tote a *casse-croûte* (lunch of crusty French bread, fresh fruit, and French wine) to the beach for a picnic. For breakfast, treat yourself to fresh-baked croissants and café au lait.

Outside of Nouméa, most relais and local restaurants offer simple French provincial cooking featuring fresh seafood and locally grown vegetables and fruit.

Native feasting and dancing. To sample Melanesian specialties, attend a *bougna*. Usually held on a beach, this native feast features fruits, vegetables, pig, fish, and chicken that have been wrapped in banana leaves and baked for several hours on hot stones covered with sand.

Following the feast, visitors are entertained by grass-skirted Melanesian dancers.

After the sun goes down. Much of Nouméa's night life centers around the hotels and their discos. You might also enjoy seeing a European or Polynesian floor show; the latter includes the Tahitian *tamure* and Wallisian saber dances. At Hotel Le Surf's casino you can try your hand at baccarat, roulette, or blackjack.

Festival Time

Join New Caledonians as they revel on their special holidays. Two of the most colorful to enjoy are Bastille Day and Anniversary Day. Important occasions include the following:

January—April

Mardi Gras. In February or early March, costumed children parade through Nouméa's streets to the Place des Cocotiers, where prizes are given for the most original costumes.

Easter. This day marks the beginning of the winter sports season.

Events are usually held weekly.

May—August

Arts Season. During the first week in May, works of artists from all over the South Pacific are displayed at the Museum of Nouméa.

Bastille Day. New Caledonians herald France's July 14th independence day with a torchlight parade and fireworks in Nouméa on the night of July 13. Celebrating continues the following day with special sports events and local festivities.

September—December

Anniversary Day. On September 24, a military parade at Anse Vata Beach and sports events commemorate the 1853 raising of the French flag in New Caledonia. Week-long activities include a cycling race around Grande Terre.

All Saints Day ("Toussaint"). On November 1, families journey to cemeteries to leave armloads of flowers at graves.

Pére Noël Day. Pére Noël arrives in Nouméa on December 24 by an unusual means of transportation—the conveyance is always a surprise.

Shop for French perfume, tapa cloth

Strolling the streets of Nouméa, you'll discover a multitude of boutiques. Each store prides itself in having the latest in fashions.

Imports from France include women's lingerie, shoes, clothing, men's ties and shirts, and perfume. You'll also want to look at Italian sandals and London sportswear. Chinese and Tahitian dressmakers can whip up beachwear from locally made "pareo" cloth in 1 or 2 days.

Don't miss the local handicrafts such as woodcarvings, woven place mats and other articles made from pandanus bark, shell and mother-of-pearl necklaces, tapa cloth, and handpainted fabrics.

Shops open early in New Caledonia and close for a lengthy lunch hour. Shop hours are 7 to 11 A.M. and 2 to 6 P.M. Monday through Friday. Most stores are closed Saturday afternoons and Sundays.

Fun in the sun

New Caledonia has one of the world's largest barrier reefs, Grand Récif, offering an ideal playground for water sport enthusiasts. Snorkeling and scuba diving are excellent in the warm, clear, reef-protected lagoons. Both snorkeling and diving equipment are available for rent locally; check with your hotel.

Many resort hotels and relais have small boats available for visitors' use. Larger boats can be chartered in Nouméa for diving, cruising, or fishing. Best fishing months are November through February for marlin, sailfish, tuna, bonito, and mahi mahi.

If you want to play tennis, you'll find courts in Nouméa at Chateau Royale, Mont Coffyn Tennis Club, Olympique, and City Council Tennis Court. You'll also find courts at some relais on Grande Terre.

Nouméa, the Capital

Often labeled "the Paris of the Pacific," Nouméa as a city blends a light-hearted zestful quality with a bit of French sophistication. *La vie française* permeates almost every facet of Nouméa: the good French restaurants, the Paris-style boutiques, streets named for Republic heroes, Frenchmen playing *pétanque* (see page 77), the predominance of the French language.

Attractively situated on a hilly peninsula on Grande Terre's southwest tip, Nouméa overlooks a succession of lovely, curving bays and a magnificent, almost landlocked harbor. The site was chosen as the country's capital and main port in 1854 by Commandant Tardy de Montravel, a French naval officer.

As you explore the city, stop in the New Caledonia Government Tourist Office located at 25 Ave. du Marechal Foch.

Exploring the city center

Downtown Nouméa offers many walking and browsing possibilities. Stroll the shady, narrow streets lined with French colonial-style, wooden buildings fitted with shuttered windows and rusting metal roofs. Interspersed with this early architecture, you'll find white, concrete modern structures.

Place de Cocotiers. Start your city explorations at Place de Cocotiers ("Coconut Palm Tree Place") or Central Square. Bordered by palms and flamboyant trees (laden with red flowers in November and December), this pedestrians' oasis extends 4 blocks through the center of the city.

It is actually two adjoining squares, one marked by a turn-of-the-century bandstand, the other by a fountain. Between the two stands the Fontaine Monumentale, focal point of Place de Cocotiers.

The Market Place. Nouméa comes to life early (5 A.M.) at the local market. Housewives and chefs haggle with food vendors over the best buys in everything from breadfruit and coconuts to squawking poultry and live fish. Fishermen wheel their catch in tanks to the market, where the fish are lifted out alive for customers. (Local law forbids the sale of dead fish unless cooked.) The market is located near the Place de Cocotiers, at the corner of Rue Anatole France and Rue Georges Clemenceau.

The Museum of Nouméa. This modern building covers an entire city block bordering Baie de la Moselle on Avenue du Maréchal Foch between Rue August Brun and Rue Tourville. The museum is open Tuesday to Friday from 9 A.M. to 5:30 P.M. and Saturday and Sunday from 9 to 11 A.M. and 2 to 5 P.M.

The main exhibit hall contains artifacts from New Caledonia and many other South Pacific islands. Another part of the museum houses an art gallery.

Along the waterfront

You'll leave the city center behind when you take the relaxing drive south along the Rue Jules Garnier, skirting boat-filled bays, to the beach resort area. The best beaches are Anse Vata and nearby Baie des Citrons, both a short 15-minute ride from Place de Cocotiers.

On the peninsula separating the Baie des Citrons and Anse Vata, you'll find the famed Aquarium de Nouméa. The aquarium offers insight into a tropical marine world —observe dangerous creatures that haunt reef waters as well as some beautiful fish. In the Hall of Fluorescent Corals you'll see these marine deposits glowing eerily under ultraviolet light.

Aquarium de Nouméa is open daily except Mondays from 1:30 to 5 P.M.

Nearby excursions

Having explored Nouméa, you will discover more of New Caledonia's charm by taking brief trips through the countryside and to outlying islands.

Villages and vistas. Near Mount Dore, 26 km/16 miles northeast of Nouméa, visitors often stop at the Mission of St. Louis to see its large church and Melanesian village of thatch-roofed bungalows.

Amédée Lighthouse. At night Amédée Lighthouse's intense beacon guides ships through the narrow coral passage into the calm lagoon near Nouméa. Built in France, the metallic lighthouse was shipped to Nouméa in sections, reassembled, and put to work in 1865.

Tour companies operate day cruises (lunch included) to tiny Amédée Island, 18 km/11 miles south of Nouméa.

Ouen Island. This get-away-from-it-all island is just a 15-minute flight or a 2½-hour cruise southeast from Nouméa.

Stay overnight at the Turtle Club, the island's one small resort, or just spend the day enjoying the beach before you return to the mainland.

Touring Grande Terre

The hinterlands of the island of New Caledonia provide an unexpectedly peaceful world of gentle, sometimes spectacular, beauty.

If you don't wish to explore on your own, you can take a guided tour from Nouméa. Air Calédonie schedules regular flights to several villages on the east and west coasts.

Along the west coast

From Nouméa, the road rambles nearly 483 km/300 miles along the Coral Sea coast to Poum, its northernmost point. On this route you enter the world of the "stockman," New Caledonia's counterpart to the gaucho or cowboy. Herds of cattle and horses graze on broad savannas punctuated with stands of white-barked niaouli trees.

For a shorter trip, take an overnight trip to Bourail (171 km/106 miles northwest of Nouméa). You'll see some of New Caledonia's small towns, Melanesian villages, cattle ranches, and mining districts along the way.

East coast destinations

The jungle vegetation and Melanesian thatched villages of New Caledonia's east coast contrast with Nouméa's urban activities and Rivieralike climate. You have three alternatives for east coast exploration—the Yaté area, the Thio area, and the coast road north from Houaïlou.

Yaté area. Yaté, known as the Paradis Botanic, lies about 64 km/40 miles east of Nouméa in the Plaine des Lacs region. More than 2,000 different kinds of plants— many found nowhere else in the world—thrive here.

Thio area. From Nouméa it's a 2-hour drive (140 km/ 87 miles) to New Caledonia's major mining center. Head northwest along the coast and turn east at Boulouparis to climb through the mountainous Chaîne Centrale. The descent to the east coast brings you to Thio. Sheared mountain tops and deeply scarred slopes reveal the town's major industry.

In the Canala area north of Thio, deep green coffee trees heavy with bright red berries and mandarin orange trees line the road. Many Melanesian tribes live in thatch-roofed villages in this area.

Complete your loop trip by traversing the mountain range once more, returning to the west coast just north of La Foa.

To the north. If you have time for a longer journey along the east coast, you can strike inland just north of Bourail, following a winding mountain road across the Chaîne Centrale to the east coast town of Houaïlou, then turn northward.

As you pass through rich, verdant fields and vine-entwined forests, you'll see little villages tucked into clearings. The well-preserved, beehive-shaped communal hut at Baye was built over a century ago.

Outer Islands

Several of New Caledonia's satellite islands can be easily reached by plane or boat. On these islands, visitors relax on quiet beaches and meet friendly villagers.

Excursion to Isle of Pines

Called Kounié Island by its inhabitants, the Isle of Pines is probably the best known of the outer islands. Located 126 km/78 miles southeast of Nouméa, the Isle of Pines has a dry climate with temperatures consistently lower than on Grande Terre. By air, it's a 35-minute flight from Nouméa.

The island's coast is one of those places you dream about—quiet and serene. Powdery white sand rims transparent, turquoise lagoons. Standing along the shores are majestic *Araucaria cookii,* a species of pine that inspired Captain Cook to name the island for them. Silhouetted against the sky, these trees become 61-meter/200-foot columns trimmed with short 2-meter/6-foot-long bristling branches.

In the late 1800s French prisoners were exiled to this island. You can still see the prison ruins.

Currently, there are no overnight accommodations on the Isle of Pines.

The seldom-visited Loyalty Islands

Not many tourists visit the main Loyalty Islands of Maré, Lifou, and Ouvéa that lie off New Caledonia's east coast. They are about an hour's flight from Nouméa's Magenta Airport.

The people of these islands maintain many traditional customs and follow deep-rooted folklore. Only local people may acquire land on these Melanesian reserve islands.

Ouvéa, smallest of the islands, has the only tourist accommodations in the group—a 16-bungalow hotel.

Know Before You Go

The following practical information will help you plan your trip to New Caledonia.

Entry/exit procedures. You will need a valid passport and a confirmed onward travel ticket for a stay no longer than 30 days. A tourist visa may be obtained at nominal cost, plus four photos, from a French consulate or embassy for stays up to 90 days.

Travelers arriving from an infected area will need smallpox, yellow fever, and cholera vaccinations. Vaccinations are also recommended against typhoid and paratyphoid fevers. (Since health requirements change from time to time, check with your local public health department before going.)

New Caledonia has no airport departure tax.

Customs. Travelers may bring into New Caledonia duty free 200 cigarettes, 50 cigars, or 8 ounces of tobacco; one bottle of liquor; and personal effects.

Currency. The French Pacific Franc (CFP). Coin denominations are 1, 2, 5, 10, 20, 50, and 100, while notes come in denominations of 500, 1000, and 5000. Export of local currency is restricted to CFP500.

Tipping. There is no tipping.

Time. New Caledonia is GMT (Greenwich mean time) +11. For example, when it is noon Sunday in Nouméa, it is 5 P.M. Saturday in San Francisco, 1 P.M. Sunday in Auckland, and 11 A.M. Sunday in Sydney.

Weather and what to wear. Nicknamed the "Island of Eternal Spring," New Caledonia enjoys a balmy, semitropical environment tempered by the trade winds. However, definite seasonal variations do exist. Summer extends from January through March with temperatures averaging 27°C/81°F. During these humid months, an occasional hurricane or thunderstorm pummels the area. The winter months from April through December are drier and cooler—a better time to visit. Temperatures average 21°C/70°F during these months, though they can drop as low as 14°C/57°F.

You can wear informal, lightweight attire the year around. Bring a light raincoat and sweater for cooler weather. You'll need beach shoes for reef exploring.

For more information. To obtain more information on New Caledonia, write to the Office du Tourisme, Box 688, Nouméa. In Australia, write to the New Caledonia Tourist Office, 39 York Street, Sydney, NSW 2000.

VANUATU

NOTE: *In July 1980 the New Hebrides gained their independence and changed their name to Vanuatu.*

Vanuatu (formerly known as the New Hebrides) provides the visitor an off-the-beaten-path experience. In this land of smoking volcanoes people still perform primitive rituals, and the Melanesian culture remains alive. Dotting the countryside are aging colonial-style plantation houses and the rusting scrap of World War II military operations.

A Land in Constant Motion

The Vanuatu archipelago forms an elongated, y-shaped chain of islands stretching north-south for 724 km/450 miles through the southwest Pacific Ocean. Nearest neighbors include New Caledonia to the southwest; the Fiji Islands to the east; and the Solomons to the northwest.

With a total land mass of 14,767 square km/5,701 square miles, Vanuatu consists of 13 large islands and 60 smaller islands and islets. Principal urban centers are Vila (the administrative capital) on the island of Efate and Luganville on Espiritu Santo.

Volcanic in origin, the islands in the Vanuatu chain are geologically young and still growing. There are five active volcanoes: two on Ambrym and one each on Tanna, Lopevi, and the ocean floor near Tongoa.

Earth tremors are common in Vanuatu, and seismograph records indicate that the archipelago is in nearly constant motion. Most of the tremors—except for a few major ones each month—are not even felt by the people, and damage is rare.

Jungles, orchids, and native birds

Edged by a narrow coastal plain, most of Vanuatu's islands are mountainous with slopes rising steeply from the sea. The highest mountain is Mount Tabwemasana (1,879 meters/6,165 feet) on Espiritu Santo.

Dense black-green jungles resembling those of the Solomons and Papua New Guinea cover the mountain sides. Along the coast you'll see patches of cultivated land and narrow, winding beaches edged with palms.

Brightening the islands are vividly colored flowers —bougainvillea, hibiscus, orchids, and plumeria—and birds such as bright green pigeons and multihued parrots. Fifty-four types of native birds include warblers, fantails, robins, mynas, peregrine falcons, Australian goshawks, island thrushes, and trillers.

Charted by Captain Cook

Pedro de Quiros, a Portuguese navigator sponsored by the King of Spain, discovered Vanuatu in April 1606. Thinking he had found the sought-after "Southern Continent," he anchored off an island which he named "Terra Australis del Espiritu Santo." Though he attempted to establish a permanent settlement on the island, his efforts failed as a result of illness and disagreements with native villagers.

Some 160 years later, the French navigator Louis de Bougainville sailed through the islands, landing at Aoba. He determined that Quiros's discovery was not the "Southern Continent."

Captain Cook charted the islands in 1774, naming them after the Hebrides located west of his Scottish homeland. Following Cook came another navigator, Captain William Bligh, who sighted several previously undiscovered islands in 1789.

After sandalwood forests were discovered in the early 1800s, greedy traders destroyed both property and lives. "Blackbirders" also visited the New Hebrides, kidnapping islanders for use as laborers on sugar plantations in Australia. The missionaries arriving in the wake of these wrongdoings felt the wrath of native hostility, but they remained to build churches, schools, and settlements.

Foreign settlers, predominantly English and French, purchased land in the New Hebrides and established coconut plantations in the late 19th century. In 1887, a Joint Naval Commission was formed to protect British and French subjects. So began the British-French connection that led to the creation of the Condominium (joint administration) of the New Hebrides in 1906.

During World War II, Luganville on Espiritu Santo served as a key staging area for U.S. troops advancing on the Solomons.

The creation of a new government

For a number of years following World War II, the New Hebrides continued to be ruled jointly by French and British Resident Commissioners in a condominium form of government. Duality applied in matters large and small—there were two separate school systems, two separate medical services, and two flags—the British Union Jack and French Tricolor. In judicial matters, four separate courts of law functioned: British; French; a court of New Hebridean native affairs; and the Joint Court, for settling matters of internal concern such as land claims.

In January 1978, a new government began to take shape, and in July 1980 the New Hebrides gained total self government. With this independence they changed the name of the country to Vanuatu. The current government consists of a Representative Assembly, a Prime Minister elected by the assembly, and a Council of Ministers who in turn are appointed by the Prime Minister. All internal affairs are governed by these ministers.

Children play *beneath upright slit log drum topped by carved, painted mask. Primitive native art and carvings depict island legends and indicate social ranking.*

Anchored boats *dot Vila's harbor. From waterfront business area, narrow streets climb steep slopes to hillside viewpoints.*

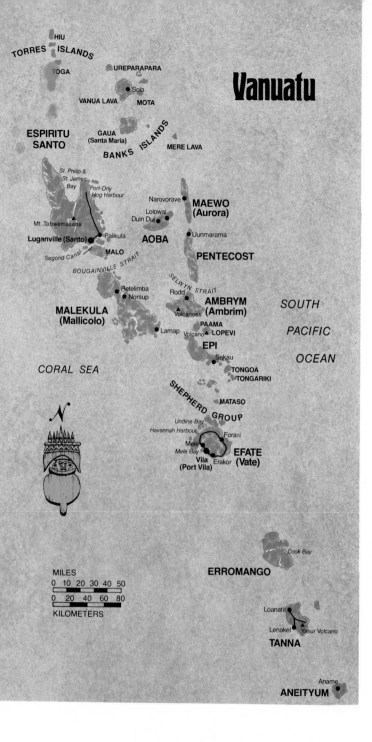

Vanuatu

HIU
TORRES ISLANDS
TOGA
UREPARAPARA
Sola
VANUA LAVA
MOTA
ESPIRITU SANTO
GAUA (Santa Maria)
BANKS ISLANDS
MERE LAVA
St. Philip & St. James Bay
Port-Orly
Hog Harbour
Narovorave
MAEWO (Aurora)
Lolowai
Duin Dui
Mt. Tabwemasana
Palikula
Uunmarama
Luganville (Santo)
AOBA
Segond Canal
MALO
PENTECOST
BOUGAINVILLE STRAIT
Retelimba
Norsup
SELWYN STRAIT
Rodd
MALEKULA (Mallicolo)
Volcanoes
AMBRYM (Ambrim)
SOUTH
PAAMA
LOPEVI
Lamap
Volcano
PACIFIC
EPI
Sakau
OCEAN
CORAL SEA
TONGOA
TONGARIKI
MATASO
SHEPHERD GROUP
Undine Bay
Havannah Harbour
Forari
Mele
Mele Bay
EFATE (Vate)
Vila (Port Vila)
Erakor

MILES
0 10 20 30 40 50
0 20 40 60 80
KILOMETERS

Cook Bay
ERROMANGO

Loanatit
Lenakel
Yasur Volcano
TANNA

Aname
ANEITYUM

People of Vanuatu

Native islanders account for more than 90 percent of Vanuatu's population of 112,000. Most are Melanesian, but a few Polynesian clans—descendants of early Pacific migrations—live on several of the country's islands.

Nonindigenous islanders include Europeans, Wallis and Kiribati islanders, Tahitians, Fijians, Australians, New Zealanders, Chinese, and some Vietnamese agricultural workers.

A rural society

Nearly 80 percent of the local people reside in rural communities; the rest live in either Vila or Luganville. The customs, traditions, and language of the rural villagers vary from island to island—and even from village to village on the same island.

Most rural inhabitants live in round or rectangular huts known as "leaf houses" constructed of bamboo walls topped by steeply pitched roofs covered with leaves. Often these leaf roofs almost touch the ground.

One of the chief occupations is the raising of pigs. Not valued as food, these animals are prized for their fine circle of tusks. Possessing pigs gives a person capital and power within the tribal system. The pigs are used in trade and even as a bride-price.

Some rural villagers still dress in the attire of their ancestors—grass skirts for the women and penis sheaths called "nambas" for the men. Other villagers and city dwellers have adopted western-style clothing. The women wear loose fitting, floral print Mother Hubbard dresses and the men don shirts and shorts or slacks. Some townspeople retain the dress of their homeland; you may see Indian women draped in saris or Vietnamese wearing oriental-style pajamas and conical hats.

Language. French and English are the major languages of Vanuatu. However, Pidgin English (Bichelamar in French) is the *lingua franca*, the common language allowing people of different tribes to communicate even though their native dialects might differ. (Several hundred different dialects are spoken in Vanuatu.) Pidgin English is even used in the Representative Assembly.

Vanuatu's Pidgin English is a mixture of basic English plus French words and local expressions.

Religion. Missions have been established by many religious groups—including Presbyterian, Anglican (Melanesian Mission), Roman Catholic, Seventh-day Adventist, Church of Christ, and Apostolic Church—all working to convert the native people to Christianity. However, tribespeople living inland on the islands of Malekula, Espiritu Santo, Pentecost, and Tanna still follow indigenous ancestral customs.

Sports. In Vanuatu's towns, you see people enjoying golf, cricket, and *pétanque* (see page 77). Other popular sports include basketball and horseback riding. Soccer is played throughout the country wherever a flat piece of ground can be found.

Wealth of the land

Vanuatu's chief export is copra, followed by manganese, fish, and timber. The manganese is mined at Forari on Efate.

Other exports include small amounts of cocoa, coffee, and beef. Cattle were first introduced to the islands to control weeds and grass on the coconut plantations.

The growing tourist industry also contributes additional income to the Vanuatu economy.

An impressive number of overseas companies have established their headquarters in Vanuatu since the country has no direct income or capital gains tax.

Planning Your Trip

Vanuatu's first visitors arrived by canoe after an arduous journey across the Pacific Ocean. Today, you can arrive by international air carrier or ship.

Several major airlines—including the country's air carrier, Air Vanuatu, land at Bauerfield Airport, 6 km/4 miles from Vila on Efate. By air, the country is an hour's flight from either Nouméa, New Caledonia, or Nadi, Fiji; it's a 2-hour trip from Honiara in the Solomons.

Many cruise ships and passenger/cargo liners stop in Vanuatu on South Pacific voyages, docking at Vila or at Luganville on Espiritu Santo.

Getting around Vanuatu

Beyond the towns of Vila or Luganville, the best way to really explore Vanuatu is by tours originating in Vila. Air tours feature volcano viewing, flights over the smaller islands near Vila, and an aerial view of Efate. You can also take land trips around Espiritu Santo and Efate, and fly to Tanna on a tour.

There is a minibus service in Vila. Travelers can obtain rental cars in Vila and Luganville. Except for short stretches of paved road on Efate and Espiritu Santo, all the roads are crushed coral. Traffic moves on the right.

Vila and Luganville have the only taxi service.

When studying maps of Vanuatu, you'll see that some islands and towns have two names—one English, one French. We use the English names in this book; the map

LAND DIVING
Pentecost Island-style

Each year during the harvest period (generally May), the men and boys of Pentecost Island gather to perform the land-diving ceremony. After climbing to various levels of a 21-meter/70-foot tower, they then dive headfirst from it. Liana vines tied around their ankles stop the fall just short of the ground.

Certain procedures are followed in building the tower. It is constructed on a hillside around a large tree. All brush is cleared in front of the tower, and the ground is dug up to soften it. (Throughout the jumping ceremony, villagers rake the ground.)

Each diver builds his own diving platform at the desired height and location. He carefully selects the vines for his legs, calculating the length so his head just brushes the ground at the end of his jump.

After the vines are secured around his ankles, the diver climbs the tower. With the vines fastened to his platform, he falls. The vines extend fully just before he reaches the ground. The platform he has constructed breaks with the pull of the vines tied to it, minimizing the vines' recoil on his legs.

According to legend, land diving originated when a woman trying to escape her husband climbed a banyan tree. He followed her, and when he had nearly caught up with her, she jumped from the tree. He followed, not realizing that she had tied lianas from the tree around her ankles before jumping. She survived her fall, but he perished. Today, only the men have the right to land dive.

If the weather permits and the Pentecost Islanders agree to have visitors, tour operators will take groups on 1-day outings to the island to witness this ceremony. During the last several jumps, no photography has been allowed.

on page 84 also shows the French version in parentheses.

Flying. Air Melanesiae, the local airline, flies from Bauerfield Airport in Vila to Aneityum, Erromango, Malekula, Aoba, Pentecost, Espiritu Santo, Sola in the Banks Islands, Tanna, and Tongoa.

Cruising. Tour operators offer short boat excursions from Vila. Local people ride interisland copra boats between islands in the Vanuatu chain; the boats sail "almost weekly" from Vila.

Where to stay

You will find most of Vanuatu's accommodations in the Vila area on Efate. Travelers who prefer large, resort-type accommodations will enjoy the Hotel Le Lagon or Port Vila Inter-Continental Island Inn. Both are located on the shores of beautiful, sheltered Erakor Lagoon less than 3 km/2 miles from town.

If you want to stay in or near the downtown Vila area, you can choose from several small hotels including the Hotel Rossi, Hotel Olympic, Marina Motel, and Kaviti Hotel.

Ten km/6 miles west of town on Mele Island, you will discover Hide Away Island Resort's island-style bungalows. Other small, bungalow-style hotels on Efate include Vila Chaumières and Erakor Island Resort.

On Espiritu Santo, Luganville has one small hotel, the Santo Hotel. You'll find simple bungalow-style accommodations on Erromango (Metesons Guest House) and on Tanna (Tanna Bungalows and Whitegrass Bungalows).

International cuisine

Vanuatu's restaurants feature an international array of offerings. French cuisine predominates, but you also can sample Chinese, Vietnamese, or Italian dishes. Among local island favorites are marinated fish, coconut crab, prawns, lobster, and flying fox (a bat).

In Vila popular restaurants include Le Pandanus,

Tanna Island children *herd goats on Mount Yasur lava flow. Island's active volcano attracts visitors, who journey to rim by jeep and foot. Painted red crosses, symbols of John Frum cargo cult, dot Tanna's countryside.*

Festival Time

Vanuatu's holidays reflect many of the country's local Melanesian traditions. Important occasions you can witness include these:

January–April

John Frum Day. On February 14 members of the John Frum cargo cult on Tanna hold dances, parades, and a feast for the expected return of John Frum. It is believed that at some time in the future shiploads of goods will arrive. (See page 89.)

May–August

Pentecost Island land diving. Men and boys of Pentecost Island gather, generally in May, to perform this ceremony. They dive headfirst from high platforms—restrained only by vines around their ankles. They believe this tradition ensures a good harvest. (See page 85.)

Toka. Featuring dancing and a pig kill, this native feast is usually held at the end of August on Tanna.

September–December

Agricultural Show. Artifacts, local produce, pets, flowers, plants, and cattle are on display in September during a 2-day show in Vila, Luganville, and on Tanna. Rodeos and dances are also held.

Christmas holidays. Special church services, choir singing, and holiday balls take place December 23 to 25.

L'Houstalet, and Kwang Tong. Hotels that have restaurants include the Hotel Le Lagon, Port Vila Inter-Continental, Hotel Rossi, Hotel Olympic, Kaiviti Hotel, Hide Away Island Resort, and Erakor Island Resort.

Duty-free treasures...

Vanuatu is a duty-free port with prices on imports that compare favorably with those in other free-port areas in the Pacific. (No sales tax nibbles away at your wallet here.)

Stores in Vila and Luganville sell cassette recorders, stereo equipment, transistor radios, cameras, watches, French perfume and clothing, and Chinese curios.

You can purchase colorful and varied Vanuatu handicrafts in both Vila and Luganville. Articles made in outlying Melanesian villages include carved, brightly painted, tree fern masks from Ambrym; grass skirts from Tanna; and baskets and mats from Pentecost. Also available are carved wooden objects from Tongoa and Espiritu Santo.

Most prices in stores are fixed.

Shop in Vila and Santo stores between 7:30 and 11:30 A.M. and 2 and 5 P.M. Monday through Friday, or on Saturday between 7:30 and 11:30 A.M. Larger stores close on Saturday afternoons and Sundays.

...Outdoor pleasures

Warm waters, calm lagoons, and miles of beaches provide Vanuatu with a perfect setting for a variety recreational activities. You can swim, water-ski, snorkel, ride horseback on the beach, hunt for shells, or rent a small boat.

Skin and scuba diving. Beautiful reefs and marine life lure divers into the country's waters. An added diving bonus is the opportunity to explore shipwrecks in Vila Harbour as well as the World War II ship relics—*President Coolidge* and *U.S.S. Tucker*—that lie at the bottom of the Segond Canal off Espiritu Santo.

Compressors are available in both Vila and Luganville. Check locally for information on diving guides and diving tours.

Golf. In Vila golfers can play at 9-hole courses at the Hotel Le Lagon and Port Vila Inter-Continental Island Inn. Luganville also has a golf course.

Tennis. Tennis buffs will find courts in Vila at the Hotel Le Lagon, Port Vila Inter-Continental Island Inn, and Vila Tennis Club (small fee). Luganville also has courts available.

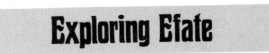

Exploring Efate

The small, oval island of Efate (Vate in French), lies near the center of the Vanuatu chain. On the southwest coast is Vila (Port Vila in French), the nation's capital and largest urban center (17,000 residents).

Vila, the capital

Vila's main business district clings to a narrow stretch of land bordering a harbor punctuated by two islets.

Inland from the waterfront, narrow streets climb steep slopes graced with flowering bougainvillea. On the hillsides you'll see a few wooden, colonial mansions with wide verandas, relics of another era. Alongside Vila's old colonial-style buildings have sprouted new concrete structures. As the town grows, the new buildings are fast replacing the old.

Cultural Centre. Located on the waterfront next door to the Hotel Rossi, Vila's Cultural Centre houses fascinating displays of primitive art, island crafts, plants, and other wildlife.

Public market. Activity starts early at Vila's public market, located on Rue Higginson along the shady waterfront opposite the government buildings. Market days are Wednesdays, Fridays, and Saturdays from 6 A.M. to noon.

Smiling village women dressed in colorful Mother Hubbards will try to sell you giant coconut crabs, fish, and home-grown fruits and vegetables. Prices in the market are now fixed, and there is no bargaining.

Art gallery. Another good browsing spot is the studio and art gallery of Nicolai Michoutouchkine and Aloi Pilioko at the edge of the Erakor Lagoon just a short distance from the Hotel Le Lagon. The wood and thatch building houses more than 800 pieces of interesting Oceanic art.

Other town sights. For a good view of Vila, climb the hill from the waterfront to the government office buildings. Since many French people live in this area it has become known as the "Quartier Français."

South of these government buildings, still more government offices are housed in a large, rambling wooden building bordering a well-tended lawn called "Independence Park." On weekends avid cricket fans gather here to see their favorite sport played. Many of the town's British residents make their homes nearby.

Boat cruises. Several tour operators offer short cruises from Vila. Enjoy a trip aboard a glass-bottomed boat to the harbor's outer reef or sail to Mele Bay.

Touring the island

Efate has about 145 km/90 miles of all-weather roads encircling the island. By metropolitan standards, these roads range from fair to poor condition.

From Vila you can take short trips or longer full-day excursions. Local operators offer organized tours of the island and a flightseeing trip.

Traveling around the island, you'll see rugged terrain, dense vine-tangled jungles, coco palm-bordered lagoons, native villages, coconut plantations, and white and black sand beaches.

Havannah Harbour. Near the north end of Efate this quiet expanse of water sheltered U.S. Navy ships during World War II.

East coast. You'll pass some of Efate's most beautiful beaches on your drive along the east coast. A short distance south of Forari, visitors can enjoy the hospitality of the Manuro Club. You can participate in water activities, have a quiet lunch or dinner, or just relax on the beach. The club is located only 55 km/34 miles from Vila on the southeastern coast.

Visiting Other Islands

For different glimpses of the country, travel to some other Vanuatu islands.

Espiritu Santo's urban center of Luganville offers a small town where touches of World War II are still visible. You can take a tour from Vila to Espiritu Santo or fly there on your own.

Another island to explore is Tanna, where you can climb an active volcano and peer into its fiery depths. On Pentecost Island you might be fortunate enough to witness a land-diving ceremony (usually held in May). Both of these trips are best taken on a tour.

A trip to Espiritu Santo

Until World War II, the quiet island of Espiritu Santo —located in the northern part of the Vanuatu chain— remained little changed from the sight that greeted Pedro de Quiros in 1606.

During the war, Allied military forces used southern Espiritu Santo as a staging area—hospitals, barracks, roads, and airfields were built. Jungles were cleared and market gardens planted to feed the American and New Zealand troops based here. At one time nearly 200,000 men were stationed on Espiritu Santo.

The military personnel have since departed, but war reminders are still evident in the crushed coral roads, houses built of abandoned war materials, and vine-covered quonset huts. Jungle has claimed the market gardens and hidden most of the rusting military scrap.

Espiritu Santo (also called Santo by the locals) is a heavily wooded island 113 km/70 miles long and 72 km/ 45 miles wide. Largest island in Vanuatu, it's just an hour's flight from Vila.

Luganville. Vanuatu's second largest town (population 5,000) grew from the former U.S. military base on southern Espiritu Santo. Like the island, Luganville is sometimes called Santo, which creates some confusion. Planes land near Luganville at Pekoa Airport, an ex-bomber base.

Luganville stretches 10 km/6 miles along the shore fronting the Segond Canal. Chinese trading stores line the town's main street, and numerous cargo ships tie up at the wharf. Luganville is one of Vanuatu's main copra exporting ports. Cattle raising also has become an important industry.

A day's tour from Vila includes a flight to the island; a visit to Palikula, port for a sizable Japanese fishing fleet; and a stop at the Santo Golf Club. It also includes a visit to a coconut experimental station, the old American military hospital, and the site of the Rene River bridge which was destroyed by an earthquake in 1971.

The town has one small hotel and rental cars are available.

Beyond Luganville. You will find beautiful beaches 50 km/31 miles north of Luganville at Hog Harbour. Here translucent blue waters roll onto sugar-white sand bordered by coconut palms.

If you wish to venture into Espiritu Santo's jungle interior, a local guide is necessary. Bush tribes still live here in tiny villages clinging to mist-enshrouded mountain sides.

Tanna's volcano

Near the southern end of the Vanuatu archipelago, the island of Tanna is one of the most fertile islands in the chain. Here you'll find an active volcano, a "cargo cult," and a large herd of wild horses.

From Vila, a 75-minute flight brings visitors to Tanna. You can take a round-trip day excursion or stay overnight on Tanna in bungalow-style accommodations. Each of the two hostelries has a restaurant. Tanna Bungalows also features traditional entertainment.

Volcano trek. Airplanes land at the airstrip near Lenakel village on the island's west coast. A waiting jeep transports visitors the 29 km/18 miles to the active volcano of Yasur. On your journey you'll pass coconut and coffee plantations, rain forests, and villages.

Surrounded by a moonscapelike plain of black ash, quiet Lake Siwi shimmers near the base of Yasur. Occasionally, ground orchids break the monotony of the desolate landscape; these flowers apparently thrive in the sulfur fumes pervading the region.

A guide from a nearby village accompanies the group on the 45-minute trek to the rim of the volcano. Your reward: a close-up glimpse of bubbling, red-hot lava.

Occasionally you'll hear an awesome rumbling as it spews from the volcano's depths.

Visitors are asked not to remove any stones from the mountain. It is considered taboo because of the stones' importance to the spiritual beliefs of the people.

John Frum movement. Sulphur Bay, the nearby village that owns Yasur, is the home of the John Frum cargo cult. Painted red crosses—symbols of the movement—dot the village and the countryside. (You can photograph these crosses, but don't touch them.)

These villagers, and others on Tanna, believe that someday "John Frum" will send them cargos of refrigerators, jeeps, and other riches. The movement began when the islanders became disillusioned with the missionaries and white people who seemed to possess all the material wealth in the area. The islanders believed the material possessions were brought "free" by cargo ship. Military cargo shipped to Vanuatu during World War II further prompted these islanders to believe that they, too, would soon receive riches from the flying bird in the sky or the ship much larger than their canoes. No one really knows who John Frum was—he may have been an American G.I.

Wild horses. A jeep tour takes visitors to White Grass, a plateau on northern Tanna where more than 500 wild horses run and graze. The stallions and mares are descendants of stock introduced by missionaries.

Know Before You Go

The following practical information will help you plan your trip to Vanuatu.

Entry/exit requirements. All visitors need a valid passport and an onward ticket. No visa is required for a stay of 30 days or less.

Travelers arriving from an infected area will need smallpox and yellow fever vaccinations. Since a malaria risk does exist outside of Vila, check with your doctor before your trip for anti-malarial treatment. (Note: Since health requirements change from time to time, check with your local public health department before leaving on your trip.)

Departing air passengers pay an airport departure tax of VT 600 in local currency.

Customs. You are allowed to bring in duty free 1 carton of cigarettes, 50 cigars, or 8¾ ounces of tobacco, plus 2 bottles of liquor.

Currency. The New Hebrides Vatu. Coin denominations are 2, 5, 10, 20, and 50, and notes come in denominations of 100, 200, 500, and 1000.

Tipping. Tipping is not customary in Vanuatu; it offends the local people's sense of hospitality.

Time. Vanuatu is GMT (Greenwich mean time) +11. For example, when it is noon Sunday in Vila, it is 5 P.M. Saturday in San Francisco, 1 P.M. Sunday in Auckland, and 11 A.M. Sunday in Sydney.

Weather and what to wear. Located 14 to 20° south of the equator, the Vanuatu islands enjoy a semitropical climate marked by two seasons. The cool, dry winter runs from May through October with temperatures averaging 27°C/81°F. During the warm rainy, humid summer (November through April), temperatures rise to around 29°C/84°F. Yearly rainfall totals about 3048 mm/120 inches, and humidity averages 83 percent. The southern islands in the chain enjoy cooler weather and less rain than their northern neighbors.

Casual, lightweight attire is perfect for the Vanuatu's tropical climate. Bring along a sweater if you journey there during the cool season. You'll want sunglasses and sturdy walking shoes if you plan to hike up Tanna's volcano.

For more information. Write to Vanuatu Visitors Bureau, P.O. Box 209, Vila, Vanuatu for further information on the country.

PAPUA NEW GUINEA

In Papua New Guinea visitors see startling contrasts between developing modern society and relatively unchanged primitive cultures.

Only in recent years has this country emerged from a dominant Stone Age culture to become an independent nation. Even today, primitive tribal traditions persist in secluded valleys and on isolated plateaus.

The rugged topography of Papua New Guinea—sometimes shortened to PNG—has not only insulated most of its people from the outside world, but it has also isolated them from each other. More than 700 different languages are spoken in the country, and some 700 different cultures have developed during centuries of isolation.

As a visitor, you'll want to discover some of these cultures. From Port Moresby, the capital, or one of the country's other major urban centers, you can take a tour back in time when you explore Papua New Guinea.

Within the Tropics

Papua New Guinea lies wholly in the tropics just a few degrees south of the equator, only 161 km/100 miles north of Australia's Cape York Peninsula.

Most of the country is located on the eastern half of New Guinea, the world's second largest noncontinental island. (Irian Jaya, a province of Indonesia, shares the island.) Large and small islands scattered off the mainland's east coast include the Admiralty Islands, New Britain, New Ireland, the Trobriands, Louisiade Archipelago, and—in the North Solomons—Bougainville and Buka. Papua New Guinea's land area totals 461,693 square km/178,213 square miles.

Highlands and lowlands

Soaring, jagged mountains with deep ravines and valleys characterize the country's topography. Extending across the central part of the mainland (called the Highlands), a massive mountain spine forms a complex chain of knife-edged ranges, high plateaus and valleys, and steep ravines.

Numerous great rivers drain the rugged pinnacles.

Two of the largest are the Sepik River, flowing north into the Bismarck Sea, and the Fly River, emptying into the Gulf of Papua on the southern coast. Where silt-laden rivers reach the flat coastal plains, large mangrove and sago swamps have been created.

Wildlife abounds in Papua New Guinea. Perhaps most famous are the birds of paradise.

Discovered en route to the "Spice Islands"

In the 16th century, Spanish and Portuguese sailors first spotted the island of New Guinea while en route to the Moluccas—the rich "Spice Islands." The first European to land was Jorge de Meneses, Portuguese governor of the Moluccas, who arrived in 1526. He called the island "Ilhas dos Papuas," meaning Island of the Fuzzy-Haired Men. Twenty years later Spanish navigator Inigo de Retes sailed along the north coast and named the island "Nueva Guinea" because of its resemblance to the Guinea coast of Africa.

Spanish, English, and Dutch explorers all visited New Guinea during the 16th and 17th centuries, but few people settled here until the 18th century.

In 1828, the Dutch annexed the western half of New Guinea (now Indonesia's Irian Jaya). Germany annexed the northeast part of the island in 1884, naming it German New Guinea. One week later, the British claimed the southeastern portion of the island plus the smaller islands to the east; they called their protectorate British New Guinea. In 1906, Australia assumed responsibility for this protectorate, changing its name to the Territory of Papua. After World War I, Australia also became the administrator of (German) New Guinea.

In 1942, during World War II, Japanese troops invaded the territories of Papua and New Guinea, but they were soon halted by the Australian and American Forces under the command of General Douglas MacArthur.

Today, the former territories of Papua and New Guinea are one nation administered by a freely elected government. Papua New Guinea achieved independence from Australia on September 16, 1975, and is now a sovereign state within the British Commonwealth of Nations.

Papua New Guinea's People

Nearly 3 million people inhabit Papua New Guinea; most are Melanesians. About 34,800 residents are of Australian, European, or Chinese ancestry.

Lifestyles—primitive and modern

Each of Papua New Guinea's 700 cultural groups has its own customs, culture, and language. Some of these people have felt the influences of modern civilization for a number of years; others scarcely knew a world outside their village existed until a short time ago.

Housing for Papua New Guinea's rural people ranges from A-framed, thatch-roofed stilt houses to round houses with dome-shaped thatch roofs. The land and

Sepik youths *process sago, a starchy food derived from sago palm. Travelers take cruises up Sepik River to view tropical wildlife, visit stilt villages, and shop for primitive art.*

Highlands tribesman *costumed for a sing sing paints face, wears feathered headdress, nose and neck ornaments. Villagers in native dress congregate for market days and Highland tribal celebrations.*

rivers provide such dietary staples as sago palm, taro, yams, and fish. More westernized city dwellers live in western-style houses and shop at the local supermarket.

Dress. Clothing in Papua New Guinea reflects both traditional and modern customs. Some Papua New Guineans wear western-style dress—loose fitting shirts and shorts or *lap-laps* (wrapround skirts) for men, "meri" blouses (long tops) and skirts for women.

Still others (living in the Highlands or Trobriands) retain their traditional tribal dress of grass skirts or apronlike string skirts. Many women wear *bilums* on their heads; in these multipurpose woven bags, they carry everything including produce and children.

Language. There are many different languages in Papua New Guinea. English, the official national language, is widely spoken particularly in business and government. Two other important languages are Pidgin and Motu.

Religion. Even though Papua New Guineans are now Christianized, superstition and magic still play an integral role in their daily lives. Their beliefs—based largely on ancestor and spirit worship *(puri-puri)*—are reflected in much of their art and customs.

Sports. Papua New Guineans touched by western civilization have become sports minded. Major activities include football, cricket, softball, and golf. Around Port Moresby you'll find teams competing in canoe races.

Mining and forestry exports

Since 1972, when Bougainville Copper Ltd. began production, copper has become an important export for the country. An enormous open-cut copper mine is located at Panguna on Bougainville. Other mining exports include small amounts of gold and silver.

Forestry products are also a leading export item, along with copra, palm oil, and tea.

Planning Your Trip

Papua New Guinea, a newly developing South Pacific destination, can be reached by both air and sea.

Several major airlines—including the country's air carrier, Air Niugini—serve Jacksons Airport at Port

Moresby. (It's an 11 km/7 mile bus or taxi trip into town from the airport.) Flights serve Papua New Guinea from Australia, the Philippines, the Solomons, Hong Kong, Singapore, Indonesia, Japan, and Hawaii.

A few passenger and cargo/passenger liners make at least one PNG town a port of call. Seaport towns include Port Moresby, Rabaul, Lae, Madang, and Wewak.

Getting around the country

Because of the rugged and mountainous terrain, few roads have been developed. Many existing roads are narrow and extremely difficult to maintain because heavy rains frequently cause problems.

The easiest way to travel within Papua New Guinea is by air. Several local airlines offer scheduled and charter service to a number of airports and landing strips.

Taxi service is available in towns. However, cabs are in short supply so be prepared for a wait.

Renting a car. If you wish to explore the towns and their neighboring environs on your own, rent a car (or hire a car and driver) in Port Moresby, Lae, Rabaul, Mt. Hagen, Goroka, Madang, Wewak, Kieta, and Popondetta. Traffic moves on the left side of the road. It's advisable to reserve your car ahead of time.

Bus travel. Regular bus service links Goroka (Highlands) and Lae (coast), and Goroka and Mt. Hagen

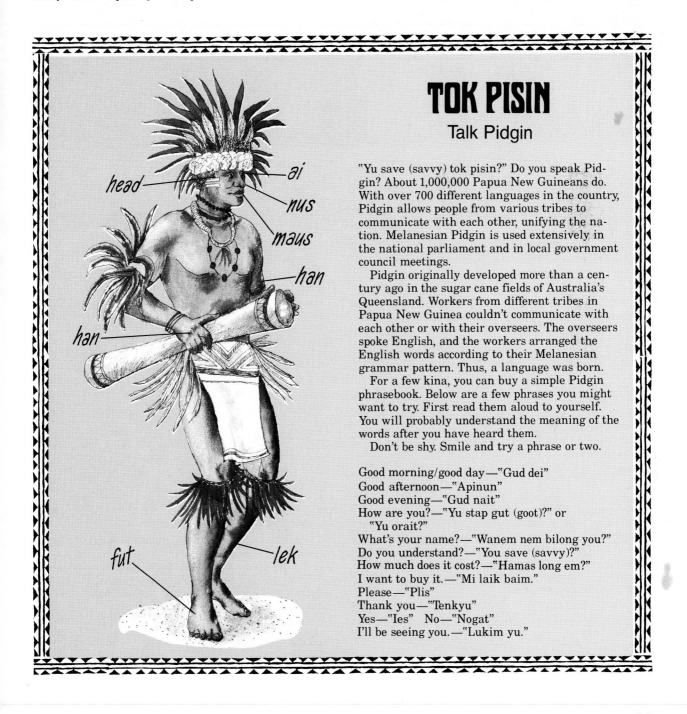

TOK PISIN
Talk Pidgin

"Yu save (savvy) tok pisin?" Do you speak Pidgin? About 1,000,000 Papua New Guineans do. With over 700 different languages in the country, Pidgin allows people from various tribes to communicate with each other, unifying the nation. Melanesian Pidgin is used extensively in the national parliament and in local government council meetings.

Pidgin originally developed more than a century ago in the sugar cane fields of Australia's Queensland. Workers from different tribes in Papua New Guinea couldn't communicate with each other or with their overseers. The overseers spoke English, and the workers arranged the English words according to their Melanesian grammar pattern. Thus, a language was born.

For a few kina, you can buy a simple Pidgin phrasebook. Below are a few phrases you might want to try. First read them aloud to yourself. You will probably understand the meaning of the words after you have heard them.

Don't be shy. Smile and try a phrase or two.

Good morning/good day—"Gud dei"
Good afternoon—"Apinun"
Good evening—"Gud nait"
How are you?—"Yu stap gut (goot)?" or
 "Yu orait?"
What's your name?—"Wanem nem bilong you?"
Do you understand?—"You save (savvy)?"
How much does it cost?—"Hamas long em?"
I want to buy it.—"Mi laik baim."
Please—"Plis"
Thank you—"Tenkyu"
Yes—"Ies"   No—"Nogat"
I'll be seeing you.—"Lukim yu."

Field workers pick tea *on Highlands plantation. Grown and harvested for export, tea contributes substantially to economy. Other main exports include lumber, minerals, copra, palm oil, rubber, spices, and pyrethrum (used in insecticides).*

(Highlands). Each trip takes about a day journeying mostly over unpaved roads.

Boating. Cargo/passenger service with limited accommodations is offered along the northeast coast between Madang and Lae. Contact Lutheran Shipping M.V. "Totol," Box 789, Madang.

Tours. Many visitors to Papua New Guinea see the country by arranged tour. Operators in both the United States and Australia offer packaged tours to and around Papua New Guinea. You also can arrange ahead (or on arrival) for a tour of the country originating in Port Moresby. Other major towns schedule short local tours of nearby points of interest. For further information on tour possibilities, check with your travel agent.

Hotels, lodges, and mountain huts

Papua New Guinea offers a wide selection of small to moderate-size accommodations. You will find comfortable hotels, motels, lodges, and guest houses scattered throughout the country. Travelers can stay in the major towns, in the jungle foothills, in the Highlands, near the Sepik River, or beside a beach. Architectural styles range from low-rise modern structures to individual thatch-roofed mountain huts.

Dining and entertainment

Hotel dining rooms offer a good menu selection as well as an occasional buffet. You also can sample Chinese, Australian, or Indonesian dishes at local restaurants.

Occasionally the Hotel Madang and Smuggler's Inn (in Madang) and the Bird of Paradise Hotel (in Goroka) present a small sing sing featuring costumed entertainers in traditional native singing and dancing. The native feast accompanying these sing sings might include roast pork, sweet potatoes, tropical fruits, and vegetables. Many feast items are cooked in a *mumu* (oven made of hot stones buried in the ground). Sometimes hotels hold a sing sing without a feast.

Tourist officials caution visitors in outlying towns against wandering alone too far from the hotel after dark. Every country has its rascals.

A plethora of primitive art

Papua New Guinea craftspeople are noted for their excellent creations of primitive art. Regional arts and crafts include carvings, ceremonial masks and figures from the Sepik; crocodile carvings from the Trobriands; basketware from Buka; and arrows, bows, and decorated axes from the Highlands.

You can buy Papua New Guinea artifacts in the villages where they are made or at shops in the major towns. Shops are open from 8 A.M. to 4:30 P.M. Monday through Friday, and on Saturday mornings. In Port Moresby the government-run Village Arts Store, on Rigo Road about 2 km/1 mile from the airport, offers a representative selection of artifacts from all over the country. Store hours are 8 A.M. to 5 P.M. Monday to Saturday, 9 to 4 on Sunday.

The export of artifacts is government controlled, and no traditional village artwork over 20 years old may be

FESTIVAL TIME

One of the best ways to see some traditional aspects of Papua New Guinean life is to attend a local celebration or festival.

January–April

Chinese New Year. The Chinese communities celebrate this occasion near the end of January with traditional festivities.

May–August

Frangipani Festival. In early May, Rabaul celebrates the arrival of the first flowers after the 1937 volcanic eruption with an annual festival. Events include a sing sing and string band competitions.

Port Moresby Show. Held in June on the Queen's Birthday weekend, this event includes sing sings and agricultural displays.

Madang Music Festival. Musicians gather in Madang in August for a week-long schedule of performances.

September–December

Independence Day. Celebrations take place throughout Papua New Guinea on the weekend nearest September 16.

Hiri Moale. This September festival in Port Moresby marks the early voyages of the Motu people along the Papuan coast.

Annual Arts Festival. In September Port Moresby and Lae alternate in hosting this 2-week event featuring guest performers from other Third World countries.

Tolai Warwagira. During a fortnight of festivities in November, Rabaul schedules fireworks displays, sing sings, and choral group performances.

Morobe Show. An October weekend of festivities in Lae includes cultural and agricultural displays plus a major sing sing.

Pearl Festival. In November a weekend-long celebration in Samarai, Milne Bay Province, features beauty contests, art and crafts displays, and canoe races.

---

taken out of the country. Your port of debarkation might want a certificate of fumigation for artifacts purchased.

Outdoor pleasures

The warm, clear waters off Papua New Guinea provide a variety of excellent snorkeling and scuba diving opportunities. Many of the diving centers have diving clubs that hold weekly outings. In addition, specialized tour companies operating out of Madang and Port Moresby offer qualified instructors, scuba gear, and compressors.

Game fishermen catch small marlin, sailfish, mackerel, and tuna as close as 6 km/4 miles from Port Moresby. For further information, write Moresby Game Fishing Club, P.O. Box 5028, Boroko, Port Moresby.

Golfers can try the 18-hole course at Port Moresby Golf Club. Other courses are located at Goroka, Lae, Madang, Minj, Wau, Rabaul, Kavieng, Popondetta, Mt. Hagen, Wewak, and Kieta.

You can also enjoy tennis, squash, boating, waterskiing, horseback riding, lawn bowling, and swimming.

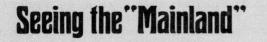

Seeing the "Mainland"

Most visitors spend their time on the Papua New Guinea mainland, an extensive area covering the eastern part of the island of New Guinea. From Port Moresby, the country's main air and sea gateway, visitors can take 2 to 14-day tours of the country or travel independently to Lae, Goroka, and Mt. Hagen (to tour the Highlands) or Madang and Wewak (to cruise on the Sepik River).

Port Moresby, the capital

Most visitors stay only briefly in Port Moresby, the country's capital and government center, before continuing on to other Papua New Guinea destinations. Located on the mainland's southern coast, the city overlooks Fairfax Harbour. Many of its 130,000 residents live near the harbor or in suburbs spreading over low hills and valleys behind it. The new government buildings are in Waigani Valley, north of the old part of town.

Visitor accommodations include the Boroko Hotel, Davara Hotel, Gateway Hotel, Islander Hotel, Papua Hotel, and Port Moresby TraveLodge.

Touring Port Moresby. Within walking distance of most hotels is popular, palm-edged Ela Beach. On Sunday mornings, the local police band performs here.

Every day is market day at Koki Market, located near the water's edge east of Ela Beach on Healy Parade. Townspeople and villagers, including out-islanders who have arrived by canoe, gather to exchange gossip and sell and purchase supplies. Stall displays feature such items as parrot fish strung on racks, big green cassowary bird eggs, and mud crabs.

The National Museum and Art Gallery is located in Waigani Valley, a suburb 13 km/8 miles north of the town center. Open daily except Saturdays, it houses one of the largest displays of traditional Papua New Guinea pottery in the world.

Sogeri Plateau. The cool Sogeri Plateau, just an hour's drive northeast of Port Moresby, offers numerous places to explore. You can see plantations, waterfalls, the Bomana War Cemetery, and Varirata National Park.

Lae, a garden town

The garden town of Lae, on the Huon Gulf, is a 45-minute flight north of Port Moresby. The country's second largest city (53,000 people), Lae originally developed around an airfield that serviced the Morobe gold fields during the 1930s gold rush. Destroyed during World War II, the town has been completely rebuilt. Travelers can stay at the Huon Gulf Motel, Lae Lodge, and the Melanesian Hotel.

Touring Lae. Within walking distance of town center are Lae's lovely Botanical Gardens. Early morning is the best time to view the water lilies and glimpse some of Papua New Guinea's colorful tropical birds flitting through the jungle forest. Other town sights include Lae War Memorial and several colorful markets.

Bulolo and Wau. You can drive or take a tour to Bulolo and Wau, located 122 km/76 miles southwest of Lae. These now-quiet towns bustled with activity during the 1930s gold rush. Some dredging equipment remains.

The fascinating Highlands

As you travel the Highlands Highway and side roads, you'll see tiny settlements of round houses near sweet potato fields fenced off by sharp stakes. You'll pass villagers—wearing brief apron skirts and carrying bows and arrows—walking their pigs alongside the road. Occasionally travelers come upon an impromptu sing sing—a colorfully costumed tribal celebration in song and dance.

You can get to the Highlands on a short flight from Lae, Port Moresby, or Madang; or by a long drive on the Highlands Highway out of Lae. Several PNG tour operators offer excursions through the Highlands. Try to schedule Highland tours at least 30 days in advance.

Goroka accommodations include the Bird of Paradise Hotel and Lantern Lodge; space is booked up to a year in advance for the annual Eastern Highlands Show (sing sing). Mt. Hagen hotels include Hagen Park, Plumes and Arrows, Highlander, Kimininga, and Baiyer River. Ambua Lodge has opened at Tari Gap in the Southern Highlands, home of the "wig men."

Goroka. Largest town in the Highlands, Goroka is located at an elevation of 1,524 meters/5,000 feet in the Bismarck Range. Market gardens and coffee plantations surround this town of 11,000 people. If you journey to the Highlands from Lae, Goroka will probably be your first stop. It's a 40-minute flight or 8-hour bus trip from Lae to Goroka.

From Goroka, take a tour to Kominufa village to see the mud men of Asaro Valley. Covered in dried grey river mud and wearing ugly helmet masks made of mud, fiber, dog teeth, and pig tusks, these men perform their traditional chants and macabre dance for tour groups.

Kundiawa. In the heart of the Chimbu province 97 km/60 miles west of Goroka, you'll find Kundiawa. It's been less than 50 years since the first westerners explored this primitive and thickly populated region. The hardworking Chimbu people cultivate patchwork vegetable gardens on the steep mountain slopes.

On a tour of the area you might see Chimbu bush plays—spectacular performances of mime, dance, and song depicting scenes of everyday tribal life.

Mt. Hagen. Nestled in the Wahgi Valley amid coffee and tea plantations, Mt. Hagen is the provincial capital of the Western Highlands. A small town of 15,000, its population soars on the big market days (Wednesdays, Fridays, Saturdays) when the tribespeople converge from outlying districts.

The Highland Show. The big event of the year in the Highlands is the Eastern Highlands Show. Previously, this annual show has alternated between Goroka and Mt. Hagen, but it is now planned yearly in Goroka, probably in late September.

More than 60,000 tribespeople from all over Papua New Guinea gather to participate in and enjoy this 2-day event. Some come by foot, traveling for weeks to the show; others arrive by plane, bus, or truck.

Highlight of the show is the sing sing. Over 4,000 tribespeople dance and sing while swaying to ancient chants and the beat of drums. Costuming is spectacular. Many performers wear huge headdresses of brilliantly colored bird of paradise plumes, fur neck pieces, shell jewelry, and body paint in bright yellow, blue, and red.

Madang, a tropical Venice

Situated on a coral promontory 241 km/150 miles northwest of Lae, Madang has one of the country's most beautiful settings. A string of palm-covered tropical islands protects its fine deepwater harbor, and placid waterways meander through the town. Madang has been called the Venice of Papua New Guinea.

Originally settled by Germans, this sleepy tropical port was invaded by the Japanese during World War II. Today Madang is a starting point for some tours into the Sepik region and Highlands.

Accommodations include the Coastwatchers Motel, Hotel Madang Resort, and Smuggler's Inn Motel.

The wonderous Sepik

Navigable for about 1,127 km/700 miles, the Sepik River drains an immense northern region of grasslands, swamps, and jungle. Its expansive area is home for a remarkable collection of animals, reptiles, insects, birdlife, and flowering plants.

Cruising the Sepik. Travelers can take half-day, all-day, and several-day water tours on the Sepik and its tributaries. Day tours by rivercraft leave from Angoram, Amboin, and Ambunti. One popular 3-day cruise on the "Melanesian Explorer" houseboat leaves Madang and goes up the Sepik to Ambunti, or heads downriver from Ambunti to Madang. River accommodations at Kaminimbit and Karawari include boat tours on the river.

Airstrips are located at Angoram, Amboin, Ambunti, Hayfield, and Wewak. A road links Wewak with Pagwi and Angoram.

Wewak and Maprik. Wewak, on the coast northwest of Madang, is the East Sepik's administrative capital. It offers the principal road accesses to the Sepik River.

Lodging includes the Sepik Motel, Wewak Hotel, and the Windjammer Beach Motel.

From Wewak, you can journey by road inland to the Maprik area, which is known as *"haus tambaran* (spirit house) country." You'll see full-scale models of these A-framed spirit houses with their murals and interesting carvings at the Maprik Cultural Center.

Primitive art. The Sepik people produce some of the finest examples of primitive art in the world including intricate carvings and decorated pottery.

Exploring Offshore Islands

In addition to Papua New Guinea's massive mainland area, the country includes numerous offshore islands. Those of interest to visitors include New Britain,

Bougainville (in the North Solomons), and the Trobriands. All are easily accessible by air.

New Britain, the largest of these islands, lies due east of Madang. Rabaul, the island's main town, sits at the head of one of the Pacific's best natural harbors, surrounded by a backdrop of several volcanic cones—some of which are still active.

In 1942 the Japanese invaded Rabaul and made it their center of operations in the Southwest Pacific. A large number of interesting war relics remain.

Accommodations in Rabaul include Hamamas Hotel, Motel Kaivuna, Kulau Lodge, and Rabaul TraveLodge.

Bougainville, located northeast of the mainland at the northern end of the Solomon Islands chain, is famed for its enormous open-cut copper mine at Panguna. While visiting this island which also has World War II battlegrounds, you can stay in Kieta at the Arovo Holiday Island Pty Ltd.

The Trobriand archipelago, lying off the mainland's southeastern coast, contains 22 coral islands—some of them so flat they're at ocean level. These islands possess both natural beauty and a carefree population.

Know Before You Go

The following practical information will help you plan your trip to Papua New Guinea.

Entry/exit procedures. Visitors to Papua New Guinea need a valid passport, a confirmed onward ticket, and sufficient funds for their stay. Upon their arrival at Port Moresby's Jackson Airport, tourists are issued a visa for stays of 30 days or less.

You'll need inoculations against smallpox, cholera, and yellow fever only if you come from an infected area. Since a malaria risk does exist, it is advisable to take antimalarial tablets. Check with your doctor for treatment a few weeks before departure. (Note: Since health requirements change from time to time, check with your local public health department before leaving on your trip.)

Departing international air passengers pay an airport departure tax of K20.

Customs. Travelers may bring in duty free 200 cigarettes or an

equal amount of cigars or tobacco, 1 litre of liquor, perfume for personal use, and gifts totaling no more than K200 (U.S. $290, A $240, N.Z. $275).

Currency. The Papua New Guinea currency is the kina. Coins are toea (1, 2, 10, 20); 100 toea equal 1 kina. Note denominations are 2, 5, 10, and 20.

Tipping. Tipping is neither customary nor encouraged.

Time. Papua New Guinea is GMT (Greenwich mean time) +10. For example, when it is noon Sunday in Port Moresby, it is 6 P.M. Saturday in San Francisco, 2 P.M. Sunday in Auckland, and noon Sunday in Sydney.

Weather and what to wear. Because Papua New Guinea lies within the tropics, the climate is typically humid. There are two principal seasons: the season of the northwest monsoon (from December to April)—hot, with sudden squalls, heavy rains, high winds; and the season of the

southeast trade winds (from May to November)—drier and cooler.

The rainfall varies. Lae averages about 457 cm/180 inches per year, whereas Port Moresby receives only about 102 cm/40 inches. Day coastal temperatures range from a minimum of 26°C/79°F to a maximum of 32°C/90°F. Night temperatures can drop to 19°C/67°F. The less humid Highlands have sunny warm days and cool nights.

As in much of the South Pacific, you'll be comfortable in lightweight summer clothes in most areas. In the Highlands you'll need warmer clothing for the evening. Bathing suits and shorts (except walking shorts and knee-high socks for men) should not be worn in towns or villages. Other articles to pack include walking shoes, an umbrella, sunglasses, suntan lotion, a rainhat, and beach shoes for reef walking.

For more information. Write to the PNG National Tourist Authority, P.O. Box 7144, Boroko, Port Moresby, for further information.

SOLOMON ISLANDS

Nowhere in the South Pacific are memories of 20th century wartime history more prevalent than in the Solomon Islands. Guadalcanal, Tulagi, the "Slot," and Iron Bottom Sound are all familiar names from the annals of World War II. The formidable Japanese offensive was stalled on Guadalcanal in 1943, changing the course of the war in the Pacific.

As you tour the Solomons, you'll still see vestiges of war—tanks overgrown with creeping vines, shell-torn landing craft ravaged by the seas, trenches gouging the land, and redoubts jutting from the hillsides. However, the islands' exotic flowers, towering palms, blue lagoons, and friendly people lessen the grimness of these war reminders.

Two Chains of Islands

The Solomon Islands cover an extensive area stretching for more than 1,448 km/900 miles across the Pacific in a northwest-southeast direction. The wide seaway of New Georgia Sound, called "The Slot," divides the island group into two chains.

The Solomons lie about 1,408 km/875 miles due east of Papua New Guinea, and 1,284 km/798 miles northwest of Vanuatu.

Guadalcanal, with an area of 6,477 square km/2,500 square miles, is the largest island in the Solomon group. Other large main islands include Choiseul, Malaita, New Georgia, San Cristobal, and Santa Isabel.

Islands vary from large, mountainous, volcanic land masses to small atolls that are mere flat coral outcroppings. Steep mountains cut through the volcanic islands, sloping sharply to the sea on one side and descending more gradually in a series of foothills on the other. Swift-flowing rivers drain these peaks. Where limestone deposits exist, the rivers may disappear to surge through underground channels.

Some of the volcanoes remain active. In the Santa Cruz Islands southeast of San Cristobal, Tinakula Volcano briefly erupted in 1971. Although Savo Volcano last erupted in 1840, it still is considered potentially dangerous with numerous hot springs and thermal areas. A submarine volcano (Kavachi) near New Georgia occasionally erupts from the sea, then disappears once more underwater.

Mangrove swamps, rain forests

Extensive mangrove swamps rim the coastal areas of the islands and dense rain forests cover much of the interior. Ferns, mosses, orchids, climbing and creeping vines, and flowering shrubs such as hibiscus thrive in the rain forests.

Wild pigs, opossums, and bush rats forage through the forests, while crocodiles and lizards lurk in the coastal mangrove swamps. Though the Solomons have many snakes, few are venomous.

Over 140 species of birds—including king and pygmy parrots, sunbirds, kingfishers, cockatoos, and a variety of pigeons—dwell in the Solomons. In addition to an interesting bird population, you'll also see a colorful assortment of butterflies.

One bird of special note—the burrowing megapode—lives on Savo Island. Although this bird is smaller than a domestic fowl, it lays an egg twice the size of a normal chicken egg. The megapode then buries the egg in a burrow. The egg eventually hatches from the heat of the sun or the warmth of an adjacent thermal spring. You can see these birds on a 1-day boat tour from Honiara to Savo Island.

Numerous sharks prowl the open seas around the Solomon Islands.

Discovered by Mendaña

In 1567 the Spanish explorer Alvaro de Mendaña sailed from Peru in search of a southern continent. He reached the Solomons the following year, discovering Guadalcanal, Ysabel (Santa Isabel), and San Cristobal. In an effort to encourage Spanish migration, he hinted at the existence of gold in the area by naming the group the Solomon Islands. (Much speculation existed regarding the site of "King Solomon's lost mines.")

Mendaña returned to the Solomons in 1595 with a group of settlers to establish a colony at Graciosa Bay in the Santa Cruz Islands. Disputes and sickness plagued the group. After Mendaña fell ill and died, the colonists sailed for the Philippines.

In the following centuries, other explorers including Abel Tasman and Louis Antoine de Bougainville sighted or stopped at the islands.

During the 1800s whalers, traders, and missionaries all found their way to the Solomons. Their reception was not always cordial. Massacre and murder reigned here during this period. Some of the attacks on Europeans were in retaliation for "blackbirding"—the kidnapping of islanders for use as laborers on South Pacific plantations.

To provide protection for Europeans in the Solomons, Great Britain declared the South Solomons a Protectorate in 1893. The remainder of the Solomon Islands became part of the Protectorate between 1898 and 1900.

Early in the 20th century, private companies started a variety of plantations, but in later years—up until

Rusting debris *marks Guadalcanal landing beach where Allied troops stormed ashore in 1942. Abandoned relics litter countryside, providing vivid reminders of heavy fighting in Solomons during World War II.*

War memorial *near Rabaul honors Commonwealth military men who died in World War II battles in New Britain area. Center of Japanese operations in 1942, Rabaul was bombed by Allies, rebuilt after war.*

AD MAJOREM DEI GLORIAM

IN THIS PLACE ARE RECORDED
THE NAMES OF OFFICERS
AND MEN OF THE BRITISH
COMMONWEALTH OF NATIONS
WHO DIED DURING THE
1939-1945 WAR IN THE NEW
BRITAIN AREA, ON LAND, AT
SEA AND IN THE AIR, BUT TO
WHOM THE FORTUNES OF WAR
DENIED THE KNOWN AND
HONOURED BURIAL GIVEN TO
THEIR COMRADES IN DEATH

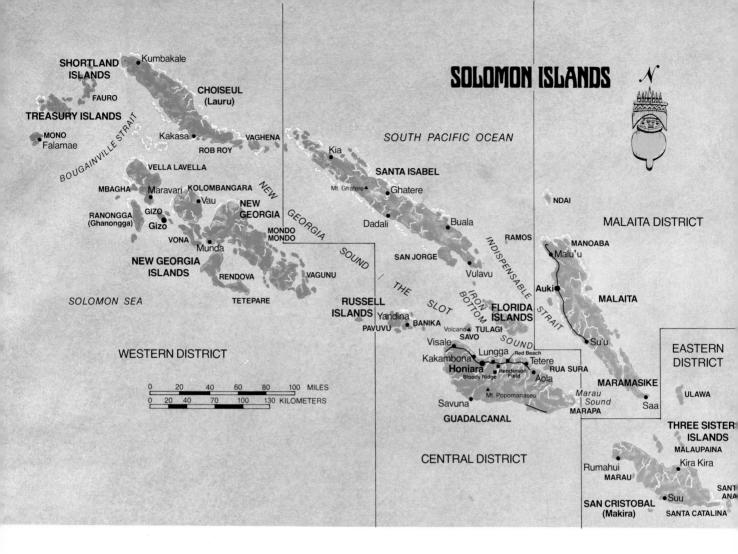

SOLOMON ISLANDS

SOUTH PACIFIC OCEAN

SHORTLAND ISLANDS — Kumbakale — FAURO — CHOISEUL (Lauru) — VAGHENA — Kia — SANTA ISABEL — Mt. Ghatere — Ghatere — NDAI — MALAITA DISTRICT — MANOABA — Malu'u — Auki — MALAITA — Su'u — EASTERN DISTRICT — ULAWA

TREASURY ISLANDS — MONO — Falamae — Kakasa — ROB ROY — VELLA LAVELLA — Dadali — Buala — RAMOS

MBAGHA — Maravari — KOLOMBANGARA — NEW GEORGIA — San Jorge — Vulavu — MARAMASIKE — THREE SISTERS ISLANDS — MALAUPAINA — Kira Kira

RANONGGA (Ghanongga) — GIZO — Vau — SAN JORGE — VONA — Gizo — NEW GEORGIA — MONDO MONDO — RUSSELL ISLANDS — Yandina — BANIKA — FLORIDA ISLANDS — Volcano — TULAGI — SAVO — Visale — Lungga — Red Beach — Tetere — RUA SURA — SANTA ANA

NEW GEORGIA ISLANDS — RENDOVA — VAGUNU — PAVUVU — Kakambona — Honiara — Bloody Ridge — Henderson Field — Aola — SANTA CATALINA

SOLOMON SEA — TETEPARE — THE SLOT — IRON BOTTOM SOUND — INDISPENSABLE STRAIT

WESTERN DISTRICT — Savuna — Mt. Popomanaseu — GUADALCANAL — Marau Sound — MARAPA — Saa

CENTRAL DISTRICT — Rumahui — MARAU — SAN CRISTOBAL (Makira) — Suu — BOUGAINVILLE STRAIT

0 20 40 60 80 100 MILES
0 20 40 70 100 130 KILOMETERS

1940—the British Solomon Islands were largely neglected except for coconut plantings.

Then came World War II. In April 1942, the Japanese invaded the Solomons, and the islands became the focal point of fierce battles between Japanese troops and the Allies. These confrontations continued until the Japanese were driven out in early 1943. Many Solomon islanders, fiercely loyal to the Allied cause, distinguished themselves in battle.

One of the most important World War II naval battles—the Battle of the Coral Sea—took place near the Solomon Islands. The U.S. Marines captured a Japanese airstrip under construction on Guadalcanal. After its completion, Henderson Air Field played an important role in the Guadalcanal Campaign.

Until World War II, most Solomon islanders had little contact with the outside world. With the advent of war, however, they learned of aircraft (believed by some to be a huge kind of bird), and other marvels such as canned foods, bottled drinks, kerosene lamps, radios, and modern weapons.

On July 7, 1978, the Solomon Islands gained their independence after 85 years of British rule. The country is governed by an elected 38-member national parliament headed by a prime minister and by elected provincial assemblies in each of the Solomons' five provinces.

Solomon Islands People

Approximately 197,000 people reside in the Solomon Islands. Of that number about 184,000 are Melanesian and 8,000 Polynesian; Europeans, Micronesians (Gilbertese), and Chinese are also represented.

Most of the Melanesians live on the larger islands, while the Polynesians inhabit the smaller islands and atolls. The most heavily populated islands are Malaita and Guadalcanal.

Most live in villages

Except for a few urban centers—Honiara on Guadalcanal, Auki on Malaita, and Gizo in the New Georgia group—most Solomon islanders reside in small, thatched hut villages. Many of these villages lie near the coasts of the islands and their inhabitants are known as "saltwater" people. "Bush" people dwell inland on Guadalcanal and Malaita.

Villagers maintain a traditional way of life that has been in existence for hundreds of years. They grow their own fruits and vegetables, and hunt and fish for addi-

(Continued on page 102)

THE COCONUT PALM
A Tropical Supermarket

Symbol of the South Pacific, the coconut palm tree is more than a decorative addition to scenic views of the South Seas. It is a tropical supermarket of useful products that contribute substantially to island life. During your South Pacific travels, you'll discover its many uses. When you're standing in its shade, however, remember that a coconut can fall without warning.

The fruit of the tree—the coconut—is an important ingredient in many native recipes. For the local population, these nuts are no farther away than a quick climb up a tree. (Visitors usually find tree climbing a little more difficult than the local people do.)

Savor coconut in cakes, puddings, and fish cream sauces. For a refreshing cool drink, sip the slightly sweet liquid of the green immature coconut. Villagers living on arid islands and atolls without rivers or streams often drink this instead of water.

The tree itself offers another gourmet treat—heart of palm salad. But a tree must be sacrificed in the preparation of this dish, sometimes known as "millionaire's salad."

The coconut tree provides building materials for islanders. Hardwood tree trunks become the uprights and rafters of huts as well as the masts and spars of boats. Palm fronds are used to thatch the hut roofs.

From the coconut tree villagers create many useful household items. The coconut shell serves as a bowl, cup, or cooking vessel. Carved shells become buttons, bracelets, and other ornamental objects. Palm fronds are woven into handsome mats, hats, and baskets. Visitors purchase many of these locally made products to take home as useful souvenirs.

Copra—the South Pacific's economic mainstay—comes from the coconut palm. Islanders halve the nuts and dry them, either naturally in the sun or artificially in kilns. As you travel through the countryside, you'll see halved coconuts spread out to dry in the sun, and occasional small roadside kilns.

The islanders take the dried meat to the nearest port, where it is shipped to a crushing mill. Here the oil—about 70 percent of the meat—is extracted. The resulting high grade vegetable oil is used in the manufacture of soap, margarine, cosmetics, and other products.

The coconut palm's origin in the South Pacific is somewhat of a mystery. Not considered indigenous by botanists, the tree may have originated in the Indo-Oceanian area. Migrating tribes took these coconuts with them to plant upon arrival in their new homeland. Some coconuts may have been dispersed naturally by drifting ocean currents. Today the tree grows on large commercial plantations as well as in natural groves.

tional food items. Any needed cash can be obtained through the sale of copra or surplus produce. Transportation is by canoe or foot.

Solomon islanders need little clothing in their warm, tropical climate. Village men wear western-style shorts or a wrap-around skirt known as a *lap-lap*. Women prefer cotton dresses or just a skirt. Honiarians have adopted western-style casual dress.

Language. Although English is the official language taught in school, few people speak it. Since more than 80 different languages and dialects are spoken in the Solomons, most inhabitants communicate by Pidgin English, which combines an English derived vocabulary with Melanesian grammar.

Religion. Nearly 90 percent of the people follow a form of Christianity combined with traditional native customs. Most villages have a church, and services are conducted daily.

Sports. In Honiara (and main centers on other islands) you can join local residents as they cheer for their favorite team. Rugby and association football are both very popular spectator sports. Rugby season runs from November to April and association football is played between April and October. League games take place on Saturday afternoons.

Other island sports include cricket, volleyball, basketball, and amateur boxing.

An agricultural economy

The Solomon Islands depend primarily on agricultural products for income. Chief cash crops include copra, cocoa, timber, and spices. There is a limited amount of commercial fishing and a growing interest in cattle raising.

Planning Your Trip

Once relatively isolated from tourist routes, today the Solomon Islands can be reached easily by either air or sea.

Several international air carriers including Solomon Island Airways—flying from other South Pacific countries—make regularly scheduled stops at Honiara on Guadalcanal. From the airport (Henderson Field), travelers board a bus or taxi for the 11-km/7-mile trip into town.

Both South Seas cruise ships and passenger/cargo liners make occasional stops at Point Cruz in Honiara, the Solomons' major port of call.

Pilot supervises *baggage loading on small plane at Munda airport in New Georgia Islands. Quonset hut serves as ticket office and waiting room. Small planes provide vital link in interisland transportation.*

Getting around the Solomons

Visitors to the Solomons spend most of their time in and around Honiara, the country's capital located on the island of Guadalcanal. Here you'll find several comfortable hotels, good shopping for native crafts, and many wartime historical sights.

For your town and island exploration, you can rent a car or hire a taxi. Since cabs are not metered, negotiate the fare in advance. Other transportation options include scheduled buses, serving Honiara and its nearby suburbs, and chauffeur-driven cars available through the rental car agencies.

Local tour operators offer trips around Honiara and Guadalcanal and excursions to the western Solomons,

Savo Island, Tulagi, and Malaita. Since transportation facilities are limited on these outer islands (Malaita is the only other island with bus and taxi service), tours provide the best way to see them.

Air travel. Solomon Islands Airways Ltd. (Solair) schedules regular trips from Honiara to some 20 airstrips in the Solomons. From Honiara a flightseeing tour takes visitors over World War II battlegrounds on and near Guadalcanal.

Boat trips. Both private and government interisland cargo boats, carrying some passengers, travel to many of the islands. Schedules are subject to alteration or cancellation, and the boats can be crowded not only with people but also with their pigs, dogs, and chickens. There are limited cabin accommodations.

From Honiara you can board a boat for a scenic trip along the Guadalcanal coast, take a canoe up the Matanikau River at the edge of Honiara, or see marine life from a glass-bottomed boat. One tour operator offers an overnight boat trip to Gizo in the New Georgia group stopping at 10 ports en route.

Hotels and guest houses

In the Solomon Islands, visitor accommodations are limited, modest in size, and relatively simple.

In Honiara, you choose from medium-size Hotel Mendana or Honiara Hotel, each with swimming pool and restaurant, or the small Hibiscus Lodge where each room has its own cooking facilities and refrigerator.

If you're seeking a hotel away from the downtown area, try the Tambea Village Hotel Resort 48 km/30 miles west of Honiara on a quiet beach. Guests stay in Melanesian-style bungalows and enjoy water sports. Anuha Island Resort, a 15-minute flight northeast of Honiara, is the Solomons' first full-fledged resort.

On the other islands, visitors stay in simple facilities ranging from two to six rooms. Tavanipupu Island Resort, 129 km/80 miles southeast of Guadalcanal on an island in Marau Sound, has several cottages with kitchens. Ngarando Resthouse, on Mohawk Bay in the Reef Islands 579 km/360 miles southeast of Honiara, is a fully equipped house with kitchen facilities.

Other accommodations include the Auki Lodge in the town of Auki on Malaita; and the Munda Rest House in Munda and the Gizo Hotel in Gizo, both in the New Georgia Islands group.

Dining and entertainment

In Honiara you'll find a variety of restaurants both at the hotels and in town. The Tambea Village Hotel Resort features an occasional Melanesian feast or barbecue. The feast might also include an evening of Melanesian dancing and music. At the Munda Rest House in the New Georgia Islands group, a native bamboo band may perform upon request.

Some tours include visits to local villages, where you'll sample native food and hear local music.

Shop for woodcarvings

Solomon Island craftsmen are noted for excellent woodcarvings enhanced by intricate patterns of pearl shell inlay. Traditional carvings still have an important ceremonial significance in parts of the country.

Carvings feature *nguzunguzus* (canoe prow heads symbolizing a protective spirit), model canoes, fish, turtles, birds, dance sticks (used in ritual dances), food bowls, and busts or full human figures. Woven fiber bags and traditional shell money are also of interest.

Several things should be noted before shopping for handicraft items. The asking price is considered reasonable for the workmanship involved; therefore, shoppers are requested not to bargain. Only replicas of Solomon Island artifacts can be freely exported; genuine artifacts may not be taken out of the country without special permission.

You'll find craft items for sale in Honiara shops and in some of the villages. The Women's Clubs of the Solomon Islands sell handicrafts at the Solomon Islands Museum on Mendana Avenue in Honiara.

A few duty-free shops in Honiara cater to visitors. Those who have sufficient time can have a reasonably priced suit made by one of Honiara's Chinese tailors.

You'll find most shops open from 8 A.M. to 12:30 P.M. and 2 to 5 P.M., Monday through Friday, and from 8 to 12:30 Saturday. Chinese shops stay open longer hours.

If you wish to avoid the risk of having woodcarvings or straw items confiscated by customs when you return home, the Customs Department office at Point Cruz in Honiara will fumigate articles for a small fee and issue a verifying certificate.

Recreational possibilities

In the Solomons most recreational activities center around the Honiara area. Private clubs offer opportunities for tennis, lawn bowling, snooker, darts, and golf; you also can go sailing and skin diving. Temporary club memberships are issued on request to visitors. Check locally with the Solomon Islands Tourist Authority.

If you enjoy water sports, arrange to go fishing, snorkeling, or boating at one of several resorts in the Solomon Islands including Tambea Village Hotel Resort, Munda Rest House, Ngarando Resthouse, and Tavanipupu Island Resort.

Skin diving. Numerous sunken World War II relics lie off the Solomon Islands. Iron Bottom Sound, located between Guadalcanal and the Florida Islands, is the world's largest graveyard of ships and planes.

The Skin Divers Association in Honiara sponsors diving trips on weekends. Information is available from the Solomon Islands Tourist Authority. Local tour operators also sponsor skin diving trips which include a professional diving guide and the use of scuba equipment. Tambea Village Hotel Resort has a dive service and scuba gear for hire.

Fishing. Fishermen catch sailfish, yellow-fin tuna, marlin, kingfish, bonito, and barracuda in the Solomons. Deep-sea fishing trips are arranged through the Point Cruz Yacht Club in Honiara. Tambea Village Hotel Resort also has facilities for fishing, and local tour operators have fishing boats available for charter.

Skin divers can enjoy spear fishing.

Golf. The Honiara Golf Club, located 6 km/4 miles from town, has a 9-hole golf course.

Exploring the Solomons

Some of the fiercest battles of the World War II South Pacific campaign were fought in the Solomon Islands from mid-1942 through February 1943. Even today you'll still find numerous rusting battle relics on beaches, in jungles, and at the bottom of bays.

Besides touring the battlegrounds, visitors can enjoy the village life of Solomon islanders, a slow-paced existence that has remained relatively unchanged despite war and modern influences.

Honiara, the capital

The capital and main port of the Solomons—Honiara—was a wartime creation. Before World War II, its site on the north coast of Guadalcanal was merely a coconut plantation. The country's capital was Tulagi, on the island of the same name just north of Guadalcanal.

War destroyed the town of Tulagi. In 1945 Honiara—offspring of a collection of military quonset huts west of Henderson Air Field—became the new capital.

Today, little remains of the World War II quonsets. Instead, Honiara displays a modern look with air-conditioned, concrete and glass buildings. The business district extends along a narrow coastal plain on either side of Point Cruz, a peninsula containing the town's wharf area. It was named in 1568 by explorer Alvaro de Mendaña, who landed on Guadalcanal and erected a cross on the peninsula.

Before embarking on your town and island explorations, stop at the Solomon Islands Tourist Authority office in Coronation Gardens on Mendana Avenue. Here you can pick up maps and a booklet describing local walks and drives.

Solomon Islands Museum. As you stroll down tree-lined Mendana Avenue, Honiara's main thoroughfare, stop at this interesting museum in Coronation Gardens across the street from the Hotel Mendana.

Open daily, the museum offers an opportunity for learning about various facets of the Solomon Islands. It displays traditional artifacts including weapons, tools, and fishing gear; war relics from Guadalcanal and the surrounding area; geological exhibits; and collections of butterflies and shells.

Botanical gardens. Walk through these gardens in the coolness of early morning or late afternoon. You'll find them in a wooded valley at the west end of town off Mendana Avenue.

Paths wind through a rain forest and alongside a small meandering stream trickling through a series of pools. You'll see lily ponds and a herbarium.

Other sights. Another place to visit is the public market; its colorful array of fruits and vegetables is located on Mendana Avenue near the bay. A short distance east of the market, you'll cross a bridge and discover Chinatown sprawling along the Matanikau River.

Drive into the hilly residential area behind the town for a good view of Iron Bottom Sound, graveyard of countless sunken planes and ships.

Touring Guadalcanal

Guadalcanal's one main road follows the island's northern coast on either side of Honiara for a total length of about 97 km/60 miles. Winding through lush coconut and cocoa plantations, it passes peaceful villages, deserted beaches, and mission schools. Traveling this road, you'll see some of Guadalcanal's World War II battlegrounds—the scene of heavy fighting between Allied and Japanese forces during 1942 and 1943. Today, the rusting relics of battle still lie on beaches and in grasslands near the road.

East of Honiara, you'll cross the Lungga River just before Henderson Field. Just across the bridge, a sign on your right indicates a foxhole where the airfield commandant took refuge during enemy attacks.

Allied forces had an underground field hospital near Lungga River. Some organized tours guide visitors through this facility.

Henderson Field. Located 11 km/7 miles east of Honiara, Henderson Field is the country's international airport. Begun by the Japanese in July 1942, the airfield was captured a month later by the U.S. Marines. After its completion, Henderson Field (named in memory of a Marine Corps hero of Midway) played an important role in the Allied campaign in the Solomons and other Pacific islands to the north.

Bloody Ridge. Looking south from Henderson Field, you'll see a low hill which became known as Bloody Ridge (or Edson's Ridge) during the Guadalcanal Campaign. Here one of the bloodiest battles between the U.S. Marines and Japanese forces occurred.

On September 12–14, 1942, the Japanese launched a counterattack in an effort to retake the airfield. The U.S. Marines, commanded by Colonel Merritt A. Edson, held their positions on Bloody Ridge and the Japanese were defeated.

Red Beach. Continuing east past Henderson Field, you'll come to the turnoff for Red Beach (Tenaru Beach). On August 7, 1942, the first U.S. Marines landed here on Guadalcanal—10,000 men and their equipment.

Rusting landing debris still litters the long, narrow strand of dark grey sand. A large landing barge juts into the waves and an antiaircraft gun points seaward.

West of Honiara. Traveling westward from Honiara, you pass through Kakambona village, the Japanese army command post during the Guadalcanal Campaign. The U.S. Marines attacked and captured it on January 23, 1943.

As you continue west, you'll see the rusted superstructure of a wrecked Japanese wartime supply ship lying close to the beach. Farther on you come to Cape Esperance with its steel tower and warning light.

Just before you reach Tambea Village Hotel Resort, you pass Kamimbo Bay. Many Japanese troops made their Guadalcanal escape from here at the end of the campaign in February 1943.

Malaita's manmade islands

For a different aspect of the Solomon Islands, take a trip to Malaita, 105 km/65 miles northeast of Honiara. Though most of the island's villages lie along the coastal plain or in the hills, a few are scattered off the coast on man-made islands situated in quiet lagoons.

Construction of these islands began more than 17 generations ago. They were built offshore as a retreat from warring hill tribes who knew nothing about using canoes or boats. These island settlements also provided easy access to fishing grounds and relief from mosquitoes.

Malaita islanders made the islands by stacking blocks of coral in the shallow waters of the lagoons. This coral area was then filled with rocks, sand, and soil, transported by canoe or log raft. As the villages grow, the islands' area also increases. Many of the homes are built on stilts over the water. Gardening takes place in nearby drained mangrove swamps.

A trip to Langa Langa Lagoon. From Honiara, you can take a tour to the Malaita manmade islands. You'll fly to Auki, Malaita's largest town, where a bus transports visitors south to Langa Langa Lagoon on Malaita's west coast. Here you'll board a boat to visit either Alite or Laulasi village.

Just before you reach your destination, a canoe bearing a custom priest will pass your boat. Waving his twig of leaves, he wants to ensure that no evil spirits accompany your group.

You leave your boat at the dock, then proceed onto the island where a threatening warrior party blocks your way. Appeased by a gift from the tour leader, your group will be allowed to pass.

On the tour, men will be allowed to see the men's custom houses and women will visit the women's custom houses. The structures are off limits to members of the opposite sex.

You'll also see shell money made. Village women gather in a special hut to make this money, still used on ceremonial occasions and as part of the "bride price."

Near the end of the tour you join in a native meal, served in a basket made of leaves. Sweet potatoes, cooked chicken, and fresh fruit are among the foods you'll sample. While you eat, villagers entertain with local songs and dances.

Visitors are expected to respect traditional beliefs and customs. Avoid wearing either black or red. Islanders believe these colors harm their fishing abilities and their skill in making shell money.

Other island explorations. If you stay on Malaita for several days, you might want to see other manmade islands. The Lau Lagoon, north of Malu'u near the northern end of Malaita has larger artificial islands then those of Langa Langa Lagoon. You reach this area by boat or canoe from the end of the road at Gwaunatolo.

Know Before You Go

The following practical information will help you plan your trip to the Solomon Islands.

Entry/exit procedures. All travelers will need a valid passport. Citizens of the United States and most British Commonwealth countries do not need a visa for a stay of 30 days or less. An onward travel ticket is also required.

Visitors coming from an infected area are required to have vaccinations against smallpox, yellow fever, and cholera. Since a malaria risk does exist, it is advisable to take antimalarial tablets. Check with your doctor a few weeks before your departure for treatment. (Note: Since health requirements change from time to time, check with your local public health department before leaving on your trip.)

Departing air passengers pay an airport departure tax of Solomon Islands $5.

Customs. Visitors may bring in duty free personal effects such as clothing, jewelry, a camera, portable tape recorder, 200 cigarettes, two bottles of liquor or three bottles of wine, plus other dutiable goods not exceeding Solomon Islands $30 in value. If you bring in a portable radio, you must declare it specifically on arrival.

Currency: The Solomon Islands currency is the Solomon Islands dollar (S $).

Tipping. There is no tipping in the Solomons, and visitors are requested to honor this custom.

Time. The Solomon Islands are 11 GMT (Greenwich mean time) +11. For example, when it is noon Sunday in Honiara, it is 5 P.M. Saturday in San Francisco, 1 P.M. Sunday in Auckland, and 11 A.M. Sunday in Sydney.

Weather and what to wear. The best time to visit the Solomons is between April and November when humidity is low and southeast trade winds cool the islands. Heavy rains and an occasional typhoon plague the area between November and April. Daytime temperatures seldom exceed 31°C/88°, and evening temperatures rarely drop below 22°C/72°F.

You'll be comfortable in light-weight summer clothes the year around. Visitors should refrain from wearing bathing suits or skimpy resort attire in towns and villages.

Don't forget to pack your umbrella, sunglasses, and beach shoes for reef walking.

For more information. Write the Solomon Islands Tourist Authority, P.O. Box 321, Honiara, for further information on the Solomon Islands.

MICRONESIA

Guam, Northern Marianas, Caroline and Marshall Islands

The word Micronesia means "small islands." It's an apt description of the islet-studded northwest Pacific, where more than 2,000 small islands are sprinkled across about 8 million square km/3 million square miles of ocean.

The entire land area of the 2,141 islands in this vast region totals only 1,834 square km/708 square miles. The islands range from low-lying coral specks inhabited by few as 8 people to rugged volcanic masses where the population is more than 10,000. Less than 100 of the islands and atolls are inhabited. Total population exceeds 100,000.

These far-reaching islands are divided into three island groups—the Mariana Islands, the Marshall Islands, and the Caroline Islands. Each group is subdivided—Palau, Yap, Truk, Kosrae, and Ponape (Carolines); Marshall Islands (Marshalls); and the Northern Marianas and Guam (Marianas).

The First Inhabitants

How did Micronesia's first settlers discover these tiny specks of land in the vast Pacific? Why and when did they settle here? Where did they come from? Scientists still are seeking the answers to these questions.

Carbon dating of artifacts found in the Marianas indicates that people lived in this part of Micronesia as early as 1500 B.C. Many scientists believe that Micronesia's first inhabitants migrated from the Malay Peninsula. Competent seamen and navigators, they sailed north and east across the uncharted seas of Micronesia, discovering islands as they went.

Their reasons for migration were probably similar to those of other groups who arrived in various regions of the Pacific during the same period. Perhaps they left an overcrowded land at war, or they may have been lured by an urge for adventure.

The first Micronesians were of medium stature with brown skin and straight-to-wavy black hair. Their physical characteristics were Malaysian with Polynesian traces. Since the first settlers arrived, several foreign powers have ruled Micronesia. Intermarriage has resulted, and today's Micronesians show traces of Filipino, Mexican, Spanish, Japanese, German, and American ancestry.

Early Foreign Rule

Since Ferdinand Magellan discovered Guam in 1521, many Micronesian islands have been dominated by one foreign power or another. Spain was the first, taking possession of the Marianas in 1565. Spanish galleons stopped regularly at the islands on their trade routes between Mexico and the Philippines.

Missionaries bring Christianity

In 1668 Spanish missionaries and a garrison of Spanish soldiers settled on Guam. They faced many setbacks and much fighting before dominating the strong-willed Chamorros, local inhabitants of the Marianas. Most of the male Chamorro population was killed before the survivors finally agreed to embrace the Catholic religion. The widowed women and their daughters then married the Filipino, Mexican, and Spanish troops stationed in the islands by the Spanish Empire.

The art of canoe building and many of the ancient

Guiding canoe *through shallow green waters of Truk lagoon, villagers travel by water between Micronesian coastal communities.*

Chamorro ceremonies and traditions died with the men. Despite intermarriage with Spanish troops, the island women retained the Chamorro language, foods, and weaving skills.

Islands sold to Germany

Following their 1898 defeat in the Spanish-American War, Spain sold the Caroline and the Mariana islands (except Guam) to Germany, which had already established a protectorate over the Marshall Islands. After capturing Guam during the Spanish-American War, the United States was given the island during the peace settlement.

Seeking profits from the sale of Micronesian copra, the Germans set up copra production quotas for all the islanders. However, the German reign was short. Soon after the outbreak of World War I, Japanese troops captured the islands of Micronesia. In 1920 the League of Nations mandated the islands to Japan.

Development under Japanese rule

For the next quarter century, the Japanese worked hard to develop the Micronesian islands as an important part of the Japanese Empire. They cleared fields and planted sugar cane, rice, and pineapple. They built attractive towns with Japanese-style houses, temples, shrines, and geisha houses. They constructed many roads, railroads, docking facilities, water and electrical systems, and hospitals.

In 1935 Japan withdrew from the League of Nations and prohibited foreign travel through the islands of Micronesia. Under a cloak of secrecy, they erected a vast complex of naval and air bases and war fortifications. Ships of the Imperial Navy sailed from Kwajalein in the Marshall Islands to attack Pearl Harbor in 1941. The Americans later wrested Kwajalein from the Japanese in a bloody battle.

Little remains of the advanced culture which the Japanese brought to Micronesia. What bombs didn't destroy, the jungle has reclaimed.

World War II strikes Micronesia

World War II did not spare the Micronesian islands. Bombing and bloody fighting occurred on many of them, and even those not actually invaded were touched by the war. Ponape was bombed, but damage wasn't heavy. Yap also escaped extensive damage; however, you'll find wrecks of Japanese fighter planes near Yap's airport. Many pieces of ancient Yapese stone money were crushed to build roads, and others were used whole as anchors.

Before the war, Koror in the Palau district was a bustling community, the capital of Japanese Micronesia and a Japanese vacation spot. Bombs reduced this town to rubble, and only a few foundations remain. Much of the Japanese fleet lies at the bottom of Truk Lagoon— victim of a surprise, pre-dawn American air attack on Feb. 17, 1944.

Saipan was a bustling commercial food processing center before the war. During bitter and costly fighting, much of the island's vegetation was destroyed. Near the end of the war, Saipan was one of the final major Jap-

anese strongholds taken by the Americans. During a month of desperate fighting, 3,144 Americans died. Many Japanese jumped to their deaths from cliffs at the northern end of the island rather than be captured by American forces.

Micronesia Today

In 1947 all the islands of Micronesia except Guam were included in the Trust Territory of the Pacific Islands— a United Nations trusteeship administered by the United States. Guam remained a U.S. territory.

The United States still maintains important military bases on Guam and Kwajalein. Both Bikini and Eniwetok in the Marshalls were used for post-World War II nuclear bomb testing. Radiation still is present on these islands, so the people of Bikini and Eniwetok cannot return to their home islands for some time to come.

Trusteeship to end soon

With the termination of the U.N. Trusteeship over the islands of Micronesia, political changes have occurred.

The Marianas (except Guam) are now a United States commonwealth whose residents are U.S. citizens.

The rest of Micronesia has become three separate sovereign states with full self-government and a "free association" status with the United States, which includes economic and defense provisions from the United States. These three independent groups are the Federated States of Micronesia (Ponape, Yap, Truk, and Kosrae), Republic of the Marshall Islands, and the Republic of Palau (Koror, Babelthuap, Peleliu, Angaur, Kayangel, Sonsorol, Tobi, and Pulo Anna).

In this book we divide the islands of Microneisa geographically, not politically.

Discovering today's Micronesia

Following the devastation of World War II, most Micronesians reverted to a simple village life where they farm their fields and fish the lagoons to satisfy their daily needs.

When you visit Micronesia, you'll meet these quiet, gentle, friendly people who have endured repeated invasions by foreign powers. You'll see remnants of occupation in the old Spanish fortresses on Guam, the remains of a Japanese hospital on Saipan, and the old American landing strips on Tinian. You'll also discover relics of ancient Micronesia: *latte* stones, believed to be supports for early Chamorro houses; Yapese stone money; and traditional Palau men's houses, virtually unchanged in architectural style over the centuries.

The past mingles with the changing present in Micronesia. Here you'll find motorboats and canoes; *carabao* (water buffalo) and motorbikes; lagoon-caught fish and canned food from the local grocery store; and disco as well as traditional dancing.

DIVING
A Fascinating Underwater World

Not all the delights of the tropical Pacific lie on the land. For the person who enjoys exploring the underwater world of the sea, the Pacific offers a fascinating and colorful variety of marine attractions.

You'll see an array of corals in varying shades of red, blue, purple, black, and white. There are staghorn coral growths, black coral trees, and clumps of brain coral. Exploring the watery depths you can see a variety of marine terrain— crevasses, caves, and overhangs. In some places vertical dropoffs plunge to depths of 305 meters/ 1,000 feet.

Darting among the colorful coral formations are brilliantly colored fish in all shapes and sizes —square, tubular, and flat. There are squirrel fish and groupers, parrot fish and butterfly wonders. Their colors—ranging from blue stripes on orange to black barred with silver—shimmer in clear water where visibility averages at least 30 meters/100 feet. In these waters, underwater photography is excellent.

For the shell collector, there are myriad choices. Families of shells represented in Pacific waters include augers, miters, helmets, olives, and cones.

Snorkelers also can enjoy the Pacific's fascinating underwater world, since colorful fish and coral are found just below the water's surface. Ideal water temperatures exist for both the snorkeler and diver. Year-round temperatures are a warm 27°C/80°F.

Besides interesting flora and fauna, the tropical Pacific waters are filled with sunken relics waiting to be discovered and explored. Over the centuries the reefs have claimed many sailing ships. World War II vessels and planes lie ghost-like at the bottom of the sea near the Solomons and other Pacific islands. More than 60 ships of the Japanese Imperial fleet rest at the bottom of Truk Lagoon. They were sunk during World War II in a surprise bombing attack. The lagoon has been declared a historical monument.

Other areas where divers find colorful marine life and an occasional sunken ship are the waters off Fiji's islands, Palau, French Polynesia, and New Caledonia. Most tropical Pacific islands have reef-protected lagoons ideal for exploring.

Be alert. When you venture into the tropical Pacific's underwater world, you should be wary of several things.

Coral cuts can be painful, and they become

infected easily. Some divers and snorkelers wear long-sleeved shirts and long pants while exploring reef areas. Reef walkers should always wear protective footwear. If you do get a coral cut, clean it carefully.

A variety of stinging fish and shells inhabit tropical waters. Never grab a fish with your bare hands, no matter how harmless it may look. You should also be careful in picking up shells, for the occupants of some will fight back. The shells are equipped with small stingers which inject a paralyzing toxin into their prey—usually small fish. This toxin can be painful, even deadly.

Tours and lessons. Many operators offer organized package diving tours to tropical Pacific island destinations. These tours usually include hotels or other accommodations and daily excursions. In some cases, participants stay aboard a chartered dive boat for several days at a time so they can make more than one dive per day. The boats are equipped with air compressors, diving tanks, and hot showers. Most diving tours are designed for experienced divers.

Novices can obtain diving instructions and rent diving gear at many Pacific island resorts. Instruction ranges from simple snorkeling lessons without air tanks to 5-day basic certification courses in scuba-diving.

Guam boutique *displays locally made sportswear fashioned from bright, tropical print fabrics. Open 7 days a week, shops cluster along shore of Agana Bay.*

Scuba divers *glide through Palau's clear blue waters, viewing an incredible marine world. Vividly colored tropical fish dart among coral formations, past underwater cliffs and caverns. Visitors can rent snorkel and scuba equipment.*

MARIANA, CAROLINE, & MARSHALL ISLANDS

The islands of Micronesia stretch across the western Pacific like the beads of a far-flung coral necklace. Though bearing some of the deepest scars of World War II, they are among the most unspoiled and varied islands in the Pacific. Most are unknown to outsiders. However, a few—such as Saipan, Truk, Yap, Peleliu, Kwajalein, Ulithi, and Majuro—stir the memories of many Pacific war veterans.

How have these lesser-known islands maintained their solitude and lack of development? For many years they were off limits to the casual visitor. Once restrictions were eased, the prospective visitor faced problems of transportation and accommodations.

But times have changed. Now frequent flights transport travelers into the area. Modern accommodations range from small but comfortable hotels to large, luxury resorts. Local tour options offer varied sightseeing opportunities. Yet despite these new tourist developments, most of the islands remain unspoiled and uncrowded.

A Multitude of Islands

Micronesia's islands wind through vast reaches of ocean, extending about 2,200 km/1,367 miles from north to south and about 3,701 km/2,300 miles from east to west. More than 2,000 specks of land cluster into three island groups—the Marianas, the Carolines, and the Marshalls. Total land area covers only about 1,833 square km/708 square miles. Guam, the largest island in Micronesia, is the main center for exploring the other islands.

High islands and coral atolls

The many islands of Micronesia range from substantial high volcanic islands to tiny, low-lying coral islands and atolls. As island topography varies, so does the vegetation. On the high islands, mangrove swamps cluster at lower elevations and forests cover the uplands. Expanses of sand dotted with groups of coconut palms mark the atolls.

Island wildlife includes bats, large monitor lizards, deer, and coconut crabs. Crocodiles live in the Palau swamplands.

Micronesia's People

Micronesia is actually an umbrella term covering a collection of islands whose people have many similarities but also some striking differences. They all share the uncomplicated life patterns associated with tropical island villages and a deep love for the island on which they were born.

The indigenous population of the islands is Micronesian, descended from people who migrated from Southeast Asia as long ago as 1500 B.C. Islanders who live nearer the Philippines and the Asian mainland more closely resemble Filipinos and Asians. The people on the more easterly islands near Polynesia have Polynesian characteristics. Locally, the people of each island are known by the district in which they live—Yapese, Marshallese, Palauan. The native people from Guam and the Northern Marianas are known as Chamorros.

Contrasts of culture

Customs differ by island group, with strong allegiances within each group to local folklore, ancestors, leaders, and social structure. Isolated islands have produced their own local adaptations and inventions—such as different ways of assembling canoes. Social organization may be matrilineal in one group, caste conscious in another, and chief-dominated in a third.

Architecture. The ways of the modern world have influenced today's Micronesian house builders. Traditional construction methods and materials have been supplanted by tin, plank, plywood, and concrete.

Occasional devastating typhoons menace all buildings. In some island districts, many families now dwell in typhoon relief houses—plywood rectangles supplied by the government.

Despite modernized construction and destructive typhoons, thatch-roofed huts and traditional architecture still exist. Distinctive examples are the men's houses of Yap and Palau.

Language. Nine distinct languages and many dialects are spoken in Micronesia. The Chamorros, in the Northern Marianas and Guam, and the Palauans speak a language similar to Malay. The language of Yap, Ulithi, Truk, Ponape, Kosrae, and the Marshall Islands is considered to be Micronesian. The Kapingamarangian and Nukuoroan people in the Ponape district speak a Polynesian tongue. You'll also find English and Japanese spoken.

Dress. Except in the Yap district, traditional dress generally has disappeared from the district center islands. Shirts, T-shirts, and trousers are male garb. Most women wear bright print dresses.

(Continued on page 112)

In the Yap district men commonly wear the *thu* (loin cloth), while women can still be seen in voluminous Yapese grass skirts.

Religion. Either Catholicism or Congregationalism is followed by a large percentage of Micronesians. Other religious groups represented included Episcopalians, Jehovah's Witnesses, Lutherans, Mormons, and Seventh-Day Adventists.

A subsistence economy

Copra is the main cash crop in Micronesia's basically subsistence economy. The sugar cane fields and pineapple plantations developed by the Japanese were allowed to revert to jungle after the war. Attempts are now being made to diversify agriculture and to develop a fishing industry.

Supplementing the receipts from agricultural products is income generated by government and tourism—and on Guam, the military.

Guam

The largest land mass between Hawaii and the Philippines is Guam, hub of United States activity in the North Pacific. Although about one-third of the island's real estate is occupied by the military, there's still plenty of open space for island residents (112,000 including the military population).

Located at the southern end of the Marianas chain, Guam covers an area of 541 square km/209 square miles. A hilly island, it has savannalike expanses punctuated by jungle-filled valleys and ravines. Bays, beaches, and rocky cliffs mark its rugged coast. Guam offers the visitor a year-round warm climate, warm surf, uncrowded beaches, and a number of resort hotels.

Guam has become a pleasant stopover point for travelers returning from a temple tour of the Orient. For many Americans and Japanese, it holds memories of World War II. Guam has become a favorite for Japanese honeymooners—a tropical haven for them in terms of reasonable flight time and air fare.

Getting there and getting settled

Guam gained a reputation as a "crossroads of the Pacific" during the days when Spanish galleons plied the hemp routes between Acapulco and Manila. Today a number of international air carriers schedule regular flights to Guam International Airport from the Orient, Southeast Asia, South Pacific, and United States. From the airport it's a 5-km/3-mile taxi ride into Agana, the island's main town. Many hotels have courtesy cars for airport pickup.

Some passenger/cargo liners also stop at Guam.

In and around Guam. Bus service operates weekdays between the resort hotel area and downtown Agana. Taxis are relatively expensive. The best way to tour the rest of Guam is by rental car or on an organized tour. Local operators offer a variety of tours.

If you are touring Guam on your own, you'll want to obtain a copy of the sightseeing map issued by the Guam Visitors Bureau. The map is keyed to 150 route signs placed by the GVB to guide visitors to places of interest. The GVB office is located at 1220 Pale San Vitores Road in Tamuning.

Where to stay. Guam offers a number of new resort hotels along Ipao Beach on Tumon Bay, about 10 minutes from the airport. Amenities include restaurants, shops, and various water sport and beach activities. Beachfront hotels include the Fujita Guam Tumon Beach Hotel, Guam Dai-Ichi, Guam Hilton, Guam Hotel Okura, Guam Reef Hotel, Guam Horizon Hotel, Pacific Islands Hotel, Pacific Islands Club, Guam Plaza, and Terraza Tumon Villa. Near Merizo is another beach resort, Cocos Island.

Away from the beach area in downtown Agana are the Cliff Hotel, Downtown Hotel, and Micronesian Hotel.

Dining pleasures. You'll find a surprisingly wide choice of cuisine—Japanese, Indonesian, Chinese, Italian, Korean, Polynesian, German, Spanish, and American—at Guam restaurants. Dining spots you might want to try are Kurumaya Restaurant for teppan-style cooking, Istemewa for Indonesian dishes, Kim Chee's Cabana for Korean specialties, Salzburg Chalet for Austrian cooking, Don Pedros for Spanish fare, and Po Po's for Polynesian delicacies.

Inquire at your hotel if any of the villages on Guam plan a fiesta during your stay. Usually held in honor of a village patron saint, these weekend, all-day affairs offer a great variety of local foods. You can sample barbecued ribs, red rice (colored with achote seed), taro, yams, chicken kelaguen (with lemon, onions, and coconut meat), roast pig, and bananas baked in coconut milk. Some hotels hold fiesta-type dinners regularly.

Shopping bargains. Guam's duty-free port status makes it a bargain center for international products. You can buy pearls, cameras, electronic equipment, watches, perfumes, liquor, and tropical resort clothing and sportswear. Shoppers find good selections of merchandise both in hotel shops and in Agana's stores.

At the public market on Marine Drive near Paseo Park you can browse for local handicraft items including shell products, ceramics, woodcarvings, and stick dolls.

Most stores are open Monday to Saturday from 10 A.M. to 9 P.M. and on Sunday from noon to 6.

A recreational playground. Water sports are the most popular recreational activities in Guam. An average year-round temperature of 28°C/82°F makes swimming, surfing, and water-skiing pleasant.

Snorkelers take advantage of miles of shallow reef-protected waters. Skin divers enjoy exploring shipwrecks in Apra Harbor—the German vessel *Cormoran* was scuttled here during World War I, and the Japanese ship *Tokai Maru* sunk during World War II. Snorkelers can rent or buy equipment at Agana stores, diving centers, and hotel shops. You'll find diving gear for rent at both the Coral Reef Marine Center and the Marianas Divers in Agana.

You can rent sailboats and canoes at hotel stands along the beach on Tumon Bay.

Reeling them in. Game fish including tuna, skipjack, mahi mahi, and sailfish abound in the waters off Guam.

FESTIVAL TIME

Residents of Micronesia observe all the national holidays of the United States. In addition, they celebrate a number of annual local events.

Almost every month, one or more of the villages on Guam holds a religious festival honoring its patron saint. These festivals usually include a parish procession on Saturday, and a special mass and community feast on Sunday. To learn about village fiestas during your visit, check with the Guam Visitors Bureau upon arrival.

Other major celebrations in Micronesia include the following:

January—April

New Year's Day. On January 1 the New Year is celebrated throughout Micronesia with family gatherings and feasts.

Saipan Laguna Regatta. In mid-February sailboat races off Saipan draw Pacific-wide participation.

Discovery Day. Ferdinand Magellan's 1521 landing at Umatac Bay is celebrated at Umatac village on Guam on March 7.

Marianas Covenant Day. The people of the Northern Marianas honor this public holiday on March 24.

Annual Saipan Ocean Swim. People from all over the Pacific congregate to compete in this swim meet held in Saipan's lagoon in March or April.

May—August

Law Day. On May 1 Micronesians gather for speeches, ceremonies, and sports events.

San Jose Fiesta. In early May the people of Tinian and Saipan honor the patron saint of the people of San Jose with processions, feasts, sports contests, and dances.

San Isidro Fiesta. Saipan's patron saint also is honored in May with religious ceremonies, a feast, and traditional songs and dances in Chalan Kanoa village.

Liberation Day. In addition to celebrating United States' independence on July 4, the people of Saipan commemorate their liberation from the Japanese. Events include beauty contests, a parade, dances, and sports and carnival events.

Micronesia Day. The 1965 founding of the Congress of Micronesia is observed throughout Micronesia on July 12.

Guam's Liberation Day. On July 21 the people of Guam cele-brate the shaping of Guam's history, the 1944 liberation from the Japanese, and the 1977 constitutional convention. Activities include athletic events, contests, and concerts.

Palau District Annual Fair. In August, a week-long fair in Koror features sports events, parades, traditional music and dance performances, and displays of Palauan-made shell, wood, and woven handicraft items.

September—December

Fiesta of San Francisco de Borja. In early October Rota honors its patron saint with food, music, dancing, cockfights, mass, and a silent procession.

United Nations Day. Most districts celebrate the founding of the United Nations with parades, sports events, and traditional dances on October 24.

All Saints Day and All Souls Day. On November 1 and 2, Micronesians clean and decorate graves and hold mass.

Feast of the Immaculate Conception. Guam's patron saint is honored on December 8 with a fiesta and Roman Catholic mass and a procession in Agana.

Charter fishing boats can be hired at the boat basin in central Agana and the charter pier in Merizo at the southern end of the island.

Land sports. Athletes who prefer to keep both feet on dry land can play tennis at a number of courts throughout the town. Many courts are lighted for night play. You'll find that a number of the resort hotels along Ipao Beach on Tumon Bay have tennis courts.

Guam's two golf courses open to the public are the Country Club of the Pacific and Windward Hills Golf and Country Club, both with 18-hole courses. They are located between Talofofo and Yona on Guam's southeastern coast—about a 30-minute drive south from Tumon Bay.

Strolling around Agana

Agana, Guam's main town, is located about midway along the west coast of the island. Once a sleepy village, today Agana is caught in an era of scrambling growth. Dozens of new buildings line Marine Drive, the main road into town from the airport.

Although much of downtown Agana is now new, you still catch glimpses of the island's architectural heritage on a short stroll through the downtown area.

Dulce Nombre de Maria Cathedral. Begin your walk at Guam's largest cathedral, located off O'Hara Street several blocks east of Marine Drive. The church was built on the site of an earlier structure destroyed during World War II.

Skinner Plaza. One block south of the cathedral, you come to Skinner Plaza dedicated to Guam's first civilian governor—Carlton Skinner. Bordered by flame trees, the park has a fountain and two monuments to local war heroes.

Spanish bridge. Continuing south another block from the plaza, you'll find an old Spanish bridge in a parklike setting. Built in 1800 and restored after World War II, the bridge was once part of a road leading from a Spanish fort at Umatac to Agana.

Plaza de Espana. Now return to the Plaza de Espana, located next to the cathedral. In this park, you'll see some of Guam's best examples of early Spanish architecture. For 160 years Guam was ruled from buildings on this site.

The Azotea is all that remains of the Spanish Governor's Palace; once his back porch, the veranda today still is used on special occasions. The small, round building with wrought ironwork nearby was called the "Chocolate House"; it dates from 1736. Here the wives of Spanish governors served hot chocolate to elite guests.

Guam Museum. You'll discover an interesting collection of artifacts reflecting Guam's history in this small museum located behind the Azotea. Built in 1736, the building was originally a guardhouse. The museum is open from 1 to 4:30 P.M. daily except Saturday.

Latte Stone Park. Located across the street from Plaza de Espana, this park honors an ancient civilization. The rough-hewn limestone columns called *latte* (pronounced lah-*tee*) stones are believed to be foundation supports for early Chamorro houses. The stones were moved to this park from the Fena River area in south central Guam.

Government House. If you hike up the hill from Latte Stone Park, you'll come to the present governor's official residence.

Fort Apugan. Adjacent to Government House stand the remains of a Spanish fortress built in 1800 (also called Fort Santa Agueda). During World War II, Japanese guns commanded the harbor from this high site. The fort offers visitors a panoramic view of the Agana area.

A trip around Guam

You can see even more of Guam's historical sights on a day excursion from Agana around the southern end of the island. On this loop trip, you'll wind along spectacular coasts, travel over mountain passes, and meander through valleys dotted with banana plantations. Besides seeing ancient Spanish ruins and charming Chamorro villages, you'll be reminded of the impact of World War II on this tiny island. You'll see invasion beaches at Asan and Agat Bay; Japanese bunkers; and coastal defense emplacements.

Agat stone bridge. Just south of Agat near Nimitz Beach, a sign directs you to the ruins of a stone bridge built in the 1700s. It was part of the old Spanish coastal road to Umatac.

Umatac. At Umatac, a small Chamorro village clusters along the shores of a cove. A monument honors Ferdinand Magellan, who discovered Guam in 1521 and reputedly landed here. Visit the ruins of Fort Nuestra Señora on the hill overlooking the town. The old Spanish sentry box still stands above the bay.

Merizo. Located near the south end of the island, Merizo boasts the oldest Spanish building continuously occupied in Guam—the parish house alongside the village church. It was built in 1856.

In Merizo you can arrange for boats to take you waterskiing, scuba diving, fishing, coral garden viewing, or sightseeing along the coast or out to nearby Cocos Island (a good picnicking and sunning spot). Cocos Island Resort is Guam's newest and most complete resort development.

Inarajan. Returning along the east coast, you pass through Inarajan, a town whose Spanish influence is evident in its narrow streets and old buildings.

The villagers have recreated a century-old Chamorro village in the area. In bamboo and palm-thatched huts, village elders demonstrate "life crafts" such as making salt from seawater, weaving hats and mats, and grinding corn. This replica village is open every afternoon.

Two Lovers' Point. Back on the west coast of Guam, the road north from Agana takes you past the hotels on Tumon Bay to the turnoff for Two Lovers' Point. From this clifftop you'll have an excellent view along the coastline. According to island legend, two lovers jumped to their death from the 102-meter/334-foot cliff rather than live apart.

The Northern Marianas

The Northern Marianas stretch northward from Guam for about 644 km/400 miles. Largest islands in the group—and the only ones with airstrips—are Saipan, Rota, and Tinian. Other populated islands include Pagan, Agrihan, and Alamagan. Total population of the district is 17,000.

A few basic facts

Local airlines—South Pacific Island Airways and Air Micronesia—provide regularly scheduled service between Guam and Saipan, Rota, and Tinian.

There is also ferry service between Saipan and Tinian. Field trip vessels make irregular stops in the Northern Marianas.

Island visitor transportation includes taxis, organized tours, and rentals (cars, jeeps, mopeds, bikes). There is public transportation between hotels and stores.

Places to stay. Saipan offers a variety of large, resort-type accommodations and smaller hotels. You can choose from the Saipan Grand Hotel, Hafadai Beach Hotel, Marianas Hotel, Royal Taga Hotel, Saipan Beach, and Hyatt Regency Saipan.

Rota's moderately sized hotels include Blue Peninsula Hotel (23 rooms), Rota Coconut Village (20 rooms), and Rota Pau-Pau Hotel (50 rooms). On Tinian you can stay in small establishments such as the Fleming Hotel (15 rooms).

(Continued on page 117)

Yapese women *dressed in voluminous grass skirts relate traditional tales in song and dance. Distinctive customs, architecture, and dress characterize the culture of Yap.*

Ponape woman *squats in partially dammed stream to wash clothes. Numerous swift-flowing rivers drain island's lush, mountainous slopes.*

GUAM

MI 0 ... 5 ... 10
KM 0 ... 10 ... 20

Anderson Air Force Base
Yigo
Two Lovers' Point
Dededo
Tumon Bay
Tamuning
Agana
Asan   Toto
Sinajana
Ordot   Mangilao
Apra Harbor   Chalan Pago
Pago Bay
Santa Rita
Agat Bay   Yona
Agat
Talofofo
Talofofo Bay
Umatac
Merizo   Inarajan
COCOS

SAIPAN

Banzai Cliff
San Roque   Suicide Cliff
Tanapag Harbor   Tanapag
Garapan   Capitol Hill
Mt. Tagpochau
Oleai
Susupe   San Vincente
Chalan Kanoa
San Antonio   *Magicienne Bay*

Enola Gay   World War II airstrips
(atomic bomb
loading pit)
Cattle Ranch

TINIAN

San Jose
House of Taga

MI 0 ... 5 ... 10
KM 0 ... 10 ... 20

AGUIJAN

ROTA

Latte stone
Songsong

0 1 2 3 4
0 2 4 6 8

Sosanjaya Bay

PONAPE

Net   Cultural Center
Kolonia
Sokehs   Uh
Nan
Kiti
Metala

0 ... 5 ... 10 MI
0 ... 10 ... 20 KM

PAGAN

SAIPAN
TINIAN
ROTA

GUAM

JOHNSTON ISLA

N

MICRONESIA

BIKINI ATOLL

ENIWETOK ATOLL

YAP

PALAU
KOROR   BABELTHUAP
PELELIU

TRUK

PONAPE
KOSRAE

KWAJALEIN ATOLL

MAJURO ATOLL

NUKUORO ATOLL

PALAU

KAYANGEL
Ngarchelong
Ngardmau
Ngaremlengui   Ngaraard
BABELTHUAP
Ngatpang
Melekeiok
Aimeliik   Ngchesar
Airai
Koror
KOROR
ISLAND
FLOATING
GARDENS
ISLANDS

PELELIU

ANGAUR

0 ... 5 ... 10 MI
0 ... 10 ... 20 KM

YAP

RUMUNG
YAP
MAP
Fanif
YAP
Weloy   Gagil
Colonia
Dalipebinaw
Kanifay   Ruul   GAGIL-TOMIL
Giliman

MI 0 1 2 3 4
KM 0 2 4 6 8 10

TRUK

FALAS   FALO
MOEN
ROMANUM
DUB
TOL   PARAM
PATA   UDOT   ETEN
FALA   FEFAN
BEGUETS   TARIK   UMA
POLLE

0 ... 5 ... 10 MI   0 ... 10 ... 20 KM

RONGRONG
MI 0 ... 5 ... 10
KM 0 ... 10

Laura
MAJURO ISLAND
Uli
Da

MAJURO

Recreation. All the islands are noted for beautiful, secluded beaches and warm lagoon waters. Popular sports include scuba diving, sailing, swimming, water-skiing, and fishing.

Saipan has a 9-hole golf course. You'll find tennis courts on some islands, but bring your own racket.

Shopping. While browsing in shops, look for local craft items like shell handbags and necklaces, and woven products.

Saipan, the largest island

Largest of the Northern Marianas, Saipan covers an area of 122 square km/47 square miles. The island is bounded on the west by gentle, reef-protected beaches, on the east by a rugged rocky coast, and on the north by dramatic inland and coastal cliffs. Many of Saipan's palm trees were destroyed during the war. The island is now extensively covered with a mass of *tangan-tangan,* a nondescript tree that holds soil in place.

Touring Saipan has a special poignancy. Here you'll see many relics of World War II—tanks, landing craft, gun emplacements, ghost towns, the old Japanese command post, and war memorials.

Garapan. Now overgrown by tangan-tangan, this village was once a major seaport for the Japanese with a population of about 15,000. You still can see the ruins of the prewar Japanese hospital and old Japanese jail where Amelia Earhart may have been imprisoned.

Command post. Near the northern end of Saipan above Marpi Point, you can see the concrete-reinforced natural cave which was the final Japanese command post on the island to fall to American forces in one of the most bitterly fought amphibious battles of World War II.

From here you can also view Suicide Cliff and Banzai Cliff. Hundreds of Japanese, including entire families, plunged to their deaths from these cliffs rather than be taken prisoner during the 1944 battle for Saipan.

Several memorials, recently erected by the Japanese, now stand atop the cliffs.

Tinian, Saipan's neighbor

From Saipan, you can travel to Tinian just 5 km/3 miles to the south. Crumbling airstrips at the northern end of the island are reminders of Tinian's importance during World War II.

From one of these airstrips the B-29 *Enola Gay* took

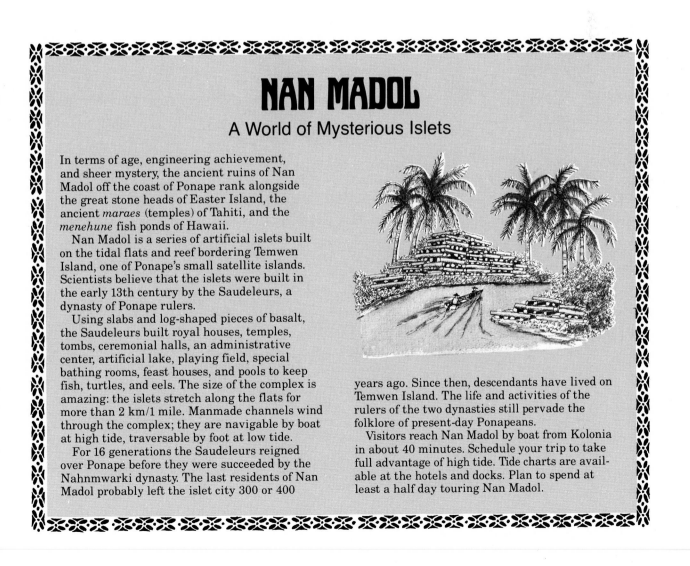

NAN MADOL
A World of Mysterious Islets

In terms of age, engineering achievement, and sheer mystery, the ancient ruins of Nan Madol off the coast of Ponape rank alongside the great stone heads of Easter Island, the ancient *maraes* (temples) of Tahiti, and the *menehune* fish ponds of Hawaii.

Nan Madol is a series of artificial islets built on the tidal flats and reef bordering Temwen Island, one of Ponape's small satellite islands. Scientists believe that the islets were built in the early 13th century by the Saudeleurs, a dynasty of Ponape rulers.

Using slabs and log-shaped pieces of basalt, the Saudeleurs built royal houses, temples, tombs, ceremonial halls, an administrative center, artificial lake, playing field, special bathing rooms, feast houses, and pools to keep fish, turtles, and eels. The size of the complex is amazing: the islets stretch along the flats for more than 2 km/1 mile. Manmade channels wind through the complex; they are navigable by boat at high tide, traversable by foot at low tide.

For 16 generations the Saudeleurs reigned over Ponape before they were succeeded by the Nahnmwarki dynasty. The last residents of Nan Madol probably left the islet city 300 or 400

years ago. Since then, descendants have lived on Temwen Island. The life and activities of the rulers of the two dynasties still pervade the folklore of present-day Ponapeans.

Visitors reach Nan Madol by boat from Kolonia in about 40 minutes. Schedule your trip to take full advantage of high tide. Tide charts are available at the hotels and docks. Plan to spend at least a half day touring Nan Madol.

Fishermen *haul nets into shallow water along Saipan's shore. Reef-protected western coast of island offers long stretches of empty beach. Rugged cliffs, rocky shores, and secluded pocket beaches mark eastern shore.*

Rusting wreckage *of Japanese fighter plane lies half buried in coral sands on Elato Atoll in Caroline Islands southeast of Yap. Atoll dwellers paddle outrigger canoes to visit neighboring islets.*

off to drop the atomic bomb on Hiroshima in August 1945. A peace memorial now marks the plane's departure point.

At the southern end of the island, you'll find remnants of an earlier era in Tinian's history. The House of Taga, near the island's main village of San Jose, includes some of the best-preserved Micronesian latte stones.

The island's central plateau supports a flourishing beef cattle industry.

Rota, a tiny island

Tiny Rota—only 83 square km/32 square miles—is located between Guam and Tinian. A quiet island with good beaches, it also has historic reminders.

An ancient Chamorro village at Mochon Beach near the northern tip of the island has latte stones. Nearby is a latte stone quarry.

The Caroline Islands

Lying south of Guam, the Caroline Islands stretch from the Palau district in the west to the Kosrae district in the east. Other island districts in the Carolines include Yap and Truk.

A few basic facts

Local airlines providing regularly scheduled service to the district centers of Yap, Palau, Truk, and Ponape include Air Micronesia, Air Nauru, and South Pacific Island Airways. Field trip vessels also make irregular stops at various islands in the group.

Rental cars are available at hotels in the district centers, but roads can be rough. Motorbikes and four-wheel-drive vehicles also may be rented. Local operators sponsor sightseeing tours by bus and boat.

Places to stay. On Yap, accommodations are available at two small hotels—the ESA Hotel and Rai View Hotel. Palau visitors can choose from a variety of hotels on Koror, most of them small. They include the New Koror Carp Island Resort, NACL Hotel, Nikko Palau Hotel, and Palau Hotel.

Truk hotels, on Moen Island, include the Christopher Inn and Truk Continental. All of Ponape's accommodations are small—Cliff Rainbow Hotel, Hifumi Inn, Kawaii Inn, Hotel Nan Madol. Hotel Pohnpei, South Park Hotel, and the Village.

Shopping for craft items. Palau is known for finely carved, wooden storyboards, an ancient art still maintained by skillful craftsmen. In Koror you can see prisoners carving them at the jail.

Other craft items of special note include carved wooden dance paddles and war clubs from Ponape, and grass skirts from Yap.

Recreational activities. Water sports are popular throughout the Caroline Islands. Skin divers head for Truk Lagoon and the islands of Palau. Tennis players find courts on both Koror and Ponape. Deep-sea fishing is excellent in many areas.

Yap, where traditions remain

Heading southwest from Guam, you'll come to the Yap district in the Western Carolines. The district center of Yap is actually four islands separated by narrow sea channels. Reminiscent of New Caledonia, Yap is noted for its red earth, fine beaches, and palm groves. Its interior stretches of dry uplands are clothed in grass, ferns, and scrub. Colonia is the island's urban center. Yap's road system is not lengthy, but the roads are good.

Least developed of any of Micronesia's island groups, the Yap district also seems the least interested in such development. Traditional culture is deeply ingrained in the Yapese way of life—customs, architecture, and dress have remained unchanged for centuries.

In local villages you can see examples of Yap's famous, doughnut-shaped stone money and some of the traditional *falus* (men's houses).

Falus. A number of well-preserved falus still stand in various parts of the main island. Centuries old in design, they rest on stone foundations, the floor a short distance above the ground. Open sided to allow the cooling trade winds to sweep through, the falus have steep, thatched roofs towering 15 meters/50 feet high. Symbolic decorations mark the thatch above the entrance.

Stone money. Northernmost in the cluster of Yap's four islands is the one claiming to have the largest piece of stone money: 4 meters/12 feet in diameter. Balabat village, on the south edge of Colonia, has Yap's largest stone money bank. You'll also find two falus in the same area. The quiet village of Dalipebinaw, on the west coast of the main island, claims to have some of the region's oldest and most valuable stone money.

Palau, world of green islets

In the Palau district you'll see a fascinating collection of black-green, jungle-clad hills, coastal mangrove swamps, and a seemingly endless number of clear, placid channels threading between countless islands.

Travelers flying into the Palau district (a 1-hour flight southwest of Guam) land on the big island of Babelthuap, then travel south to the neighboring island of Koror, the district center.

Seeing Koror. Busy Koror has a varied array of stores, handicraft shops, nightclubs, boat docks, and busy fisheries. Sprawling over flatlands and across undulating hills, the town is nearly submerged in lush greenery.

While in Koror, visit the local museum, housed in the former Japanese Communications Center. Its collection includes artifacts from many Micronesian islands, World War II relics, and some fascinating photographs of the Koror area as it looked at the height of its development under the Japanese.

You'll also find an *abai* (Palauan men's house) on the grounds of the museum. The Palauans decorate the thatch above the abai entrance with intricately carved and decorated storyboards. These long wood planks illustrate scenes from local legends.

Palau's Floating Islands. South of Koror are Palau's Floating Garden Islands—land masses that resemble huge green pin cushions. About 200 islands lie in clusters, creating a labyrinth of channels and protected bays. The best way to see the islands is by boat.

Rounded limestone knobs undercut by centuries of tidal action, the Floating Garden Islands are smothered in trees, shrubs, and vines that grow in an impenetrable mass right to the waterline. Few of the islands are inhabited because of the dense growth, the steep rise of rock from the water, and the sharp undercut that makes landing on most islands extremely difficult.

Visiting Babelthuap. Despite Babelthuap's intriguing appearance, most Palau visitors bypass Babelthuap en route to Koror.

On Babelthuap you can explore fascinating caves, some a part of island lore, others used as hangars for Japanese seaplanes. Island villages have preserved Palauan culture in an almost unchanged state. You'll discover jungle waterfalls that may be among the most beautiful in the tropical Pacific and stone pillars marking the ruins of what may have been a giant abai large enough to shelter more than 1,000 people.

Most of Babelthuap's attractions must be reached by boat, since little remains of the old Japanese road system.

Truk, a fascinating lagoon

In the eastern Carolines, a collection of verdant islands lie within the protective reef enclosing Truk Lagoon. Roughly triangular in shape, the lagoon measures 64 km/40 miles at its widest point and encloses an area of 2,130 square km/822 square miles. This lagoon and the marine world beneath its surface are Truk's key attractions. Arriving travelers land on Moen Island, but most of Truk's interesting spots are found elsewhere.

Exploring the lagoon. For the scuba diver, the lagoon holds a dual fascination: the natural world of coral and tropical fish counterbalanced by submerged World War II wreckage. More than 60 ships of the Japanese Imperial fleet were sunk in the lagoon during a surprise bombing attack in February 1944.

The superstructures of some of the hulls rest just below the water surface, and some masts jut above the water. Nondivers can share a little of this underwater world by snorkeling or cruising over the wrecks in a glass-bottomed boat.

Because the lagoon has been declared a monument, salvage and souvenir taking of relics are prohibited by law. Divers should obtain a permit from the Truk Office of Tourism before diving around the ships.

Excursion to Dublon Island. Since Truk was Japan's major Micronesian naval installation, the Japanese developed the area with airfields, seaplane ramps, underground hangars, submarine pens, huge docking facilities, hospitals, extensive communications installations, gun emplacements, and roadways.

Before the war, more than 40,000 Japanese lived on Dublon Island, the Japanese naval command headquarters. If you take a boat excursion to the island today, you'll discover that the jungle has reclaimed much of the prewar development. Trees and vines nearly cover the remains of the roads and buildings.

On a walking tour from the docks, you'll stroll along one of the overgrown roads past the ruins of a Japanese hospital, an elaborate geisha house, and other installations that partially survived the war.

Ponape, a mountainous island

One high island—Ponape—and eight atolls comprise the Ponape district, located in the easternmost part of the Carolines.

Compared with other Micronesian islands, Ponape is large: 303 square km/117 square miles. Ponape Island is actually the slightly submerged remains of a classic, shield-shaped volcano, now encircled by a coral reef that protects a narrow lagoon.

Its rugged central mountains, 17 of which rise above 488 meters/1,600 feet, taper off to the sea. Cutting their flanks are long, deep valleys marked by turbulent rivers and dramatic, cascading waterfalls.

Dense, mossy rain forests, almost perpetually in the clouds, clothe Ponape's upper elevations. The island's lowlands are planted with breadfruit and coconut trees. Extensive mangrove swamp areas border the coastline; some of the swamps are planted in taro.

Kolonia, the only town. Ponape's only town is Kolonia (not to be confused with Colonia on Yap), the government and commercial center for the district. Rising across the lagoon that fronts the town is the profile of Sokehs, a soaring promontory sometimes called the "Diamond Head" of Ponape.

In and near Kolonia, you'll find a few fragmentary mementos of former governing powers: a moss-covered Spanish fort, an agricultural station begun by the Germans, an encircling road and fortifications built by the Japanese.

Ponape's cultural center. A visitor can easily spend a half day or more at Ponape's Nett Cultural Center. Inspired by Hawaii's Polynesian Cultural Center, a young Ponapean returned to his homeland and organized a cultural center for Ponape with the cooperation of the people of his community.

Visitors arrive at the center by car or canoes that they paddle themselves. At the center—a simple collection of thatched sheds set in a shady spot beside the river—you'll see Ponapeans demonstrate local dances and handicrafts. They'll make and serve you some *sakau*, Ponape's tongue-numbing, potent brand of *kava* (see page 61).

Other sights. A prime target for Ponape visitors is Nan Madol. For more information on this intriguing ancient city, see page 117.

The Marshall Islands

The Marshall Islands—a collection of 29 low-lying atolls and 5 small coral islands—lie east of the Caroline Islands and the Marianas. Total land area covers only about 181 square km/70 square miles.

A few basic facts

Air Micronesia, Air Nauru, and Air Tungaru provide transportation to and from the Marshalls. The Airline of the Marshall Islands provides regularly scheduled domestic flights to many of the atolls in the Marshalls.

You'll find taxis at the airport. You can explore the island of Majuro by rental car or on a tour.

Accommodations. Majuro has only two small hotels— the Eastern Gateway Hotel (28 rooms) and the Hotel Majuro (30 rooms).

Buying craft items. Favorite souvenirs are local woodcarvings such as small canoes and stick charts. Charts of this type were used in ocean navigation by early Micronesians.

Recreational possibilities. Swimming, shell collecting, snorkeling, scuba diving, and fishing are prime attractions on Majuro. Visitors can rent small boats from hotel concessionaires. Cruisers may be chartered for deep-sea fishing trips.

Touring Majuro

Located near the southern end of the Marshall Islands, Majuro is the major tourist center for the group. Majuro Atoll itself is a meandering thread of reef and palm-studded sand surrounding a huge turquoise lagoon.

Outside the reef, the ocean waves pound endlessly; inside, the calm waters of the lagoon lap gently on the white sand beaches. The lagoon itself sparkles like a lake. At its highest point, the land surrounding the lagoon is only a few feet above sea level.

Majuro's strip of land is only a kilometer/½ mile wide at its widest point, but it stretches so far along the western edge of the lagoon that Majuro boasts the longest road in Micronesia. Beginning near the airport, the road extends 56 km/35 miles to the beautiful little mission village at Laura Point on Majuro's northern tip.

Know Before You Go

The following practical information will help you plan your trip to Micronesia.

Entry/exit procedures. United States citizens need only proof of citizenship. Other visitors will need a current passport. All visitors are required to have an onward travel ticket.

Travelers arriving from an infected area will need smallpox, yellow fever, and cholera inoculations. Typhoid, paratyphoid, and tetanus shots are also recommended. (Since health requirements change from time to time, check with your local public health department before leaving on your trip.)

There is no departure tax.

Currency. The United States dollar is used throughout Micronesia.

Tipping. On Guam a 10 to 20 percent tip is expected. Tipping is beginning to be customary on other Micronesian islands.

Time. Because the islands of Micronesia are scattered across a great expanse of the Pacific Ocean, they are included in several time zones. Agana, Guam, the principal arrival point in Micronesia, is GMT (Greenwich mean time) +10.

For example, when it is noon on Sunday in Agana, it is 6 P.M. Saturday in San Francisco, 2 P.M. Sunday in Auckland, and noon Sunday in Sydney.

Weather and what to wear. Micronesia's islands share a common tropical climate: hot, with high humidity. Temperatures rarely drop below 21°C/70°F or exceed 32°C/90°F, but humidity can make them seem higher. The fall and winter months—November to April north of the equator—are the best months to visit. The rainy period can extend from May to October. Typhoons are possible almost any time, but usually occur only once or twice a year.

Lightweight summer clothing is worn throughout the year in Micronesia. Short shorts are considered inappropriate in some of the more remote areas. Don't forget to pack sunglasses, suntan lotion, and a plastic raincoat for sudden showers. You'll need beach shoes for reef walking and insect repellent to ward off mosquitoes.

For more information. For more information on Micronesia you can write several different sources.

Information on Guam is available from the Guam Visitors Bureau, P.O. Box 3520, Tamuning, Guam 96911.

For information on other islands within Micronesia, write the Micronesia Regional Tourism Council, Inc., P.O. Box 4222, Agana, Guam 96910; the Marianas Visitors Bureau, P.O. Box 861, Saipan, Commonwealth of the Marianas 96950; Palau Tourist Commission, P.O. Box 256, Koror, Republic of Palau 96940; Ponape Tourist Commission, P.O. Box 66, Kolonia, Ponape State 96941; Truk Tourist Commission, P.O. Box 910, Moen, Truk State 96942; Department of Resources and Development, Government of Kosrae, Lelu, Kosrae 96944; and Yap Tourist Commission, Colonia, Yap State 96943.

OTHER ISLANDS

Easter Island, Lord Howe Island, Norfolk Island, Nauru, Kiribati, Tuvalu

In addition to the varied and fascinating tropical islands already described, the South Pacific offers other interesting off-beat destinations. Each year inveterate island collectors go out of their way to visit these "untouched" islands.

Relatively undeveloped islands just beginning to experience tourism include Easter, Lord Howe, Norfolk, Nauru, Kiribati, and Tuvalu. Each offers the traveler different experiences, yet all feature simple but comfortable accommodations, limited island transportation, and a pace of life geared to a relaxing visit.

Most of these islands are some distance from well-traveled routes, but a visit to one or more of them can become the highlight of a South Pacific journey. Here are brief overviews of some of these intriguing destinations.

Easter Island

At the southeastern tip of the Polynesian triangle lies windswept Easter Island, one of the South Pacific's most isolated destinations. Surrounded by limitless ocean, Easter Island is regarded by some travelers as one of the loneliest islands in the world. Its closest neighbor is Pitcairn Island, 1,900 km/1,181 miles to the west. Chile, Easter Island's governing country, lies 3,701 km/2,300 miles east on the South American continent.

Triangular in shape, Easter Island—called Rapa Nui in Polynesian—is 117 square km/45 square miles of rocky grasslands, extinct volcanic cones, and steep ocean cliffs. Looming like ancient sentinels, the famed stone statues gaze with brooding eyes over this desolate landscape.

Easter Island is a vast storehouse of archeological treasures. Nearly 1,000 of these huge monoliths (called *moai*) dot the island; some are over 18 meters/60 feet high. The island also contains hundreds of petroglyphs and cave paintings, and the foundations of ancient buildings. Scientists still are trying to unravel the mystery of the island's ancient civilization and its culture.

Migration, discovery, and exploitation

Some scientists theorize that during ancient migrations two separate groups of Polynesians—the "Long Ears," who wore jewelry that elongated their ear lobes, and the "Short Ears"—arrived and settled on Easter Island.

The more artistic Long Ears carved the statues. Some scholars feel that the Long Ears wanted the Short Ears to do their manual labor—hauling the heavy statues and clearing the island of rocks. The two groups eventually fought and the Short Ears killed off the Long Ears. The victors then toppled many of the statues, and carving ceased.

When the first European navigator—Dutch Admiral Jacob Roggeveen—arrived on Easter Sunday, 1722, many of the statues had been toppled. In 1770 Felipe Gonzalez claimed the island for the King of Spain. Other explorers to visit the island were Captain James Cook in 1774 and French navigator Jean La Pérouse in 1785.

Six Peruvian slave ships arrived at Easter Island in 1862, and their crews hauled more than 1,000 islanders off to work Peru's guano islands. Most died en route. When the 15 survivors were finally released to return home, they brought smallpox with them. Within a short time an epidemic reduced the island's remaining population of 4,000 to a few hundred.

In 1888 Chile annexed Easter Island. Today's 1,800 residents mainly live off the desolate land, growing vegetables and fruit inside small gardens walled against the drying effects of the constant winds. Fish, pigs, and sheep provide other dietary staples. The island's main industry is sheep ranching. Since the island has no rivers or streams, water is sometimes scarce.

Hanga Roa, the island's only village, is located not far from the airport.

Visiting Easter Island today

LAN-Chile, the Chilean airline, stops at Easter Island on regularly scheduled flights between Chile and Tahiti

Brooding *stone statues (called* moai*) gaze over lonely, rolling hills of remote Easter Island, easternmost outpost of Polynesia.*

Kiribati Islander *carries outrigger canoe from thatched boathouse. Small boats provide main transport between scattered islets and atolls.*

and Fiji. Easter Island visitors stay in the modern 60-room Hanga Roa Hotel or at a local family's guest house.

Horses provide the most popular form of local transportation. They can be rented in the Hanga Roa village area. The island has few motor vehicles, and car rentals are expensive.

Visitors can explore the island independently or join a full or half-day guided tour.

Statues and other sights

Whether you take a tour or explore on your own, you'll find a number of interesting sights. At Ahu Akivi, northeast of Hanga Roa, you'll see seven statues that were replaced on their *ahu* (stone platform) during a 1960 restoration project.

On the eastern side of the island, you'll find Rano Raraku. From the crater walls of this extinct volcano, islanders obtained the stone which they fashioned skillfully into huge statues with elongated ears and jutting chins. The statues remain as they were left—some half carved, others completed. They stand in groups or alone, both inside and outside the crater; some are upright, some haphazardly tilted, some sprawled on the ground.

Besides the island's statues, you can see the ruins of ancient huts—their long, boat-shaped stone foundations still intact. The island also contains hundreds of petroglyphs and cave paintings.

For more information on Easter Island, write the Chilean National Tourist Board, 510 W. Sixth Street, Suite 1210, Los Angeles, CA 90014.

Lord Howe Island

Qualifying as a hideaway is Lord Howe Island, 670 km/416 miles northeast of Sydney. The friendly islanders move at a relaxed pace—and so will you when you visit this small island. A dependency of the Australian state of New South Wales, Lord Howe is 11 km/7 miles long and 3 km/2 miles wide. Many island visitors return regularly every year for a vacation.

An interesting topography

Aside from its peace and quiet, Lord Howe Island is distinguished for its coral reef—the most southerly one in the world. Two massive mountains dominate the south end of the island. Heavily forested, the island has fine stands of Kentia (or Howea) palms and banyan trees.

Lord Howe Island derives its name from the lord who was Secretary of State for the Colonies in the British Cabinet in 1788, the year the island was discovered by Lieutenant Lidgbird Ball.

Visiting the island

Regular air service connects Lord Howe with Sydney and Brisbane in Australia and with Norfolk Island.

Since Lord Howe has few motor vehicles, the best method of island transportation is a bicycle. Rentals are available.

Tour opportunities feature glass-bottomed boat trips and around-the-island bus excursions. Other activities you might want to try are deep-sea fishing, swimming, scuba diving, snorkeling, tennis, mountain climbing, golf, and lawn bowls.

Accommodations on Lord Howe Island include a number of simple lodges and motels, some apartments, and a few cottages.

For further information about the island, write the Lord Howe Island Promotion Committee, c/o N.S.W. Department of Tourism, 140 Phillip Street, Sydney, New South Wales 2000, Australia.

Norfolk Island

Lying 1,448 km/900 miles off the east coast of Australia, Norfolk Island possesses an interesting but not always pleasant past.

At first glance the tiny island resembles Cornwall. Just 8 km/5 miles long and 5 km/3 miles wide, it is reminiscent of England in its greenness, its pastoral qualities, and its peaceful atmosphere. Rugged basalt cliffs edge the island's irregular coastline; inland, cows and horses roam the rolling green hills. The native Norfolk Island pines, many of them planted by convict laborers, majestically crown the ridges and mark the roadways.

A former penal colony

Life was not always as peaceful on the island as it is today. When Captain James Cook discovered Norfolk in 1774 it was uninhabited. However, a few weeks after the founding of Sydney, Australia, in 1788, a small convict settlement was established on Norfolk Island for felons of the British Empire. This settlement was difficult to supply, and it was abandoned in 1814.

The island became a penal settlement again in 1825, when hardened criminals were sent to Norfolk Island. Tales of brutality, floggings, executions, and violence in the penal colony spread throughout the Pacific. By 1855, surviving prisoners were shipped to Tasmania and the penal settlement was closed.

As a result of overcrowding on Pitcairn Island, descendants of the mutineers of *Bounty* fame migrated to Norfolk Island to settle in 1856. Norfolk became a Territory of the Commonwealth of Australia in 1913. The administrative center is located at Kingston on the island's southern coast.

Many of today's 1,600 island residents are descendants of the first settlers from Pitcairn. These friendly, hospitable people live in modest wooden houses tucked amid groves of Norfolk pines. They tend gardens yielding bananas, yams, melons, potatoes, oranges, and peaches. Norfolk residents speak English and a language called Norfolk—a combination of west country English and Tahitian.

Discovering Norfolk's attractions

Norfolk Island can be reached easily by plane from Auckland, New Zealand; Sydney and Brisbane, Australia; and Lord Howe Island. On the island, you can rent a car or bicycle, or tour by taxi. Horses are also available for inland excursions. Local tour operators offer glass-bottomed boat cruises and around-the-island trips.

Accommodations range from self-contained apartments to small hotels and lodges, inns, and guest houses.

At the south end of the island near Kingston you'll find walls and buildings built by convict labor during the penal settlement era. Many of the fine colonial Georgian buildings have been restored and are now used for government administrative offices. You'll also see the remains of high prison walls topped with broken glass, the gallows gate, the guard's barracks, officer's baths (Roman-style), and Bloody Bridge (where many prisoners died). The epitaphs on the headstones in the prison cemetery tell of the harshness of this era in Norfolk Island history.

On Douglas Drive near the airport, you'll discover remnants of the island's Melanesian Mission established in the late 18th century. All that remains today is the vicarage and handsomely designed St. Barnabas Chapel —an architectural gem with stained-glass windows and handworked timbers. The Mission moved to the Solomon Islands in 1920.

For further information on Norfolk Island, write the Norfolk Island Government Tourist Bureau, P.O. Box 211, Norfolk Island, South Pacific.

Nauru

The Republic of Nauru—just 21 square km/8 square miles in area—is one of the smallest sovereign states in the world. Located about 644 km/400 miles west of the Gilberts, Nauru is distinguished from other South Pacific islands by having one of the highest per capita incomes in the world. This income is derived from the mining of phosphate deposits that cover about 85 percent of the island.

The land and its people

Island residents live in a narrow green belt along the shore. Less than a kilometer/½ mile inland lies a barren, phosphate-rich plateau. After the phosphate has been mined, grotesque coral pinnacles remain, giving the area an appearance of devastation. In the shadows of late afternoon, the pinnacles resemble stark gravestones. Acre upon acre of coral pillows—rising to 18 meters/60 feet—are all that remain after the phosphate has been ripped away.

The Nauruans who live on this mineral-rich island are friendly, humorous, helpful people. Every man, woman, and child receives an annual income of several thousand dollars plus free health services. Workers from other South Pacific islands and the Orient actually

mine the phosphate. The government invests excess money earned from phosphate mining for security against the time when the phosphate deposits are exhausted.

Taking a trip to Nauru

The Republic of Nauru has its own airline, Air Nauru, that operates regular flights linking Nauru with a number of other Pacific islands as well as Australia, New Zealand, Japan, the Philippines, and Taiwan.

The island's only hotel is the 32-room Meneng Hotel. Arriving travelers must have confirmed hotel reservations or confirmation of home-stay accommodations.

For further information on Nauru, write the Secretary for Island Development and Industry, Republic of Nauru; or Nauru's Honorary Consulate, 841 Bishop Street, Suite 506, Honolulu, HI 96813.

Kiribati and Tuvalu

Until recently Kiribati (formerly the Gilbert Islands) and Tuvalu (formerly the Ellice Islands) were one British Crown Colony. They have now separated into two colonies and have gained their independence.

The three island groups of Kiribati have a total land area of only 684 square km/264 square miles. Smaller in area, Tuvalu covers only 26 square km/10 square miles.

The people of Kiribati are predominantly Micronesians who speak both Gilbertese and English. The Tuvaluans are Polynesians; they speak both English and their own Polynesian dialect. The people of both countries must eke a living from the sparse land of the atolls, which are nothing more than bits of coral rock covered with hard sand. The islands' scanty soil is just enough to grow taro, coconut, and pandanus. The rest of their food must come from the sea.

Travelers reach Kiribati and Tuvalu on regularly scheduled flights from Fiji and Nauru. Air Tungaru, Kiribati's airline, Air Nauru, and Fiji Air provide the area's air service.

Kiribati visitors can stay at the Otintai Hotel (30 rooms) and the Kiribati Hotel (10 rooms) on Tarawa, the Captain Cook Hotel (36 rooms) on Kiritimati (Christmas Island), or the Robert Louis Stevenson Hotel (8 rooms) on Abemama. Tuvalu accommodations are available at the small Vaiaku Lagi Hotel (7 rooms) on Funafuti.

The remoteness of these islands makes them an interesting place to visit. Visitors can go fishing, swimming, picnicking, or shell collecting. There are also World War II battlegrounds to explore. During your visit, you'll learn how the islanders have adapted to an atoll existence.

For more information on Kiribati, write to the Government of the Republic of Kiribati, Ministry of Natural Resources, Box 261, Bairiki, Tarawa, Kiribati. You can get information on Tuvalu by writing the Ministry of Commerce and Natural Resources, Tuvalu Government, Vaiaku, Funafuti Island, Tuvalu.

Additional Readings

Battleground South Pacific by Robert Howlett with photos by Bruce Adams. Rutland, Vermont, and Tokyo, Japan: Charles E. Tuttle Co., 1971. A pictorial presentation of well-known World War II combat areas in the South Pacific.

A Descriptive Atlas of the Pacific Islands by T. F. Kennedy. New Zealand: A. H. & A. W. Reed Ltd., 1974. A comprehensive atlas including maps of Polynesia, Melanesia, Micronesia, Australia, New Zealand, and the Philippines.

Easter Island by Bob Putigny with photos by Olivier de Kersauson, Michel Folco, and Jean-Paul Duchêne. Papeete, Tahiti: Les Éditions du Pacifique, 1976. Color photos and text cover this remote Polynesian island.

Explorations of Captain James Cook in the Pacific, As Told by Selections of His Own Journals, 1768–1779 edited by A. Grenfell Price. Massachusetts: Peter Smith Publishers. Explorer's account of South Pacific journeys.

Fodor's Australia, New Zealand, and the South Pacific edited by Robert C. Fisher and Leslie Brown. New York: David McKay Company Inc., 1978. A travel guide containing facts about many South Pacific countries.

Guam: Past & Present by Charles Beardsley. Rutland, Vermont, and Tokyo, Japan: Charles E. Tuttle Co., 1964. This general handbook tells of the island's discovery, history, culture, and geography.

Isles of the South Pacific by Maurice Shadbolt and Olaf Ruhen. Washington, D.C.: The National Geographic Society, 1968. Color photographs and text cover the islands of Polynesia and Melanesia.

Men From Under the Sky by Stanley Brown. Rutland, Vermont, and Tokyo, Japan: Charles E. Tuttle Co., 1973. A historical account of the arrival of the first westerners in Fiji.

Micronesia: The Breadfruit Revolution by Byron Baker and Robert Wenkam. Honolulu, Hawaii: East-West Center Press, 1971. The islands of the Marshalls, Carolines, and Marianas are covered through text and photographs.

Moorea by James Siers. Wellington, New Zealand: Millwood Press, 1976. A photographic guide to the history, people, and sights of this French Polynesian island.

New Guinea by Milton and Joan Mann. Tokyo, Japan, and Palo Alto, California: Kodansha International Ltd., 1972. A first-hand account of travels through Papua New Guinea.

Pacific Islands Year Book edited by Stuart Inder. Sydney, Australia: Pacific Publications, 1979. A standard reference book on the islands of the Pacific.

Pan Am's World Guide. New York: McGraw-Hill Book Co., 1978. An encyclopedia of travel containing basic facts on many South Pacific countries as well as Europe, Africa, the Middle East, Orient, Asia, North, Central and South America, and the Caribbean.

Papua New Guinea Handbook and Travel Guide edited by Stuart Inder. Sydney, Australia: Pacific Publications, 1978. A standard reference guide to this South Pacific country.

Polynesia in Colour by James Siers. Rutland, Vermont, & Tokyo, Japan: Charles E. Tuttle Co., 1970. Text and photographs cover Fiji, the Samoas, Tonga, the Cooks, New Caledonia, and Tahiti.

Rarotonga by James Siers. Wellington, New Zealand: Millwood Press, Ltd., 1977. The people of the Cook Islands are portrayed in color photos.

Samoa in Colour by James Siers. Rutland, Vermont, and Tokyo, Japan: Charles E. Tuttle Co., 1970. Photographs and text tell of the Samoan people and their islands.

Samoa, A Photographic Essay by Frederic Koehler Sutter. Honolulu, Hawaii: The University Press of Hawaii, 1971. Color photographs and detailed captions depict Samoan daily life.

South Pacific by Jack and Dorothy Fields. Tokyo, Japan, and Palo Alto, California: Kodansha International Ltd., 1972. A pictorial with photographs and text covering 14 island groups in Melanesia, Micronesia, and Polynesia.

South Pacific Travel Digest by Charles and Babette Jacobs. Palm Desert, California: Paul Richmond and Co., 1978. A guide to sights, transportation, hotels, restaurants, and shopping in the South Pacific. Books may be ordered (by mail or phone) from Travel Digests, 30695 Ganado Drive, Rancho Palos Verdes, CA 90274; phone (213) 541-6161.

Tin Roofs & Palm Trees, a Report on the New South Seas by Robert Trumbull. Seattle & London: University of Washington Press, 1977. A portrait of the South Pacific's emerging island states.

Setting sun *streaks the Pacific sky with vibrant tones of gold, pink, and purple as lone stroller walks along the shore.*

Index

Photographers

Dave Bartruff: 43 bottom, 54, 75 top. **Jack Cannon:** 10, 59 bottom. **Joan Erickson:** 62 top. **Jack Fields:** 2, 31 all, 35, 51 top, 75 bottom, 83 all, 86, 94, 99 all, 107, 110 bottom, 115 all, 118 bottom. **Shirley Fockler:** 18 top, 23 all, 26, 38 right, 46, 51 bottom, 91 top, back cover top right. **James Gebbie:** 43 top, 91 bottom. **Jane Keator:** 67, 70. **Milt and Joan Mann:** 110 top, 123 bottom. **Richard Rowan:** 15 top, 78. **Elliott Varner Smith:** 7 bottom, 62 bottom, 102, 118 top, back cover top left. **Joan Storey:** 7 top right, 18 bottom, 59 top, 126, back cover bottom. **Darrow M. Watt:** 15 bottom. **Basil Williams:** 7 top left, 38 left, 123 top.

COMBINED INDEX

A comprehensive index to all three volumes
appears on the following pages. This is in addition
to the individual book indexes which appear on
page 127 of each title.

Australia

Sweeping "sails" of Sydney Opera House
soar above harbor waters.

New Zealand

Fattened lambs funnel through a loading
chute at Pirinoa.

Islands of the South Pacific

Samoan girls splash in pool at base of
waterfall near Apia.

BRIAN BRAKE, PHOTO RESEARCHERS, INC.

NEW ZEALAND TOURIST OFFICE

BASIL WILLIAMS

Combined Index